CLYMER®
HONDA
4-STROKE OUTBOARD SHOP MANUAL
2-130 HP • 1976-1999

The World's Finest Publisher of Mechanical How-to Manuals

INTERTEC PUBLISHING

P.O. Box 12901, Overland Park, KS 66282-2901

Copyright ©1999 Intertec Publishing

FIRST EDITION
First Printing December, 1999

Printed in U.S.A.

CLYMER and colophon are registered trademarks of Intertec Publishing.

ISBN: 0-89287-738-3

Library of Congress: 99-69557

Tools shown in Chapter Two courtesy of Thorsen Tool, Dallas, Texas. Test equipment shown in Chapter Two courtesy of Dixson, Inc., Grand Junction, Colorado.

Technical photography by Mark Rolling.

Technical illustrations by Mitzi McCarthy, Michael St. Clair, Michael Rose and Robert Caldwell..

Technical assistance provided by Jerry Whittle Marine, Lewisville, TX.

Cover photo courtesy of Trailerboats Magazine.

All rights reserved. Reproduction or use, without express permission, of editorial or pictorial content, in any manner, is prohibited. No patent liability is assumed with respect to the use of the information contained herein. While every precaution has been taken in the preparation of this book, the publisher assumes no responsibility for errors or omissions. Neither is any liability assumed for damages resulting from use of the information contained herein. Publication of the servicing information in this manual does not imply approval of the manufacturers of the products covered.

All instructions and diagrams have been checked for accuracy and ease of application; however, success and safety in working with tools depend to a great extent upon individual accuracy, skill and caution. For this reason, the publishers are not able to guarantee the result of any procedure contained herein. Nor can they assume responsibility for any damage to property or injury to persons occasioned from the procedures. Persons engaging in the procedure do so entirely at their own risk.

1. General Information
2. Tools and Techniques
3. Troubleshooting
4. Routine Maintenance and Tune-up
5. Timing, Synchronization and Adjustments
6. Fuel System Repair
7. Electrical and Ignition
8. Base Engine
9. Gearcase Repair
10. Jet Drives
11. Rewind Starter
12. Power Trim/Tilt Systems
13. Midsection
14. Remote Control
15. Index
16. Wiring Diagrams

Intertec Book Division

President Raymond E. Maloney
Vice President, Book Division Ted Marcus

EDITORIAL

Director
Randy Stephens

Senior Editor
Mark Jacobs

Editors
Mike Hall
Tom Fournier
Frank Craven
Paul Wyatt

Associate Editors
Robert Sokol
Carl Janssens

Technical Writers
Ron Wright
Ed Scott
George Parise
Mark Rolling
Michael Morlan
Jay Bogart
Ronney Broach

Warehouse and Production Manager
Terry Distin

Editorial Production Manager
Shirley Renicker

Senior Editorial Production Coordinator
Dylan Goodwin

Editorial Production Coordinator
Sandy Kreps

Editorial Production Assistants
Greg Araujo
Dennis Conrow
Shara Meyer
Susan Hartington

Technical Illustrators
Steve Amos
Robert Caldwell
Mitzi McCarthy
Michael St. Clair

MARKETING/SALES AND ADMINISTRATION

Product Development Manager
Michael Yim

Marketing Assistant
Melissa Abbott

Art Director
Andrew Brown

Associate Art Director
Chris Paxton

Sales Manager/Marine
Dutch Sadler

Sales Manager/Manuals
Ted Metzger

Sales Manager/Motorcycles
Matt Tusken

Sales Coordinator
Paul Cormaci

Telephone Sales Supervisor
Joelle Stephens

Telemarketing Sales Representative
Susan Kay

Customer Service/Fulfillment Manager
Caryn Bair

Fulfillment Coordinator
Susan Kohlmeyer

Customer Service Supervisor
Terri Cannon

Customer Service Representatives
Stephanie Fuller
Ardelia Chapman
Donna Schemmel
Dana Morrison
April LeBlond

The following books and guides are published by Intertec Publishing.

CLYMER SHOP MANUALS
Boat Motors and Drives
Motorcycles and ATVs
Snowmobiles
Personal Watercraft

ABOS/INTERTEC/CLYMER BLUE BOOKS AND TRADE-IN GUIDES
Recreational Vehicles
Outdoor Power Equipment
Agricultural Tractors
Lawn and Garden Tractors
Motorcycles and ATVs
Snowmobiles and Personal Watercraft
Boats and Motors

AIRCRAFT BLUEBOOK-PRICE DIGEST
Airplanes
Helicopters

AC-U-KWIK DIRECTORIES
The Corporate Pilot's Airport/FBO Directory
International Manager's Edition
Jet Book

I&T SHOP SERVICE MANUALS
Tractors

INTERTEC SERVICE MANUALS
Snowmobiles
Outdoor Power Equipment
Personal Watercraft
Gasoline and Diesel Engines
Recreational Vehicles
Boat Motors and Drives
Motorcycles
Lawn and Garden Tractors

Contents

QUICK REFERENCE DATA IX

CHAPTER ONE
GENERAL INFORMATION
Manual organization......................... 1
Notes, cautions and warnings.................. 1
Torque specifications........................ 2
Engine operation............................ 2
Fasteners................................... 2
Lubricants.................................. 8
Gasket sealant.............................. 10
Galvanic corrosion.......................... 11
Protection from galvanic corrosion 13
Propellers.................................. 14

CHAPTER TWO
TOOLS AND TECHNIQUES
Safety first................................ 21
Basic hand tools............................ 21
Test equipment............................. 26
Service hints............................... 28
Special tips................................ 30
Mechanics' tips............................. 31

CHAPTER THREE
TROUBLESHOOTING 33
Troubleshooting test equipment............... 33
Troubleshooting preparation 41
Starting difficulty.......................... 44
Fuel system testing......................... 46
Starting system............................. 57
Ignition system............................. 65
Warning systems............................ 82
Charging system............................ 89
Fuses and wire harnesses 93
Trim system troubleshooting 94
Base engine 103
Cooling system............................. 111
Gearcase.................................. 114
Electronic fuel injection system.............. 117

CHAPTER FOUR
LUBRICATION, MAINTENANCE AND TUNE-UP 142
Routine maintenance 142
Electrical and ignition system 153
Cooling system maintenance 155
Fuel system................................ 156
Submersion................................ 159
Tune-up 160

CHAPTER FIVE
TIMING, SYNCHRONIZATION AND ADJUSTMENTS 177

Timing adjustments 177	Neutral start system adjustment 198
Throttle control/cable adjustments 178	Trim sender adjustment 200
Carburetor adjustments 187	Timing belt tensioner 200
Shifting system adjustments 193	

CHAPTER SIX
FUEL SYSTEM REPAIR 202

Fuel tank and fuel hose components 203	Carburetor repair 225
Silencer cover and carburetor/ throttle body 215	EFI components 230

CHAPTER SEVEN
ELECTRICAL AND IGNITION 242

Starting system 242	Warning system components 261
Charging system 253	Battery maintenance and testing 261
Ignition system 255	

CHAPTER EIGHT
BASE ENGINE 270

Base engine removal and installation 270	Base engine disassembly 335
Flywheel 287	Base engine inspection and measurement 359
Timing belt 294	Primary gearcase repair 373
Rocker arm removal/installation 308	Break-in procedure 373
Cylinder head 308	
Oil pump 331	

CHAPTER NINE
GEARCASE REPAIR 395

Gearcase operation 395	Water pump 410
Propeller 397	Gearcase repair 415
Gearcase removal and installation 400	

CHAPTER TEN
JET DRIVES 465

Jet drive operation 465	Intake housing liner replacement 469
Jet drive components 465	Impeller removal/installation 469
Thrust control 465	Impeller shimming 469
Jet drive repair 467	Bearing housing removal 471
Jet drive removal/installation 468	Bearing housing installation 473
Intake housing removal/installation 468	Correcting steering torque 474

CHAPTER ELEVEN
REWIND STARTER 475

Rewind starter operation 475	Rewind starter disassembly,
Rewind starter removal, repair,	inspection and assembly 483
assembly and installation 477	

CHAPTER TWELVE
POWER TRIM/TILT SYSTEMS...490
Gas-assisted manual tilt system
  removal/installation 490
Single hydraulic cylinder trim/tilt systems
  removal/installation 492
Three cylinders trim/tilt systems
  removal/installation 494
Trim/tilt system components 496
Trim position sender removal/installation 496
Trim control unit removal/installation 497
Electric trim/tilt motor removal/installation....... 497
Manual relief valve replacement 500
Electric trim/tilt motor repair 500
Filling procedure 503
Bleeding procedure 504

CHAPTER THIRTEEN
MIDSECTION...506
Minor repairs 506
Major repairs 507
Tiller control components 518

CHAPTER FOURTEEN
REMOTE CONTROL..521
Throttle/shift cable removal/installation 521
Remote control disassembly and assembly 524

INDEX...533

WIRING DIAGRAMS..537

Quick Reference Data

MAINTENENCE INTERVALS

Models	Required maintenance
BEFORE AND AFTER EVERY USE	
All models	Check oil level and condition
BF20, BF2A, BF50, BF5A	Check gearcase lubricant level
BF75, BF8A, BF100	–
BF9.9A, BF15A	–
All models	Check propeller fasteners for tightness
All models	Check fuel line condition
MONTHLY OR AFTER EACH 20 HOURS OF USE	
BF2A, BF20, BF5A, BF50	Check throttle linkages
6 MONTHS OR 50 HOURS OF USE	
Models	Required maintenance
All models	Check gearcase lubricant condition
BF20, BF2A, BF50, BF5A	Inspect or change spark plugs
6 MONTHS OR 100 HOURS OF USE	
All models	Lubricate swivel bracket **
Manual start models	Check the starter rope condition
Manual start models	Lubricate starter rope **
All models	Lubricate motor cover fasteners and latches **
Tiller control models	Lubricate tiller arm control pivot **
All models without power trim	Lubricate tilt lock mechanism **
All models with clamp bolts	Lubricate engine clamp bolts **
All models	Lubricate throttle linkages *
All models	Change engine oil *
BF20, BF2A, BF50, BF5A	Check shear pin condition
All models	Check idle speed
All models	Check battery condition
All models	Check for loose bolts or nuts
All models	Check battery cable terminals
All models	Check fuel filters
ANNUALLY OR 200 HOURS OF USE	
All models with external filter	Change oil filter
All models	Change gearcase lubricant *
All models	Check and adjust valve clearance *
All models	Clean fuel tank
All models	Check or replace fuel lines
BF75, BF100	Check and adjust timing *
All models	Replace fuel filters
All models	Check and adjust timing/balancer belt
(Excludes models BF20, BF2A, BF50, BF5A)	–
All models	Check thermostat operation
BF20A, BF25A, BF30A	Check and correct carburetor syncronization *
BF35A, BF40A	–
BF45A, BF50A	–
BF75A, BF90A	–

ADDITIONAL MAINTENENCE REQUIREMENTS

Model	Required maintenance	Maintenance interval
BF20, BF2A	Clean combustion chamber	Every 300 hours of use
BF115, BF130	Replace high pressure filter	Every 2 years or 400 hours of use

* Perform this maintenance after the first month or 15 hours of usage when the engine is new or recently repaired.
** Perform this maintenance more often when the engine is used in saltwater.

SPARK PLUG RECOMMENDATIONS

Model	Standard spark plug	Alternate spark plug
BF20, BF2A	–	–
(2 hp models)	–	–
(BF20S, BF20L models)	NGK BMR-4A *	–
BF20, BF2A	–	–
(2 hp models)	–	–
(BF2AS, BF2AL models)	NGK BMR-4A *	ND W14MR-U **
BF50, BF5A	NGK BPR5ES *	ND W16EPR-U **
(5 hp models)		
BF75, BF8A, BF100	NGK DR-5HS *	NGK DR-4HS *
(7.5, 8, 9.9 hp models)		
BF9.9A	NGK DR-5HS *	ND X16FSR-U **
BF15A	NGK DR-6HS *	ND X20FSR-U **
BF20A, BF25A, BF30A	NGK DR7EA *	ND X22ESR-U **
BF35A, BF45A	NGK DR7EA *	ND X22ESR-U **
BF75A, BF90A	NGK DR7EA *	ND X22ESR-U **
(75, 90 hp models)		
BF115A, BF90A	NGK ZFR7F *	ND KJ22CR-L8

* Designates NGK brand spark plug
** Designates Nippon Denso brand spark plug

SPARK PLUG GAP

Model	Gap specification
BF20, BF2A	0.6-0.7 mm (0.024-0.028 in.)
(2 hp models)	–
BF50, BF5A	0.7-0.8 mm (0.028-0.031 in.)
(5 hp models)	–
BF75, BF8A, BF100	0.6-0.7 mm (0.024-0.028 in.)
(7.5, 8, 9.9 hp models)	–
BF9.9A, BF15A	0.6-0.7 mm (0.024-0.028 in.)
BF20A, BF25A, BF30A	0.6-0.7 mm (0.024-0.028 in.)
BF35A, BF40A, BF45A, BF50A	0.6-0.7 mm (0.024-0.028 in.)
BF75A, BF90A	0.6-0.7 mm (0.024-0.028 in.)
(75, 90 hp models)	–
BF115A, BF130A	0.7-0.8 mm (0.028-0.031 in.)

MAXIMUM ENGINE SPEED SPECIFICATIONS

Model	Maximum RPM range	Overspeed control range
BF20, BF2A	4000-5000	*
BF50, BF5A	4000-5000	*
75LD (1976 &1977 models)	5000-6000	*
BF75	4700-5200	*
BF8A	4950-5500	*
BF100	5200-5700	*
BF9.9A	4500-5500	*
BF15A	5000-6200	*
BF20A	5000-6000	6300-6900
BF25A	5000-6000	6300-6900
BF30A	5500-6000	6300-6900
BF35A	4600-5600	6400-6800
BF40A	5000-6000	6400-6800
BF45A	5000-6000	6400-6800
BF50A	5500-6000	6400-6800
BF75A	5000-6000	6300-6900
BF90A	5000-6000	6300-6900
BF115A	5000-6000	6300-6400
BF130A	5000-6000	6300-6400

* Overspeed control circuits are not used on these models.

CLYMER
HONDA
4-STROKE OUTBOARD SHOP MANUAL
2-130 HP • 1976-1999

Introduction

This Clymer shop manual covers service and repair of 2-130 hp Honda four-stroke outboard motors manufactured during 1976-1999. Coverage is also provided for models equipped with jet drive propulsion.

Step-by-step instructions and hundreds of illustrations guide you through tasks ranging from routine maintenance to complete overhaul.

This manual can be used by anyone from a first-time owner to a professional technician. Easy-to-read type, detailed drawings and clear photographs provide all the information needed to perform a procedure correctly.

Having a well-maintained outboard motor will increase your enjoyment of your boat as well as ensure your safety offshore. Keep this manual handy and use it often. Performing routine, preventive maintenance will save you time and money by helping to prevent premature failure and unnecessary repais.

Chapter One

General Information

This detailed, comprehensive manual contains complete information on maintenance, tune-up, repair and overhaul. Hundreds of photos and drawings guide you through every step-by-step procedure.

Troubleshooting, tune-up, maintenance and repair are not difficult if you know what tools and equipment to use and what to do. Anyone not afraid to get their hands dirty, of average intelligence and with some mechanical ability, can perform most of the procedures in this book. See Chapter Two for more information on tools and techniques.

A shop manual is a reference. You want to be able to find information fast. Clymer books are designed with you in mind. All chapters are thumb tabbed and important items are indexed at the end of the book. All procedures, tables, photos, etc., in this manual assume that the reader may be working on the machine or using this manual for the first time.

Keep this book handy in your tool box. It will help you to better understand how your machine runs, lower repair and maintenance costs and generally increase your enjoyment of your marine equipment.

MANUAL ORGANIZATION

This chapter provides general information useful to marine owners and mechanics.

Chapter Two discusses the tools and techniques for preventive maintenance, troubleshooting and repair.

Chapter Three describes typical equipment problems and provides logical troubleshooting procedures.

Following chapters describe specific systems, providing disassembly, repair, assembly and adjustment procedures in simple step-by-step form. Specifications concerning a specific system are included at the end of the appropriate chapter.

NOTES, CAUTIONS AND WARNINGS

The terms NOTE, CAUTION and WARNING have specific meanings in this manual. A NOTE provides additional information to make a step or procedure easier or clearer. Disregarding a NOTE could cause inconvenience, but would not cause damage or personal injury.

A CAUTION emphasizes areas where equipment damage could result. Disregarding a CAUTION could cause permanent mechanical damage; however, personal injury is unlikely.

A WARNING emphasizes areas where personal injury or even death could result from negligence. Mechanical damage may also occur. WARNINGS *are to be taken seriously.* In some cases, serious injury or death has resulted from disregarding similar warnings.

TORQUE SPECIFICATIONS

Torque specifications throughout this manual are given in foot-pounds (ft.-lb.) and either Newton meters (N•m) or meter-kilograms (mkg). Newton meters are being adopted in place of meter-kilograms in accordance with the International Modernized Metric System. Existing torque wrenches calibrated in meter-kilograms can be used by performing a simple conversion: move the decimal point one place to the right. For example, 4.7 mkg = 47 N•m. This conversion is accurate enough for mechanics' use even though the exact mathematical conversion is 3.5 mkg = 34.3 N•m.

ENGINE OPERATION

All marine engines, whether 2- or 4-stroke, gasoline or diesel, operate on the Otto cycle of intake, compression, power and exhaust phases.

4-stroke Cycle

A 4-stroke engine requires two crankshaft revolutions (4 strokes of the piston) to complete the Otto cycle. **Figure 1** shows gasoline 4-stroke engine operation. **Figure 2** shows diesel 4-stroke engine operation.

2-stroke Cycle

A 2-stroke engine requires only 1 crankshaft revolution (2 strokes of the piston) to complete the Otto cycle. **Figure 3** shows gasoline 2-stroke engine operation. Although diesel 2-strokes exist, they are not commonly used in light marine applications.

FASTENERS

The material and design of the various fasteners used on marine equipment are not arrived at by chance or accident. Fastener design determines the type of tool required to work with the fastener. Fastener material is carefully selected to decrease the possibility of physical failure or corrosion. See *Galvanic Corrosion* in this chapter for more information on marine materials.

Threads

Nuts, bolts and screws are manufactured in a wide range of thread patterns. To join a nut and bolt, the diameter of the bolt and the diameter of the hole in the nut must be the same. It is just as important that the threads on both be properly matched.

The best way to determine if the threads on two fasteners are matched is to turn the nut on the bolt (or the bolt into the threaded hole in a piece of equipment) with fingers only. Be sure both pieces are clean. If much force is required, check the thread condition on each fastener. If the thread condition is good but the fasteners jam, the threads are not compatible.

Four important specifications describe every thread:
  a. Diameter.
  b. Threads per inch.
  c. Thread pattern.
  d. Thread direction.

Figure 4 shows the first two specifications. Thread pattern is more subtle. Italian and British

GENERAL INFORMATION

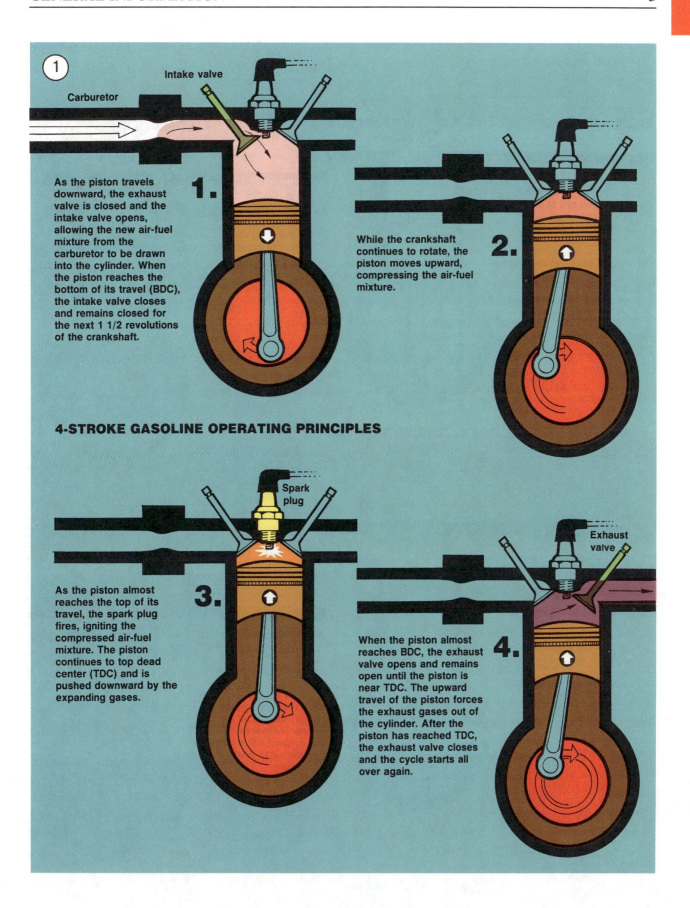

4-STROKE GASOLINE OPERATING PRINCIPLES

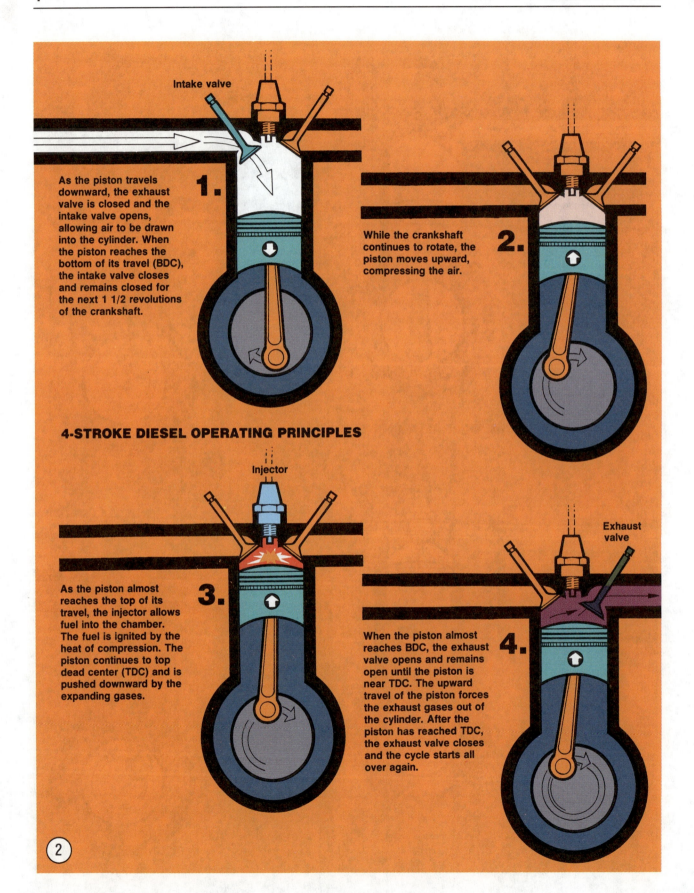

GENERAL INFORMATION

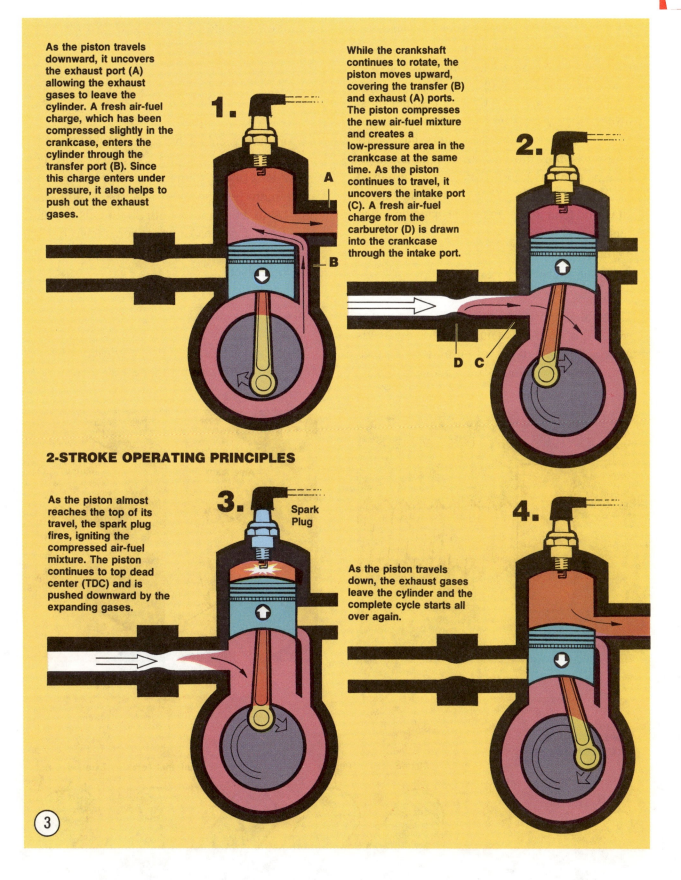

2-STROKE OPERATING PRINCIPLES

1. As the piston travels downward, it uncovers the exhaust port (A) allowing the exhaust gases to leave the cylinder. A fresh air-fuel charge, which has been compressed slightly in the crankcase, enters the cylinder through the transfer port (B). Since this charge enters under pressure, it also helps to push out the exhaust gases.

2. While the crankshaft continues to rotate, the piston moves upward, covering the transfer (B) and exhaust (A) ports. The piston compresses the new air-fuel mixture and creates a low-pressure area in the crankcase at the same time. As the piston continues to travel, it uncovers the intake port (C). A fresh air-fuel charge from the carburetor (D) is drawn into the crankcase through the intake port.

3. As the piston almost reaches the top of its travel, the spark plug fires, igniting the compressed air-fuel mixture. The piston continues to top dead center (TDC) and is pushed downward by the expanding gases.

4. As the piston travels down, the exhaust gases leave the cylinder and the complete cycle starts all over again.

standards exist, but the most commonly used by marine equipment manufacturers are American standard and metric standard. The threads are cut differently as shown in **Figure 5**.

Most threads are cut so that the fastener must be turned clockwise to tighten it. These are called right-hand threads. Some fasteners have left-hand threads; they must be turned counterclockwise to be tightened. Left-hand threads are used in locations where normal rotation of the equipment would tend to loosen a right-hand threaded fastener.

Machine Screws

There are many different types of machine screws. **Figure 6** shows a number of screw heads requiring different types of turning tools (see Chapter Two for detailed information). Heads are also designed to protrude above the metal (round) or to be slightly recessed in the metal (flat) (**Figure 7**).

Bolts

Commonly called bolts, the technical name for these fasteners is cap screw. They are normally described by diameter, threads per inch and length. For example, 1/4-20 × 1 indicates a bolt 1/4 in. in diameter with 20 threads per inch, 1 in. long. The measurement across two flats on the head of the bolt indicates the proper wrench size to be used.

Nuts

Nuts are manufactured in a variety of types and sizes. Most are hexagonal (6-sided) and fit

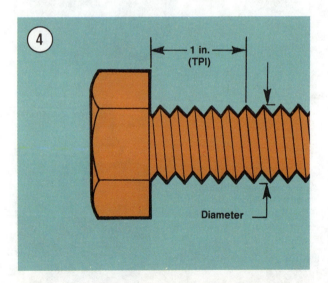
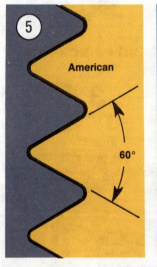
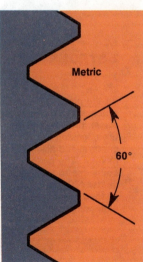
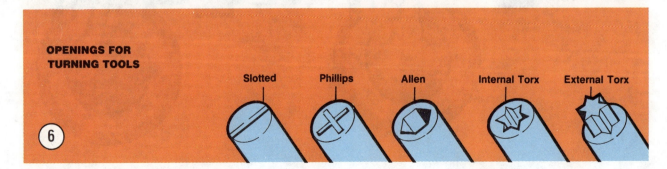

GENERAL INFORMATION

on bolts, screws and studs with the same diameter and threads per inch.

Figure 8 shows several types of nuts. The common nut is usually used with a lockwasher. Self-locking nuts have a nylon insert that prevents the nut from loosening; no lockwasher is required. Wing nuts are designed for fast removal by hand. Wing nuts are used for convenience in non-critical locations.

To indicate the size of a nut, manufacturers specify the diameter of the opening and the threads per inch. This is similar to bolt specification, but without the length dimension. The measurement across two flats on the nut indicates the proper wrench size to be used.

Washers

There are two basic types of washers: flat washers and lockwashers. Flat washers are simple discs with a hole to fit a screw or bolt. Lockwashers are designed to prevent a fastener from working loose due to vibration, expansion and contraction. **Figure 9** shows several types of lockwashers. Note that flat washers are often used between a lockwasher and a fastener to provide a smooth bearing surface. This allows the fastener to be turned easily with a tool.

Cotter Pins

Cotter pins (**Figure 10**) are used to secure special kinds of fasteners. The threaded stud

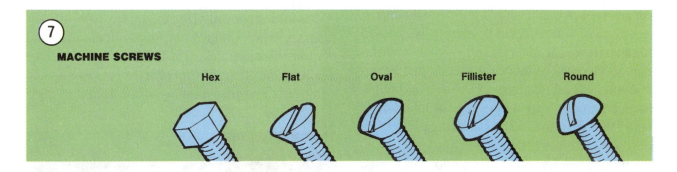

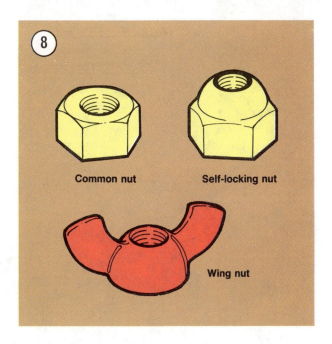

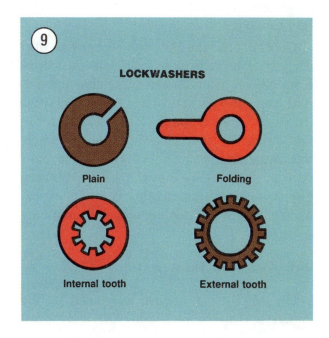

must have a hole in it; the nut or nut lock piece has projections that the cotter pin fits between. This type of nut is called a "Castellated nut." Cotter pins should not be reused after removal.

Snap Rings

Snap rings can be of an internal or external design. They are used to retain items on shafts (external type) or within tubes (internal type). Snap rings can be reused if they are not distorted during removal. In some applications, snap rings of varying thickness can be selected to control the end play of parts assemblies.

LUBRICANTS

Periodic lubrication ensures long service life for any type of equipment. It is especially important to marine equipment because it is exposed to salt or brackish water and other harsh environments. The *type* of lubricant used is just as important as the lubrication service itself; although, in an emergency, the wrong type of lubricant is better than none at all. The following paragraphs describe the types of lubricants most often used on marine equipment. Be sure to follow the equipment manufacturer's recommendations for lubricant types.

Generally, all liquid lubricants are called "oil." They may be mineral-based (including petroleum bases), natural-based (vegetable and animal bases), synthetic-based or emulsions (mixtures). "Grease" is an oil which is thickened with a metallic "soap." The resulting material is then usually enhanced with anticorrosion, antioxidant and extreme pressure (EP) additives. Grease is often classified by the type of thickener added; lithium and calcium soap are commonly used.

4-stroke Engine Oil

Oil for 4-stroke engines is graded by the American Petroleum Institute (API) and the Society of Automotive Engineers (SAE) in several categories. Oil containers display these ratings on the top or label (**Figure 11**).

API oil grade is indicated by letters, oils for gasoline engines are identified by an "S" and oils for diesel engines are identified by a "C." Most modern gasoline engines require SF or SG graded oil. Automotive and marine diesel engines use CC or CD graded oil.

Viscosity is an indication of the oil's thickness, or resistance to flow. The SAE uses numbers to indicate viscosity; thin oils have low numbers and thick oils have high numbers. A "W" after the number indicates that the viscosity testing was done at low temperature to simulate cold weather operation. Engine oils fall into the 5W-20W and 20-50 range.

Multi-grade oils (for example, 10W-40) are less viscous (thinner) at low temperatures and more viscous (thicker) at high temperatures. This allows the oil to perform efficiently across a wide range of engine operating temperatures.

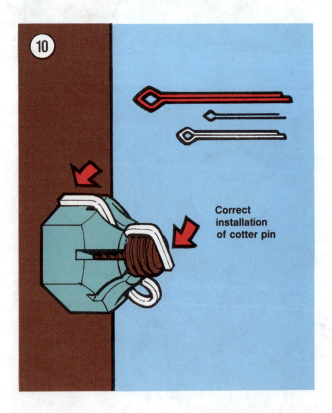

Correct installation of cotter pin

GENERAL INFORMATION

2-stroke Engine Oil

Lubrication for a 2-stroke engine is provided by oil mixed with the incoming fuel-air mixture. Some of the oil mist settles out in the crankcase, lubricating the crankshaft and lower end of the connecting rods. The rest of the oil enters the combustion chamber to lubricate the piston, rings and cylinder wall. This oil is then burned along with the fuel-air mixture during the combustion process.

Engine oil must have several special qualities to work well in a 2-stroke engine. It must mix easily and stay in suspension in gasoline. When burned, it can't leave behind excessive deposits. It must also be able to withstand the high temperatures associated with 2-stroke engines.

The National Marine Manufacturer's Association (NMMA) has set standards for oil used in 2-stroke, water-cooled engines. This is the NMMA TC-W (two-cycle, water-cooled) grade (**Figure 12**). The oil's performance in the following areas is evaluated:

   a. Lubrication (prevention of wear and scuffing).
   b. Spark plug fouling.
   c. Preignition.
   d. Piston ring sticking.
   e. Piston varnish.
   f. General engine condition (including deposits).
   g. Exhaust port blockage.
   h. Rust prevention.
   i. Mixing ability with gasoline.

In addition to oil grade, manufacturers specify the ratio of gasoline to oil required during break-in and normal engine operation.

Gear Oil

Gear lubricants are assigned SAE viscosity numbers under the same system as 4-stroke engine oil. Gear lubricant falls into the SAE 72-250 range (**Figure 13**). Some gear lubricants are multi-grade; for example, SAE 85W-90.

Three types of marine gear lubricant are generally available: SAE 90 hypoid gear lubricant is designed for older manual-shift units; Type C gear lubricant contains additives designed for electric shift mechanisms; High viscosity gear lubricant is a heavier oil designed to withstand the shock loading of high-performance engines or units subjected to severe duty use. Always use a gear lubricant of the type specified by the unit's manufacturer.

Grease

Greases are graded by the National Lubricating Grease Institute (NLGI). Greases are graded by number according to the consistency of the grease; these ratings range from No. 000 to No. 6, with No. 6 being the most solid. A typical multipurpose grease is NLGI No. 2 (**Figure 14**). For specific applications, equipment manufacturers may require grease with an additive such as molybdenum disulfide (MOS^2).

GASKET SEALANT

Gasket sealant is used instead of pre-formed gaskets on some applications, or as a gasket dressing on others. Two types of gasket sealant are commonly used: room temperature vulcanizing (RTV) and anaerobic. Because these two materials have different sealing properties, they cannot be used interchangeably.

RTV Sealant

This is a silicone gel supplied in tubes (**Figure 15**). Moisture in the air causes RTV to cure. Always place the cap on the tube as soon as possible when using RTV. RTV has a shelf life of one year and will not cure properly when the shelf life has expired. Check the expiration date

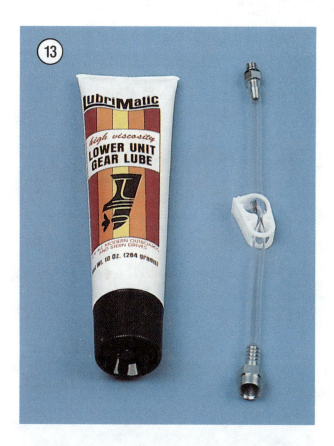

GENERAL INFORMATION

on RTV tubes before using and keep partially used tubes tightly sealed. RTV sealant can generally fill gaps up to 1/4 in. (6.3 mm) and works well on slightly flexible surfaces.

Applying RTV Sealant

Clean all gasket residue from mating surfaces. Surfaces should be clean and free of oil and dirt. Remove all RTV gasket material from blind attaching holes because it can create a "hydraulic" effect and affect bolt torque.

Apply RTV sealant in a continuous bead 2-3 mm (0.08-0.12 in.) thick. Circle all mounting holes unless otherwise specified. Torque mating parts within 10 minutes after application.

Anaerobic Sealant

This is a gel supplied in tubes (**Figure 16**). It cures only in the absence of air, as when squeezed tightly between two machined mating surfaces. For this reason, it will not spoil if the cap is left off the tube. It should not be used if one mating surface is flexible. Anaerobic sealant is able to fill gaps up to 0.030 in. (0.8 mm) and generally works best on rigid, machined flanges or surfaces.

Applying Anaerobic Sealant

Clean all gasket residue from mating surfaces. Surfaces must be clean and free of oil and dirt. Remove all gasket material from blind attaching holes, as it can cause a "hydraulic" effect and affect bolt torque.

Apply anaerobic sealant in a 1 mm or less (0.04 in.) bead to one sealing surface. Circle all mounting holes. Torque mating parts within 15 minutes after application.

GALVANIC CORROSION

A chemical reaction occurs whenever two different types of metal are joined by an electrical conductor and immersed in an electrolyte. Electrons transfer from one metal to the other through the electrolyte and return through the conductor.

The hardware on a boat is made of many different types of metal. The boat hull acts as a conductor between the metals. Even if the hull is wooden or fiberglass, the slightest film of water (electrolyte) within the hull provides conductivity. This combination creates a good environment for electron flow (**Figure 17**). Unfortunately, this electron flow results in galvanic corrosion of the metal involved, causing one of the metals to be corroded or eaten away by the process. The amount of electron flow (and, therefore, the amount of corrosion) depends on several factors:

a. The types of metal involved.
b. The efficiency of the conductor.
c. The strength of the electrolyte.

Metals

The chemical composition of the metals used in marine equipment has a significant effect on the amount and speed of galvanic corrosion. Certain metals are more resistant to corrosion than others. These electrically negative metals are commonly called "noble;" they act as the cathode in any reaction. Metals that are more subject to corrosion are electrically positive; they act as the anode in a reaction. The more noble metals include titanium, 18-8 stainless steel and nickel. Less noble metals include zinc, aluminum and magnesium. Galvanic corrosion becomes more severe as the difference in electrical potential between the two metals increases.

In some cases, galvanic corrosion can occur within a single piece of metal. Common brass is a mixture of zinc and copper, and, when immersed in an electrolyte, the zinc portion of the mixture will corrode away as reaction occurs between the zinc and the copper particles.

Conductors

The hull of the boat often acts as the conductor between different types of metal. Marine equipment, such as an outboard motor or stern drive unit, can also act as the conductor. Large masses of metal, firmly connected together, are more efficient conductors than water. Rubber mountings and vinyl-based paint can act as insulators between pieces of metal.

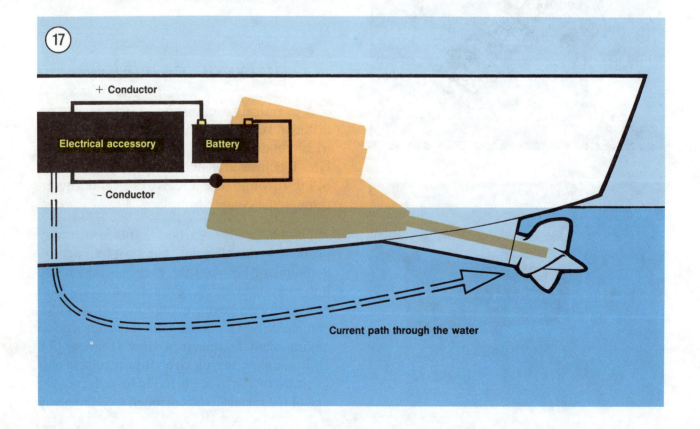

GENERAL INFORMATION

Electrolyte

The water in which a boat operates acts as the electrolyte for the galvanic corrosion process. The better a conductor the electrolyte is, the more severe and rapid the corrosion.

Cold, clean freshwater is the poorest electrolyte. As water temperature increases, its conductivity increases. Pollutants will increase conductivity; brackish or saltwater is also an efficient electrolyte. This is one of the reasons that most manufacturers recommend a freshwater flush for marine equipment after operation in saltwater, polluted or brackish water.

PROTECTION FROM GALVANIC CORROSION

Because of the environment in which marine equipment must operate, it is practically impossible to totally prevent galvanic corrosion. There are several ways by which the process can be slowed. After taking these precautions, the next step is to "fool" the process into occurring only where *you* want it to occur. This is the role of sacrificial anodes and impressed current systems.

Slowing Corrosion

Some simple precautions can help reduce the amount of corrosion taking place outside the hull. These are *not* a substitute for the corrosion protection methods discussed under *Sacrificial Anodes* and *Impressed Current Systems* in this chapter, but they can help these protection methods do their job.

Use fasteners of a metal more noble than the part they are fastening. If corrosion occurs, the larger equipment will suffer but the fastener will be protected. Because fasteners are usually very small in comparison to the equipment being fastened, the equipment can survive the loss of material. If the fastener were to corrode instead of the equipment, major problems could arise.

Keep all painted surfaces in good condition. If paint is scraped off and bare metal exposed, corrosion will rapidly increase. Use a vinyl- or plastic-based paint, which acts as an electrical insulator.

Be careful when using metal-based antifouling paints. These should not be applied to metal parts of the boat, outboard motor or stern drive unit or they will actually react with the equipment, causing corrosion between the equipment and the layer of paint. Organic-based paints are available for use on metal surfaces.

Where a corrosion protection device is used, remember that it must be immersed in the electrolyte along with the rest of the boat to have any effect. If you raise the power unit out of the water when the boat is docked, any anodes on the power unit will be removed from the corrosion cycle and will not protect the rest of the equipment that is still immersed. Also, such corrosion protection devices must not be painted because this would insulate them from the corrosion process.

Any change in the boat's equipment, such as the installation of a new stainless steel propeller, will change the electrical potential and could cause increased corrosion. Keep in mind that when you add new equipment or change materials, you should review your corrosion protection system to be sure it is up to the job.

Sacrificial Anodes

Anodes are usually made of zinc, a far from noble metal. Sacrificial anodes are specially designed to do nothing but corrode. Properly fastening such pieces to the boat will cause them to act as the anode in *any* galvanic reaction that occurs; any other metal present will act as the cathode and will not be damaged.

Anodes must be used properly to be effective. Simply fastening pieces of zinc to your boat in random locations won't do the job.

You must determine how much anode surface area is required to adequately protect the equipment's surface area. A good starting point is provided by Military Specification MIL-A-818001, which states that one square inch of new anode will protect either:

a. 800 square inches of freshly painted steel.
b. 250 square inches of bare steel or bare aluminum alloy.
c. 100 square inches of copper or copper alloy.

This rule is for a boat at rest. When underway, more anode area is required to protect the same equipment surface area.

The anode must be fastened so that it has good electrical contact with the metal to be protected. If possible, the anode can be attached directly to the other metal. If that is not possible, the entire network of metal parts in the boat should be electrically bonded together so that all pieces are protected.

Good quality anodes have inserts of some other metal around the fastener holes. Otherwise, the anode could erode away around the fastener. The anode can then become loose or even fall off, removing all protection.

Another Military Specification (MIL-A-18001) defines the type of alloy preferred that will corrode at a uniform rate without forming a crust that could reduce its efficiency after a time.

Impressed Current Systems

An impressed current system can be installed on any boat that has a battery. The system consists of an anode, a control box and a sensor. The anode in this system is coated with a very noble metal, such as platinum, so that it is almost corrosion-free and will last indefinitely. The sensor, under the boat's waterline, monitors the potential for corrosion. When it senses that corrosion could be occurring, it transmits this information to the control box.

The control box connects the boat's battery to the anode. When the sensor signals the need, the control box applies positive battery voltage to the anode. Current from the battery flows from the anode to all other metal parts of the boat, no matter how noble or non-noble these parts may be. This battery current takes the place of any galvanic current flow.

Only a very small amount of battery current is needed to counteract galvanic corrosion. Manufacturers estimate that it would take two or three months of constant use to drain a typical marine battery, assuming the battery is never recharged.

An impressed current system is more expensive to install than simple anodes but, considering its low maintenance requirements and the excellent protection it provides, the long-term cost may actually be lower.

PROPELLERS

The propeller is the final link between the boat's drive system and the water. A perfectly

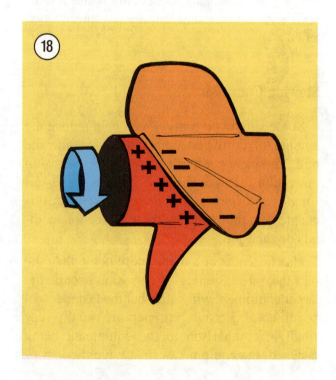

GENERAL INFORMATION

maintained engine and hull are useless if the propeller is the wrong type or has been allowed to deteriorate. Although propeller selection for a specific situation is beyond the scope of this book, the following information on propeller construction and design will allow you to discuss the subject intelligently with your marine dealer.

How a Propeller Works

As the curved blades of a propeller rotate through the water, a high-pressure area is created on one side of the blade and a low-pressure area exists on the other side of the blade (**Figure 18**). The propeller moves toward the low-pressure area, carrying the boat with it.

Propeller Parts

Although a propeller may be a one-piece unit, it is made up of several different parts (**Figure 19**). Variations in the design of these parts make different propellers suitable for different jobs.

The blade tip is the point on the blade farthest from the center of the propeller hub. The blade tip separates the leading edge from the trailing edge.

The leading edge is the edge of the blade nearest to the boat. During normal rotation, this is the area of the blade that first cuts through the water.

The trailing edge is the edge of the blade farthest from the boat.

The blade face is the surface of the blade that faces away from the boat. During normal rotation, high pressure exists on this side of the blade.

The blade back is the surface of the blade that faces toward the boat. During normal rotation, low pressure exists on this side of the blade.

The cup is a small curve or lip on the trailing edge of the blade.

The hub is the central portion of the propeller. It connects the blades to the propeller shaft (part of the boat's drive system). On some drive systems, engine exhaust is routed through the hub; in this case, the hub is made up of an outer and an inner portion, connected by ribs.

The diffuser ring is used on through-hub exhaust models to prevent exhaust gases from entering the blade area.

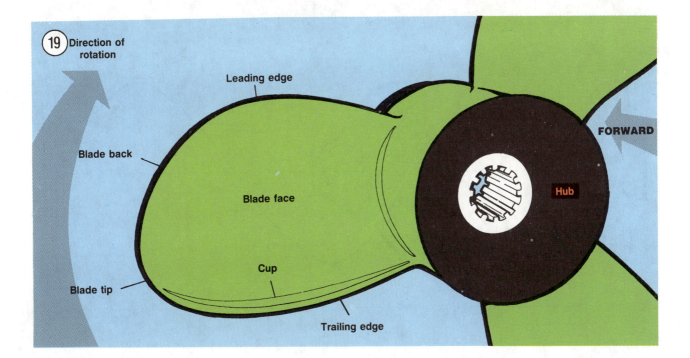

Propeller Design

Changes in length, angle, thickness and material of propeller parts make different propellers suitable for different situations.

Diameter

Propeller diameter is the distance from the center of the hub to the blade tip, multiplied by 2. That is, it is the diameter of the circle formed by the blade tips during propeller rotation (**Figure 20**).

Pitch and rake

Propeller pitch and rake describe the placement of the blade in relation to the hub (**Figure 21**).

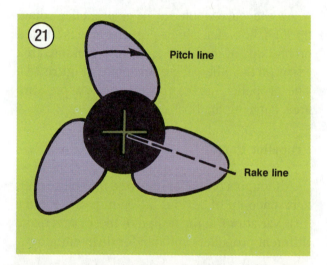

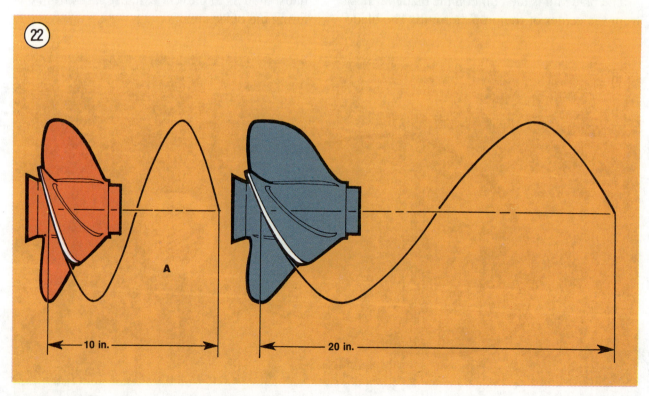

GENERAL INFORMATION

Pitch is expressed by the theoretical distance that the propeller would travel in one revolution. In A, **Figure 22**, the propeller would travel 10 inches in one revolution. In B, **Figure 22**, the propeller would travel 20 inches in one revolution. This distance is only theoretical; during actual operation, the propeller achieves about 80% of its rated travel.

Propeller blades can be constructed with constant pitch (**Figure 23**) or progressive pitch (**Figure 24**). Progressive pitch starts low at the leading edge and increases toward to trailing edge. The propeller pitch specification is the average of the pitch across the entire blade.

Blade rake is specified in degrees and is measured along a line from the center of the hub to the blade tip. A blade that is perpendicular to the hub (A, **Figure 25**) has 0° of rake. A blade that is angled from perpendicular (B, **Figure 25**) has a rake expressed by its difference from perpen-

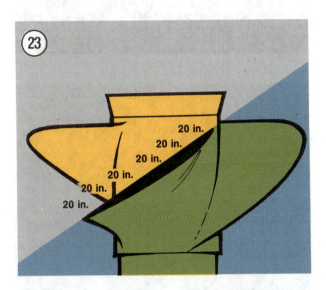

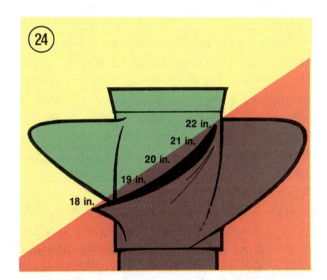

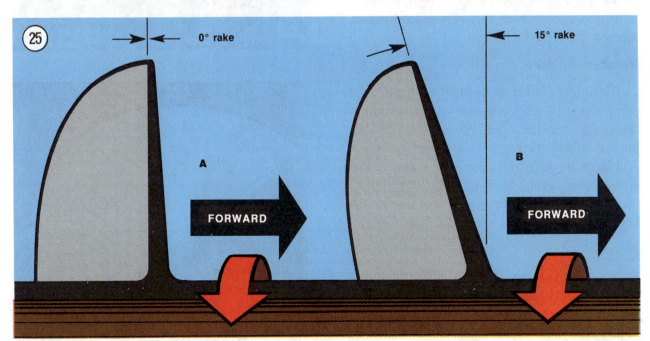

dicular. Most propellers have rakes ranging from 0-20°.

Blade thickness

Blade thickness is not uniform at all points along the blade. For efficiency, blades should be as thin as possible at all points while retaining enough strength to move the boat. Blades tend to be thicker where they meet the hub and thinner at the blade tip (**Figure 26**). This is to support the heavier loads at the hub section of the blade. This thickness is dependent on the strength of the material used.

When cut along a line from the leading edge to the trailing edge in the central portion of the blade (**Figure 27**), the propeller blade resembles an airplane wing. The blade face, where high pressure exists during normal rotation, is almost flat. The blade back, where low pressure exists during normal rotation, is curved, with the thinnest portions at the edges and the thickest portion at the center.

Propellers that run only partially submerged, as in racing applications, may have a wedge-shaped cross-section (**Figure 28**). The leading edge is very thin; the blade thickness increases toward the trailing edge, where it is the thickest. If a propeller such as this is run totally submerged, it is very inefficient.

Number of blades

The number of blades used on a propeller is a compromise between efficiency and vibration. A one-blade propeller would be the most efficient, but it would also create high levels of vibration. As blades are added, efficiency decreases, but so do vibration levels. Most propellers have three blades, representing the most practical trade-off between efficiency and vibration.

Material

Propeller materials are chosen for strength, corrosion resistance and economy. Stainless steel, aluminum and bronze are the most commonly used materials. Bronze is quite strong but

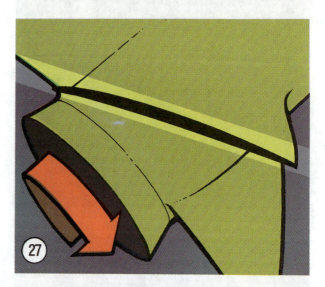

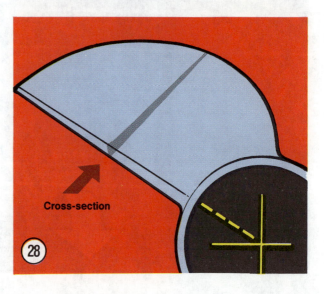

GENERAL INFORMATION

rather expensive. Stainless steel is more common than bronze because of its combination of strength and lower cost. Aluminum alloys are the least expensive but usually lack the strength of steel. Plastic propellers may be used in some low horsepower applications.

Direction of rotation

Propellers are made for both right-hand and left-hand rotation although right-hand is the most commonly used. When seen from behind the boat in forward motion, a right-hand propeller turns clockwise and a left-hand propeller turns counterclockwise. Off the boat, you can tell the difference by observing the angle of the blades (**Figure 29**). A right-hand propeller's blades slant from the upper left to the lower right; a left-hand propeller's blades are the opposite.

Cavitation and Ventilation

Cavitation and ventilation are *not* interchangeable terms; they refer to two distinct problems encountered during propeller operation.

To understand cavitation, you must first understand the relationship between pressure and the boiling point of water. At sea level, water will boil at 212° F. As pressure increases, such as within an engine's closed cooling system, the boiling point of water increases—it will boil at some temperature higher than 212° F. The opposite is also true. As pressure decreases, water will boil at a temperature lower than 212° F. If pressure drops low enough, water will boil at typical ambient temperatures of 50-60° F.

We have said that, during normal propeller operation, low-pressure exists on the blade back. Normally, the pressure does not drop low enough for boiling to occur. However, poor blade design

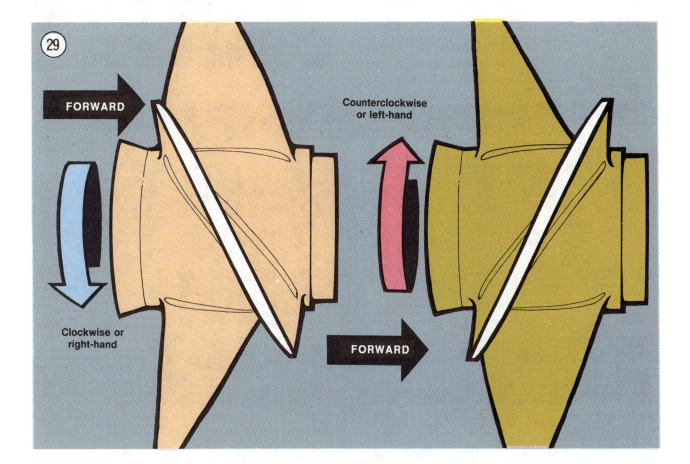

or selection, or blade damage can cause an unusual pressure drop on a small area of the blade (**Figure 30**). Boiling can occur in this small area. As the water boils, air bubbles form. As the boiling water passes to a higher pressure area of the blade, the boiling stops and the bubbles collapse. The collapsing bubbles release enough energy to erode the surface of the blade.

This entire process of pressure drop, boiling and bubble collapse is called "cavitation." The damage caused by the collapsing bubbles is called a "cavitation burn." It is important to remember that cavitation is caused by a decrease in pressure, *not* an increase in temperature.

Ventilation is not as complex a process as cavitation. Ventilation refers to air entering the blade area, either from above the surface of the water or from a through-hub exhaust system. As the blades meet the air, the propeller momentarily over-revs, losing most of its thrust. An added complication is that as the propeller over-revs, pressure on the blade back decreases and massive cavitation can occur.

Most pieces of marine equipment have a plate above the propeller area designed to keep surface air from entering the blade area (**Figure 31**). This plate is correctly called an "antiventilation plate," although you will often *see* it called an "anticavitation plate." Through hub exhaust systems also have specially designed hubs to keep exhaust gases from entering the blade area.

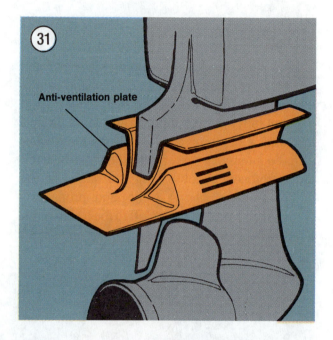

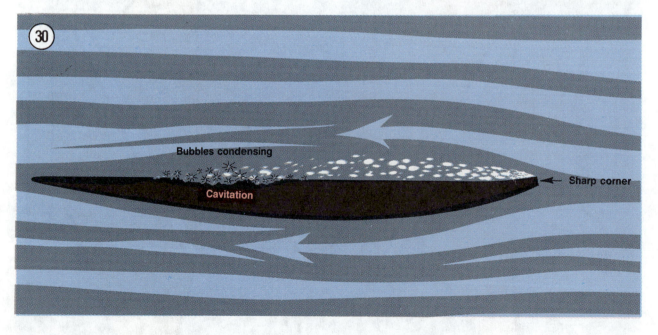

Chapter Two

Tools and Techniques

This chapter describes the common tools required for marine equipment repairs and troubleshooting. Techniques that will make your work easier and more effective are also described. Some of the procedures in this book require special skills or expertise; in some cases, you are better off entrusting the job to a dealer or qualified specialist.

SAFETY FIRST

Professional mechanics can work for years and never suffer a serious injury. If you follow a few rules of common sense and safety, you too can enjoy many safe hours servicing your marine equipment. If you ignore these rules, you can hurt yourself or damage the equipment.

1. Never use gasoline as a cleaning solvent.
2. Never smoke or use a torch near flammable liquids, such as cleaning solvent. If you are working in your home garage, remember that your home gas appliances have pilot lights.
3. Never smoke or use a torch in an area where batteries are being charged. Highly explosive hydrogen gas is formed during the charging process.
4. Use the proper size wrenches to avoid damage to fasteners and injury to yourself.
5. When loosening a tight or stuck fastener, think of what would happen if the wrench should slip. Protect yourself accordingly.
6. Keep your work area clean, uncluttered and well lighted.
7. Wear safety goggles during all operations involving drilling, grinding or the use of a cold chisel.
8. Never use worn tools.
9. Keep a Coast Guard approved fire extinguisher handy. Be sure it is rated for gasoline (Class B) and electrical (Class C) fires.

BASIC HAND TOOLS

A number of tools are required to maintain marine equipment. You may already have some of these tools for home or car repairs. There are also tools made especially for marine equipment repairs; these you will have to purchase. In any case, a wide variety of quality tools will make repairs easier and more effective.

Keep your tools clean and in a tool box. Keep them organized with the sockets and related drives together, the open end and box wrenches together, etc. After using a tool, wipe off dirt and grease with a clean cloth and place the tool in its correct place.

The following tools are required to perform virtually any repair job. Each tool is described and the recommended size given for starting a tool collection. Additional tools and some duplications may be added as you become more familiar with the equipment. You may need all standard U.S. size tools, all metric size tools or a mixture of both.

Screwdrivers

The screwdriver is a very basic tool, but if used improperly, it will do more damage than good. The slot on a screw has a definite dimension and shape. A screwdriver must be selected to conform with that shape. Use a small screwdriver for small screws and a large one for large screws or the screw head will be damaged.

Two types of screwdriver are commonly required: a common (flat-blade) screwdriver (**Figure 1**) and Phillips screwdrivers (**Figure 2**).

Screwdrivers are available in sets, which often include an assortment of common and Phillips blades. If you buy them individually, buy at least the following:

a. Common screwdriver—5/16 × 6 in. blade.
b. Common screwdriver—3/8 × 12 in. blade.
c. Phillips screwdriver—size 2 tip, 6 in. blade.

Use screwdrivers only for driving screws. Never use a screwdriver for prying or chiseling. Do not try to remove a Phillips or Allen head screw with a common screwdriver; you can damage the head so that the proper tool will be unable to remove it.

Keep screwdrivers in the proper condition and they will last longer and perform better. Always keep the tip of a common screwdriver in good condition. **Figure 3** shows how to grind the tip to the proper shape if it becomes damaged. Note the parallel sides of the tip.

Pliers

Pliers come in a wide range of types and sizes. Pliers are useful for cutting, bending and crimping. They should never be used to cut hardened objects or to turn bolts or nuts. **Figure 4** shows several types of pliers.

Each type of pliers has a specialized function. General purpose pliers are used mainly for holding things and for bending. Locking pliers are used as pliers or to hold objects very tightly, like a vise. Needlenose pliers are used to hold or bend small objects. Adjustable or slip-joint pliers can

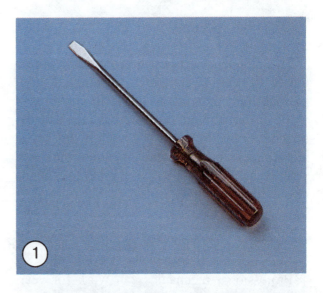

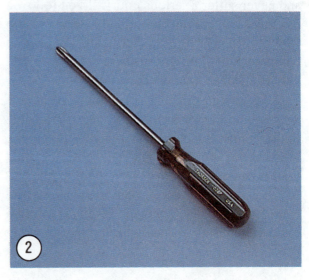

TOOLS AND TECHNIQUES   23

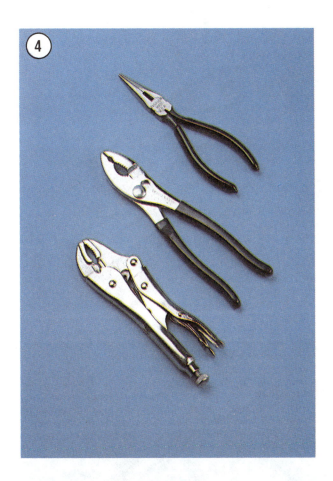

be adjusted to hold various sizes of objects; the jaws remain parallel to grip around objects such as pipe or tubing. There are many more types of pliers. The ones described here are the most commonly used.

Box and Open-end Wrenches

Box and open-end wrenches are available in sets or separately in a variety of sizes. See **Figure 5** and **Figure 6**. The number stamped near the end refers to the distance between two parallel flats on the hex head bolt or nut.

Box wrenches are usually superior to open-end wrenches. An open-end wrench grips the nut on only two flats. Unless it fits well, it may slip and round off the points on the nut. The box wrench grips all 6 flats. Both 6-point and 12-point openings on box wrenches are available. The 6-point gives superior holding power; the 12-point allows a shorter swing.

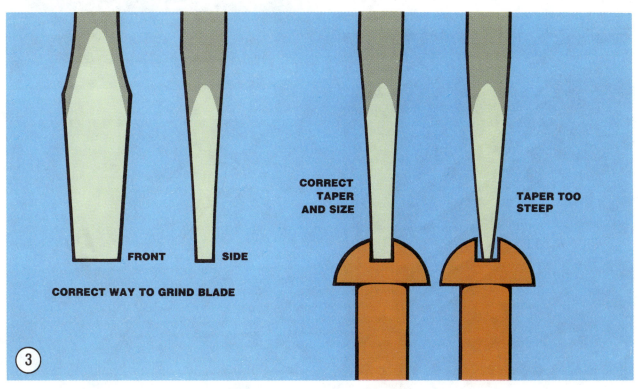

CHAPTER TWO

Combination wrenches, which are open on one side and boxed on the other, are also available. Both ends are the same size.

Adjustable Wrenches

An adjustable wrench can be adjusted to fit nearly any nut or bolt head. See **Figure 7**. However, it can loosen and slip, causing damage to the nut and maybe to your knuckles. Use an adjustable wrench only when other wrenches are not available.

Adjustable wrenches come in sizes ranging from 4-18 in. overall. A 6 or 8 in. wrench is recommended as an all-purpose wrench.

Socket Wrenches

This type is undoubtedly the fastest, safest and most convenient to use. See **Figure 8**. Sockets, which attach to a suitable handle, are available with 6-point or 12-point openings and use 1/4, 3/8 and 3/4 inch drives. The drive size indicates

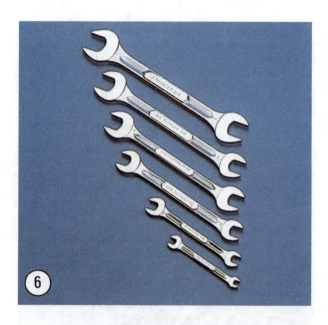

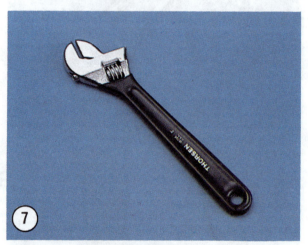

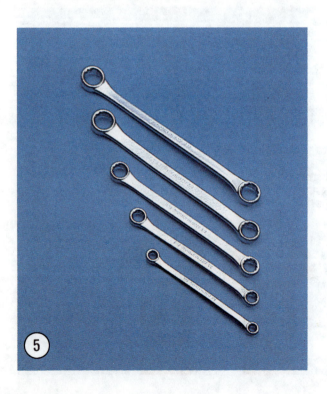

TOOLS AND TECHNIQUES

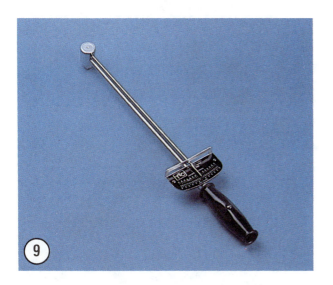

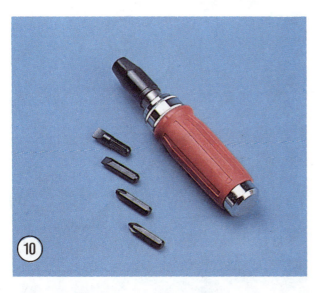

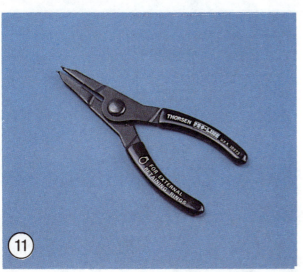

the size of the square hole that mates with the ratchet or flex handle.

Torque Wrench

A torque wrench (**Figure 9**) is used with a socket to measure how tight a nut or bolt is installed. They come in a wide price range and with either 3/8 or 1/2 in. square drive. The drive size indicates the size of the square drive that mates with the socket. Purchase one that measures up to 150 ft.-lb. (203 N•m).

Impact Driver

This tool (**Figure 10**) makes removal of tight fasteners easy and eliminates damage to bolts and screw slots. Impact drivers and interchangeable bits are available at most large hardware and auto parts stores.

Circlip Pliers

Circlip pliers (sometimes referred to as snap-ring pliers) are necessary to remove circlips. See **Figure 11**. Circlip pliers usually come with several different size tips; many designs can be switched from internal type to external type.

Hammers

The correct hammer is necessary for repairs. Use only a hammer with a face (or head) of rubber or plastic or the soft-faced type that is filled with buckshot (**Figure 12**). These are sometimes necessary in engine tear-downs. *Never* use a metal-faced hammer as severe damage will result in most cases. You can always produce the same amount of force with a soft-faced hammer.

Feeler Gauge

This tool has either flat or wire measuring gauges (**Figure 13**). Wire gauges are used to measure spark plug gap; flat gauges are used for all other measurements. A non-magnetic (brass) gauge may be specified when working around magnetized parts.

Other Special Tools

Some procedures require special tools; these are identified in the appropriate chapter. Unless otherwise specified, the part number used in this book to identify a special tool is the marine equipment manufacturer's part number.

Special tools can usually be purchased through your marine equipment dealer. Some can be made locally by a machinist, often at a much lower price. You may find certain special tools at tool rental dealers. Don't use makeshift tools if you can't locate the correct special tool; you will probably cause more damage than good.

TEST EQUIPMENT

Multimeter

This instrument (**Figure 14**) is invaluable for electrical system troubleshooting and service. It combines a voltmeter, an ohmmeter and an ammeter into one unit, so it is often called a VOM.

Two types of multimeter are available, analog and digital. Analog meters have a moving needle with marked bands indicating the volt, ohm and amperage scales. The digital meter (DVOM) is ideally suited for troubleshooting because it is easy to read, more accurate than analog, contains internal overload protection, is auto-ranging (analog meters must be recalibrated each time the scale is changed) and has automatic polarity compensation.

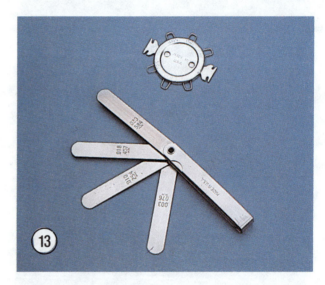

TOOLS AND TECHNIQUES

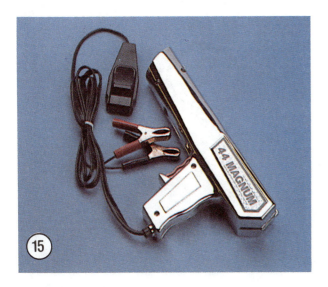

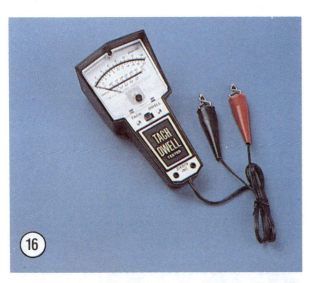

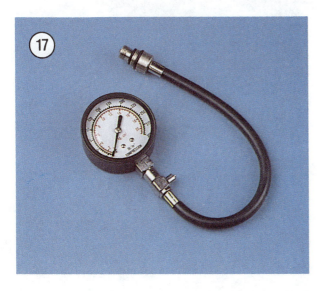

Strobe Timing Light

This instrument is necessary for dynamic tuning (setting ignition timing while the engine is running). By flashing a light at the precise instant the spark plug fires, the position of the timing mark can be seen. The flashing light makes a moving mark appear to stand still opposite a stationary mark.

Suitable lights range from inexpensive neon bulb types to powerful xenon strobe lights. See **Figure 15**. A light with an inductive pickup is best because it eliminates any possible damage to ignition wiring.

Tachometer/Dwell Meter

A portable tachometer is necessary for tuning. See **Figure 16**. Ignition timing and carburetor adjustments must be performed at the specified idle speed. The best instrument for this purpose is one with a low range of 0-1000 or 0-2000 rpm and a high range of 0-6000 rpm. Extended range (0-6000 or 0-8000 rpm) instruments lack accuracy at lower speeds. The instrument should be capable of detecting changes of 25 rpm on the low range.

A dwell meter is often combined with a tachometer. Dwell meters are used with breaker point ignition systems to measure the amount of time the points remain closed during engine operation.

Compression Gauge

This tool (**Figure 17**) measures the amount of pressure present in the engine's combustion chamber during the compression stroke. This indicates general engine condition. Compression readings can be interpreted along with vacuum gauge readings to pinpoint specific engine mechanical problems.

The easiest type to use has screw-in adapters that fit into the spark plug holes. Press-in rubber-tipped types are also available.

Vacuum Gauge

The vacuum gauge (**Figure 18**) measures the intake manifold vacuum created by the engine's intake stroke. Manifold and valve problems (on 4-stroke engines) can be identified by interpreting the readings. When combined with compression gauge readings, other engine problems can be diagnosed.

Some vacuum gauges can also be used as fuel pressure gauges to trace fuel system problems.

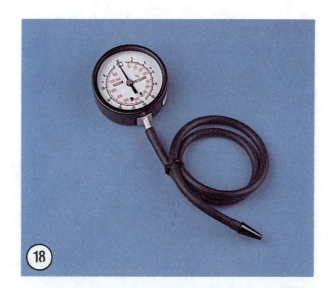

Hydrometer

Battery electrolyte specific gravity is measured with a hydrometer (**Figure 19**). The specific gravity of the electrolyte indicates the battery's state of charge. The best type has automatic temperature compensation; otherwise, you must calculate the compensation yourself.

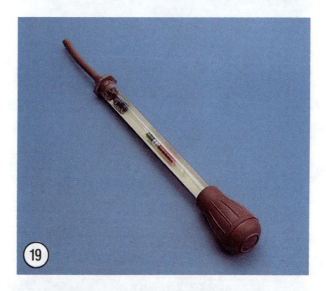

Precision Measuring Tools

Various tools are needed to make precision measurements. A dial indicator (**Figure 20**), for example, is used to determine run-out of rotating parts and end play of parts assemblies. A dial indicator can also be used to precisely measure piston position in relation to top dead center; some engines require this measurement for ignition timing adjustment.

Vernier calipers (**Figure 21**) and micrometers (**Figure 22**) are other precision measuring tools used to determine the size of parts (such as piston diameter).

Precision measuring equipment must be stored, handled and used carefully or it will not remain accurate.

SERVICE HINTS

Most of the service procedures covered in this manual are straightforward and can be performed by anyone reasonably handy with tools.

TOOLS AND TECHNIQUES

It is suggested, however, that you consider your own skills and toolbox carefully before attempting any operation involving major disassembly of the engine or gearcase.

Some operations, for example, require the use of a press. It would be wiser to have these performed by a shop equipped for such work, rather than trying to do the job yourself with makeshift equipment. Other procedures require precise measurements. Unless you have the skills and equipment required, it would be better to have a qualified repair shop make the measurements for you.

Preparation for Disassembly

Repairs go much faster and easier if the equipment is clean before you begin work. There are special cleaners, such as Gunk or Bel-Ray Degreaser, for washing the engine and related parts. Just spray or brush on the cleaning solution, let it stand, then rinse away with a garden hose. Clean all oily or greasy parts with cleaning solvent as you remove them.

> *WARNING*
> *Never use gasoline as a cleaning agent. It presents an extreme fire hazard. Be sure to work in a well-ventilated area when using cleaning solvent. Keep a Coast Guard approved fire extinguisher, rated for gasoline fires, handy in any case.*

Much of the labor charged for repairs made by dealers is for the removal and disassembly of other parts to reach the defective unit. It is frequently possible to perform the preliminary operations yourself and then take the defective unit in to the dealer for repair.

If you decide to tackle the job yourself, read the entire section in this manual that pertains to it, making sure you have identified the proper one. Study the illustrations and text until you have a good idea of what is involved in completing the job satisfactorily. If special tools or replacement parts are required, make arrangements to get them before you start. It is frustrating and time-consuming to get partly into a job and then be unable to complete it.

Disassembly Precautions

During disassembly of parts, keep a few general precautions in mind. Force is rarely needed to get things apart. If parts are a tight fit, such as

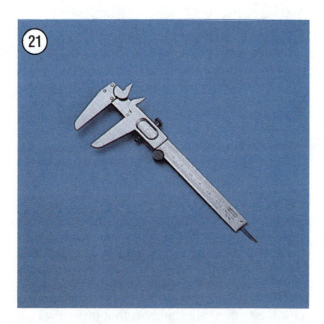

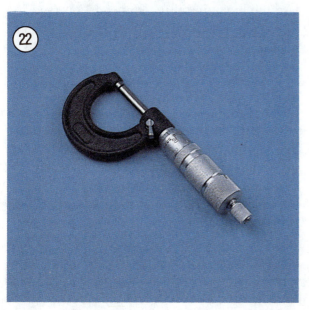

a bearing in a case, there is usually a tool designed to separate them. Never use a screwdriver to pry apart parts with machined surfaces (such as cylinder heads and crankcases). You will mar the surfaces and end up with leaks.

Make diagrams (or take an instant picture) wherever similar-appearing parts are found. For example, head and crankcase bolts are often not the same length. You may think you can remember where everything came from, but mistakes are costly. There is also the possibility you may be sidetracked and not return to work for days or even weeks. In the interval, carefully laid out parts may have been disturbed.

Cover all openings after removing parts to keep small parts, dirt or other contamination from entering.

Tag all similar internal parts for location and direction. All internal components should be reinstalled in the same location and direction from which removed. Record the number and thickness of any shims as they are removed. Small parts, such as bolts, can be identified by placing them in plastic sandwich bags. Seal and label them with masking tape.

Wiring should be tagged with masking tape and marked as each wire is removed. Again, do not rely on memory alone.

Protect finished surfaces from physical damage or corrosion. Keep gasoline off painted surfaces.

Assembly Precautions

No parts, except those assembled with a press fit, require unusual force during assembly. If a part is hard to remove or install, find out why before proceeding.

When assembling two parts, start all fasteners, then tighten evenly in an alternating or crossing pattern if no specific tightening sequence is given.

When assembling parts, be sure all shims and washers are installed exactly as they came out.

Whenever a rotating part butts against a stationary part, look for a shim or washer. Use new gaskets if there is any doubt about the condition of the old ones. Unless otherwise specified, a thin coat of oil on gaskets may help them seal effectively.

Heavy grease can be used to hold small parts in place if they tend to fall out during assembly. However, keep grease and oil away from electrical components.

High spots may be sanded off a piston with sandpaper, but fine emery cloth and oil will do a much more professional job.

Carbon can be removed from the cylinder head, the piston crown and the exhaust port with a dull screwdriver. *Do not* scratch either surface. Wipe off the surface with a clean cloth when finished.

The carburetor is best cleaned by disassembling it and soaking the parts in a commercial carburetor cleaner. Never soak gaskets and rubber parts in these cleaners. Never use wire to clean out jets and air passages; they are easily damaged. Use compressed air to blow out the carburetor *after* the float has been removed.

Take your time and do the job right. Do not forget that the break-in procedure on a newly rebuilt engine is the same as that of a new one. Use the break-in oil recommendations and follow other instructions given in your owner's manual.

SPECIAL TIPS

Because of the extreme demands placed on marine equipment, several points should be kept in mind when performing service and repair. The following items are general suggestions that may improve the overall life of the machine and help avoid costly failures.

1. Unless otherwise specified, use a locking compound, such as Loctite Threadlocker, on all bolts and nuts, even if they are secured with lockwashers. Be sure to use the specified grade

TOOLS AND TECHNIQUES

of thread locking compound. A screw or bolt lost from an engine cover or bearing retainer could easily cause serious and expensive damage before its loss is noticed.

When applying thread locking compound, use a small amount. If too much is used, it can work its way down the threads and stick parts together that were not meant to be stuck together.

Keep a tube of thread locking compound in your tool box; when used properly, it is cheap insurance.

2. Use a hammer-driven impact tool to remove and install screws and bolts. These tools help prevent the rounding off of bolt heads and screw slots and ensure a tight installation.

3. When straightening the fold-over type lockwasher, use a wide-blade chisel, such as an old and dull wood chisel. Such a tool provides a better purchase on the folded tab, making straightening easier.

4. When installing the fold-over type lockwasher, always use a new washer if possible. If a new washer is not available, always fold over a part of the washer that has not been previously folded. Reusing the same fold may cause the washer to break, resulting in the loss of its locking ability and a loose piece of metal adrift in the engine.

When folding the washer, start the fold with a screwdriver and finish it with a pair of pliers. If a punch is used to make the fold, the fold may be too sharp, thereby increasing the chances of the washer breaking under stress.

These washers are relatively inexpensive and it is suggested that you keep several of each size in your tool box for repairs.

5. When replacing missing or broken fasteners (bolts, nuts and screws), always use authorized replacement parts. They are specially hardened for each application. The wrong 50-cent bolt could easily cause serious and expensive damage.

6. When installing gaskets, always use authorized replacement gaskets *without* sealer, unless designated. Many gaskets are designed to swell when they come in contact with oil. Gasket sealer will prevent the gaskets from swelling as intended and can result in oil leaks. Authorized replacement gaskets are cut from material of the precise thickness needed. Installation of a too thick or too thin gasket in a critical area could cause equipment damage.

MECHANIC'S TECHNIQUES

Removing Frozen Fasteners

When a fastener rusts and cannot be removed, several methods may be used to loosen it. First, apply penetrating oil, such as Liquid Wrench or WD-40 (available at any hardware or auto supply store). Apply it liberally and allow it penetrate for 10-15 minutes. Tap the fastener several times with a small hammer; do not hit it hard enough to cause damage. Reapply the penetrating oil if necessary.

For frozen screws, apply penetrating oil as described, then insert a screwdriver in the slot and tap the top of the screwdriver with a hammer. This loosens the rust so the screw can be removed in the normal way. If the screw head is too chewed up to use a screwdriver, grip the head with locking pliers and twist the screw out.

Avoid applying heat unless specifically instructed because it may melt, warp or remove the temper from parts.

Remedying Stripped Threads

Occasionally, threads are stripped through carelessness or impact damage. Often the threads can be cleaned up by running a tap (for internal threads on nuts) or die (for external threads on bolts) through threads. See **Figure 23**.

Removing Broken Screws or Bolts

When the head breaks off a screw or bolt, several methods are available for removing the remaining portion.

If a large portion of the remainder projects out, try gripping it with vise-grip pliers. If the projecting portion is too small, file it to fit a wrench or cut a slot in it to fit a screwdriver. See **Figure 24**.

If the head breaks off flush, use a screw extractor. To do this, centerpunch the remaining portion of the screw or bolt. Drill a small hole in the screw and tap the extractor into the hole. Back the screw out with a wrench on the extractor. See **Figure 25**.

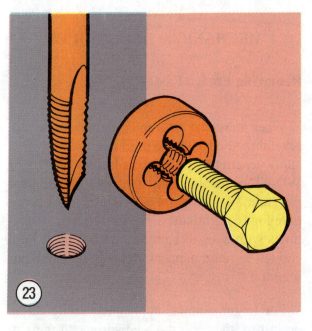

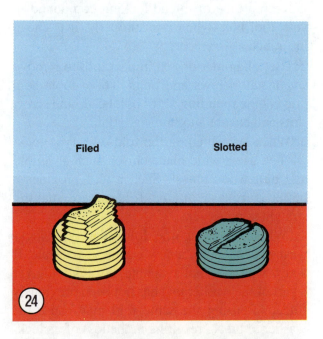

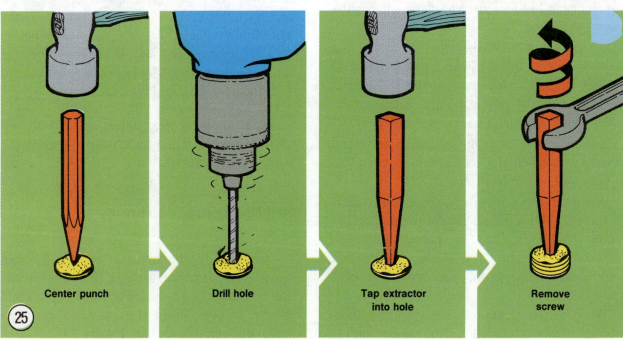

Chapter Three

Troubleshooting

The modern outboard engine is quite reliable when compared to earlier models. It provides impressive performance and better fuel economy than models produced just a few years ago.

The use of advanced electronic ignition control and precisely controlled fuel systems helps these engines perform at a top level.

As reliable as outboards have become, problems will eventually occur. This chapter provides the information and instructions to pinpoint the source of most problems. Troubleshooting procedures are used to determine the system that is likely at fault. Component testing procedures are used to determine which component of the system is likely at fault. You will be directed to the appropriate chapter for repair or replacement of the faulty component.

Refer to **Tables 1-19** for test specifications and other information. **Tables 1-19** are located at the end of this chapter.

TROUBLESHOOTING TEST EQUIPMENT

Most troubleshooting and test procedures can be performed with common test equipment. Commonly used test equipment includes the volt/ohm meter, ammeter, vacuum/pressure gauges, compression tester, and the gearcase pressure tester. This section provides instruction on the use of this equipment. To ensure safe and accurate test results, read and understand all test precautions and procedures before using any of the test equipment.

Many of the required tools are available from your local Honda outboard dealership. Most of the tools and equipment required for troubleshooting are available at automotive supply stores or from tool suppliers. A list of tool suppliers is included at the end of this section.

Volt/Ohm Meter

The modern outboard provides excellent performance, improved economy and smoother operation than earlier outboards. Advanced electronic engine control systems are responsible for many of these improvements. The expanded use of advanced electronic control systems has resulted in the increased use of the volt/ohm meter when troubleshooting your outboard. A thorough understanding of the proper use of the volt/ohm meter is essential for accurate testing.

Use a volt/ohm meter to read voltage, resistance, amperage and to perform other test functions. Always refer to the applicable test procedures for specific test procedures as listed in this chapter.

CHAPTER THREE

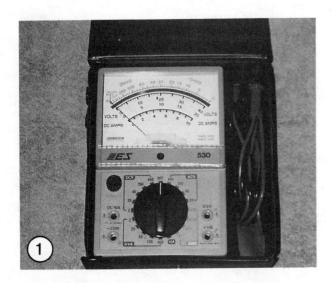

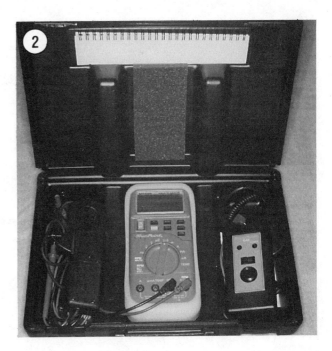

WARNING
Use caution when working with electrical meters and test leads. Never touch the conductive (metal) portion of the test lead during a voltage test. Never test electrical components while standing in water or when the components are wet. High voltage may be present in any electrical component of the engine. An electrical shock can result in severe injury or death.

Types of Volt/Ohm Meters

Two basic types of volt/ohm meters are commonly used. The most common is the *analog* volt/ohm meter (**Figure 1**). The other regularly used type is the *digital* volt/ohm meter (**Figure 2**). For most tests, either type of meter may be used. In some instances, a particular type is required to ensure accurate test results. Use either type unless a specific type is indicated in the instructions. Review the following information for the selected type prior to performing tests.

Analog Volt/Ohm Meter

The main parts of the *analog volt/ohm meter* are the meter face (A, **Figure 3**), indicator or needle (B, **Figure 3**), selector (C, **Figure 3**) and test leads (D, **Figure 3**).

The face of the meter provides a scale to read the measured values on the meter. Values are determined by reading the point to which the needle moves on the meter face. The needle is aligned with the 15 mark, indicating a value of 15 ohms in **Figure 4**. When the needle is positioned between markings or numbers on the meter face, the measured value

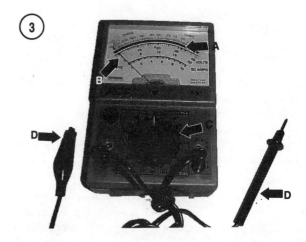

TROUBLESHOOTING

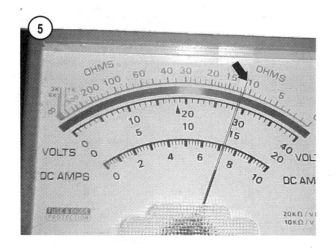

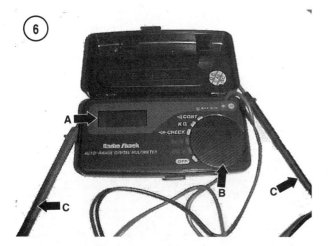

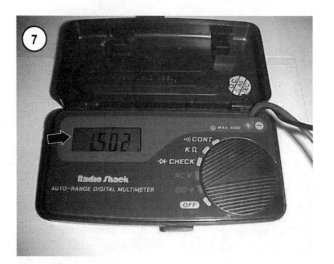

is between the value indicated with markings or numbers. The needle is positioned midway between the 11 and 12 markings in **Figure 5** indicating a value of 11.5 ohms.

NOTE
Variations in the meter face markings exist among the meters available. Always refer to the instructions provided with the meter for specific instructions.

Most *analog volt/ohm meters* require that a function and scale or range be selected prior to performing any testing. Refer to *Function Selection* in this chapter to determine the correct function to select. Refer to *Scale or Range Selection* in this chapter to determine the correct scale to select.

Digital Volt/Ohm Meter

The main parts of a *digital volt/ohm meter* are the display screen, (A, **Figure 6**) selector (B, **Figure 6**) and test leads (C, **Figure 6**).

The value measured by the digital meter is displayed on the screen (**Figure 7**), making it easier to use than an analog meter.

Be aware that some testing cannot be accurately performed using a digital volt/ohm meter. In these cases an analog volt/ohm meter must be used. Test procedures will indicate when a specific type of meter is required.

Select the proper function before performing any test. Most digital volt/ohm meters are *auto scaling* and you do not need to select the proper scale or range manually. Refer to *Function Selection* in this chapter to determine the correct function to select. Refer to *Scale or Range Selection* in this chapter to determine the correct scale or range to select.

Test lead connection

Always identify the test lead polarity prior to performing any test. The negative (–) meter lead is usually black and the positive (+) meter lead is usually red.

The positive (+) and negative (–) lead connections are marked on the meter (**Figure 8**) to identify the correct polarity of the test leads. The leads must be correctly connected to the meter and the test connections to ensure correct polarity and accurate test results. Test lead connection points and polarity are listed in all procedures and specifications.

CAUTION
Make certain that all test lead connection points are clean prior to performing any test. Dirty or corroded leads and/or connections will lead to inaccurate test results.

Volt/Ohm Meter Functions

A common volt/ohm meter will measure DC voltage, AC voltage, resistance (ohms) and current (amperage). Some meters also measure peak voltage. Refer to the following sections for a description for each meter function.

Voltage Measurement

Voltage is best described as the pressure of the electrical current in a wire. It can be compared to the water pressure present in a garden hose when the water valve is turned on. Electrical pressure, or voltage, can be measured using a voltmeter. Both DC (direct current) and AC (alternating current) can be measured with most meters.

DC voltage

Direct current (DC) describes electrical current that is flowing in one direction in a wire or circuit.

When performing a test using the DC volts function, the positive (+) test lead is usually connected to a specified terminal or other point on the engine. The negative (–) test lead is usually connected to an engine ground (engine block).

WARNING
A battery emits explosive hydrogen gas, especially when charging. Use extreme caution when working around the battery. Never smoke or allow sparks to occur near the battery.

Use a voltmeter to check the battery voltage. Connect the positive test lead to the positive battery terminal and the negative test lead to the negative battery terminal (**Figure 9**).

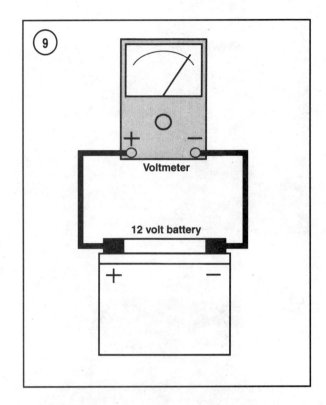

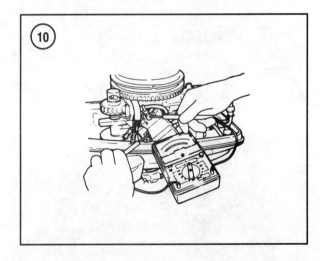

AC voltage

Alternating current (AC) is current that alternates directions in the wire or circuit. A common test using the AC volts function of the multimeter is checking charge coil output. To check charge coil output, connect the positive test lead to one charge coil wire and the negative test lead to a good engine ground (**Figure 10**). In most cases, AC voltage can be checked without removing existing connections. AC measurements are typically nec-

TROUBLESHOOTING

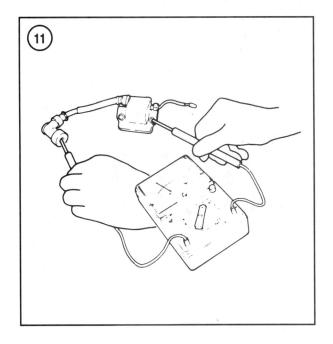

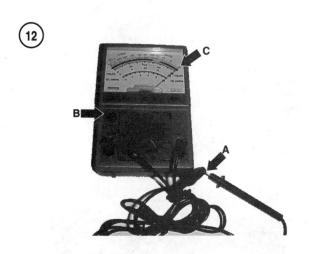

essary when troubleshooting the charging and ignition systems on your outboard motor.

Resistance

Resistance is the measurement of resistance to electrical current flow in a circuit. The length of the wire, size of the wire and the type of material from which the wire is constructed can all affect current flow. With a given water pressure, a certain volume of water will flow from a garden hose in a set amount of time. Using the same water pressure but with a longer hose or hose with a smaller diameter, less water would flow from the garden hose in the set amount of time. This occurs because the longer hose or smaller diameter hose provides resistance to water flow. To flow the same amount of water through the longer or smaller diameter hose requires a higher water pressure from the source (water valve).

The longer the wire or circuit, the greater the resistance to electrical current flow. Other factors can affect resistance to electric current flow. The size and type of material used in the wire or circuit, temperature of the wire or circuit and the presence of dirt or other contaminants on the contacts can effect electrical current flow.

Higher temperatures will generally increase the measured resistance. In many cases the listed specifications are at a given temperature. Measure the resistance at normal room temperature unless a given temperature is listed.

The unit used to measure resistance to current flow is the *ohm*. The higher the resistance the greater the ohms reading; the lower the resistance, the lower the ohms reading.

In most cases, all leads must be disconnected from the circuit when measuring resistance. This is necessary to isolate the selected circuit from all other circuits.

To measure the resistance of a wire or circuit, connect the positive test lead to one end of the wire and the negative test lead to the other end (**Figure 11**). Polarity of the test leads is generally not important; however, some resistance tests require the correct test lead polarity.

Calibrating an Analog Ohmmeter

Always calibrate or zero an analog ohmmeter before performing any resistance test. Failure to calibrate the meter will likely result in an inaccurate resistance measurement.

1. Connect the ohmmeter test leads together (A, **Figure 12**).
2. Rotate the adjusting knob (B, **Figure 12**) until the indicator or needle is aligned with the zero mark on the meter face (C, **Figure 12**). Clean the test leads and plug terminals and replace the meter battery if you are unable to properly calibrate the meter.
3. During testing, do not move the adjusting knob unless the meter scale is changed. If a different scale is selected, calibrate the meter again.

Checking Internal Resistance (Digital Ohmmeter)

Check the internal resistance of a digital ohmmeter before performing a resistance test. Failure to check and compensate for the meter's internal resistance can result in an inaccurate resistance measurement.

1. Connect the meter test leads together (A, **Figure 13**).

2. Switch the meter ON and record the resistance indicated on the meter display (B, **Figure 13**).

3. Subtract this value (Step 2) from the resistance reading obtained during actual testing.

Ohmmeter Guidelines

Some specifications list continuity or no continuity as a test result. Refer to the following descriptions when performing ohmmeter tests.

Continuity or closed circuit

Current can flow through a wire or circuit if *continuity*

is present. A zero or very low (near zero) reading (**Figure 14**) indicates continuity. Continuity is commonly referred to as a closed circuit.

Some meters offer a continuity test feature (**Figure 15**) that provides an audible or visual signal if low resistance is present.

No continuity or open circuit (infinity)

No continuity is indicated by an infinity (∞) of very high reading (**Figure 16**). No continuity means that electricity cannot flow and is most often caused by a broken wire. This condition is also referred to as an open circuit.

Amperage

Amperage is the volume of electrical current flowing through a wire, circuit or component. An ammeter (**Figure 17**) is used to measure the current flow through an electrical circuit. Most multimeters are capable of measuring a small amount of current (approximately 10 amps maximum). To prevent damage, never exceed the capability of the meter.

A common amperage test is the starter motor current draw test (**Figure 17**). To perform this test, connect the positive test lead to the positive battery terminal and the negative test lead to the starter motor. This type of connection is referred to as a series connection.

DVA or Peak Voltage

Some meters are capable of reading DVA or peak volt pulses. Many ignition system components produce short AC voltage pulses. A conventional multimeter is incapa-

ble of accurately measuring these short-duration electrical pulses. A peak-reading voltmeter has special circuits that allow the meter to capture the maximum voltage produced

TROUBLESHOOTING

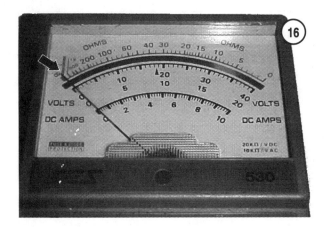

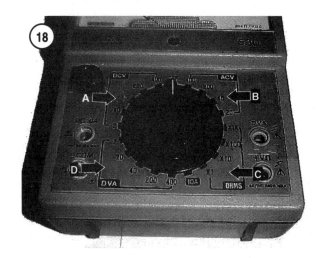

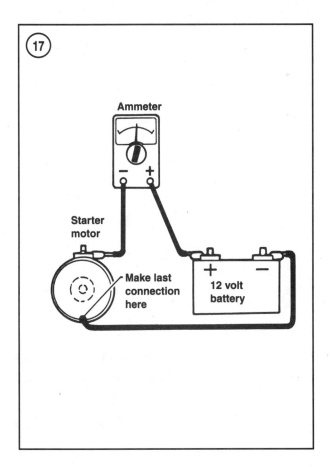

during these short duration pulses and display the voltage as DVA or peak volts.

Function Selection

Use the selector to choose volts, ohms, amperage or other functions the meter is capable of measuring. Also, select the correct scale to use for the specific test. Although most meters are equipped with a dial switch to select the desired function and range, the scales available vary among the different meters.

DC volts or DVC

Select the DC volts function (A, **Figure 18**) if DC, DCV or VDC is listed within the specification. This allows measurement of direct current voltage. Always follow procedures to ensure accurate test results. Turn the selector to the DC voltage section and align the knob with the desired scale or range.

AC volts or VAC

Select the AC volts function (B, **Figure 18**) if AC, ACV or VAC is listed within the specification. This allows measurement of alternating current voltage. Always follow procedures to ensure accurate test results.

Ohms or resistance

Select the ohms or resistance (res.) function (C, **Figure 18**) if either is listed in the specifications. This allows measurement of the resistance of the wire or circuit. Follow the test procedures closely to ensure accurate test results.

DVA or peak volts

Select the DVA or Peak V function (D, **Figure 18**) if they are listed in the specifications. This allows measurement of the peak voltage from a pulsating voltage source. Follow the test procedures closely to ensure accurate test results.

CHAPTER THREE

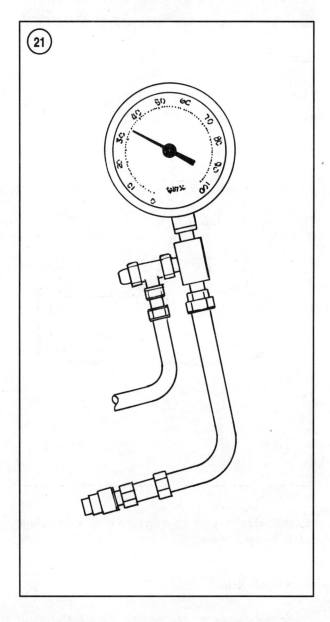

Range or scale selection

Accurate reading of the meter requires proper range or scale selection. The correct range lists a value consistent with the test specification.

Many variations exist from one meter to the next regarding the ranges on the selector. To determine the selection of the range or scale to use, refer to the tables at the end of this chapter. This table lists the preferred range and alternate ranges to use for various test specifications.

Abbreviations are used with many of the listed scales. When using the ohm function, a *K* is used to designate 1000 ohm increments. For example, if 10 K is displayed on the selector, it indicates it is the 10,000-ohm range or scale.

The range of voltage measurements is relatively small and abbreviations for voltage specifications are seldom used. In cases where the voltage specification lists a value less than one volt, the millivolt (Mv) abbreviation is used. A millivolt (Mv) is equal to 0.001 volt. A digital Volt/Ohm meter is required when measuring voltages in the millivolt range.

Diode testing

Diodes are electrical devices that perform like electrical check valves. They allow electrical current to flow easily in one direction and provide resistance if the current attempts to flow in the opposite direction.

To test a diode, select the R × 1 ohm or diode test function. Connect the ohmmeter to the diode and note the meter reading. Reverse the meter leads and again note the meter reading. A low (or zero) reading should be noted in one polarity and a high (infinity) reading should be noted with the leads reversed. If both readings are high or if both readings are low, the diode has failed and requires replacement.

TROUBLESHOOTING

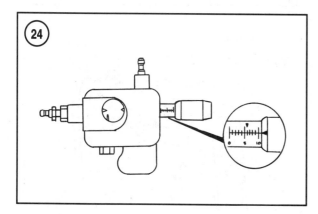

Vacuum/Pressure Gauges

Vacuum and pressure gauges (**Figure 19**) are used to test the fuel, lubrication, hydraulic and other engine systems. These gauges are available from most tool suppliers. Refer to the tools and techniques section of this manual for additional information.

A special vacuum gauge set (**Figure 20**) (Honda part No. 07LMJ-001000A) is used to check and calibrate the carburetors on multiple carburetor models. This type of gauge set is available from most tool suppliers.

Fuel injected models (models BF115A and BF130A) require a special gauge (**Figure 21**) (Honda part No. 7406-004000A) to measure the high-pressure fuel system. Specific instructions on the use of these gauges are provided in this chapter.

Compression Tester

A compression tester (**Figure 22**) measures the pressure that builds in the combustion chamber at a specified cranking speed. Compression testers are available at most automotive supply stores and tool suppliers. Use a gauge that is capable of reading pressure in the range of 0-16.0 kg/cm^2 (0-228.0 psi). Accurate measurements are essential to properly diagnose engine performance problems. Always use a good quality compression tester.

Gearcase Pressure Tester

Gearcase pressure testers (**Figure 23**) find the source of water or lubricant leakage from the gearcase and other components. These are considered specialty tools and are not generally available at automotive supply stores. They can be purchased through many tool suppliers. Specific instructions on the use of these testers are provided in this chapter.

Spark Gap Tester

Spark gap testers (**Figure 24**) are used to determine if spark is present at the spark plug lead connection. Spark gap testers are available from a variety of sources. Check with a tool supplier or automotive parts store. Some models have an adjustable spark gap setting (**Figure 24**) and are useful with models that require a minimum spark gap test.

TROUBLESHOOTING PREPARATION

Before troubleshooting the engine, always verify the model name, product identification number and the serial number. Repair and test procedures vary by model, horsepower and sometimes serial number. It is absolutely essential that the engine is correctly identified before testing or servicing the engine. Most test specifications are listed

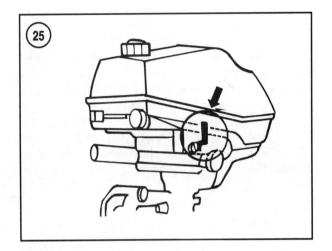

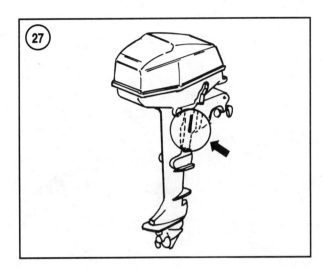

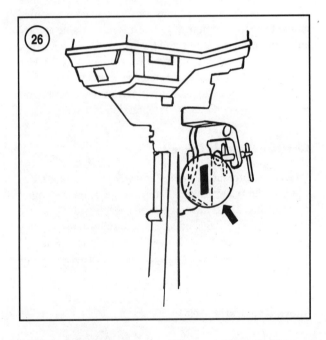

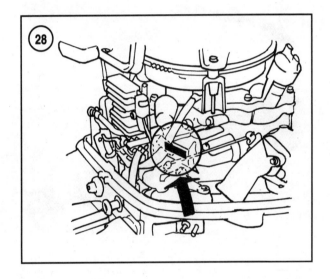

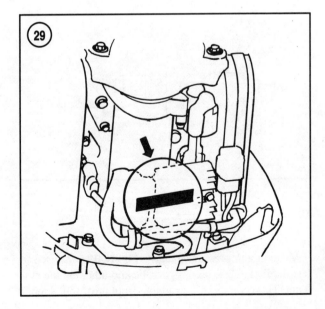

the tables at the end of this chapter. In most cases, the model and serial number are required to identify the proper specifications.

Serial Number Location

Refer to the engine serial number when selecting replacement parts locating the correct test and repair specifications. Some models have an additional serial number attached to the swivel housing/frame assembly. This number may be different from the engine serial number and is needed when selecting repair or maintenance parts for the swivel housing/gearcase assemblies. Always record both serial numbers (when applicable) and the product identification number if so equipped.

TROUBLESHOOTING

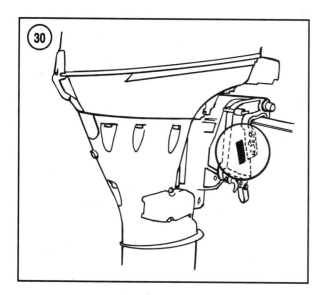

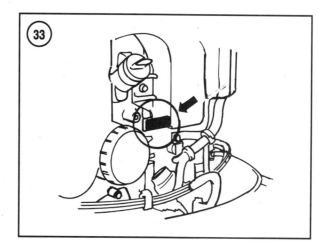

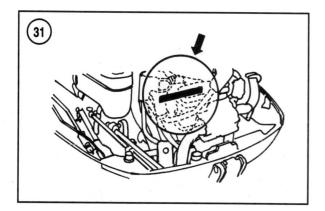

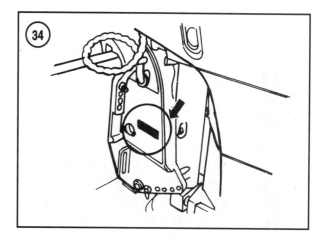

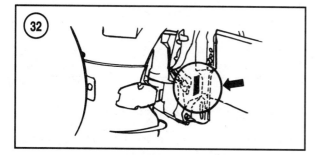

Serial number and product identification number locations vary widely among the models. Refer to the information provided below along with **Figures 25-34** to locate your engine serial and product identification number.

On two hp models BF20 and BF2A, the engine serial number is stamped into the lower port side of the cylinder block (**Figure 25**) and on the starboard side clamp bracket (**Figure 26**).

On five hp models BF50 and BF5A, the engine serial number is stamped into an identification plate mounted to the starboard side of the swivel housing (**Figure 27**).

On 7.5-9.9 hp models BF75, BF8A and BF100, the engine serial number is stamped into an identification plate mounted to the starboard swivel housing (**Figure 27**).

On 9.9 and 15 hp models BF9.9 and BF15, the engine serial number is stamped into the front port side of the cylinder block (**Figure 28**). The swivel housing/frame serial number is stamped into an identification plate mounted to the starboard swivel housing (**Figure 27**).

On 20-30 hp models BF20A and BF25A, the engine serial number is stamped into the cylinder block near the starter motor mounting area (**Figure 29**). The product identification number is stamped into a tag mounted to the starboard side clamp bracket (**Figure 30**).

On 35-50 hp models BF35A, BF40A, BF45A, and BF50A, the engine serial number is stamped into the rear portion of the cylinder block (**Figure 31**). The product identification number is stamped into a tag mounted to the starboard side clamp bracket (**Figure 32**).

On 75-115 hp models BF75A, BF90A, BF115A and BF130A, the engine serial number is stamped into the cylinder block near the oil filter-mounting pad (**Figure 33**). The product identification number is stamped into a tag mounted to the port side clamp bracket (**Figure 34**).

Preliminary Inspection

Most engine malfunction can be corrected by correcting a few simple items. Check the following and if the problem still exists, refer to **Tables 1-3** for starting, ignition, and fuel system troubleshooting. They list the suggested testing or adjustments to correct most problems. All test procedures are listed in this chapter along with helpful troubleshooting tips.

1. Inspect the engine for loose, disconnected, dirty or corroded wires.
2. Fill the fuel tank with fresh fuel.
3. Ensure the battery and cable connections are tight and clean (Chapter Seven).
4. Fully charge the battery, if needed (Chapter Seven).
5. Check the condition of the spark plugs (Chapter Four).
6. Use proper equipment and test for spark at each cylinder. See *Spark Test Procedure* in this chapter.
7. Install the engine stop switch lanyard (if so equipped).
8. Verify that the boat hull is clean and in good condition.
9. Verify that the correct propeller is used.

Operating Requirements

The three basic requirements for an internal combustion engine to run (**Figure 35**) include a fresh supply of fuel and air in the proper proportion, adequate compression in the combustion chamber and a source of ignition at the proper time. If any of these requirements are missing, the engine will not run. If any of these components are inadequate, the engine may not run properly.

Additional troubleshooting procedures and tips are listed by symptom in the following section.

STARTING DIFFICULTY

If the engine is hard to start, the problem may be in the engine or starting system or you could be following an improper starting procedure. Refer to the owner's manual for the correct starting procedure. If the correct starting procedure is followed, but the engine still starts hard, continue as follows.

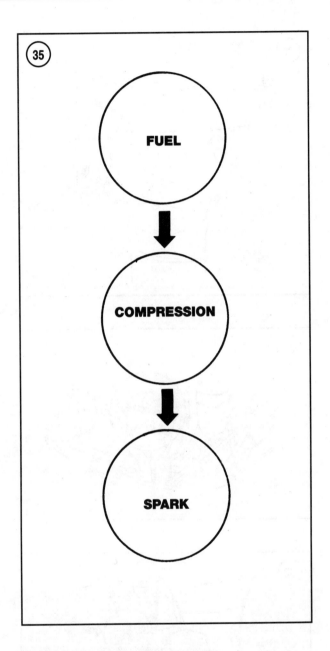

Determining a Fuel or Ignition Fault

It can be difficult to determine if a starting problem is related to fuel, ignition or other causes. It is usually easiest to first verify that the ignition system is operating. Check the fuel system if the ignition system is operating but the engine will not start or is starting with difficulty. Refer to *Spark Test Procedures* in this chapter to determine if spark is present at the spark plugs.

WARNING
High voltage is present in the ignition system. Never touch wires or wire connections while the engine is running. Never perform

TROUBLESHOOTING

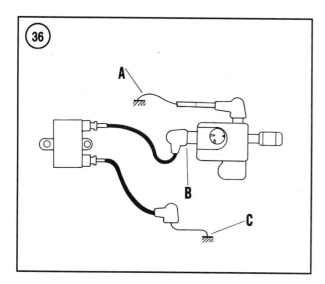

6. Observe the spark gap tester as you operate the electric or manual starter. The presence of a strong blue spark at the spark gap tester while cranking indicates that the ignition system is operating for that cylinder. Record the test results.

7. Repeat Steps 3-6 for all remaining cylinders. Clean and install all spark plugs following the instructions listed in Chapter Four. Connect all spark plug leads to the correct spark plug. Ensure that all leads are routed correctly. Install the propeller following the instructions listed in Chapter Nine.

8. Refer to *Ignition System Troubleshooting* in this chapter if spark is weak or not present on any of the cylinders. Refer to *Checking the fuel system* in this chapter if the ignition system is operating properly but the engine does not start.

Checking the Fuel System

Fuel-related problems are common on outboard engines. Fuels available today have a relatively short shelf life and become stale within a few weeks under some conditions. These fuels work fine for an automobile because the fuel is consumed in a week or so. Because a marine engine may sit idle for several weeks, the fuel can become stale or sour.

As fuel evaporates, a gummy deposit may form in the carburetor or other fuel system components. These deposits may clog fuel filters, fuel lines, fuel pumps, fuel injection components and small passages within the carburetor.

Fuel stored in the fuel tank tends to absorb water vapor from the air over time. This water separates from the fuel and settles at the bottom of the tank, leading to the formation of rust in the fuel tank. This rust likely migrates to and blocks fuel filters and other fuel system passages. Inspect the fuel in the fuel tank if the engine refuses to start and the ignition system is not at fault. An unpleasant or unusual odor usually indicates the fuel has exceeded its shelf life and should be replaced.

Refer to *Inspecting the fuel* in this chapter.

ignition system testing in wet conditions. Electric shock can cause serious bodily injury or death. Never perform electrical testing when fuel or fuel vapors are present.

Spark test

This test checks for output from the ignition system at the spark plug connector. A spark gap tester is required to perform this test. This section provides typical instructions for using a spark gap tester. Refer to the instructions that came with the spark gap tester for specific instructions.

Refer to *Checking the fuel system* in this chapter if spark plugs produce adequate spark but the engine is starting with difficulty.

1. Note all spark plug connector locations and lead routing to ensure proper connections after testing is complete. Disconnect the spark plug leads from all cylinders. Refer to Chapter Four for instructions and remove the spark plugs from all cylinders.

2. Refer to Chapter Nine for instruction to remove the propeller from the gearcase.

3. Connect the ground lead (A, **Figure 36**) of the spark gap tester to a suitable engine ground, such as a cylinder head attaching bolt.

4. Connect the spark plug lead from one of the cylinders to the appropriate terminal (B, **Figure 36**) on the spark gap tester.

5. Connect all remaining spark plug connectors (C, **Figure 36**) to a suitable engine ground such as a cylinder head attaching bolt. Shift the engine into neutral (on shifting models).

> *WARNING*
> *Use extreme caution when working with the fuel system. Fuel is extremely flammable; if ignited, it can result in serious bodily injury or death. Never smoke or allow sparks to occur around fuel or fuel vapors. Wipe up any spilled fuel at once with a shop towel and dispose of the shop towel in an appropriate manner. Check all fuel hoses, connections and fittings for leaks after any fuel*

system repair. Correct all fuel system leakage before returning the engine to service.

Inspecting the fuel

Check the condition of the fuel if the engine has been stored for some time and refuses to start. All Honda Outboards are equipped with fuel bowl drains (**Figure 37**). Refer to Chapter Six to locate the fuel bowl drain locations for your model. To check the fuel, carefully drain the fuel from the fuel bowl into a suitable container. A glass container allows easier viewing of the fuel for the presence of water or other contaminants.

Unusual odor, debris, cloudy appearance or the presence of water are a sure sign of contaminated fuel. If any contamination is noted, dispose of all the fuel in the fuel tank in an environmentally friendly manner. Contact a local marine dealership or automotive repair facility for information on the proper disposal of this fuel.

Clean and inspect the entire fuel system if water or other contaminants are found in the fuel bowl. Refer to Chapter Six for complete fuel system disassembly, inspection and assembly procedures. Problems will likely reappear if all contaminants are not removed from the fuel system. Replace all fuel system filters to ensure a reliable repair.

If no fuel can be drained from the fuel bowl, inspect the carburetor or vapor separator tank (EFI models) along with the fuel pump and fuel lines. Typically the fuel inlet needle is stuck closed or plugged with debris. Carburetor and vapor separator tank repair instructions are provided in Chapter Six. Be sure to inspect all fuel filters in the system for the presence of debris.

Models BF20 and BF2A are equipped with a fuel valve at the carburetor. Check the position of the valve before removing the carburetor and/or other components for inspection.

A faulty choke valve (**Figure 38**) or binding choke valve control linkage (**Figure 39**) can result in hard starting conditions with a cold or warmed up engine. Check for proper operation of these components if other faults are not found. Refer to *Fuel System Component Testing* in this chapter to test these components.

FUEL SYSTEM TESTING

This section provides testing procedures for all carburetor equipped engines. Test procedures are provided for fuel tanks, hoses, pumps, carburetors and choke valve components.

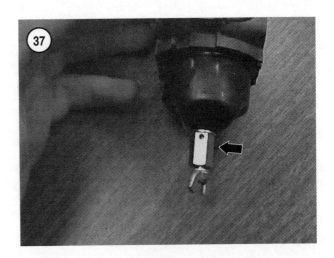

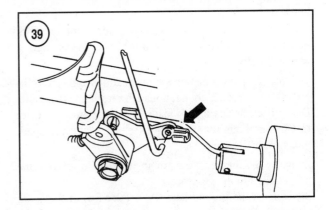

Refer to *Electronic Fuel Injection System* in this chapter to test the fuel system components on 115 and 130 hp models.

NOTE
Always ensure that the fuel tank vent is open before testing the fuel tank. The vent is integrated into the fill cap on most portable fuel

TROUBLESHOOTING

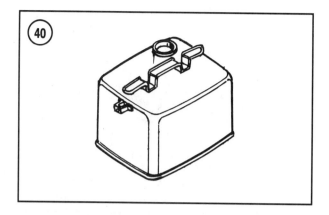

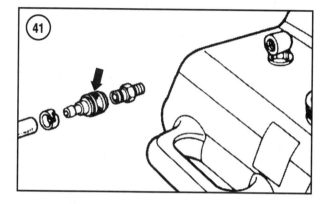

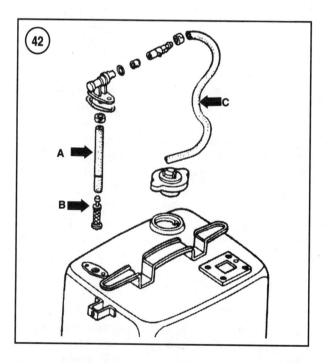

tanks. A boat-mounted fuel tank venting system is used in applications with integral fuel tanks.

Fuel Tank and Fuel Hose Testing

A faulty fuel tank or related component usually causes a surge, misfire or rough operation at higher engine speeds. The problem is due to inadequate fuel delivery to the engine. A problem with the fuel tank may occur only at higher engine speeds as the fault may allow adequate fuel for operation at lower engine speeds.

Most outboards use portable fuel tanks (**Figure 40**) that can be easily removed from the boat for refilling or cleaning. Some boats are equipped with built-in fuel tanks that are not easily removed for service.

The most effective method to check the fuel tank is to temporarily run the engine on a known-good portable fuel tank and hose, filled with fresh fuel. New portable fuel tanks are available at most marine dealerships and many department stores. Follow the tank manufacturer's instructions to connect the fuel line to the portable tank (**Figure 41**). Ensure that the inside diameter of the fuel hose and fuel fittings on the test fuel tank is 6.4 mm (1/4 in.) or larger. Otherwise, fuel starvation symptoms may still occur at higher engine speeds.

A problem with the fuel, fuel tank pickup, fuel hoses, primer bulb, fuel tank vent or antisiphon device is indicated if the engine performs properly on a known-good fuel supply. A blocked fuel filter, faulty fuel pump, blocked fuel passage in the carburetor or fault with other engine components is indicated if the fault is still present with a known-good fuel supply.

NOTE
The engine must be operated at full throttle for several minutes to accurately check for a fuel tank-related fault. With 25 hp and larger engines, it is usually necessary to operate the engine under actual running conditions to check for a problem with the fuel tank. With the smaller engines, use a test propeller and test tank to check for fuel tank-related faults.

NOTE
Models BF20, BF2A are equipped with an integral fuel tank. Removal and inspection of the fuel tank is necessary if a fuel tank-related problem is suspected. A mechanical fuel pump is not used, as this engine uses a gravity feed fuel delivery system.

Fuel Tank Pickup

The fuel tank pickup (A, **Figure 42**) affixes to the fuel tank, serving as a means to draw fuel from near the bottom of the fuel tank. Most applications use a simple tube that extends from the fuel tank hose connection to near the bottom of the fuel tank. Some fuel tanks are equipped with a screen or filter (B, **Figure 42**) located at the bottom of the tube to capture debris that may be present in the fuel tank. This screen or filter may become obstructed by debris or contaminants, restricting fuel flow. Debris or contaminants can also block the tube type fuel tank pickups.

Partial disassembly of the fuel tank is necessary to inspect the fuel tank pickup. Inspection of the fuel tank pickup is a relatively easy process where portable fuel tanks are used. Refer to Chapter Six for portable fuel tank inspection and repair instructions.

With applications using a built-in fuel tank, the inspection of the fuel tank pickup is usually more difficult. Accessibility to the fuel tank and its components may be limited. Seating, storage areas and even the structure of the boat must be removed on some boats to access the fuel tank.

Many variations exist in the type and design of these built-in fuel tanks. Contact the boat manufacturer for information on repair and a source for replacement parts for a built-in fuel tank.

Fuel Hoses

CAUTION
Automotive-type replacement fuel hoses may not meet the requirements for the outboard. Fuel leakage may occur and result in a fire and/or explosion. Always use the hose sold by the manufacturer when fuel hose replacement is required.

Fuel hose failure can result in fuel leakage or, in some cases, an internal fuel restriction. Visually inspect the fuel hose (C, **Figure 42**) for cracked surfaces or a weathered appearance and replace the hose if either condition is noted. Pinch the fuel hose until it collapses, then release it. Replace the fuel hose if it is difficult to squeeze, feels excessively soft or tends to stick together on the internal surfaces. Replace the fuel hose if you detect any source of leakage.

CAUTION
Avoid using couplings or other patching methods to repair a damaged fuel hose. The coupling or patch may result in restricted fuel flow and lead to fuel starvation. A hose that requires a temporary repair will likely fail again and result in a potential fuel or air leak.

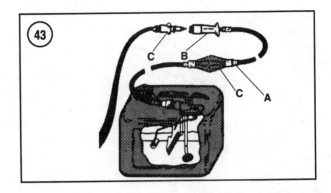

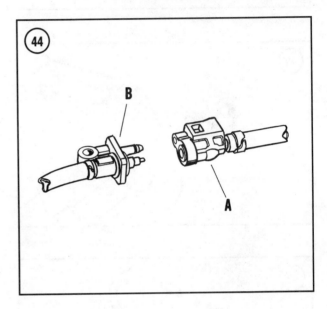

To check for an internal fuel hose restriction, disconnect the hose from both the fuel tank and the engine. Thoroughly drain any fuel from the fuel hose into a suitable container. Pump the primer bulb as necessary to remove the fuel from the hose. Refer to (**Figure 43**) to assist with the identification and orientation of the fuel hose components.

1. Remove all fuel hose clamps (A, **Figure 43**) then remove any remaining fuel hose connectors (B, **Figure 43**). Remove the primer bulb (C, **Figure 43**) and test as indicated.

2. Direct one end of the disconnected hose to a clear area and use compressed air to blow through the hose. Replace the hose if air does not flow freely through the hose.

3. Inspect all fuel hoses from the fuel tank to the engine, and all fuel hoses on the engine if a restriction is found. The condition that caused the internal hose restriction may cause failure of other fuel system hoses.

4. Replace all damaged hose clamps and ensure that they are securely tightened upon assembly. Check the entire

TROUBLESHOOTING

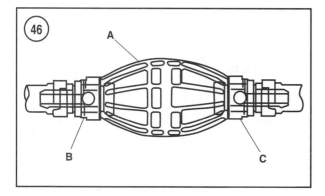

Have an assistant operate the engine while the fuel starvation symptoms are present. Carefully press the connector tighter against the connection point and hold it in position. Perform this step with both the engine and fuel tank connectors. A problem with the connector is evident if the symptoms cease within a few minutes. The problem is generally due to a worn or damaged seal or clamp connection that requires replacement of the connector. Replace both connectors (A and B, **Figure 44**) to ensure a reliable repair.

Worn or damaged components and the presence of debris can result in an internal fuel restriction in the connector. To check for this condition, temporarily run the engine with the engine side of the fuel tank to engine hose connected directly to the fuel pump inlet connector (**Figure 45**). Squeeze the primer bulb and check for fuel leakage. Correct any leakage before running the engine. Ensure that the temporary fuel hose is routed so it does not contact any moving component and does not interfere with any shift or throttle control mechanisms. Run the engine to check for proper operation. Replace both connectors if the symptoms disappear. Reconnect all fuel hoses and install new fuel hose clamps. Always check for and correct any fuel leakage prior to operating the engine.

When a fuel restriction is present at the tank side connectors, the primer bulb tends to collapse at higher engine speeds. In most cases, the problem is with the hose end connector and replacement is required.

Primer Bulb

The primer bulb (**Figure 46**) is essentially a hand-operated fuel pump integrated into the fuel supply hose. The primer bulb fills the carburetor fuel bowl or vapor separator tank (EFI models) with fuel prior to starting the engine. This pump is useful as the fuel in the bowl tends to evaporate during periods of nonuse preventing quick starting of the engine.

Pump the primer bulb only if the engine has not been used for several hours or more to prevent a potential flooding condition. Gently squeeze the primer bulb until it becomes firm then start the engine. Never use excessive force when pumping the primer bulb. You should feel the fuel pumping within the fuel hoses while pumping the primer bulb.

The major components of the primer bulb include the bulb (A, **Figure 46**), inlet fuel check valve (B, **Figure 46**) and outlet fuel check valve (C, **Figure 46**).

CAUTION
Avoid using excessive force when pumping the primer bulb. The pressure in the line

fuel system for fuel leaks and correct them before operating the engine.

Quick Connect Fittings

Quick connect fittings (A, B, **Figure 44**) are used with most outboards to connect the fuel tank hose to the engine. Sometimes they are used to connect the fuel hose to the portable fuel tank. The female connection (A, **Figure 44**) clamps to the fuel hose leading to the fuel tank. The male connection (B, **Figure 44**) attaches to the engine and connects to a fuel hose leading to the fuel filter and fuel pump. A problem with the connector may result in fuel leakage, air leakage and, in some cases, a fuel restriction.

If air leakage is present at the fitting, (at the engine or fuel tank) the fuel pump draws air and fuel into the fuel hose, resulting in insufficient fuel for the engine (fuel starvation). In most cases, the symptoms will worsen at higher engine speeds. In most (but not all) cases, a fuel leak will be detected at the connection points (A and B, **Figure 44**) when the primer bulb is pumped.

may exceed the normal fuel system pressures and lead to fuel leakage or a flooding condition.

Primer bulb malfunction can lead to an inability to prime the fuel system or it may cause a restriction within the fuel system. Hard starting or poor performance can result from a problem with the primer bulb.

If the primer bulb does not pump fuel, you will notice that the bulb does not become firm when the fuel system is sufficiently primed. Also, suspect a problem if you do not feel the fuel flowing when the bulb is pumped.

When the primer bulb restricts fuel flow the primer bulb will tend to collapse when the engine speed is increased. This condition can also occur at lower speeds if the fuel restriction is severe.

Fuels available today may contain ingredients that tend to cause deterioration of many of the fuel system components including the primer bulb. Replace the primer bulb if you notice that it sticks together on the internal surfaces when the primer bulb is fully compressed. Thoroughly inspect the fuel hose and other fuel system components if you note this condition.

> *WARNING*
> *Use extreme caution when working with the fuel system. Fuel is extremely flammable and if ignited can result in serious bodily injury or death. Never smoke or allow sparks to occur around fuel or fuel vapors. Wipe up any spilled fuel at once with a shop towel and dispose of the shop towel in an appropriate manner. Check all fuel hoses, connections and fittings for leaks after any fuel system repair. Correct all fuel system leaks before returning the engine into service.*

Testing the primer bulb check valves requires a common hand-operated pressure/vacuum pump (**Figure 47**). These are available at many automotive parts stores and through tool suppliers.

1. Disconnect both ends of the fuel line that connects the fuel tank to the engine. Remove and discard the clamps from both fuel line connections (B and C, **Figure 46**). Remove both fuel lines from the primer bulb.
2. Squeeze the primer bulb until it is fully collapsed. Replace the primer bulb if it does not freely expand when released or it sticks in the collapsed position. Replace the primer bulb if it has cracked surfaces or is hard to squeeze.
3. Use the *arrow* on the primer bulb for correct orientation then connect a hand-operated pressure pump to the inlet side fuel hose connection (**Figure 47**). Clamp the pump hose securely to the primer bulb hose fitting. Gently pump the hand-operated pump. Air *must* exit the outlet

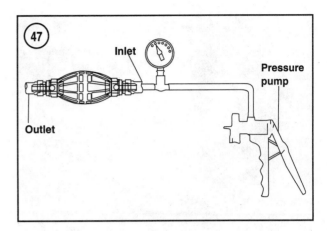

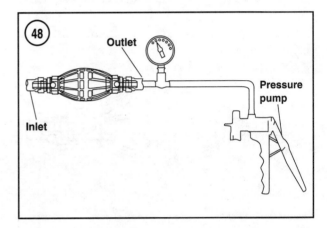

side (**Figure 47**) as the pressure pump is operated. Replace the primer bulb if incorrect test results are noted.

4. Use the *arrow* on the primer bulb for correct orientation then connect a hand-operated pressure pump to the outlet side fuel hose connection (**Figure 48**). Clamp the pump hose securely to the primer bulb fuel fitting. Gently pump the hand-operated pump. Air *must not* exit the inlet side fuel fitting, as the pump operates. Replace the primer bulb if incorrect test results are noted.

5. With the pressure pump connected to the outlet side fuel hose connection (**Figure 48**), submerge the primer bulb in water. Gently pump the hand-operated pressure pump. Replace the primer bulb if you note bubbles or other indications of a leak. Thoroughly dry the primer bulb.

6. Use the *arrow* on the primer bulb for correct orientation then install the inlet and outlet fuel hoses to the primer bulb. Install new hose clamps to both fuel hose connections and securely tighten them. Operate the primer bulb and check for correct operation and for fuel leakage. Correct all fuel leakage prior to using the outboard.

TROUBLESHOOTING

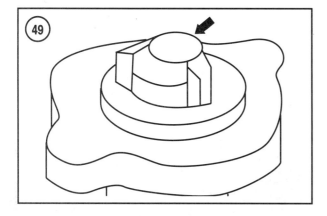

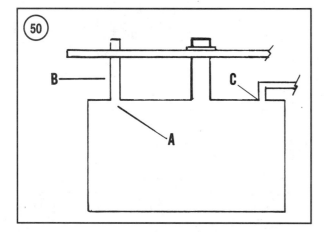

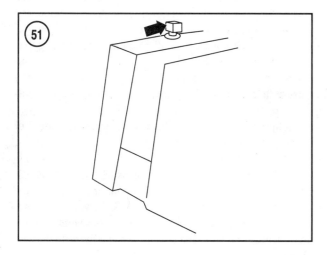

Fuel Tank Vent

Fuel tank venting is required for fuel to flow from the fuel tank to the engine. Inadequate venting of the tank allows a vacuum to form as fuel is drawn from the tank. With continued running, the vacuum becomes strong enough that the fuel pump is unable to draw fuel from the tank resulting in fuel starvation. This usually results in performance problems at higher engine speeds. At times, the symptoms occur at lower speeds. If the fuel tank vent is completely shut off the engine may stall and not restart.

The vent for portable fuel tanks and the 2-horsepower models is incorporated into the fill cap (**Figure 49**). This allows the vent to close, preventing fuel spillage when carrying the fuel tanks or the engine.

The vent system for applications with built-in fuel tanks include a vent hose connection (A, **Figure 50**) at the fuel tank, the vent hose (B, **Figure 50**) and the hull-mounted vent fitting (C, **Figure 50**). This type of venting system is always open. It is not uncommon for insects or spiders to obstruct the vent passages. Take this into consideration when a fuel tank venting problem is suspected.

Fuel starvation symptoms generally occur shortly after the fuel tank has been completely filled. Usually the engine performs properly for a short time before the symptoms appear. Engine performance gradually decreases as the vacuum formed in the fuel tank increases.

When you suspect inadequate fuel tank venting, simply loosen the fuel tank fill cap slightly to allow venting. Clean and inspect the fuel tank vent hose and all fittings on built-in fuel tank applications if the fuel starvation symptoms disappear when the cap is loosened. Check the position of the vent screw on the fill cap with applications using portable fuel tanks. Replace the fill cap if the screw is fully opened yet the symptoms persist until the cap is loosened.

NOTE
The two-horsepower models are equipped with an integral or engine-mounted tank. This engine is very portable and requires no fuel line connections to run. The fuel tank vent is integrated into the fuel tank fill cap.

Antisiphon Devices

Antisiphon devices are commonly used on applications with the fuel tank(s) built into the boat. These devices are installed to prevent fuel in the tank from siphoning out in the event of a leak in the fuel hose. The most common type is the spring-loaded check valve, mounted to the tank at the fuel hose connection (**Figure 51**). Other applications use a manual shutoff type valve or solenoid activated shutoff valve mounted at the fuel hose connection. These safety devices are useful and bypassing them is not recommended. If testing indicates a problem with an antisiphon device, replace it. They are available at most marine dealerships and marine supply businesses.

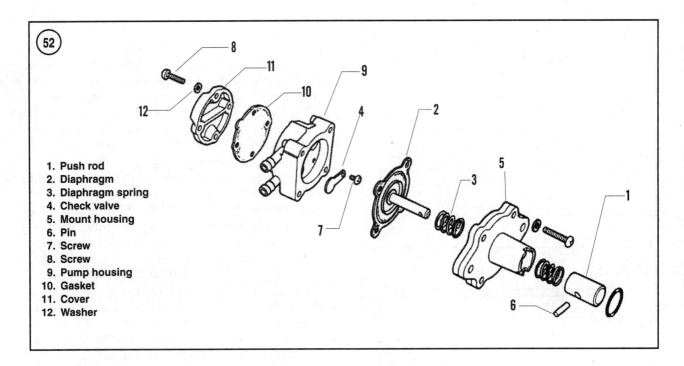

1. Push rod
2. Diaphragm
3. Diaphragm spring
4. Check valve
5. Mount housing
6. Pin
7. Screw
8. Screw
9. Pump housing
10. Gasket
11. Cover
12. Washer

CAUTION
Never run an outboard without cooling water. Use either a test tank or a flush/test device. Always remove the propeller before running the engine on a flush/test device. Install a test propeller to run the engine in a test tank.

The most effective way to check for a faulty antisiphon device is through a process of elimination. Run the engine on a known-good portable fuel tank under actual running conditions. A fault is indicated with the fuel tank pickup, fuel hoses, primer bulb, fuel tank vent or antisiphon device if the engine performs properly. If testing or inspection indicates these components operate properly, a faulty antisiphon may be the cause of the malfunction. Remove and replace the antisiphon device following the instructions that are provided with the new component. Some antisiphon devices can be cleaned. Thoroughly inspect the device for worn, damaged or corroded components. Replace the valve if any questionable condition is noted.

Clean the fuel tank if significant amounts of debris are found in the antisiphon device or fuel tank pickup to prevent a repeat failure. Inspect all fuel system hoses and filters for blockage if debris is found in the fuel tank, fuel tank pickup or antisiphon device. Always check for and correct any fuel system leakage before returning the engine to service.

Fuel Pump Testing

A diaphragm type fuel pump (**Figure 52**, typical) is used on 5 horsepower and larger models to move the fuel from the fuel tank to the carburetor or vapor separator tank (115 and 130 hp models).

A lobe on the camshaft contacts a pushrod (1, **Figure 52**) which operates the fuel pump. The pushrod moves the diaphragm (2, **Figure 52**) and collapses the diaphragm spring (3) with each camshaft rotation. The moving diaphragm causes fuel to flow into and out of the pump chamber. The inlet and outlet check valves (4, **Figure 52**) ensure that the fuel flows toward the carburetor(s) or vapor separator tank.

Failure of the fuel pump can result in inadequate fuel delivery to the engine, fuel leakage or, in some rare cases, excessive fuel pressure.

Test the fuel pump using fuel pressure gauges to check the fuel pressure. Use a graduated container (suitable for holding fuel) and a stopwatch to check the volume of fuel delivered during a specific time frame. These methods, although accurate, are time consuming and the potential for fuel leakage is always present.

An easier, faster and more effective means to check the fuel pump is to have an assistant operate the engine under actual running conditions. Vigorously pump the primer bulb when fuel starvation or other symptoms appear. Thoroughly inspect any fuel filters for debris or blockage if the symptoms disappear when pumping the primer bulb. Thoroughly inspect the fuel pump if the filters are in

TROUBLESHOOTING

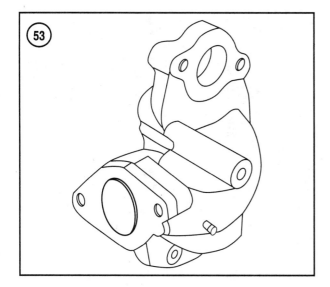

acceptable condition. Refer to Chapter Six for fuel pump removal, inspection and repair.

A faulty fuel pump that results in excessive fuel pump pressure is rare. A flooding condition likely occurs if excessive fuel pressure is present. Inspect the fuel pump if flooding is present and no other problems are found. In these cases, an inspection of the fuel pump usually reveals mechanical damage to internal fuel pump components.

Carburetor Testing

A problem with a carburetor can result in hard starting, rough idle or an inability to run at idle speed. Other symptoms include rough operation or shaking at various engine speeds, a bogging or sagging sensation during acceleration, poor performance at higher engine speeds and spark plug fouling.

Problems such as these can result from the following causes:
1. A flooding carburetor.
2. Incorrect carburetor adjustment.
3. Incorrect carburetor synchronization.
4. Plugged carburetor passages.
5. Air leaks at the carburetor mounting surfaces.
6. Running the engine at high-elevation reservoirs.
7. Malfunctioning choke valve.

CAUTION
Always correct any problems with the fuel, fuel tank and fuel pump prior to troubleshooting the carburetor(s).

This section provides troubleshooting tips and procedures to help pinpoint the cause of carburetor-related problems.

If hard starting, rough idle or stalling at idle are noted, check for a choke valve malfunction, flooding carburetor(s), maladjusted carburetor or plugged carburetor passages.

If poor performance at various speeds is noted, check the carburetor adjustment and carburetor synchronization. Also check for a malfunctioning choke valve and restricted carburetor passages.

If bogging or hesitation during acceleration is present, check the carburetor adjustment, dashpot adjustment, carburetor synchronization and a choke valve malfunction. Also check for plugged or restricted carburetor passages, flooding carburetor(s) or a damaged or incorrect propeller.

If spark plug fouling occurs, check for a choke valve malfunction, carburetor adjustment and synchronization, flooding or plugged carburetor passages. Spark plug fouling can also occur if the outboard motor is operated at high elevation without performing the necessary adjustments to compensate for the altitude.

WARNING
Use extreme caution when working with the fuel system. If ignited, fuel is extremely flammable can result in serious bodily injury or death. Never smoke or allow sparks to develop around fuel or fuel vapors. Wipe up any spilled fuel at once with a shop towel and dispose of the shop towel in an appropriate manner. Check all fuel hoses, connections and fittings for leaks after any fuel system repair. Correct all fuel system leaks before returning the engine into service.

Flooding carburetor

A flooded carburetor can be the result of debris in the fuel inlet needle valve or a possibly worn or damaged needle valve and seat. A misadjusted, damaged or fuel-saturated float may also cause carburetor flooding. A flooding condition allows excessive amounts of fuel to enter the engine, resulting in stalling or poor low-speed operation. In many cases, the engine is able to use the fuel at higher engine speeds and may perform well at higher speeds.

Many variations exist within the type and appearance of the carburetor (**Figure 53**) and cover/silencer (**Figure 54** typical). Refer to Chapter Six for specific information on the removal of the silencer/cover for your specific model.

Follow Steps 1-5 to check for a flooded carburetor.

1. Refer to Chapter Six to remove the silencer/cover (**Figure 54** typical) from the front of the carburetor.
2. Open the choke valve and look into the front opening of the carburetor (**Figure 53**).
3. Open the fuel valve on models BF20, BF2A or gently squeeze the primer bulb on the other models. Fuel flowing into the carburetor opening indicates a flooding condition.
4. Remove and repair the carburetor(s) following the procedures listed in Chapter Six if the carburetor is flooded.
5. Install the silencer cover (**Figure 54**) following the instructions in Chapter Six. Close the fuel valve on models so equipped. Correct any fuel leakage before running the engine.

Carburetor adjustment

Improper carburetor adjustment may result in hard starting, poor performance and rough operation at any engine speed. In most cases, however, the symptoms are present at lower engine speeds only.

Do not confuse the pilot screw with the idle speed or carburetor synchronization screw. The location of the pilot screw (**Figure 55**) varies by model and carburetor. Refer to Chapter Six for assistance locating the pilot adjusting screw.

Note the position of the adjusting screw slot (**Figure 55**). Count the number of turns as you *slowly* rotate the screw clockwise until it is lightly seated. Record the number of turns necessary to seat the pilot screw. Adjust the pilot screw according to the instructions listed in Chapter Five. If the adjustment is correct, the problem with the engine is likely due to other causes and changing the adjustment only masks the real problem with the engine.

Carburetor synchronization

Improper carburetor synchronization can result in hard starting, poor performance and rough engine operation at various engine speeds. Engines equipped with a single carburetor require that the carburetor opening be precisely timed to the spark timing advancement. Multiple carburetor engines require the same precise timing and also require that all carburetors open and close simultaneously. Carburetor synchronization on multiple carburetor engines requires the use of a special vacuum gauge set (**Figure 56**). Check and correct if necessary the carburetor synchronization when the symptoms are not caused by other carburetor problems. Refer to Chapter Five for carburetor adjustments and synchronization procedures.

Plugged carburetor passages

Plugged jets, passages, orifices or vents within the carburetor can result in excessive fuel (rich condition) or inadequate fuel (lean condition) for the engine. The symptoms can occur at any engine speed range depending

TROUBLESHOOTING

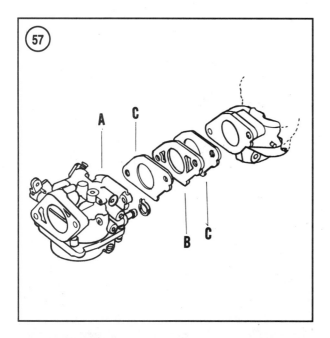

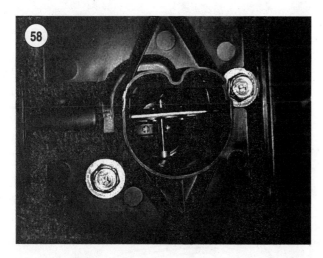

1. A hissing or squealing noise emanating from the engine.
2. Rough idle characteristics.
3. Bogging or sagging hesitation during acceleration.
4. Poor high-speed performance.
5. Spark plug overheating (see Chapter Four).

Continued operation under lean fuel conditions can lead to piston and valve damage requiring repair to the base engine.

To locate a leakage point, use a common spray lubricant such as WD 40. Run the engine in a test tank or with a flush test adapter. See Chapter Four for instruction on using the flush/test adapter. With the engine running at idle speed, carefully spray the lubricant around the carburetor mounting base (A, **Figure 57**) and spacer mounting base (B, **Figure 57**). An increase in idle speed or any change in the idle when the lubricant is sprayed indicates leakage at the carburetor mount surfaces.

Remove the carburetor, spacer, and gaskets. Inspect the gaskets and mounting surfaces following the instructions listed in Chapter Six. Always replace the carburetor mounting gaskets (C, **Figure 57**) anytime the carburetor is removed.

Altitude adjustments

Air density decreases as altitude increases. The less dense air reduces the efficiency of the engine and reduces the horsepower output. The less dense air affects the engine carburetor calibration, causing the air/fuel mixture to become excessively rich. Therefore, if the engine is operated at higher elevation, the carburetor jets or adjustment must be changed to compensate for the less dense air. Contact a Honda marine dealership in the area where the engine is operated for jet and adjustment recommendations.

CAUTION
Once the engine is rejetted for high elevation, it must again be rejetted before operation at low altitude. Power head damage will occur if the engine is operated with an excessively lean air/fuel mixture.

Choke Valve Testing

The choke valve provides an enriched fuel mixture to start a cold engine. The valve (**Figure 58**) is positioned to allow it to almost completely block the front opening of the carburetor. When activated, the choke valve causes a significant decrease in the amount of air flowing into the engine, resulting in a rich air/fuel mixture.

on the location and extent of the blockage. In many cases, a surging or misfire is noted at higher engine speeds. Remove, clean and inspect the carburetor(s) if all other fuel system components are operating correctly. Complete carburetor removal, cleaning, inspection and repair are provided in Chapter Six.

Air leakage at the carburetor mounting surfaces

Air leakage at the carburetor mounting surfaces (**Figure 57**) allows air to be drawn into the engine along with the air/fuel mixture. The resulting dilution of the air/fuel mixture causes the engine to operate lean.

Typical symptoms include:

A malfunctioning choke valve (**Figure 58**) can result in hard starting, rough idle, spark plug fouling or poor performance. The cause is usually the result of a sticking or binding linkage or control mechanism. In some instances, the choke solenoid on remote control models is faulty.

Tiller-controlled models utilize linkage to activate the choke valve when the choke knob is pulled out or activated.

Remote control models (20 horsepower and larger) use a solenoid-type motor (**Figure 59**) to activate the choke valve. Electric current from the key switch or choke switch (on some models) is supplied to the choke solenoid when activated. A magnetic field is generated that moves the choke linkage (**Figure 59**) thereby closing the choke valve. When the switch is released, the field collapses allowing a spring to move the linkage and open the choke valve.

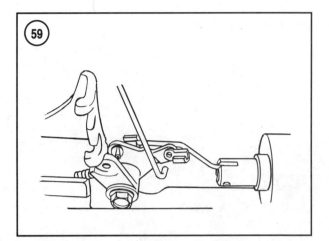

Tiller controlled models

1. Remove the silencer/cover (**Figure 54**) following the procedure listed in Chapter Six.
2. Position the choke control knob (**Figure 60**, typical) to the IN or retracted position. Check the choke valve (**Figure 58**) position. The valve should be fully open.
3. Position the choke knob (**Figure 60** typical) in the OUT or fully extended position. The valve should be closed.
4. Perform the following if improper valve position is noted in Step 2 or Step 3.
    a. Clean all debris or contaminants from the linkage.
    b. Inspect for bent or damaged linkages and replace as required.
    c. Lubricate the linkage following the instructions listed in Chapter Four.
    d. Adjust the choke linkage following the instructions listed in Chapter Five.
5. Install the silencer/cover (**Figure 54**) following the instructions listed in Chapter Six.
6. Check proper operation of the choke valve. Check for and correct any fuel leakage.

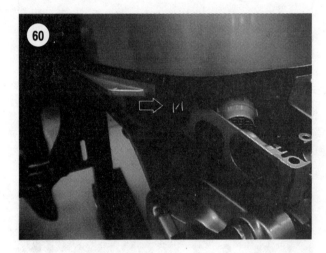

Remote control models

1. Remove the silencer/cover following the instructions listed in Chapter Six.
2. Position the key switch in the RUN position (do not start the engine).
3. Note the position of the carburetor(s) choke valves (**Figure 58**). The valve should be in the fully open position.

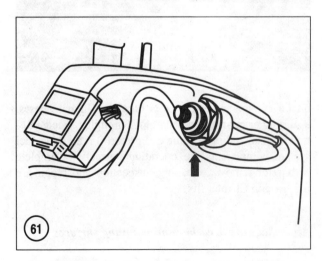

4. Have an assistant push straight in on the key switch (**Figure 61**) or activate the choke valve switch as you observe the choke valve. The choke valve should now be in the closed position.

TROUBLESHOOTING

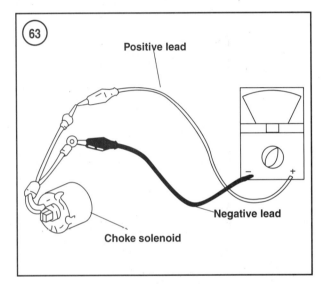

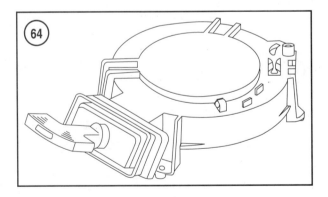

5. Return the key switch to the OFF position. Perform the following if improper valve position is noted in Step 3 or Step 4:
   a. Clean all debris or contaminants from the linkage.
   b. Inspect for bent or damaged linkages and replace as required.
   c. Refer to *Choke Solenoid Resistance Test* and test as indicated.

   d. Lubricate the linkage following the instructions listed in Chapter Four.
   e. Adjust the choke linkage following the instructions listed in Chapter Five.

6. Install the silencer/cover (**Figure 54**) following the instructions listed in Chapter Six.
7. Check for proper engine operation. Check for and correct any fuel leaks.

Choke Solenoid Resistance Test

A volt/ohm meter is required to test the resistance of the coil in the choke solenoid. Refer to *Troubleshooting Test Equipment* (in this chapter) to review volt/ohm meter usage. Refer to the wiring diagrams located at the end of this manual to identify the wire colors used for the choke solenoid (**Figure 62**). Trace the wire color to the component on the engine.

1. Locate and disconnect both wire terminals that connect the main engine wire harness to the choke solenoid. Note the size and location of any plastic tie straps along the choke solenoid wires. Carefully cut and remove any tie straps that hinder free access to the leads.
2. Select the ohms or resistance function of the volt/ohm meter. Refer to **Table 4** for choke solenoid resistance specifications.
3. Connect the positive (+) meter test lead to the brown wire of the choke solenoid. Connect the negative test lead to the black wire of the choke solenoid (**Figure 63**).
4. Compare the measured resistance with the specification listed in **Table 4**. Replace the solenoid if the measured resistance is not as specified. Refer to Chapter Seven for choke solenoid replacement.
5. Clean all terminals, then connect all leads to the proper terminals. Install new plastic tie straps to replace any that were removed for testing.

STARTING SYSTEM

A manual rewind starter is used on 2-8 hp models. A manual starter and an electric starter are used on 9.9-30 hp models. On 35 hp and larger models, only an electric starter is used.

Manual Rewind Starter

All 2-30 hp models are equipped with a manual rewind starter.

The components of a manual starter (**Figure 64**, typical) include the housing, sheave or spool, drive pawl (engagement mechanism), neutral interlock mechanism, starter rope, rope guide and the handle.

The most common failure is a frayed or broken starter rope. Other failures are caused by a broken rewind spring and a worn or damaged drive pawl (engagement mechanism).

Electric Starting Systems

The major components of the electric starting system include the battery, start button or key switch, electric starter motor, electric starter relay, neutral switch and the wiring.

The electric starter motor (**Figure 65**, typical) is similar in design to what is commonly used on automotive applications. The starter motor used on 9.9-50 hp models (**Figure 65**) is different from the electric starter motor used on 75-130 hp models (**Figure 66**). With either design, its mounting position on the base engine allows the starter drive (**Figure 67**) to engage a flywheel-mounted ring gear when operated. This rotates the crankshaft with sufficient speed to start the engine. A neutral switch is used to prevent the starter motor from operating if the engine is in gear. Release from the flywheel ring gear occurs when the starter switch or button is released.

The electric starter motor provides the torque necessary to rotate the engine. This requires substantial electric current. An undercharged battery is the leading cause of starting system problems. Battery maintenance and testing procedures are provided in Chapter Seven.

Electric Starter Operation

Operation of the start circuit begins at the ignition switch or start button (A, **Figure 68**). The switch or button is connected to the positive terminal of the battery (B, **Figure 68**). Engaging the switch or button directs current through the neutral switch (C, **Figure 68**) then to the electric starter relay (D, **Figure 68**). One (large) terminal of the starter relay is connected with a large diameter cable to the positive terminal of the battery (B, **Figure 68**). The other large terminal connects a large diameter cable to the starter motor. The starter motor attaches to and grounds to the cylinder block.

When current is applied to the starter relay from the neutral switch, it causes switching in the relay that allows current to flow through the relay thereby connecting the battery terminal directly to the starter motor.

When the key switch or button is released, the starter relay opens the connection, causing current flow to the

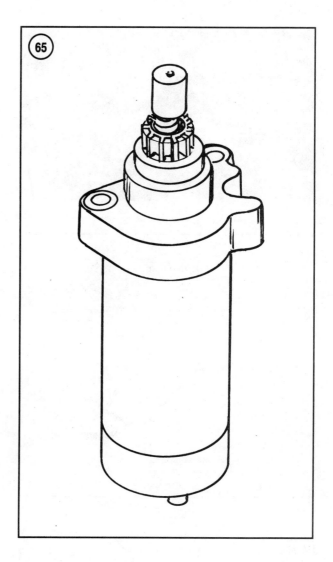

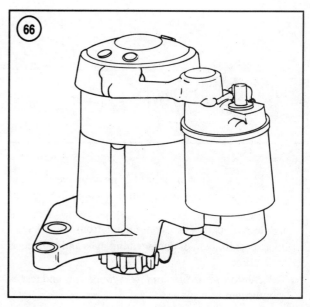

TROUBLESHOOTING

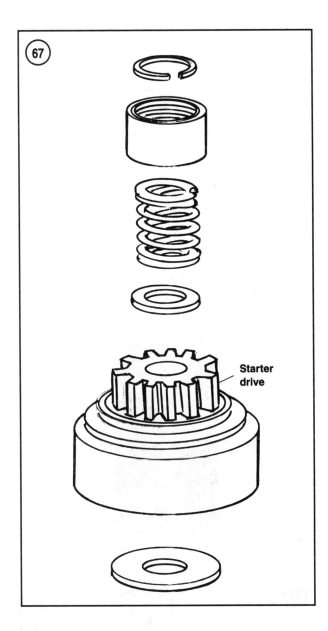

Starter drive

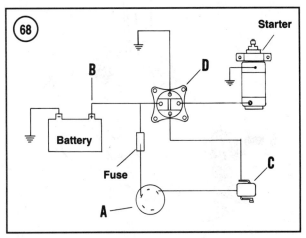

starter motor to cease. The starter motor drive then moves away from the flywheel, disengaging the starter motor.

CAUTION
Never operate the starter motor continuously for more than 10 seconds or the motor will overheat. Allow at least 2 minutes for the motor to cool between starting attempts. Also, operating the starter motor with an undercharged battery or a battery with insufficient capacity can cause overheating and subsequent failure.

Electric Starting System Testing

This section contains electric starting system testing of:
1. Starter cranking voltage.
2. Ignition switch.
3. Start button.
4. Electric starter relay.
5. Neutral switch.

Starting system malfunctions can result from many causes. To determine which test is required, refer to **Table 1** located at the end of this chapter.

WARNING
Use extreme caution when working around batteries. Do not smoke or produce sparks. Batteries produce hydrogen gas that can explode and result in severe bodily injury or death.

Starter Cranking Voltage Test

This test measures the voltage delivered to the starter motor while cranking the engine. The battery condition must be checked and corrected, if necessary, prior to performing this test. A volt/ohm meter is required to check the starter motor cranking voltage. Refer to *Troubleshooting Test Equipment* (in this chapter) to review volt/ohm meter usage. Refer to Chapter Seven for battery maintenance procedures. Rule out a seized engine or gearcase before replacing any component(s) due to a non-cranking condition.

1. Remove the propeller following the instruction listed in Chapter Nine. Shift the engine into neutral.
2. Select the voltage function on the volt/ohm meter. Connect the positive test lead to the large terminal lead on the starter motor (**Figure 69**). Connect the negative test lead to a suitable engine ground or the negative terminal of the battery.

3. Disconnect all spark plug leads and connect them to a suitable engine ground. Observe the volt/ohm meter as you operate the starter motor.
4. The cranking voltage should be 9.5 volts or more.
   a. If the voltage is less than 9.5 volts, make sure the battery is fully charged. Also inspect all wiring for loose or corroded connections.
   b. If the cranking voltage is 9.5 volts or more, but the engine does not crank or cranks slowly, repair or replace the starter motor. See Chapter Nine.

NOTE
Your Honda outboard may not be equipped with Honda-manufactured controls. Refer to the aftermarket manufacturer's instruction for repair and test procedures on their control system components.

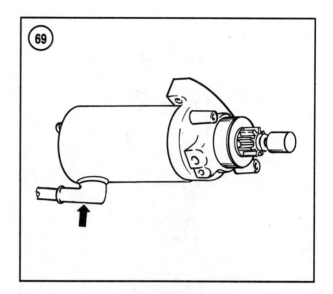

Ignition Switch Testing

The ignition switch provides the connection that allows electric current to flow to the neutral switch and the starter relay. In addition, this switch turns the ignition system ON or OFF and supplies electrical current to other components on the engine. Use a volt/ohm meter to test the ignition switch operation. Refer to *Troubleshooting Test Equipment* in this chapter for information on volt/ohm meter usage.

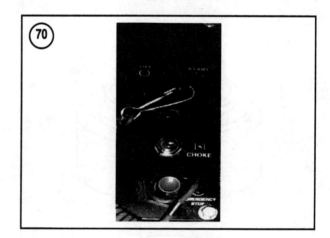

The ignition switch can be mounted in the control station dashboard, integrated into the remote control box or the tiller handle (75 and 90 hp with tiller control).

Access to the switch lead is required for testing. Removal of the dash-mounted panel (**Figure 70**) (on models so equipped) allows easy access to the switch leads. Removal and partial disassembly of the control box is necessary if the switch is integrated into the remote control box (**Figure 71**). Refer to Chapter Fourteen to access the switch leads. Refer to Chapter Thirteen for switch removal if the ignition switch is integrated into the tiller arm control (**Figure 72**).

1. Disconnect both battery cables from the battery terminals. Shift the engine into neutral. Refer to the appropriate chapter to access the ignition switch leads and terminal connections. Note all ignition switch wire connections and routing prior to disconnecting the leads to ensure correct connections on assembly. Disconnect all ignition switch leads and terminals prior to performing any test.
2. Select the ohms or resistance function on the volt/ohm meter. Select the R × 1 scale on the meter. Connect the positive test lead to the white/black or battery (*batt.*) switch lead (A, **Figure 73**). Connect the negative test lead to the black/white or *start* (St.) switch lead (B, **Figure73**).

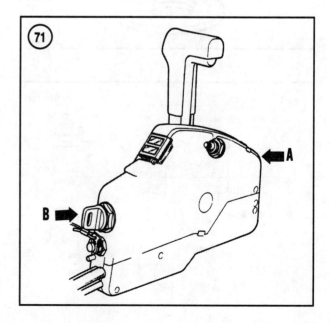

TROUBLESHOOTING

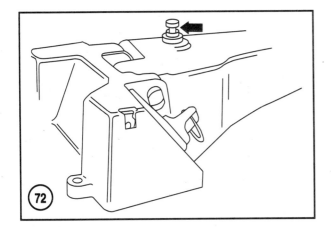

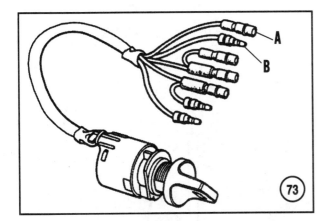

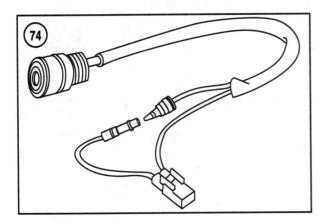

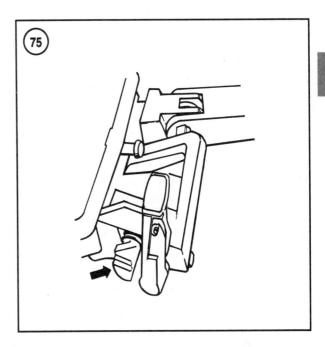

3. Turn the ignition switch OFF and note the ohmmeter. No continuity should be noted.

4. Turn the ignition switch to RUN and note the ohmmeter. No continuity should be noted.

5. Turn the ignition switch to START and note the meter. Continuity should now be present.

6. Replace the ignition switch if it does not function as specified.

7. Clean corrosion, dirt or other debris from the key switch terminals. Connect all wires to the correct terminals to ensure they are routed correctly. Install the key switch following the procedure listed in the appropriate chapter.

8. Clean then connect the battery cables to the correct terminals.

Start Button Test

The start button (**Figure 74**) is used to activate the electric starter motor on tiller handle control models with electric start. It allows electrical current to flow to the neutral switch and electric starter relay. A start button (**Figure 74**) is still used on 9.9 and 15 hp models with the optional remote control kit.

Use a volt/ohm meter to test the start button. Refer to *Troubleshooting Test Equipment* in this chapter for information on volt/ohm meter usage.

The start button is mounted to the lifting/carrying bracket on 9.9-25 hp models (**Figure 75**) to allow easy access for the operator. Access to the start button leads is required for testing. Refer to Chapter Seven for start button removal and installation.

1. Disconnect both battery cables from the battery terminals. Shift the engine into neutral. Refer to the wiring diagrams located at the end of this manual to identify the wiring used for the start button. Trace the wires to the start button on the engine.

2. Refer to the appropriate chapter to gain access to the start button switch lead. Note the wire connection points and wire routing prior to disconnecting any leads. Carefully disconnect both terminals or lead connectors from the start button.

3. Select the ohms or resistance function on the volt/ohm meter. Select the R × 1 scale on the volt/ohm meter.

4. Connect the positive test lead to the white/black lead of the starter button. Connect the negative test lead to the black/white lead of the starter button (**Figure 76**).

5. Note the ohmmeter. No continuity should be noted with the start button in the released position.

6. Next, depress the start button (**Figure 76**) and note the meter. Continuity should now be present.

7. Replace the start button if it does not perform as specified. See Chapter Seven.

Electric Starter Relay Operation

The electric starter relay (**Figure 77**) provides current to the starter motor using the shortest possible path. This ensures that the maximum amount of current reaches the starter motor.

When the ignition switch or start button is used, current flows through the neutral switch (when neutral gear is selected) to the starter relay. This current passes through a coil in the relay and then to engine ground through a ground lead. The current flowing through the coil creates a strong magnetic field that causes contacts in the relay to join together. This allows a large amount of current to flow from the battery through the relay and to the starter motor. When the ignition switch returns to the run position or the start button disengages, the current flowing to the starter relay ceases, causing the magnetic field to dissipate. A spring in the relay separates the internal contacts, halting the current flow to the starter motor. The starter relay alone cannot provide enough current to start 75-130 hp models under all conditions. A starter solenoid (**Figure 78**) is used in addition to the starter relay, providing the additional electrical current required for these larger engines. This starter motor-mounted solenoid engages via a wire connection to the starter relay. With this arrangement the starter relay only supplies enough current to switch on the starter solenoid. Refer to Chapter Seven for starter solenoid removal and testing procedures.

WARNING
Use extreme caution when working around batteries. Batteries produce hydrogen gas that can explode and result in severe bodily injury or death. Never make the final con-

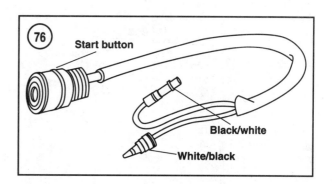

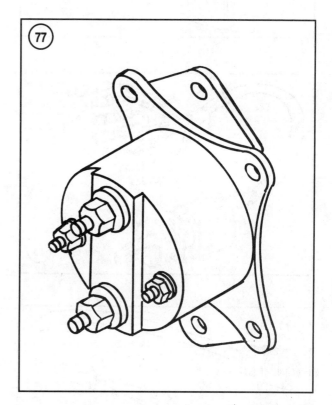

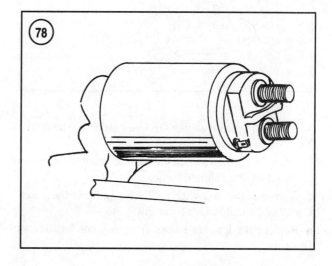

TROUBLESHOOTING

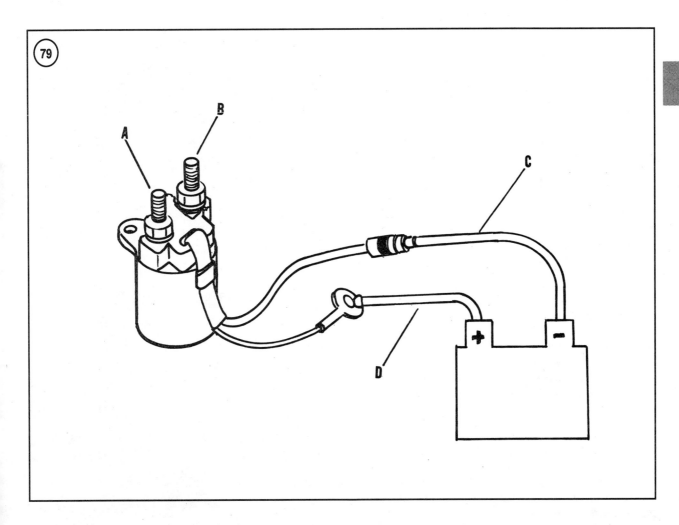

79

nection to the positive battery terminal; an arc may occur and lead to fire or explosion.

Starter Relay Test

A volt/ohm meter, fully charged battery and short jumper leads are required to test the starter relay. Refer to *Troubleshooting Test Equipment* in this chapter for information on using volt/ohm meter. Refer to the wiring diagrams located at the end of this manual to identify the wiring used for the starter relay. Trace the wire color to the component on the engine.

1. Remove the starter relay following the procedure listed in Chapter Seven.
2. Select the ohms or resistance function on the volt/ohm meter. Select the R × 1 scale on the volt/ohm meter. Place the starter relay on a suitable work surface that is far from any flammable substance.
3. Connect the positive test lead securely to one of the large relay terminals (A, **Figure 79**). Connect the negative test lead to the other large relay terminal (B, **Figure 79**) and note the meter reading. No continuity should be noted.
4. Connect a jumper wire to the positive terminal of the 12-volt battery. Touch the other end of the jumper wire to the black/white wire terminal connector (D, **Figure 79**) of the relay.
5. Connect the black wire terminal (C, **Figure 79**) of the relay to the negative terminal of a 12-volt battery using a jumper wire and observe the meter. Continuity should be noted with the battery connected to the relay..
6. Replace the relay if it does not perform as specified. See Chapter Seven.

Neutral Switch

The neutral switch (**Figure 80**) prevents the starter motor from operating if the engine shifts into gear. The switch opens the circuit connecting the ignition switch or start button to the starter relay and prevents the electric starter motor from operating.

The neutral switch is mounted to the engine on 20-130 hp electric start models with remote or tiller arm controls.

The switch is operated by shift linkage or other control mechanisms.

Removal of the switch is required for testing. Neutral switch appearance and mounting locations vary by model. Refer to the information provided in Chapter Seven to locate the neutral switch.

Use a volt/ohm meter to test the switch.

Refer to the wiring diagrams located at the end of this manual to identify the wiring used for the neutral switch. Trace the wire color to the component on the engine. (**Figure 80** and **Figure 81** typical)

NOTE
Improper shift adjustment, damaged linkage or cables or an out-of-position neutral switch can result in improper neutral switch operation.

CAUTION
Do not confuse the neutral switch used with the electric starting system with the neutral switch used on 8 hp manual start models (Model BF8A). This switch is a component of the ignition system. Refer to IGNITION SYSTEM in this chapter for test procedures with this type of neutral switch.

Neutral Switch Test

1. Shift the engine into neutral gear. Remove both battery cables from the battery.

2. Locate the neutral switch wire connectors or terminals. Note the wire connection and wire routing to ensure correct connections and routing on assembly.

3. Carefully unplug the neutral switch electrical connector(s) from the main engine wire harness.

4. Select the ohms or resistance function on the volt/ohm meter. Select the R × 1 scale on the volt/ohm meter.

5. Connect the positive test lead to one of the black/white wire terminals (A, **Figure 82**) at the switch connector. Connect the negative test lead to the other black/white wire terminal (B, **Figure 82**) at the switch connector.

6. With the switch in the released (plunger extended) position, no continuity should be noted.

7. Depress the neutral switch plunger (C, **Figure 82**) and note the meter. Continuity should now be present.

8. Replace the neutral switch if it does not perform as described. See Chapter Seven.

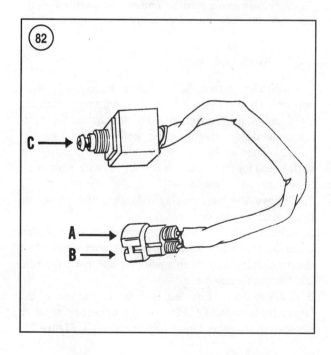

TROUBLESHOOTING

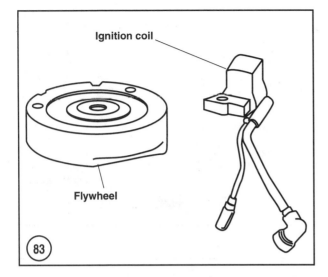

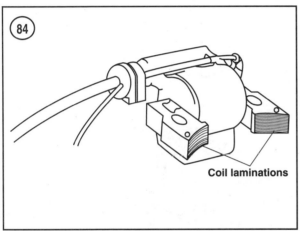

IGNITION SYSTEM

Outboard engines consistently run at a higher speed than most internal combustion engines; this places a greater burden on the ignition system. Proper engine operation is only possible if the ignition system is operating correctly. Spark must be generated at the plug(s) several thousand times per minute and each spark must occur at exactly the right time. This section provides a brief description of the various systems used along with information to help identify ignition system components followed by troubleshooting and testing procedures.

System Description

Models BF20, BF2A, BF50 and BF5A

All two hp models utilize a CDI (capacitor discharge ignition) system. This type of system does not require the use of a battery or charging system to operate. The major components include the flywheel, coil unit, spark plug lead/cap and of course the spark plug.

The flywheel (**Figure 83**) is attached to the top end of the crankshaft. Magnets are positioned within the outer surface of the flywheel.

A cylinder block-mounted ignition coil (**Figure 83**) is positioned in close proximity to the magnets of the flywheel.

As the flywheel magnets pass by the ignition coil, a strong magnetic field forms in the coil laminations (**Figure 84**). Electric current is created in the primary circuit of the ignition coil. Transistorized circuits within the ignition coil complete a circuit that allows current to flow through the primary circuit as the magnetic field passes through the coil. Electrical current flowing through the primary circuit allows the magnetic field surrounding the coil to strengthen. Using the internal transistorized circuits, the primary circuit is switched off. Switching the primary circuit off causes the magnetic field to collapse. The collapsing field causes a very high voltage to develop in the secondary circuit. The secondary circuit is connected to the spark plug lead and spark plug.

This system operates at the speed of the flywheel unlike most 4-stroke engines with ignition systems that operate at the speed of the camshaft. An extra or wasted spark occurs during the exhaust stroke and poses no problems, provided the system timing is correct.

Timing advancement with increasing engine speed is performed by the internal transistorized circuits and timing adjustments are not required.

Pushing the stop button grounds the primary ignition circuit and prevents the ignition system from operating.

Except for the spark plug, this system requires no maintenance or adjustments and is extremely reliable. Most problems are the result of debris or corrosion buildup between the coil lamination (**Figure 84**) and the flywheel (**Figure 83**). The spacing between the ignition coil and the flywheel is adjustable and proper spacing is required for accurate system operation. Refer to Chapter Seven for information on the removal, installation and adjustment of the ignition coil unit. Other problems are caused by dirty or contaminated wire connections. A faulty stop switch or associated wiring can result in no start or an ignition misfire. See *Component Test Sequence* in this chapter for information on troubleshooting this ignition system.

Models BF75 and BF100 prior to serial No. 1200000

These models use a breaker points ignition system. The major components are the flywheel (**Figure 85**), ignition charge coil, camshaft pulley, breaker points and condenser, ignition coil and timing advance mechanism (**Figure 87**).

The flywheel (**Figure 85**) is securely attached to the top end of the crankshaft. Magnets are positioned on the inner diameter of the flywheel and are used to create the electric current needed to operate the ignition system.

An ignition charging coil (**Figure 85**) is positioned under the flywheel and in close proximity to the flywheel magnets.

The breaker points and condenser are positioned under the camshaft pulley (**Figure 86**). They complete a circuit that allows the current created by the ignition charge coil to flow through the primary circuit in the ignition coil. Opening and closing the breaker points with a cam located under the camshaft pulley (**Figure 86**) switches the circuit on and off.

Electrical current generates as the flywheel magnets pass near the ignition charge coil. This electrical current flows through the primary circuit in the ignition coil (**Figure 86**) and causes a magnetic field to form within the coil. Rotation of the camshaft pulley (**Figure 86**) causes the pulley-mounted cam to open the breaker points (**Figure 86**). Interruption of the primary circuit then occurs and the magnetic field in the ignition coil collapses. This collapsing action causes the magnetic field to pass through the secondary coil, allowing high-voltage current to flow from the coil to the spark plugs.

A condenser (**Figure 86**) extends the life of the breaker points by preventing arcing at the breaker point contacts. In addition, the condenser allows the magnetic field in the coil to collapse much faster causing, a higher voltage potential at the spark plug.

Proper engine operation requires the spark at the plug to occur earlier at higher engine speeds. A centrifugal weight advance mechanism causes the points to open earlier relative to the camshaft with increased engine speed. This timing advance results in improved performance and fuel economy.

Spark occurs at both spark plugs simultaneously, essentially wasting one of the sparks. No problems result from firing both sparks simultaneously, provided the system is properly adjusted. When one of the cylinders is at the firing position, the other cylinder is on its exhaust stroke.

Grounding the primary circuit when the stop button is pushed stops the ignition system.

Regular maintenance is required to ensure proper ignition system operation. An opening in the camshaft pulley allows access to the breaker points.

This system is very reliable and most problems are related to misadjusted, dirty, burnt or corroded breaker point contacts. Other problems may be related to failure of the condenser, ignition charge coil or ignition coil. See

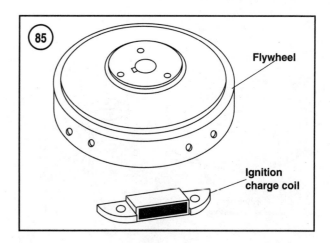

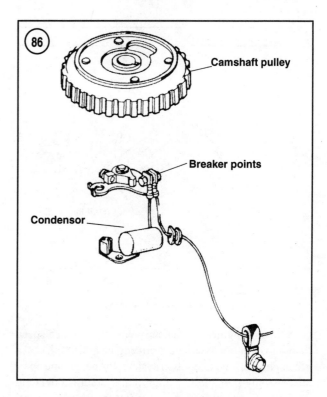

Component Test Sequence in this chapter for information on troubleshooting this ignition system.

Models BF75, BF8A, BF100, BF9.9A and BF15A serial No. 1200001-on

These models are equipped with a capacitor discharge ignition system (CDI) that provides a stronger spark and requires less maintenance than earlier models with breaker-type ignition systems. Major components of the ignition system are the flywheel, ignition charge coil, CDI unit and ignition coils. Other components include the

TROUBLESHOOTING

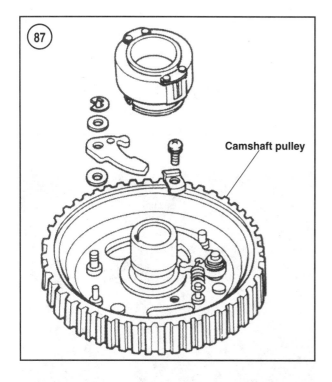

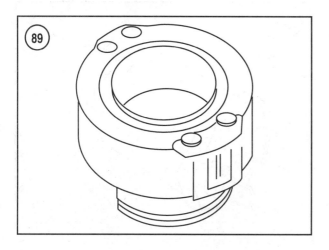

camshaft pulley, pulser coil and trigger magnet mechanism.

The flywheel (**Figure 85**) attaches to the top end of the crankshaft. Magnets are positioned on the inner diameter of the flywheel and create the electric current needed to operate the ignition system.

An ignition charging coil (**Figure 85**) is positioned under the flywheel in close proximity to the flywheel magnets.

Rotation of the flywheel magnets next to the ignition charge coil causes AC (alternating current) to form and flow from the ignition charge coil to the CDI unit. The CDI unit converts the AC to DC (direct current) for storage in an internal capacitor.

A pulser coil (**Figure 88**) sits under the camshaft pulley (**Figure 87**) in close proximity to the trigger magnet mechanism (**Figure 89**) mounted to the camshaft pulley.

The CDI unit (**Figure 90**) stores the electrical current created by the ignition system and releases it at the proper time.

Rotation of the camshaft pulley causes the trigger magnet mechanism to pass near the pulser coil, creating a trigger pulse in the pulser coil. The trigger pulse is sent to the CDI unit causing the voltage stored in the CDI unit to release into the primary ignition coil. This rapid current buildup creates a magnetic field that passes into the secondary coil which creates the voltage necessary to jump the spark plug gap(s).

Proper engine operation requires the spark at the plug to occur earlier at higher engine speeds. A centrifugal weight advance mechanism rotates the magnetic trigger mechanism, allowing the trigger pulse to occur earlier relative to the camshaft with increased engine speed. This timing advance results in improved performance and fuel economy.

Spark occurs at both spark plugs simultaneously, essentially wasting one of the sparks. No problems result from firing both sparks simultaneously, provided the system is properly adjusted. When one of the cylinders is at the firing position, the other cylinder is on its exhaust stroke.

Grounding the ignition charging coil circuit stops the ignition system with the stop button or ignition switch.

This system is extremely reliable and requires little maintenance except for spark plug maintenance. Problems are generally related to dirty or corroded contacts. Problems with the ignition stop circuit may result in a no-start or misfire condition. See *Component Test Sequence* in this chapter for information on troubleshooting this ignition system.

20-50 hp models

These models are equipped with a solid state CDI (capacitor discharge ignition) ignition system that requires very little maintenance (other than periodic replacement of the spark plugs).

Major components of the ignition system are the flywheel, ignition charge coil, CDI unit and ignition coils. Other components include the camshaft pulley, pulser coil and trigger magnet mechanism. The flywheel (A, **Figure 85**) is attached to the top end of the crankshaft. Magnets positioned on the inner diameter of the flywheel are used to create the electric current needed to operate the ignition system.

An ignition charging coil (B, **Figure 85**) is positioned under the flywheel and in close proximity to the flywheel magnets. Rotation of the flywheel magnets next to the ignition charge coil causes AC (alternating current) to form and flow from the ignition charge coil to the CDI unit (**Figure 91**). The CDI unit coverts the AC to DC (direct current) for storage in a capacitor inside the CDI unit.

A pulser coil (**Figure 92**) is positioned under the camshaft pulley (**Figure 87**) in close proximity to the trigger magnet mounted to the camshaft pulley. As the trigger magnet passes the pulser coil, a trigger pulse is sent to the CDI unit (**Figure 91**) which causes the stored voltage to be released into the primary ignition coil. The rapid buildup of electricity in the primary ignition coil (**Figure 93**) causes a magnetic field to build inside the secondary coil, which creates the spark necessary to jump the spark plug gap(s).

The stop circuit grounds the ignition charging coil output and prevents current from flowing to the CDI unit.

The CDI unit (**Figure 91**) provides overspeed protection and other features to protect the engine, should overheating or low oil pressure occur.

Ignition problems with this system are generally related to dirty or corroded contacts. Problems with the ignition stop circuit may result in a no-start or misfire condition. See *Component Test Sequence* in this chapter for information on troubleshooting this ignition system.

75-130 hp models

These models are equipped with a battery-powered CDI (capacitor discharge ignition) ignition system that requires very little maintenance (other than periodic replacement of the spark plugs).

Major components of this ignition system include the alternator rotor (**Figure 94**), crankshaft pulley (**Figure 95**) on 115 and 130 hp models, pulser coils (**Figure 96**),

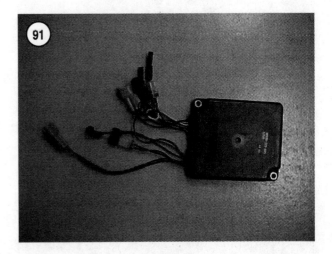

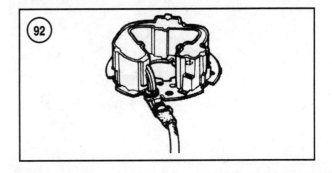

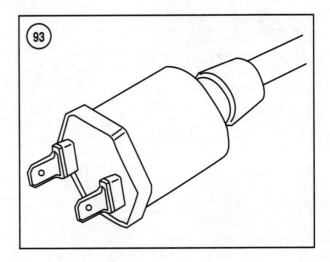

TROUBLESHOOTING

69

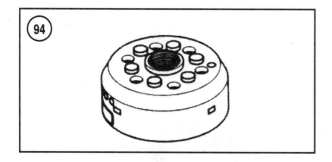

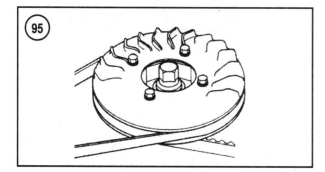

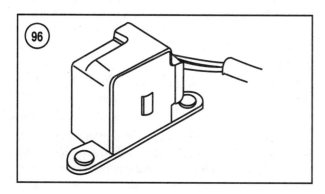

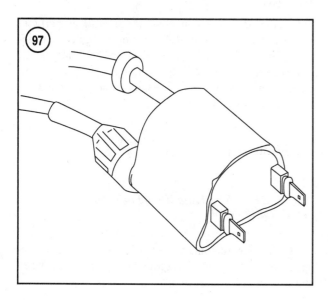

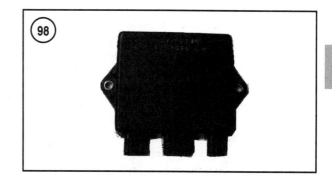

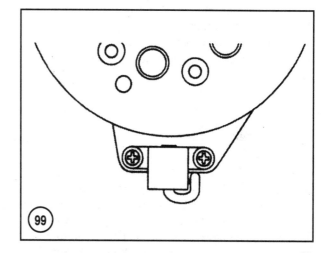

ignition coils (**Figure 97**) and the engine control unit (**Figure 98**).

When the ignition is switched ON, battery voltage is supplied to the engine control unit where it is increased and stored within an internal capacitor.

The pulser coils are attached to the cylinder block in close proximity to the alternator rotor or crankshaft pulley (**Figure 99**). One of the pulser coils triggers the ignition pulse for cylinders 1 and 4. The other pulser coil triggers the ignition pulse for cylinders 2 and 3. Magnetic raised areas (A, **Figure 100**) on the pulley cause electrical pulses to form as they pass by the pulser coils. These pulses are sent to the engine control unit (**Figure 98**) and determine engine speed and crankshaft position.

When a pulse is created in the pulser coil for cylinders 1 and 4, switching circuits within the engine control unit release the current stored in the capacitor and direct it to the cylinder 1 and 4 primary coil. As this surge of current passes through the coil, it causes a magnetic field to rapidly form in the ignition coil. The building magnetic field passes through the secondary coil, causing a very high voltage at both spark plugs.

This system creates an additional or wasted spark that occurs during one of the cylinders' exhaust stroke. Because burning of the fuel is complete, the extra spark creates no problems if the system is operating correctly.

Proper engine operation requires the spark at the plug to occur earlier at higher engine speeds. These models' engine control units automatically advance the spark timing as engine speed increases. The electronic ignition advance systems eliminate the problems associated with mechanical timing advance. In addition, timing adjustments are not required with these models.

Other functions performed by the engine control unit (**Figure 98**) include:
1. Fuel injection control (115 and 130 hp models).
2. Overspeed protection.
3. Electric fuel pump control (115 and 130 hp models).
4. Low oil pressure and overheat power reduction.
5. Emergency stop (lanyard switch).

Refer to *Electronic Fuel Injection System* in this chapter for additional information covering the engine control unit on 115 and 130 hp models.

Ignition problems with this system are generally related to dirty or corroded contacts. Problems with the ignition ON circuit may result in a no-start or misfire condition. Ignition problems such as no-start conditions or ignition misfires may result from debris or corrosion deposits on the crankshaft pulley or pulser coil. Improper clearance adjustment (B, **Figure 100**) of the pulser coil-to-pulley may cause a no-start or ignition misfire as well. See *Component Test Sequence* in this chapter for information on troubleshooting this ignition system.

Component Test Sequence

Always refer to *Troubleshooting Preparation* in this chapter prior to performing any testing. Many times ignition problems are the result of dirty, loose, corroded or damaged wire connections. Wasted time and the replacement of good components can result from not performing a few preliminary steps.

Refer to **Table 3** under the listed symptom to determine the component or system that requires testing.

Stop Circuit Test

Any malfunction with the stop circuit usually results in an inability to start the engine. In some cases the engine starts, yet it suffers an ignition misfire at various engine speeds. A fault may result in an inability to switch off the engine. This section provides troubleshooting and testing procedures for the engine stop circuit.

Various means are used to stop or interrupt the ignition systems. On 2-5 hp models and BF75, BF100 models

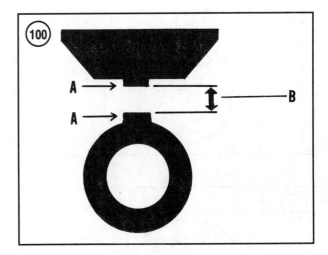

(prior to serial No. 1200000), the engine stop circuit operates by grounding the primary ignition coil circuit. The engine stops by grounding the ignition charging coil output on models BF8A, BF75, BF100 (serial No. 1200001-on) along with all 9.9-50 hp models. All 75-130 hp models use a battery-powered ignition system; switching off the power source stops the engine. Additionally, the ignition is interrupted internally within the ECU when the lanyard switch lead and key switch black/red wire are grounded.

Major components of the stop circuits include the engine stop button, ignition switch (on models so equipped), emergency switch (lanyard switch) and associated wiring.

Refer to *Spark Test* in this chapter to determine if spark is present prior to testing the stop circuit. A problem with the stop circuit is unlikely if spark is present; however, testing may find intermittent faults. All tests are performed without running the engine.

Determining if the stop circuit is operating properly requires a volt/ohm meter. Refer to the wiring diagrams located at the end of this manual to help locate the components described in the following test procedures. Identify the wiring for the stop circuit and trace the wires to the component on the engine.

Continuity Test

Models BF75, BF8A and BF100 prior to serial No. 1200000

The black wire connecting the ignition coil to the engine stop switch is used to ground the ignition coil when the stop switch is activated.

TROUBLESHOOTING

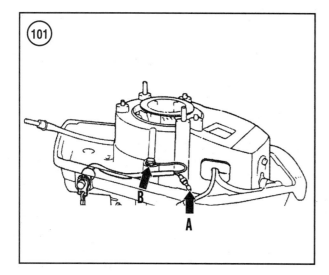

101

1. Disconnect both battery cables (electric start and/or battery charging models). Remove the spark plug and connect the spark plug lead to a suitable engine ground.
2. Locate and disconnect the black wire lead from the ignition coil connection.
3. Select the ohms function on your volt/ohm meter. Select the R × 1 scale on the meter. Connect the positive test lead to the disconnected black lead (A, **Figure 101**). Connect the negative test lead to a suitable engine ground or an unpainted cylinder block bolt (B, **Figure 101**).
4. Observe the meter reading without activating the stop switch. No continuity should be noted.
5. Observe the meter while you depress the stop switch. Continuity should not be present.
6. Check all wire terminal connections and test the stop switch following the procedure listed in this chapter if the switch does not operate as described. Test all other components of the ignition system if no spark is present and the stop circuit operates correctly.
7. Connect all leads to the correct locations then install the spark plug and spark plug lead.

Models BF50 and BF5A

The black/red wire connecting the ignition coil to the stop switch is used to ground the ignition when the stop switch is activated.
1. Remove the spark plug and ground the spark plug lead.
2. Locate and disconnect the black/red lead connecting the stop switch to the engine. Be careful to avoid inadvertently selecting the warning system lead that is also colored black/red.
3. Select the ohms function of your volt/ohm meter. Select the R × 1 scale on the meter. Connect the positive test lead to the disconnected black/red lead (A, **Figure 101**) connected to the stop switch. Connect the negative test lead to a suitable engine ground or an unpainted cylinder block bolt (B, **Figure 101**).
4. Observe the meter reading without activating the stop switch. No continuity should be noted.
5. Observe the meter as you depress the stop switch. Continuity should now be noted.
6. Check all wire terminal connections and test the stop switch following the procedure listed in this chapter if the switch does not operate as described. Check all other components of the ignition system if no spark is present and the stop circuit operates correctly.
7. Connect all leads to the correct locations then install the spark plug and spark plug lead.

Models BF75, BF100 (Serial No. 1200001-on) BF8A, BF9.9A, BF15A

The black or black/red wire connecting the CDI unit to the stop switch is used to interrupt the ignition by grounding the charge coil output.
1. Disconnect both battery leads (electric start and/or battery charging models). Remove both spark plugs and ground the spark plug leads.
2. Locate and disconnect the black or black/red wire connecting the stop switch to the CDI unit.
3. Isolate the ignition charge coil from the ignition system as follows:
   a. On models BF75, BF100 locate and disconnect the black ignition charge coil lead at the CDI unit.
   b. On models BF8A locate and disconnect the brown ignition charge coil lead at the CDI unit.
   c. On models BF9.9A, BF15A, locate and disconnect the black/green (black/red on some models) ignition charge coil leads from the engine wire harness.
4. Select the ohms function on your volt/ohm meter. Select the R × 1 scale on the meter.
5. Connect the positive test lead to the black or black/red lead connecting the stop switch to the CDI unit (A, **Figure 102**). Connect the negative test lead to a suitable engine ground or an unpainted cylinder block bolt (B, **Figure 102**).
6. Observe the meter reading without activating the stop switch. No continuity should be noted.
7. Push or activate the stop switch and observe the meter. Continuity should now be noted. Observe the meter readings. (On models so equipped, activate the lanyard switch.) Continuity should be noted.
8. Test the stop switch and/or lanyard switch (on models so equipped) following the procedure listed in this chapter if the switch does not operate as described. Test the wire

harness for a short to ground. Test all other components of the ignition system if no spark is present and the stop circuit operates correctly.

9. Connect all leads to the correct locations then install the spark plugs and leads. Clean then connect the battery cables to the proper connection.

Models BF20A, BF25A, BF30A and 35-50 hp models)

The stop switch or key switch is connected to the CDI unit by the black/red wire. The stop switch or key switch interrupts ignition by grounding the charge coil output.

1. Disconnect both battery cables from the battery terminals (electric start and battery charging models). Remove all spark plugs and ground all spark plug leads.
2. Locate and disconnect the black/red wire from the wire terminal bracket (**Figure 103**, typical).
3. Select the ohms function on your meter. Select the R × 1 scale on the meter.
4. Connect the positive test lead to the disconnected black/red stop switch wire (**Figure 104**). Connect the negative test lead to a suitable engine ground or an unpainted cylinder block bolt (B, **Figure 102**).
5A. *Models equipped with a key switch*—Turn the key switch to the ON position. No continuity should be noted. Next, turn the key switch to OFF while noting the meter. Continuity should now be present.
5B. *Models equipped with a stop button*—Observe the meter without activating the stop switch. No continuity should be noted. Next, push the stop button while noting the meter. Continuity should now be present.
6. On models equipped with a lanyard switch, activate the lanyard switch while noting the meter. Continuity should be noted.
7. Test the key switch, stop switch and/or lanyard switch (as necessary) as described in this chapter if the switch does not function as described. Also check the stop circuit for a short to ground.
8. Connect all wires, then install the spark plugs and plug wires. Connect the battery cables to the battery.

Models BF75, BF90, BF115 and BF130

NOTE
An inaccurate result will occur if the wrong black/red wire is tested. Ensure that the test is performed using the black/red wire connected to the tiller or remote control.

1. Remove both battery cables from the battery. Remove the spark plugs and ground the spark plug leads.

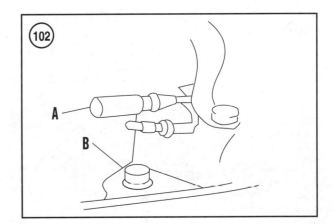

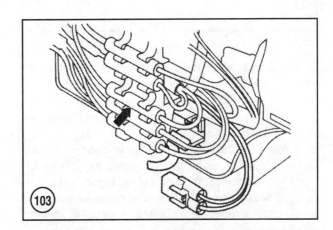

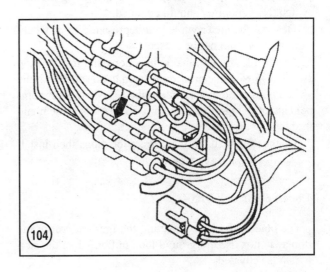

2. Note all wire connections and routing, then locate and disconnect the black/red wire from the wire terminal bracket (**Figure 105**).
3. Select the R × 1 scale on the meter. Connect the positive test lead to the black/red wire connected to the key switch side of the circuit. Connect the negative test lead to

TROUBLESHOOTING

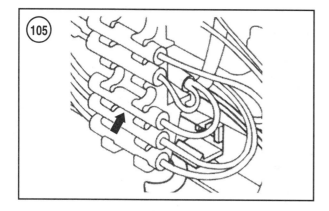

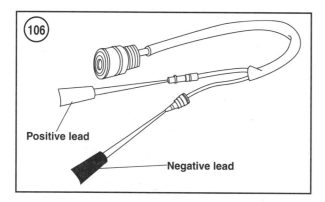

a suitable engine ground or an unpainted cylinder head bolt.

4. Position the key switch in the ON position and observe the meter readings. No continuity should be noted.

5. Position the key switch in the OFF position and observe the meter readings. Continuity should now be noted.

   a. Position the key switch in the ON position. Observe the meter reading as you activate the lanyard switch. The meter should indicate continuity.

6. Test all wire connections, lanyard switch and key switch following the procedures listed in this chapter if the stop circuit does not perform as described.

7. Clean the wire terminals and connection points then connect the black/red wires to the correct location on the wire terminal bracket. Clean and connect both battery cables to the battery.

Voltage Test

Models BF75, BF90, BF115 and BF130

These models are equipped with a battery-powered ignition system. A black/yellow wire is used to provide battery voltage to the ignition system. A black/red wire is used to switch the ignition system OFF when the key switch is positioned in the OFF position or the lanyard switch is activated. A failure in either wire or associated circuit can result in a no-spark condition.

NOTE
An inaccurate result will occur if the wrong black/yellow wire is tested. Ensure that the test is performed using the black/yellow wire connected to the tiller or remote control.

1. Remove the spark plugs and ground the spark plug leads. Note all wire connections and routing, then locate and disconnect the black/yellow wires from the wire terminal bracket (**Figure 105**, typical).

2. Select the *DC volts* function on your volt/ohm meter. Select either the 20- or 40-volt scale on the meter. Connect the positive test lead to the black/yellow wire connected to the key switch side of the circuit (**Figure 105**). Connect the negative test lead to a suitable engine ground or and unpainted cylinder head bolt.

3. With the key switch in the OFF position, observe the meter reading. The meter should indicate zero (0) volts.

4. Turn the key switch to the ON position. The meter should now indicate 12.0-13.0 volts.

5. Check the battery condition, fuses, all wire connection and test the key switch following the procedures listed in this chapter if the switch does not perform as described.

6. Clean the terminal and connection on the wire terminal bracket, then connect all black/yellow wire terminals. Install the spark plugs and plug wires.

Stop Button Test

Refer to the wiring diagrams located at the end of this manual to assist with identification and location of the stop button. Identify the wiring used, then trace the wire to the stop button on the engine. Removing the stop button is not required for testing.

1. Disconnect both battery cables from the battery. Remove the spark plugs and ground the spark plug leads.

2. Locate the stop switch lead connection on the engine and carefully disconnect or unplug both connections from the engine.

3. Select the ohms function on your volt/ohm meter. Select the R × 1 scale on the meter. Connect the positive test lead to one of the wires connected to the stop button. Connect the negative test lead to the other wire of the stop button (**Figure 106**).

4. Without pushing or activating the stop button, observe the meter reading. No continuity should be noted.

5. Observe the meter reading as you push or activate the stop button. The meter should now indicate continuity.

6. Check the entire wire harness for bare wires, dirty, corroded or abraded areas and repair as required. Replace the stop button if it does not perform as described. Refer to Chapter Seven for stop button replacement. Repeat Steps 1-6 after the repair to ensure proper operation.

7. Install the spark plugs and leads. Clean and connect the battery cables to the battery.

Lanyard Switch Test

The lanyard switch is located on the engine on tiller-controlled models and is integrated into the remote control on remote-controlled models. Access to the lanyard switch wire is required for proper testing. Removal and partial disassembly of the remote control is required on models so equipped. Refer to Chapter Thirteen to remove and install the lanyard switch on tiller controlled models. Refer to Chapter Fourteen to remove and disassemble the control box. Refer to the wiring diagrams located at the end of this manual to assist with identifying and locating the lanyard switch.

NOTE
Models BF20, BF2A are equipped with the lanyard switch integrated into the stop switch. This does not effect the testing of the components.

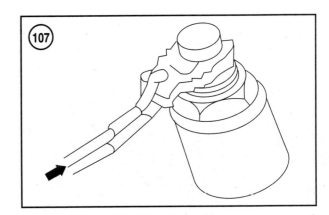

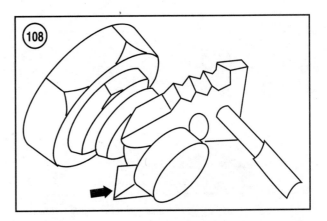

1. Disconnect both battery cables at the battery terminals. Remove the spark plugs and ground the plug leads.
2. Locate the lanyard switch wires. Note the location and routing of the switch wires and carefully disconnect both wires from the engine wire harness or remote control wiring connectors.
3. Select the R × 1 scale on your volt/ohm meter. Connect the positive test lead to one of the lanyard switch leads. Connect the negative test lead to the other lanyard switch lead (**Figure 107**).
4. Ensure that the lanyard switch cord connector is properly clipped to the switch (**Figure 108**) and the switch is in the normal or run position.
5. Observe the meter reading. The meter should indicate no continuity.
6. Pull the lanyard from the switch (**Figure 108**) while noting the meter. The meter should indicate continuity when the lanyard is pulled from the switch.
7. Inspect the lanyard switch wires and connectors for worn or damaged areas or loose or corroded connections. Replace the lanyard switch if the wiring and connectors are in good condition, but the lanyard does not operate as described.

NOTE
*See **Neutral Switch** in this chapter for an 8 hp engine (model BF8A) with serial No. 1300001-on that is experiencing an ignition problem.*

Spark Plug Connector

A defective spark plug cap can result in a no-start condition, or in many instances, an ignition misfire at higher engine speeds. Inspect the cap for corrosion or a weathered appearance. Replace all of the spark plug caps and the wires to ensure a reliable repair. If the cap is defective, arcing is noted in most cases around the cap-to-spark plug connection while cranking or running the engine.

Most models have a device integrated into the cap to reduce electrical interference caused by the ignition system. Spark plug cap resistance specifications are provided for the 35-50 hp models. Specifications are not provided for the other models. Test the cap resistance when testing the ignition coils on 35-50 hp models.

TROUBLESHOOTING

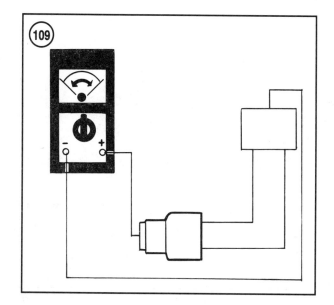

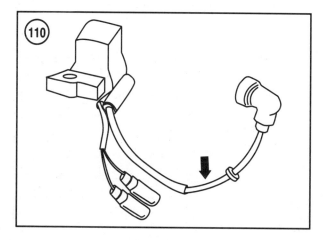

Spark Plug Lead

The spark plug lead (**Figure 110**) is integrated into the ignition coil on 35-50 hp models. Attempts to remove the wire will result in subsequent coil failure. Worn or damaged insulator jacket surfaces allow arcing to the cylinder block or other surfaces. This condition results in an ignition misfire. Inspect the spark plug lead for cracks in the insulating jacket, abraded surfaces or weathered surfaces. Replace the ignition coil/lead assembly if you note any of these defects.

Ignition Coil Resistance Tests

Resistance testing checks for open circuits or short circuits in the primary and secondary circuits of the ignition coil. In the vast majority of cases, a fault within the ignition coil appears when the resistance is tested. Ignition coil test specifications are listed in **Table 5** for both primary and secondary resistance. Perform all resistance tests at normal room temperature to ensure accurate test results.

A resistance test only indicates a short or open circuit. Faults within the coil may result in internal arcing that prevents a good spark at the spark plug. When this condition is present, you may notice a clicking noise emanating from the coil as you attempt to start the engine. A spark test tool usually indicates the lack of good, strong blue spark when the engine is cranked. A resistance test may or may not indicate an internal short. Refer to *Checking for spark* in this chapter for instruction on using a spark test tool.

Primary resistance test

1. Disconnect both battery cables from the battery. Remove the spark plugs from the engine. Refer to Chapter Eight and remove the flywheel to gain access to the test points on 2 and 5 hp models. Note the wire location and routing, then disconnect the ignition coil wires.
2. Select the *Ohms or Resistance* function on your volt/ohm meter.
3A. On 2 and 5 hp models, connect the positive test lead to the black coil wire and the negative test lead to the coil lamination (**Figure 111**).
3B. On BF75 and BF100 models, connect the positive test lead to the primary wire terminal and the negative test lead to the ignition coil laminations (**Figure 112**).
3C. On BF9.9A, BF15A, BF90A, BF115A and BF130A models, connect the positive test lead to one terminal of the coil and the negative test lead to the remaining terminal (**Figure 113**).

1. Disconnect both battery cables from the battery. Remove the spark plugs. Carefully twist the cap counterclockwise to unscrew the cap from the spark plug lead.

2. Select the *ohms* function on your volt/ohm meter. Select the 10K scale on the meter. Connect the positive test lead to the coil end of the spark plug cap. Connect the negative (–) meter test lead to the spark plug end of the spark plug cap (**Figure 109**).

3. The resistance should be 7,500-12,500 ohms. Repeat the test for the remaining spark plug caps. Replace all spark plug caps if any incorrect readings are noted.

4. Thread the spark plug cap onto the spark plug lead and tighten securely. Install the spark plugs. Clean and connect the battery cables to the battery.

CHAPTER THREE

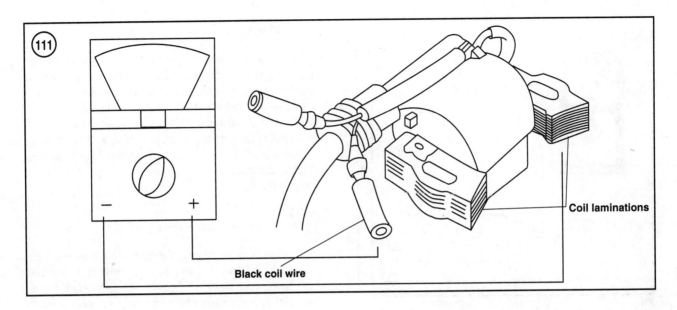

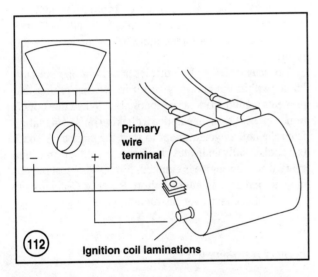

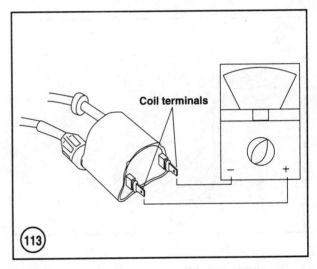

3D. On 20-50 hp models, connect the positive test lead to one of the coil primary terminals (A, **Figure 114**) and the negative test lead to the remaining coil primary terminal (B, **Figure 114**).

4. Compare the resistance to the primary resistance specifications listed in **Table 5**. Replace the ignition coil if the resistance is not as specified. Refer to Chapter Seven.

5. Install the spark plugs and connect the coil leads to the spark plugs. Clean and connect the battery cables to the battery.

Secondary resistance test

CAUTION
On 2-15 and 35-50 horsepower models, inaccurate test results may result if the spark

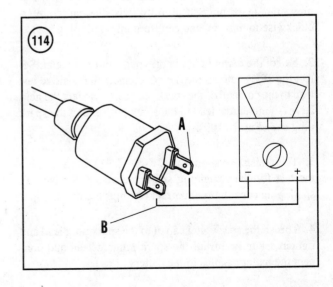

TROUBLESHOOTING

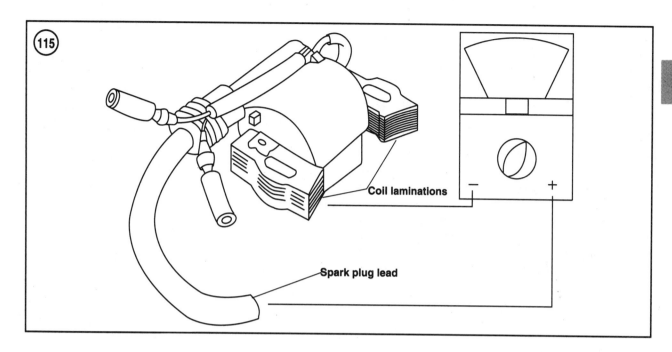

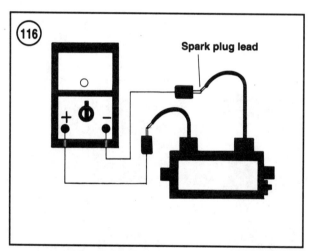

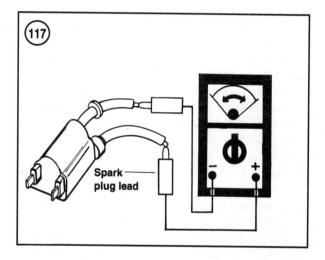

plug cap is not removed prior to performing the secondary resistance test.

1. Disconnect the battery cables from the battery. Remove the spark plugs. On 2 and 5 hp models, remove the flywheel to access the test points. See Chapter Eight. Note the wire locations and routing, then disconnect the ignition coil wires.

2A. On 2 and 5 hp models, remove the spark plug cap prior to measuring the coil resistance. Connect the positive test lead to the spark plug lead and the negative test lead to the coil laminations (**Figure 115**).

2B. On BF75 and BF100 models, remove the spark plug caps. Connect the positive test lead to one spark plug lead and the negative test lead to the other spark plug lead (**Figure 116**).

2C. On BF9.9A and BF15A models, remove the spark plug caps. Connect the positive test lead to one spark plug lead (A, **Figure 117**) and the negative test lead to the other spark plug lead (B, **Figure 117**).

2D. On 20-30 hp models, connect the positive test lead to the green wire terminal (A, **Figure 118**) and the negative test lead to the spark plug cap (B, **Figure 118**).

2E. On 35-50 hp models, remove the spark plug caps. Connect the positive test lead to the green wire terminal (A, **Figure 119**) and the negative test lead to the spark plug lead connection (B, **Figure 119**).

2F. On 75-130 hp models, connect the positive test lead to one of the spark plug leads (A, **Figure 120**) and the negative test lead to the other spark plug lead (B, **Figure 120**).
3. Compare the resistance with the secondary resistance specifications listed in **Table 5**. Replace the ignition coil if the resistance is not as specified. Refer to Chapter Seven.
4. Install the spark plugs and connect the coil wires. Clean and connect the battery cables to the battery.

Pulser Coil Resistance Test

A pulser coil triggers the ignition system on all 9.9-130 hp models and models BF75 and BF100 serial No. 1200001-on. A fault with the pulser coil can result in a no spark or intermittent ignition misfire. Most faults can be readily detected by performing a resistance test. Bear in mind that a fault with the trigger magnet may cause intermittent pulser coil operation. A thorough inspection of the magnet may reveal a cracked or damaged magnet. In addition, corrosion or other deposits on the magnet can cause intermittent pulser coil operation and subsequent ignition misfire. Removal of the camshaft pulley is required on 7.5-50 hp models to access the trigger magnets. Refer to the wiring diagrams located at the end of this manual to assist with identifying and locating the pulser coil. Identify the wiring used for the pulser coil and trace the wires to the pulser coil on the engine. Remove the electrical component cover (**Figure 121**) to access the pulser coil-to-wire harness connector.
1. Disconnect both battery cables from the battery terminals. Remove the spark plugs and connect the spark plug leads to a ground.
2. Locate and disconnect the pulser coil-to-wire harness connection(s).
3. Refer to **Table 6** for pulser coil resistance specifications. Select the ohms function on your volt/ohm meter.
4. Connect the meter test leads to the wires (**Figure 122**, typical).
5. Compare the resistance with the specification listed in **Table 6**. Replace the pulser coil(s) if the resistance does not meet the listed specification. Refer to Chapter Seven for pulser coil removal and installation.
6. Install the spark plugs and connect the spark plug leads. Clean and connect the battery cables to the battery terminals.

Ignition Charge Coil

An ignition charge coil is used to power the ignition system on all 7.5-50 hp models. This coil also powers overheating and low oil pressure warning systems. A fault

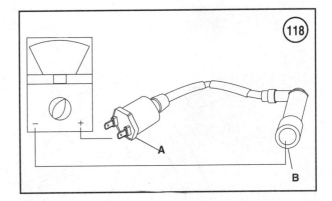

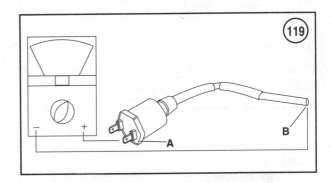

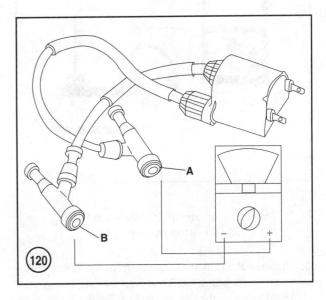

with the ignition charge coil generally results in a no-spark condition. On occasion, the only symptom is an ignition misfire at higher engine speeds.

Testing the coil involves using a volt/ohm meter to measure the resistance of the coil winding. The long wire that comprises the coil creates high resistance values. Ambient temperature significantly effects resistance readings when testing the charge coil. Perform these tests at room

TROUBLESHOOTING

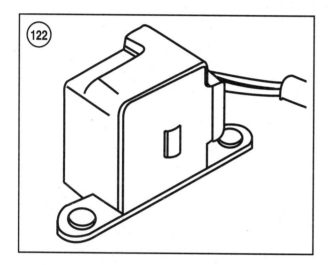

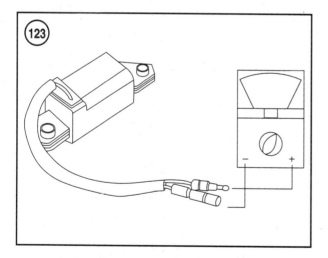

temperature unless a specific temperature is indicated. Ignition charge coil resistance specifications are listed in **Table 7**.

Ignition charge coil resistance test

The ignition charge coil is located under the flywheel and removal of the flywheel is required should it need replacement. Resistance measurements can be performed without removing the flywheel provided that the ignition charge coil wires are accessible. Refer to the wiring diagrams located at the end of this manual to assist with locating and identifying the ignition charge coil wires.

1. Disconnect both battery cables from the battery. Remove the spark plugs and connect the spark plug leads to a suitable engine ground.
2. Locate the ignition charge coil wire connector or terminal location and carefully disconnect the wires from the engine harness.
3. Select the ohms function on your volt/ohm meter.
4. Connect the meter test leads (**Figure 123**, typical) to the wire terminals. Measure and record the resistance.
5. Compare the resistance with the specifications listed in **Table 7**.
6. Replace the ignition charge coil if the resistance measurement is not within the listed specifications. Refer to Chapter Seven for ignition charge coil removal and replacement.
7. Connect the ignition charge coil wire connector or terminals to the engine wire harness. Make certain that all wires are connected to the proper terminals and the wire is properly routed to avoid interference. Install the spark plugs and leads. Clean the terminals and connect the battery cables to the battery.

WARNING
Improper removal and installation of the camshaft pulley can result in valve train damage and/or internal damage to the engine. Always refer to the appropriate section of this manual to remove or install the camshaft pulley.

Breaker Points Components

Breaker points (**Figure 124**) trigger the ignition system on models BF75 and BF100 (prior to serial No. 1200000). As with other breaker point ignition systems, a condenser (**Figure 125**) is used to enhance the performance of the ignition system. This section provides test procedures for these components.

A fault with the breaker points can result in a no-spark condition or an ignition misfire at any engine speed. Visual inspection of the breaker points usually reveals the cause of any malfunction with the breaker points.

1. Disconnect both battery cables from the battery. Remove the spark plugs and connect the spark plug leads to a suitable engine ground.
2. Remove the camshaft pulley cover (A, **Figure 126**) to access the opening in the camshaft pulley (C, **Figure 126**). Do not remove the camshaft pulley at this time.
3. Manually rotate the flywheel until the opening in the camshaft pulley (B, **Figure 126**) is positioned directly over the breaker points (**Figure 124**).
4. Inspect the breaker point contact surfaces (**Figure 127**) for burned, pitted, misaligned or corroded surfaces. Inspect the cam surface and the rub block on the breaker points for worn or damaged surfaces. Replace the breaker points along with the condenser (**Figure 125**) if you observe any of these conditions. Refer to Chapter Seven for breaker points removal and installation. Refer to Chapter Five for breaker point adjustment.
5. Install the camshaft pulley cover (A, **Figure 126**) as described in Chapter Eight. Install the spark plugs and attach the leads. Clean the terminals and connect both battery cables to the battery.

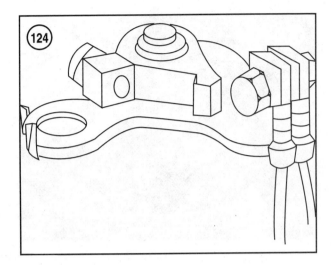

Condenser

A fault with the condenser (**Figure 125**) can result in a no-spark condition or an ignition misfire at any engine speed. A common symptom with a faulty condenser is an engine surge that is remarkably similar to an engine running out of fuel. In some cases, a faulty condenser will cause the breaker point contacts (**Figure 127**) to rapidly wear or burn.

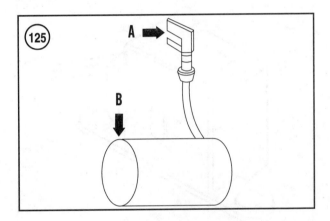

In most instances, it is in the interest of saving time and money to replace the condenser if it is suspected of causing an ignition problem. Testing the capacitance of the condenser is possible, provided the volt/ohm meter used has that capability.

1. Disconnect both battery cables from the battery. Remove the spark plugs and connect the spark plug leads to an engine ground.
2. Remove the camshaft pulley cover (A, **Figure 126**) to gain access to the camshaft pulley opening (B, **Figure 126**).
3. Manually rotate the flywheel until the camshaft pulley opening (B, **Figure 126**) is directly over the condenser (**Figure 125**).
4. Note the connection point and routing of the wire to the condenser (A, **Figure 125**). Use a small wrench and carefully disconnect the wire from the breaker points. Use extreme care to avoid dropping the attaching hardware. Route the condenser wire out of the opening in the camshaft pulley.

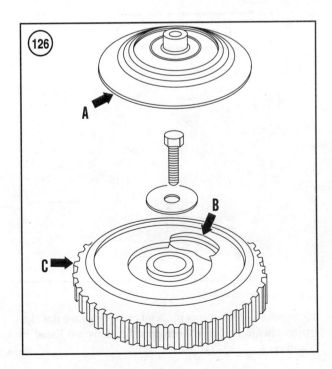

TROUBLESHOOTING

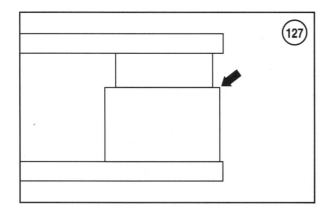

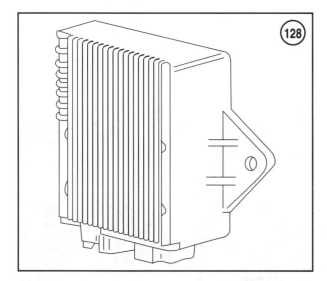

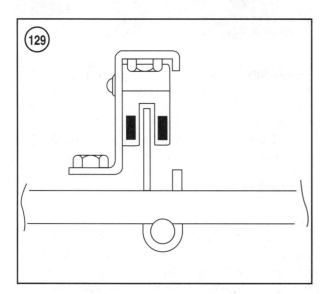

5. Follow the instructions that came with your volt/ohm meter and select the *capacitance* function on your meter.

6. Connect the positive test lead to the condenser lead (A, **Figure 125**). Touch the negative test lead to the case of the condenser (B, **Figure 125**). The capacitance should be 0.24 microfarad.

7. Refer to Chapter Seven to replace the condenser if necessary.

8. Pay particular attention to the wire routing and connect the condenser lead (A, **Figure 125**) to the breaker points. Tighten the fastener securely.

9. Refer to Chapter Eight and install the camshaft pulley cover. Install the spark plugs and leads. Clean the terminals and connect the battery cables to the battery.

CDI Unit Test

A CDI unit is used to control the ignition system on 5-90 hp models (except BF75 and BF100 models prior to serial No. 1200000). Failure of the CDI unit can result in a no-spark condition on one or all cylinders. In some rare instances, the only symptom is an intermittent ignition misfire. Erratic timing fluctuations may also occur in very rare instances. Failure of the ignition control circuits within the ECU (engine control unit) on 115 and 130 horsepower models can cause the same symptoms. In addition, the ECU (**Figure 128**) controls fuel delivery and idle speed. Refer to *Electronic Fuel Injection* in this chapter for information on testing the ECU. An inability to idle or poor performance can result if the ignition timing control circuit fails.

Testing the CDI unit uses a process of elimination. If an ignition fault is verified (no spark at the coil) and all other components of the ignition system operate correctly, the problem is likely due to a faulty CDI unit. Replace the CDI unit after testing indicates no faults with the following components:

 Engine stop circuits.
 Ignition charge coil.
 Pulser coil.
 Ignition coil.
 Neutral switch (Model BF8A serial No. 1300001-on).
 All ignition system wiring and connectors.
Refer to Chapter Seven for CDI unit replacement.

Neutral Switch

The neutral switch is used (**Figure 129**) on BF8A models (Serial No. 1300001-on) to prevent the engine from starting unless the shifter is in neutral. The switch opens a circuit leading to the CDI unit when shifted into forward or reverse gear. A faulty or maladjusted switch can result in no spark at the plug or an ignition misfire. Use a volt/ohm meter to test the operation of the neutral switch. Refer to the wiring diagrams located at the end of this manual to assist with locating and identifying the neutral switch. Identify the wiring used for the switch and trace the wires to the component on the engine.

1. Disconnect both battery cables from the battery. Remove the spark plugs and connect the spark plug leads to an engine ground.
2. Select the *ohms* function on your volt/ohm meter. Select the R × 1 scale on the meter.
3. Note the wire terminal connection and wire routing, then disconnect the blue and black/white wire connectors for the neutral switch.
4. Connect the positive test lead to the blue wire terminal leading to the switch. Connect the negative test lead to the black/white wire terminal leading to the switch.
5. Observe and record the meter reading as you shift the engine into forward, neutral and reverse gears.
6. No continuity should be noted when the shift selector is in forward or reverse gear.
7. Continuity should be noted with the shift selector is in neutral.
8. Check for proper shift adjustment as described in Chapter Five if the neutral switch does not perform as described. If the switch is adjusted correctly, but does not operate as specified, replace the switch as described in Chapter Seven.
9. Install the spark plugs and connect the spark plug leads. Clean the terminals and connect the battery cables to the battery.

WARNING SYSTEMS

Warning systems are used on 5-130 hp models to warn of a problem with the engine. Continuing to operate the engine despite an activated warning system may lead to serious damage. Components used and the mode of operation vary by model and type of control mechanism.

Models BF50, BF5A, BF75, BF8A, BF100, BF9.9A, and BF15A

These models use a warning system that indicates if low oil pressure occurs while operating the engine. They do not provide warning if the engine overheats. Electrical current to operate the oil pressure warning system is provided by the ignition system, ensuring power to the system anytime the engine is running.

The oil pressure indicator light (**Figure 130**) is mounted to the front side of the lower engine cover. The oil pressure switch (**Figure 131**) provides control of the light. On

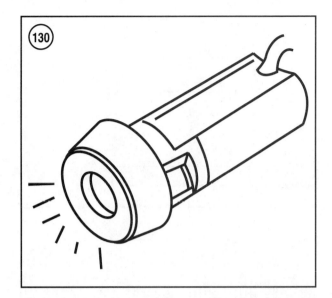

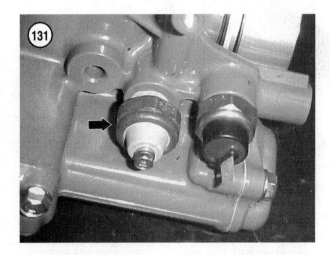

models BF50, BF5A the switch is mounted to the lower starboard side of the base engine. On models BF75, BF8A, and BF100, the switch is mounted to the upper starboard side of the base engine. On models BF9.9A and BF15A, the switch is mounted to the upper port side of the base engine near the front of the engine.

When the oil pressure reaches 0.2-0.4 kg/cm^2 (2.8-5.7 psi) the oil pressure switch closes an internal connection. This allows current from the ignition to flow through the light causing it to glow green.

On models BF8A, BF9.9A and BF15A, the circuit that connects the oil pressure indicator light passes through the CDI unit. This provides power reduction by retarding the timing advancements if low oil pressure is detected.

Flickering of the light at lower engine speeds is a normal occurrence under some conditions (low idle speed). With increasing engine speeds, a subsequent increase in

TROUBLESHOOTING

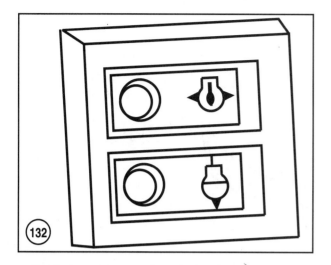

Models BF20A, BF25A, BF30A, BF35A, BF40A, BF45A, BF50A, BF75A and BF90A

These models use a system that indicates if the oil pressure is low when operating the engine. In addition, they provide an indication to the operator if the engine overheats. Electrical current to operate these systems comes from the ignition charge coil on tiller control models (BF20A, BF25A, BF30A Models) ensuring power to the system anytime the engine is running. The battery charging system provides the electrical current to power the system on models BF35A, BF40A, BF45A, BF50A and remote control models BF20A, BF25A and BF30A.

The type and location of the warning lights varies by model. Tiller-controlled models BF20A, BF25A and BF30A are equipped with an oil pressure indicator light (**Figure 130**) mounted in the front portion of the lower engine cover. All remote control models and tiller control models BF35A, BF40A, BF45A and BF50A are equipped with a warning light unit (**Figure 132**) mounted to the remote control or the tiller handle. It indicates low oil pressure and/or overheating.

Control of the light(s) is provided by the oil pressure switch (**Figure 131**) and the overheat switch (**Figure 133**).

Tiller Control Models BF20A, BF25A, BF30A

Current from the ignition system is supplied to the light via a circuit passing through the CDI unit. The oil pressure switch (**Figure 131**) is mounted to the upper port side of the base engine, near the ignition coils. This switch circuit is normally closed. Internal switching opens the circuit if there is adequate oil pressure. This allows electrical current to flow from the ignition charging coil through the CDI unit and through the oil pressure indicator light (**Figure 130**) causing it to glow green. Should low oil pressure occur, the circuits within the oil pressure switch (**Figure 131**) will close. This causes the current to flow through the oil pressure switch instead of the oil pressure light. The light turns off if low oil pressure is detected.

The overheat switch (**Figure 133**) indicates an overheat condition. This switch mounts to rear port side of the base engine between the No. 1 and No. 2 spark plugs. The circuits within this switch are open provided the engine is not overheating.

Should an overheat condition occur, the overheat switch circuits will close. A connection to the CDI unit allows it to create an ignition misfire, gradually reducing engine speed to a maximum of approximately 2800 rpm when overheat is detected. Full power gradually is restored when the overheating condition ceases.

the current provided by the ignition system causes the light to glow much brighter than at lower speed. At engine speeds of 2000 rpm and higher, the light should glow brightly. Never operate the engine unless the light comes on within a few seconds after starting the engine.

Failure of the light to glow can be caused by the following conditions. Check and/or correct each as indicated.

1. Low oil level (see Checking Oil Level in Chapter Four).
2. Faulty oil pump (see Checking Oil Pressure in this chapter).
3. Faulty oil pump check valve (see Checking Oil Pressure in this chapter).
4. Blocked oil pickup screen (see Checking Oil Pressure in this chapter).
5. Faulty oil pressure switch (see Oil Pressure Switch Testing in this chapter).
6. Faulty oil pressure indicator light (see Oil Pressure Indicator Light Testing in this chapter).

Remote Control Models BF20A, BF25A, BF30A and Tiller or Remote Control Models F35A, BF40A, BF45A, BF50A, BF75, BF90A

Current from the battery charging system powers the oil pressure and overheat indicator lights. An oil pressure switch (**Figure 131**) is mounted to the upper port side of the base engine, near the ignition coils. The circuits within the switch are normally open if sufficient oil pressure is present. During normal operation, current from the battery charging system flows through the oil pressure indicator light on the control station mounted warning light unit (**Figure 132**). Current flowing through the light causes it to glow green. If a low oil pressure condition is detected, the circuits within the oil pressure switch close. Due to a connection to the indicator light circuit, the current flows through the oil pressure switch instead of the oil pressure indicator light, turning the light off.

The overheat switch (**Figure 133**) indicates an overheat condition. This switch is mounted to the rear port side of the base engine, between the No. 1 and No. 2 spark plugs. The circuits within this switch are open, provided the engine is not overheating. A connection to the battery charging system provides the electric current to power the overheat indicator light. The normally open circuit within the overheat switch prevents a complete circuit for the light, keeping it switched off. If an overheat condition occurs, the circuits within the overheat switch close. This completes the electrical circuit and allows the current to flow through the overheat indicator light, causing it to turn on and glow red. In addition, a remote control mounted warning buzzer (**Figure 134**) sounds when the overheat warning light is switched on.

Should engine overheating occur or low oil pressure be detected, a connection to the CDI unit allows the CDI unit to gradually reduce engine speed to a maximum of 2800 rpm. This is accomplished by creating an ignition misfire. Full power gradually is restored when the overheating condition ceases.

Failure of the oil pressure indicator light to glow can be caused by the following conditions.
1. Low oil level (see Chapter Four).
2. Faulty oil pump (see *Checking Oil Pressure* in this chapter).
3. Faulty oil pump check valve (see *Checking Oil Pressure* in this chapter).
4. Blocked oil pickup screen (see *Checking Oil Pressure* in this chapter).
5. Faulty oil pressure switch (see *Oil Pressure Switch Testing* in this chapter).
6. Faulty oil pressure indicator light (see *Oil Pressure Indicator Light Testing* in this chapter).

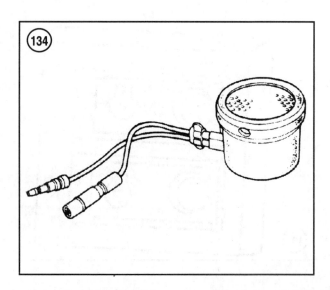

7. Fault with the battery charging system (see *Charging Systems* in this chapter).
8. Fault with the CDI Unit or wiring.

Incorrect or continuous operation of the overheat indictor light can be caused by the following conditions.
1. Faulty cooling system (see *Cooling System* in this chapter).
2. Faulty overheat switch (see *Overheat Switch Testing* in this chapter).
3. Faulty overheat indictor light (see *Overheat Indicator Light Testing* in this chapter).
4. Faulty CDI unit or wiring.

Models BF115, BF130

These models use a system that detects low oil pressure or an overheating condition. In addition, an indicator light alerts the operator that it has detected a fault with the electronic fuel injection system or the battery charging system. Refer to *Electronic Fuel Injection* in this chapter for information on the EFI system indicator light. Refer to battery charging system (in this chapter) for information on the battery charging indicator light.

The battery and/or charging system on these models provides the electrical current to operate the warning system on these models.

The oil pressure switch (**Figure 131**) is mounted to the upper starboard side of the base engine near the No. 1 cylinder intake runner. Circuits within this switch are normally open when the engine is running. This allows current to flow through the oil pressure indicator light on the warning light unit (**Figure 132**) causing it to glow green. If low oil pressure is detected, the circuits within the switch close. This allows the current to flow through

TROUBLESHOOTING

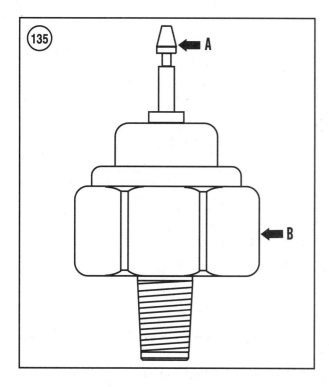

135

the oil pressure switch instead of the oil pressure indicator light, resulting in an unlit light. A connection to the ECU (**Figure 128**) allows it to reduce power by creating an ignition misfire. In addition, the warning buzzer (**Figure 134**) sounds continuously. Engine speed is gradually reduced to approximately 1800 rpm. Normal power gradually returns if the low oil pressure condition ceases.

The overheat switch (**Figure 133**) is mounted to the upper port side of the cylinder head. It connects directly to the ECU (**Figure 128**), allowing constant monitoring of the engine temperature. If an overheating condition occurs, the ECU switches on the overheat light (located on the control mounted warning light unit, **Figure 132**), causing it to glow red. The control station-mounted warning buzzer (**Figure 134**) sounds continuously as well. The ECU (**Figure 128**) enables the power reduction circuits, causing the engine speed to gradually reduce to a maximum of 1800 rpm. If overheating is still present 10 seconds after first detected, further power reduction limits the engine to 1000 rpm. The ECU stops the engine if overheating is still detected after an additional 10 seconds. Full power gradually returns if the overheating condition ceases.

Failure of the oil pressure indicator light to glow can be caused by the following conditions.

1. Low oil level (see *Checking Oil Level* in Chapter Four).

2. Faulty oil pump (see *Checking Oil Pressure* in this chapter).
3. Faulty oil pump check valve (see *Checking Oil Pressure* in this chapter).
4. Blocked oil pickup screen (see *Checking Oil Pressure* in this chapter).
5. Faulty oil pressure switch (see *Oil Pressure Switch Testing* in this chapter).
6. Faulty oil pressure indicator light (see *Oil Pressure Indicator Light Testing* in this chapter).
7. Fault with the battery charging system (see *Charging Systems* in this chapter).
8. Fault with the CDI Unit or wiring.

Incorrect or continuous operation of the overheat indictor light can be caused by the following conditions.

1. Faulty cooling system (see *Cooling System* in this chapter).
2. Faulty overheat switch (see *Overheat Switch Testing* in this chapter).
3. Faulty overheat indictor light (see *Overheat Indicator Light Testing* in this chapter).
4. Faulty ECU or wiring. (see *Electronic Fuel Injection* in this chapter).

Continuous sounding of the warning horn (**Figure 134**) can be caused by any of the conditions that cause the oil pressure indicator light to not glow green. Likewise, any condition that causes the overheat indicator light to glow red can cause the warning horn to sound continuously.

Oil pressure switch testing

Testing the operation of the oil pressure switch requires the use of a volt/ohm meter. Additional testing requires the use of an oil pressure gauge.

Locate the oil pressure switch using the information provided earlier in this section along with the wiring diagrams located at the end of this manual.

1. Disconnect both battery cables from the battery (if so equipped). Remove the spark plugs and connect the spark plug leads to a suitable engine ground.
2. Locate and disconnect the wire leading to the oil pressure switch.
3. Select the *ohms* function on your volt/ohm meter. Select the R × 1 scale on the meter.
4. Connect the positive test lead to the wire terminal connection on the oil pressure switch (A, **Figure 135**). Observe the meter reading as you touch the negative (–) meter test lead to the body of the oil pressure switch (B, **Figure 135**).
   a. On models BF50, BF5A, BF75, BF8A and BF100, no continuity should be noted.

b. On all other models except BF2A, continuity should be noted.

5. Check the operation of the oil pressure indicator light following the procedure listed in this section. Check all wiring for loose, damaged or corroded contacts.

6. If no faults are found in Step 4, refer to *Oil Pressure Test* in this chapter and perform the test as indicated.

7. Replace the oil pressure switch if the oil pressure measurements are correct and the oil pressure indicator light will not glow. Refer to Chapter Seven for oil pressure switch replacement.

8. Install the spark plugs and connect the spark plug leads. Clean the terminals and connect the battery cables to the battery.

Overheat Switch Testing

Testing the overheat switch requires a volt/ohm meter, a container of water, liquid thermometer and heat source. Use the information provided in this section and the wiring diagrams located at the end of this manual to locate the overheat switch. Identify the wire color used and trace the wire to the component on the engine.

1. Disconnect both battery cables from the battery. Remove the spark plugs and connect the spark plug lead to a suitable engine ground.

2. Locate the overheat switch on the engine. Note the wire terminal connections and wire routing, then disconnect the wire(s) from the switch. Refer to Chapter Seven and remove the switch from the engine.

3. Suspend the overheat switch in the container so that the tip of the switch is just below the water surface (**Figure 136**).

4. Select the ohms function on your volt/ohm meter and the R × 1 scale. Connect the positive test lead to one of the switch leads and the negative test lead to the remaining switch lead (**Figure 136**).

5. No continuity should be present with the water cool.

6. Begin heating the water while observing the meter. Discontinue the test if the water boils before the meter reading change.

7. Note the temperature at which the meter reading changes to continuity. The switch should close at 88-92° C (190-198° F).

8. While observing the meter, allow the water to cool. Note the water temperature at which the meter indicates no continuity. The switch should open at 77-83° C (171-181° F).

9. Replace the overheat switch if it does not operate as described.

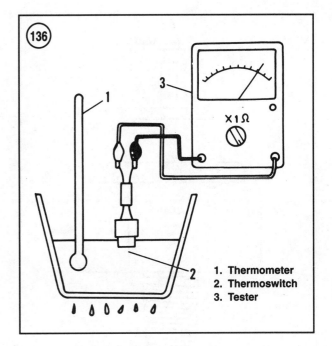

1. Thermometer
2. Thermoswitch
3. Tester

Oil Pressure Indicator Light Testing

Testing the oil pressure indicator light requires a 9-volt battery. This light is located near the front portion of the lower engine cover. Remove the light if you cannot access the wire terminals to the light. The wire colors used for the light vary by model. Refer to the wiring diagrams located at the end of this manual to assist with locating the light and wires. If necessary, trace the indicated wire color to the component on the engine.

1. Disconnect both battery cables from the battery (if so equipped). Remove the spark plugs and connect the plug leads to a suitable engine ground.

2. Note the wire connections and wire routing, then carefully disconnect the wires from the oil pressure indicator light.

3. Connections vary by model. Refer to the following to determine the connection to the 9-volt battery.

   a. On models BF50 and BF5A, connect the black/red wire terminal to the positive terminal of the 9-volt battery. Connect the black/yellow wire terminal to the negative terminal of the 9-volt battery (**Figure 137**).

   b. On other models, connect the yellow wire plug-type connector to the positive terminal of the 9-volt battery. Connect the red wire terminal or eyelet-type connector to the negative terminal of the 9-volt battery (**Figure 137**).

4. When the battery is connected, the light should glow. If not, replace the light.

TROUBLESHOOTING

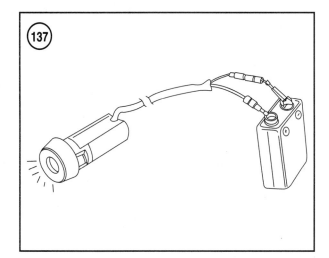

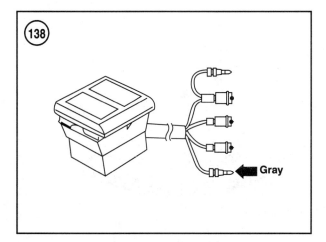

It is necessary to remove the warning light unit from the remote control, tiller handle or dash mounted panel to access the wire terminals. See Chapter Seven.

1. Disconnect both battery cables from the battery. Note the wire terminal connections and wire routing, then disconnect all wires connected to the warning light unit. Remove the warning light from its mounting location.

2. Using a jumper wire, connect the gray wire terminal (**Figure 138**) to the positive terminal of the battery.

3. Using a jumper wire, connect the negative battery terminal to the red wire terminal on the light unit. The red light should glow.

4. Remove the jumper wire from the red wire terminal and connect it to the black wire terminal on the light unit. Now the green light should glow.

5. Without removing the jumper leads, connect an additional jumper lead to the negative terminal of the battery (C, **Figure 138**) and the yellow wire terminal on the light unit. The green light should turn off and the red light should remain lit.

6. Replace the control mounted warning light unit if it fails to operate as described.

7. Install the light unit. Ensure that the wires are routed correctly. Install the spark plugs and connect the leads. Clean the terminals, and connect the battery cables to the battery.

Warning Buzzer Testing

Testing the warning buzzer requires a fully charged 12-volt battery and two jumper wires. Removing the warning buzzer may be necessary to access the wire connections. Warning buzzer mounting locations vary by model and type of control.

1. Disconnect both battery cables from the battery.

2. Remove the buzzer from its mounting location to access the wire connections.

3. Note the wire terminal connections and wire routing, then carefully disconnect both warning buzzer wires from the wire harness.

4. Using a jumper wire, connect the positive battery terminal to the black/yellow wire terminal (**Figure 139**).

5. Connect the negative terminal of the battery to the yellow/green wire terminal (**Figure 139**).

6. The warning buzzer should sound loudly when the battery is connected to it. If the buzzer fails to sound a loud tone when the battery is connected, replace the buzzer.

5. If removed, install the switch. Clean the terminals and connect the light wire terminals. Ensure the wires are routed correctly. Install the spark plugs and connect the spark plug leads. Clean and connect the battery cables to the battery.

> *WARNING*
> *Use extreme caution when working around batteries. Do not smoke or create sparks around batteries. Batteries produce hydrogen gas that can explode, resulting in severe bodily injury or death. Never make the final connection of a circuit to the battery terminal, as an arc may occur and lead to fire or explosion.*

Control Mounted Warning Light Unit Testing

Testing this component requires a fully charged 12-volt battery and three jumper wires.

Overspeed Control

Operation of outboard engines at speeds greater than recommended can lead to increased engine wear and, in many cases, engine failure. Excessive engine speed is generally the result of operation with the wrong or damaged propeller. Refer to Chapter One for information on selecting the correct propeller for your engine.

Take care when operating your outboard in shallow water or areas with underwater objects (stumps and large rocks). The engine may swing up if allowed to contact the bottom or other underwater objects. This may allow the propeller to leave the water, causing the engine to unload. When unloaded at higher engine speeds, the engine can quickly exceed the maximum recommended speed.

Overspeed control circuits are integrated into the CDI units on models BF20A, BF25A, BF30A, BF35A, BF40A, BF45A, BF50A, BF75A and BF90A. The overspeed control circuits are integrated into the ECU (engine control unit) on models BF115A and BF130A.

A fault with the overspeed control circuits can result in an ignition misfire at speeds within the recommended rpm, a no-spark condition or engine stall. In some cases, the overspeed control will not operate.

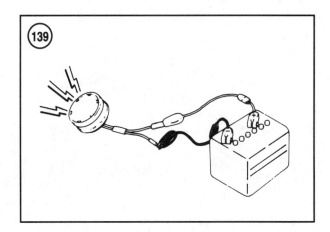

Testing the overspeed control system

Testing the overspeed control circuit requires a good tachometer and a qualified assistant to operate the boat. Follow the manufacturer's recommendation to connect and operate the tachometer. Never use the dash-mounted tachometer to determine the actual engine speed, as a discrepancy of 200 rpm or more is common. Refer to **Table 8** to determine the maximum recommended engine speed for your model. Connect the shop tachometer and have an assistant operate the engine at full throttle while you observe the tachometer reading. Never allow the engine speed to exceed the maximum rpm. Note the speed at which the misfire or rough engine operation is detected.

An engine speed in excess of the rpm limiting range indicates a fault with the CDI or ECU and replacement is required. Refer to the following to determine the correct rpm limiting range.

On models BF20A, BF25A, BF30A, BF75A and BF90A, the overspeed control circuit must activate at 6300-6900 rpm.

On models BF35A, BF40A, BF45A and BF50A, the overspeed control circuit must activate at 6400-6800 rpm.

On models BF115A and BF130A, the overspeed control circuit must activate at 6300-6400 rpm.

On other models that are not equipped with overspeed control circuits, check the propeller for damage or the

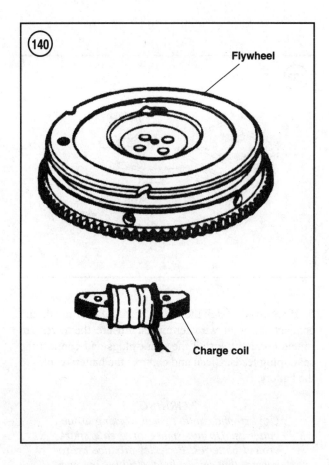

wrong pitch/diameter and correct as required. Other conditions that can contribute to excessive engine speed are a damaged gearcase, protrusions on the bottom of the boat, excessive engine mounting height and, in some instances, damaged components within the gearcase and intermediate gears. Refer to gearcase in this chapter if you suspect gearcase damage.

Always check the fuel and ignition system first if an engine misfire is detected while operating at speeds below

TROUBLESHOOTING

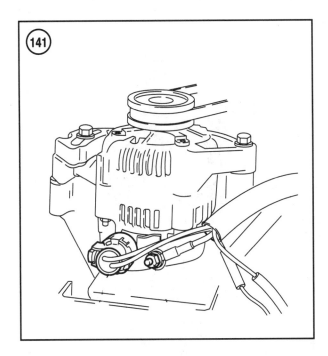

141

the maximum recommended engine speed. Replace the CDI unit or ECU if ignition misfire is detected and all other components of the ignition system operate correctly.

CHARGING SYSTEM

System Description

Information is provided in this section to help you understand the charging system function and to assist with component identification.

Models BF50 and BF5A

On these models, an optional lighting kit is available. It provides electrical current to operate onboard lighting and can be used to charge onboard batteries. Components used include the flywheel, battery charging coil (**Figure 140**), rectifier, wiring and the battery.

> **CAUTION**
> *Avoid using gel-type batteries on models BF50, BF5A and Models BF75, BF8A, BF100 and BF9.9 (prior to serial No. 1200000) unless the optional rectifier/regulator is installed to control the system output. Permanent battery damage can occur if it is allowed to overcharge.*

Manual Start Models BF75, BF8A, BF100, BF9.9A, BF15A, BF20A, BF25A and BF30A

The battery charging system charges a battery that provides current for on-board accessories. Also the charging system powers various engine controls and warning system components. Components used include the flywheel, battery charging coil (**Figure 140**), rectifier/regulator, wiring and the battery.

Electric Start Models (Except Models BF115A and BF130A)

These models use a fully regulated charging system to restore the battery charge level after starting the engine. In addition, the charging system powers the various engine controls and warning system components. Components used include the flywheel (A, **Figure 140**), battery charging coil (B, **Figure 140**), rectifier/regulator, wiring and the battery.

Models BF115A and BF130A

As these models use advanced electronic control systems, a greater demand is placed on the charging system. To address this, a high capacity belt-driven (automotive style) alternator is used (**Figure 141**). This unit is fully regulated and is capable of providing the current to operate the engine control system and charge onboard batteries.

All components of this charging system (except the wiring) are enclosed within the alternator housing (**Figure 141**) to improve reliability.

System Operation

All models (excluding BF115A, BF130A)

When the engine is running, the magnets located within the inner ring of the flywheel (**Figure 140**) pass next to the cylinder block-mounted battery charging coil (**Figure 140**). Magnetic lines of force (from the flywheel-mounted magnets) pass through the battery charging coil, creating pulsating alternating current.

As alternating current cannot be used to charge the onboard battery, a rectifier or rectifier/regulator is used to convert the alternating current to direct current.

Models BF115A, BF130A

Rotation force drives the alternator (**Figure 141**) via a grooved drive belt. Major components of the alternator include the rotor (A, **Figure 142**), stator (B, **Figure 142**) and the regulator (C, **Figure 142**).

Current passes through contact brushes (E, **Figure 142**) into the a winding in the rotor (A, **Figure 142**) creating a magnetic field. As the rotor rotates inside the stator (B, **Figure 142**), alternating current (AC) is created. A rectifier bridge in the alternator (D, **Figure 142**) converts the alternating current (AC) to direct current (DC) for storage in the onboard battery.

An internal voltage regulator controls output voltage by varying the strength of the magnetic field in the rotor. This is accomplished by limiting the amount of current flowing through the contact brushes into the rotor.

System Testing

A charging system malfunction generally causes the battery to be undercharged. Modern boats are equipped with numerous electric accessories such as electric trolling motors, depth finders, radio, stereo, live well and lighting. Frequently, the current required to operate these accessories exceeds the output of the charging system and results in a discharged battery.

Installing an auxiliary battery and a switch device (**Figure 143**) may be necessary to power accessories and to prevent a discharged cranking battery.

CAUTION
Charging system damage will occur if the battery cable(s) or any charging system wire(s) are disconnected while the engine is running. Ensure that any battery-switching device does not break the charging system circuit.

Perform a *System Output Test* as described in this chapter to determine if the charging system is operating properly. If a charging system malfunction occurs, test the individual components of the system to determine which components have failed. Test all of the components as described; more than one part could be faulty.

WARNING
Use extreme caution when working around batteries. Batteries produce hydrogen gas that can explode and result in severe bodily injury or death. Never make the final connection of a circuit to the battery terminal as an arc may occur and lead to fire or explosion.

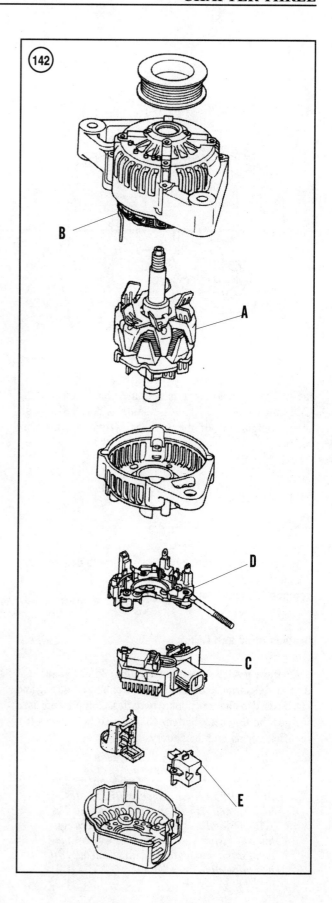

TROUBLESHOOTING

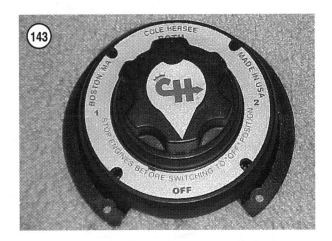

CAUTION
Never run an outboard without cooling water. Use either a test tank or flush/test device. Remove the propeller before running the engine on a flush/test device. Use a suitable test propeller to run the engine in a test tank.

WARNING
Stay clear of the propeller shaft while running an outboard on a flush/test device. Remove the propeller before running the engine to help avoid serious bodily injury or death. Disconnect all spark plug leads and both battery cables before removing or installing the propeller.

System Output Test

This test requires the use of a volt/ohm meter and a flush/test device or suitable test tank. Always inspect the battery terminals, all wire terminals, plugs and other charging system connections for corrosion, debris or damage and correct them as required prior to performing this test. Refer to Chapter Four for flush/test device or test tank instructions.

1. Select the DC voltage function on your volt/ohm meter. Select the 20- or 40-volt scale on the meter. Switch all electrical accessories off.
2. With the engine switched OFF, connect the positive test lead to the positive terminal on the battery.
3. Connect the negative test lead to an engine ground, such as a clean cylinder head bolt.
4. Note the voltage displayed on the meter.
5. Start the engine and run it at idle speed. Note the voltage displayed on the meter.
6. Carefully raise the engine speed to approximately 2000 rpm. Note the voltage displayed on the meter.
7. Repeat Steps 5 and 6 with electrical accessories switched ON one at a time. Note the voltage displayed on the meter.
8. Turn the engine OFF and refer to the following information to determine test results.

Compare the voltage recorded in Step 4 with the voltage displayed in Steps 5 and 6.

When the voltage reading recorded in Steps 5 and 6 is greater (0.2 volts or more) than the voltage reading in Step 4, the charging system is operating. Replace the battery if it does not hold a charge. Refer to Chapter Seven for battery testing procedures.

Very little (less than 0.2 volt) increase in voltage indicates that the charging system is not charging the battery properly.

Voltage readings recorded in Steps 5 and 6 exceeding 13.8 volts indicate an overcharge condition.

If the system is not charging the battery with all electrical accessories switched off, test the battery charge coil and the rectifier/regulator (except Models BF115A and BF30A) following the procedures listed in this section. Should a no charge condition occur only with all accessories switched on, the charging system is likely operating properly. Refer to *System Testing* in this section for additional information.

Overcharging conditions are often the result of a faulty rectifier/regulator (except models BF115A and BF130A). Test this component following the procedure listed in this section. An overcharge condition can also result from a faulty battery or corroded terminals and wiring. Refer to Chapter Seven for battery testing. Always clean and repair any faults with wiring or terminals prior to testing the charging system.

On models BF115A and BF130A, the warning light for the charging system should illuminate for both an undercharge and overcharge condition. Refer to *Warning Systems* in this chapter if a condition exists and the warning light does not illuminate.

Check all wiring for loose, dirty or corroded connections prior to testing the charging system. On these models, a damaged or blown fuse can result in an undercharge or no charge condition. Refer to *Fuses and Wire Harnesses* in this chapter for additional information.

Remove, inspect and repair the alternator (**Figure 141**) if either an overcharge or undercharge exists and you note no faulty wiring or connectors. Refer to Chapter Seven for alternator repair procedures.

Battery Charging Coil Resistance Test

This test requires a volt/ohm meter and, with some models, some short jumper leads. Refer to the wiring diagrams located at the end of this manual to determine the wire color used. To ensure the correct wires are selected, trace the wire color to the component on the engine. Removal of the charge coil is not required, provided you have access to the coil wire connection. Refer to Chapter Seven to remove the battery charging coil as required.

1. Disconnect both battery cables from the battery. Remove the spark plugs and connect the spark plug leads to a suitable engine ground.
2. Locate the wire terminals connecting the battery charging coil to the engine wire harness. Note the wire connection points and wire routing, then carefully disconnect both battery charging coil wires.
3. Select the ohms function on your volt/ohm meter.
4. Ensure that the wire terminals are clean, then connect the meter test leads (**Figure 144**, typical) to the battery charge coil wire colors indicated in **Table 9**. Record the meter readings for each connection.
5. Compare the recorded meter readings with the specifications listed in **Table 9**. Replace the battery charge coil if your measurements are not within the listed specification. Refer to Chapter Seven for battery charge coil replacement.
6. Carefully route the wire and connect the battery charge coil wires to the engine wire harness. Install the spark plugs and connect the leads. Clean the terminals, then connect the battery cables to the battery.

Rectifier/Regulator Testing

Models using just a rectifier do not control the charging system output. Models using a rectifier/regulator do provide a system to control charging system output.

Models BF50 and BF5A use a rectifier on all models, unless the optional rectifier/regulator is installed in place of the rectifier.

Models BF75, BF8A, BF100 and BF9.9 (prior to serial No. 1200000) use a rectifier. The models with serial No. 1200000-on are equipped with a rectifier/regulator in place of the rectifier.

All other models (except Models BF115A and BF130A) utilize a rectifier/regulator that offers charging system output control.

Refer to the test procedures in this section and perform the tests as described. Test procedures for either component are similar with the only difference being the wire colors used and the number of tests required. All test specifications are provided in **Table 10** and **Table 11**.

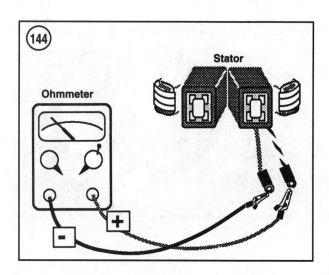

Rectifier and rectifier/regulator resistance test

This test requires a volt/ohm meter and short jumper leads. Rectifier or rectifier/regulator appearance and wire colors used vary. Refer to the wiring diagrams at the end of this manual for the selected model to determine the wire color used. To ensure the correct wires are selected, trace the wire color to the component on the engine. Removal of the rectifier or rectifier/regulator is not required, provided you have adequate access to the wires. Refer to Chapter Seven to remove the rectifier or rectifier/regulator as required.

1. Disconnect both battery cables from the battery. Remove the spark plugs and connect the spark plug leads to a engine ground.
2. Locate all wires connected to the rectifier or rectifier/regulator. Note the wire connection points and wire routing, then carefully disconnect wires from the engine wire harness.
3. Select the *ohms* function on your volt/ohm meter.
4. Ensure that the wire terminals are clean, then connect the meter test leads to the rectifier or rectifier/regulator wire lead colors indicated in **Table 10** and **Table 11** (**Figure 145**, typical). Record the meter readings for each connection.
5. Compare the meter readings with the specifications. Replace the rectifier or rectifier/regulator if you note any incorrect readings. Refer to Chapter Seven for replacement procedures.
6. Carefully route the wires, then connect the rectifier or rectifier/regulator wires to the engine wire harness. Install the spark plugs and connect the leads. Clean the terminals, and connect the battery cables to the battery.

TROUBLESHOOTING

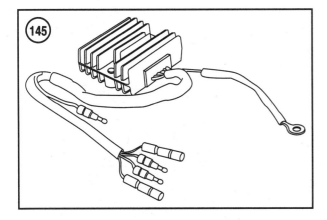

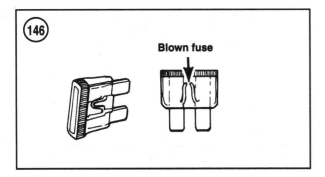

Optional Carburetor Heating Kit

Models BF75A and BF90A may be equipped with an optional carburetor heating kit. It helps to prevent ice from forming on the carburetor when using these models in very cold climates. The charging system provides power to operate this system. A malfunction with this system can result in an inability to heat the carburetor, or in some cases, can prevent the charging system from operating properly. Major components include a carburetor heater control unit, thermosensor and four individual heating elements. No test specifications or procedures for these components are available.

Locate, disconnect and tape back all wires connecting to the system components if you suspect a fault with this system is causing a problem with the charging system. Always test the charging system prior to checking the operation of this system.

Use a thermomelt stick (see *Cooling System* in this chapter) to determine if the heating elements are working properly. If any of the heating elements are warming up as the engine is running (cold conditions only), the carburetor heater control unit and thermosensor are operating properly. If none are working (and the conditions are very cold), the fault is likely with the thermosensor or carburetor heater control unit. Replace the thermosensor or the carburetor control unit if the heating elements still fail to operate. If some of the elements are heating and others are not, replace those that are not heating.

FUSES AND WIRE HARNESSES

Wire harness and fuse arrangements vary among the models. Refer to the wiring diagrams located at the end of this manual to determine component usage for the selected model.

> *WARNING*
> *A fire and/or explosion can result if sparks are produced by an electrical fault in the vicinity of fuel vapor. Never replace a fuse without thoroughly inspecting the wiring harness for chafing, bare wires or other damage. Never install a fuse with a higher capacity than the original fuse.*

Fuse Testing

The type, number, size, appearance and location of the fuses used varies by model. The symptom that a faulty fuse causes may also vary by model. A damaged or blown fuse (**Figure 146** and B, **Figure 147**) can usually be identified by a visual inspection; however, testing with an ohmmeter is sometimes necessary.

Refer to the wiring diagrams located at the end of this manual to determine the number of fuses used and the wire colors to which they are connected. Locate and test all fuses on the engine to prevent a false diagnosis. Trace the wire color to the fuse on the engine and test it following the procedure indicated in this chapter.

1. Disconnect both battery cables from the battery. Remove the spark plugs and connect the spark plug lead to a engine ground. Carefully remove the fuse from the bracket or fuse holder on the wire harness.
2. Select the ohms function on your volt/ohm meter. Select the R × 1 scale on the meter. Connect the positive test lead to one end of the fuse terminal. Connect the negative test lead to the other fuse terminal. Note the meter test readings.
3. Zero or nearly zero ohms should be present if the fuse is in good condition. If no continuity is noted, the fuse is blown.
4. Before replacing a defective fuse, inspect the routing and condition of the wiring to the fuse holder (A, **Figure 147**). Correct or repair as needed.
5. Clean the fuse contacts and install the fuse into the holder or bracket. Install the spark plugs and spark plug

leads. Clean the terminals and connect the battery cables to the battery.

Wire Harness Testing

Due to the harsh environment in which boats are operated, problems can occur with the wire harness. A problem with the engine may occur one time out and disappear the next. If an electrical problem exists and all components test correctly, test the wire harness. Check both the engine and instrument harness (remote control models). Perform tests using a common volt/ohm meter. With the test leads attached, twist, bend and pull on the wire connectors of suspect circuits. This is often the way intermittent faults are located.

Perform Steps 1-5.
1. Select the ohms or resistance function of the meter. Select the R × 1 scale.
2. Select a lead (wire color) to test. Refer to the wiring diagrams at the end of this manual to determine the proper pin connection to select for the wire color. Connect the positive test lead to one end of the wire harness connector (**Figure 148**).
3. Connect the negative test lead to the selected wire harness connector. Continuity must be present.
4. Check and repair all connectors or wiring if an open circuit or high resistance reading is indicated.

TRIM SYSTEM TROUBLESHOOTING

System Descriptions and Troubleshooting Tips

This section provides descriptions of the types of trim systems used along with helpful troubleshooting tips.

Tilt Pin and Lockdown Hook

Trim and tilt systems used on Honda outboards vary by model and horsepower. Two-hp models BF20 and BF2A use a tilt pin only. 5-30 hp models use a tilt pin and hold down hook (**Figure 149**, typical). In either case, it allows the engine to run slightly tilted (in or out) to change the running attitude of the boat or enhance shallow water operation. The hold down hook operates (on models so equipped) in reverse gear to prevent the propeller thrust from moving the engine up or out. If a malfunction occurs, you may notice that the unit does not hold down when in reverse or cannot be tilted up when in forward or neutral. Should this symptom occur, check the adjustment and inspect the system for damaged or excessively worn components. Repair procedures are provided in Chapter

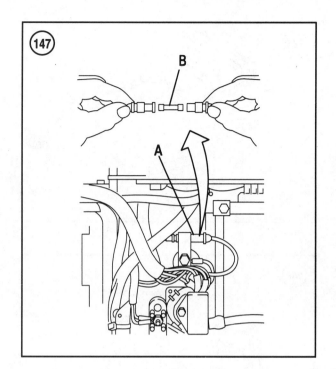

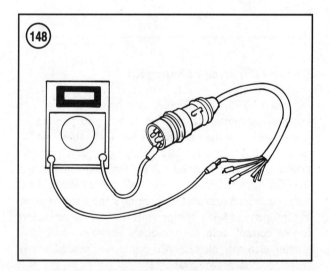

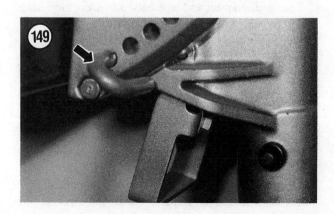

TROUBLESHOOTING

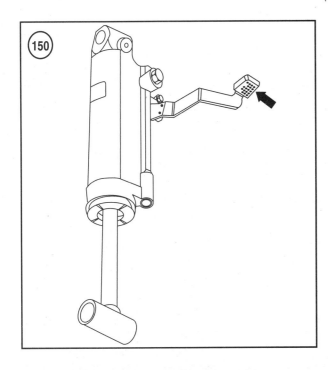

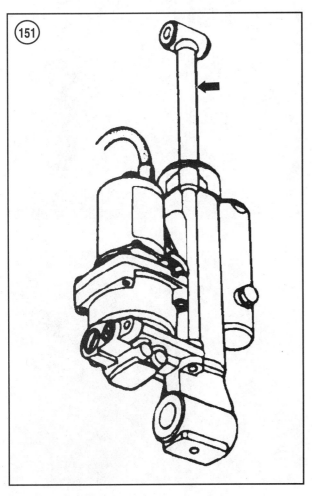

Thirteen. Adjustment procedure for the hold down hook is provided in Chapter Five.

Gas Accumulator Type Tilt Systems

The gas accumulator type tilt system is used on tiller control BF35A, BF40A, BF45A and BF50A models (**Figure 150**) that are not equipped with power trim and tilt. This unit is mounted between the engine clamp brackets. It provides hydraulic assist when tilting the engine for towing or beaching the boat. The tilt function activates when the operator moves the lever (**Figure 150**). This system holds the engine trim position during normal operation hydraulically. Shock dampening is provided for in case of impact with an underwater object to help minimize impact damage. The typical symptoms of a fault include:

1. Not holding trim angle.
2. Coming up in reverse or when slowing down.
3. Leaking fluid.

This unit is not serviceable. First check the lever position if a problem is noted. Replace the assembly if the lever is in the normal position and a fault still exists. See Chapter Twelve.

Single Hydraulic Cylinder Power Trim System

The single cylinder trim system is used on tiller or remote control models BF35A, BF40A, BF45A, and BF50A equipped with power trim. This trim system provides the capability to move the engine up/out against propeller thrust, allowing the operator to change the running attitude of the boat while underway. The major components include the *electric motor, relays, hydraulic pump and hydraulic cylinder.* A bi-directional electronic motor drives the hydraulic pump. Reversing motor direction reverses pump rotation, thereby changing the direction of trim cylinder (**Figure 151**) movement. As the unit is trimming up, fluid moves to the up side of the cylinder. Fluid returns to the pump from the down side of the cylinder. As the unit trims down, fluid moves to the down side of the cylinder. Fluid returns to the pump from the up side of the cylinder.

For manual operation, a relief valve (**Figure 152**) allows the engine to moved up or down without running the electric motor. Access the valve through an opening on the port side clamp bracket (**Figure 153**). Always verify that the valve is fully seated clockwise before performing other tests.

Check the fluid level following the procedure provided in Chapter Four before performing any test. Refer to *Electrical Testing* in this section for electrical troubleshooting procedures. Instructions are provided in Chapter Twelve for trim electrical repair along with removal and installation procedures for major components of the trim system.

Repairing to the hydraulic portion of the system usually involves using special service tools and equipment. Have major hydraulic component repairs performed by a professional. Remove the trim system as instructed in Chapter Twelve and contact a Honda dealership for information. Run the trim system to ensure that the electric motor runs properly. Refer to the *Electrical Testing* in this chapter if the electric motor is not operating.

Common symptoms indicating a possible hydraulic malfunction include:

1. The engine does not move up.
2. The engine does not move down.
3. The engine leaks down while tilted up or when underway.
4. The engine trails out when slowing down or when in reverse.
5. Hydraulic fluid leaks from the system.

Three Hydraulic Cylinder Trim Systems

Tiller or remote control models BF75A, BF90A, BF115A and BF130 with power trim use a three-cylinder trim system (**Figure 154**). The entire hydraulic system mounts between the engine clamp brackets. A benefit derived from mounting the pump outside the boat instead of inside the boat include: fewer hydraulic hoses and connections; a cleaner, lighter system; and a system with faster response. Disadvantages of the system are a greater exposure to the corrosive environment and greater difficulty pinpointing which component is faulty during hydraulic testing.

The major components of this system include the bi-directional electric motor and pump (A, **Figure 154**), fluid reservoir (B, **Figure 154**), trim rams (C, **Figure 154**) and tilt cylinder (D, **Figure 112**). Relays mounted on the engine control electric motor/pump rotational direction and fluid directional movement within the system. When trimming up from a down position, fluid is moved into the up cavity of both trim rams and the tilt cylinder. The end of the trim rams (C, **Figure 154**) contact against the striker plate on the engine swivel bracket. Fluid pressure causes all three cylinders to extend, thereby moving the engine up/out. At the point the trim rams are fully extended, the tilt cylinder remains the only means to move the engine up/out.

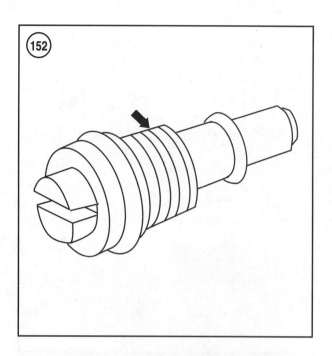

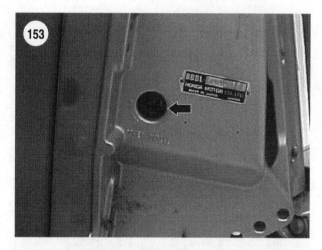

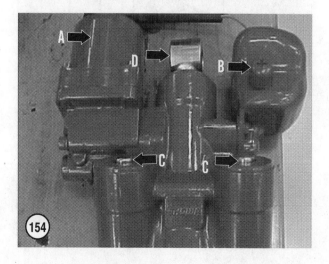

TROUBLESHOOTING

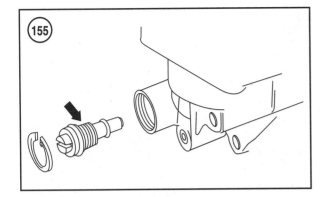

NOTE
Lubricate the end of the trim rams (C, Figure 154) to prevent noisy operation when trimming up.

When trimming down, the motor changes direction causing fluid to flow to the down side or cavity of the cylinders. As the only cylinder connected to the engine at both ends, the tilt cylinder provides all down movement.

A manual relief valve (**Figure 155**) allows manual engine movement without operating the pump. Access the manual relief valve through an opening on the port clamp bracket. The fluid fill/check point (**Figure 156**) is located on the fluid reservoir and can only be accessed when the engine is tilted up. Always check this manual relief valve and fluid level before testing or replacing components. The normal position of this manual relief valve is fully seated clockwise. To activate this manual relief valve use a screwdriver and rotate the valve (**Figure 155**) counterclockwise three complete turns. Refer to Chapter Four to check the trim fluid level.

Refer to *Electrical Testing* (in this chapter) for electrical troubleshooting procedures.

Have major hydraulic component repair performed by a professional. Remove the entire system following the procedure provided in Chapter Twelve and contact a Honda dealership for repair information. Make sure the electric motor is operating before beginning any hydraulic test. Refer to *Electrical Testing* in this chapter if the electric trim motor does not operate.

Common symptoms indicating a possible hydraulic malfunction include:
1. The engine does not move up.
2. The engine does not move down.
3. The engine leaks down from a full-tilt position.
4. The engine leaks down when underway.
5. The engine trails out when slowing down.
6. Hydraulic fluid leaks from the system.

Refer to *Hydraulic Testing* in this chapter to determine if repair to the hydraulic system is required.

WARNING
The hydraulic system fluid is under high pressure. Use extreme caution when removing valves or fittings. Always use safety goggles when working with the hydraulic system. Avoid touching areas where hydraulic fluid is leaking.

Hydraulic System Testing

Testing the hydraulic system requires a pressure gauge capable of measuring between 40 kg/cm^2 (569 psi) and 120 kg/cm^2 (1707 psi) or Honda part No. 07KPJ-VD6020A. Special adapters are also required when checking up and down pressures on the three hydraulic cylinder trim systems. These are available through a Honda dealership by ordering part No.07SPJ-ZW1020A (up pressure adapter) and 07SPJ-ZW1010A (down pressure adapter).

NOTE
Pressure testing is not provided for the single hydraulic cylinder trim system. It is usually better to have the unit repaired by a qualified technician.

This test measures the maximum UP and DOWN pressures. Perform this test if the outboard will not move UP or hold in the UP position. Before performing the test, confirm that the electrical system is operating properly, the manual relief valve is in the normal position, the trim system fluid level is correct and that the battery is fully charged.

1. Activate the manual relief valve and tilt the engine to the fully up position. Make sure the engine is supported

using blocks or overhead cables. Check the fluid level following the procedure in Chapter Four.

2. Remove the clip (A, **Figure 157**) from the manual relief valve (B, **Figure 157**). Remove the manual relief valve through the access hole. Quickly install the down pressure adapter (A, **Figure 158**) into the manual relief valve fitting (B, **Figure 158**).

3. Thread the hydraulic pressure gauge (C, **Figure 158**) to the adapter and tighten it securely.

4. Using caution, remove the supports for the engine. Run the trim system down while observing the gauge until all hydraulic cylinders are fully retracted. Record the maximum down pressure. Wait two minutes and read the pressure again.

5. Correct pressure readings should be within 40-75 kg/cm^2 (569-1067 psi) and should not drop significantly over a two-minute period. Position the engine in the fully up position and provide support for the engine.

6. Slowly remove the gauge and adapter to relieve pressure with a suitable container positioned below the fitting. Quickly install the up pressure adapter and gauge (A and C, **Figure 158**) to minimize fluid loss. Check and correct the fluid level.

7. Run the trim in the up direction while observing the gauge until all hydraulic cylinders are fully extended. Record the maximum up pressure. Wait two minutes and read the pressure again.

8. Correct readings should be within 90-120 kg/cm^2 (1280-1707 psi) and should not drop significantly over a two-minute period.

9. Remove the pressure gauge and adapter. Install the manual relief valve and clip (B and A, **Figure 157**). Check and correct the fluid level as indicated in Chapter Four.

10. Have the trim system inspected and repaired if the pressure readings are not within the specified range or you note a significant pressure drop.

On three-cylinder models, replace the hydraulic pump assembly if the unit leaks down or does not hold a trim or tilt position. Replace the pump/valve assembly if the unit does not move the engine when activated.

Electrical Testing

The major electrical components of the trim system are the electric motor, relays, trim position sender and switches. When the trim switch is toggled to the UP position, the bi-directional electric motor rotates in the direction that moves fluid toward the UP side of the hydraulic cylinders. When the DOWN direction is selected, the relays simply reverse the motor direction.

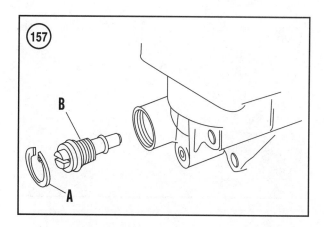

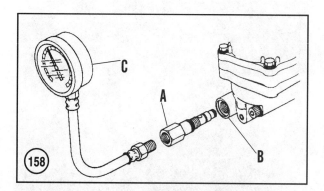

Selection of trim direction is accomplished with a remote control, dash mounted or tiller arm mounted trim switch (**Figure 159**). The relay unit (**Figure 160**) activates and reverses the circuits that supply current to the electric motor.

The white or white/black wire of the switch assembly carries voltage from the battery. When the switch is toggled to the UP selection, the white or white/black wire connects to the blue wire that connects to the UP relay cir-

TROUBLESHOOTING

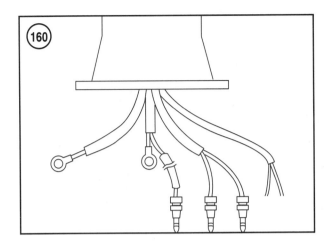

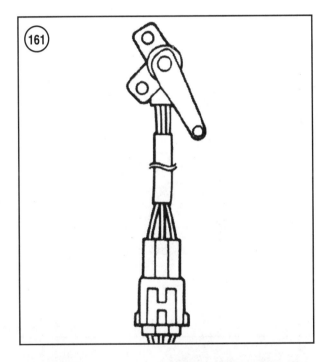

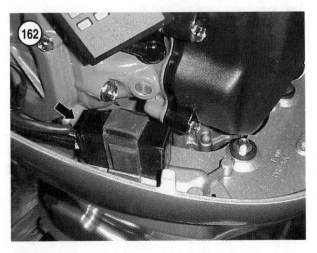

cuit. When the switch is toggled to the DOWN selection, the white or white/black wire is connected to the green wire that is connected to the down relay circuit.

When a relay receives voltage, it in turn supplies voltage to the electric motor. The other relay supplies the connection to ground for the electric motor until it is activated. Both relay circuits must make the proper connection for the electric motor to operate. Both relay circuits are incorporated into one relay unit.

A trim-sending unit (**Figure 161**) is used with a dash-mounted gauge to give the operator an indication of the current trim position. On models BF35A, BF40A, BF45A and BF50A, the signal from the trim sending unit is used with the trim control unit (**Figure 162**) to activate the overtrim alarm system. A remote control mounted switch provides a signal to the trim control unit to indicate that the throttle has reached a predetermined position. The warning buzzer sounds intermittently if the trim position sensor indicates that the engine is trimmed beyond the desired point and the throttle is opened.

A fuse is provided in the circuit that connects the positive battery terminal to the trim switch. Refer to the wiring diagrams at the end of this manual to help locate the fuse. Test this fuse if the electric motor will not operate in the up or down direction. Refer to *Fuse Testing* in this chapter.

Test the electrical system if the electric trim motor cannot be heard running when either the UP or DOWN switch is activated. Test the fuses, trim switches and trim relay. Thoroughly check the wire harness for loose, corroded or damaged wire connectors. Follow the procedure listed in Chapter Twelve to remove, repair and install the electric motor if a thorough inspection indicates no faults with the wiring.

Test the trim position sender if the dash-mounted gauge (on models so equipped) is not operating or is providing false readings. Always check and correct the sensor adjustment prior to replacing the sensor.

Incorrect operation of the overtrim system (on models so equipped) can result from a fault with the trim position sensor, throttle switch or trim control unit. Incorrect operation can cause the warning buzzer not to sound when overtrimmed, or can cause the buzzer to sound if a proper trim angle is selected. Test the trim position sensor and throttle switch.

Replace the trim control unit if all components are adjusted and test correctly.

WARNING
Use extreme caution when working around batteries. Never smoke or allow sparks to occur around batteries. Batteries produce hydrogen gas that can explode and result in

severe bodily injury or death. Never make the final connection to the positive battery terminal; an arc may occur and lead to fire or explosion.

Trim System Relay Testing

Trim relay testing requires using a volt/ohm meter, a fully charged battery and two jumper leads. Refer to the wiring diagrams located at the end of this manual to properly locate the trim relay wires. To ensure that the proper wires are selected, trace the wires to the component on the engine. Perform the test in two segments.

Relay resistance

1. Disconnect the battery cables. Remove the spark plugs and connect the spark plug leads to an engine ground.
2. Locate the trim relay on the engine. Note the wire connection points and wire routing, then carefully disconnect all leads connecting the trim relay to the engine wire harness. Refer to Chapter 12 and remove the trim relay from the engine.
3. Select the ohms function on your volt/ohm meter.
4. Connect the meter test leads to the trim relay wires (**Figure 163**, typical) indicated in **Table 12**. Record the meter readings for each connection indicated.
5. Replace the trim relay as described in Chapter 12 if the resistance is not specified.

Relay operation

Perform the following test to complete the testing of the trim relay. Perform the test with the relay removed from the engine.
1. Connect one jumper lead to the white wire connector (**Figure 164**) of the trim relay. Connect the other end of the jumper lead to the positive terminal of a battery.
2. Connect one jumper lead to the black wire connector of the trim relay. Connect the other end of the jumper lead to the negative terminal (**Figure 164**) of a fully charged battery.
3. Select the volts function on your volt/ohm meter. Select the 20- or 40-volt scale on the meter.
4. Connect the negative test lead to the negative terminal (**Figure 164**) on the battery.
5. Observe the meter reading as you alternately touch the positive test lead to the dark blue and dark green wire terminals of the trim relay.
6. Battery voltage should be noted when the positive test lead touches the dark blue and the dark green terminals.

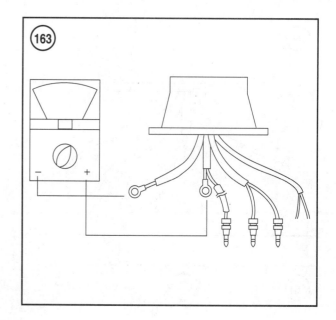

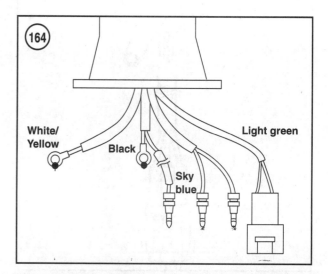

TROUBLESHOOTING

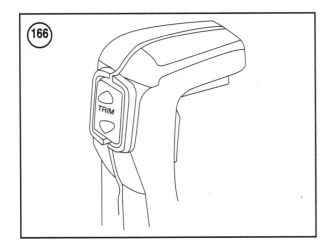

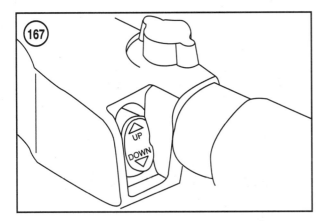

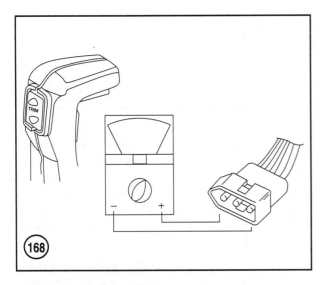

wires are routed correctly. Install the trim relay to the engine as described in Chapter Twelve. Install the spark plugs and connect spark plug leads. Clean the terminals and connect the battery cables to the battery.

Trim Switch Test

A faulty trim switch can result in an inability to operate the trim system in the UP, DOWN or both directions. Other symptoms may include operation of the trim system in either direction without the operator even touching the switch.

Intermittent faults with the trim switch may occur and it is difficult to pinpoint the cause. If an intermittent problem occurs, thoroughly check the wires leading to the switch (especially on remote control models) for damage and repair as required. If no defects are noted, repeat switch testing several times before accepting the switch as satisfactory.

Testing the trim switch requires a volt/ohm meter. Trim switch mounting location varies by model. Trim switches are mounted to the lower port side of the engine cover (**Figure 165**) on all models with power trim.

On remote control models, the switch is mounted on the shift/throttle handle (**Figure 166**). Tiller control models are equipped with a trim switch mounted to the tiller control bracket (**Figure 167**).

Access the trim switch wire connectors for testing. When testing the engine cover-mounted or tiller control-mounted trim switches, removal of the switch is not required. In either case, refer to the wiring diagrams located at the end of this manual and identify the wire color used for the switch. To ensure that the proper wire is selected, trace the wire to the switch on the engine. Check both the engine cover-mounted and tiller control-mounted switches to ensure that both are operating properly.

When testing remote control-mounted trim switches, a partial disassembly of the remote control is required to access the wire connectors for the switch (**Figure 168**). Refer to Chapter Fourteen for remote control removal and disassembly.

1. Remove both battery cables from the battery.
2. Locate the trim switch wires for the both switches. Refer to Chapter Fourteen to access the remote control mounted trim switch. Note the wire connection points and wire routings. Carefully disconnect the wire connecting the trim switch to the wire harness.
3. Select the ohms function on your volt/ohm meter. Select the R × 1 scale on the meter.
4. Refer to **Table 13** for specifications and connect the meter test lead to the wire color terminal as indicated

7. Replace the trim relay as described in Chapter Twelve if it does not perform as it should.

8. Remove all jumper leads. Clean then connect all trim relay wire leads to the engine wire harness. Ensure that all

(**Figure 168**). Note the meter reading with the switch in the position indicated. Perform the test with all wire color terminals and switch positions and record the test results.

5. Compare your test results with the specifications listed in **Table 13**. Replace the switch if you note any incorrect test results. Refer to Chapter Twelve to replace engine mounted trim switches. Refer to Chapter Fourteen to replace remote control mounted trim switches.

6. Clean the terminals and connect the trim switch wire terminals to the harness connectors. Ensure that all wires are routed properly. Clean the terminals and connect the battery cables to the battery.

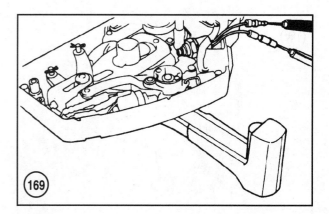

Trim Position Sender Test

A fault with the trim position sender can result in inaccurate operation of the dash-mounted trim gauge or incorrect operation of the overtrim warning system (Models BF35A, BF40A, BF45A and BF50A). This switch mounts inside the port side clamp bracket (**Figure 169**). Removal of the trim position sender is not required for testing, provided that the sender wires are accessible.

Refer to the wiring diagrams located at the end of this manual to identify the wire color used for the sender. To ensure that the correct wires are selected, trace the wires to the component on the engine. Use a digital volt/ohm meter to test the internal circuit resistance as indicated in the following procedures.

1. Position the engine in the fully down position. Disconnect both battery cables from the battery.
2. Locate the wire connectors for the trim position sender to the engine wire harness. Note the wire connection points and the wire routing.
3. Select the *Ohms* function on your volt/ohm meter.
4. Connect the meter test lead to the wire color terminals (**Figure 170**) indicated in **Table 14**. Record the meter readings for each wire and test lead connection.
5. Compare your meter readings with the specifications listed in **Table 14**. Check the installation of the sender as indicated in Chapter Twelve. Replace the trim position sender if the installation is correct yet you obtained incorrect readings.
6. Clean the terminals and connect the sender wires to the engine wire harness. Ensure that the wires are routed correctly. Clean the terminals, then connect the battery cables to the battery.

Throttle Switch

A faulty throttle switch (**Figure 169**) can result in no operation or incorrect operation of the overtrim warning

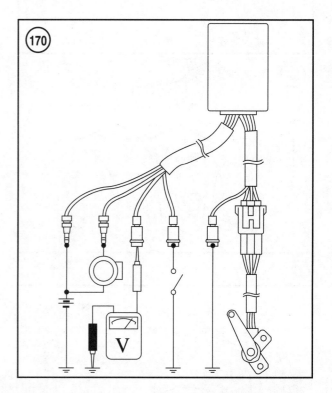

system. Access to the switch wire connectors is required for testing. Refer to Chapter Fourteen to access the switch connector. Refer to the remote control wiring diagrams located at the end of this manual to assist with wire identification. To ensure that the correct wires are selected for testing, trace the wire colors to the component in the remote control.

1. Remove both battery cables from the battery. Refer to Chapter 14 and disassemble the remote control enough to access the throttle switch wire connectors.

2. Note the switch wire connection points and wire routing. Carefully disconnect the switch wires from the wire harness.

TROUBLESHOOTING

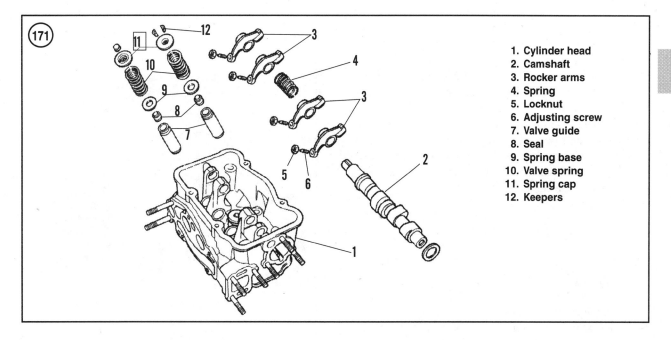

171.
1. Cylinder head
2. Camshaft
3. Rocker arms
4. Spring
5. Locknut
6. Adjusting screw
7. Valve guide
8. Seal
9. Spring base
10. Valve spring
11. Spring cap
12. Keepers

3. Select the R × 1 ohms function on your volt/ohm meter. Connect the positive test lead to the light green/black wire terminal on the switch. Connect the negative test lead to the black/green wire terminal on the switch.
4. No continuity should be noted when the switch is in the extended (released) position.
5. Depress the switch while noting the meter. Continuity should be noted with the switch depressed.
6. Replace the switch if it does not function as described.
7. Ensure that all wires are correctly routed and connect the switch wire terminal to the control wire harness. Assemble and install the control following the procedures listed in Chapter Fourteen. Clean the terminals, then connect the battery cables to the battery.

BASE ENGINE

All Honda outboard engines use a 4-stroke engine. Four-stroke engines offer several advantages over the more commonly used 2-stroke design. These advantages include:
1. Smoother running at all engine speeds.
2. Better fuel economy.
3. Reduced exhaust emissions.
4. Reduced oil usage.

Disadvantages of the 4-stroke engine include an increase in weight over a comparable 2-stroke design. In addition, the 4-stroke engine is generally more complex in design. All Honda outboards (except models BF20, BF2A, BF50 and BF5A) use an overhead camshaft (**Figure 171**) to reduce the weight and complexity.

Problems with the base engine can be as simple to repair as excessive carbon deposits (requiring chemical additives) or as difficult as a seized piston (requiring major base engine repairs).

This section covers troubleshooting and testing to determine if a problem is present in the base engine. Areas covered include: compression testing, engine noises, valve train component failure, lubrication failure, detonation, preignition, engine seizure, water entering the cylinder(s) and oil in the cylinder(s).

Engine Noises

Noise occurs in the base engine during normal operation. A ticking noise or a heavy knocking noise that intensifies when under load (accelerating) is a reason for concern. Refer to the following information for typical causes of engine noise.

Should you determine that a worn or damaged component is causing an engine noise, consider having a professional technician listen to the engine. In many cases, only the trained ear of the technician can determine if and what component(s) have failed. Repairs to the base engine are time-consuming and costly. Many times an inspection of the engine components reveals no problems. Often a loose bracket or fastener on the engine is causing the noise.

Ticking noises

A ticking noise is common if valve adjustment is required or a valve train component has failed. Valve adjusting procedures are provided in Chapter Four. See *Valve Train Component Failure* (in this chapter) for additional troubleshooting tips.

A ticking noise can also result from a damaged piston. Inspect the spark plug for damage or aluminum deposits and perform a compression test as described in this chapter. Complete base engine disassembly and repair is required if metal deposits are found on the spark plug. You must remove the cylinder head to inspect the valves, piston, cylinder walls and related components if you note any problems with the compression.

CAUTION
Ignoring suspicious noises may result in increased damage.

Whirring noises

A whirring noise that is most pronounced as the throttle is *decreased* is usually related to a problem with crankshaft and rod bearings.

Sometimes using a mechanic's stethoscope can identify the cylinder creating the noise. Compare the noise emanating from one area of the engine with the noise from the same area but different cylinder. Test the oil pressure (see *Oil Pressure Testing* in this section) to ensure that the noise is not caused by lack of lubrication. Be aware that the cooling fan (**Figure 172**) used on some models can generate a fair amount of noise. Use the stethoscope to ensure that the noise is emanating from the engine before proceeding with engine repair.

WARNING
Use extreme caution when working on or around a running engine. Never wear loose fitting clothing. Make sure that no one gets near the flywheel or any drive belts. Never position anyone near the propeller or propeller shaft while the engine is running.

Knocking noises

Use a mechanic's stethoscope to determine if the noise is emanating from the base engine or other component on the engine. The noise is more pronounced in the crankcase area if a problem exists in the crankshaft and connecting rod components. Special insulated pliers are available that allow spark plug lead removal while running the engine. The noise may lessen when the spark plug lead is removed on the suspect cylinder. This procedure is difficult to perform and may result in damage to the electrical system if the spark plug leads are not promptly grounded. A better method is to remove one spark plug lead and attach it to an

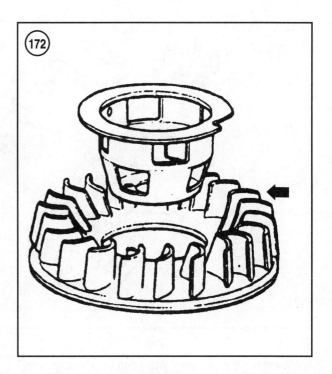

engine ground. Start the engine and listen to the noise. Install the spark lead and repeat the process for another cylinder. If, with one lead grounded, you notice the noise is less than another cylinder, the grounded cylinder may be damaged.

Always perform an oil pressure check when you detect knocking noises. When combined with low or unstable oil pressure, knocking noises generally indicate a problem with the base engine. Major repair may be required. Refer to *Oil Pressure Testing* in this section for repair procedures.

Lubrication System Failure

If lubrication is insufficient, engine damage to the internal components will result. Knocking or other types of noise are almost always present with lubrication system failures. The engine may stop and not crank with the starter. On occasion, the engine cranks after cooling, but likely slows down and stops again. When the engine is restarted, it may run rough or not idle. Performance is lacking as well. The engine eventually seizes and requires extensive and expensive repair.

If you suspect that the engine ran with insufficient lubrication, perform a compression test. The pistons and cylinder walls may be scuffed, scored or damaged.

Lubrication failure can result from an oil pump failure, insufficient oil in the oil pan or cylinder block, or contamination of the oil with fuel or water. Other causes include

TROUBLESHOOTING

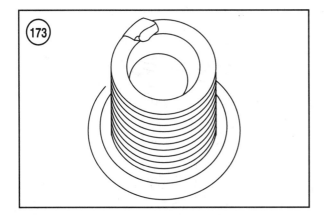

running the engine with old or dirty oil, and in some cases, running the engine with the wrong type of oil.

Stop the engine if you suspect a lubrication failure or if the warning system activates. Check the oil level and condition following the instructions listed in Chapter Four. Perform an oil pressure check if you note no problems with the oil level or condition. Refer to *Oil Pressure Testing* in this section for the procedure to follow.

Detonation and Preignition

Detonation and preignition damage occurs less frequently with 4-stroke engines than with 2-stoke engines. Still, detonation and preignition can occur. The resulting damage is similar for either, yet the causes are slightly different.

Detonation

Detonation damage is the result of the heat and pressure in the combustion chamber becoming too great for the fuel being used. Fuel normally burns at a controlled rate that causes the expanding gasses to drive the piston down. When conditions in the engine allow the heat and pressure to get too high, the fuel may explode violently. These violent explosions in the combustion chamber cause serious damage to internal engine components. Carbon deposits, overheating, lean fuel mixture, over-advanced timing and lugging are some of the conditions that may lead to detonation. Never use a fuel with a lower than recommended octane rating. Its use may cause detonation under normal operating conditions. The piston suffers most of the adverse effects of detonation. If detonation occurs, the engine has a pinging noise not unlike the pinging sometimes heard in automobiles. Outboards are considerably noisier than automobiles, so the noise is seldom detected. The engine likely has a rough idle and may seize if the damage is great enough. A compression test likely reveals one or more cylinders low on compression. Inspect the spark plug. The presence of aluminum deposits or melted electrodes (**Figure 173**) indicates probable detonation damage. To avoid repeat failures, address the listed causes for detonation prior to returning the engine to service.

Preignition

Preignition is the result of a glowing object in the combustion chamber that causes early ignition. The wrong heat range spark plugs, carbon deposits and inadequate cooling are some of the causes of preignition. Preignition can lead to severe damage to the internal engine components. The primary component that is damaged is the piston. The damage is very similar to detonation, as the early ignition causes the heat and pressure to become too great for the fuel being used. It explodes violently, causing a melted effect on the piston dome. It is not uncommon to have a hole form in the dome of the piston where pre-ignition has occurred. As with detonation damage, the engine runs poorly, particularly at idle. When the compression test is performed, one or more cylinders may have low compression. Inspecting the spark plugs likely reveals aluminum deposits (**Figure 173**) consistent with detonation failures. Base engine repair procedures are provided in Chapter Eight. To avoid repeat failures, address and correct the causes of preignition before putting the engine back into service.

Engine Seizure

The base engine can seize at any speed. Normally the engine does not seize up at high speed as the engine typically loses power gradually. The primary reason for the seizure is an internal problem, such as a failed crankshaft and rod bearing or detonation/preignition damage. An immediate seizure can result from a valve train component failure as well. In either case, the starter will be unable to turn the engine over. Always inspect the gearcase or jet pump before removing the base engine. Gearcase or jet pump failures prevent the base engine from rotating. Refer to *Gearcase* in this chapter to inspect the gearcase for metal contamination or the jet pump for a seized impeller or drive shaft. The gearcase or jet pump can also be removed to check for gearcase seizure as instructed in Chapter Nine. Refer to Chapter Ten for jet pump removal and repair information. Repair the gearcase or jet pump if the base engine turns over freely with the component removed. Refer to Chapter Eight for powerhead removal, repair and installation procedures.

Water Entering the Cylinder

Water can enter the cylinder from a number of areas. Water in the fuel, water entering the front of the carburetor or throttle body, leaking exhaust covers/gaskets, leaking cylinder head and/or gaskets and cylinder block internal leaks are some common causes. The typical symptom of water intrusion is rough running, particularly at idle. The engine may run correctly at higher speeds. Verify water intrusion when the spark plugs are removed. Water is likely present on the spark plugs, and a white deposit may be present. Remove the cylinder head following the instructions listed in Chapter Eight. Compare the wet cylinder(s) with the dry cylinders. A cylinder with water intrusion usually has significantly less carbon deposits on the piston, cylinder walls and cylinder dome. Rust or corrosion may be present on the valves and/or other components. Complete base engine repair is not required if the cause and damage is confined to the cylinder head. Leakage in the cylinder block can be difficult to find. Casting flaws, pinholes and cracks may or may not be visible. Replacement of the cylinder block and/or cylinder head is required when water is entering the cylinder and no visible gasket leakage can be found. Continued operation with water intrusion will result in engine failure.

Blown Cylinder Head Gasket

A blown cylinder head gasket results from a failure of the gasket that seals the cylinder head to the cylinder block. Symptoms of a blown head gasket include, water in the oil, water entering the cylinder(s), overheating (particularly at higher engine speeds), rough running (particularly at lower engine speeds) and noises coming from the cylinder head to cylinder block mating surface. Refer to *Compression Testing* in this section and perform a compression test if you suspect a blown head gasket. Low or uneven compression may or may not indicate a blown head gasket. A slight leakage can cause the listed symptoms, yet it may not be detected by a compression test. Only removal and inspection of the gasket and mating surfaces will indicate a failure. Refer to Chapter Eight for the cylinder head removal procedure.

Oil Entering the Cylinders

Oil entering the cylinders is almost always the result of storing the engine improperly. When positioned incorrectly, oil from the crankcase or oil pan can flow past the piston rings and enter the combustion chambers. This can lead to a seized or hydraulically locked engine, fouled

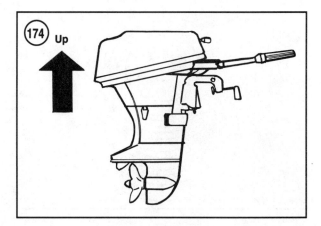

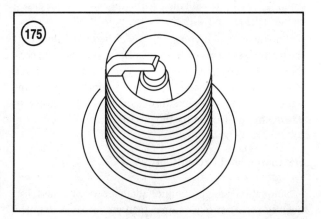

spark plugs, low oil level and high oil consumption. The preferred position for the engine is upright (**Figure 174**). Small engines are sometimes transported while lying on their side. If transporting or storing the engine in the upright position is not possible, refer to the following information.

a. On 2-15 hp models, place the outboard on the side that positions the spark plug facing up.

b. On all other models, position the outboard in a vertical or tilted-up position.

To verify that excessive oil is entering the cylinders, remove the spark plugs and securely ground the spark plug leads to the engine. If the spark plugs are oily, place a shop towel over the spark plug holes and slowly rotate the flywheel to blow excess oil from the cylinders. Correct the oil level as described in Chapter Four. Clean and install the spark plugs.

Next, start the engine and warm it to normal operating temperature. Stop the engine, allow it to cool and remove the spark plugs. If the plugs are oily or fouled (**Figure 175**), excessive oil is entering the cylinders. Refer to Chapter Four for spark plug inspection instructions.

TROUBLESHOOTING

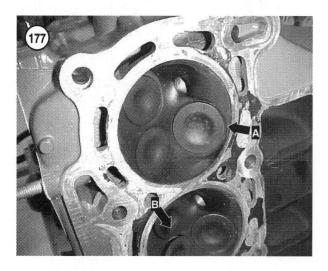

Valve Train Components

Valve train problems can result in an inability to start the engine, rough engine operation, backfiring in the exhaust or intake or a ticking noise. Subjects covered in this section include timing belt failure, worn valves guides, sticking, worn or damaged valves, camshaft failure and rocker arm failure.

Timing Belt Failure

Failure of the timing belt (**Figure 176**) can result in an inability to start the engine or rough running of the engine. If the belt is sufficiently worn, it may allow the belt to jump over one or more of the teeth on the crankshaft pulley. This results in improper valve timing. A broken timing belt prevents camshaft operation and results in a no-start condition.

Refer to Chapter Five for the timing belt adjustment procedures. If the timing belt has jumped, replace the timing belt following the procedure listed in Chapter Eight. Inspection and periodic replacement of the timing belt is required.

Refer to Chapter Four for additional information. Refer to Chapter Five for timing belt tensioner adjustment.

> *CAUTION*
> *Internal damage to the valves and piston can result from attempting to start the engine with incorrect valve timing or a broken timing belt.*

Sticking, Worn or Damaged Valves

Corrosion or heavy carbon deposits can cause a valve (A, **Figure 177**) to stick in the open position. Worn or damaged valves or valve contact surfaces (B, **Figure 177**) result in similar symptoms. Either condition results in lost compression and rough running or backfiring. Backfiring or popping noises coming from the intake usually are the result of a stuck, damaged or worn intake valve. A backfiring or popping noise coming from the exhaust is usually the result of a stuck, damaged or worn exhaust valve.

If you detect backfiring, perform a compression test following the procedures listed in this section. Try running the engine with one spark plug lead grounded at a time. The backfire ceases when the spark plug lead is grounded on the defective cylinder. Only disassembly and inspection of the valve verifies this condition. In some cases, the valve contacts the top of the piston, resulting in a bent valve or damage to the top of the piston. Removal and inspection procedures for valves and related components are covered in Chapter Eight.

Stuck valves are generally the result of improper long-term storage, water entering the cylinders or submersion of the engine. Using the wrong type of oil, improper fuel system operation or lugging the engine all contribute to increased deposits or wear of the valve and seat area. Refer to Chapter Four for information regarding oil usage. Refer to Chapter One to select the correct propeller to prevent lugging the engine. Refer to Chapter Five and Chapter Six to ensure that the fuel system is adjusted properly.

Camshaft Failure

Failure of any of the camshaft lobes (**Figure 178**) can cause the same symptoms as a sticking or damaged valve. Typically the lobe fails in such a manner (rounded lobe) that the valve is constantly closed. On all models (except

BF20, BF2A, BF50 and BF5A) the camshaft can be inspected without major disassembly of the base engine. Removal of the rocker cover (**Figure 179**) allows you to visually inspect the camshaft lobes for a rounded condition. Refer to Chapter Eight for rocker cover removal and cylinder head repair procedures. Failure of the camshaft is generally the result of insufficient lubrication (wrong type or dirty oil). Continuous operation in cool water can cause an increase in oil dilution with fuel byproduct. Diluted oil can contribute to camshaft lobe failure. More frequent oil changes reduce the chance of having this type of failure. Refer to Chapter Four for oil recommendations.

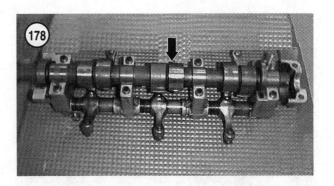

Rocker Arm Failure

Failure of a rocker arm (**Figure 179**) and related components can result in noise coming from the rocker cover area or in some case loss of compression on the corresponding cylinder. Remove the rocker cover and visually inspect all rocker arms for broken or damaged components. Repair the damaged component following the procedure listed in Chapter Eight.

Failure of the rocker arms is generally the result of running the engine at higher than recommended speeds. Refer to **Table 8** for maximum recommended engine speeds. A different propeller may be required to correct the cause of this failure.

Lubrication System Failure

Failure of the lubrication system can result in severe engine failure. Failure of the system can result from an incorrect oil level, failure of the oil pumping system or using contaminated or inadequate oil. All of these conditions and oil pressure test procedures are covered in this section.

CAUTION
Damage can occur in a matter of seconds if the lubrication system fails. To help prevent serious engine damage, slow down and stop the engine at once if the warning system indicates low oil pressure.

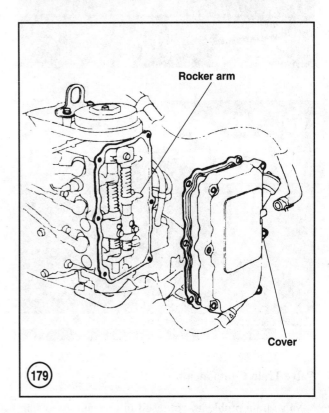

Incorrect oil level

An incorrect oil level can result from improperly filling the engine with oil or using improper procedures when checking the engine oil level.

An insufficient oil level can result in an inadequate supply of oil to the oil pump and/or overheating oil. The oil cools the crankshaft and other internal engine components.

An excessive oil level allows the crankshaft and other components to whip the oil, causing bubbles or foam to form. This foam-contaminated oil may cause low oil pressure and activate the warning system. In some cases, the oil pressure remains above the point necessary to keep the warning system from activating, yet the engine is not receiving adequate lubrication. Foam-contaminated oil does not provide the lubrication required by the engine.

Refer to Chapter Four when checking or filling the engine oil.

In most cases, oil leaks are easily detected and corrected. Common leakage points are at the rocker cover area (**Figure 179**), oil filter mounting surface, fuel pump

TROUBLESHOOTING

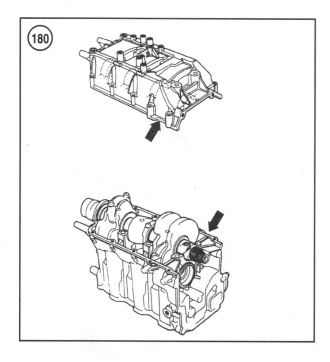

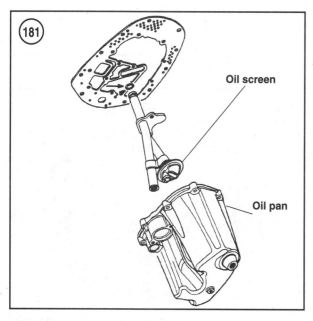

mounting surface or crankcase mating surface (**Figure 180**). Carefully clean the engine with a degreasing agent. Run the engine until it reaches operating temperature. Turn the engine off, then inspect the mating surfaces for fresh oil leakage.

All engines consume some oil while running. Some of the oil that lubricates the cylinder walls or valves is drawn into the combustion chamber and subsequently burned. Oil consumption rates vary by model, condition of the engine and how the engine is used. Engines with worn internal components generally burn more oil than new engines. Damage to the piston and cylinder walls from detonation or preignition can cause increased oil consumption as well. New or recently rebuilt engines generally consume more oil during the break-in period. After the break-in period, the oil consumption should return to normal. Normal usage varies widely and oil usage specifications are not provided.

A typical symptom of excessive oil burning/consumption is a blue smoke coming from the exhaust during hard acceleration or high-speed operation. Inspection of the spark plug usually reveals oil fouling (**Figure 175**). Perform a compression test following the procedure listed in this section. Worn or damaged components generally cause low compression results.

If frequent low oil levels are encountered and neither high oil consumption or external leak is noted, a leakage at the oil pan area (**Figure 181**, typical) is the usual cause. Inspection of the oil pan and cylinder block mating surfaces and gaskets is then required. Refer to Chapter Eight for engine removal and in inspection procedures.

Failure of the Oil Pump System

Failure of the oil pump system results from a worn or damaged oil pump (**Figure 182**), worn or damaged bearing surface (**Figure 183**) within the base engine, or a blocked, damaged or loose oil screen (**Figure 181**).

Perform an oil pressure test to determine if a problem exist with the oil pumping system. See *Oil Pressure Testing* in this chapter.

> *NOTE*
> *Oil pressure test specifications are not provided for models BF20, BF2A, BF75, BF8A and BF100. If the oil pressure does not reach the value required to switch on the oil pressure indicator light, inspect the oil pump and strainer. Refer to Chapter Eight for oil pump and related component inspection.*

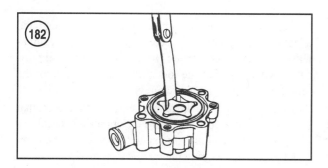

CAUTION
Never run an outboard without providing cooling water. Use either a test tank or flush/test device. Remove the propeller before running the engine on a flush/test device. Use a suitable test propeller to run the engine in a test tank.

WARNING
Stay clear of the propeller shaft while running an outboard on a flush/test device. Remove the propeller before running the engine to help avoid serious bodily injury or death. Disconnect all spark plug leads and both battery cables before removing or installing the propeller.

Oil Pressure Test

An oil pressure gauge (**Figure 184**) and accurate shop tachometer are required to perform an oil pressure test. Perform the test while running the engine on a flush test device or in a suitable shop tank. Take all necessary precautions to prevent injury to yourself or others. Refer to *Oil Pressure Switch Test* (in this chapter) to determine the location of the oil pressure switch. Refer to **Table 15** for oil pressure specification and use an oil pressure gauge capable of reading 0-7 kg/cm^2 (0-100 psi). Use an adapter with the same threads as the oil pressure switch to attach the gauge to the engine.

1. Run the engine in a test tank or on a flush/test adapter until it reaches normal operating temperature.
2. With the engine switched OFF, note the wire location points and wire routing. Remove the wire from the oil pressure switch.
3. Using a suitable wrench, remove the oil pressure switch from the engine. Install the adapter (**Figure 184**) into the threaded hole for the oil pressure switch and firmly tighten. Attach the oil pressure gauge to the adapter.
4. Following the manufacturer's instructions to attach the shop tachometer to the engine.
5. Start the engine and check for leakage at the gauge attaching points.
6. With the engine shifted into neutral, advance the throttle until the tachometer indicates the engine speed specified in **Table 15**. Record the oil pressure reading on the gauge. Switch the engine OFF.
7. Compare the oil pressure with the specification. Oil pressure below or above the listed specification indicates a problem with the oil pump system. Inspect the oil pump and related components following the procedure listed in Chapter Eight.

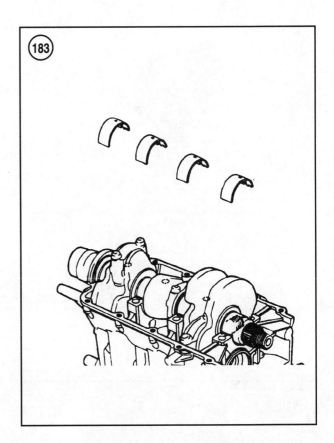

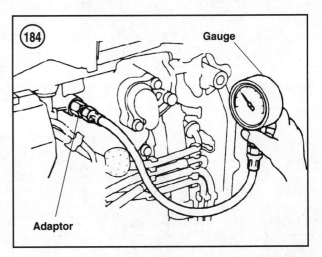

8. Remove the shop tachometer, oil pressure gauge and adapter. Apply ThreeBond sealant type 1215 (or equivalent) to the threaded portion (**Figure 185**) of the oil pressure switch. Install the oil pressure switch into the threaded hole and tighten securely.
9. Connect the wire to the oil pressure switch. Ensure that the wire is routed correctly. Start the engine and check for oil leakage at the oil pressure switch area. Correct any oil leakage before returning the engine into service.

TROUBLESHOOTING

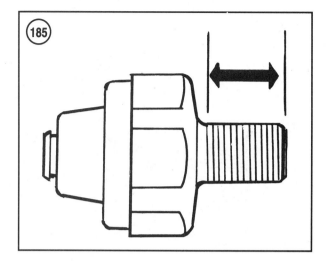

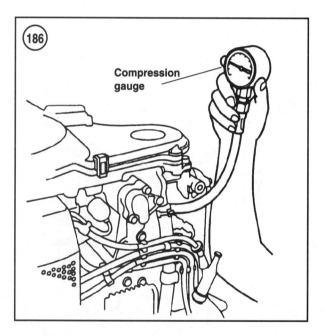

Compression Testing

A compression gauge (**Figure 186**) and adapter are required to perform a compression test. They are available at automotive parts stores and from tool suppliers. A small squirt can of engine oil may also be required.

1. Remove the spark plugs and connect the spark plug leads to an engine ground.

2. Install the adapter and compression gauge (**Figure 186**) into the No. 1 spark plug hole. Position the throttle in the wide-open position during testing.

3. Stand clear of the remaining spark plug openings during testing. Observe the compression gauge as you operate the manual or electric starter. Ensure that the engine has made a minimum of 10 revolutions and the cranking speed is at or above the rated rpm (**Table 16**). Record the compression reading.

4. Repeat Step 2 and Step 3 for the remaining cylinders. Record all compression readings.

5. Compare the recorded readings with the specification listed. Perform Step 6 if any of the readings are below the listed specification. Go to Step 8 if all readings are within the listed specification.

6. Squirt approximately one teaspoon of engine oil into any cylinder with low compression. Rotate the engine several revolutions to distribute the oil in the cylinder. Repeat Step 2 and Step 3 for each suspect cylinder.

7. Compare the second compression readings with the first compression reading. A higher second reading indicates that the low compression is the result of a problem with the piston, piston rings or cylinder walls. A problem with the valve or valve seat is indicated if no increase in compression is noted. Refer to Chapter Eight to repair the base engine.

8. Position the throttle in the closed position. Remove the compression gauge and adapter. Install the spark plugs and connect the spark plug leads.

COOLING SYSTEM

CAUTION
Never run an outboard without providing cooling water. Use either a test tank or flush/test device. Remove the propeller before running the engine on a flush/test device. Use a suitable test propeller to run the engine in a test tank.

WARNING
Stay clear of the propeller shaft while running an outboard on a flush/test device. Remove the propeller before running the engine to help avoid serious bodily injury or death. Disconnect all spark plug leads and both battery cables before removing or installing the propeller.

System Description

The cooling system for Honda outboards is relatively simple. On all models (except BF20 and BF2A) water is pumped by the drive shaft driven, gearcase or jet pump mounted water pump (**Figure 187**). The water is pumped to the exhaust area of the powerhead, then to the cylinder block and heads. The water exits the powerhead near the powerhead mounting surface and travels out through the drive shaft housing. As the water travels through the

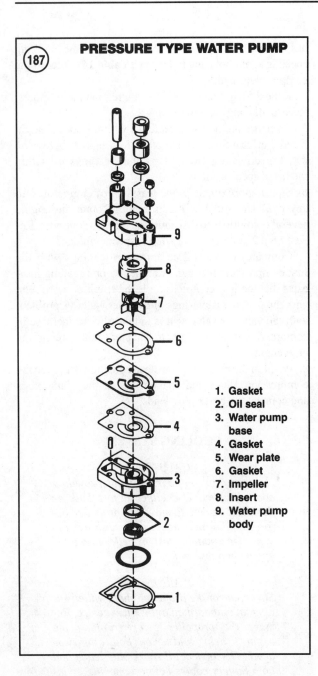

PRESSURE TYPE WATER PUMP

1. Gasket
2. Oil seal
3. Water pump base
4. Gasket
5. Wear plate
6. Gasket
7. Impeller
8. Insert
9. Water pump body

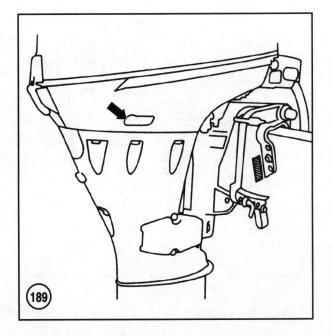

powerhead, it absorbs heat and carries it away. If the engine is overheating, the problem is that water is not flowing through the powerhead in sufficient volume or is not absorbing the heat. All models (except BF20 and BF2A) are equipped with a thermostat (**Figure 188**) to help maintain a minimum powerhead temperature and improve low speed running characteristics. They work by restricting exit water until a minimum water temperature is attained. A stream of water is visible at the rear of the lower motor cover (**Figure 189**) when water exits the powerhead. The fitting for the stream commonly becomes blocked by debris and may cease flowing. Clean the passage with a small, stiff wire brush. Inspect the cooling system if the water stream is still not present. Models BF75A, BF90A, BF115A and BF130A are equipped with a water pressure control valve (**Figure 190**) to provide adequate water pressure in the cylinder block at low speeds. Blockage in the valve can result in overheating at higher engine speeds. In addition, models BF115A and BF130A are equipped with a flushing adapter to allow flushing of salt, sand and other debris from the engine. To prevent water leakage from the valve while running the engine a flush

TROUBLESHOOTING

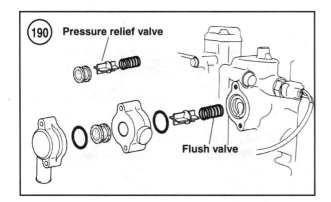

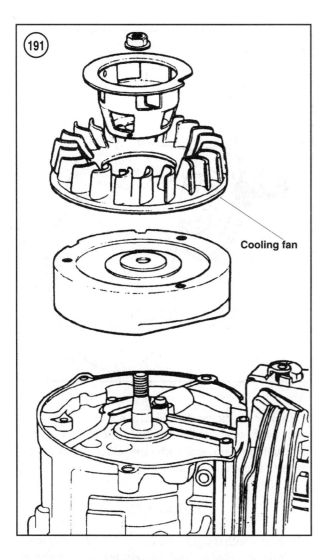

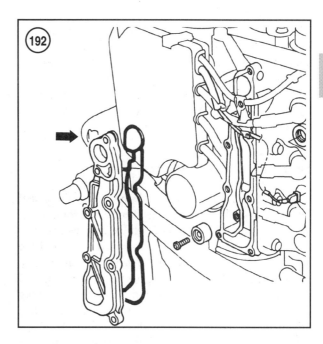

check valve is used. Water exits the flush adapter fitting (**Figure 190**) if the valve does not seat properly.

Models BF20 and BF2A are air-cooled. A flywheel mounted cooling fan (**Figure 191**) blows air through the cylinder block cooling fins to remove excess heat. Overheating on these models is generally the result of debris blocking the cooling fins or contaminants preventing proper heat transfer. To prevent engine overheating, inspect and clean the cooling fan and cooling fins on a regular basis. With these models, a gearcase-mounted water pump cools the exhaust gasses as they pass through the drive shaft housing. As with other models, never run the engine without supplying it with cooling water.

Cooling System Inspection

If the overheat warning horn sounds or the water stream is not present at the rear of the engine, perform the following:

1. Inspect and repair the water pump in the gearcase or jet pump. Refer to Chapter Nine for gearcase repair and Chapter Ten for jet pump repair
2. Inspect and test the thermostat (if so equipped) if overheating occurs and the water pump is in good condition. Refer to *Thermostat Testing* in this section.
3. If no faults can be found with the water pump, thermostat or water pressure relief valve (if so equipped), inspect the exhaust water jacket portion (**Figure 192**, typical) of the cooling system for debris and deposit buildup. Rocks, pieces of the water pump, sand, shells or other debris, may restrict water flow. Salt, calcium or other deposits can form in the cooling passages and restrict water flow.
4. The other problem with deposit buildup is that the insulating quality of the deposit prevents the water from absorbing the heat from the powerhead. Use a cleaner specifically designed to dissolve this type of deposit.

Make sure that the cleaner used is suitable for use on aluminum material. Always follow the manufacturer's instructions when using these products. These cleaners are usually available at marine specialty stores.

5. It is necessary to remove the water jackets when inspecting cooling passages. Refer to Chapter Eight for water jacket removal and installation.

Verifying Engine Temperature

If you suspect overheating, always verify the actual temperature of the engine using Thermomelt sticks (**Figure 193**). Thermomelt sticks resemble crayons and they are designed to melt at a given temperature. Hold the sticks against the cylinder head near the temperature sender or switch. On smaller engines that are not equipped with an overheat alarm, hold the stick near the spark plug mounting area. Try to check the temperature immediately after or during the suspected overheat condition. Hold different temperature sticks to the powerhead to determine the temperature range the engine is reaching. Stop the engine if the temperature exceeds 90° C (194° F) to avoid damage to the powerhead. Perform a complete cooling system inspection if overheating is occurring. Test the overheat switch if an alarm or gauge indicates overheating and the thermomelt sticks indicate normal temperature. Troubleshooting an overheating problem with a flush/test attachment is difficult, as the water supplied through the hose masks problems with the cooling system. Perform this test with the engine in the water or use a test tank.

Thermostat Testing

Test the thermostat(s) if the engine is overheating or running too cool. To test a thermostat, you will need a thermometer, piece of string and container of water that can be heated. Refer to Chapter Eight to help locate the thermostat cover and related components.

1. Remove the thermostats following the instructions provided in Chapter Eight. Discard the thermostat cover gasket. With a string tied to the thermostat, suspend the thermostat in the container of water (**Figure 188**).
2. Place the thermometer in the container and begin heating the water. Continue to heat the container while observing temperature and thermostat.

3A. *Models BF20A, BF25A and BF30A*—The thermostat should begin to open at approximately 72° C (162° F) and be fully open at approximately 82° C (180° F).

3B. *All other models*—The thermostat should begin to open at approximately 52° C (126° F) and be fully open at approximately 62° C (144° F).

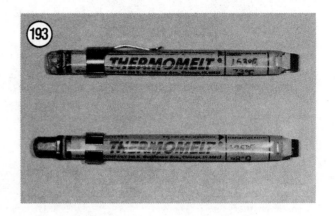

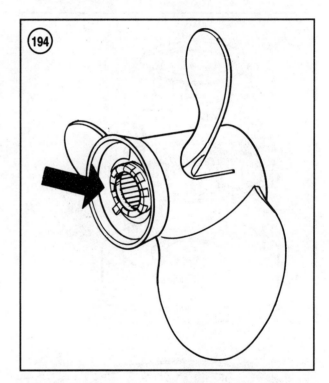

4. Replace the thermostat if it does not fully open or if it opens below or above the specified temperature.
5. Install the thermostat with new gaskets following the instruction provided in Chapter Eight.

GEARCASE

Problems with the gearcase can include water or lubricant leakage, failed internal components, noisy operation or shifting difficulty. The keys to preventing gearcase problems are to avoid contact with underwater objects, shift the engine at idle speed only and perform regular maintenance. Maintenance procedures for the gearcase are located in Chapter Four.

TROUBLESHOOTING

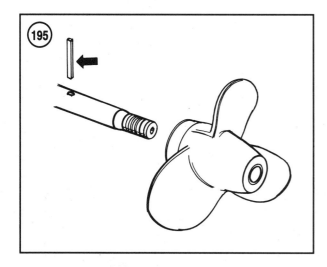

A slipping propeller hub can lead you to believe that a problem exists with the gearcase when only minor repair to the propeller is required. The typical symptom is an inability to accelerate the boat onto plane without over-speeding the engine. Other times the engine seems as though it is not shifting into gear at all.

Propeller Hub Slipping

The propeller hub (**Figure 194**) is installed in the propeller to cushion the shifting action and helps absorb minor impacts. If the propeller hub is spinning in its bore, the engine speed increases as the throttle increases; however, the boat does not increase in speed. In most cases, the boat does not accelerate. Some smaller engines use a shear pin (**Figure 195**) that is designed to break on impact. Symptoms indicating a broken shear pin are similar to a spun propeller hub.

Make a reference mark on the propeller shaft aligned with a reference mark on the propeller. Operate the boat and compare the reference marks after you remove the engine from the water. Have the propeller repaired if the reference marks do not align after running the engine.

Water in the Gearcase

A small amount of water may be present in the gearcase lubricant if the gearcase has not received normal maintenance for several years and has been stored while submerged in water. Pressure test the gearcase to determine the source of water intrusion any time water is found in the gearcase lubricant. Refer to *Pressure Testing* in this section. Failure to correct the leakage eventually leads to extensive damage to the internal components or complete failure of the gearcase. When a repair is required, refer to Chapter Nine.

Lubricant Leakage

The presence of gearcase lubricant on the exterior or around the gearcase requires a pressure test to determine the source of the leakage. Refer to *Pressure Testing*. Failure to correct the leakage results in gear and bearing damage due to lack of lubrication. Refer to Chapter Nine for gearcase repair procedures.

Pressure Testing

You need a gearcase pressure tester to perform this test. Drain the gearcase lubricant and dispose of it in a responsible manner. Air pressure is then applied to the internal cavities of the gearcase. The pressure gauge indicates if leakage is present. Submerge the entire gearcase in water to check for bubbles to determine the point of leakage. Gearcase removal and installation procedures are provided in Chapter Nine. Locations of the drain and vent plugs vary by model. Refer to Chapter Nine for assistance with locating these plugs.

1. Place a suitable container below the gearcase. Position the gearcase so that the drain (**Figure 196**) is at the lowest point relative to the container. The engine may need to be tilted slightly. Remove the drain and vent plug (**Figure 196**) and allow the gearcase to drain completely.
2. Install the pressure tester into the vent opening. Install the drain plug.
3. Slowly apply pressure with the pressure tester. Push, pull and turn all shafts while observing the pressure gauge as the pressure slowly increases. Stop increasing pressure when it reaches approximately 100 kPa (14.5 psi).
4. If the unit does hold this pressure for at least 10 seconds, remove the gearcase following the procedure listed in Chapter Nine. Submerge the gearcase with the pressure applied. Replace the seal and/or seal surface at the location that bubbles appear. Refer to Chapter Nine for repair procedures.
5. Loosen the drain plug to allow the air to slowly bleed from the gearcase. Refill the gearcase with fresh lubricant following the procedures listed in Chapter Four.

Metal Contamination in the Lubricant

Fine metal particles form in the gearcase during normal usage. The gearcase lubricant may have a *metal flake* appearance when inspected during routine maintenance. The fine metal particles tend to cling to the end of the drain plug, causing great concern to anyone who is performing routine maintenance. Carefully apply some of the material to your finger and thumb and rub them together. Inspect the gearcase if any of the material is large enough to feel. Removing the propeller shaft bearing carrier allows a view of the internal components. Refer to Chapter Nine for removal, inspection and assembly procedures.

Gearcase Vibration or Noise

Gearcase noise does occur from normal usage. The normal noise is barely noticeable. A rough, growling noise or a loud high-pitched whine is reason to suspect damaged or faulty components.

Knocking or grinding noise

If a knocking or grinding noise comes from the gearcase, the cause is likely damaged gears or other components. The gears may have suffered damage as the result of underwater impact or high speed shifting. On occasion a knocking noise can come from the gearcase, leading one to believe the base engine has a failure. Always inspect the gearcase lubricant before inspecting the base engine. Inspect the gearcase lubricant for metal contamination. In most cases, the gearcase lubricant indicates if internal components have failed. Refer to Chapter Nine for removal and repair procedures.

High-pitched whine

If a high-pitched whine is present, it normally indicates a bearing problem or, in some cases, the gears running out of alignment. The only way to verify that a problem exists is to disassemble and inspect the internal components. Have a professional listen to the gearcase before proceeding with a repair.

Gearcase vibration

Vibration in the engine can originate in the gearcase. In almost all cases, the vibration is due to a bent propeller shaft or damaged propeller. A propeller can appear perfect, but still be out of balance. The best way to determine this is to have the propeller trued and balanced at a reputable propeller repair station, or simply try a different (yet suitable) propeller for the engine. A bent propeller shaft is normally the result of an impact with an underwater object. Always check for a bent propeller shaft when vibration is present following the procedures in Chapter Nine. If the propeller shaft is bent, disassemble and inspect the

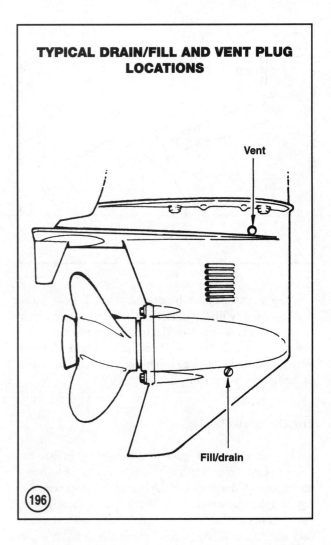

gearcase as other internal components may also be damaged. Never operate the outboard motor if severe vibration is occurring. Excessive vibration can compromise the durability of the entire outboard motor.

WARNING
Remove all spark plug leads and disconnect both battery cables before removing, installing or working around the propeller.

Shifting difficulty

Hard shifting is usually the result of improper shift cable adjustment. Refer to Chapter Five and adjust the shift cables and linkage as described. Gearcase removal, disassembly and inspection are required if shifting problems are not corrected with adjustment. Refer to Chapter Nine for gearcase repair procedures.

TROUBLESHOOTING

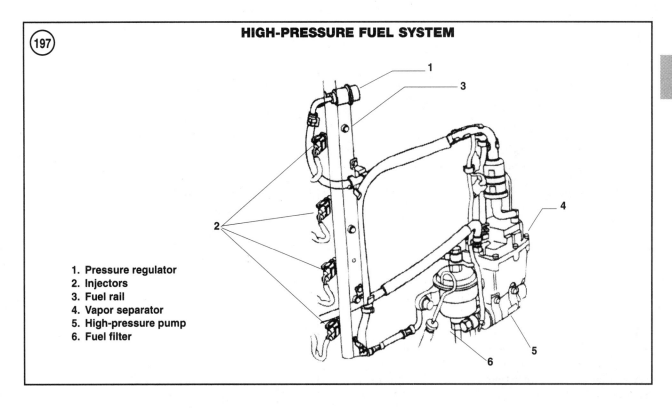

HIGH-PRESSURE FUEL SYSTEM

1. Pressure regulator
2. Injectors
3. Fuel rail
4. Vapor separator
5. High-pressure pump
6. Fuel filter

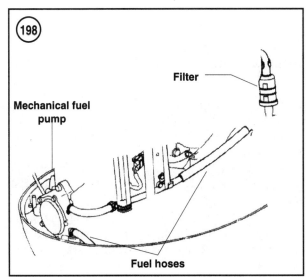

ELECTRONIC FUEL INJECTION SYSTEM

Compared with carburetor-equipped outboards, advanced electronic fuel injection provides quicker starting, automatic altitude compensation, improved fuel economy and smoother overall operation. This section provides an explanation of the EFI system, EFI troubleshooting tips and component testing.

A problem with the electric fuel injection system can cause rough engine operation, reduced power, a bogging or hesitation during acceleration, or in some cases, a no-start condition.

Troubleshooting the system is relatively simple if one system at a time is checked. Remember to check the base engine and the ignition system before proceeding with EFI system testing. Much time and expense can be wasted replacing EFI components only to find that a cylinder has low compression or a simple ignition problem.

Troubleshooting the EFI system is separated into two sections that include the *Fuel Supply System* and the *Electronic Control System*.

Always check the fuel supply system first. Most EFI problems are directly related to failed fuel system components. Perform test on the electronic control systems if all components of the fuel supply system test correctly.

Fuel System

This section covers troubleshooting the high-pressure side of the fuel system. The components include the high-pressure fuel pump, vapor separator tank, fuel rail, fuel injectors, and fuel pressure regulator (**Figure 197**). The low-pressure side of the system includes the mechanical fuel pump, fuel lines and fuel filters (**Figure 198**). The low-pressure components are similar to those used on carburetor-equipped engines. Refer to *Fuel Tank and Fuel Pump* in this chapter to test the low-pressure fuel components.

> *WARNING*
> *Use extreme caution when working with the fuel system. Fuel can spray out under high pressure. Always use the required safety gear. Never smoke or perform any test around an open flame or other source of ignition. Fuel and/or vapor can ignite or explode, resulting in damaged property, severe bodily injury or death.*

High-Pressure Fuel System Testing

The basic test to perform on a fuel-injected engine is the fuel rail pressure test. This test verifies that fuel is supplied to the fuel injectors at the required pressure. While this test can ensure that the fuel pump and regulator are operating under controlled conditions, it cannot determine if fuel pressure is adequate at all engine operating ranges. Leaking fuel lines, restricted passages and a blocked filter can inhibit fuel flow and reduce fuel pressure in the low- and high-pressure systems. If one of these conditions exists, the fuel rail pressure may be correct at a lower speed, but it drops sharply as the throttle opening increases. Engine performance falters as the pressure drops. If this symptom is present, check all fuel filters, antisiphon valve, fuel tank pickup and low-pressure pump following the procedures provided in this chapter.

Fuel rail pressure test

Honda part No 07406-004000A or a suitable fuel pressure gauge capable of measuring 314 kPa (46 psi) is required. Purchase the fuel pressure gauge from a local Honda Outboard dealership. A special adapter is included that threads into a hole in the fuel rail (**Figure 199**). A dangerous fuel leak can occur if the gauge does not seal properly to the fuel rail. In addition, the fuel fitting sealing washer must be replaced if the fitting is loosened.

Perform this test with the engine running at idle speed on a flush/test device, in the water or in a suitable test tank. The engine can run at all speeds with the gauge attached to verify fuel pressure. Ensure that the gauge is properly secured and does not interfere with control mechanisms. Remove the gauge when the testing is complete.

1. Disconnect both battery cables from the battery. Locate the fuel pressure test fitting on the lower portion of the fuel rail (**Figure 200**).

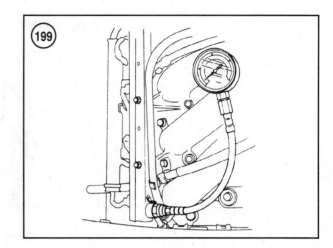

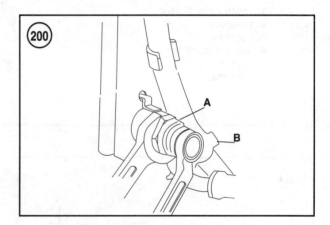

2. Place a shop towel below the fuel pressure test fitting. Work slowly and carefully while working with the fuel pressure test fitting. Fuel will likely spray from the fitting when loosened.
3. Place a wrench on the larger fitting (A, **Figure 200**) while slowly loosening the smaller fitting (B, **Figure 200**) no more than one turn.
4. After the fuel pressure bleeds off, wipe up any spilled fuel then remove the smaller fitting from the larger portion of the fitting. Remove and discard the sealing washer from the fitting.
5. Thread the fuel pressure gauge into the fuel pressure test fitting on the fuel rail. Hold the larger fitting (A, **Figure 200**) with a wrench as you securely tighten the fuel pressure gauge fitting.
6. Locate the fuel pressure regulator vacuum hose (**Figure 201**). Remove the hose from the regulator and plug the hose with a suitable object such as a golf tee.
7. Clean the terminals, then connect the battery cables to the battery. Supply a source of cooling water for the engine. Have an assistant start the engine as you inspect the fuel rail connections for potential fuel leaks. Stop the en-

TROUBLESHOOTING

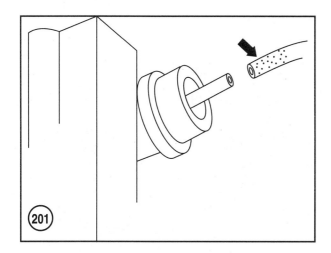

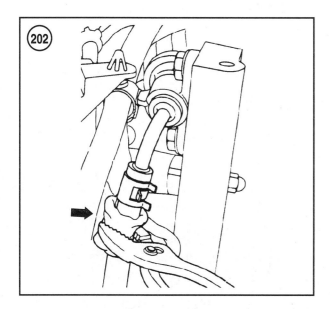

gine immediately and correct any fuel leaks before proceeding with the test.

8. Observe the measured fuel pressure and record the readings. Correct pressure is 265-314 kPa or 38-46 psi at idle speed (700-800 rpm).

9. If low fuel pressure is noted in Step 8, locate the fuel pressure regulator-to-vapor separator hose (**Figure 202**). While observing the fuel pressure gauge, slowly pinch the regulator hose with pliers until you note an increase in fuel pressure. If the pressure increases to within the specified pressure, replace the fuel pressure regulator.

10. With the engine still running, carefully remove the plug from the fuel pressure regulator vacuum hose. Observe the fuel pressure gauge as you attach the hose to the fuel pressure regulator. A slight decrease in pressure should be noted as the hose is attached. Replace the fuel pressure regulator if the pressure does not decrease.

11. Observe the fuel pressure gauge and have an assistant switch the engine off. The fuel pressure should not drop significantly over a 1-minute time span. If the pressure drops significantly, check for a leaking injector, leaking fuel hose(s), or a faulty electric fuel pump check valve.

   a. Test and inspect the low-pressure system, vapor separator tank and all filters if fuel pressure is too low at idle speed or decreases significantly as the throttle is opened.

   b. Check for blocked or restricted hoses if fuel pressure is above the specification. Replace or inspect the fuel pressure regulator and regulator filter if the hoses are not blocked.

12. Disconnect both battery cables from the battery. Place a shop towel below the fuel gauge fitting. Use a wrench to hold the large portion of the fitting (A, **Figure 200**) as you slowly loosen the fuel pressure gauge fitting.

13. When the fuel pressure is relieved, remove the fuel gauge fitting from the fuel rail and clean all spilled fuel from the engine. Drain any fuel from the gauge into a suitable container for disposal.

14. Install a new sealing washer onto the small fuel pressure fitting (B, **Figure 200**). Install the small fitting into the threaded hole in the fuel rail and hand-tighten. Hold the large fitting (A, **Figure 200**) with a wrench and securely tighten the small fitting.

15. Clean the terminals, then connect the battery cables to the battery terminals. Start the engine. Immediately correct any fuel leakage before returning the engine to service.

Vapor Separator Tank

A water-cooled vapor separator tank provides a consistent supply of fuel (in liquid form) to the electric fuel pump. The water cooling effect reduces chance of forming vapor bubbles in the fuel system. It houses a float, needle seat and vent system, allowing any vapor or air bubbles to be purged from the system.

A flooding vapor separator tank allows excessive fuel to enter the intake portion of the engine. This condition normally leads to rough running at lower engine speeds, and excessive exhaust smoke. Spark plug fouling may also occur.

Check for the presence of fuel in the vapor separator tank if a no-start condition exists and no or very little fuel pressure is measured when tested.

Flooding Vapor Separator Tank

1. Locate the hose from the vent fitting on top of the tank (**Figure 203**). Remove the hose from the fitting.
2. Connect a suitable hose to the fitting and direct the other end to a clean container suitable for holding fuel.
3. Slowly squeeze the primer bulb while observing the connected hose and container.
4. Completely disassemble, inspect and reassemble the vapor separator tank following the procedure described in Chapter Six if fuel flows from the hose when squeezing the primer bulb.
5. Return any captured fuel to the fuel tank. Connect the vent hose to the fitting on the vapor separator tank using a new hose clamp. Correct any fuel leakage before returning the engine to service.

Checking for Fuel in the Vapor Separator Tank

1. Remove both battery cables from the battery. Place a container under the fuel hose connecting the vapor separator tank to the electric fuel pump (**Figure 204**).
2. Carefully pull the hose from the vapor separator tank. Loosen the drain screw then allow all the fuel to drain from the vapor separator tank. Securely tighten the drain screw. Gently squeeze the primer bulb while observing the hose fitting.
3. If fuel does not flow from the hose fitting when the primer bulb is squeezed, disassemble the vapor separator tank following the instructions in Chapter Six.
4. Connect the hose to the tank fitting and install a new hose clamp. Squeeze the primer bulb until firm. Inspect for and correct fuel leaks before returning engine back to service. Clean the terminals then connect the battery cables to the battery.

Testing High-Pressure Pump Operation

Perform this test if a no-start condition exists and you detect low fuel pressure. The engine control unit (ECU) controls the fuel pump. The pump operates for a few seconds when the key is switched to the ON position, then it stops. The pump runs again when the ECU detects flywheel rotation. The pump is relatively quiet, yet it can be heard running with a stethoscope. You can also feel vibration from the pump while it is running. Verify that spark is present at all ignition coils before performing this test.

1. Turn the ignition key to the ON position. Immediately check to see if the pump is operating. If the pump runs, refer to high-pressure fuel test.

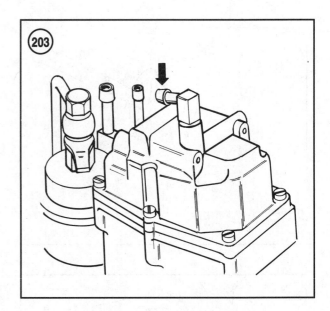

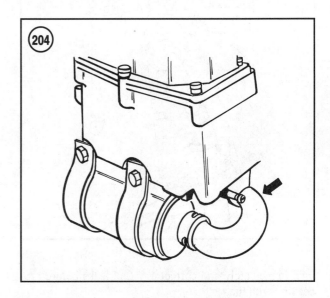

2. If the pump does not run, check for battery voltage at the fuel pump following the procedure listed in this section.

Testing For Fuel Injector Operation

Use a mechanic's stethoscope to check for fuel injector operation. Run the engine in the water, on a flush/test device or in a test tank. Locate the fuel injectors and touch the stethoscope probe to the body of all fuel injectors (**Figure 205**). All fuel injectors should create a distinct clicking sound when operating. If no noise is detected, or the noise it creates is noticeably different from the other injectors, the injector is faulty. Additional testing includes

TROUBLESHOOTING

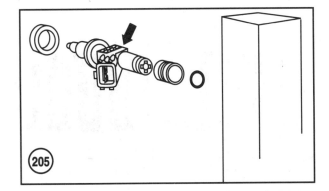

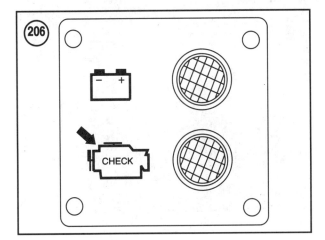

the *fuel injector circuit test* provided in this section. A fault with the ignition system, wiring or engine control unit (ECU) can cause the injector not to function. Check these components prior to replacing an injector.

NOTE
High-power electrical equipment such a stereos or communication radios can cause electrical interference that may affect the electronic fuel injection system. Switch these devices off when you detect trouble with the engine. Avoid using these devices when the engine is running if normal engine operation resumes with these devices switched OFF.

Electric Control Unit

This section provides testing procedures for the engine control unit (ECU) portion of the EFI System. Test procedures for the various system sensors and other electrical components are also provided in this section.

The ECU directly controls both the fuel injectors and the ignition system on all EFI models. It uses input from various engine-mounted sensors to compute the proper fuel delivery and spark timing for any given condition. Engine idle speed and operation of the high-pressure electric pump are controlled by the ECU as well.

Incorporated into the ECU are special circuits that enable self-diagnosis. A dash-mounted warning light (**Figure 206**) illuminates when a malfunction is detected with the fuel system sensors or internal ECU circuits and goes out when the malfunction is corrected. The ECU provides a substitute value for a sensor with a malfunction to allow continued engine operation. Engine performance or running quality may suffer, yet it will allow you to motor back to port.

The dash-mounted warning light (**Figure 206**) is also used to read any stored trouble codes.

Perform the *Reading Trouble Codes* test if the dash-mounted engine warning light illuminates while running the engine or if you observe problems with the engine not caused by fuel system malfunctions, low compression or ignition faults.

NOTE
A short blink on the dash-mounted engine warning light should occur when the key is switched to the ON position. Check for a defective light bulb if no blink is indicated. A fault with the ECU or wiring may prevent proper operation of the light.

Reading Trouble Codes

Use a jumper wire or preferably Honda part No. 07WPZ-0010100 to direct the ECU to display trouble codes on the dash-mounted engine warning light. Trouble codes are indicated by a series of flashing lights. Reading the codes can be tricky. A repeating short-duration light separated by a long-duration light-off period (**Figure 207**) indicates a code 1. Two short-duration flashes separated by a long-duration light-off period (**Figure 208**) indicate a code 2. A long-duration flash quickly followed by four short-duration flashes (**Figure 209**) indicates a code 14.

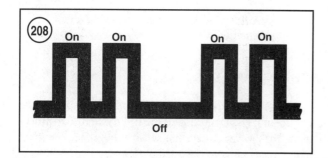

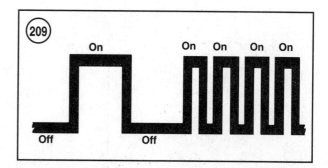

The short-duration flashes indicate the first digit of a stored trouble code. Long duration flashes indicate the second digit of the trouble code. All trouble codes repeat in numerical sequence when the self-diagnosis system is enabled. **Table 17** lists and explains the trouble codes.

1. Locate and remove the electrical component cover (**Figure 210**). Locate the diagnostics-enable wire connector (**Figure 211**). Remove the wire connector cap or cover.
2. Plug the special wire connector (Honda part No. 07WPZ-0010100) onto the plug or carefully connect a jumper wire to each red wire terminal on the wire harness connector.
3. Switch the key switch to the ON position.
4. Read the flashing lights and determine any stored trouble codes, following the instructions listed earlier. Record all indicated trouble codes. Switch the ignition OFF then disconnect the special wire connector or jumper wire from the wire harness connector. Install the wire connector cap or cover, then install the electrical component cover.
5. Refer to **Table 17** to determine which component or circuit malfunction is indicated. Test the indicated sensor or components following the procedure listed in this section.
6. Refer to *Clearing Trouble Codes* in this section after repairs are complete to erase the codes from the ECU memory.

CAUTION
Review all steps for clearing trouble codes prior to starting the procedure. Steps 2-5 must be completed in 20 seconds or less to properly clear the codes from the ECU.

Clearing Trouble Codes

1. Locate and remove the electrical component cover (**Figure 210**). Locate the diagnostics-enable wire connector (**Figure 211**). Remove the wire connector cap or cover.
2. Position the key switch in the OFF position. Plug the special wire connector Honda part No. 07WPZ-0010100 onto the plug, or carefully connect a jumper wire to each red wire terminal on the wire harness connector.

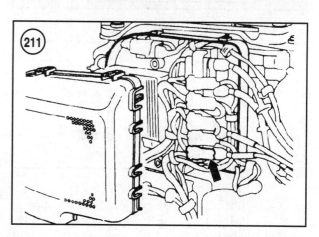

3. Turn the key switch to the ON position. Press the engine stop button (**Figure 212**) for 1 second, then release the button for 1 second. Repeat this five times.
4. Lighting of the dash-mounted engine warning light followed by a double sounding of the warning buzzer indicates that the codes have been cleared.
5. Turn the key switch to the OFF position. Remove the special wire connector or jumper wire, then install the wire connector cap or cover. Install the electrical component cover (**Figure 210**).

TROUBLESHOOTING

located at the end of this manual to locate the fuel injectors and wiring. Identify the wire color used for the injectors, then trace the wires to the component on the engine.

1. Disconnect both battery cables from the battery.
2. Locate the fuel injector and wire harness connector(s). Note the position of the wire harness connector and the wire routing. Carefully disconnect the wire harness from a selected injector.
3. Select the ohms function on your volt/ohm meter. Select the R × 1 scale on the meter.
4. Clean any corrosion or debris from the injector or harness terminals prior to performing this test. Touch the positive test lead to one of the terminals on the injector. Touch the negative test lead to the other injector terminal (**Figure 213**). Record the meter readings. Repeat Steps 2-4 for any remaining injectors.
5. Injector resistance should be 11.1-12.3 ohms. Replace any injector that reads beyond this specification.
6. Pay careful attention to the position of the injector in relation to the wire harness connector during installation. Ensure that the terminals are clean, then connect the wire harness to the fuel injector.
7. Clean the terminals, then connect the battery cables to the battery.

Checking Battery Voltage At The Fuel Pump

This test determines if the circuits that provide electric current to the fuel pump are operating correctly. This test requires a volt/ohm meter. Ensure that the engine battery is fully charged prior to performing this test.

1. Locate and carefully disconnect the engine wire harness from the electric fuel pump connector (**Figure 214**).
2. Select the volts function on your volt/ohm meter. Select the 20- or 40-volt scale on the meter.
3. Connect the positive test lead to the blue/yellow wire terminal connector on the main engine harness. Connect the negative test lead to the black wire terminal connector on the main engine harness.
4. Have an assistant turn the key switch to the ON position as you observe the voltmeter. Battery voltage should be present for approximately 2 seconds when the key switch is turned ON.
5. If the correct voltage is present, but the fuel pump does not operate, replace the fuel pump. Refer to Chapter Six for fuel pump replacement. If battery voltage is not present in Step 4, continue to Step 6.
6. Calibrate the ohmmeter on the R × 1 scale. Connect the positive lead to the blue/yellow wire terminal of the main

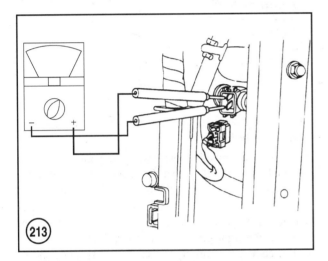

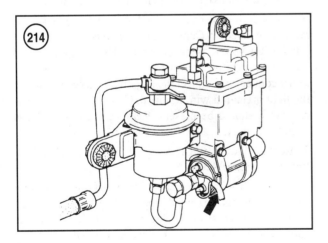

Injector Circuit Testing

Fuel injectors are electronically operated fuel valves. This portion of the test checks the internal resistance of the fuel injectors. Perform this test if an injector is not operating. Use a *digital* volt/ohm meter to check the resistance of the fuel injector. Refer to the wiring diagrams engine harness. Connect the negative lead to an engine ground.

7. Continuity should be noted. If no continuity is noted, repair the open circuit in the wire or connector in the main engine harness.

8. Test the system relay as described in this chapter. Check the main wire harness connectors and the harness for damaged wiring if the system relay is operating correctly, but the correct voltage is not present during Step 4. If the wiring, connectors and relay are in acceptable condition, but the incorrect voltage is present during Step 4, the ECU requires replacement.

9. Clean the terminals and connect the wire harness to the fuel pump connector.

System Relay Test

When the key switch is positioned in the RUN position, the system relay (**Figure 215**) provides electric current to the engine control unit, fuel injectors and the ignition coils. In addition, this relay provides electric current to the dash-mounted engine warning light, charging system indicator light, and the voltage regulator in the alternator. The key switch supplies the current to activate the relay.

Dedicated switches in the system relay supply current to the electric fuel pump. Using a connection to the electric starter motor relay, the system relay activates the electric fuel pump when the starter motor is operated. Using a connection to the system relay, the ECU activates the electric fuel pump circuit while the engine is running.

Testing the relay requires a fully charged battery, two jumper leads and a volt/ohm meter. Refer to the wiring diagrams located at the end of this manual to locate the system relay and its wire connectors. Identify the wire colors used and trace the wires to the relay on the engine. The following test procedures check the actual operation of the relay.

1. Disconnect both battery terminals from the battery. Locate the system relay on the engine (**Figure 215**).
2. Note the wire harness orientation and wire routing, then carefully disconnect the system relay from the engine wire harness.
3. Select the ohms function of a volt/ohm meter. Select the R × 1 scale.
4. Connect the positive test lead to the white/yellow wire terminal connector. Connect the negative test lead to the yellow/black wire terminal connector. Using a jumper lead, connect the positive battery terminal to the black/yellow wire terminal connector. Using a jumper lead, connect the negative battery terminal to the black wire terminal. Observe the meter reading. Continuity or

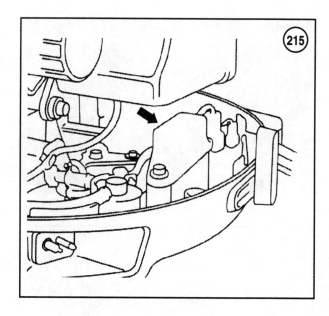

very low resistance should be present. Remove the jumper leads from the battery.

5. Connect the positive test lead to the white/black wire terminal connector. Connect the negative test lead to the blue/yellow wire terminal connector. Using a jumper lead connect the positive battery terminal to the yellow/black wire terminal connector. Connect the negative battery terminal to the light green/red wire terminal. Observe the meter reading. Continuity or very low resistance should be present. Remove the jumper leads from the battery.

6. Connect the positive test lead to the white/black wire terminal connector. Connect the negative test lead to the blue/yellow wire terminal connector. Using a jumper lead connect the positive battery terminal to the *white* wire terminal connector. Connect the negative battery terminal to the light green/red wire terminal. Continuity or very low resistance should be present. Remove the jumper leads from the battery.

7. Replace the relay if it does not operate as described. Refer to Chapter Seven.

8. Ensure all wire connections are positioned correctly and that all wires are routed properly. Clean the terminals, then connect the system relay connectors to the engine harness connectors and the battery cables to battery.

NOTE
When using a digital volt/ohm meter, connect the test leads together and read the displayed resistance. This indicates the amount of internal resistance in the meter and leads. Subtract the displayed measurement from the test results to determine the actual resistance of a circuit.

TROUBLESHOOTING

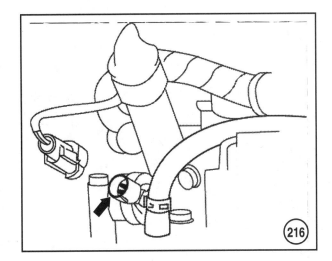

Idle Air Control (IAC) Motor Testing

Testing of the idle air control motor (**Figure 216**) is required if you note unstable or incorrect idle speed. Other symptoms include engine stalling when shifted into gear, or stalling when the throttle returns to the idle position. A malfunctioning idle air control motor can contribute to engine starting difficulty.

Use a digital volt/ohm meter to test the resistance of the idle air control motor. To assist with locating the idle air control motor and its wire connections, refer to the wiring diagrams located at the end of this manual. Identify the wire colors used and trace the wires to the component on the engine. Check for dirty, loose or damaged wires or connectors.

1. Disconnect both battery cables from the battery. Locate the idle air control motor (**Figure 216**) on the engine. Note the position of the wire connectors and the wire routing. Carefully disconnect the 2-pin connector from the idle air control motor.

2. Select the ohms function on your digital volt/ohm meter. Select the R × 1 scale on the meter.

3. Connect the positive test lead to one of wire connector terminals on the idle air control motor. Observe the meter reading as you touch the negative test lead to the other terminal on the idle air control motor. Record the meter reading. The meter readings should indicate 10-13 ohms.

4. Connect the negative meter lead to a known-good engine ground. Observe the meter readings as you touch the positive meter lead to either wire connector terminal. Repeat this step, touching the other wire terminal connector. The meter should indicate an open circuit or very high resistance when touching either wire terminal connector.

5. Replace the idle air control motor if you note incorrect test results in Step 3 or Step 4. Idle air control motor replacement is provided in Chapter Six.

6. Clean the terminals and carefully connect the wire harness connector to the idle air control wire connector. Ensure that the wire connector is correctly attached and all wires are routed properly. Clean the terminals, then connect the battery cables to the battery.

Air Pressure Sensor Testing

The air pressure sensor (**Figure 217**) provides the input used by the engine control unit to determine intake manifold air pressure. Manifold air pressure and fuel requirements are affected by operating altitude as well as engine load. Fuel delivery based on manifold air pressure allows for the lowest possible exhaust emissions, optimum fuel economy and smooth operation. The engine control unit alters fuel delivery to the engine to compensate for changes in manifold air pressure.

Excessive exhaust smoke, spark plug fouling, poor performance or a lean running condition can result from a faulty pressure sensor.

Testing involves checking sensor input voltage and associated wires. When the trouble code for the air pressure sensor illuminates and there are no wire or input voltage faults, you must replace the sensor. Jumper leads and a digital volt/ohm meter are required to perform this test.

1. Remove the spark plugs and connect the spark plug lead to an engine ground.

2. Find where the wire harness connects to the air pressure sensor (**Figure 217**). Note the wire connector position and wire routing. Carefully disconnect the wire harness connector from the sensor connector.

3. Select the DC volts function on the digital volt/ohm meter. Select the 10- or 20-volt scale on the meter. Connect the positive meter lead to the brown/yellow wire har-

ness terminal. Connect the negative meter lead to an engine ground.

4. Turn the key switch ON and observe the meter reading. The meter should indicate 4.75-5.25 volts DC.

5. Connect the positive test lead to the brown/yellow wire harness terminal. Connect the negative test lead to the green wire harness terminal connector. Observe the meter readings. The meter should indicate 4.75-5.25 volts DC.

6. Connect the positive test lead to the white/red wire harness terminal. Connect the negative test lead to the green wire harness terminal connector. Observe the meter readings. The meter should indicate 4.75-5.25 volts DC.

7. Replace the air pressure sensor if the voltage in Steps 3-6 is not as specified.

8. Check for loose, damaged or corroded wires or connections between the air pressure sensor and ECU if any of the voltage readings in Steps 3-6 are not as specified. If the wiring and connections are not at fault, the ECU may be defective.

9. Carefully connect the wire harness connector to the air pressure sensor connector. Ensure the wires are routed properly. Install the spark plugs and connect the spark plug leads.

Air Temperature Sensor Testing

Air temperature directly influences air density, therefore changing fuel delivery requirements. Cooler air requires more fuel; warmer air requires less fuel. Poor performance, excessive smoke, plug fouling and a lean operating condition can result from a defective air temperature sensor. The air temperature sensor (**Figure 218**) provides input to the engine control unit (ECU) to indicate the temperature of incoming air. Required fuel delivery changes can then occur.

You need a digital volt/ohm meter and air thermometer to test this sensor. The test is divided into two sequences. The first verifies correct input voltage to the sensor. The second tests the air temperature sensor resistance. Perform both tests if you observe a fault with the air temperature sensor.

Voltage test

1. Remove the spark plugs and connect the spark plug lead to a suitable ground (clean cylinder head or cylinder block bolts).

2. Locate the air temperature sensor on the engine (**Figure 218**). Note the orientation of the sensor to the wire harness connection as well as the wire routing. Carefully disconnect the wire harness connector from the sensor.

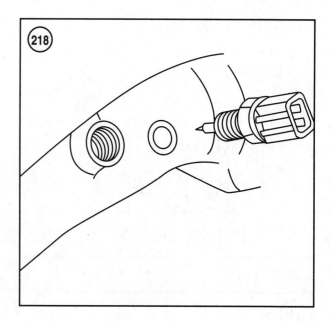

3. Select the DC volts function on your digital volt/ohm meter. Select the 10- or 20-volt scale on the meter. Connect the positive meter lead to the red/yellow color wire terminal on the sensor connector. Connect the negative meter lead to an engine ground.

4. Turn the key switch ON and note the voltage reading. The voltage should be between 4.30-5.25 volts DC. Test the system relay, all wires and connectors, fuses and key switch if the voltage is not as specified. A fault with the engine control unit (ECU) is indicated when incorrect voltage readings are indicated and all listed components test correctly.

5. Turn the key switch OFF. Remove both battery cables from the battery. Perform the *air temperature sensor resistance test* as described in this chapter.

Resistance test

1. Refer to Chapter Six and remove the air temperature sensor from the engine.

2. Place the sensor on a work surface. Select the ohms function on your digital volt/ohm meter. Connect the positive meter lead to one of the intake air temperature sensor terminals (**Figure 218**). Connect the negative meter lead to the other sensor terminal.

3. Place the air thermometer in close proximity to the sensor. Note the air temperature and the resistance displayed on the meter. Compare these measurements to the specifications listed in **Table 18**.

4. Use a hair dryer or heat lamp to heat the air around the sensor. Again note the resistance and air temperature.

TROUBLESHOOTING

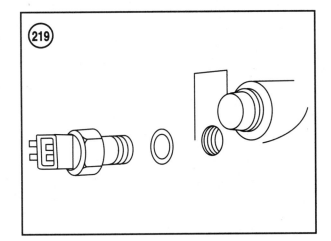

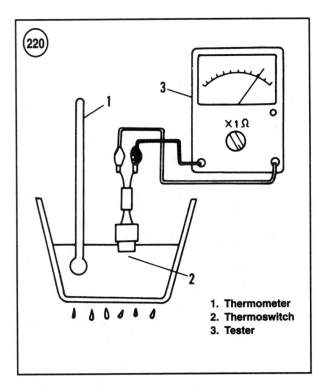

1. Thermometer
2. Thermoswitch
3. Tester

5. Place the meter, air temperature sensor and thermometer in a cool area for a few minutes. Take the temperature and resistance reading again and compare them to the specifications listed in **Table 18**.

6. Replace the sensor if the readings are not within the specifications listed for the measured temperature.

7. Install the air temperature sensor following the procedure listed in Chapter Six. Clean the connector terminals, then carefully connect the wire harness connector to the sensor. Ensure that the wires are routed correctly. Install the spark plugs and connect the spark plug leads. Clean the terminals, then connect the battery cables to the battery.

Engine Temperature Sensor Testing

Engine temperature has a direct influence on engine fuel requirements. A cool engine requires more fuel than one that has reached operating temperature. Poor performance, excessive smoke, plug fouling and rough operation can all result from a faulty engine temperature sensor. The engine temperature sensor (**Figure 219**) provides input to the engine control unit (ECU) to indicate the operating temperature of the engine. Required fuel delivery changes can then occur.

A digital volt/ohm meter, a liquid thermometer and a container of water that can be heated are required to test this sensor. The test is divided into two sequences. The first sequence verifies correct input voltage to the sensor. The second sequence tests the engine temperature sensor resistance. Perform both tests if an engine temperature sensor trouble code is present.

Voltage test

1. Remove the spark plugs and connect the spark plug leads to an engine ground.
2. Locate the air temperature sensor on the engine (**Figure 219**). Note the orientation of the sensor to the wire harness connection and the wire routing. Carefully disconnect the wire harness connector from the sensor.
3. Select the DC volts function on your digital volt/ohm meter. Select the 10- or 20-volt scale on the meter. Connect the positive meter lead to the red/white color wire terminal on the sensor connector. Connect the negative meter lead to a suitable engine ground (clean cylinder head or cylinder block bolt).
4. Turn the key switch to the ON position and note the voltage reading. The voltage should be 4.30-5.25 volts DC. Test the system relay, all wires and connectors, fuses and key switch if you note an incorrect reading. Incorrect voltage readings when all listed components test correctly indicates a fault with the engine control unit (ECU).
5. Turn the key switch OFF. Remove both battery cables from the battery. Perform the *Temperature Sensor Resistance Test* following the procedures listed in this section.

Resistance test

1. Refer to Chapter Six and remove the air temperature sensor from the engine. Suspend the sensor in a suitable container of water (**Figure 220**).

2. Select the ohms function on your digital volt/ohm meter. Connect the positive meter lead to one of the intake air temperature sensor terminals. Connect the negative meter lead to the other sensor terminal.

3. Place the liquid thermometer in the container next to the sensor. Allow a few minutes for the thermometer to stabilize. Refer to **Table 18** for the specifications, then note the temperature and the displayed resistance reading on the meter. Compare these measurements to the specifications.

4. Observe the thermometer and the reading on the meter as you begin to heat the water. Note the meter reading as the water temperature matches the temperatures listed in **Table 18**. Record the readings.

5. Allow the water to cool, then place ice (or cold water) in the water. Take resistance measurements as the sensor cools to the temperatures listed in **Table 18**.

6. Replace the sensor if the readings do not fall within the specifications listed. A wire or ECU is at fault if an engine temperature sensor code continues to set, but the sensor operates correctly.

7. Install the engine temperature sensor as described in Chapter Six. Clean the connector terminals, then carefully connect the wire harness connector to the sensor. Ensure that the wires are routed correctly. Install the spark plugs and connect the spark plug leads. Clean the terminals, then connect the battery cables to the battery.

Exhaust Port Temperature Sensor Testing

This sensor indicates the engine temperature near the exhaust port of the No. 1 cylinder. The engine control unit switches on the warning buzzer, warning lights and activates power reduction if it detects overheating.

A malfunction with this sensor or sensor circuit may result in the warning system operating at normal engine temperatures. It is possible for a sensor malfunction to not indicate an overheating condition.

You need a digital volt/ohm meter, liquid thermometer and a container of water that can be heated to test this sensor. The test is divided into two test sequences. The first verifies correct input voltage to the sensor. The second tests the engine temperature sensor resistance. Perform both tests if an exhaust port temperature sensor trouble code is noted.

Voltage test

Refer to the wiring diagrams located at the end of this manual to assist with locating the exhaust port tempera-

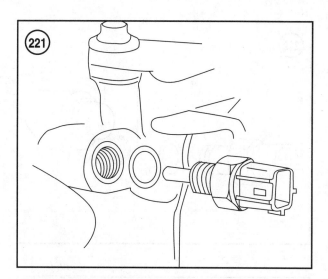

ture sensor. Identify the wire colors used and trace the wire to the component on the engine.

1. Remove the spark plugs and connect the spark plug lead to an engine ground.

2. Locate the exhaust port temperature sensor (**Figure 221**) on the engine. Note the position of the sensor to the wire harness connection and the wire routing. Carefully disconnect the wire harness connector from the sensor.

3. Select the DC volt function on your digital volt/ohm meter. Select the 10- or 20-volt scale on the meter. Connect the positive meter lead to the red/green wire terminal on the sensor connector. Connect the negative meter lead to an engine ground.

4. Turn the key switch ON and note the voltage reading. The voltage should be between 4.30-5.25 volts DC. Test the system relay, all wires and connectors, fuses and key switch if you note any incorrect readings. The engine control unit (ECU) is defective if an incorrect voltage reading is indicated but all other listed components test correctly.

5. Turn the key switch OFF. Remove both battery cables from the battery. Perform the *exhaust port temperature sensor resistance test* following the procedures listed in this section.

Resistance test

Refer to the wiring diagrams located at the end of this manual to locate the exhaust port temperature sensor. Identify the wire colors used and trace the wire to the component on the engine.

1. Refer to Chapter Six and remove the exhaust port temperature sensor from the engine. Suspend the sensor in a suitable container of water (**Figure 220**).

2. Select the ohms function on your digital volt/ohm meter. Connect the positive meter lead to one of the intake air

TROUBLESHOOTING

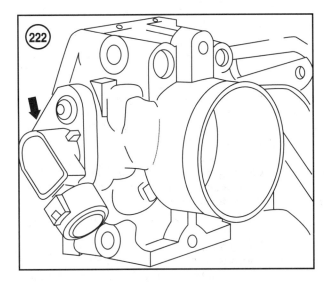

Throttle Position Sensor Test

An immediate increase in fuel delivery is required to ensure good throttle response during acceleration. The throttle position sensor (**Figure 222**) provides a voltage signal to the engine control unit (ECU) relative to the throttle opening. This allows the electronic control unit to provide an immediate increase in fuel delivery if the throttle is opened suddenly. This signal and other sensors ensure the proper fuel and timing advance is provided for a given operating condition.

A faulty throttle position sensor can result in a bog or hesitation during rapid acceleration, unstable idle speed, excessive exhaust smoke or rough engine operation. Testing is required if a trouble code indicates a fault with the throttle position sensor. Testing requires a digital volt/ohm meter.

Refer to the wiring diagrams located at the end of this manual to locate the sensor wires. Identify the wire colors used and trace it to the component on the engine.

1. Remove the spark plugs and connect the spark plug lead to an engine ground.
2. Locate the wire harness connection to the throttle position sensor (**Figure 222**). Note the wire connector position and wire routing. Carefully disconnect the wire harness connector from the sensor connector.
3. Select the DC volts function on your digital volt/ohm meter. Select the 10- or 20-volt scale on the meter. Connect the positive meter lead to the brown/yellow wire harness terminal. Connect the negative meter lead to the green wire harness terminal.
4. Turn the key switch ON, and observe the meter readings. The voltage should be 4.75-5.25 volts DC. Switch the key switch OFF.
5. Replace the throttle position sensor if a trouble code indicates a fault with this sensor and the voltage is not correct in Step 4. Sensor replacement is provided in Chapter Six.
6. If you obtain incorrect readings in Step 4, check all wires and connectors (throttle position sensor to ECU) for corroded or damaged wires or terminals. A faulty engine control unit is indicated if all wires and terminals are in good condition, but an incorrect reading persists in Step 4.
7. Clean the terminals, then carefully connect the wire harness connector to the throttle position sensor. Ensure that the wires are routed correctly. Clean the terminals and connect the battery cables to the battery.

temperature sensor terminals. Connect the negative meter lead to the other sensor terminal.

3. Place the liquid thermometer in the container next to the sensor. Allow a few minutes for the thermometer to stabilize. Refer to **Table 18** for the specification, then note the temperature and the resistance reading displayed on the meter. Compare these measurements with the specifications listed.
4. Observe the thermometer and the reading on the meter as you begin to heat the water. Note the meter reading as the water temperature begins to match the temperature listed in **Table 18**. Record the readings. Remove the sensor and thermometer from the water before it starts to boil.
5. Allow the water to cool, then place ice (or cold water) in it. Take a resistance measurement as the water cools to the temperatures listed in **Table 18**.
6. Replace the sensor if the readings do not fall within the specifications listed for the measured temperature. A wire or ECU may be damaged if an exhaust port temperature sensor code continues to set and no fault is found with the sensor.
7. Install the exhaust port temperature sensor as described in Chapter Six. Clean the connector terminals, then carefully connect the wire harness connector to the sensor. Ensure that the wires are routed correctly. Install the spark plugs and connect the spark plug leads. Clean the terminals, then connect the battery cables to the battery.

TABLE 1 STARTING SYSTEM TROUBLESHOOTING

Symptom	Cause(s)	Corrective Action
Electric starter does not energize	Engine not in neutral gear	Shift into neutral gear
	Weak or discharged battery	Fully charge and test battery
	Dirty or corroded battery terminals	Thoroughly clean battery terminals
	Faulty neutral start switch	Test neutral switch operation
	Faulty starter switch	Test starter switch
	Faulty starter relay	Test starter relay
	Loose or faulty starter wires	Clean and check wire connections
	Faulty starter motor	Inspect and repair starter motor
	Improperly installed starter	Check for proper installation
	Improperly installed wires	Check for proper wire installation
Starter engages flywheel but rotates slowly	Weak or discharged battery	Fully charge and test battery
	Dirty or corroded battery terminals	Thoroughly clean battery terminals
	Loose or faulty starter wires	Clean, tighten and repair wire connections
	Faulty starter motor	Inspect and repair starter motor
	Improperly installed starter	Check for proper installation
	Engine is in gear	Check and correct shift system
Starter engages flywheel (flywheel does not rotate)	Weak or discharged battery	Fully charge and test battery
	Dirty or corroded battery terminals	Thoroughly clean battery terminals
	Loose or faulty starter wires	Clean tighten and repair wire connections
	Dirty or dry starter clutch/bendix	Clean and lubricate starter clutch/bendix
	Faulty starter motor	Inspect and repair starter motor
	Improperly installed starter	Check for proper installation
	Improper valve timing or adjustment	Check valve timing and adjustment
	Seized gearcase assembly	Check for gearcase failure
	Seized base engine	Manually rotate flywheel
	Water in the cylinder(s)	Check for water in the cylinder(s)
	Oil in the cylinder(s)	Check for oil in the cylinder(s)
	Faulty starter motor	Repair starter motor
Noisy starter operation	Dirty or dry starter clutch/bendix	Clean and lubricate starter clutch/bendix
	Improperly installed starter	Check for proper installation
	Worn or dry starter bearings	Repair starter motor
	Corroded or damaged flywheel gear	Check condition of flywheel gear teeth
	Worn or damaged clutch/bendix	Check condition of starter clutch/bendix
	Internal damage in base engine	Check for problem in base engine
	Internal damage in gearcase	Check for problem in gearcase
Rewind starter does not engage flywheel	Worn or damaged drive pawl	Inspect and repair rewind assembly
	Worn or damaged starter rope	Inspect and/or replace starter rope
	Corroded or dry rewind mechanism	Inspect and repair rewind assembly
	Broken or damaged friction spring	Inspect and/or replace friction spring
	Loose or damaged starter pulley	Inspect starter pulley

(continued)

TROUBLESHOOTING

TABLE 1 STARTING SYSTEM TROUBLESHOOTING (continued)

Symptom	Cause(s)	Corrective Action
Rewind starter engages flywheel, but does not rotate	Worn or damaged rewind mechanism	Inspect and repair rewind assembly
	Worn or frayed starter rewind rope	Inspect and/or replace starter rope
	Corroded or dry rewind mechanism	Inspect and repair rewind assembly
	Improper valve timing or adjustment	Check valve timing and adjustment
	Water in the cylinder(s)	Check for water in the cylinder(s)
	Oil in the cylinder(s)	Check for oil in the cylinder(s)
	Seized or damaged base engine	Manually rotate flywheel
	Seized or damaged gearcase	Check for problem in gearcase
	Engine is in gear	Shift engine into neutral
	Misadjusted neutral only start mechanism	Adjust the neutral only start mechanism
Rewind starter rope does not rewind	Worn or frayed starter rope	inspect and/or replace starter rope
	Broken or damaged rewind spring	Inspect and repair rewind assembly
	Worn or damaged rewind mechanism	Inspect and repair rewind assembly
	Dry or corroded rewind mechanism	Inspect and repair rewind assembly

TABLE 2 FUEL SYSTEM TROUBLESHOOTING

Symptom	Causes	Corrective Action
Engine does not start	Old or contaminated fuel	Supply the engine with fresh fuel
	Fuel pump malfunction	Check for proper pump operation
	Plugged carburetor jets	See plugged carburetor jets
	Improper carburetor adjustment	Check carburetor adjustment
	Blocked fuel filter	Check all fuel filters
	Closed fuel tank vent	Check for and correct closed vent
	Air leaks in the fuel hoses	Check fuel hoses
	Fuel leaking from system	Check for fuel leaks
	Flooding carburetor	Check for flooding carburetor
	Improper choke operation	Check for proper choke operation
	Electric pump failure	Check fuel pump operation (EFI models)
	Faulty idle air control motor	Check idle air control motor operation
	Faulty system relay	Check system relay (EFI models)
	Faulty fuel injectors	Check fuel injectors
	Faulty throttle position sender	Check for trouble code
	Faulty engine temp sender	Check for trouble code
	Faulty air pressure sender	Check for trouble code
	Faulty engine control unit	Test using a known good unit

(continued)

TABLE 2 FUEL SYSTEM TROUBLESHOOTING (continued)

Symptom	Causes	Corrective Action
Rough Idle	Old or contaminated fuel	Supply the engine with fresh fuel
	Fuel pump malfunction	Check for proper pump operation
	Plugged carburetor jets	See plugged carburetor jets
	Improper carburetor adjustment	Check carburetor adjustment
	Air leaks in the fuel hoses	Check fuel hoses
	Flooding carburetor	Check for flooding carburetor
	Improper choke operation	Check for proper choke operation
	Faulty idle air control motor	Check idle air control motor operation
	Faulty fuel injectors	Check fuel injectors
	Faulty throttle position sender	Check for trouble code
	Faulty engine temp sender	Check for trouble code
	Faulty air pressure sender	Check for trouble code
	Faulty engine control unit	Test using a known good unit
	Flooding vapor separator tank	Check the vapor separator tank
Engine dies at idle	Old or contaminated fuel	Supply the engine with fresh fuel
	Fuel pump malfunction	Check for proper pump operation
	Plugged carburetor jets	See plugged carburetor jets
	Improper carburetor adjustment	Check carburetor adjustment
	Blocked fuel filter	Check all fuel filters
	Closed fuel tank vent	Check for and correct closed vent
	Air leaks in the fuel hoses	Check fuel hoses
	Fuel leaking from system	Check for fuel leaks
	Flooding carburetor	Check for flooding carburetor
	Improper choke operation	Check for proper choke operation
	Electric pump failure	Check fuel pump operation (EFI models)
	Faulty idle air control motor	Check idle air control motor operation
	Faulty fuel injectors	Check fuel injectors
	Faulty throttle position sender	Check for trouble code
	Faulty air pressure sender	Check for trouble code
	Faulty engine control unit	Test using a known good unit
	Flooding vapor separator tank	Check the vapor separator tank
Idle speed too high	Improper carburetor adjustment	Check carburetor adjustment
	Improperly adjusted throttle cable	Check cable adjustment
	Binding throttle linkages	Check linkages
	Faulty idle air control motor	Check for trouble code
	Faulty engine temperature sender	Check for trouble code
Hesitation during acceleration	Old or contaminated or fuel	Supply the engine with fresh fuel
	Fuel pump malfunction	Check for proper pump operation
	Plugged carburetor jets	See plugged carburetor jets
	Improper carburetor adjustment	Check carburetor adjustment
	Blocked fuel filter	Check all fuel filters
	Closed fuel tank vent	Check for and correct closed vent
	Air leaks in the fuel hoses	Check fuel hoses
	Fuel leaking from system	Check for fuel leaks
	Flooding carburetor	Check for flooding carburetor
	Improper choke operation	Check for proper choke operation
	Electric pump failure	Check fuel pump operation (EFI models)
	Faulty fuel injectors	Check fuel injectors
	Faulty throttle position sender	Check for trouble code

(continued)

TROUBLESHOOTING

TABLE 2 FUEL SYSTEM TROUBLESHOOTING (continued)

Symptom	Causes	Corrective Action
Hesitation during acceleration (continued)	Faulty engine temp sender	Check for trouble code
	Faulty air pressure sender	Check for trouble code
	Faulty engine control unit	Test using a known good unit
	Improper valve timing	Check and correct valve timing
Misfire at high engine speed	Old or contaminated or fuel	Supply the engine with fresh fuel
	Fuel pump malfunction	Check for proper pump operation
	Plugged carburetor jets	See plugged carburetor jets
	Improper carburetor adjustment	Check carburetor adjustment
	Blocked fuel filter	Check all fuel filters
	Closed fuel tank vent	Check for and correct closed vent
	Air leaks in the fuel hoses	Check fuel hoses
	Fuel leaking from system	Check for fuel leaks
	Improper choke operation	Check for proper choke operation
	Electric pump failure	Check fuel pump operation (EFI models)
	Faulty fuel injectors	Check fuel injector
	Faulty air pressure sender	Check for trouble code
	Faulty engine control unit	Test using a known good unit
Excessive exhaust smoke	Improper carburetor adjustment	Check carburetor adjustment
	Fuel leaking from system	Check for fuel leaks
	Flooding carburetor	Check for flooding carburetor
	Improper choke operation	Check for proper choke operation
	Faulty fuel injectors	Check fuel injectors (EFI models)
	Faulty throttle position sender	Check for trouble code (EFI models)
	Faulty air temperature sender	Check for trouble code (EFI models)
	Faulty engine temp sender	Check for trouble code (EFI models)
	Faulty air pressure sender	Check for trouble code (EFI models)
	Faulty engine control unit	Test using a known good unit (EFI models)
	Flooding vapor separator tank	Check the vapor tank (EFI models)

TABLE 3 IGNITION SYSTEM TROUBLESHOOTING

Symptom	Causes	Corrective Action
Does not start	Emergency stop switch activated	Check stop switch position
	Shorted stop circuit	Test stop circuit
	Low battery voltage	Test battery voltage
	Faulty ignition charge coil	Test ignition charge coil
	Faulty ignition coil	Test ignition coil
	Faulty CDI unit	See *CDI Unit* Chapter Three
	Faulty ECU	See ECU Chapter Three
	Faulty breaker points	Test breaker points (models BF75, BF100)
	Misadjusted breaker points	Adjust breaker points (see Chapter Seven)
	(continued)	

Table 3 IGNITION SYSTEM TROUBLESHOOTING (continued)

Symptom	Causes	Corrective Action
Dies at idle	Shorted stop circuit	Test stop circuit
	Faulty breaker points	Test breaker points (models BF75, BF100)
	Misadjusted breaker points	Adjust breaker points (see Chapter Seven)
	Faulty ignition charge coil	Test ignition charge coil
	Faulty ignition coil	Test ignition coil
	Faulty CDI unit	See CDI Unit Chapter Three
	Overheated engine	Check overheat sensor
	Low oil pressure	Check oil pressure switch
Idle speed too high	Misadjusted breaker points	Adjust breaker points (see Chapter Seven)
	Faulty CDI Unit	See CDI Unit Chapter Three
Hesitation during acceleration	Misadjusted breaker points	Adjust breaker points (see Chapter Seven)
	Faulty CDI unit	See CDI Unit Chapter Three
	Faulty ignition charge coil	Test ignition charge coil
	Faulty ignition coil	Test ignition coil
	Overheated engine	Check overheat switch
	Low oil pressure	Check oil pressure switch
Poor high speed performance	Partially shorted stop circuit	Test stop circuit
	Faulty ignition charge coil	Test ignition charge coil
	Faulty ignition coil	Test ignition coil
	Faulty CDI unit	See CDI Unit Chapter Three
	Faulty ECU	See ECU Chapter Three
	Faulty breaker points	Test breaker points (models BF75, BF100)
	Misadjusted breaker points	Adjust breaker points (see Chapter Seven)
	Overheated engine	Check overheat switch
	Low oil pressure	Check oil pressure switch

Table 4 CHOKE SOLENOID RESISTANCE SPECIFICATIONS

Model	Resistance (ohms)
Models BF20A, BF25A and BF30A	2.8-3.4
Models BF35A, BF40A, BF45A and BF50A	2.8-3.4
Models BF75A and BF90A	2.8-3.4

Table 5 IGNITION COIL RESISTANCE SPECIFICATIONS

Model	Resistance (ohms)
Primary winding resistance	
BF20, BF2A (2 hp models)	0.70-0.90
BF50, BF5A (5 hp models)	0.70-0.90
BF75, BF8A, BF100 (7.5, 8, 9.9 hp models)	0.50-0.61
BF9.9A, BF15A	0.35-0.43
BF20A, BF25A, BF30A	0.19-0.23
BF35A, BF40A, BF45A, BF50A	0.19-0.23
BF75A, BF90A (75, 90 hp models)	0.35-0.43
BF115A and BF130A	0.60-0.72
(continued)	

TROUBLESHOOTING

TABLE 5 IGNITION COIL RESISTANCE SPECIFICATIONS (continued)

Model	Resistance (ohms)
Secondary winding resistance	
BF20, BF2A (2 hp models)	6300-7700
BF50, BF5A (5 hp models)	6300-7700
BF75, BF8A, BF100 (7.5, 8, 9.9 hp models)	6000-10,000
BF9.9A and BF15A	8010-9790
BF20A, BF25A and BF30A	10,300-15,900
BF35A, BF40A, BF45A, BF50A	2800-3400*
BF75A, BF90A (75, 90 hp models)	23,100-34,700 *
BF115A and BF130A	25,000-38,000 *

* Resistance specification with the spark plug cap installed.

TABLE 6 PULSER COIL RESISTANCE SPECIFICATIONS

Model	Resistance (ohms)
BF75, BF8A, BF100 (7.5, 8, 9.9 hp models)	108-132
BF9.9A and BF15A	351-429
BF20A, BF25A and BF30A	290-355
	290-355
BF35A, BF40A, BF45A, BF50A	288-352
BF75A and BF90A	168-252
(75 and 90 hp models)	168-252
BF115A and BF130A	970-1170

TABLE 7 IGNITION CHARGE COIL RESISTANCE SPECIFICATIONS

Model	Resistance (ohms)
BF75, BF100	2.0
(7.5, 9.9 hp models)	
(Breaker point ignition)	–
BF75 , BF8A, BF100	297-363
(7.5, 8, 9.9 hp models)	
(Breakerless Ignition)	
BF9.9A and BF15A	207-253
BF20A, BF25A, BF30A	278-363
BF35, BF40A, BF45A	168-227
BF50A	

TABLE 8 MAXIMUM ENGINE SPEED SPECIFICATIONS

Model	Maximum rpm range	Overspeed control range
BF20, BF2A	4000-5000	*
BF50, BF5A	4000-5000	*
75LD (1976 &1977 models)	5000-6000	*
BF75	4700-5200	*
BF8A	4950-5500	*
BF100	5200-5700	*
BF9.9A	4500-5500	*
BF15A	5000-6200	*
BF20A	5000-6000	6300-6900
BF25A	5000-6000	6300-6900
BF30A	5500-6000	6300-6900
BF35A	4600-5600	6400-6800
BF40A	5000-6000	6400-6800
BF45A	5000-6000	6400-6800
BF50A	5500-6000	6400-6800
BF75A	5000-6000	6300-6900
BF90A	5000-6000	6300-6900
BF115A	5000-6000	6300-6400
BF130A	5000-6000	6300-6400

* Overspeed control circuits are not used on these models.

TABLE 9 BATTERY CHARGING COIL RESISTANCE

Model	Test Lead Connection	Resistance (ohms)
BF50, BF5A (5 hp models)	(+) Pink – (-) Yellow	0.2-0.4
BF75, BF8A, BF100 (7.5, 8, 9.9 hp models)	(+) Blue – (-) Blue	0.12-0.15
BF9.9A and BF15A		
5 amp system *	(+) Green – (-) Green	0.33-0.41
10 amp system *	(+) Green – (-) Green	0.20-0.24
BF20A, BF25A and BF30A		
(6 amp electric start models) *	(+) Gray – (-) Gray	0.45-0.54
(12 amp optional system) *	(+) Gray – (-) Gray	0.27-0.33
BF35, BF40A, BF45A and BF50A		
(6 amp system) *	(+) Gray – (-) Gray **	0.20-0.26
(12 amp system) *	(+) Gray – (-) Gray **	0.17-0.23
BF75A and BF90A (75, 90 hp models)	(+) Gray – (-) Gray	0.46-0.69

* Refer to Chapter Three to assist with battery charge coil identification.
** Two same color terminals are used. Perform the test using each combination of same color leads.

TROUBLESHOOTING

TABLE 10 RECTIFIER TEST SPECIFICATIONS

Model	Test Lead Connections	Test Results (ohms)
BF50, BF5A (5 hp models)		
	(+) Pink – (-) Red *	Open
	(+) Pink – (-) Green *	100-50 k
	(+) Pink – (-) Yellow *	Open
	(+) Pink – (-) Pink	Open
	(+) Green – (-) Yellow *	Open
	(+) Green – (-) Red	Open
	(+) Green – (-) Pink *	Open
	(+) Red – (-) Pink *	100-50 k
	(+) Red – (-) Green	200-100 k
	(+) Red – (-) Yellow *	100-50 k
	(+) Yellow – (-) Red *	Open
	(+) Yellow – (-) Green *	100-50 k
	(+) Yellow – (-) Pink *	Open
	(+) Yellow – (-) Yellow	Open
BF75, BF8A, BF100 (7.5, 8, 9.9 hp models) (Serial No. 1199999 and prior)		
	(+) Green – (-) Blue*	Open
	(+) Red – (-) Blue*	Continuity
	(+) Blue – (-) Red*	Open
	(+) Blue – (-) Green*	Continuity

* Two same color leads are used. Perform the test using each same color lead.

TABLE 11 RECTIFIER/REGULATOR TEST SPECIFICTIONS

Model	Test Lead Connections	Resistance (ohms)
BF75, BF8A, BF100 (Serial No. 1200001 and On)		
	(+) Blue – (-) Blue	Open
	(+) Blue – (-) Red *	Open
	(+) Blue – (-) Green*	Open
	(+) Red – (-) Blue*	1000-200 k
	(+) Red – (-) Green	500-100 k
	(+) Green – (-) Blue*	100-50 k
	(+) Green – (-) Red	Open
BF9.9A and BF15A		
	(+) Gray – (-) Gray *	Open
	(+) Gray – (-) Red *	Open
	(+) Gray – (-) Green*	Open
	(+) Red – (-) Gray *	1000-200 k
	(+) Red – (-) Green	500-100 k
	(+) Green – (-) Gray *	100-50 k
	(+) Green – (-) Red	Open

(continued)

Table 11 RECTIFIER/REGULATOR TEST SPECIFICTIONS (continued)

Model	Test Lead Connections	Resistance (ohms)
BF9.9A and BF15A (electric start)		
	(+) White/black – (-) Black *	500-100 k
	(+) White – (-) Black *	500-100 k
	(+) White/black – (-) Gray	1000-200 k
	(+) White – (-) Gray	1000-200 k
	(+) Black – (-) White/Black *	Open
	(+) Black – (-) White *	Open
	(+) Black – (-) Gray *	100-50 k
	(+) Gray – (-) White *	Open
	(+) Gray – (-) White/Black *	Open
	(+) Gray – (-) Black *	Open
	(+) Gray – (-) Gray	Open
BF20A, BF25A BF30A, BF35A, BF45A and BF50A		
	(+) Gray – (-) Gray *	Open
	(+) Gray – (-) White/black *	1000-200 k
	(+) Gray – (-) White *	1000-200 k
	(+) Gray – (-) Black *	500-50 k
	(+) White – (-) Gray	Open
	(+) White – (-) Black	Open
	(+) White/black – (-) Black	Open
	(+) White/black – (-) Gray *	Open
	(+) Black – (-) Gray *	Open
	(+) Black – (-) White/black	500-100 k
	(+) Black – (-) White	500-100 k
BF75A and BF90A (75, 90 hp models)		
	(+) Black – (-) White	Open
	(+) Black – (-) Gray *	Open
	(+) Gray – (-) White *	Open
	(+) Gray – (-) Gray *	Open
	(+) Gray – (-) Black *	500-15 k
	(+) White – (-) Gray *	500-15 k
	(+) White – (-) Black	500-20 k

* Two same color leads are used. Perform the test using each same color lead.

Table 12 POWER TILT/TRIM SYSTEM RELAY TEST SPECIFICATIONS

Model	Test lead connections	Test results (ohms)
BF35A, BF40A, BF45A and BF50A		
	(+) White/yellow – (-) Black	Open
	(+) Light Blue – (-) Black	90-120
	(+) Light Green – (-) Black	90-120
	(+) Blue – (-) Black	Continuity
	(+) Green – (-) Black	Continuity

(continued)

TROUBLESHOOTING

TABLE 12 POWER TILT/TRIM SYSTEM RELAY TEST SPECIFICATIONS (continued)

Model	Test lead connections	Test results (ohms)
BF75A, BF90A, BF115A and BF130A	(+) White – (-) Black	Open
	(+) Light blue – (-) Black	36-40
	(+) Blue – (-) Black	Continuity
	(+) Light green – (-) Black	35-40
	(+) Green – (-) Black	Continuity

TABLE 13 TRIM SWITCH

Switch Position	Test Lead Connections	Test Results
BF35A, BF40A, BF45A, BF50A		
Neutral	(+)White/black – (-)Light blue	Open
Neutral	(+)White/black – (-)Light green	Open
Up	(+)White/black – (-)Light green	Continuity
Up	(+)White/black – (-)Light blue	Open
Down	(+)White/black – (-)Light green	Open
Down	(+)White/black – (-) Light blue	Continuity
BF75A, BF90A, BF115A, BF130A		
Neutral	(+)Red – (-)Purple	Open
Neutral	(+)Red – (-)Green	Open
Up	(+)Red – (-)Purple	Continuity
Up	(+)Red – (-)Green	Open
Down	(+)Red – (-)Purple	Open
Down	(+)Red – (-)Green	Continuity

TABLE 14 TRIM POSITION SENSOR

Model	Test Lead Connections	Resistance (ohms)
BF35A, BF40A, BF45A and BF50A	(+) Orange – (-) Black	4000-6000
	(+) Yellow/blue – (-) Black	2700-4300
BF75A, BF90A, BF115A and BF130A	(+) Yellow/blue – (-) Black	2700-4300
	(+) Light green/black – (-) Black	4000-6000

TABLE 15 OIL PRESSURE SPECIFICATIONS

Model	kg/cm² (psi)
BF20, BF2A (2 hp models)	*
BF50, BF5A (5 hp models)	0.60 (8.53) at 1300 rpm 3.00 (42.66) at 5000 rpm
BF75, BF8A, BF100 (7.5, 8, 9.9 hp models)	*
BF9.9A, BF15A	0.60 (8.54) at 1050-1150 rpm
BF20A, BF25A, BF30A	1.1 (15.6) at 850-950 rpm
BF35A, BF40A, BF45A, BF50A	1.5 (21.3) at 850-950 rpm
BF75A, BF90A (75, 90 hp models)	1.5 (21.3) at 900-1000 rpm
BF115A, BF130A	1.0-1.4 (14.0-21.0) at 700-800 rpm

* Oil pressure specification is not provided for these models. Refer to *Oil Pressure Test* in Chapter Three for additional information.

TABLE 16 COMPRESSION SPECIFICATIONS

Model	Compression kg/cm (psi)
BF20, BF2A (2 hp models)	6.5 (92.0) at 800 rpm
BF50, BF5A (5 hp models)	3.5-5.5 (50-78) at 600 rpm
BF75 (7.5 hp models)	10.0 (142.0) at 600 rpm
BF100 (9.9 hp models)	10.6 (151.0) at 600 rpm
BF9.9A, BF15A	10.0-12.0 (143.0-171) at 100 rpm
BF20A, BF25A, BF30A	14.0-16.0 (199-228) at 100 rpm
BF35A, BF50A	14.0-16.0 (199-228) at 500 rpm
BF75A, BF90A (75, 90 hp models)	14.0.16.0 (199-228) at 300 rpm
BF115A, BF130A	14.0-16.0 (199-228) at 300 rpm

TABLE 17 EFI SYSTEM TROUBLE CODES

Indicated Code Number	System or Component Indicated
3	Air pressure sensor or wiring
4	Ignition system pulser coil or wiring
6	Engine temperature sensor or wiring
7	Throttle position sensor or wiring
8	Ignition system pulser coil or wiring
10	Air temperature sensor or wiring
14	Idle air control motor or wiring
24	Exhaust port temperature sensor
3 and 7 (simultaneous)	Faulty brown/yellow wire from the ECU
3,6,7,10,24 (simultaneous)	Faulty green wire to the sensors

TROUBLESHOOTING

TABLE 18 TEMPERATURE SENSOR SPECIFICATIONS (ENGINE, AIR, EXHAUST PORT SENSORS)

Temperature	Resistance Specification (ohms)
-20° C (-4°F)	15,000-18,000
0° C (32° F)	5000-7500
20° C (68° F)	3000-4000
50° C (122° F)	1000-1100
100° C (212° F)	300-400

TABLE 19 TORQUE SPECIFICATIONS STANDARD TORQUE

Fastener Size	Torque
5 mm bolt/nut	40-70 kg/cm (35-61 in. lbs.)
6 mm bolt/nut	80-120 kg/cm (69-104 in. lbs.)
8 mm bolt/nut	20-28 N m (15-21 ft. lbs.)
10 mm bolt/nut	35-40 N m (26-30 ft. lbs.)

Chapter Four

Lubrication, Maintenance and Tune-Up

When operating properly, your Honda outboard provides smooth operation, reliable starting and excellent performance. Regular maintenance and frequent tune-ups help keep it in top shape and running great.

During operation, certain components of the engine wear or become contaminated. When maintenance is neglected, the engine performance decreases and the life of the engine can be substantially reduced. Performing routine maintenance and necessary tune-ups helps ensure your Honda outboard performs as it should and delivers a long, trouble-free life.

This chapter provides the maintenance procedures for all systems and components on the engine as well as a description of the required lubricants. Certain components or systems on the engine require maintenance at more frequent intervals than others. **Table 1** lists the maintenance items and intervals for all engine systems and components. **Tables 2-10** provide the necessary specifications. **Tables 1-10** are located at the end of this chapter.

Because of their unique application, outboards may suffer complete or partial submersion. Special instructions and procedures must be followed to minimize damage to the engine. Refer to *Submersion* under the *Routine Maintenance* section of this chapter.

Engines used in saltwater or polluted water are especially susceptible to corrosion. Additional maintenance can minimize the damage caused by corrosion. For special maintenance requirements, refer to *Corrosion Prevention* under *Routine Maintenance* section in this chapter.

ROUTINE MAINTENANCE

The most common routine maintenance is checking and/or changing the lubricating fluids, cleaning debris and contaminants from the engine and the application of grease or other lubricants to certain engine components. Refer to *Lubricants* in this chapter for oil, grease and gear lubricant specifications and recommendations.

Performing Maintenance

Make sure that you have the proper equipment and lubricants before performing routine maintenance. Using the wrong type of lubricant can cause serious engine damage or shorten the life of the engine. Refer to *Lubrication* in this section to determine what types of lubricant(s) you need for your engine.

Refer to **Table 1** to identify the maintenance items and intervals.

Always keep a log of what maintenance was performed and when it was done. Try to log the number of running hours after each use. Without a maintenance/running hours log or a dash-mounted hour meter (**Figure 1**), it is almost impossible to accurately determine the hours of usage. Be aware that a dash-mounted hour meter runs even when the key switch is left ON and the engine is not running. Note this event in the maintenance log if it occurs.

NOTE
Variations in maintenance requirements exist among the models. When working with

LUBRICATION, MAINTENANCE AND TUNE-UP

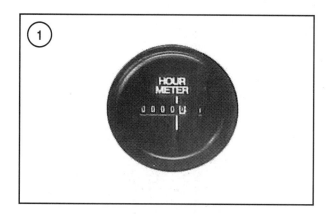

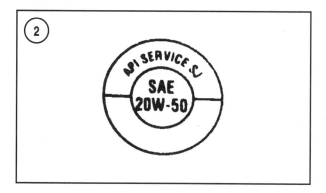

smaller engines, many of the required maintenance procedures do not apply. To determine your engine's unique maintenance requirements, refer to **Table 1**. Visually inspect your engine to determine if listed systems or components are present.

Lubrication

Lubrication is the most important maintenance element for any outboard. Lubricant for the base engine, gearcase and other areas helps prevent excessive component wear, guards against corrosion and provides smooth operation of turning or sliding surfaces (tilt tubes and swivel brackets).

CAUTION
Never use non-detergent oil or two-stroke outboard motor oil in your Honda outboard; it does not provide adequate lubrication for the internal engine components. Operating the engine without adequate lubrication results in severe base engine damage or engine seizure.

Engine oil

Checking the oil level before every use combined with regular oil changes is the best way to prolong the life of your engine. Always use a high-quality grade of oil in your Honda outboard. A few extra dollars spent on premium oil is money well spent. Look for the API classification emblem (**Figure 2**) on the oil container when selecting oil for your engine. **Table 3** lists the approximate oil capacity for your Honda outboard.

The viscosity index (weight) indicates the flow rate of the oil. For most models Honda recommends a 10W-30 or 10W-40 viscosity oil that meets API service classification SG, SH or SJ. This weight and grade of oil is suitable under most operating conditions. All oil weight recommendations are based on the average ambient air temperature where the engine is operated. Refer to **Table 2** to select the correct oil viscosity for your Honda outboard.

On models so equipped, the oil filter traps dirt, debris and other contaminants during engine operation. Although it is not specifically recommended, always change the oil filter at the same time as the oil. When the filter is not changed, contaminated oil remaining in the filter immediately flows into the fresh oil at start up.

CAUTION
Never use automotive gear lubricant or transmission lubricant in the gearcase. These types of lubricants are usually not suitable for marine applications. The use of anything other than the recommended lubricants can lead to increased wear and corrosion of internal components.

Gearcase Lubricant

Use Quicksilver gearcase lubricant or a high grade SAE 90 marine gearcase lubricant that meets GL5 specifications. Read the information on the container to ensure that it meets the specification before using it in your outboard. **Table 4** lists the approximate gearcase lubricant capacity for your Honda outboard.

Check the gearcase lubricant level and condition at regular intervals as indicated in **Table 1**. Correct any problems before they lead to gearcase component failure.

Tilt and Trim Fluid

Honda recommends a premium grade Type A automatic transmission fluid (ATF) for all power trim and tilt systems. Look carefully at the container to ensure that

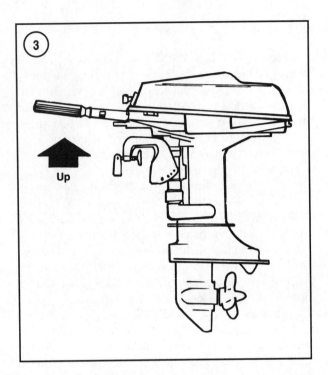

DEXRON or DEXRON II is selected. Other types of ATF may not be compatible with the seals or other components in the system.

Corrosion Prevention

The use of a corrosion prevention spray on the external engine components can substantially reduce corrosion damage. Regular use is highly recommended if the engine is operated in saltwater or polluted water. Corrosion prevention sprays are available from most marine dealerships or marine supply stores. Follow the instructions on the container for the proper use of these products.

Base Engine Oil Level and Condition Check

Always check the oil level before and after each use. Accurate oil level measurements are only possible if the engine has been switched off for 30 minutes or more and if the engine is in a vertical position (**Figure 3**).

On models BF20, BF2A, BF50, BF5A, BF75, BF8A and BF100A, the oil dipstick is integrated into the oil fill cap (**Figure 4**). Twist the cap counterclockwise to remove it from the engine. On all other models, the oil dipstick is separate from the oil fill cap. Simply pull the oil dipstick to remove it from the engine (**Figure 5**).

Refer to the following to locate your oil dipstick on your Honda outboard.

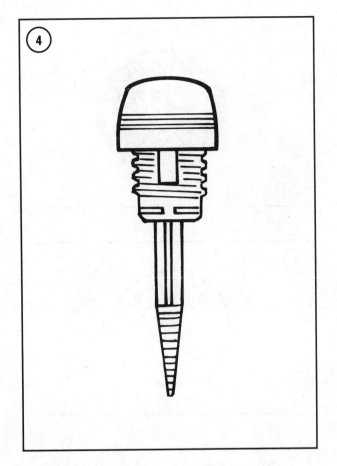

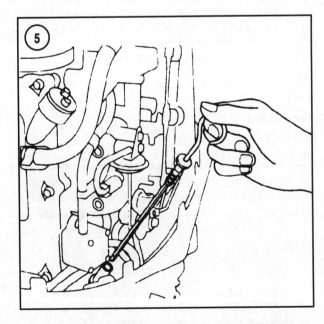

On models BF20 and BF2A, the oil dipstick/fill cap is located on the lower port side of the engine and near the tiller control handle (**Figure 6**).

LUBRICATION, MAINTENANCE AND TUNE-UP

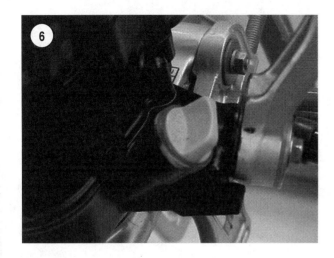

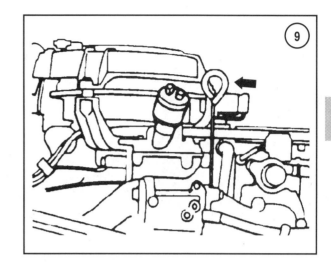

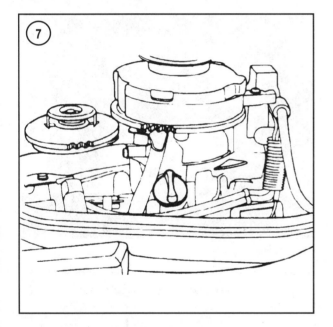

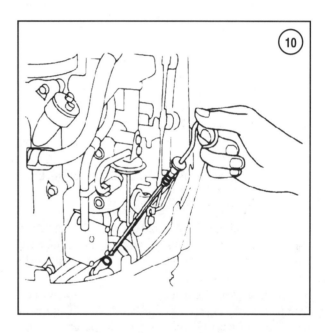

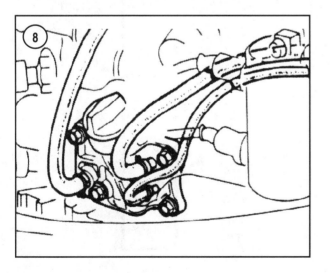

On models BF50 and BF5A, the oil dipstick /fill cap is located on the port side of the engine between the flywheel and tiller control handle (**Figure 7**).

On models BF75, BF8A and BF100, the oil dipstick/fill cap is located on the lower starboard side of the base engine (**Figure 8**).

On models BF9.9A and BF15A, the oil dipstick is located on the upper port side of the engine near the flywheel (**Figure 9**).

On models BF20A, BF25A and BF30A, the oil dipstick is located on the lower rear starboard side of the base engine (**Figure 10**).

On models BF35A, BF40A, BF45A and BF50A, the oil dipstick is located on the lower rear starboard side of the base engine (**Figure 11**).

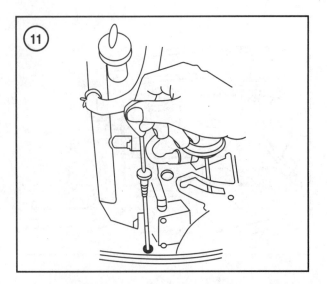

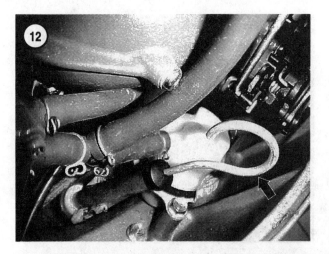

On models BF75A and BF90A, the oil dipstick is located on the lower starboard side of the base engine near the fuel pump (**Figure 12**).

On models BF115A and BF130A, the oil dipstick is located on the lower starboard side of the base engine below the No. 4 intake runner (**Figure 13**).

1. Position the engine vertically with the ignition switched OFF.
2. Refer to **Figures 6-13** and locate the oil dipstick for your engine.
3. Remove the oil dipstick and wipe it clean.
4. Insert the oil dipstick into the opening. Do not thread the dipstick into the opening. On models with the dipstick integrated into the fill cap, allow the oil dipstick/fill cap to rest on the cylinder block.
5. Pull the dipstick from the engine. Note the oil level on the dipstick (A, **Figure 14**). Inspect the oil for water, a milky appearance, or significant fuel odor. Refer to Chapter Three if you observe any of these conditions.
6. Add oil to the engine and repeat Steps 3-5 until the oil level is at or near the full mark on the oil dipstick (B, **Figure 14**). Do not overfill the engine with oil. It is far better for the oil level to be *slightly* below the full mark than to be above the full mark. Drain any excess oil from the engine following the procedures listed in *Changing Engine Oil* in this section.
7. Fully insert the oil dipstick and twist clockwise on models with a combination oil dipstick/fill cap until the oil dipstick is fully seated.

CAUTION
Avoid serious damage to the base engine. Never run your engine with the oil level over the full mark on the oil dipstick. Overfilling

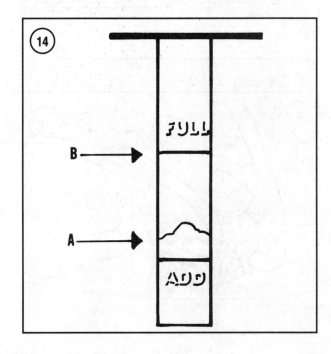

LUBRICATION, MAINTENANCE AND TUNE-UP

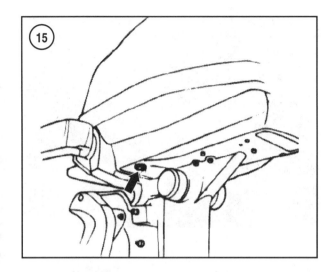

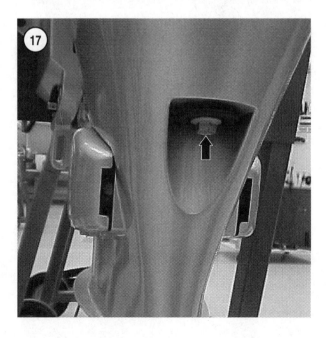

the engine with oil can result in foaming oil and inadequate lubrication.

Engine Oil Drain Location

Refer to **Table 2** to determine the correct oil viscosity and **Table 3** to determine the quantity of oil for you Honda outboard motor. The location of the oil drain varies among the models. Refer to the following information to locate the oil drain.

1. On models BF20 and BF2A, drain the oil from the oil dipstick/fill cap located on the lower port side of the engine near the tiller handle (Figure 6).
2. On models BF50 and BF5A, the oil drain is located on the lower port side of the engine near the tiller handle (**Figure 15**).
3. On models BF75, BF8A, BF100, BF9.9A and BF15A, the oil drain is located on the starboard side of the drive shaft housing (**Figure 16**).
4. On models BF20A, BF25A and BF30A, the oil drain is located on the rear portion of the drive shaft housing (**Figure 17**).
5. On models BF35A, BF40A, BF45A and BF50A, the oil dipstick is located under a cover on the rear portion of the drive shaft housing (**Figure 18**). Swing the cover open to access the drain plug. The cover also helps direct the oil to the drain container.
6. On models BF75A, BF90A, BF115A and BF130A, the oil drain is located under a cover on the lower starboard side of the drive shaft housing (**Figure 19**). Remove the cover retaining bolt to access the oil drain.

Oil Fill Cap Location

Refer to the following information to locate the oil fill cap.

148 CHAPTER FOUR

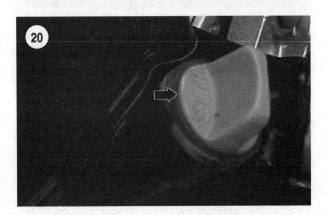

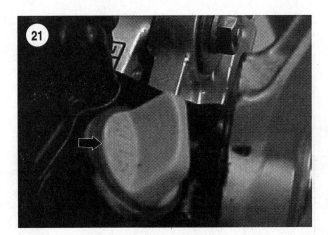

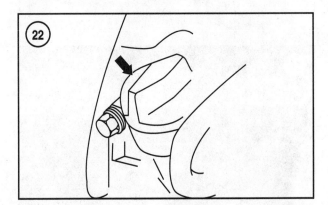

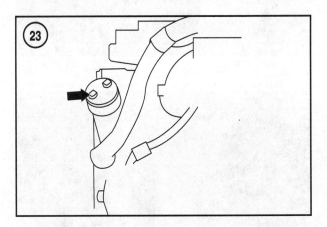

1. On models BF20 and BF2A, the dipstick/fill cap is located on the lower port side of the engine near the tiller control handle (**Figure 20**).

2. On models BF50 and BF5A, the dipstick/fill cap is located on the port side of the engine between the flywheel and tiller handle (**Figure 21**).

3. On models BF75, BF8A and BF100, the dipstick/fill cap is located on the lower starboard side of the engine (**Figure 22**).

4. On models BF9.9A and BF15A, the fill cap is located on the upper starboard side of the engine near the dipstick (**Figure 23**).

5. On models BF20A, BF25A and BF30A, the fill cap is located on the upper rear starboard side of the engine (**Figure 24**).

6. On models BF35A, BF40A, BF45A and BF50A, the fill cap is located on the upper rear starboard side of the engine (**Figure 25**).

7. On models BF75A and BF90A, the fill cap is located on the port side of the engine just above the oil filter (**Figure 26**).

8. On models BF115 and BF130A, the fill cap is located on the upper front starboard side of the engine (**Figure 27**).

Oil Change

1. Remove both battery cables from the battery.

2. Position the engine vertically with the ignition switched OFF.

3. Refer to **Figures 6-13** to locate the oil dipstick for your engine.

LUBRICATION, MAINTENANCE AND TUNE-UP

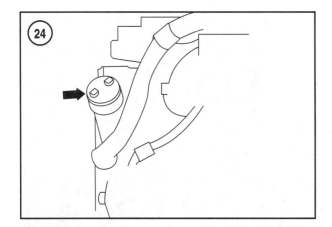

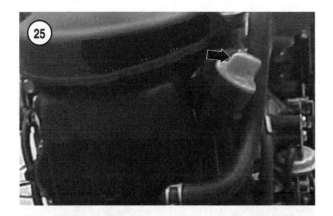

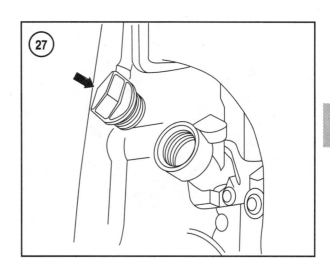

ting and tighten it to the specification listed in **Table 10**. Install or close the oil drain cover (on models so equipped).

    a. On models with a dipstick/fillcap, position the engine over the container with the oil dipstick/fill cap opening (**Figure 20**) at the lowest point. Maintain this position until all oil drains from the engine. Tighten the oil dipstick/fillcap.

6. Inspect the oil for the presence of water, milky appearance or significant fuel odor. Refer to Chapter Three for information if any of these conditions are noted.

7. Refer to **Table 3** to determine the oil capacity. Reduce this amount by 20% to determine the initial amount of oil to add to the engine.

8. Refer to (**Figures 20-27**) and locate the oil fill cap for your engine. Add the quantity of oil noted in Step 7 through this opening.

9. Refer to *Oil Level and Condition Check* in this section and follow the procedure to check and correct the oil level.

10. Clean the battery terminals, then connect the battery cables to the battery. Check for oil leaks and correct them prior to running the engine.

Oil Filter Change

    Purchase a filter from your local Honda dealership prior to starting this operation. A oil filter removal tool (**Figure 28**) is required to remove the oil filter. These are available from most automotive parts stores and tool suppliers. Take the filter with you when selecting the tool to ensure a correct fit. You will also need a container to position under the filter during removal. Always dispose of the filter in a responsible manner.

4. Remove the oil dipstick from your engine and wipe it clean. Refer to *Oil Filter Change* and perform Steps 2-6 when changing the oil and the oil filter.

5. On models so equipped, remove or swing down the oil drain cover (**Figure 18**). Position a suitable container under the oil drain fitting. Remove the oil drain fitting. When all oil has drained from the engine, replace the fit-

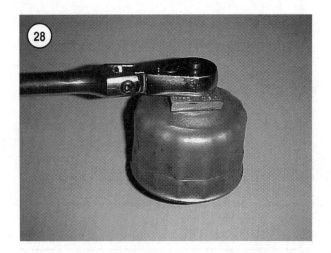

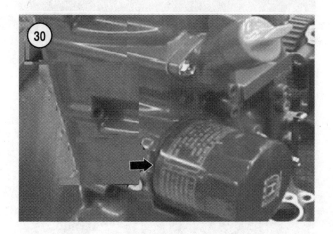

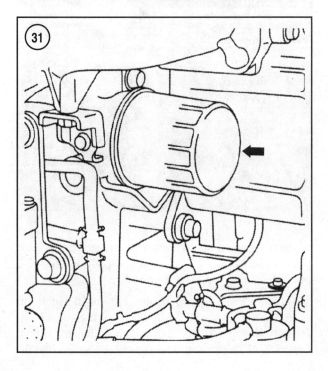

Variations exist among the models regarding the location of the oil filter. Refer to the following information to locate the oil filter on your Honda outboard.

On models BF20A, BF25A, BF30A, BF35A, BF40A and BF50A, the oil filter is located on the lower port side of the base engine (**Figure 29**).

On models BF75A and BF90A, the oil filter is located on the lower front and starboard side of the base engine (**Figure 30**).

On models BF115A and BF130A, the oil filter is located on the rear and port side of the base engine (**Figure 31**).

1. Remove both battery cables from the battery.
2. Clean debris from the oil filter to cylinder block mating area. Place a small container under the oil filter to cylinder block mating surface.
3. Using an oil filter removal tool, turn the filter one turn counterclockwise. Use your hand to remove the oil filter. Clean up any spilled oil.
4. Inspect the used oil filter for the presence of the sealing ring (**Figure 32**). Remove the sealing ring from the cylinder block if it is not stuck to the oil filter. Dispose of the used oil filter and sealing ring in a responsible manner.
5. Carefully clean all debris from the oil filter to cylinder block mounting surfaces (**Figure 33**). Apply a light coat of oil to the sealing ring on the new oil filter (**Figure 32**) and carefully thread the new oil filter onto the oil filter fitting.
6. Using an oil filter removal tool, tighten the new filter to the specification listed in **Table 9**.
7. Clean the battery terminals, then connect the cables to the battery.
8. Check for and correct oil leaks immediately after starting the engine. Refer to *Engine Oil Level and Condition Check* for the procedures and correct the oil level as indicated.

LUBRICATION, MAINTENANCE AND TUNE-UP

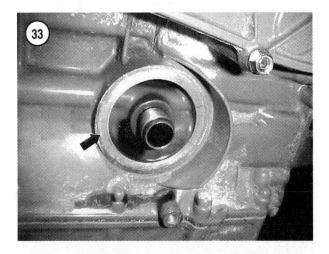

Gearcase Lubricant Level and Condition

Significant differences exist in gearcase appearance and size among the various models. The procedures listed are similar, with the primary difference being the plug locations. Drain and vent plug locations may vary from the illustration. Refer to Chapter Nine for specific information on drain and vent plug location. Refer to **Table 4** for approximate gearcase lubricant capacity.

1. Set the engine upright for at least 2 hours before checking the lubricant.
2. Remove both battery cables from the battery terminals.
3. Position a container under the gearcase. Slowly remove the drain plug (A, **Figure 34**) and drain a small sample (a teaspoonful or less) of fluid from the gearcase. Quickly replace the drain plug and tighten securely. Pressure test the gearcase to determine the source of leakage if you observe water or a milky appearance in the fluid sample.
4. Rub a small amount of the fluid sample between your finger and thumb. Disassemble and inspect the Gearcase if the sample feels gritty. Refer to Chapter Nine.
5. Remove the oil vent plug (B, **Figure 34**). The lubricant level should be even with the bottom of the threaded vent plug opening. Add lubricant into the drain plug opening until fluid flows from the vent plug. If over an ounce is required to fill the unit, perform a pressure test as described in Chapter Three.
6. Allow the gearcase to sit in a shaded area for 2 hours and recheck the lubricant level. Top off again if necessary.
7. Clean the battery terminals and connect the cables to the battery.

CAUTION
Inspect the sealing washers on both gearcase plugs. Replace missing or damaged sealing washers to prevent water or lubricant from seeping past the threads.

NOTE
A small amount of very fine particles are usually present in the gear lubricant. These fine particles form during normal gearcase operation, and their presence does not indicate a problem. The presence of large particles indicates a potential problem with the gearcase.

Gearcase Lubricant Change

Significant differences exist within the various models as to Gearcase appearance. Vent and drain plug location may vary from the illustration. Refer to Chapter Nine for specific information on the plug locations.

1. Remove both battery cables from the battery terminals.

2. Place a container under the gearcase. Remove the drain plug (A, **Figure 34**) and oil vent plug (B, **Figure 34**).

3. Take a small sample of the gearcase lubricant and inspect it as described under *Lubricant Level and Condition* in this chapter.

4. Allow the gearcase to drain completely. Tilt the engine slightly to ensure that the drain opening is at the lowest point.

5. Use a pump-type dispenser and *slowly* pump quicksilver gearcase lubricant or a suitable substitute into the drain plug opening (B, **Figure 34**) until lubricant flows out the vent plug opening. Without removing the pump from the drain opening, install the vent plug (A, **Figure 34**) and tighten it securely. Remove the pump from the drain opening and *quickly* install the drain plug (A, **Figure 34**). Tighten the drain plug securely.

6. Allow the engine to remain upright for 2 hours in a shaded location and check the fluid level. Top it off, if necessary.

7. Clean the battery terminals and then connect the battery cables to the battery. Dispose of the old gearcase lubricant in a responsible manner.

Propeller Shaft and Propeller

Refer to Chapter Nine for the procedure, then remove the propeller nut. Inspect the propeller for damage and the propeller shaft for twisted splines or a bent shaft. Replace the propeller shaft if the shaft is bent or the splines are twisted. Refer to Chapter Nine for propeller shaft replacement. Have the propeller refinished at a reputable propeller repair shop if it is damaged. Clean all corrosion or deposits from the propeller shaft splines and the splined section of the propeller. Apply high-quality marine all-purpose grease to the splines before installing the propeller.

Jet Drive Lubrication

The jet unit attaches to the drive shaft housing at the same location as the gearcase. The engine is identical to the standard drive models from the drive shaft housing upward.

Jet drive units require maintenance at frequent intervals. The drive shaft bearing must be lubricated after each operating period. Lubrication is also required after every 10 hours of use and when preparing the engine for extended storage. Use high-quality all-purpose marine grease or grease that meets or exceeds NLGI No. 1 rating.

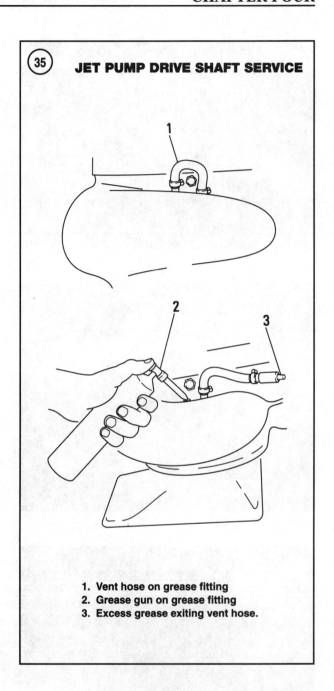

35 JET PUMP DRIVE SHAFT SERVICE

1. Vent hose on grease fitting
2. Grease gun on grease fitting
3. Excess grease exiting vent hose.

NOTE
Slight discoloration of the expelled jet drive grease is normal during the break-in period. You must inspect the seals and internal components if the expelled grease is contaminated with metal filings, is dark gray in color or contains significant amounts of water.

1. Locate the capped hose on the port side of the jet drive (**Figure 35**).

LUBRICATION, MAINTENANCE AND TUNE-UP 153

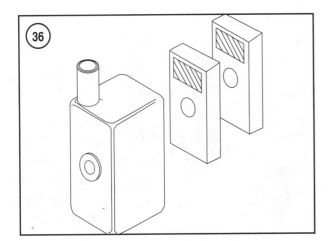

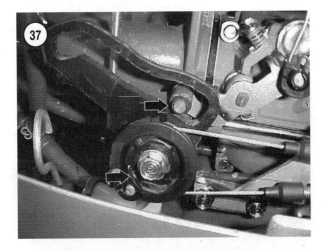

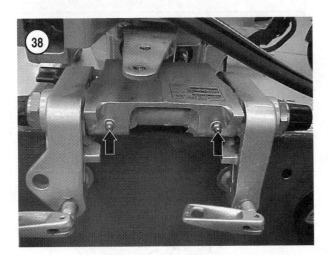

2. Disconnect the vent hose from the grease fitting.

3. Connect a grease gun to the fitting on the jet drive and inject grease until grease exits the capped end of the disconnected hose.

4. Inspect the grease. Disassemble and inspect the seals and bearings if you observe water or contaminants in the expelled grease.

5. Wipe the expelled grease from the capped hose and connect the hose to the jet drive grease fitting (**Figure 35**).

Breather Elements

Models BF115A and BF130A are equipped with a breather tube filter (**Figure 36**) that requires periodic inspection. Note any wire or hose routing to the breather element housing, then disconnect the required hoses or wiring. Remove the retaining bolt, then the breather housing. Note the orientation of the markings on the filter elements as you remove them from the housing. Replace the filter elements if they are contaminated. Installation is the reverse of removal.

Throttle Linkages

Apply high-quality all-purpose grease to the pivot points of the throttle linkages (**Figure 37**) to ensure smooth operation. Only a small amount of grease is required; use just enough to lubricate the throttle connector. Apply penetrating corrosion prevention oil on all pivot surfaces if you are unable to easily apply grease.

CAUTION
The steering cable must be retracted before injecting grease into the fitting. The cable can become hydraulically locked if grease is injected with the cable extended.

Steering Controls/Pivot Points

Apply a high-quality all-purpose grease to the pivot points of steering connections (**Figure 38**). Grease fittings are provided for most pivot points. Pump in the grease until the old or contaminated grease is expelled from the pivot point.

Some steering cables have a grease fitting. Regular lubrication of the steering cable dramatically increases its life. Pump high quality marine all-purpose grease into the fitting until you feel a slight resistance. Avoid overfilling the steering cable.

ELECTRICAL AND IGNITION SYSTEM

Many problems with a modern outboard are directly related to a lack of maintenance to the electrical systems. Components requiring maintenance include:

1. Cranking battery.
2. Wiring and electrical connections.
3. Starter motor.

Battery Maintenance

Unlike automobiles, boats may sit idle for weeks without running. Without proper maintenance, the battery loses its charge and begins to deteriorate. Marine engines are exposed to a great deal more moisture than automobiles, resulting in more corrosion forming on the battery terminals. Clean the terminals and *charge* the battery at 30 day intervals during storage. Refer to Chapter Seven for complete battery testing, maintenance and charging procedures.

Wiring and Connections

Periodically inspect the main harness connector (**Figure 39**) for contaminated or faulty pin connections. Carefully scrape contaminants from the contacts. Use a good quality marine all-purpose grease on the main harness plug to seal out moisture and prevent corrosion.

CAUTION
Use only enough grease to provide a light coating on the electrical contacts. The grease may seep into some electrical components (such as relays) and cause a malfunction.

Electric Starter Motor

Maintaining the electric starter motor involves cleaning external electrical terminals and applying a good quality marine all-purpose grease to the pinion shaft (**Figure 40**). Refer to Chapter Seven when removal or repair of the electric starter motor is required.

Trim/Tilt System Fluid Check

Check the fluid level if you suspect a leak or if you note a trim system malfunction. Models BF35A, BF40A, BF45A and BF50 use a single cylinder trim/tilt system (**Figure 41**). Models BF75A, BF90A, BF115A and BF130A use a 3-cylinder trim/tilt system (**Figure 42**). Regardless of the system used, all models use dexron automatic transmission fluid (ATF) as the operating fluid. Use a suitable block of wood or overhead cable to secure the engine when checking the trim/tilt fluid level.

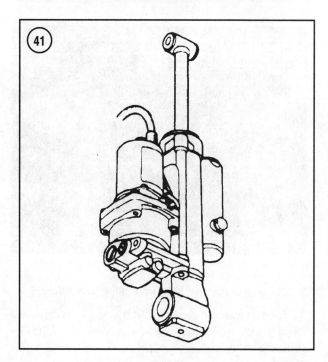

LUBRICATION, MAINTENANCE AND TUNE-UP

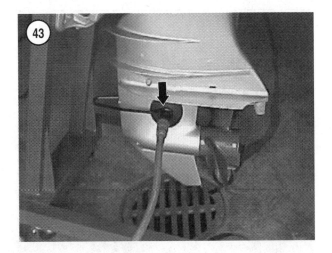

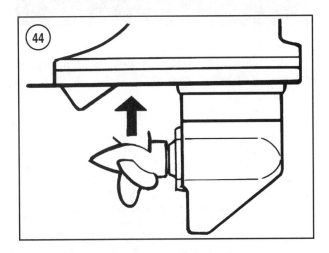

1. Operate the trim/tilt system or open the manual relief valve and move the engine to the fully UP position. Securely tighten the manual relief valve if opened.
2. Secure the engine in position with an overhead cable or other reliable means. Locate the trim fluid cap on the trim/tilt system (**Figure 41** or **Figure 42**). Clean all debris from the trim fluid cap area.
3. Slowly and carefully remove the oil fill cap from the trim system reservoir.
4. Carefully clean all debris from the cap-mounting surface. Take all necessary steps to prevent debris from entering the fluid reservoir.
5. Note the fluid level. Add fluid until the level is even with the bottom of the trim fluid cap opening (**Figure 41** or **Figure 42**). Clean the trim fluid reservoir cap and carefully thread it onto the reservoir. Securely tighten the oil fill cap.
6. Remove the overhead cable or supporting blocks, then lower the engine. Run the trim system to the fully UP and fully DOWN positions several times to purge air from the system. Repeat Steps 1-5 if using more than 2 oz. (59 mL) of fluid to correct the fluid level.

COOLING SYSTEM MAINTENANCE

Inspect the cooling system for proper operation every time the engine is run. A stream of water at the lower back area of the engine indicates that the water pump is operating. Never run the engine if it overheats or you suspect the water pump is not operating efficiently. Inspect the water pump if overheating occurs or the engine runs warmer than normal. Water pump inspection and repair procedures are provided in Chapter Nine.

Flush the cooling system at regular intervals to help prevent corrosion and deposit buildup in the cooling passages. Flush the cooling system after each operation when running salt, brackish water or polluted water. Running the engine in salt- or sand-laden water substantially reduces the life of the water pump components. You must inspect the water pump frequently when operating your engine under these conditions.

Use a standard flush/test adapter (**Figure 43**) or test tank for propeller drive models. Use a special jet flush adapter available from a Honda outboard dealership (part No. 6EO-28193-00-94) to operate jet models on a water hose.

Some models have the water pickup located below the antiventilation plate (**Figure 44**). They require a special adapter that can be purchased from most marine dealerships. Use full water pressure and never run the engine at high speed on a flush/test adapter.

Flushing the Cooling System

1. Use a test tank filled with clean water or a flush/test adapter with a freshwater supply.

2. Attach a flush/test adapter to the gearcase (**Figure 43**) or jet drive if a test tank is not available.

3. Turn the water on. Make certain that the flush/test adapter is positioned over the water pickup area of the gearcase. Start the engine and run it at a fast idle in neutral until the engine reaches normal operating temperature.

4. Continue to run the engine for a minimum of 10 minutes until the water exiting the engine is clear. Monitor the engine temperature. Stop the engine if it begins to overheat.

5. Throttle the engine back to idle for a few minutes, then stop the engine. Remove the flush adapter or remove the engine from the test tank.

WARNING
Use extreme caution when working with or around fuel. Never smoke around fuel or fuel vapor. Make sure no flame or source of ignition is present in the work area. Flame or sparks can ignite the fuel or vapors and result in fire or explosion.

FUEL SYSTEM

Topics covered in this section include fuel requirements, problems associated with old or stale fuel, fuel filter servicing, inspection of fuel hoses and clamps and basic fuel system inspection. Refer to **Table 1** for required maintenance items and recommended intervals.

Fuel Requirements

Always use a name-brand fuel from a facility that sells a large amount of fuel. Today's fuel has a relatively short shelf life. Some fuels begin to lose potency in as little as 15 days. Consider this when purchasing fuel for you outboard. Plan on using the fuel in 60 days or less to reduce fuel-related problems with your outboard.

Your Honda outboard is designed to use unleaded fuel. Unleaded fuels burn cleaner than leaded fuels; this results in fewer emissions, reduced deposits and longer engine life. Use regular grade fuel with an average octane rating of 86 or higher for all models. This fuel should meet the requirements for your engine when used under normal conditions. Using premium-grade fuel offers few advantages over regular grade fuel, under most operating condition. However, premium fuel normally contains a higher concentration of detergents that help keep the internal components of the base engine and fuel system clean. Use a higher-octane fuel when using the engine for commercial or heavy-duty service. Premium or high-octane fuel

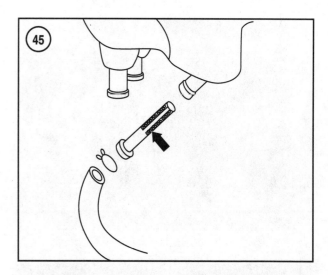

provides added protection against damaging detonation that may occur under heavy loads.

CAUTION
Never run your outboard on old or stale fuel. Engine damage could result from fuel that has deteriorated. Varnish-like deposits form in the fuel system as fuel deteriorates. These deposits can block fuel flow and result in lean fuel mixture. Burnt valves or other damage can result from operating with an excessively lean fuel mixture. Dispose of fuel that has been stored for a long time without proper treatment. Fuel should not be stored for more than 60 days, even with proper treatment. Contact a local marine dealership or automotive repair facility for information on disposal of old or stale fuel.

LUBRICATION, MAINTENANCE AND TUNE-UP

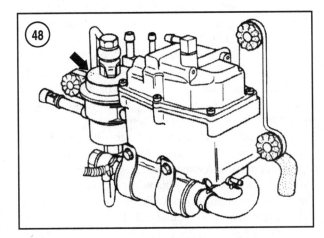

Fuel Additives

Use fuel additives such as Sta-Bil to help prevent gum or varnish-like deposits forming in the fuel system during a lay-up period. Other additives such as octane boosters are not required under normal conditions. Be aware that some additives may adversely affect fuel system components.

Fuel Filters

Clean, inspect or change fuel filters at the intervals listed in **Table 1**. Refer to the following information to assist with fuel filter location(s).

Models BF20 and BF2A use a single filter mounted in the fuel tank and connected to the fuel tank fitting (**Figure 45**).

Models BF50, BF5A, BF20A, BF25A, BF30A and all 2-cylinder models use a single fuel filter mounted to the fuel line (**Figure 46**). It is positioned in the hose connecting the fuel tank to the fuel pump.

Models BF35A, BF40A, BF45A, BF50A, BF75A and BF90A use a canister type fuel filter (**Figure 47**). It is located on the lower starboard side of the base engine and sits in a recessed area of the lower engine cover.

Models BF115A and BF130A use a cartridge-type fuel filter (**Figure 47**). It is located on the rear port side of the engine and sits in a bracket mounted to the lower engine cover. On these models an additional fuel filter is provided for the high-pressure side of the fuel system. It is located on front lower port side of the engine and connected to the vapor separator tank (**Figure 48**).

Inspect the fuel filter at the intervals specified in **Table 1**. Do not attempt to clean the fuel filter. Cleaning the filter will damage it and result in fuel leakage or a contaminated fuel system.

NOTE
Some boats are equipped with a large spin-on type fuel filter that separates much of the water from the fuel. It is located between the primer bulb and fuel tank. Service this unit when servicing other fuel filters on the engine.

Visually inspect the fuel filter(s) and replace it if it contains contaminants or it has become dark in color. Inspect the fuel tank(s) and other fuel lines for contamination if water or other contaminants are found in the filter. Visual inspection is not possible for the high-pressure fuel filter used on models BF115 and BF130. Replace this filter at the intervals specified in **Table 1**. Refer to Chapter Six to replace the fuel filter.

WARNING
Avoid the potential for fuel leakage and its associated dangers. Correct all fuel leakage prior to operating or storing the engine. Models BF20 and BF2A are equipped with an integral or engine-mounted fuel tank. A shutoff valve mounted to the carburetor and the vent on the fuel tank cap can be closed, should it become necessary to lay the engine on its side. Always inspect these components to ensure they are not leaking when the engine is stored in this manner.

Fuel Hoses and Clamps

At the recommended intervals, check the entire fuel system for leaking hoses or connections. Check the conditions of all fuel line clamps. Remove and replace plastic locking tie clamps if they are damaged or have become brittle.

Carefully tug on the fuel lines to ensure a tight fit on all connections. Inspect the spring-type fuel clamps for corrosion or lack of spring tension. Replace any clamps that are in questionable condition.

Replace fuel lines that are hard or brittle, are leaking, or have a spongy feel. Only use the recommended hoses available from a Honda dealership. Other fuel hoses available at auto parts stores may not meet the demands placed upon these hoses, or may not meet coast guard requirements.

Preparing Your Engine for Storage

The objective when preparing the engine for long-term storage is to prevent any corrosion or deterioration during the storage period. This section provides the procedures to prepare your engine for storage and to return the engine to service.

All major systems require some preparation before storage. If done correctly, the engine should operate properly when returned to service.

Refer to **Table 1** to determine any necessary maintenance.
1. Change the gearcase lubricant.
2. Check and top off the fluid in the hydraulic tilt or trim system.
3. Lubricate the propeller shaft.
4. Remove the battery and service it as described in Chapter Seven.
5. Check all electrical harnesses for corrosion or faulty connections and repair them as required.
6. Lubricate all steering, throttle and control linkages.
7. Lubricate all pivot and swivel shafts on the midsection of the engine.
8. Lubricate jet pump if applicable.
9. Check the condition and clean all sacrificial anodes.
10. Drain the fuel from the fuel tank and treat any residual fuel with a fuel stabilizer such as Sta-Bil.
11. Clean the exterior of the gearcase, drive shaft housing and swivel brackets to remove vegetation, dirt or deposit buildup.
12. Wipe down the components under the cover and apply a good corrosion prevention spray such as CR66 or its equivalent.
13. Change all fuel filters.
14. Flush the cooling system following the procedure listed in this chapter.
15. Treat the internal engine components with a storage-sealing agent specified for outboard engines following the procedure listed in this chapter. This step can prevent corrosion in the engine during the storage period. These storage agents are available from most marine dealerships and marine supply stores.

Preparing the Engine for Storage

1. Remove the silencer cover from the carburetors as described in Chapter Six.
2. Run the engine at idle speed in a test tank or on a flush/test adapter for 10 minutes or until the engine reaches operating temperature.
3. Raise the engine speed to approximately 1500 rpm. Spray the storage-sealing agent into all carburetor openings. Try to spray the agent evenly into all carburetors (on multiple carburetor engines). Spray in 5-10 second intervals. Continue to spray the agent into the engine until you note heavy smoking from the exhaust. This indicates the agent has passed through the engine. Stop the engine.
4. Remove the engine from the test tank or remove the flush/test adapter. Remove each spark plug and spray the sealing agent into each spark plug hole. Crank the engine over a few times to distribute sealing agent.
5. Change the engine oil and oil filter as described in this chapter. Drain each carburetor float bowl (vapor separator on EFI models). Disconnect the fuel hose from the engine and route it to a container suitable for holding fuel. Slowly pump the primer bulb to move the residual fuel in the fuel hoses to the float bowl for drainage. Install the drain plugs and tighten them securely. Connect the fuel hose to the engine. Treat any remaining fuel in the fuel tanks with fuel stabilizer.
6. Apply a light oil to the threads then install the spark plugs. Store the engine upright. Check all water drains on the gearcase and the water stream fitting on the lower engine cover for the presence of debris. They must be clear to ensure that water is not trapped in the cooling system. Disconnect the battery cables. Refer to Chapter Seven for battery storage information.

Returning Engine to Service

When the time comes to use the outboard, a few items need attention. Perform all scheduled maintenance. It is wise to service the water pump and replace the impeller as described in Chapter Nine. This vital component may have deteriorated during extended storage.

Change or correct all lubricant levels. Supply the engine with fresh fuel. Open the fuel valve or pump the primer bulb and check for a flooded carburetor following the procedure described in Chapter Three.

LUBRICATION, MAINTENANCE AND TUNE-UP

Install the battery as instructed in Chapter Seven. Supply the engine with cooling water, then start the engine. Run the engine at low speed for the first few minutes and avoid running at wide-open throttle until the engine reaches operating temperature. Check for proper operation of the cooling, electrical and warning systems and make corrections as required. Avoid continued operation if the engine is not functioning properly. Refer to Chapter Three for troubleshooting and testing procedures if there are further problems.

SUBMERSION

If the engine has been completely submerged, three factors need to be considered. Was the engine running when the submersion occurred? Was the engine submerged in salt, brackish or polluted water? How long ago was the engine retrieved from the water?

Complete disassembly and inspection of the base engine is required if the engine was submerged while running. Internal damage to the base engine (bent connecting rod) is likely if this occurs. Refer to Chapter Eight for base engine repair procedures.

Many components of the engine suffer the corrosive effects of submersion in salt, brackish or polluted water. The symptoms may not occur for some time after the event. Salt crystals form in many areas of the engine and promote intense corrosion. The wire harness and its connections are usually affected early. It is difficult to remove all of the salt crystals from the harness connectors. Replace the wire harness and clean all electrical component connections to ensure a reliable repair. The starter motor, relays and any switch on the engine will likely fail if it is not thoroughly cleaned or replaced.

Refer to *Submerged Engine Servicing* in this section for required service procedures.

If the engine is submerged in freshwater, refer to *Submerged Engine Servicing* in this section and follow the procedures as indicated. Replace the wire harness and any components if the terminal connectors are corroded.

Retrieve and service the engine as soon as possible. Vigorously wash all debris from the engine with freshwater upon retrieval. Complete base engine disassembly and inspection is required if sand, silt or other gritty material is in the engine cover. Refer to Chapter Eight for base engine repair procedures.

Service the engine quickly to ensure that it is running within two hours of retrieval. Submerge the outboard motor in a barrel or tank of clean freshwater if it cannot be serviced within this two-hour time frame. This is especially important if the engine was submerged in salt, brackish or polluted water. This *protective submersion* prevents exposure to air and decreases the potential for corrosion. This will not preserve the engine indefinitely, however. Service the engine within a few days of protective submersion.

If the engine was retrieved but not serviced in a prompt manner, completely disassemble and inspect the base engine.

WARNING
Use extreme caution when working with the fuel system. Never smoke around fuel or fuel vapors. Make sure that no flame or source of ignition is present in the work area. Flame or sparks can ignite the fuel or vapors and result in fire or explosion.

CAUTION
Models BF75A, BF90A, BF115A and BF130A use a flywheel mounted to the bottom of the base engine. Water can enter the flywheel cavity if the engine is submerged. Always remove the starter motor and inspect the flywheel cavity for water contamination immediately after retrieval. Fully tilt the engine to allow the water to drain from the starter mounting area.

Submerged Engine Servicing

Follow Steps 1-10 as soon as you retrieve the engine from the water.

1. Remove the engine cover and *vigorously* wash all material from the engine with freshwater. Completely disassemble and inspect the base engine internal components if there is sand, silt or gritty material inside the engine cover.

2. Dry the exterior of the engine with compressed air or other means. Remove the spark plugs and ground all spark plug leads. Remove the propeller.

3. Refer to Chapter Seven to assist with carburetor drain, fuel filter(s) locations and fuel hose routing. Drain all water and residual fuel from the fuel system. Remove any water from the carburetor cover. Replace all fuel filters on the engine.

4. Refer to the procedure listed in this section, then drain the oil and remove the oil filter (on models so equipped). Position the engine so that the spark plug openings face down.

5. Slowly rotate the flywheel clockwise (as viewed from the flywheel end) to force the water from the cylinder(s). Rotate the flywheel several times, noting whether or not the engine turns over freely. Completely disassemble and

inspect the internal components of the base engine if there is interference or hard rotation.

6. Position the engine with the spark plug holes facing up. Pour approximately one teaspoon of engine oil into each spark plug opening. Repeat Step 5 to distribute the oil within the cylinder.

7. Note all wire connection points and wire routing. Disconnect all electrical connections and inspect the terminals. With compressed air, dry all exterior surfaces and wire connectors. Remove, disassemble and inspect the electric starter motor following the procedure provided in Chapter Seven. Replace the ignition contact points along with the condenser (on models so equipped).

8. Following the procedures listed in this section, install fresh oil and a new oil filter (on models so equipped).

9. Fill the fuel tank with a fresh supply of fuel. Start the engine and run it at low speed for a few minutes. Refer to Chapter Three if the engine will not start. Stop the engine immediately and investigate if you notice unusual noises. Start the engine and continue to run it at low speeds for at least 30 minutes to dry any residual water from the engine. Promptly investigate any unusual noises or unusual running conditions.

10. Change the engine oil and filter (on models so equipped) to remove any residual water. Perform ALL routine maintenance items before returning the engine to service. Perform a compression test to ensure that the base engine is operating correctly. Install the propeller.

Corrosion Prevention

Reducing corrosion damage is an effective way to increase the life and reliability of your engine. A simple and effective way to reduce corrosion inside the engine cooling system is by flushing the cooling system after running the engine. Refer to *Cooling System Flushing* in this chapter.

Sacrificial anodes (**Figure 49**) are used on some models to lessen corrosion damage to exposed surfaces. The anode material is more corrosively active than the other exposed engine components. Essentially the anodes sacrifice themselves in order to protect the engine from corrosion damage.

These sacrificial anodes are mounted to an exposed portion of the gearcase and, on some models, are mounted to an internal cooling passage. Refer to Chapter Eight and Chapter Nine to determine if and where anodes are located on your engine.

Clean and inspect the sacrificial anodes (**Figure 49**) at the recommended intervals. Inspect and clean the anodes more often if you run or store the engine in salt, brackish

or polluted water. Use a stiff brush to clean deposits and other material from the anode. Replace the anode when it has lost 40% or more of its material. Never paint or cover the anode with a protective coating. Doing so dramatically decreases its ability to protect the underwater components. Clean the mounting area before installing a new anode to ensure a proper connection.

Inspect the anode mounting area if engine components are corroded but the anode is not. It is likely that corrosion or contaminants may prevent the anode from making adequate contact with the mounting surface. Clean the area thoroughly if you observe this condition.

TUNE-UP

A complete tune-up consists of a series of adjustments, tests, inspections and part replacements that return the outboard motor to original factory specifications. A partial tune-up often results in unsatisfactory performance and can cause engine damage and reduced engine life. Therefore, always complete all of the applicable instructions provided in this section.

Compression Test

No tune-up is complete without a compression test. An engine with low or weak compression on one or more cylinders simply cannot be tuned properly. If not corrected, the tune-up is unlikely to improve the performance of your engine. Refer to *Compression Test* in Chapter Three and perform the test as indicated. Correct any condition that is causing low or weak compression prior to performing the remaining tune-up procedure.

LUBRICATION, MAINTENANCE AND TUNE-UP

Spark Plugs

Spark plug inspection or replacement is the most important part of a complete tune-up. No other component on the engine can effect the engine running characteristics more than the spark plug. Spark plugs are repeatedly subjected to very high heat, pressure, and exposure to the corrosive by-products of combustion.

As all Honda outboards are of a four-stroke design, the spark plug life is far better than that of most two-stroke engines. Nevertheless, spark plugs operate in a harsh environment and eventually require cleaning or replacement.

Replacement spark plugs must be of the correct size, reach and heat range to operate properly in the engine. Spark plug recommendations are listed in **Table 5**. Alternate spark plug numbers are listed and can be used if the standard plug is not readily available.

Inspecting the spark plug reveals much about the condition of the engine and allows you to correct some problems before expensive engine damage occurs. Remove the spark plug(s) and compare them to the ones listed in **Figure 50**. Be sure you correct any problem with the engine before installing new spark plugs. Otherwise, the problem may recur. Follow the listed procedures for spark plug removal, inspection, cleaning, gap adjustment and installation.

Spark plug removal

Caution
When the spark plug(s) are removed, dirt or other foreign material surrounding the spark plug hole(s) can fall into the cylinder(s). Foreign material inside the cylinders can cause engine damage when the engine is started.

1. Clean the area around the spark plug(s) using compressed air or an appropriate brush
2. Disconnect the spark plug lead(s) by twisting the boot back and forth on the spark plug insulator while pulling outward. Pulling on the lead instead of the boot can cause internal damage to the lead
3. Remove the spark plugs using the correct size spark plug socket. Arrange the spark plugs in order of the cylinder from which they were removed.

Spark plug inspection

Remove the plugs and compare them to the plugs shown in **Figure 50** for standard gap plugs and **Figure 51** for surface gap plugs. Spark plugs can give you an indication of problems in the engine, sometimes before the symptoms occur. Refer to the information provided in **Figure 50** and **Figure 51** for spark plug inspection.

Spark plug cleaning

Although cleaning and correcting the gap on the plugs usually corrects spark plug-related problems, it is recommended you replace them with new plugs. New spark plugs are relatively inexpensive and offer a considerably longer life than a cleaned and gapped plug.

When a spark plug must be re-used, clean the plug with a suitable wire brush and solvent to dissolve the deposits. Special spark plug cleaning devices are available which use a forced abrasive blast (small sand blaster) to remove stubborn deposits.

Remove all debris from the plug with compressed air prior to gapping and installing the spark plug.

Spark plug gap adjustment

Use a gapping tool (**Figure 52**) to adjust the spark plug gap to the specification listed in **Table 6**. Never tap the plug against a hard object to close the gap. The ceramic insulator can crack and possibly break away. Gapping tools are available at most automotive part stores and allow you to change the gap without damaging the plug.

1. Refer to **Table 6** to determine the correct Spark Plug Gap.
2. Measure the gap with a feeler gauge to set to the recommended thickness. The gauge should pass between the electrodes with a slight drag at the points indicated in **Figure 53**.
3. Open the gap and reset it if the gauge cannot be inserted with only a slight drag.
4. Inspect the gap for parallel electrode surfaces (**Figure 53**) and readjust as necessary.

Spark plug installation

1. Apply a very thin coating of light oil to the spark plug threads and thread them in by hand. Use a torque wrench and tighten the spark plugs to the specification listed in **Table 9**.
2. Apply a light coating of corrosion-prevention oil to the spark plug connector and carefully slide it over the correct spark plug. Snap the connector fully onto the spark plug.
3. Clean the battery terminals, then connect the cables.

SPARK PLUG ANALYSIS

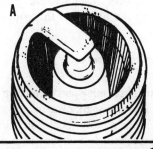
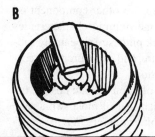
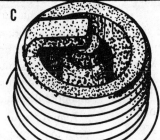

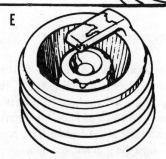
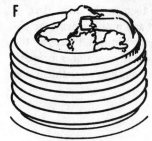

A. **Normal**—Light to tan gray color of insulator indicates correct heat range. Few deposits are present and the electrodes are not burned.

B. **Core bridging**—These defects are caused by excessive combustion chamber deposits striking and ahering to the firing end of the plg. In this case, they wedge or fuse between the electrode and core nose. They originate from the piston and cylinder head surfaces. Deposits are formed by one or more of the following:
  a. Excessive carbon in cylinder.
  b. Use of non-recommended oils.
  c. Immediate high-speed operation after prolonged trolling.

C. **Wet fouling**—Damp or wet, black carbon coating over entire firing end of plug. Forms sludge in some engines. Caused by one or more of the following:
  a. Spark plug heat range too cold.
  b. Prolonged trolling.
  c. Low-speed carburetor adjustment too rich.
  d. Induction manifold bleed-off passage obstructed.
  e. Worn or defective breaker points.

D. **Gap bridging**—Similar to core bridging, except the combustion particles are wedged or fused between the electrodes. Causes are the same.

E. **Overheating**—Badly worn electrodes and premature gap wear are indicative of this problem, along with a gray or white "blistered" appearance on the insulator. Caused by one or more of the following:
  a. Spark plug heat range too hot.
  b. Incorrect propeller usage, causing engine to lug.
  c. Worn or defective water pump
  d. Restricted water intake or restriction somewhere in the cooling system.

F. **Ash deposits or lead fouling**—Ash deposits are light brown to white in color and result from use of fuel or oil additives. Lead fouling produces a yellowish-brown discoloration and can be avoided by using unleaded fuels.

LUBRICATION, MAINTENANCE AND TUNE-UP

SURFACE GAP SPARK PLUG ANALYSIS

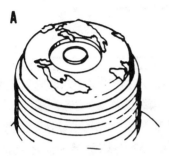
A

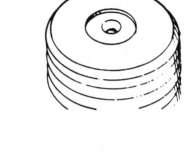
B

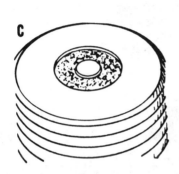
C

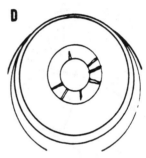
D

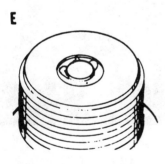
E

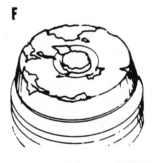
F

A. Normal—Light tan or gray colored deposits indicate that the engine/ignition system condition is good. Electrode wear indicates normal spark plug rotation.
B. Worn out—Excessive electrode wear can cause hard starting or a misfire during acceleration.
C. Cold fouled—Wet fuel deposits are caused by "drowning" the plug with raw fuel mix during cranking or overrich carburetion. Weak ignition will also contribute to this condition.
D. Carbon tracking—Electrically conductive deposits on the firing end provide a low-resistance path for the voltage. Carbon tracks form and can cause misfires.
E. Concentrated arc—Multi-colored appearance is normal. It is caused by electricity consistently following the same firing path. Arc path changes with deposit conductivity and gap erosion.
F. Aluminum throw-off—Caused by preignition. This is not a plug problem but the result of engine damage. Check the engine to determine the cause and extent of damage.

164

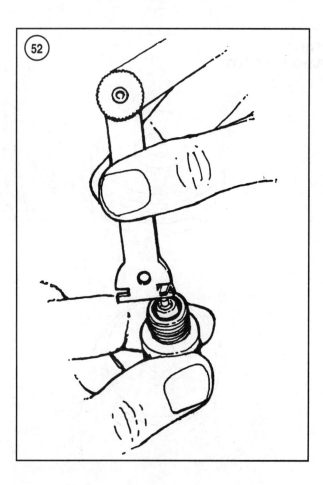

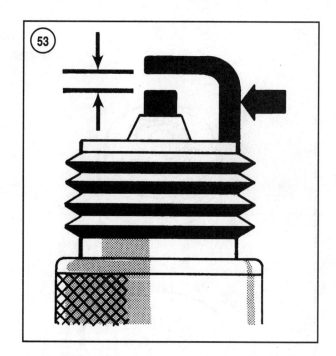

NOTE
Timing check and adjustments are required at regular intervals on models BF75 and BF100. Refer to Chapter Five for timing adjustment procedures.

Timing and Carburetor Adjustment

You can make timing adjustments easily at low engine speeds. Checking the timing at higher speeds generally requires that the engine be test ran with a timing light installed.

Carburetor calibration involves adjusting the idle mixture and idle speed for most models. Some models require pilot screw adjustment. Preliminary adjustments are provided in Chapter Six. Final corrections are best made under actual running conditions. This provides the smoothest and most efficient operation. Carburetor linkage adjustment must be performed when the carburetors are adjusted. Refer to Chapter Five for timing, carburetor, linkage and other adjustments.

LUBRICATION, MAINTENANCE AND TUNE-UP

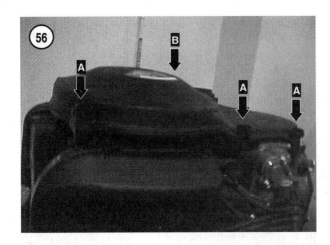

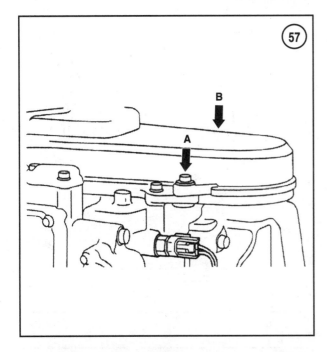

CAUTION
Never operate your Honda outboard with a damaged belt or with improper belt tension. The belt can fail, causing serious and expensive damage to the base engine.

Timing/Alternator Belt Inspection

Inspect the timing/alternator belt (**Figure 54**) (on models so equipped) at the intervals listed in **Table 1**. Use compressed air to blow debris from the area prior to removing any components. Removal of the timing belt cover is required on most models to properly inspect the belt. Refer to the following instructions to remove the cover. It is not necessary to remove the cover on all models.

1A. On models BF35A, BF40A, BF45A and BF50A, remove the attaching nuts and washers (A, **Figure 55**). Lift the cover (B, **Figure 55**) from the engine.

1B. On models BF75A and BF90A, loosen the four cover screws (A, **Figure 56**). Lift the cover (B, **Figure 56**) from the engine.

1C. On models BF115A and BF130A, loosen the bolts and washers (A, **Figure 57**). Remove the cover (B, **Figure 57**) from the engine.

2. Disconnect both battery cables from the battery. Remove all spark plugs and connect the spark plug leads to an engine ground.

3. Remove the belt cover from the engine. Inspect the belt for cracked, worn or damaged surfaces. Note the presence of oil, grease or other contaminants on the belt surfaces.

4. Manually rotate the flywheel to ensure that you inspect all areas of the belt. Note the condition of the cogs (**Figure 58**) on the timing belt.

5. Inspect the belt for excessive play at a midway point between the pulleys. Refer to Step 8 if free play is noted.

6. Refer to Chapter Eight to replace the timing belt if you find worn, damaged or contaminated areas.

7. Install the belt cover and securely tighten the screws or bolts. Install the spark plugs and spark plug leads. Clean the battery terminals, then connect the cables to the battery.

8. Some models are equipped with a belt tension device (**Figure 59**). Proper adjustment is required to ensure long belt life and reliable operation. Refer to Chapter Five for adjustment procedures if there is excessive play in the belts.

Removing Carbon from the Combustion Chamber

You must remove carbon from the combustion chamber at regular intervals on models BF20 and BF2A. Refer to Chapter Eight and remove the cylinder head from the engine (**Figure 60**). Use a soft wire brush to remove all deposits from the cylinder head, avoiding contact with any gasket surfaces. Install the cylinder head following the procedure listed in Chapter Eight.

CAUTION
Never rotate the flywheel opposite of the normal direction of rotation. Serious damage to the water pump components can occur if the flywheel rotates in the wrong direction.

Valve Clearance Adjustment

Perform valve clearance adjustment to compensate for normal valve train wear. Valve clearance adjustments must be performed when the engine is at room temperature. Adjustment performed on a warm engine will result in improper clearances.

You need feeler gauges to check and adjust the valve clearance. Try different feeler gauges until you find one that passes between the components with a slight drag. The one with the slight drag indicates the clearance between the components. Refer to **Table 7** to determine correct valve clearance.

Always inspect the condition of all belts on the engine prior to performing the adjustments. Refer to *Timing/Alternator Belt Inspection* in this section.

A special procedure must be followed to position the crankshaft and camshaft prior to checking the valve clearance. In addition, removal of several components may be required.

Valve adjustment BF20 and BF2A models

1. Refer to Chapter Eight and remove the cooling fan cover, carburetor and valve tappet cover from the engine.
2. Remove the spark plug and connect the lead to an engine ground.
3. Place your thumb over the spark plug opening. Slowly rotate the flywheel clockwise until you feel air pressure on your thumb. Continue to rotate the flywheel until the marks on the manual starter pully and ignition coil align as shown in **Figure 61**.
4. Locate the valve adjustment spacers (A, **Figure 62**) in the opening under the tappet cover (**Figure 62**). Using a feeler gauge, measure the clearance between the valve ad-

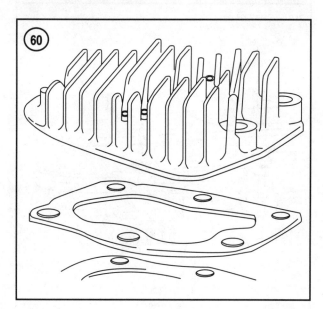

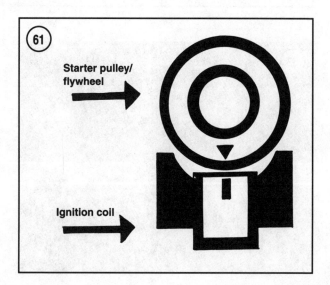

LUBRICATION, MAINTENANCE AND TUNE-UP

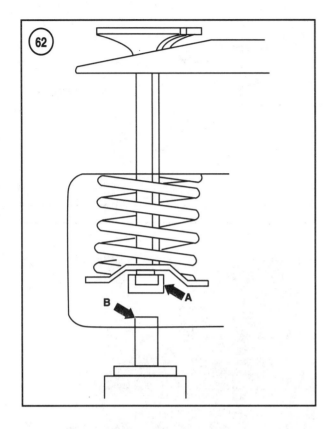

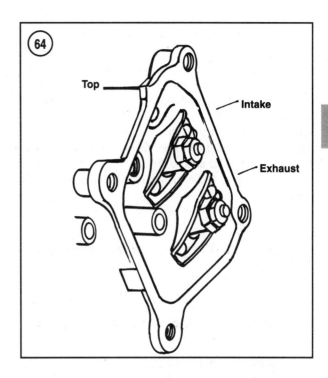

justment spacers (A, **Figure 62**) and the valve tappets (B, **Figure 62**). Use a feeler gauge that can be passed between these components with a slight drag. This feeler gauge indicates the clearance.

5. Compare the measurements with the specification listed in **Table 7**. Install a thicker valve adjustment spacer if the clearance is more than the listed specification. Install a thinner valve adjustment spacer if the clearance is less than the listed specifications. Refer to Chapter Eight for valve adjustment spacer installation. Alternate spacer thicknesses are provided in **Table 7**. Purchase them at a local Honda dealership.

6. Refer to Chapter Eight and install the cooling fan cover, carburetor and tappet cover. Install the spark plug and spark plug lead.

Valve adjustment (BF50 and BF5A models)

1. Remove the spark plug and connect the lead to an engine ground.

2. Place your thumb over the spark plug opening. Slowly rotate the flywheel clockwise until you feel air pressure on your thumb. Continue to rotate the flywheel until the marks on the flywheel and ignition coil align as shown in **Figure 63**.

3. Refer to Chapter Eight and remove the rocker arm cover. Refer to **Figure 64** to locate the intake and exhaust rocker arms.

4. Using a feeler gauge, measure the clearance between the valve stem and the rocker arm at the indicated points (**Figure 65**). Measure the clearance for both the intake and exhaust valves (**Figure 64**).

5. Refer to **Table 7** to determine the correct clearance. If adjustment is necessary, loosen the locknut and adjust the screw (**Figure 65**) until you obtain the proper clearance. Tighten the locknut to the specification listed in **Table 8**.

6. Install the rocker arm cover following the procedures in Chapter Eight. Install the spark plug and spark plug lead.

Valve adjustment (BF75, BF8A, BF100, BF9.9A and BF15A models)

1. Disconnect both battery cables from the battery. Remove the spark plugs and connect the spark plug leads to an engine ground.

2. Refer to Chapter Eleven and remove the manual rewind starter.

3. Refer to Chapter Eight for procedures and remove the rocker arm cover (**Figure 66**).

4. Place your thumb over the No. 1 (top) cylinder spark plug opening. Slowly rotate the flywheel clockwise until air pressure is felt on your thumb. Continue to rotate the flywheel until the marks on the flywheel and the starter mount boss are aligned as shown in **Figure 67**.

5. Refer to **Figure 68** and locate the intake and exhaust rocker arm for No. 1 cylinder.

6. Using a feeler gauge, measure the clearance between the valve stem and the rocker arm at the indicated points (**Figure 65**). Refer to **Table 7** to determine the correct clearance. Measure the clearance on both valves.

7. If adjustment is necessary, loosen the locknut and adjust the screw (**Figure 65**) until you get the proper clearance. Tighten the locknut to the specification listed in **Table 7**.

8. Slowly rotate the flywheel clockwise *exactly one revolution*. Locate the intake and exhaust valves for the No. 2 cylinder. Repeat Steps 6 and 7 for the No. 2 cylinder valves.

9. Refer to Chapter Eight and install the rocker arm cover. Refer to Chapter Eleven and install the manual rewind starter. Install the spark plugs and spark plug leads. Clean the battery terminals, then connect the cables to the battery.

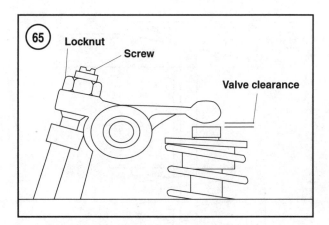

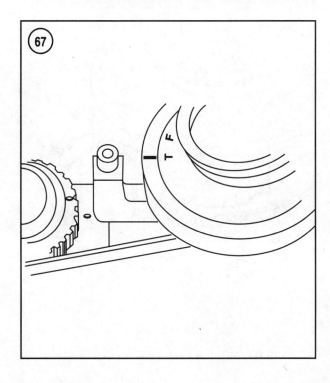

LUBRICATION, MAINTENANCE AND TUNE-UP

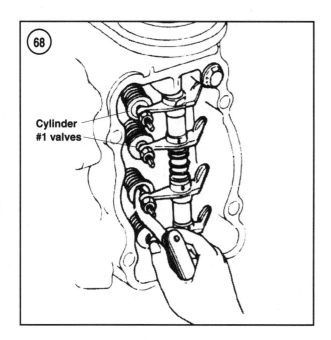

68

Cylinder #1 valves

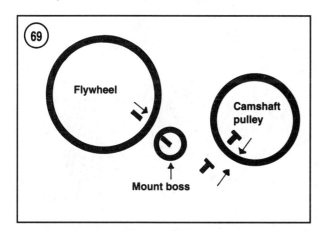

69

Flywheel

Camshaft pulley

Mount boss

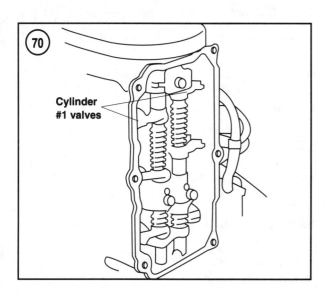

70

Cylinder #1 valves

Valve adjustment (BF20A, BF25A and BF30A models)

1. Disconnect both battery cables from the battery. Remove the spark plugs and connect the spark plug leads to an engine ground.
2. Refer to Chapter Eight and remove the flywheel cover or manual rewind starter. Remove the lifting hook from the engine.
3. Slowly rotate the flywheel clockwise until the marks on the flywheel and the cover-mounting boss align. Ensure the marks next to the T on the camshaft pulley and cylinder head align (**Figure 69**). Refer to timing belt installation in Chapter Eight if these marks will not align.
4. Refer to Chapter Eight and remove the rocker arm cover (**Figure 66**).
5. Refer to **Figure 70** and locate the intake and exhaust rocker arm for the No. 1 cylinder.
6. Using a feeler gauge, measure the clearance between the valve stem and the rocker arm at the points indicated (**Figure 65**). Refer to **Table 7** to determine the correct clearance. Measure the clearance on both valves.
7. If adjustment is necessary, loosen the locknut and adjust the screw (**Figure 65**) until the proper clearance is obtained. Tighten the locknut to the specification listed in **Table 9**.
8. Slowly rotate the flywheel clockwise until the No. 2 mark on the camshaft pulley and cylinder head align. Repeat Steps 6 and 7 for the No. 2 cylinder valves.
9. Slowly rotate the flywheel clockwise until the No. 3 mark on the camshaft pulley and cylinder head align. Repeat Steps 6 and 7 for the No. 3 cylinder valves.
10. Install the lifting hook. Refer to Chapter Eight and install the rocker arm cover and flywheel cover or manual rewind starter. Install the spark plugs and spark plug leads. Clean the battery terminals and connect the cables to the battery.

Valve adjustment (BF35A, BF40A, BF45A and BF50A models)

1. Disconnect both battery cables from the battery. Remove the spark plugs and connect the spark plug lead to an engine ground.

2. Refer to Chapter Eight and remove the flywheel cover.

3. Slowly rotate the flywheel clockwise (as indicated on the flywheel) until the mark on the flywheel and the lifting hook mounting boss align. Ensure the arrow next to the T on the camshaft pulley and cylinder head align as shown in **Figure 72**. Refer to timing belt installation in Chapter Eight if these marks do not align.

4. Refer to Chapter Eight and remove the rocker arm cover (**Figure 66**).
5. Refer to (**Figure 70**) and locate the intake and exhaust rocker arm for the No. 1 cylinder.
6. Using a feeler gauge, measure the clearance between the valve stem and the rocker arm at the points indicated (**Figure 65**). Refer to **Table 7** to determine the correct clearance. Measure the clearance on both valves.
7. If adjustment is necessary, loosen the locknut and adjust the screw (**Figure 65**) until the proper clearance is obtained. Tighten the locknut to the specification listed in **Table 9**.
8. Slowly rotate the flywheel clockwise until the No. 2 mark on the camshaft pulley and cylinder head align. Repeat Steps 6 and 7 for the No. 2 cylinder valves.
9. Slowly rotate the flywheel clockwise until the No. 3 mark on the camshaft pulley and cylinder head align. Repeat Steps 6 and 7 for the No. 3 cylinder valves.
10. Install the lifting hook. Refer to Chapter Eight and install the rocker arm cover and flywheel cover. Install the spark plugs and spark plug leads. Clean the terminals and connect the battery cables to the battery.

Valve adjustment (BF75A and BF90A models)

1. Disconnect both battery cables from the battery. Remove the spark plugs and connect the spark plug leads to an engine ground.
2. Refer to Chapter Eight and remove the flywheel cover (**Figure 66**).
3. Slowly rotate the flywheel clockwise until the arrows on the flywheel and the lower timing belt cover align. Ensure the marks next to the T on the camshaft pulley and lower timing belt cover align (**Figure 72**).
4. Refer to Chapter Eight and remove the rocker arm cover (**Figure 66**).
5. Refer to (**Figure 73**) and locate the intake and exhaust rocker arms for the No. 1 cylinder.
6. Using a feeler gauge, measure the clearance between the valve stem and the rocker arm at the points indicated (**Figure 65**). Refer to **Table 7** to determine the correct clearance. Measure the clearance on all three valves.
7. If adjustment is necessary, loosen the locknut and adjust the screw (**Figure 65**) until you obtain the proper clearance. Tighten the locknut to the specification listed in **Table 9**.
8. Slowly rotate the flywheel clockwise until the No. 2 mark on the camshaft pulley and lower timing belt cover align. Repeat Steps 6 and 7 for the No. 2 cylinder valves.
9. Slowly rotate the flywheel clockwise until the No. 3 mark on the camshaft pulley and lower timing belt cover align. Repeat Steps 6 and 7 for the No. 3 cylinder valves.

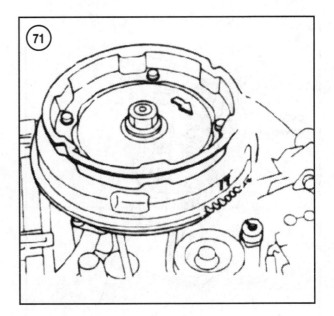

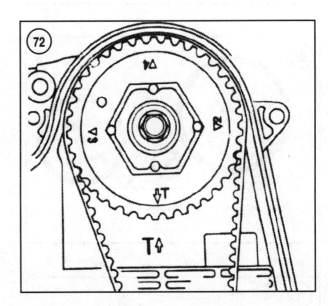

10. Slowly rotate the flywheel clockwise until the No. 4 mark on the camshaft pulley and lower timing belt cover align. Repeat Steps 6 and 7 for the No. 4 cylinder valves.

11. Refer to Chapter Eight for procedures and install the rocker arm cover and flywheel cover. Install the spark plugs and spark plug leads. Clean the battery terminals and connect the cables to the battery.

Valve adjustment (BF115A and BF130A models)

1. Remove the spark plugs and connect the spark plug lead to an engine ground.

LUBRICATION, MAINTENANCE AND TUNE-UP

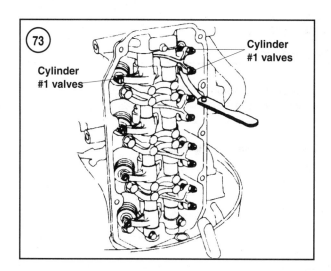

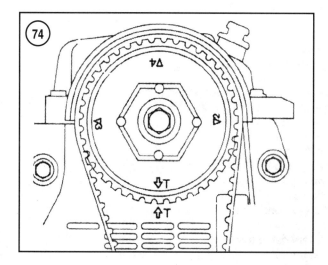

clearance. Tighten the locknut to the specification listed in **Table 8**.

8. Slowly rotate the flywheel clockwise until the No. 2 mark on the camshaft pulley and lower timing belt cover align. Repeat Steps 6 and 7 for the No. 2 cylinder valves.
9. Slowly rotate the flywheel clockwise until the No. 3 mark on the camshaft pulley and lower timing belt cover align. Repeat Steps 6 and 7 for the No. 3 cylinder valves.
10. Slowly rotate the flywheel clockwise until the No. 4 mark on the camshaft pulley and lower timing belt cover align. Repeat Steps 6 and 7 for the No. 4 cylinder valves.
11. Refer to Chapter Eight for procedures and install the rocker arm cover and flywheel cover. Install the spark plugs and spark plug leads. Clean the battery terminals and connect the cables to the battery.

CAUTION
Never run the engine without providing cooling water. Use either a test tank or flush/test adapter. Remove the propeller before running the engine.

WARNING
Stay clear of the propeller shaft while running an engine on a flush/test adapter. The propeller should be removed before running the engine or performing tests. Disconnect all spark plug leads and disconnect the battery connections before removing or installing a propeller.

2. Refer to Chapter Eight for procedures and remove the flywheel cover.
3. Slowly rotate the flywheel clockwise until the arrows on the lower timing belt cover and camshaft pulley align as indicated (**Figure 74**).
4. Refer to Chapter Eight and remove the rocker arm cover (**Figure 66**).
5. Refer to **Figure 73** and locate the intake and exhaust rocker arm for the No. 1 cylinder.
6. Using a feeler gauge, measure the clearance between the valve stem and the rocker arm at the points indicated (**Figure 65**). Refer to **Table 7** to determine the correct clearance. Measure the clearance on all three valves.
7. If adjustment is necessary, loosen the locknut and adjust the screw (**Figure 65**) until you obtain the proper

Test Running Your Outboard

The final operation to perform in a tune-up is the test run. Operate the engine on a flush/test device or in a test tank to ensure correct starting and idling prior to running it under actual conditions. Connect a shop tachometer to the engine. Have an assistant operate the boat as you observe the idle speed. Refer to Chapter Five to adjust the idle speed.

Note the tachometer reading as an assistant operates the engine at full speed. Perform this test with the average load or passengers in the boat. Make sure to operate the tilt/trim system to reach the correct trim position. Note the maximum engine speed. Refer to Chapter Three for the correct engine operating speed. Examine the propeller for damage or incorrect pitch when the maximum engine speed is below or above the recommended engine speed range. Refer to Chapter Three.

TABLE 1 MAINTENENCE INTERVALS

Models	Required Maintenance
BEFORE AND AFTER EVERY USE	
All models	Check oil level and condition
BF20, BF2A, BF50, BF5A	Check gearcase lubricant level
BF75, BF8A, BF100	–
BF9.9A, BF15A	–
All models	Check propeller fasteners for tightness
All models	Check fuel line condition
MONTHLY OR AFTER EACH 20 HOURS OF USE	
BF2A, BF20, BF5A, BF50	Check throttle linkages
6 MONTHS OR 50 HOURS OF USE	
Models	Required maintenance
All models	Check gearcase lubricant condition
BF20, BF2A, BF50, BF5A	Inspect or change spark plugs
6 MONTHS OR 100 HOURS OF USE	
All models	Lubricate swivel bracket **
Manual start models	Check the starter rope condition
Manual start models	Lubricate starter rope **
All models	Lubricate motor cover fasteners and latches **
Tiller control models	Lubricate tiller arm control pivot **
All models without power trim	Lubricate tilt lock mechanism **
All models with clamp bolts	Lubricate engine clamp bolts **
All models	Lubricate throttle linkages *
All models	Change engine oil *
BF20, BF2A, BF50, BF5A	Check shear pin condition
All models	Check idle speed
All models	Check battery condition
All models	Check for loose bolts or nuts
All models	Check battery cable terminals
All models	Check fuel filters
ANNUALLY OR 200 HOURS OF USE	
All models with external filter	Change oil filter
All models	Change gearcase lubricant *
All models	Check and adjust valve clearance *
All models	Clean fuel tank
All models	Check or replace fuel lines
BF75, BF100	Check and adjust timing *
All models	Replace fuel filters
All models	Check and adjust timing/balancer belt
(Excludes models BF20, BF2A, BF50, BF5A)	–
All models	Check thermostat operation
BF20A, BF25A, BF30A	Check and correct carburetor syncronization *
BF35A, BF40A	–
BF45A, BF50A	–
BF75A, BF90A	–

(continued)

LUBRICATION, MAINTENANCE AND TUNE-UP

MAINTENENCE INTERVALS (continued)

Models	Required maintenance
EVERY 300 HOURS OF USE BF20, BF2A	Clean combustion chamber
EVERY 2 YEARS OR 400 HOURS OF USE BF115, BF130	Replace high pressure filter

* Perform this maintenance after the first month or 15 hours of usage when the engine is new or recently repaired.
** Perform this maintenance more often when the engine is used in saltwater.

TABLE 2 ENGINE OIL VISCOSITY

Model	Temperature range C°	(F°)	SAE viscosity
BF20, BF2	-20° to over 40°	(-4° to over 104°)	10W-40
	-20° to 33°	(-4° to 91°)	10W-30
	-10° to over 40°	(14° to over 104°)	20W-40, 20W-50
BF50, BF5A	-20° to 33°	(-5° to 90°)	10W-30
	-20° to over 40°	(-4 to over 104°)	10W-40
	-10° to over 40°	(14° to over 104°)	20W-40, 20W-50
BF75, BF8A, BF100	-20° to over 40°	(-4 to over 104°)	10W-40
BF9.9A, BF15A	-20° to 33°	(-4° to 91°)	10W-30
	-20° to over 40°	(-4° to over 104°)	10W-40
	-10° to over 40°	(14° to over 104°)	20W-40, 20W-50
BF20A, BF25A, BF30A	-20° to over 40°	(-5° to over 100°)	10W-30
	10° to over 40°	(50° to over 100°)	30W
BF35A, BF40A, BF45A, BF50A	-20° to over 40°	(-5° to over 100°)	10W-30
	10° to over 40°	(50° to over 100°)	30W
BF75A, BF90A	-20° to 30°	(-4° to 86°)	10W-30
	-20° to over 40°	(-4° to over 104°)	10W-40
BF115A, BF130A	-20° to over 40°	(-4° to over 104°)	10W-40

TABLE 3 ENGINE OIL CAPACITY

Model	Capacity
BF20, BF2A (2 hp models)	0.40 L (0.42 US qt.)
BF50, BF5A (5 hp models)	0.55 L (0.58 US qt.)
BF75, BF8A, BF100 (7.5, 8, 9.9 hp models)	0.80 L (0.85 US qt.)
BF9.9A, BF15A	1.10 L (1.16 US qt.)
BF20A, BF25A, BF30A	1.90 L (2.01 US qt.)
BF35A, BF40A, BF45A, BF50A	2.40 L (2.54 US qt.)
BF75A, BF90A (75, 90 hp models)	4.00 L (4.23 US qt.)
BF115A, BF130A	5.60 L (5.92 US qt.)

TABLE 4 GEARCASE CAPACITY

Model	Capacity
BF20, BF2A (2 hp models)	0.05 L (1.057 US pt.)
BF50, BF5A (5 hp models)	0.10 L (0.211 US pt.)
BF75, BF8A, BF100 (7.5, 8, 9.9 hp models)	0.23 L (0.486 US pt.)
BF9.9A, BF15A	0.24 L (0.507 US pt.)
BF20A, BF25A, BF30A	0.29 L (0.306 US qt.)
BF35A, BF40A, BF45A, BF50A	0.52 L (0.549 US qt.)
BF75A, BF90A (75, 90 hp models	0.66 L (0.697 US qt.)
BF115A, BF130A	1.00 L (1.057 US qt.)

TABLE 5 SPARK PLUG RECOMMENDATIONS

Model	Standard spark plug	Alternate spark plug
BF20, BF2A (2 hp models) (BF20S, BF20L models)	– – NGK BMR-4A *	– – –
BF20, BF2A (2 hp models) (BF2AS, BF2AL models)	– – NGK BMR-4A *	– – ND W14MR-U **
BF50, BF5A (5 hp models)	NGK BPR5ES *	ND W16EPR-U **
BF75, BF8A, BF100 (7.5, 8, 9.9 hp models)	NGK DR-5HS *	NGK DR-4HS *
BF9.9A	NGK DR-5HS *	ND X16FSR-U **
BF15A	NGK DR-6HS *	ND X20FSR-U **
BF20A, BF25A, BF30A	NGK DR7EA *	ND X22ESR-U **
BF35A, BF45A	NGK DR7EA *	ND X22ESR-U **
(Continued)		

LUBRICATION, MAINTENANCE AND TUNE-UP

TABLE 5 SPARK PLUG RECOMMENDATIONS (continued)

Model	Standard spark plug	Alternate spark plug
BF75A, BF90A (75, 90 hp models)	NGK DR7EA *	ND X22ESR-U **
BF115A, BF90A	NGK ZFR7F *	ND KJ22CR-L8

* Designates NGK brand spark plug
** Designates Nippon Denso brand spark plug

TABLE 6 SPARK PLUG GAP

Model	Gap
BF20, BF2A (2 hp models)	0.6-0.7 mm (0.024-0.028 in.)
BF50, BF5A (5 hp models)	0.7-0.8 mm (0.028-0.031 in.)
BF75, BF8A, BF100 (7.5, 8, 9.9 hp models)	0.6-0.7 mm (0.024-0.028 in.)
BF9.9A, BF15A	0.6-0.7 mm (0.024-0.028 in.)
BF20A, BF25A, BF30A	0.6-0.7 mm (0.024-0.028 in.)
BF35A, BF40A, BF45A, BF50A	0.6-0.7 mm (0.024-0.028 in.)
BF75A, BF90A (75, 90 hp models)	0.6-0.7 mm (0.024-0.028 in.)
BF115A, BF130A	0.7-0.8 mm (0.028-0.031 in.)

TABLE 7 VALVE CLEARANCE

Model	mm (in.)
BF20, BF2A	
Intake and exhaust	0.080-0.160 (0.003-0.006)
BF50, BF5A	
Intake	0.060-0.140 (0.002-0.006)
Exhaust	0.110-0.190 (0.004-0.007)
BF75, BF100	
Intake and exhaust	0.060-0.100 (0.002-0.004)
BF8A	
Intake	0.100-0.140 (0.0040-0.0055)
Exhaust	0.180-0.220 (0.0070-0.0086)
BF9.9A and BF15A	
Intake	0.100-0.140 (0.0040-0.0055)
Exhaust	0.180-0.220 (0.0070-0.0086)
BF20A, BF25A and BF30A	
Intake	0.100-0.140 (0.040-0.0055)
Exhaust	0.180-0.0220 (0.0070-0.0086)
BF35A, BF40A, BF45 and BF50A	
Intake	0.130-0.170 (0.0051-0.0066)
Exhaust	0.210-0.250 (0.0082-0.0098)

(continued)

TABLE 7 VALVE CLEARANCE (continued)

Model	mm (in.
BF75A and BF90A	
Intake	0.180-0.220 (0.0071-0.0086)
Exhaust	0.260-0.300 (0.0102-0.0118)
BF115A and BF130A	
Intake	0.240-0.280 (0.0094-0.0110)
Exhaust	0.280-0.320 (0.0110-0.0126)

TABLE 8 ALTERNATE VALVE ADJUSTMENT SPACERS

Models	Thickness
BF20, BF2A	3.15 mm (0.124 in.)
	3.25 mm (0.128 in.)
	3.34 mm (0.131 in.)
	3.43 mm (0.135 in.)
	3.52 mm (0.139 in.)
	3.61 mm (0.142 in.)
	3.72 mm (0.146 in.)
	3.82 mm (0.150 in.)

TABLE 9 TORQUE SPECIFICATIONS

Model	N•M	(ft.-lb.)	(in.-lb.)
Spark plug			
BF20, BF2A	10-15	(7-11)	
BF50, BF5A	15-18	(11-13)	
All other models			
New plug	½ turn after hand seated		
Used plug	$1/_8$ - ¼ turn after hand seated		
Valve adjustment lock nut			
BF50, BF5A, BF75, BF8A & BF100	6-10	–	(53-89)
BF9.9A, BF15A, BF20A, BF25A & BF30A	8	–	(71)
BF35A, BF40A, BF45A &BF50A	23.0	(17)	–
BF75, BF90	23	(17)	–
BF115A and BF130A	20	(15)	–
Oil filter			
BF20A, BF25A & BF30A	11	–	(97)
BF35A, BF40A, BF45, BF50A	8	–	(71)
BF75A, BF90A, BF115A & BF130A	22	(16)	–
Oil drain plug			
BF20A, BF25A, BF30A, BF35A, BF40A,			
BF45A, BF50A, BF75A, BF90A, BF115A			
BF130A	23	(17)	–

TABLE 10 STANDARD TORQUE

Fastener Size	N•M	(ft.-lb.)	(in.-lb.)
5 mm bolt/nut	4-7	–	(35-62)
6 mm bolt/nut	8-12	–	(71-106)
8 mm bolt/nut	20-28	(15-21)	–
10 mm bolt/nut	35-40	(25-29.5)	–

Chapter Five

Timing, Synchronization and Adjustments

For optimum performance, an outboard's ignition and fuel systems must be precisely adjusted and synchronized. In addition, shift cables and linkage must be correctly adjusted or difficult shifting and gearcase damage can result.

This chapter provides the adjustment procedures for the fuel and ignition systems, shift system and trim/tilt system.

Perform all applicable adjustments in the order provided. **Tables 1-4** list torque and specifications. **Tables 1-4** are located at the end of this chapter.

TIMING ADJUSTMENTS

Timing adjustments are required on models BF75, BF8A and BF100. Ignition timing is electronically controlled on all other models and adjustment is not required.

BF75 and BF100 (prior to serial No. 1200000)

Check and adjust the ignition timing at the intervals specified in Chapter Four and/or when the breaker points or other ignition system components have been removed or disturbed. A volt/ohm meter is required to check and adjust the ignition timing.

1. Disconnect both battery cables from the battery. Remove all spark plugs and connect the spark plug leads to an engine ground.

2. Remove the rewind starter assembly from the engine. Refer to Chapter Eleven

3. Locate the ignition coil wires that lead under the flywheel. Disconnect the wires (**Figure 1**).

4. Calibrate an ohmmeter on the R × 1 scale. Connect the positive lead to the ignition coil side of one of the disconnected black wires. Connect the negative lead to a good engine ground.

5. Slowly turn the flywheel clockwise while observing the ohmmeter. The meter should indicate continuity, then change to no continuity just as the marks on the flywheel and rewind starter mount align (**Figure 2**).

6. Connect the positive meter lead to the remaining black wire (ignition coil side). Rotate the flywheel clockwise while observing the ohmmeter. The meter should again indicate continuity, then change to no continuity just as the mark on the flywheel align with the mark on the starter mount.

7. Adjust the ignition timing if the meter does not change from continuity to no continuity when the mark on the flywheel aligns with the mark on the starter mount. Refer to **Table 4** for the correct breaker point gap. To set the gap, loosen the breaker point retaining screw (**Figure 2**) and slightly move the breaker points within the adjusting slot as necessary. Securely tighten the retaining screw when finished. Rotate the camshaft pulley 180° and set the gap on the remaining breaker point set.

8. Repeat Steps 4-6 until the gap is correctly set. Several adjustments may be required.

178

9. Refer to Chapter Seven and install the camshaft pulley cover and bolt. Refer to Chapter Eleven and install the rewind starter assembly.
10. Clean the terminals and connect the black wires to the engine wire harness. Install the spark plugs and spark plug leads. Clean the battery terminals, then connect the cables to the battery.

BF75, BF8A and BF100 (serial No. 1200000-on)

Timing adjustments on these models are only required when ignition components are replaced or disturbed.
1. Disconnect both battery cables from the battery. Remove the spark plugs, and connect the spark plug leads to an engine ground.
2. Remove the rewind starter assembly from the engine. Refer to Chapter Eleven.
3. Slowly rotate the flywheel clockwise until the F mark next to the T on the flywheel (A, **Figure 3**) aligns with the mark on the rewind starter mounting boss (B, **Figure 3**).
4. Rotate the flywheel one complete revolution. Align the mark on the rewind starter mounting boss (B, **Figure 3**) with the F mark on the flywheel (A, **Figure 3**). Maintain this flywheel position.
5. Look into the opening in the camshaft pulley. The mark on the pulser coil (C, **Figure 3**) should be aligned with the mark on the advance mechanism (D, **Figure 3**).
6. If adjustment is necessary, loosen the pulser coil mounting screws and move the pulser coil enough to align the marks as described in Step 5. Securely tighten the pulser coil mounting screws and repeat Steps 3-5.
7. Refer to Chapter Seven and install the camshaft pulley and bolt. Refer to Chapter Eleven and install the rewind starter assembly onto the engine.
8. Install the spark plugs and spark plug leads. Clean the battery terminals, then connect the cables to the battery.

THROTTLE CONTROL/CABLE ADJUSTMENTS

This section provides the procedures to properly adjust the throttle linkage and cables. Always check and correct the linkage after initial adjustments if necessary. Perform other carburetor adjustments and synchronization after adjusting the linkage and cables. Perform all adjustments without running the engine.

Models BF20 and BF2A

Throttle control is accomplished by moving the front-mounted throttle lever (**Figure 4**). A cable connects

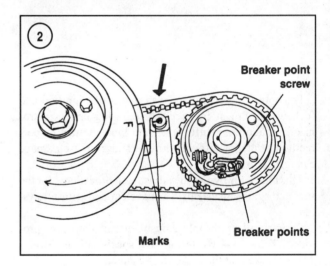

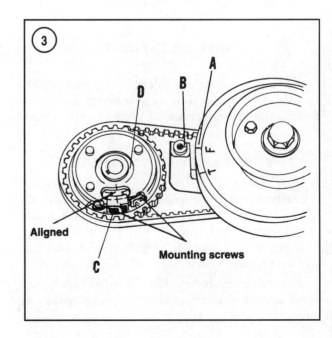

TIMING, SYNCHRONIZATION AND ADJUSTMENTS

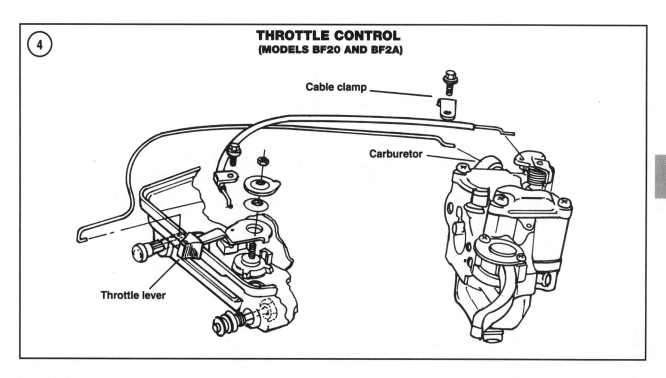

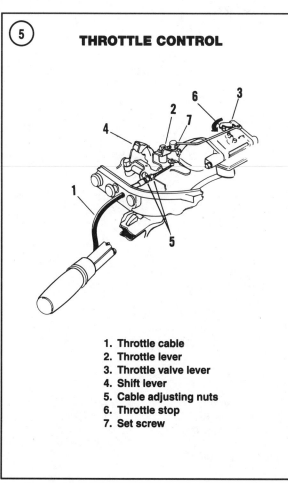

1. Throttle cable
2. Throttle lever
3. Throttle valve lever
4. Shift lever
5. Cable adjusting nuts
6. Throttle stop
7. Set screw

the throttle lever to the carburetor, allowing throttle control via the lever. To adjust the throttle cable on these models, proceed as follows.

1. Position the throttle lever in idle position.
2. Loosen the throttle cable screw and clamp (**Figure 4**).
3. Lightly push the throttle valve linkage on the carburetor toward the closed throttle position.
4. Hold the throttle cable and throttle valve linkage in this position, then securely tighten the cable clamp and screw.
5. Operate the throttle to ensure smooth operation. Ensure that you reach full throttle and idle positions. Readjust as necessary.

Models BF50 and BF5A

A cable connects the throttle handle to the throttle valve lever on the carburetor (**Figure 5**). To prevent stalling when returning the throttle rapidly to the idle position, a dashpot is used. Perform these adjustments while the engine is not running.

1. Refer to Chapter Eleven and remove the rewind starter from the engine.
2. Place the tiller mounted throttle handle in the idle or slowest speed position.
3. Measure the distance between the end of the cable housing and the point indicated on the cable bracket (1, **Figure 6**).
4. The distance should be 8.5-9.5 mm (0.33-0.37 in.). Loosen both nuts (2, **Figure 6**) and adjust the distance as

required. Securely tighten both nuts. Check for a proper measurement after adjustments.

5. Measure the distance from the dashpot contact point to the dashpot bracket at the points indicated (3, **Figure 6**).
6. Push and hold the dashpot toward the dashpot bracket and measure the distance again at the points indicated (3, **Figure 6**).
7. Subtract the second measurement from the first measurement to indicate the dashpot travel. Proper dashpot travel is 8.6-8.8 mm (0.34-0.0.35 in.). Loosen the mounting nuts (4, **Figure 6**) and adjust them until you have the correct dashpot travel measurement. Securely tighten the mounting nuts.
8. Position the shift lever in neutral. Position the throttle handle in the full throttle position. Locate the throttle lever and throttle stop adjusting screw (5 and 6, **Figure 6**).
9. Adjust the throttle stop screw until a measurement of 0.1-1.0 mm (0.0040-.039 in.) is obtained between the throttle lever and the dashpot contact (7, **Figure 6**).
10. Place the throttle handle in the idle position. Note the alignment of the mark on the throttle valve lever and the throttle stop (8, **Figure 6**).
11. The mark should be aligned with the stop in the casting. Loosen the throttle linkage adjusting screw and adjust the linkage in the slot until the mark aligns with the stop in the casting. Tighten the screw securely. Refer to Chapter Eleven and install the rewind starter onto the engine.

Models BF75, BF8A and BF100

A cable (1, **Figure 5**) connects the throttle handle to the engine-mounted throttle lever (2, **Figure 5**). A linkage rod connects the throttle lever to the throttle valve lever (3, **Figure 5**) Perform these adjustments with the engine turned off.

1. Disconnect both battery cables from the battery (electric start models).
2. Observe the throttle lever (2, **Figure 5**) and the shift lever (4, **Figure 5**) as you move the tiller control throttle handle to the Start position.
3. The throttle lever (2, **Figure 5**) should just contact the shift lever as the throttle handle just reaches the start position.
4. If adjustment is required, loosen the cable adjusting nuts (5, **Figure 5**) and move the cable until the correct operation is obtained.
5. Tighten the cable adjusting nuts securely. Place the tiller handle control in the idle position while observing the throttle stop. The throttle valve lever (3, **Figure 5**) should contact the throttle stop (6, **Figure 5**) as the throttle handle just reaches the idle setting.

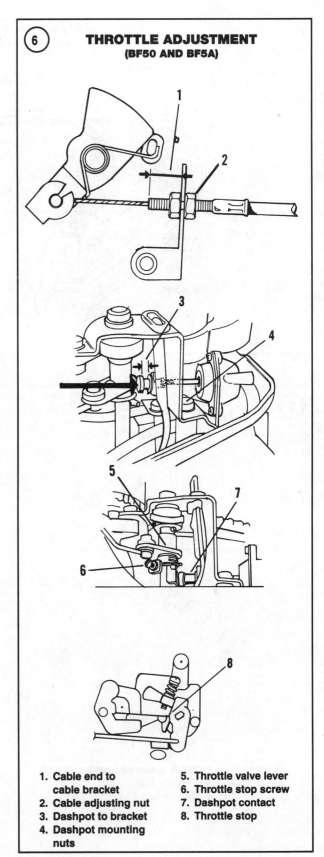

6. THROTTLE ADJUSTMENT (BF50 AND BF5A)

1. Cable end to cable bracket
2. Cable adjusting nut
3. Dashpot to bracket
4. Dashpot mounting nuts
5. Throttle valve lever
6. Throttle stop screw
7. Dashpot contact
8. Throttle stop

TIMING, SYNCHRONIZATION AND ADJUSTMENTS

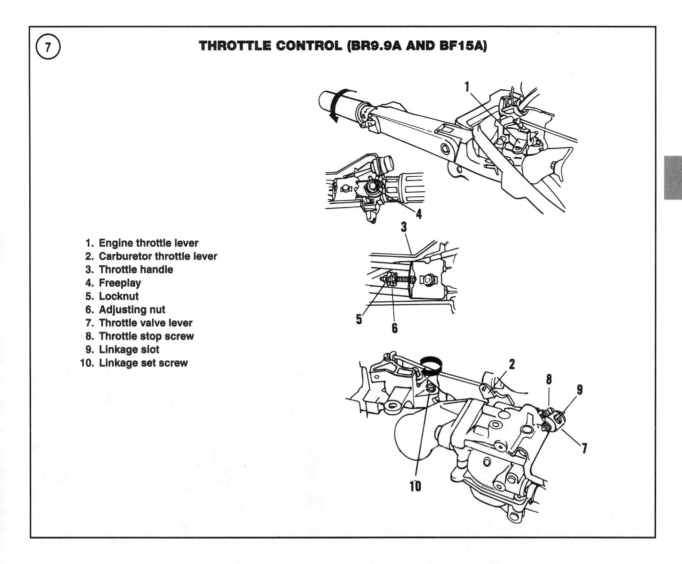

⑦ **THROTTLE CONTROL (BR9.9A AND BF15A)**

1. Engine throttle lever
2. Carburetor throttle lever
3. Throttle handle
4. Freeplay
5. Locknut
6. Adjusting nut
7. Throttle valve lever
8. Throttle stop screw
9. Linkage slot
10. Linkage set screw

6. If adjustment is necessary, loosen the throttle linkage set screw (7, **Figure 5**) and adjust the linkage until the throttle valve lever contacts the stop. Securely tighten the throttle linkage set screw.

7. Connect the battery cables to the battery on electric start models.

Models BF9.9A and BF15A

A cable connects the throttle handle to engine-mounted throttle lever (1, **Figure 7**). A linkage rod connects the throttle lever to the throttle valve lever on the carburetor (2, **Figure 7**). Perform these adjustments with the engine off.

1. Disconnect both battery cables from the battery on electric start models. Remove the spark plugs and connect the spark plug leads to an engine ground.

2. Locate the throttle cable adjusting mechanism under the tiller control handle (3, **Figure 7**). Place the throttle handle in the idle speed setting.

3. Carefully rotate the throttle handle and note the amount of free play at the points indicated (4, **Figure 7**).

4. The free play should be 0.3-3.0 mm (0.012-0.118 in.). Loosen the locknut (5, **Figure 7**) and move the adjusting nut (6, **Figure 7**) until the correct amount of free play exists. Securely tighten the adjusting nut and locknut.

5. Observe the throttle valve lever (7, **Figure 7**) and throttle stop screw (8, **Figure 7**) as you move the throttle handle to the idle speed position. There should be 0.1-1.0 mm (0.004-0.039 in.) of clearance in the throttle linkage connector slot (9, **Figure 7**).

6. Locate the engine-mounted throttle lever and hold it in the closed position. Loosen the linkage set screw (10, **Figure 7**) and move the linkage until you obtain the correct adjustment. Tighten the linkage set screw securely.

7. Install the spark plugs and spark plug leads. Clean the terminals then connect the battery cables to the battery (electric start models).

Models BF20A, BF25A, BF30A, BF35A, BF40A, BF45A, BF50A

The throttle is controlled by moving the tiller-mounted throttle handle or remote control throttle handle and its attached cable. Moving the cable results in movement of the engine-mounted throttle cam. The carburetor throttle valves open via the throttle roller contacting the moveable throttle cam. This section provides adjustment procedures for both the remote and tiller control models. Perform all adjustments with the engine off.

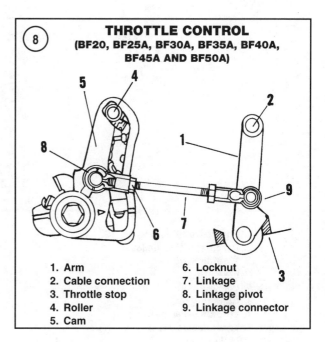

Remote control models

1. Disconnect both battery cables from the battery. Remove the spark plugs and connect the spark plug leads to an ground.

2. Disconnect the throttle cable from its attaching point on the throttle arm (1, **Figure 8**).

3. Observe the throttle arm (1, **Figure 8**), throttle stop (3, **Figure 8**), throttle roller (4, **Figure 8**) and throttle cam (5, **Figure 8**) as you move the throttle arm in the indicated direction. (**Figure 8**). With the throttle held in this position, measure the clearance between the No. 3 carburetor throttle valve lever and the throttle stop (**Figure 9**).

4. Correct adjustment allows the throttle arm to contact the full throttle stop and the throttle roller (4, **Figure 8**) to reach the end of the slot simultaneously. The clearance between the No. 3 carburetor throttle valve lever and the stop should be between 0.1 and 1.0 mm (0.004-0.039 in.).

5. If adjustment is required, loosen the locknut (6, **Figure 8**), then carefully pry the throttle linkage (8, **Figure 8**) from the throttle cam. Adjust the length of the throttle linkage (7, **Figure 8**) until you have a correct adjustment. Tighten the locknut securely and carefully snap the throttle linkage onto the throttle cam.

6. Connect the remote control throttle cable to the throttle arm. Place the remote control in the neutral (closed throttle) position. Note the alignment of the throttle roller and the triangle marks on the throttle cam (**Figure 10**). Correct adjustment allows the center of the roller and the triangle mark to align.

7. If adjustment is required, remove the clip and slide the cable pivot from the throttle lever (2, **Figure 8**). Loosen

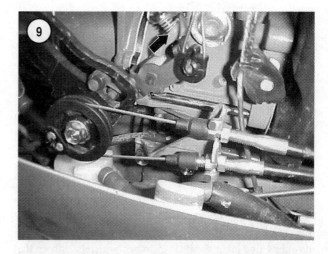

TIMING, SYNCHRONIZATION AND ADJUSTMENTS

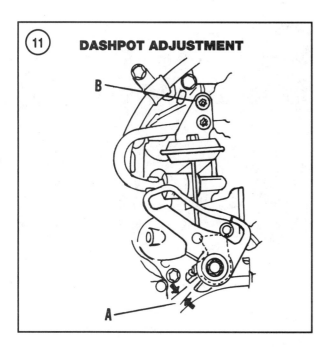

the locknut, then adjust the cable pivot until you have correctly aligned the roller and cam. Refer to Step 3 to verify that the adjustment is correct.

8. Securely tighten the locknut. Install the cable, pivot washers, and clip to the throttle lever connection point (2, **Figure 8**).

9. Observe the throttle cam and throttle roller and slowly move the throttle cam in the direction indicated (**Figure 8**) until the *throttle cam just contacts the throttle roller*. Measure the distance between the dashpot activation lever at the points indicated (A, **Figure 11**).

10. Refer to **Table 3** for the dashpot clearance specification. If adjustment is required, loosen the dashpot bracket screws (B, **Figure 11**) and move the dashpot up or down until you obtain the correct adjustment. Securely tighten the dashpot bracket screws.

11. Install the spark plugs and spark plug leads. Clean the battery terminals and connect the cables to the battery.

Tiller control models

1. Remove both battery cables from the battery. Remove the spark plugs and connect the spark plug leads to a ground. Place the throttle handle in the full-speed position.

2. Inspect the throttle arm and throttle stop (3, **Figure 8**). Correct adjustment allows the throttle arm to just contact the stop as it reaches the full speed position.

3. If adjustment is required, loosen the upper cable adjusting nuts (A, **Figure 12**). Adjust them until correct contact is made, as indicated in Step 2. Securely tighten the adjusting nuts after adjustment.

4. Move the shifter to the forward-gear position. Observe the No. 3 carburetor throttle valve stop lever (**Figure 9**) as you move the throttle handle to the full-speed position. There should be a clearance of 0.1-1.0 mm (0.004-0.039 in.) between the throttle valve lever and the stop as it reaches the full speed position.

5. If adjustment is required, carefully pry the throttle linkage connector (8, **Figure 8**) from the throttle cam (5, **Figure 8**). Loosen the locknut and adjust the length of the throttle linkage (7, **Figure 8**) until you have the correct throttle stop contact. Securely tighten the locknut. Snap the throttle linkage connector onto the throttle cam.

6. Observe the throttle roller (4, **Figure 8**) and throttle cam (5, **Figure 8**) as you move the throttle handle to idle speed. The center of the throttle roller should align with the triangle marks on the throttle cam as it reaches the idle position.

7. If adjustment is required, loosen the lower starboard side throttle cable adjusting nuts (A, **Figure 13**) and ad-

just them until the roller and triangle mark align. Securely tighten the adjusting nuts.

8. Observe the throttle cam and throttle roller and slowly move in the throttle cam in the direction indicated (**Figure 8**) until the throttle cam just contacts the throttle roller. Measure the distance between the dashpot activation levers at the points indicated (A, **Figure 11**).

9. Refer to **Table 3** for the dashpot clearance specifications. If adjustment is required, loosen the dashpot bracket screws (B, **Figure 11**) and move the dashpot up or down until the correct adjustment is obtained. Tighten the dashpot bracket screws securely.

10. Install the spark plugs and spark plug leads. Clean the battery terminals and connect the cables to the battery.

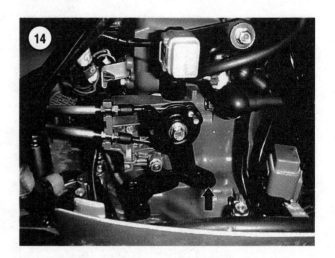

CAUTION
You may experience difficulty while attempting to shift the engine into forward gear during cable and linkage adjustment. When shifting is required for cable or linkage adjustments, never use excessive force. If the shift lever does not move easily, manually move the propeller clockwise while shifting. This step can prevent damage to internal gearcase or other shifting system components.

Models BF75A and BF90A

The throttle is controlled by moving the tiller control-mounted throttle handle or remote control-mounted throttle handle and its attached cable. Moving the cables results in movement of the starboard side-mounted throttle cam. The carburetor throttle valves open via the throttle roller contacting the moveable throttle cam. Perform all adjustments with the engine off.

1. Disconnect both battery cables from the battery. Remove the spark plugs and connect the spark plug leads to an engine ground.

2. Disconnect the throttle cable from its attaching point on the throttle arm (**Figure 14**).

3. Locate the throttle cable attaching points on the port side throttle lever. Measure the upper and lower cable connectors at the indicated points (A and B, **Figure 15**).

4. The measurements should be 14.0 mm (0.551 in.) on the upper connector (A, **Figure 15**) and 16.0 mm (0.630 in.) on the lower connector (B, **Figure 15**).

5. If adjustment is required, loosen the locknuts and adjust the nuts until the correct measurements are obtained. Securely tighten the adjusting nuts.

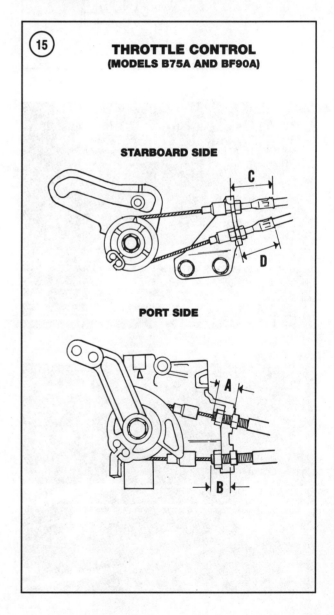

TIMING, SYNCHRONIZATION AND ADJUSTMENTS

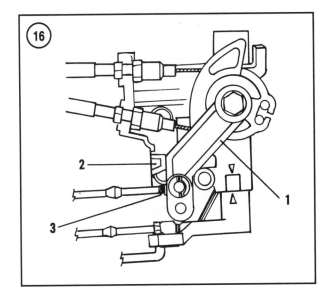

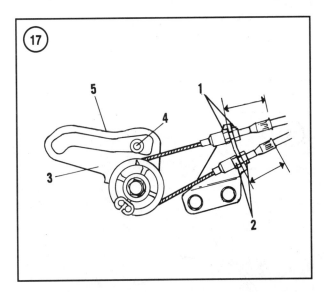

10. The throttle lever should contact the full throttle stop or boss as the full speed position is reached. If adjustment is required, place the throttle handle (remote or tiller control) in the idle or slowest speed position. Remove the throttle cable locknut then remove the pin and washers (3, **Figure 16**). Slide the cable pivot from the throttle lever. Rotate the pivot on the shift cable to adjust the cable length. Adjust the cable length until the throttle lever just contacts the throttle stop or boss as full speed is reached. Ensure that the Cable Pivot adjustment allows full thread engagement of the pivot onto the throttle cable end.

11. Place the throttle handle in idle or slowest speed. Install the washer and pin onto the cable. Securely tighten the throttle cable locknut.

12. Observe the No. 4 carburetor throttle valve lever and the full throttle stop screw (**Figure 9**) as you move the throttle handle (remote or tiller arm control) to full speed.

13. The throttle valve lever should just contact the stop screw as full throttle is reached. If adjustment is required, position the throttle in the idle speed position in neutral. Locate the throttle cam adjusting nuts (1 and 2, **Figure 17**). Loosen the upper throttle cable adjusting nut. Adjust the nut until a clearance of 0.1-1.0 mm (0.004-0.039 in.) is obtained at the stop screw with the throttle in the wide-open position. Securely tighten the upper cable adjusting nuts.

14. Position the throttle in the idle position with the gearcase in neutral. Note the position of the throttle cam and throttle roller (3 and 4, **Figure 17**). The center of the throttle roller should align with the triangle mark on the throttle cam.

15. If adjustment is required, loosen the upper and lower throttle cable adjusting nuts (1 and 2, **Figure 17**). Adjust the lower nuts until the correct roller and throttle cam alignment is obtained. Securely tighten the upper and lower adjusting nuts.

16. Position the throttle in the idle position with the gearcase in neutral. Make sure the throttle cam is in the closed-throttle position. Using a feeler gauge, measure the clearance between the throttle cam and throttle roller at the point indicated at 5, **Figure 17**. The clearance should be 0.2-0.8 mm (0.008-0.032 in.).

17. If adjustment is required, loosen the dashpot bracket screws (B, **Figure 11**) and move the dashpot up or down until the correct clearance is obtained. Tighten the dashpot bracket screws securely.

18. Install the spark plugs and attach the plug leads. Connect the battery cables to the battery.

6. Locate the throttle cable attaching points on the starboard side throttle/cam lever (**Figure 15**). Measure the upper and lower cable connectors at the indicated points (C and D, **Figure 15**).

7. The correct adjustment is 34.0 mm (1.339 in.) on the upper connector (C, **Figure 15**) and 25.0 (0.984 in.) on the lower connector (D, **Figure 15**).

8. If adjustment is required, loosen the locknuts and adjust the nuts until the correct measurements are obtained. Securely tighten the adjusting nuts.

9. Observe the port side throttle lever (1, **Figure 16**) and full throttle stop or boss (2, **Figure 16**) as you place the remote control (or tiller control) throttle handle in the full-speed (forward gear) position.

Models BF115A and BF130A

Control of the throttle is accomplished by moving the remote control-mounted throttle handle and its attached cable. Moving the cables causes the engine-mounted throttle arm and throttle cam to move. The throttle valve opens via the throttle roller contacting the moveable throttle cam. Perform all adjustments with the engine off.

1. Disconnect both battery cables from the battery. Remove the spark plugs and connect the spark plug leads to an engine ground.

2. Refer to Chapter Six and remove the silencer cover from the throttle body.

3. Locate the throttle cable attaching points on the starboard side throttle lever (**Figure 17**). Measure the upper and lower cable connectors at the indicated points (1 and 2, **Figure 17**).

4. The adjustment is correct if 17.0 mm (0.669 in.) is noted on the upper and lower connectors, as indicated (**Figure 17**).

5. If adjustment is required, loosen the locknuts and adjust the nuts until you obtain the correct measurements. Securely tighten the adjusting nuts.

6. Locate the port side of the engine throttle arm (**Figure 18**). Measure the front and rear cable connectors at the indicated points (2 and 3, **Figure 18**).

7. The adjustment is correct if 18.0 mm (0.709 in.) is noted on the front connector (2, **Figure 18**) and 16.0 mm (0.630 in.) on the rear connectors (3, **Figure 18**).

8. If adjustment is required, loosen the locknuts (4, **Figure 18**) and adjust the nuts (5, **Figure 18**) until the correct measurements are obtained. Securely tighten the adjusting nuts.

9. Observe the engine-mounted port side throttle lever (1, **Figure 18**) and the full-throttle stop (6, **Figure 18**) as you place the throttle handle in the wide-open throttle position. The throttle lever should contact the full throttle stop as the wide-open throttle position is reached.

10. If adjustment is required, place the throttle handle in the idle position with the gearcase in neutral. Remove the throttle cable locknut, pin and washers (7, **Figure 18**). Slide the cable pivot from the throttle lever (1, **Figure 18**). Rotate the pivot on the shift cable to adjust the cable length. Adjust the cable length until the throttle lever just contacts the throttle stop as wide-open throttle is reached. Make sure the cable pivot adjustment allows full thread engagement of the pivot onto the throttle cable end. Install the washer and pin onto the cable. Securely tighten the throttle cable locknut.

11. Place the throttle handle in the idle speed setting.

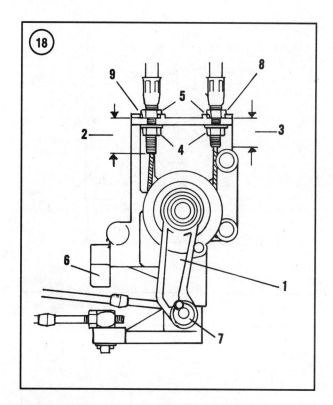

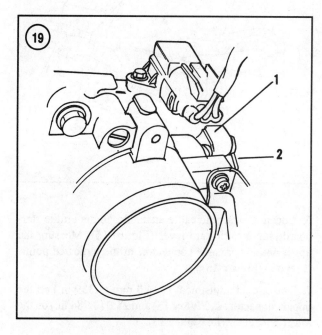

12. Observe the throttle valve lever and the full throttle stop on the throttle body (1 and 2, **Figure 19**) as you move the throttle handle to the full-speed position.

13. There should be a clearance of 0.1-1.0 mm (0.004-0.039in.) between the throttle valve lever and the full throttle stop or boss as full throttle is reached. If ad-

TIMING, SYNCHRONIZATION AND ADJUSTMENTS

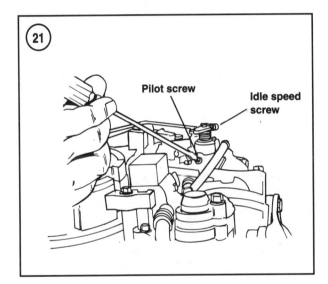

justment is required, position the throttle handle in the idle speed setting. Loosen the rear throttle lever cable adjusting nuts (8, **Figure 18**). Adjust the rear nuts until you obtain the correct clearance when the throttle handle is placed in the full-throttle position. Securely tighten the cable adjusting nuts.

14. Position the throttle handle in the idle speed setting. Note the alignment of the throttle cam and throttle roller (3 and 4, **Figure 17**). The center of the throttle roller should align with the triangle mark on the throttle cam.

15. If adjustment is required, loosen the front and rear throttle cable adjusting nuts. Adjust the front adjusting nuts (9, **Figure 18**) until you obtain the correct roller and throttle cam alignment. Securely tighten the front and rear adjusting nuts.

16. Refer to Chapter Six, then install the silencer cover to the throttle body.

17. Install the spark plugs and spark plug leads. Clean the battery terminals and connect the cables to the battery.

CARBURETOR ADJUSTMENTS

This section provides pilot screw adjustment, idle speed adjustment and carburetor synchronization procedures for all carburetor-equipped models. Idle speed is controlled by the ECU on EFI models BF115A and BF130A. Perform these adjustments in the order provided.

CAUTION
Use extreme caution when seating the pilot screw. The tapered seat will be permanently damaged if excessive force is used. Turn the screw with very light force and stop the instant resistance is felt.

NOTE
Many models have multiple carburetors. Adjust the pilot screws to the same position on all carburetors unless different settings are indicated.

Pilot Screw Adjustment

Unless specified otherwise adjust all pilot screws to the same setting. To locate the pilot screws, refer to the illustration for the selected model (**Figures 20-25**).

1. For models BF20 and BF2A refer to **Figure 20**.
2. For models BF50 and BF5A refer to **Figure 21**.
3. For models BF75, BF8A and BF100 refer to **Figure 22**.
4. For models BF9.9A and BF15A refer to **Figure 23**.
5. For models BF20A, BF25A and BF30A refer to **Figure 24**.

6. For models BF35A, BF40A, BF45A and BF50A refer to **Figure 24**.
7. For models BF75A and BF90A refer to **Figure 25**.

NOTE
Models BF115A and BF130A are equipped with electronically controlled fuel injection and pilot screw adjustment is not required.

NOTE
Special procedures are provided for adjusting the pilot screw on models BF20 and BF2A.

Use a screwdriver and carefully turn the pilot screw (**Figure 26**) clockwise until lightly seated. Refer to **Table 2** for adjustment specifications. Turn the pilot screw counterclockwise to the middle of the specified range.

Additional adjustment may be required if you note improper throttle response or if the engine is operated in high elevations. Operation in a very cold environment may require variation from the listed specification to obtain satisfactory running quality.

To determine the need for adjustment, operate the engine under actual running conditions. Run the engine for approximately 10 minutes to reach normal operating temperature. Advance the throttle rapidly from idle and check for proper throttle response.

The pilot screw can be adjusted to a slightly richer (counterclockwise) or leaner (clockwise) setting if you note a bog or hesitation during acceleration. Perform the adjustments in $1/8$-turn increments, then check the throttle response. Reverse the screw adjustment direction if the bog or hesitation worsens. Adjust all screws to the same settings on engines with multiple carburetors. The pilot screw adjustment must remain within the specification listed in **Table 2**.

A special procedure is required after the initial adjustment on some models. Refer to the following information:

Models BF20, BF2A

1. Connect a shop tachometer per the manufacturer's instructions.
2. Place the engine in a test tank or in the water under actual running conditions. Start the engine and allow it to reach normal operating temperature.
3. Observe the tachometer and slowly turn the pilot screw clockwise until the idle speed begins to drop. Note the position of the screw slot.
4. Observe the tachometer and slowly turn the pilot screw counterclockwise until the idle speed begins to drop. Note the position of the screw slot.

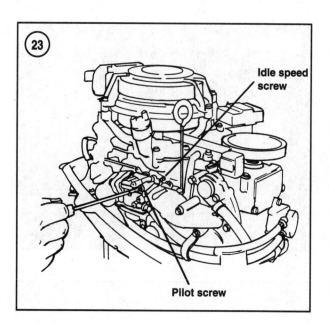

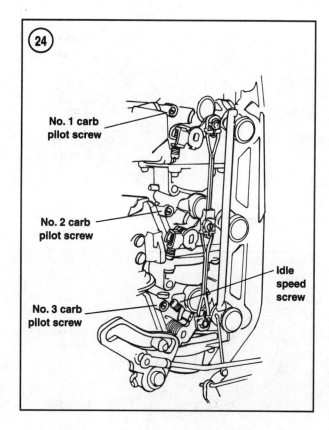

5. Observe the tachometer and slowly rotate the screw clockwise and counterclockwise until you observe the highest engine speed and the screw slot is between the positions noted in Steps 3 and 4. Remove the tachometer. Refer to *Idle Speed Adjustment* in this chapter and adjust the idle speed as indicated.

TIMING, SYNCHRONIZATION AND ADJUSTMENTS

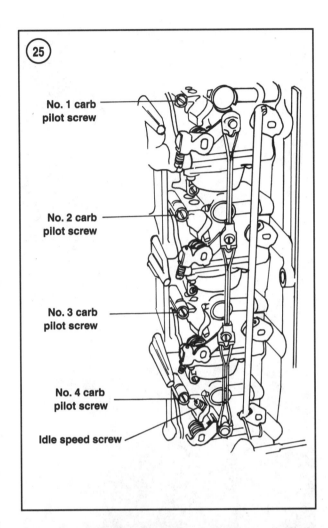

WARNING
High voltage is present when the engine is running. Stay clear of all spark plug wires. Never work while standing in water. Never work on the engine while it is running and the powerhead is wet.

CAUTION
Never run an outboard without providing cooling water. The water pump will be damaged within a few seconds if it runs dry. A damaged water pump results in insufficient water for proper cooling of the powerhead. The engine can overheat and/or suffer serious powerhead damage if it is run without sufficient cooling water.

Idle Speed Adjustment

Refer to *Pilot Screw Adjustment* in this chapter then perform the pilot screw adjustment prior to adjusting the idle speed.

To locate the idle speed screw, refer to the following illustrations:

1. For models BF20 and BF20A, refer to (**Figure 20**).
2. For models BF50A and BF5A, refer to (**Figure 21**).
3. For models BF75, BF8A and BF100, refer to (**Figure 22**).
4. For models BF9.9A and BF15A, refer to (**Figure 23**).
5. For models BF20A, BF25A and BF30A, refer to (**Figure 24**).
6. For models BF35A, BF40A, BF45A and BF50A, refer to (**Figure 24**).
7. For models BF75A and BF90A, refer to (**Figure 25**).
8. For models BF115A and BF130A, refer to (3, **Figure 19**).
9. Install a suitable tachometer to one of the spark plug leads. Follow the manufacturer's instructions to connect the tachometer.
10. Run the engine for 10 minutes at low speed to attain normal operating temperature.
11. Check the throttle lever or remote control lever to ensure they are in idle position. Refer to THROTTLE LINKAGE ADJUSTMENT in this chapter and adjust if necessary.
12. Refer to **Table 1** for the correct idle speed and gear position for your model. Perform this adjustment with the engine in a test tank or under actual running conditions. Have a qualified assistant operate the boat when the specifications list an *in gear* idle speed.
13. Shift the engine into the specified gear. Locate the idle speed adjusting screw.

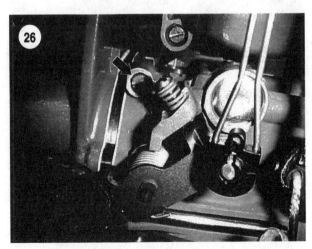

WARNING
Use extreme caution when working around a running engine. Stay clear of the flywheel and the propeller shaft.

14. Observe the idle speed on the tachometer as you adjust the screw. Stop when the idle speed is in the middle of the range listed in **Table 1**.

15. Slowly advance the throttle then bring it back down to the idle position. Observe the idle speed and readjust if necessary.

16. On models that list both an *in gear* and *out of gear* idle speed, perform the adjustments in both gear positions. Adjust the pilot screw if both specifications cannot be attained.

> *WARNING*
> *Use extreme caution when working around a running engine. Stay clear of the flywheel and the propeller shaft.*

> *WARNING*
> *High voltage is present when the engine is running. Stay clear of all spark plug wires. Never work while standing in water. Never work on the engine when the engine is running and the powerhead is wet.*

> *CAUTION*
> *Never run an outboard without providing cooling water. The water pump will be damaged within a few seconds if it runs dry. A damaged water pump results in insufficient water for proper cooling of the powerhead. The engine can overheat and/or suffer serious powerhead damage if it runs without sufficient cooling water.*

Carburetor Synchronization

Carburetor synchronization is required on all 3- and 4-cylinder models, except models BF115A and BF130A. Obtain a shop tachometer and vacuum gauge set Honda part No. 001000A before attempting this adjustment. Perform pilot screw and idle speed adjustments prior to performing carburetor synchronization. Recheck pilot screw and idle speed when synchronization is complete.

Locate all carburetor synchronization screws prior to beginning adjustment. Refer to the following to locate the synchronization screws.

1. For models BF20A, BF25A and BF30A, refer to **Figure 27** and **Figure 28**.

2. For models BF35A, BF40A, BF45A and BF50A, refer to **Figure 27** and **Figure 28**.

3. For models BF75A and BF90A, refer to **Figure 28** and **Figure 29**.

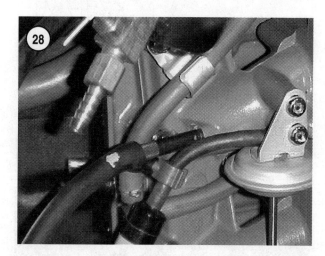

Models BF20A, BF25A, BF30A, BF35A, BF40A, BF45A, BF50A

1. Place the engine in a suitable test tank or place the boat in the water. Make sure that the water level is at least 152 mm (6.0 in.) above the upper water inlets on the gearcase.

2. Locate the three vacuum gauge fittings on the intake manifold runners (**Figure 28**). Slowly loosen, then remove all three fitting screws and sealing washers. Inspect the washers for torn or damaged surfaces. Discard the washers if you note any defects.

3. Using the fittings that accompany the gauge, attach the vacuum gauge set to all three fittings as indicated in **Figure 28**. Mark the cylinder number for the attached fitting on the gauges prior to performing any adjustments. Se-

TIMING, SYNCHRONIZATION AND ADJUSTMENTS

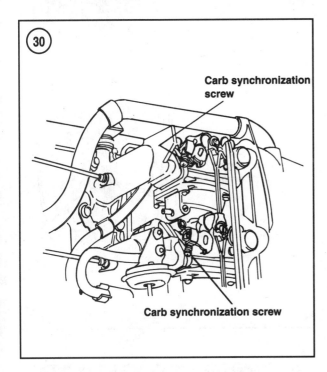

Carb synchronization screw

Carb synchronization screw

curely attach the vacuum gauge set to a location OFF the engine. Make sure all hoses and fittings are secure and cannot become entangled during engine operation.

4. Following the manufacturer's instructions, attach an accurate shop tachometer to the engine.

5. Start and run the engine for at least 10 minutes to attain normal operating temperature. Return the throttle setting to the idle position.

6. Refer to *Idle Speed Adjustment* (in this chapter) and check the engine idle speed. Correct the idle speed if necessary. Additional idle speed adjustments may be required during carburetor synchronization.

7. Note the reading on each vacuum gauge (**Figure 29**). A maximum difference of 20 mm (0.78in) Hg vacuum from the highest to lowest reading is acceptable. If correct adjustment is indicated on the vacuum gauges, go to Step 14.

8. If incorrect adjustment is indicated on the vacuum gauges, use **Figure 30** to locate the carburetor synchronization screws.

9. Watch the vacuum gage set while *slowly* rotating the No. 1 carburetor adjusting screw so the vacuum setting matches that of the No. 3 cylinder.

10. Slightly increase the engine speed for approximately 30 seconds, then return to idle speed. Wait a minute for the idle to stabilize. Observe the idle speed on the shop tachometer. Adjust the idle speed, if necessary, following the procedure listed in this chapter.

11. Watch the vacuum gauge set while *slowly* rotating the No. 2 carburetor adjusting screw so the vacuum setting matches those of the No. 1 and No. 3 cylinders.

12. Slightly increase the engine speed for approximately 30 seconds, then return to idle speed. Wait a minute for the idle to stabilize. Observe the idle speed on the shop tachometer. Adjust the idle speed, if necessary, following the procedure listed in this chapter.

13. Repeat Steps 8-10 until you obtain the correct vacuum readings and idle speed. Check and adjust the idle speed after each carburetor adjustment. The idle speed stabilizes and the idle quality improves as the vacuum readings become closer.

14. Turn the engine OFF. Remove the vacuum gauge and fittings. If needed, install new sealing washers onto the fitting screws. Install all three screws and tighten them securely.

Models BF75A, BF90A

1. Place the engine in a suitable test tank or place the boat in the water. Ensure that the water level is at least 152 mm (6.0 in.) above the upper water inlets on the gearcase.

2. Locate the four vacuum gauge fittings on the intake manifold runners (**Figure 27**). Slowly loosen, then remove all four fitting screws and sealing washers. Inspect the washers for torn or damaged surfaces. Discard the washers if defects are noted.

3. Using the fittings that accompany the gauge, attach the vacuum gauge set to all four fittings as indicated in **Figure 28**. Mark the cylinder number for the attached fitting on the gauges prior to performing any adjustments. Securely attach the vacuum gauge set to a location *off* the engine. Ensure that all hoses and fittings are secure and will not become entangled during engine operation.

4. Following the manufacturer's instructions, attach an accurate shop tachometer to the engine.

5. Start and run the engine for at least 10 minutes to attain normal operating temperature. Return the throttle setting to the idle position.

6. Refer to *Idle Speed Adjustment* in this chapter and check the engine idle speed. Correct the idle speed if necessary. Additional idle speed adjustments may be required during carburetor synchronization.

7. Note the reading on each vacuum gauge. A difference of 20 mm (0.78in) Hg vacuum from the highest to lowest reading on the gauges (**Figure 29**) is acceptable. When the gauge indicates the correct adjustment, proceed to Step 16.

8. If incorrect adjustment is indicated on the vacuum gauges, refer to **Figure 31** and locate the carburetor synchronization screws.

9. Watch the vacuum gage set while *slowly* rotating the No. 1 carburetor adjusting screw so the vacuum setting matches that of the No. 4 cylinder.

10. Slightly increase the engine speed for approximately 30 seconds, then return to idle speed. Wait a minute for the idle to stabilize. Observe the idle speed on the shop tachometer. Adjust the idle speed, if necessary, following the procedure listed in this Chapter.

11. Observe the vacuum gauge set while *slowly* rotating the No. 2 carburetor adjusting screw so the vacuum setting matches those of the No. 1 and No. 4 cylinders.

12. Slightly increase the engine speed for approximately 30 seconds, then return to idle speed. Wait a minute for the idle to stabilize. Observe the idle speed on the shop tachometer. Adjust the idle speed, if necessary, following the procedure listed in this Chapter.

13. Observe the vacuum gauge set while *slowly* rotating the No. 3 carburetor adjusting screw so the vacuum setting matches those of the No. 1, No. 2 and No. 4 cylinders.

14. Slightly increase the engine speed for approximately 30 seconds, then return to idle speed. Wait a minute for the idle to stabilize. Observe the idle speed on the shop tachometer. Adjust the idle speed, if necessary, following the procedure listed in this chapter.

15. Repeat Steps 8 through 14 until you obtain the correct vacuum readings and idle speed. Check and adjust the idle speed (**Figure 32**) after each carburetor adjustment. The idle speed stabilizes and the idle quality improves as the vacuum readings begin to balance.

16. Turn the engine *off*. Remove the vacuum gauge and fittings. If needed, install new sealing washers onto the fitting screws. Install all four screws and tighten them securely.

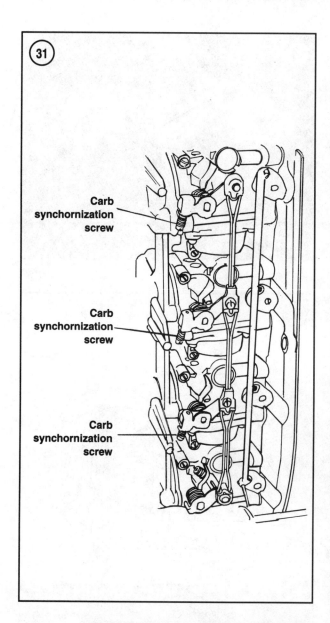

TIMING, SYNCHRONIZATION AND ADJUSTMENTS

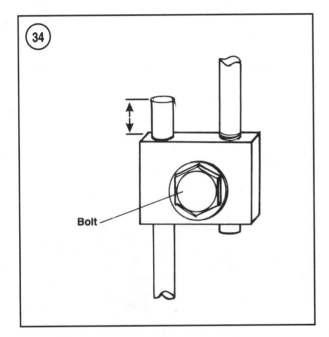

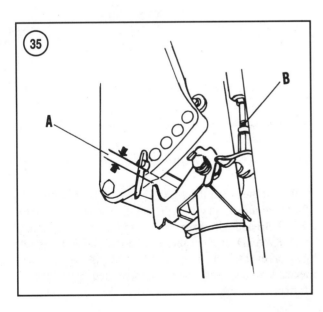

WARNING
The battery contains explosive gasses. Use extreme caution when removing or installing the battery cables. Refer to Chapter Four for the proper removal and installation of the battery terminals.

SHIFTING SYSTEM ADJUSTMENTS

This section provides the procedures to adjust the shifting system for all propeller and jet drive models. Adjustment procedures for the reverse locking mechanism are included as applicable.

Shift system adjustments require using a ruler and small feeler gauges.

WARNING
Remove all spark plug leads and both battery cables prior to removing the propeller to prevent injury.

Models BF20 and BF2A (Standard Rotation)

Shift adjustment is not required as these models use a non-shifting gearcase.

Models BF50 and BF5A (Standard Rotation)

Shift adjustment is performed at the upper-to-lower shift shaft connector. Adjustment for the reverse lock mechanism follows the shift shaft adjustment.

1. Remove the spark plug and connect the spark plug lead to an engine ground. Shift the gear selector into forward gear. Follow the procedures in Chapter Nine and remove the propeller

2. Locate and carefully pry the rubber plug from the opening on the lower port side of the drive shaft housing. Locate the shift shaft connector inside the opening (**Figure 33**).

3. Measure the distance the lower shift rod protrudes above the shift shaft connector at the point indicated in **Figure 34**. Correct adjustment is indicated when a measurement of 4.5-6.5 mm (0.177-0.26 in.) is noted.

4. If adjustment is required, loosen the bolt (**Figure 34**) enough to move the lower shift shaft up or down until a correct measurement is obtained. Securely tighten the bolt and verify the correct measurements.

5. Locate the tilt pin and reverse lock hook mechanism on the engine (**Figure 35**). Shift the gear selector to neutral. Using feeler gauges, measure the clearance between the tilt pin and reverse lock hook at the indicated points (A,

Figure 35). The clearance is 0.1-1.0 mm (0.004-0.040 in.).

6. If adjustment is required, locate the reverse hook rod and adjusting nut (B, **Figure 35**). Hold the lower nut with a wrench, then loosen the locknut. Adjust the lower nut (B, **Figure 35**) until you obtain the correct measurement. Hold the lower nut with a suitable wrench and securely tighten the locknut.

7. Shift the gear selector to reverse. Ensure that the propeller shaft does *not* rotate clockwise. Make sure that the engine will not tilt UP when shifted into REVERSE, and tilts UP when shifted into neutral or forward. Readjust if you observe incorrect operation.

8. Refer to Chapter Nine, and install the propeller. Install the spark plug and spark plug lead.

Models BF75, BF8A and BF100 (Standard Rotation)

Shift adjustment is made at the upper shift shaft-to-shift linkage connector. Adjustment of the reverse lock mechanism is not required. Damaged or worn components are usually present if you note incorrect operation of the reverse lock mechanism.

1. Remove the spark plugs and connect the spark plug leads to an engine ground. Disconnect both battery cables from the battery on electric start models.
2. Shift the gear selector into forward. Refer to Chapter Nine and remove the propeller.
3. Locate the shift lever and shift shaft on the engine. Remove the cotter pin and shift linkage pin from the shift linkage (**Figure 36**).
4. Rotate the connector on the upper end of the shift shaft clockwise until it is fully seated onto the shift shaft. Turn the connector counterclockwise 4-½ turns, then enough to align the hole in the connector with the holes in the shift linkage (**Figure 36**). Make sure that the detent roller is properly seated into the notch on the shift linkage (**Figure 36**).
5. Install the shift linkage pin through the shift linkage and shift shaft connector as indicated (**Figure 36**). Install the cotter pin and bend the ends over to secure the fit.
6. Shift the gear selector into FORWARD gear and attempt to rotate the propeller shaft counterclockwise as viewed from behind the propeller shaft. The propeller shaft should *not* turn counterclockwise.
7. Shift the gearcase into NEUTRAL and rotate the propeller shaft in both directions. The propeller shaft should turn freely clockwise and counterclockwise.
8. Shift the gearcase into REVERSE and attempt to rotate the propeller shaft clockwise as viewed from behind the

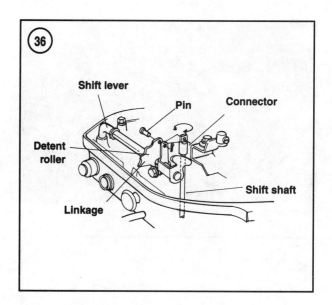

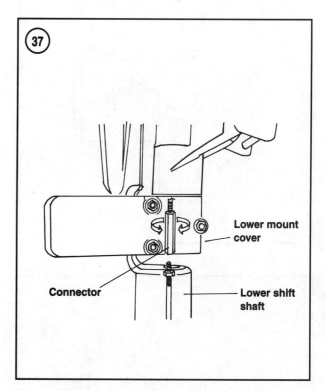

propeller shaft. The propeller shaft should *not* turn clockwise.

9. Repeat Steps 3-5 if further adjustment is necessary.
10. Make sure the engine will not tilt up when shifted into REVERSE and will tilt up when shifted into NEUTRAL or FORWARD. Inspect the reverse lock hook for damaged or excessively worn components if the tilt lock mechanism does not function as specified. See Chapter Thirteen.

TIMING, SYNCHRONIZATION AND ADJUSTMENTS

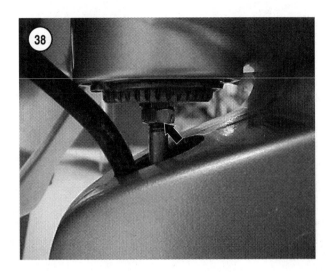

11. Install the propeller (Chapter Nine). Install the spark plugs and attach the plug leads. On electric start models, connect the battery cables to the battery.

Models BF9.9A and BF15A (Standard Rotation)

Perform shift adjustment at the upper-to-lower shift connector. Adjustment of the reverse lock mechanism is not required. Damaged or worn components are indicated if you note incorrect operation of the reverse lock mechanism.

1. Remove the spark plugs and connect the spark plug leads to an engine ground. Disconnect both battery cables from the battery on electric start models.
2. Place the gear selector into FORWARD. Refer to Chapter Nine and remove the propeller.
3. Locate the upper-to-lower shift shaft connector on the drive shaft housing (**Figure 37**). Hold the upper nut with a wrench and loosen the lower nut. Turn the upper nut until it releases from the lower shift shaft.
4. With the gear selector in FORWARD, turn the upper nut until it protrudes 3.0 mm (0.118 in.) below the lower edge of the engine mount cover.
5. Mate the lower shift shaft to the upper nut. Hold the lower shift shaft in contact with the upper nut. Ensure that the upper nut threads completely onto the lower shift shaft.
6. Turn the upper nut onto the lower shift shaft until it protrudes 6.0 mm (0.236 in.) below the lower edge of the engine mount cover. Hold the upper nut with a wrench and securely tighten the lower nut against the upper nut.
7. Place the gearcase in NEUTRAL and rotate the propeller shaft back and forth. The propeller shaft should turn freely in both directions.

8. Shift the gearcase into FORWARD gear and attempt to rotate the propeller shaft counterclockwise. The propeller shaft should *not* turn counterclockwise.
9. Shift the gearcase in REVERSE gear and attempt to rotate the propeller shaft clockwise. The propeller shaft should *not* turn clockwise.
10. Make sure the engine will not tilt up when shifted into REVERSE and will tilt up with shifted into NEUTRAL or FORWARD. Inspect the reverse lock mechanism if it does not operate as described. See Chapter Thirteen.
11. Install the propeller as described in Chapter Nine. Install the spark plugs and attach the plug leads. Connect the battery cables to the battery on electric start models.

Model BF20A, BF25A, BF30A, BF35A, BF40A, BF45A and BF50A

Make shift adjustments at the upper-to-lower shift connector (**Figure 38**). These models use the hydraulic trim/tilt system to provide a reverse lock system. Adjustment of the reverse lock system is not required. Improper use or failure of the trim/tilt system is indicated if the motor tilts up when in reverse gear. Refer to Chapter Three for troubleshooting procedures.

Shift system adjustment varies with the type of control used. Adjustment is provided for both the tiller control and remote control models. Refer to the procedures for the selected model.

Tiller control models

1. Remove the spark plugs and connect the spark plug leads to an engine ground. Disconnect both battery cables from the battery on electric start models only.
2. Locate the shift linkage detents (**Figure 36**) and the lower-to-upper shift shaft connector at the lower side of the drive shaft housing (**Figure 38**).
3. Shift the gear selector into REVERSE. Observe the shift shaft linkage detents to ensure that the roller is positioned in the R detent. Hold the upper shift shaft connector nut with a suitable wrench, then loosen the lower nut (**Figure 38**). Turn the upper nut until it fully releases from the lower shift shaft, with approximately 3.0 mm (0.118 in.) of clearance between the shafts remaining.
4. Turn the lower nut until 8.0 mm (0.315 in.) of the thread on the lower shift shaft is exposed. Hold the lower nut in this position.

5. Verify that the gearcase is still in REVERSE gear. Attempt to rotate the propeller shaft clockwise. The propeller shaft should *not* turn clockwise. If necessary, move the lower shift shaft down until the propeller shaft will not rotate clockwise.

6. Turn the upper nut until it moves down and contacts the threaded section of the lower shift shaft. Make contact between the upper nut and the lower shift shaft. Turn the upper nut until in contacts the lower nut.

7. Hold the upper nut with a wrench, then securely tighten the lower nut against the upper nut.

8. Shift the gearcase into NEUTRAL and turn the propeller shaft back and forth. The propeller shaft should turn freely in both directions.

9. Shift the gearcase into FORWARD gear and attempt to rotate the propeller shaft counterclockwise. The propeller shaft should *not* turn counterclockwise.

10. Shift the gearcase into REVERSE gear and attempt to rotate the propeller shaft clockwise. The propeller shaft should *not* turn clockwise.

11. Repeat the entire adjustment procedure if the gearcase does not shift as specified.

12. Install the propeller as described in Chapter Nine. Install the spark plugs and attach the plug leads. On electric start models, connect the battery cables to the battery.

Remote control models

1. Remove all spark plugs and connect the spark plug leads to an engine ground. Disconnect both battery cables from the battery, on electric start models.

2. Locate the shift linkage detents (**Figure 36**) and the lower-to-upper shift shaft connector at the lower side of the drive shaft housing (**Figure 38**).

3. Place the remote control handle in NEUTRAL. Observe the shift linkage detents (**Figure 36**) to ensure that the roller is positioned in the N detent. If adjustment is correct, go to Step 7.

4. If adjustment is required, locate the shift cable connection on the shift lever (**Figure 39**). Remove the locking pin and washer and slide the shift cable connector from the shift lever.

5. Position the shift lever so the roller is in the N detent on the shift linkage. Loosen the locknut on the shift cable connector. Adjust the connector to allow it to slide onto the shift lever while the roller is in the N detent. Ensure that the connector is fully threaded onto the shift cable.

6. Place the cable connector into the shift lever along with the washers. Install the locking pin. Securely tighten the locknut against the shift cable connector.

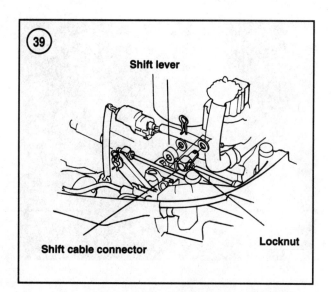

7. Place the remote control into REVERSE. Observe the shift shaft linkage detents to ensure that the roller is position in the R detent. Hold the upper shift shaft connector nut with a wrench, then loosen the lower nut (**Figure 38**). Turn the upper nut until you see that it fully releases from the lower shift shaft and has approximately 3.0 mm (0.118 in.) of clearance.

8. Turn the lower nut (**Figure 38**) until 8.0 mm (0.314 in.) of the thread on the lower shift shaft is exposed. Maintain the lower nut in this position.

9. Gently rotate the propeller shaft clockwise (as viewed from the rear) to ensure the gearcase is in REVERSE. Correct gearcase shift position prevents the propeller shaft from rotating clockwise. If necessary, move the lower shift shaft down until the propeller shaft cannot rotate clockwise.

10. Turn the upper nut until it contacts the threaded section of the lower shift shaft. Hold the upper nut against the lower shift shaft; turn the upper nut until in contacts the lower nut.

11. Hold the upper nut with a suitable wrench, then securely tighten the lower nut against the upper nut.

12. Shift the gearcase into NEUTRAL and turn the propeller shaft back and forth. The propeller shaft should turn freely in both directions.

13. Shift the gearcase into FORWARD gear and attempt to rotate the propeller shaft counterclockwise. The propeller shaft should *not* turn counterclockwise.

14. Shift the gearcase into REVERSE gear and attempt to rotate the propeller shaft clockwise. The propeller shaft should *not* turn clockwise.

15. Repeat the entire adjustment procedure if the gearcase does not shift as specified.

TIMING, SYNCHRONIZATION AND ADJUSTMENTS

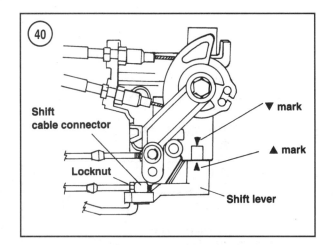

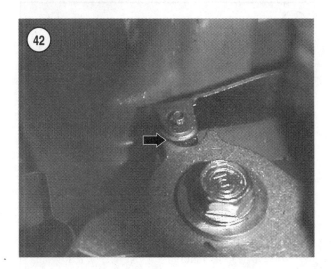

16. Install the propeller as described in Chapter Nine. Install the spark plugs and attach the plug leads. On electric start models, connect the battery cables to the battery.

Models BF75A, BF90A, BF115A, BF130A

Perform shift adjustments at the shift cable pivot connector on the engine-mounted shift lever. These models use the hydraulic trim/tilt system to provide a reverse lock system. Adjusting the reverse lock system is not required. Improper use or failure of the trim/tilt system is indicated if the motor tilts up when running in reverse. Refer to Chapter Three for troubleshooting procedures.

Shift system adjustment varies slightly with the type of control used. The adjustment procedures provide instructions for both types of controls.

1. Remove the spark plugs and connect the spark plug leads to an engine ground. Disconnect both battery cables from the battery on electric start models only.
2. Locate the shift lever and shift/throttle bracket (**Figure 40**) on the port side of the base engine.
3. Place the shift selector (tiller or remote control) in neutral. Inspect the triangle marks on the shift lever and shift/throttle bracket. The triangle marks should align perfectly when the neutral gear is selected. Go to Step 8 if this adjustment is correct.
4. If adjustment is required, loosen the locknut (**Figure 40**) from the shift cable connector.
5. Remove the locking pin and washers, then slide the shift cable pivot connector from the shift lever.
6. Rotate the pivot connector until it can be installed into the shift lever with the triangle marks aligned and the shift selector (tiller or remote control) in the NEUTRAL position. Make sure that the pivot connector is fully threaded onto the threaded section of the shift cable.
7. Slide the shift cable pivot connector and washers into the shift lever as shown in **Figure 40**. Install the locking pin.
8. Locate the neutral switch and detent roller on the engine (**Figure 41**). Note the alignment of the detent roller to the detent (**Figure 42**) on the shift lever and the alignment of the neutral switch and the shift lever.
9. The detent roller should be in the detent notch and the tip on the shift lever aligned with the tip of the neutral switch (**Figure 41**).
10. If adjustment to the detent roller is required, loosen the retaining bolt for the detent roller (**Figure 42**) and move the detent roller until the roller is positioned in the detent notch. Tighten the detent roller-retaining bolt securely.
11. If adjustment to the neutral switch-to-shift lever is required, perform Steps 5-7.
12. Shift the gearcase into NEUTRAL and turn the propeller shaft back and forth. The propeller shaft should turn freely in both directions.

13. Shift the gearcase into FORWARD gear and attempt to rotate the propeller shaft counterclockwise. The propeller shaft should *not* turn counterclockwise.
14. Shift the gearcase into REVERSE gear and attempt to rotate the propeller shaft clockwise. The propeller shaft should *not* turn clockwise.
15. Repeat the entire adjustment procedure if the gearcase does not shift as specified.
16. Install the propeller as described in Chapter Nine. Install the spark plugs and attach the plug leads. On electric start models, connect the battery cables to the battery.

Jet Models

WARNING
The linkage connecting the cable pivot bracket to the scoop lever must attach through the lever's lower hole.

On jet drive models, the shift cable connects directly to the jet drive unit. Proper adjustment of the jet drive unit allows the reverse scoop to completely clear the discharge nozzle when in FORWARD (**Figure 43**). The reverse scoop must completely cover the discharge nozzle when in REVERSE. Neutral adjustment positions the scoop halfway between these points.

To adjust the jet drive, first position the control in FORWARD. Adjust the cable until the cable pivot bracket aligns with the linkage that connects the cable bracket to the scoop arm (**Figure 44**). The scoop should contact the rubber pad on the bottom of the jet drive.

Position the shift handle in NEUTRAL. Loosen the nut (**Figure 44**) and move the stop to contact the scoop lever. Securely tighten the nut. Check for proper directional control before returning the engine to service.

NEUTRAL START SYSTEM ADJUSTMENT

This section provides the procedures to adjust the start-in-gear protection cable or neutral switch.

Models BF20 and BF2A

These models are equipped with a non-shifting gearcase; a neutral start protection system is not required.

Models BF50 and BF5A

A link rod connecting to the shift selector activates the neutral start system when in FORWARD or REVERSE gear. If the rewind starter is pulled when the engine is in

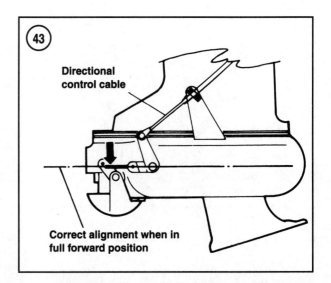

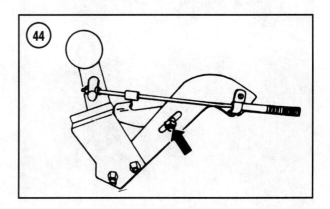

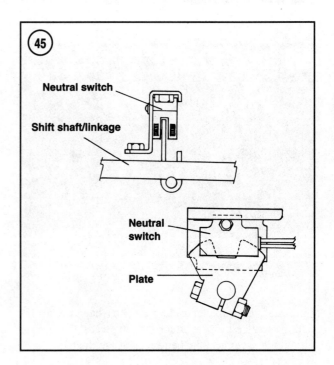

TIMING, SYNCHRONIZATION AND ADJUSTMENTS

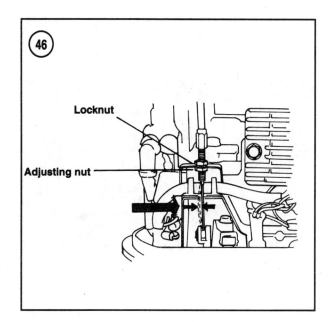

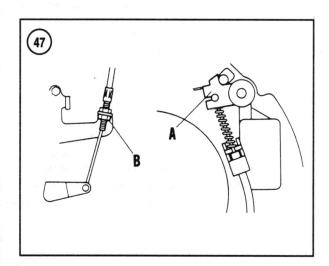

plate passes between the slot in the switch. A wire connecting the neutral switch to the CDI unit prevents spark at the plug if starting is attempted.

Adjusting the switch is not required, provided the shifting system operates correctly. Correct any loose, bent or misaligned components if the opening in the plate does not align with the slot when in NEUTRAL gear.

Models BF9.9A and BF15A (Manual Start)

1. Remove the spark plugs and connect the spark plug leads to an engine ground.

2. Position the gear selector in NEUTRAL. Lightly push the cable wire in the directions indicated in **Figure 46**, noting the amount of cable wire side movement. The wire side movement should be 2.0-3.0 mm (0.078-0.118 in.).

3. If adjustment is required, loosen the upper nut (**Figure 46**) and adjust the lower nut until the correct amount of cable wire side movement is measured. Tighten the upper nut to 10.0 N·m (89.0 in. lbs.). Refer to Step 2 and check for proper adjustment.

4. Install the spark plugs and spark plug leads.

Models BF20A, BF25A and BF30A

Manual start models

A cable connected to the shift linkage activates a rewind starter-mounted neutral start mechanism.

1. Remove the spark plugs and connect the spark plug leads to an engine ground.

2. Locate the neutral start mechanism on the rewind starter housing (**Figure 47**).

3. Place the shift selector in NEUTRAL. Check the alignment of the mark on the rewind housing and the cable slot on the mechanism (A, **Figure 47**). The cable slot should align with the mark on the rewind housing.

4. If adjustment is required, follow the cable to the bracket-mounted adjustment nuts (at the cable connection to the shift linkage).

5. Loosen the nut on the cable side of the bracket and adjust the nut on the linkage side of the bracket (B, **Figure 47**) until the mechanism is properly adjusted. Securely tighten the adjusting nuts. Verify proper adjustment. Attempt to pull the rewind starter with the engine in gear. Correct the adjustment if you are able to pull the rewind starter.

6. Install the spark plugs and spark plug leads.

gear, a spring-loaded lever in the neutral start system makes contact with a projection on a wheel that is mounted to the flywheel. This system prevents rotation. System malfunction is generally caused by worn, bent or damaged components. Adjustments to this system are not required. Refer to Chapter Eleven for additional information.

Models BF75, BF8A and BF100

These models with Serial No. 1300001-on are equipped with an engine-mounted neutral start system (**Figure 45**). While in neutral gear, an opening on a shift linkage-mounted plate (**Figure 45**) aligns with a slot in the switch. If shifted into FORWARD or REVERSE gear, the

Electric start models

These models are equipped with a neutral start switch to prevent operation of the electric starter motor when shifted into forward or reverse gear. Adjustment of the switch is not necessary. Incorrect operation is generally the result of a malfunction of the switch. Refer to Chapter Three for troubleshooting of the neutral switch. Adjust the shift cables and linkage if you note incorrect operation, but the switch tests correctly.

Models BF35A, BF40A, BF45A, BF50A

These models are equipped with a neutral start switch to prevent operation of the electric starter motor when shifted into forward or reverse gear. Adjusting the switch is unnecessary. Incorrect operation is generally caused by a switch malfunction. Refer to Chapter Three for troubleshooting and testing of the neutral switch. Adjust the shift cables and linkages if incorrect operation is noted, but the switch operates correctly.

Models BF75A, BF90A, BF115A and BF130A

Refer to *Shifting System Adjustment* in this chapter. The neutral switch should function properly if the shift system is correctly adjusted.

TRIM SENDER ADJUSTMENT

Adjustment of the sender is not required. Proper operation of the sender should occur if the sender is correctly mounted to the port clamp bracket. If improper operation is noted, refer to Chapter Three for the troubleshooting procedure for the trim sender.

TIMING BELT TENSIONER

Timing belt tension adjustment is not required, as a spring provides proper tension on the belt. Never push the pulley closer to the belt to increase timing belt tension. To properly adjust the timing belt tensioner mount, loosen (but do not remove) the pulley mounting bolt (**Figure 48**). Allow the spring to pivot the pulley toward the timing belt, then tighten the pulley bolt to 45.0 N•m (33 ft. lbs)

TABLE 1 IDLE SPEED SPECIFICATIONS

Model	RPM
BF20, BF2A	1300-1500 (in forward gear)
BF50, BF5A	1200-1400 (in forward gear)
	1500-1600 (in neutral)
BF75, BF8A, BF100	1100-1300 (in neutral)
BF9.9A, BF15A	1050-1150 (in neutral)
BF25A	850-950 (in neutral)
BF30A, BF35A, BF40A, BF45A, BF50A, BF75A, BF90A	900-1000 (in neutral)
BF115A and BF130A	700-800 (in neutral)

TIMING, SYNCHRONIZATION AND ADJUSTMENTS

TABLE 2 PILOT SCREW ADJUSTMENT SPECIFICATIONS

Model	Turns out from a light seat
BF20, BF2A	-
BF20S	
Serial No. 1000001-1007046	2 turns
Serial No. 1007047-on	1-3/4 turns
BF20L	2-1/8 turns
BF2A	1-¼ turns
BF50 & BF5A	2-3/8 turns
BF75, BF8A & BF100	1-¾ to 2 ¼
BF9.9A	2-3/4
BF15A	1- 5/8
BF20A	2 turns
BF25A	2 turns
BF30A	3 turns
BF35A, BF40A, BF45A & BF50A	2-/8 turns
BF75A	1-7/8 turns
BF90A	2-1/4 turns

TABLE 3 DASHPOT CLEARANCE

Model	Clearance
BF20A, BF25A & BF30A	6.3 mm (0.248 in.)
BF35A, BF40A, BF45A & BF50A	4.2 mm (0.165 in.)

TABLE 4 BREAKER POINT GAP

Model	Gap specification
BF75 & BF100	0.3-0.4 mm (0.012-0.016 in.)

Chapter Six

Fuel System Repair

This chapter provides instructions on removal, repair and installation of all fuel system components. Those components covered include the fuel tanks, fuel hoses, connectors and fuel pumps. Fuel filters, silencer cover, carburetor and EFI fuel components are also covered as well.

Diagrams are provided to assist with fuel hose routing and identifying component mounting locations. Refer to these when removing and installing components. Drawings are also provided for the various carburetors and fuel system components. Refer to these drawings when disassembling or assembling all fuel system components.

> *WARNING*
> *Use caution when working with the fuel system. Never smoke around fuel or fuel vapors. Make sure that no flame or source of ignition is present in the work area. Flame or sparks can ignite fuel or vapor resulting in fire or explosion.*

> *WARNING*
> *Always disconnect both battery cables before working on the engine.*

When disassembling carburetors, pay very close attention to location and orientation of the internal parts. Fuel jet size changes with the model and carburetor location on the engine. Fuel jets normally have a jet number stamped on the side or opening end. Make a drawing or note the fuel jet number and location in the carburetor. Take all necessary steps to ensure that fuel jets and other carburetor components are reinstalled in the correct location.

Replacement fuel jets can be purchased at a Honda dealership or carburetor specialty shop. Replacement fuel jets must have the same size and shape of opening as the original fuel jets.

Engines used at higher altitudes or in an extreme environment may require that alternate fuel jets be installed. Contact a Honda dealership for additional information.

Use great care and patience when removing fuel jets and other threaded or pressed in components. Clean the passage without removing the jet if they cannot be removed without damaging them.

Carburetor fuel jets are easily damaged if the screwdriver slips in the slot. Never install a damaged jet in the carburetor. The fuel or air flow characteristics may be altered and can cause performance problems or potentially serious engine damage.

To avoid potential fuel or air leakage, replace all gaskets, seals or O-rings anytime a fuel system component is assembled.

The most important step in carburetor repair is the cleaning process. Use a good quality solvent, suitable reservoir for the solvent and cleaning brush to remove the varnish-like deposits that commonly occur in a fuel system. Spray type carburetor cleaners are available at most auto parts stores and are effective in removing most deposits. Avoid using any solvents that are not suitable for aluminum. Remove all plastic or rubber components from the fuel pump, carburetor or filter assembly before clean-

FUEL SYSTEM REPAIR

ing them with solvent. Gently scrape away gasket material with a scraper. To prevent potential leakage, avoid scratching or nicking gasket surfaces. Use a stiff parts cleaning brush and solvent to remove deposits from the carburetor bowl. Never use a wire brush as delicate surfaces can become damaged. Blow out all passages and orifices with compressed air. A piece of straw from a broom works well to clean out small passages. Never use stiff wire for this purpose as the wire may enlarge the size of the passage and alter the carburetor calibration. Allow the component to soak in the solvent for several hours if the deposits are particularly difficult to remove

FUEL TANK AND FUEL HOSE COMPONENTS

An integral or engine mounted fuel tank is used on models BF20 and BF2A. A portable or built-in fuel tank may be used on all other models. Most Honda outboards use the original portable fuel tank that came with the engine. They have the Honda name on the body of the fuel tank. Purchase any required parts for these fuel tanks from a local Honda dealership.

Portable fuel tanks are manufactured by several different companies and your Honda outboard may be equipped with any of them. The types of components used, cleaning and repair procedures are similar for all brands of fuel tanks. Refer to a reputable marine repair shop or marine dealership when parts are required for other brands of fuel tanks.

A built-in fuel tank may be used on all models, except BF20 and BF2A. They are often difficult to locate in the boat and access is impossible in some cases. On some applications, removal of major boat components is required if the tank must be removed. Fortunately, access panels are installed in most boats to provide access to fuel line fittings and the fuel level sender assembly.

Major fuel tank components requiring service include the fuel pickup, fuel level sender, fuel fill fitting and the antisiphon device.

Fuel Tank Removal Models BF20 and BF2A

1. Remove the engine cover. Turn the fuel petcock to the OFF position.
2. Locate the fuel hose at the carburetor connection (2, **Figure 1**). Carefully remove the clamp from the fuel hose connection at the carburetor.
3. Squeeze the fuel hose shut, which is near the connection, with a pair of pliers. Carefully pull the fuel hose from the carburetor fuel fitting and direct the hose into a suitable container. Release the pliers from the hose and allow the fuel in the fuel tank to drain into the container. Have a shop towel handy as residual fuel may spill from the fuel hose. Immediately clean up any spilled fuel.
4. Refer to Chapter Eleven and remove the rewind starter from the engine. Remove the two nuts that attach the fuel tank to the engine, then carefully lift the fuel tank from the engine.
5. Remove the fill cap from the tank. Pour any residual fuel from the tank into a container. Dispose of all drained fuel in a responsible manner. Remove the fuel hose from the fuel tank fitting and carefully pull the filter from the fitting.
6. Thoroughly clean the fuel tank with a suitable solvent. Inspect the tank mounted filter for blockage or damage. Replace as required. Drain all solvent from the tank and dry it with compressed air. Repeat the cleaning process until the tank is completely clean. Inspect the tank for cracks or other physical damage and replace the tank if any defects are noted.
7. The installation is the reverse of removal. Inspect all fuel hoses and clamps. Replace any fuel hose that has cracks, holes or leaks. Replace any fuel hose clamp that is physically damaged, corroded or lacks spring tension. Tighten all fasteners securely. Correct all fuel leaks at once.

Portable Fuel Tank

Portable remote fuel tanks may require periodic cleaning and inspection. If water is present in the tank, inspect the remainder of the fuel system for potential contamination.

1. Remove the fuel hose connector and fuel tank cap (1 and 4, **Figure 2**). Empty the tank into a container for proper disposal.
2. Remove the screws that retain the fuel metering assembly. Carefully remove the fuel metering assembly from the tank. Never force the assembly as damage may occur. Remove and discard the gasket between the fuel metering assembly and fuel tank.
3. Check for free movement of the float arm on the fuel metering assembly. Replace the assembly if binding cannot be corrected by bending the float arm into the correct position.
4. Inspect the float. Replace the float if suffers from any physical damage or is saturated with fuel. Inspect the fuel pickup for damage or blockage. Clean or replace as required.
5. Add a small amount of solvent to the fuel tank. Block the fuel metering assembly opening with a shop towel. Install the fuel tank cap. Shake or agitate the tank for a few

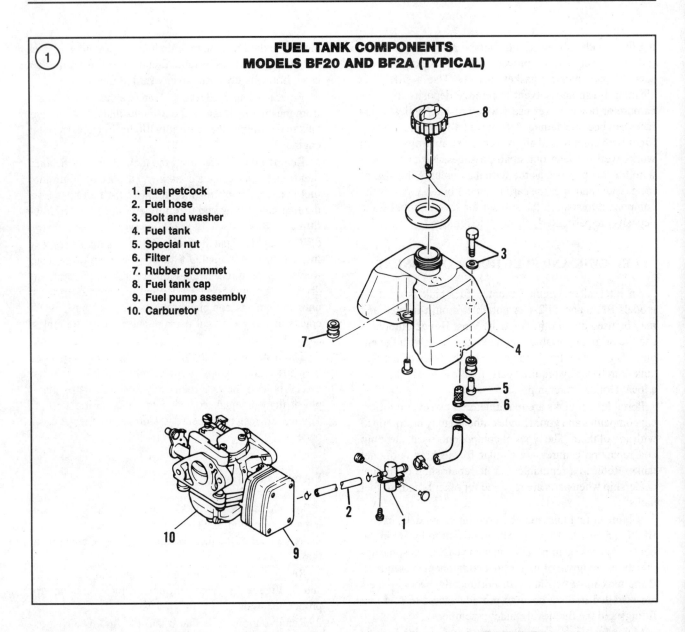

FUEL TANK COMPONENTS MODELS BF20 AND BF2A (TYPICAL)

1. Fuel petcock
2. Fuel hose
3. Bolt and washer
4. Fuel tank
5. Special nut
6. Filter
7. Rubber grommet
8. Fuel tank cap
9. Fuel pump assembly
10. Carburetor

minutes. Empty the solvent and blow the tank dry with compressed air.

Built-In Fuel Tank

The only components that can be serviced, without major disassembly of the boat, include the fuel pickup, fuel fill, fuel level sender and antisiphon device. These components are available from many different suppliers. Removal and inspection varies by model and brand. Contact the tank manufacturer or boat manufacturer for specific instructions. Always replace any gasket or seal when they are disturbed or suspected of leaking.

WARNING
Fuel leakage can lead to fire and explosion with potential bodily injury or death. Check for and correct fuel leakage after any repair is made to the fuel system.

Primer Bulb

The primer bulb or hand pump is located between the fuel tank and the engine (2, **Figure 2**). Refer to Chapter Three to test the primer bulb.

1. Disconnect the hose that connects the fuel tank to the engine. Drain the fuel from the hose into a container for proper disposal. Remove and discard the fuel hose clamps at both fuel hose connections to the primer bulb.

FUEL SYSTEM REPAIR

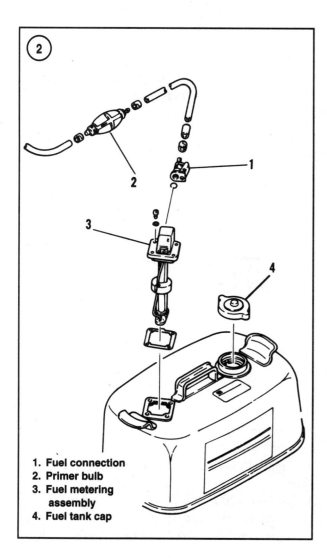

1. Fuel connection
2. Primer bulb
3. Fuel metering assembly
4. Fuel tank cap

2. Note the arrow (**Figure 3**) direction on the primer bulb, then remove the primer bulb from the fuel hoses. Drain any fuel remaining in the primer bulb into a suitable container.

3. Squeeze the primer bulb until fully collapsed. Replace the bulb if it does not freely expand when released. Replace the bulb if it appears weathered, has surface cracks or is hard to squeeze.

4. Inspect the fuel hoses for wear, damage, or leaks. Replace both fuel hoses if defects are noted.

5. Installation is the reverse of removal. Note the direction of flow (**Figure 3**) as the new bulb is installed onto the fuel hose. Arrows are present on the new bulb for correct orientation. The arrow must align with the direction of fuel flow to the engine. Carefully slide the fuel hoses onto the fittings on the primer bulb.

6. Always install new fuel clamps. Make sure that the fuel clamps are securely tightened. Squeeze the primer bulb and check for any indication of fuel leakage. Correct any fuel leakage at once.

Fuel Hoses

Fuel hoses vary by model and location on the engine. Refer to the provided illustrations for correct hose connections and routing. Use only Honda replacement hoses that meet US Coast Guard requirements for marine applications. Never install a fuel hose that is smaller in diameter than the original hose.

Inspect all fuel hoses and replace hoses that feel sticky or spongy to the touch, are hard and brittle or have surface

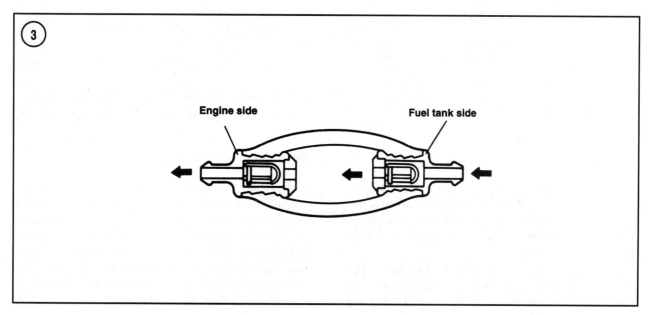

cracks. Replace hoses that have splits on the ends instead of cutting the end off and attaching the hose. To avoid hose failure or interference with other components, never cut the replacement hose shorter or longer than the original. If one fuel hose on the engine requires replacement due to wear, others likely will have similar defects. Replace all fuel hoses to help prevent potential leakage.

NOTE
Some models are equipped with check valves located in various hoses on the engine. Note the check valve orientation prior to removing the hose or valve.

Fuel Hose Connectors

Connectors used on fuel hoses include the quick connect type (**Figure 4**), spring type hose clamp (5, **Figure 5**) and plastic locking tie (**Figure 6**) clamps. The plastic locking tie clamp must be cut to be removed. Replace them with the correct Honda part. Some plastic locking ties are not suitable for the application and may fail. Use the same width as was removed. Pull the end through the clamp until the hose is securely fastened and will not rotate on the fitting. Avoid pulling the clamp too tight as the clamp may be damaged.

Inspect the quick connect clamp by squeezing the primer bulb while checking for leakage at the engine side quick connector. Replace the connector(s) if leakage is observed at the engine or fuel tank end.

Remove the spring type clamps by squeezing the ends together with a pair of pliers while carefully moving the clamp away from the fitting. Replace the clamp if it is corroded, bent, deformed or lost spring tension.

WARNING
Fuel leakage can lead to fire or explosion with potential bodily injury, death or destruction of property. Always correct fuel leakage after any repair is made to the fuel system.

Fuel Pump

Two methods are used to move fuel from the tank to the engine. Models BF20 and BF2A use gravity to feed fuel to the carburetor. Engine mounted mechanical fuel pumps (**Figure 7**) are used on all other models to move fuel from the fuel tank to the engine.

Fuel pump mounting location, number of fuel pumps used and fuel pump hose routing/connections vary by model. To assist with fuel pump location and fuel pump

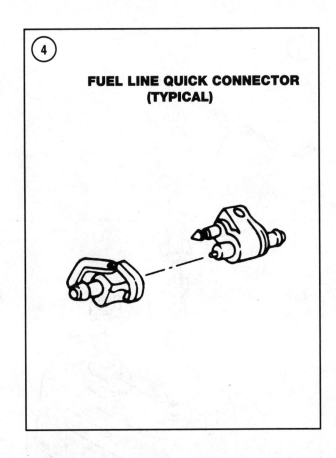

FUEL LINE QUICK CONNECTOR (TYPICAL)

hose routing/connections, refer to the following illustrations.

1. For models BF20 and BF2A refer to **Figure 8**.
2. For models BF50 and BF5A refer to **Figure 9**.
3. For models BF75, BF8A and BF100 refer to **Figure 10**.
4. For models BF9.9A and BF15A refer to **Figure 11**.
5. For models BF20A, BF25A and BF30A refer to **Figure 12**.
6. For models BF35A, BF40A, BF45A and BF50A refer to **Figure 13**.
7. For models BF75A and BF90A refer to **Figure 14**.
8. For models BF115A and BF130A refer to **Figure 15**.

Fuel Pump Repair/Replacement

Repair or replacement of engine mounted fuel pumps is possible without removing the carburetor or other fuel system components. Repair the fuel pump only if you are certain that the carburetor or other fuel system components are in good condition. Mark all components during disassembly to ensure proper position of the components upon assembly. Replace hoses that are hard or brittle. Use care to avoid damaging the fuel pump fittings. Refer to

FUEL SYSTEM REPAIR

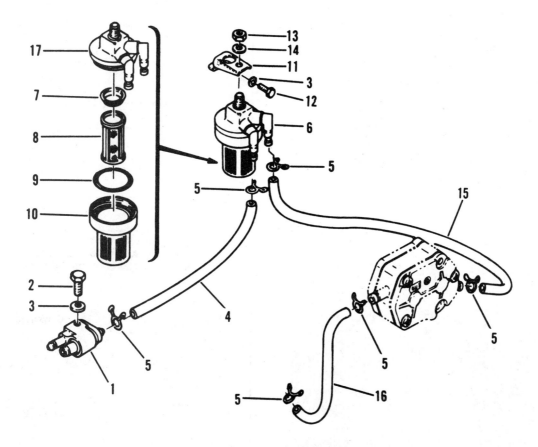

FUEL FILTER AND PUMP ASSEMBLY (TYPICAL)

1. Fuel hose connector
2. Bolt
3. Washer
4. Fuel hose
5. Hose clamp
6. Fuel filter
7. Gasket
8. Filter element
9. O-ring
10. Filter bowl
11. Filter bracket
12. Bolt
13. Nut
14. Washer
15. Fuel hose
16. Fuel hose
17. Filter housing

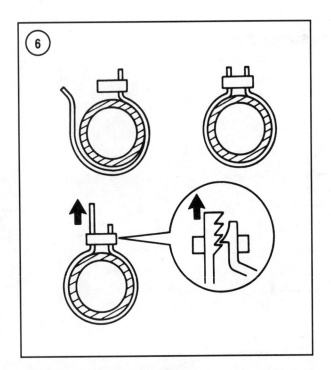

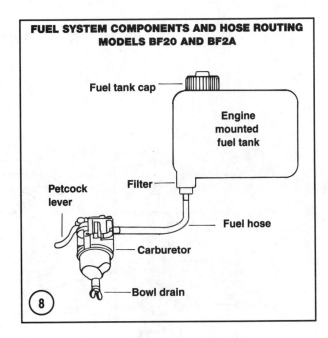

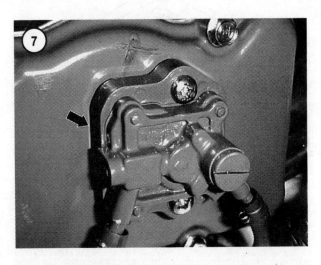

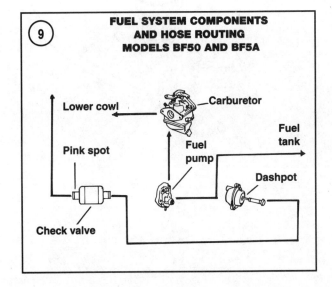

Figures 16-18 to assist with internal/external fuel pump component identification and orientation.

1. For models BF50, BF5A, BF75, BF8A, BF100 refer to **Figure 16**.
2. For models BF9.9A, BF15A, refer to **Figure 17**.
3. For all other models refer to **Figure 18**.

When repairs are performed, replace all gaskets, diaphragms, check valves and seals during assembly. Check for proper operation and fuel leaks after the repair is completed. Correct all fuel leaks at once.

Internal fuel pump components are available for models BF50, BR5A, BF75, BF8A, BR100, BF9.9A and BR15A.

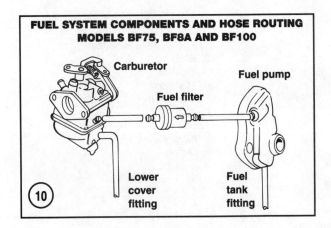

FUEL SYSTEM REPAIR

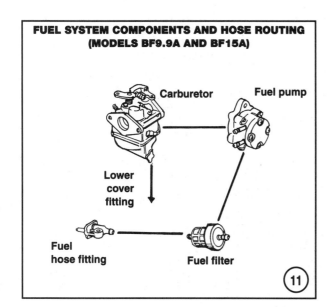

11 FUEL SYSTEM COMPONENTS AND HOSE ROUTING (MODELS BF9.9A AND BF15A)

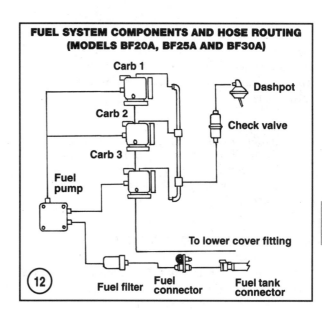

12 FUEL SYSTEM COMPONENTS AND HOSE ROUTING (MODELS BF20A, BF25A AND BF30A)

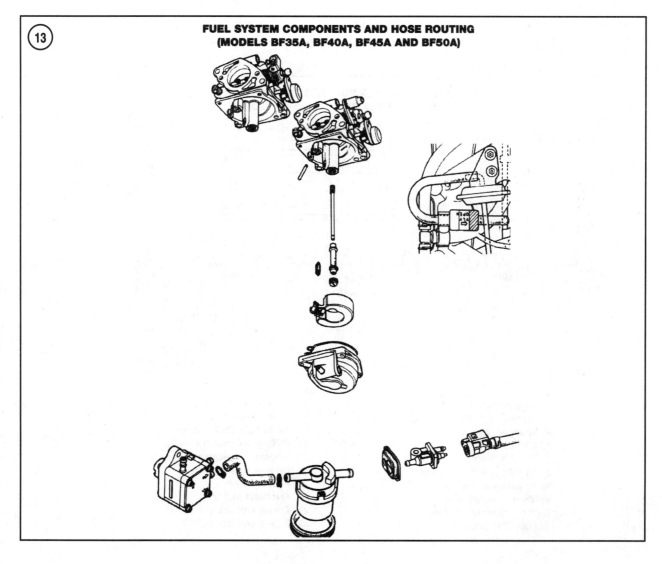

13 FUEL SYSTEM COMPONENTS AND HOSE ROUTING (MODELS BF35A, BF40A, BF45A AND BF50A)

Replacement fuel pump components are not available for other models. On all models not previously listed, replace the complete fuel pump if the pump fails. Disassembly and repair of the fuel pump is not recommended on these models.

CAUTION
Avoid lost or damaged fuel pump components. Spring pressure is in the fuel pump assembly. Provide support to keep the fuel pump in position as the mounting bolts are removed.

Models BF50, BF5A, BF75, BF8A, BF100

1. Disconnect both battery cables from the battery on electric start models. Remove the spark plugs and connect the spark plug leads to an engine ground.
2. Refer to **Figures 8-15** and locate the fuel pump(s) on the engine. Mark all fuel hoses connected to the fuel pump to ensure correct installation.

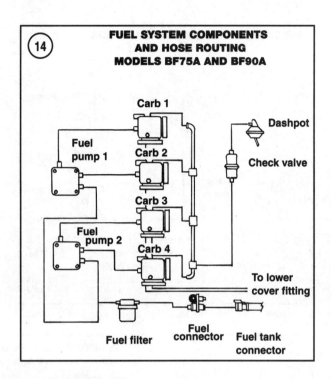

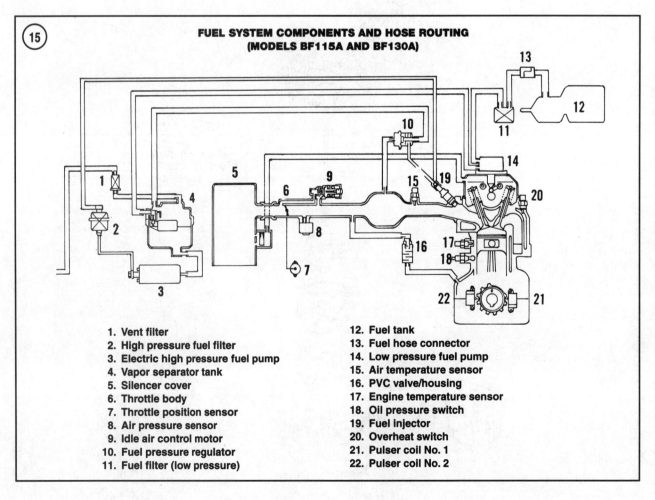

FUEL SYSTEM REPAIR

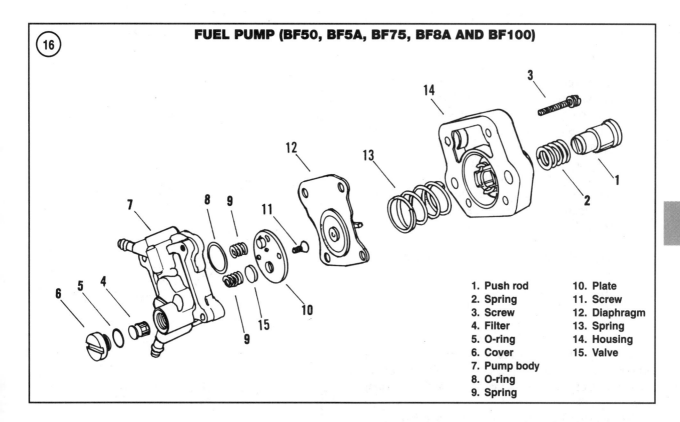

FUEL PUMP (BF50, BF5A, BF75, BF8A AND BF100)

1. Push rod
2. Spring
3. Screw
4. Filter
5. O-ring
6. Cover
7. Pump body
8. O-ring
9. Spring
10. Plate
11. Screw
12. Diaphragm
13. Spring
14. Housing
15. Valve

3. Have a shop towel and a container ready as residual fuel may spill from the disconnected hoses. Locate the hose connection at the inlet and outlet on the fuel pump(s). Cut and remove the plastic locking ties used on the hoses of some models. Using a pair of pliers remove spring type hose clamps, on models so equipped, by squeezing the ends together.

4. Pull or twist the hose to free it from the fuel pump. Use care to avoid bending or breaking the fuel pump fittings. Position the container below the hose connection to the fuel pump and carefully remove the inlet and outlet hose from the fuel pump.

5. Inspect the spring clamp, if so equipped, for corrosion or lack of spring tension and replace any faulty hose clamp.

6. Note the position of the fuel pump fittings (**Figure 19**) prior to removal. Place a shop towel under the fuel pump as fuel or oil may spill as the pump is removed from the base engine.

7. Hold the fuel pump firmly against the mounting surface then carefully remove both fuel pump mounting screws. Slowly remove the fuel pump from the base engine. Immediately place the fuel pump over a suitable container and drain any residual fuel from the fuel pump hose fittings. Clean all debris from the mounting bolts and the threaded holes in mounting surface.

8. Clean and inspect the fuel pump mating surface on the base engine. Remove and discard the fuel pump O-ring(s) from the mating surface.

9. Loosen the filter cover bolt (**Figure 16**), then remove the bolt, sealing ring and filter. Inspect the filter for damage or debris and replace if either defect is noted. Discard the filter sealing ring.

10. Place the fuel pump over a container suitable for holding fuel, then evenly loosen and remove all four fuel pump assembly screws (**Figure 16**). Separate the inner and outer fuel pump housings. Use care to avoid damaging sealing surfaces if it is necessary to pry the housings apart.

11. Hold the push rod in position then carefully push the diaphragm toward the push rod (**Figure 16**). Rotate the diaphragm 90° relative to the push rod to release the diaphragm from the push rod. Remove the diaphragm and push rod from the inner pump housing. Inspect the push rod and both springs for worn, corroded or damaged areas. Replace any defective components.

12. Note the location and orientation of all components. Remove the plate, springs, valves and O-rings (**Figure 16**) from the outer pump housing.

13. Inspect the diaphragm for holes, tears, wear or deformed areas. Replace the diaphragm if any defects are noted.

14. Clean all components in a suitable solvent and dry with compressed air. Ensure that all passages are cleaned of debris or contaminants.
15. Inspect the plate, valves, spring and both pump housings for worn, cracked, corroded or damaged surfaces. Replace the component(s) if any defects are noted.
16. Assembly is the reverse of disassembly. Assemble the fuel pump ensuring that
    a. All components are installed in exactly the same position as noted on disassembly.
    b. The diaphragm is properly attached to the push rod.
    c. The diaphragm is correctly positioned between the inner and outer pump housing.
    d. All valves and springs are placed correctly over the mounting bosses on the plate and outer pump housing.
    e. New O-ring(s) are installed in all locations.
    f. The fuel pump assembly screws are securely tightened.
17. Lubricate with engine oil or grease then place a *new* O-ring(s) onto the fuel pump mounting surface. Make sure that the O-ring(s) is properly positioned. Apply a light coating of engine oil to the threads of the mounting bolts.
18. Position the fuel pump onto the mounting surface and position it as noted prior to removal. While holding the fuel pump in position, align the mounting bolt holes, then thread the mounting bolts in until hand tight. Release the fuel pump. Tighten the mounting bolts to the specification listed in **Table 1**. Slide the fuel hoses onto the fuel pump fittings as noted prior to removal. Securely attach all hose clamps.
19. Squeeze the primer bulb as you inspect all hoses and connections for fuel leakage. Correct any fuel leakage at once. Install the spark plugs and spark plug leads. Clean the battery terminals, then connect the battery cables to the battery.
20. Operate the engine for several minutes as you inspect the fuel pump mounting area for fuel or oil leakage. Remove the fuel pump and replace the mounting surface O-ring(s) if an oil leak is detected.

Models BF9.9A and BF15A

1. Disconnect both battery cables from the battery on electric start models. Remove the spark plugs and connect the spark plug leads to an engine ground.
2. Refer to **Figures 8-15**, then locate the fuel pump(s) on the engine. Mark or make note of all fuel hoses connected to the fuel pump to ensure correct installation.
3. Have a shop towel and a container ready as residual fuel may spill out of the disconnected hoses. Locate the

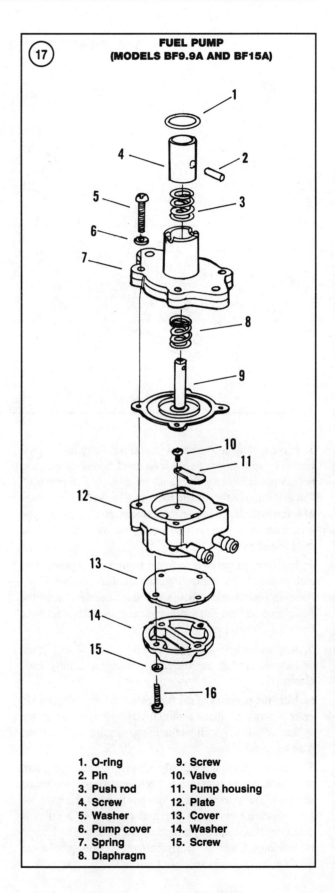

17 FUEL PUMP (MODELS BF9.9A AND BF15A)

1. O-ring
2. Pin
3. Push rod
4. Screw
5. Washer
6. Pump cover
7. Spring
8. Diaphragm
9. Screw
10. Valve
11. Pump housing
12. Plate
13. Cover
14. Washer
15. Screw

FUEL SYSTEM REPAIR

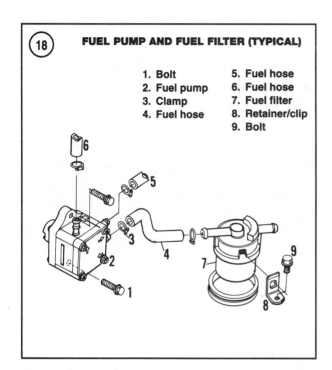

18 FUEL PUMP AND FUEL FILTER (TYPICAL)

1. Bolt
2. Fuel pump
3. Clamp
4. Fuel hose
5. Fuel hose
6. Fuel hose
7. Fuel filter
8. Retainer/clip
9. Bolt

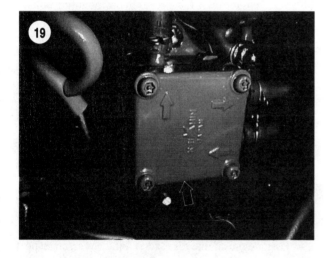

6. Note the orientation of the arrows on the fuel pump (**Figure 19**) prior to removal. Place a shop towel under the fuel pump as fuel or oil may spill as the pump is removed from the base engine.

7. Hold the fuel pump firmly against the mounting surface, then carefully remove both fuel pump mounting screws. Slowly pull the fuel pump from the base engine. Immediately place the fuel pump over a suitable container and drain any residual fuel from the fuel pump hose fittings. Clean all debris from the mounting bolts and the threaded holes in mounting surface.

8. Clean and inspect the fuel pump mating surface on the base engine. Remove and discard the fuel pump surface O-ring(s) from the mating surface.

9. Place the fuel pump over a container suitable for holding fuel then remove the four Torx screws from the inner pump housing (**Figure 17**). Separate the inner and outer fuel pump housings. Use care to avoid damaging sealing surfaces, if it is necessary to pry the housings apart.

10. Using your thumb, press the diaphragm into the inner pump housing enough to collapse the fuel pump springs and expose the pin that retains the diaphragm to the push rod. Use a small rod or screwdriver to push the pin from the push rod. Pull the diaphragm from the inner pump housing.

11. Inspect the diaphragm for holes, tears, worn surfaces or deformed areas. Replace the diaphragm if any defects are noted.

12. Remove the screws and both check valves from the outer pump housing.

13. Clean all components in a suitable solvent and dry with compressed air. Make sure all passages are cleaned of debris or contaminants.

14. Inspect the check valves, springs and both pump housings for worn, cracked, corroded or damaged surfaces.

15. Assembly is the reverse of disassembly. Assemble the fuel pump ensuring that:
   a. All components are installed in exactly the same position as noted on disassembly.
   b. The diaphragm is properly attached to the push rod.
   c. The diaphragm is correctly positioned between the inner and outer pump housing.
   d. The check valves are properly positioned on the outer pump housing and the retaining screws are securely tightened.
   e. New O-ring(s) are installed in all locations.
   f. The four Torx screws are securely tightened.

16. Lubricate with engine oil or grease and place a *new* O-ring(s) onto the fuel pump mounting surface. Make sure the O-ring(s) is properly positioned. Apply a light coating of engine oil to the threads of the mounting bolts.

hose connection at the inlet and outlet on the fuel pump(s). Cut and remove plastic locking ties used on the hoses of some models. Using a pair of pliers, remove spring type hose clamps, on models so equipped by squeezing the ends together.

4. Pull or twist the hose to free it from the fuel pump. Use care to avoid bending or breaking the fuel pump fittings. Position a container below the hose connection to the fuel pump and carefully remove the inlet and outlet hose from the fuel pump.

5. Inspect the spring clamp, if so equipped, for corrosion or lack of spring tension and replace any faulty or questionable hose clamp.

17. Position the fuel pump onto the mounting surface as noted prior to removal. While holding the fuel pump in position, align the mounting bolt holes and thread the mounting bolts in until hand tight. Release the fuel pump. Tighten the mounting bolts to the specification listed in **Table 1**. Slide the fuel hoses onto the fuel pump fittings as noted prior to removal. Securely attach all hose clamps.

18. Squeeze the primer bulb as you inspect all hoses and connections for fuel leakage. Correct all fuel leakage at once. Install the spark plugs and spark plug leads. Clean the battery terminals then connect the cables to the battery.

19. Operate the engine for several minutes as you inspect the fuel pump mounting area for fuel or oil leaks. Remove the fuel pump and replace the mounting surface O-ring(s) if an oil leak is detected.

All other models

1. Remove the spark plugs and connect the spark plug leads to an engine ground. Disconnect both battery cables from the battery on electric start models.
2. Refer to **Figure 18**, then locate the fuel pump(s) on the engine. Mark fuel hoses connected to the fuel pump to ensure correct installation.
3. Have a shop towel and a container ready as residual fuel may spill out of the disconnected hoses. Locate the hose connection at the inlet and outlet on the fuel pump(s). Cut and remove the plastic locking ties used on the hoses of some models. Using a pair of pliers, remove spring type hose clamps, on models so equipped, by squeezing the ends together.
4. Pull or twist the hose to free it from the fuel pump. Use care to avoid bending or breaking the fuel pump fitting. Position a container below the hose connection to the fuel pump and carefully remove the inlet and outlet hose from the fuel pump.
5. Inspect the spring clamp, if so equipped, for corrosion or lack of spring tension and replace any faulty or questionable hose clamp.
6. Note the position of the arrows on the fuel pump (**Figure 19**) prior to removal. Place a shop towel under the fuel pump as fuel or oil may spill as the pump is removed from the base engine.
7. Hold the fuel pump firmly against the mounting surface, then carefully remove both fuel pump mounting screws. Slowly pull the fuel pump from the base engine. Immediately place the fuel pump over a container and drain any residual fuel from the fuel pump hose fittings. Clean all debris from the mounting bolts and the threaded holes in mounting surface.

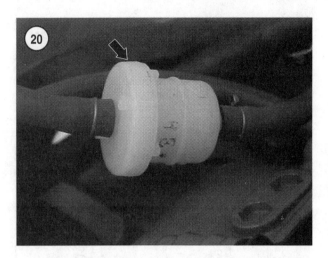

8. Clean and inspect the fuel pump mating surface on the base engine. Remove and discard the fuel pump surface O-ring(s) from the mating surface.
9. Lubricate with engine oil or grease and place a *new* O-ring(s) onto the fuel pump mounting surface. Make sure the O-ring(s) is properly positioned. Apply a light coating of engine oil to the threads of the mounting bolts.
10. Position the fuel pump onto the mounting surface as noted prior to removal. While holding the fuel pump in position, align the mounting bolt holes, and thread the mounting bolts in until hand tight. Release the fuel pump. Tighten the mounting bolts to the specification listed in **Table 1**.
11. Slide the fuel hoses onto the fuel pump fittings as noted prior to removal. Securely attach all hose clamps.
12. Squeeze the primer bulb as you inspect all hoses and connections for fuel leakage. Correct any fuel leakage at once.
13. Install all spark plugs and spark plug leads. Clean the battery terminals, then connect the cables to the battery on electric start models.
14. Operate the engine for several minutes as you inspect the fuel pump mounting area for fuel or oil leakage. Remove the fuel pump and replace the mounting surface O-ring(s) if an oil leak is detected.

Fuel Filter

Models BF20 and BF2A use a single fuel filter mounted to the fuel fitting on the fuel tank. Models BF35A, BF40A, BF45A, BF50A, BF75A and BF90A use a canister type fuel filter held into a recess in the lower starboard side motor cover (**Figure 20**). All other models use an inline fuel filter (**Figure 21**) located in the fuel hose. For models BF115A and BF130A, refer to the EFI components section of this chapter to replace the fuel filters.

FUEL SYSTEM REPAIR

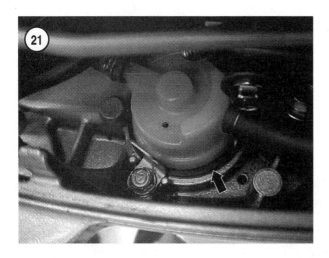

Inspect all fuel hoses and the fuel tank when debris, water or deposits are found in the fuel filter. Inspect the carburetor(s) and fuel pump if a significant amount of varnish deposits are found in the fuel filter.

Filter replacement (canister type fuel filter)

1. Disconnect both battery cables from the battery on electric start models. Remove the spark plugs and connect the spark plug leads to an engine ground.
2. Refer to **Figure 13** and **Figure 14** to locate the fuel filter.
3. Carefully pull the filter retaining clip away from the fuel filter (**Figure 21**) and lift the filter from the recess in the lower engine cover.
4. Squeeze the ends of the spring type hose clamps to remove them from the fuel filter fittings. Replace corroded or weak hose clamps. Make note of the arrow on the fuel hose fitting *prior* to removing the hoses from the fuel filter.
5. Place a container under the fuel filter. Carefully twist or pull the hoses to remove them from the filter. Discard the fuel filter.
6. Inspect the fuel hoses and fuel clamps.
7. Install the fuel filter so the arrow on the fuel hose fitting is facing toward the carburetor. Push the fuel hoses fully onto each filter fitting.
8. Install the spring type hose clamps onto each hose connection. Make sure all connections are secure and neither the filter nor fuel hoses interfere with other components of the engine. Squeeze the primer bulb as you inspect all hoses and connections for fuel leakage. Correct all fuel leakage at once.
9. Carefully lower the fuel filter into the recess as you hold the retaining clip away from the fuel filter. Release the retaining clip and check the clip to ensure correct clip position on the fuel filter as shown in **Figure 21**.
10. Install all spark plugs and spark plug leads. Clean the battery terminals and connect the cables to the battery on electric start models. Check for fuel leakage when the engine is started. Correct any fuel leakage at once.

Fuel filter replacement (inline filter)

1. Disconnect both battery cables from the battery on electric start models. Remove all spark plugs and connect the spark plug leads to an engine ground.
2. Refer to **Figure 9-12** to locate the fuel filter. Note the arrow on the fuel filter (**Figure 21**) prior to removing the fuel filter from the hoses.
3. Cut and remove plastic locking tie clamps at the hose to the filter connection. Squeeze the ends of the spring type hose clamps to remove them from the fuel filter fitting. Replace corroded or weak hose clamps.
4. Place a container for capturing fuel under the fuel filter. Carefully twist or pull the hoses to remove them from the filter. Discard the fuel filter.
5. Inspect the fuel hoses and fuel clamps.
6. Install the fuel filter so the arrow is facing toward the carburetor. Push the fuel hoses fully onto each fitting on the filter.
7. Install new plastic locking ties or good spring type hose clamps onto each hose connection. Make sure all connections are secure and neither the filter nor fuel hoses will interfere with any components on the engine. Squeeze the primer bulb as you inspect all hoses and connection for fuel leakage. Correct all fuel leakage as once.
8. Install all spark plugs and spark plug leads. Clean the battery terminals and connect the cables to the battery on electric start models. Check for fuel leakage when the engine is started.

SILENCER COVER AND CARBURETOR/ THROTTLE BODY

This section provides removal and installation procedures for the silencer cover and carburetor/throttle body. When removing only the silencer cover, follow the procedure until it is removed. Reverse the removal steps to install the silencer cover.

Have shop towels nearby and use a suitable container to capture the residual fuel from the components as the fuel hoses are removed. Refer to Chapter Five to perform all applicable linkage and carburetor adjustments. Refer to **Figures 22-28** as necessary.

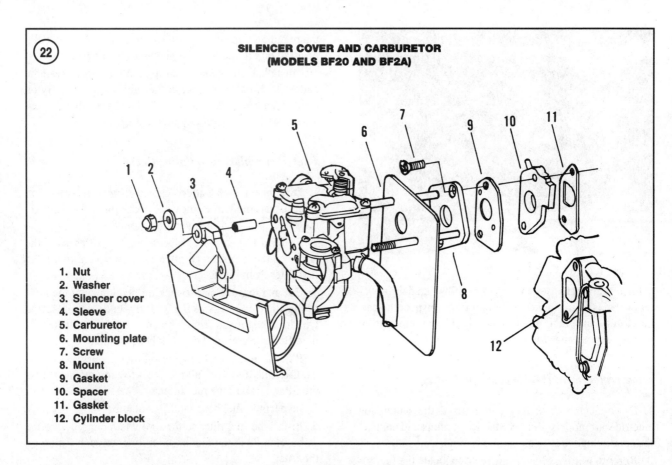

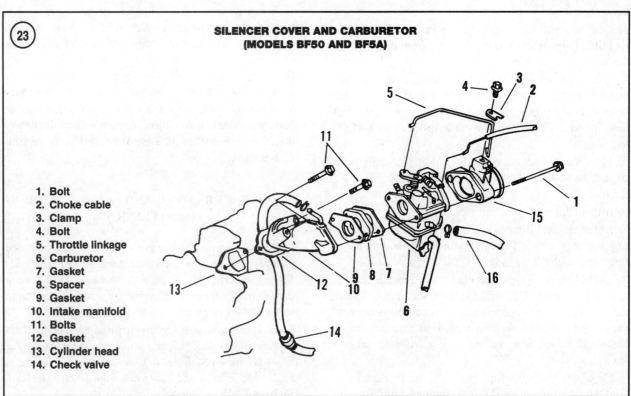

FUEL SYSTEM REPAIR

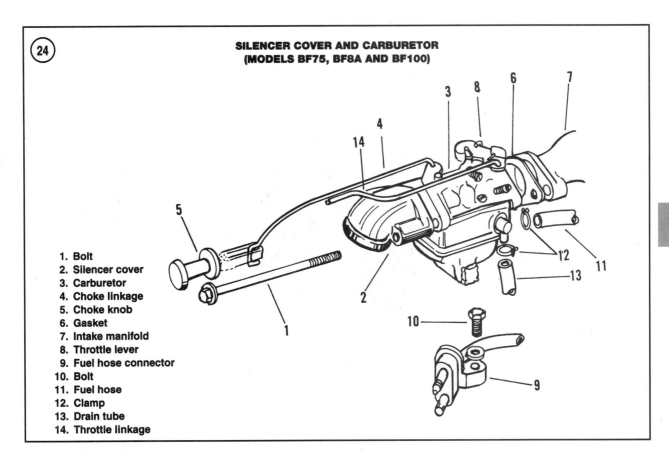

24. SILENCER COVER AND CARBURETOR (MODELS BF75, BF8A AND BF100)

1. Bolt
2. Silencer cover
3. Carburetor
4. Choke linkage
5. Choke knob
6. Gasket
7. Intake manifold
8. Throttle lever
9. Fuel hose connector
10. Bolt
11. Fuel hose
12. Clamp
13. Drain tube
14. Throttle linkage

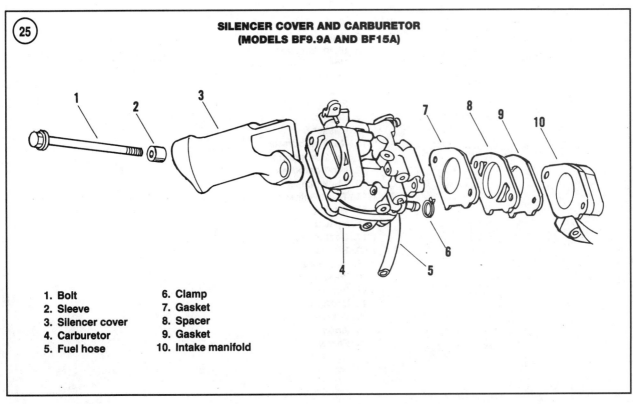

25. SILENCER COVER AND CARBURETOR (MODELS BF9.9A AND BF15A)

1. Bolt
2. Sleeve
3. Silencer cover
4. Carburetor
5. Fuel hose
6. Clamp
7. Gasket
8. Spacer
9. Gasket
10. Intake manifold

CHAPTER SIX

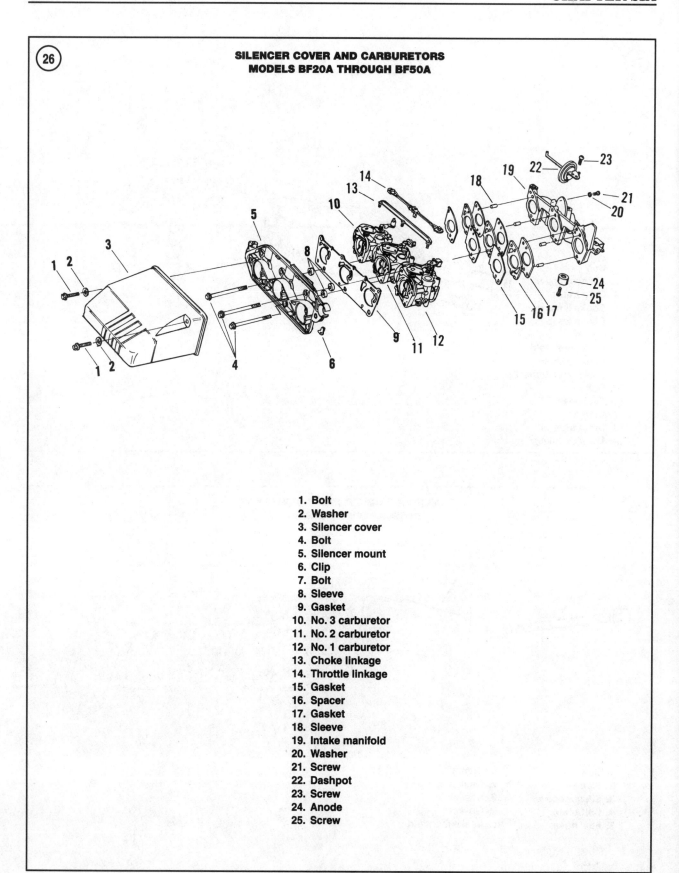

SILENCER COVER AND CARBURETORS MODELS BF20A THROUGH BF50A

1. Bolt
2. Washer
3. Silencer cover
4. Bolt
5. Silencer mount
6. Clip
7. Bolt
8. Sleeve
9. Gasket
10. No. 3 carburetor
11. No. 2 carburetor
12. No. 1 carburetor
13. Choke linkage
14. Throttle linkage
15. Gasket
16. Spacer
17. Gasket
18. Sleeve
19. Intake manifold
20. Washer
21. Screw
22. Dashpot
23. Screw
24. Anode
25. Screw

FUEL SYSTEM REPAIR

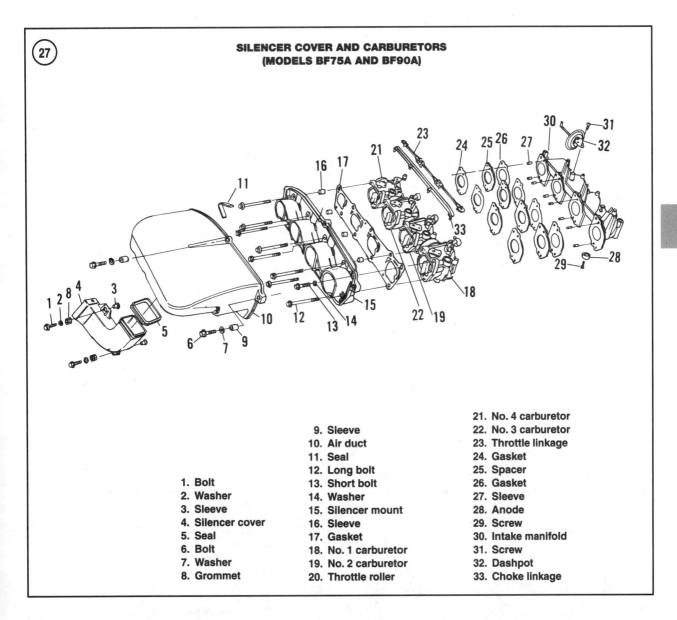

SILENCER COVER AND CARBURETORS (MODELS BF75A AND BF90A)

1. Bolt
2. Washer
3. Sleeve
4. Silencer cover
5. Seal
6. Bolt
7. Washer
8. Grommet
9. Sleeve
10. Air duct
11. Seal
12. Long bolt
13. Short bolt
14. Washer
15. Silencer mount
16. Sleeve
17. Gasket
18. No. 1 carburetor
19. No. 2 carburetor
20. Throttle roller
21. No. 4 carburetor
22. No. 3 carburetor
23. Throttle linkage
24. Gasket
25. Spacer
26. Gasket
27. Sleeve
28. Anode
29. Screw
30. Intake manifold
31. Screw
32. Dashpot
33. Choke linkage

Silencer Cover and Carburetor Removal/Installation (Models BF20 and BF2A)

1. Refer to **Figure 22** during the removal/installation procedure. Refer to *Fuel Tank and Fuel Hose Components* in this chapter and remove the fuel tank from the engine.

2. Place a container under the carburetor. Locate and remove the float bowl drain screw (**Figure 29**) and allow the fuel to drain from the carburetor. Install and tighten the float bowl drain screw. Dispose of the fuel in a responsible manner.

3. Loosen the retaining clip and disconnect the throttle cable from the throttle lever on the carburetor. Disconnect the choke linkage from the choke lever on the carburetor.

4. Loosen and remove the two nuts from the front of the silencer cover, then slide the silencer cover and sleeves from the carburetor. Note the position of all plates and gaskets prior to removing them from the base engine. Loosen the two retaining screws, then remove the spacers and gaskets from the base engine.

5. Carefully slide the carburetor, plates and gaskets from the mounting studs. Discard all gaskets. Do not damage any gasket contact surfaces. Use a blunt gasket scraper and carefully scrape all gasket material from the mounting location on the base engine. Carefully remove all gasket material from both spacer plates and the carburetor mounting base.

6. Refer to *Carburetor Repair* in this chapter and repair the carburetor as required.

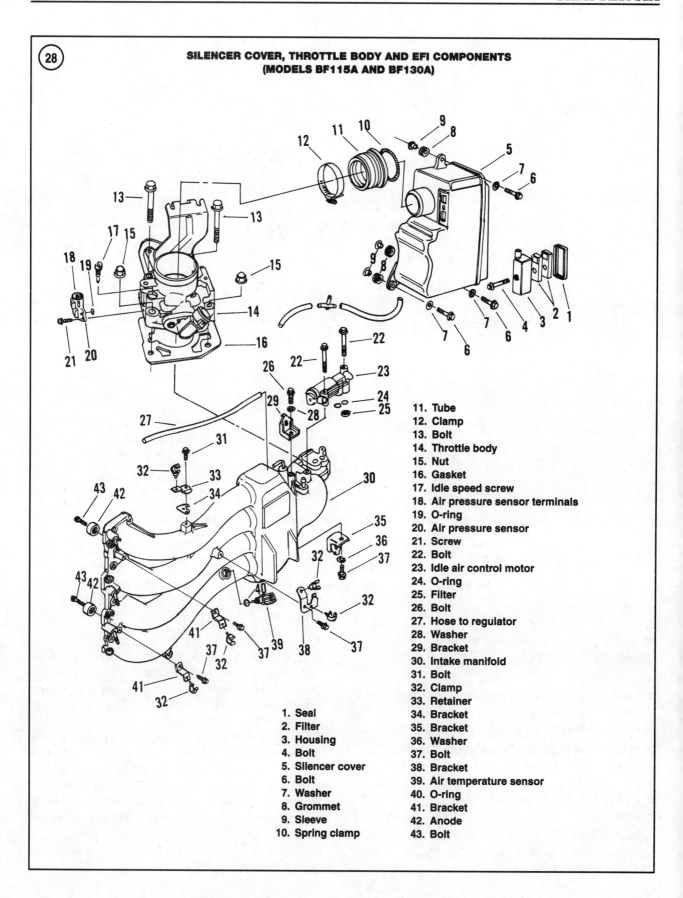

FUEL SYSTEM REPAIR

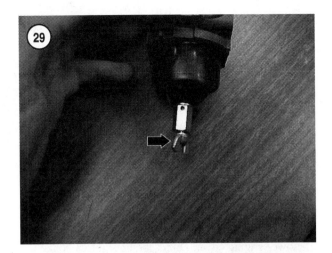

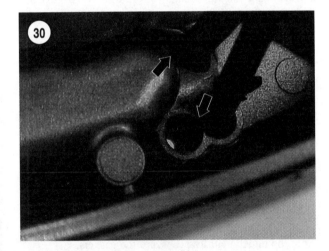

c. Securely tighten all screws and nuts to the specifications listed in **Table 1**.
d. Attach all hoses to the locations noted prior to removal.
e. Inspect all hose clamps and replace if defective.

8. Refer to Chapter Five and perform all applicable linkage and fuel system adjustments.

9. Correct any fuel leakage at once.

Silencer Cover and Carburetor Removal/Installation (Models BF50 and BF5A)

1. Refer to **Figure 23** during the removal and installation procedure. Remove the spark plugs and connect the spark plug leads to an engine ground.
2. Make notes or drawings indicating the hose routing and connection points prior to removal.
3. Remove the drain tube from its location on the lower engine cover (**Figure 30**). Direct the tube to a container to capture fuel. Locate and remove the float bowl drain screw (**Figure 31**) and drain the fuel from the carburetor.
4. Remove the fuel hose clamp then carefully pull the fuel hose connecting the fuel pump to the carburetor from the carburetor hose fitting. Drain all fuel from the hose into the container. Install and tighten the float bowl drain screw. Dispose of the fuel in a responsible manner.
5. Loosen the screws and clips then remove the throttle linkage and choke cable from the carburetor.
6. Note the position of all components *prior* to removing them from the intake manifold. Loosen the two retaining screws then pull the silencer cover, carburetor, spacer and gaskets from the intake manifold. Discard the gaskets.
7. Use a blunt gasket scraper and carefully scrape all gasket material from the mounting location on the intake manifold. Carefully remove all gasket material from the spacer plate and the carburetor mounting surface.
8. Refer to *Carburetor Repair* in this chapter and repair the carburetor as required.
9. Install these components in the reverse order of removal while doing the following:
    a. Install *new* gaskets in all locations.
    b. Make sure all gaskets and spacers are positioned as noted prior to removal.
    c. Securely tighten all screws and nuts to the specifications listed in **Table 1**.
    d. Attach all hoses to the locations noted prior to removal.
    e. Inspect all hose clamps and replace if defective.

10. Refer to Chapter Five and perform all applicable linkage and fuel system adjustments.

7. Install these components in the reverse order of removal while doing the following:
    a. Install *new* gaskets at all locations.
    b. Make sure all gaskets and spacers are positioned as noted prior to removal.

11. Install the spark plugs and spark plug leads. Squeeze the primer bulb and check for fuel leakage. Correct any fuel leakage at once.

Silencer Cover and Carburetor Removal/Installation (Models BF75, BF8A and BF100)

1. Refer to **Figure 24** during the removal and installation procedure. Disconnect both battery cables from the battery, if so equipped. Remove the spark plugs and connect the spark plug leads to an engine ground.
2. Make notes or drawings indicating the hose routing and connection points prior to removal.
3. Place a container under the carburetor. Remove the drain hose from the fitting on the float bowl. Locate and remove the float bowl drain screw (**Figure 31**) and allow the fuel to drain from the carburetor. Tighten the float bowl drain screw.
4. Remove the fuel hose clamp then carefully pull the fuel hose connecting the fuel pump to the carburetor from the carburetor hose fitting. Direct the hose into the container and drain all fuel from the hose. Dispose of the fuel in a responsible manner.
5. Loosen the throttle linkage retainer and choke rod clip and remove the throttle linkage and choke rod from the carburetor.
6. Mark or note the position of all components *prior* to removing them from the intake manifold. Loosen the two retaining screws, then pull the silencer cover, carburetor and gaskets from the intake manifold. Remove and discard the gaskets.
7. Use a blunt gasket scraper and carefully scrape all gasket material from the mounting location on the intake manifold. Carefully remove all gasket material from the spacer plate and the carburetor mounting surface.
8. Refer to *Carburetor Repair* in this chapter and repair the carburetor as required.
9. Install these components in the reverse order of removal while doing the following:
   a. Install *new* gaskets in all locations.
   b. Make sure the silencer cover, carburetor and all gaskets are positioned as noted prior to removal.
   c. Securely tighten all screws and nuts to the specifications listed in **Table 1**.
   d. Attach all hoses to the locations noted prior to removal.
   e. Inspect all hose clamps and replace if defective.
10. Refer to Chapter Five and perform all applicable linkage and fuel system adjustments.
11. Install the spark plug and spark plug leads. Squeeze the primer bulb and check for fuel leakage. Correct any fuel leakage at once. Clean the battery terminals and connect the cables to the battery, if so equipped.

Silencer Cover and Carburetor Removal/Installation (Models BF9.9A and BF15A)

1. Refer to **Figure 25** during the removal and installation procedure. Remove the spark plugs and connect the spark plug leads to an engine ground. Disconnect both battery cables from the battery on electric start models.
2. Make notes or drawings indicating the hose routing and connection points prior to removal.
3. Remove the drain hose from its mounting location in the lower engine cover. Direct the hose into a container. Locate and loosen the float bowl drain screw (**Figure 31**) and drain the fuel from the carburetor. Tighten the float bowl drain screw.
4. Loosen the throttle linkage retainer and choke rod clip, then remove the throttle linkage and choke rod from the carburetor.
5. Remove the fuel hose clamp, then carefully pull the fuel hose connecting the fuel pump to the carburetor from the carburetor hose fitting. Drain all fuel from the hose into the container. Dispose of the fuel in a responsible manner.
6. Mark or note the position of all components *prior* to removing them from the intake manifold. Loosen the two retaining screws, then pull the silencer cover alignment sleeves, silencer cover, carburetor, spacer and gaskets from the intake manifold. Discard the gaskets.
7. Use a blunt gasket scraper and carefully scrape all gasket material from the mounting location on the intake manifold. Carefully remove all gasket material from the spacer plate and the carburetor mounting surface.
8. Refer to *Carburetor Repair* in this chapter and repair the carburetor as required.
9. Install these components in the reverse order of removal while doing the following:
   a. Install *new* gaskets in all locations.
   b. Make sure all gaskets and spacers are positioned as noted prior to removal.
   c. Securely tighten all screws and nuts to the specifications listed in **Table 1**.
   d. Attach all hoses to the locations noted prior to removal.
   e. Inspect all hose clamps and replace if defective.
10. Refer to Chapter Five and perform all applicable linkage and fuel system adjustments.
11. Install the spark plugs and spark plug leads. Squeeze the primer bulb and check for fuel leakage. Correct any

FUEL SYSTEM REPAIR

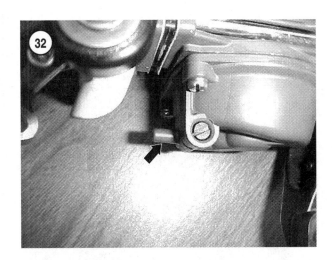

leaks at once. Clean the battery terminals, then connect the cables to the battery, if so equipped.

Silencer Cover and Carburetor Removal/Installation (Models BF20A, BF25A, BF30A, BF35A, BF40A, BF45A and BF50A)

1. Refer to **Figure 26** during the removal and installation procedure. Remove the spark plugs and connect the spark plug leads to an engine ground. Disconnect both battery cables from the battery on electric start models.
2. Make notes or drawings indicating all hose routing and connection points prior to removal.
3. Mark the silencer cover bolt locations *prior to* removing them. Note the hose routing and pull the crankcase breather hose from the top fitting on the silencer cover. Remove the upper and lower bolts and washers, then carefully pull the silencer/cover from the front carburetor mounting plate.
4. Remove *both* drain hoses from their mounting location in the lower engine cover (**Figure 30**). Connect a suitable length of fuel hose to the top carburetor drain fitting (**Figure 32**). Direct the hose into a container suitable for capturing fuel. Locate and loosen the float bowl drain screw. Allow fuel to drain from the carburetor and tighten the drain screw and remove the section of fuel hose. Repeat this procedure for the remaining two carburetors. Dispose the fuel in a responsible manner.
5. Locate the fuel hose connecting the fuel pump to the T fitting near the carburetors. Remove the fuel hose clamp, then carefully pull the fuel hose connecting the fuel pump to the carburetor from the carburetor hose fitting. Drain all fuel from the hose into the container. Dispose of the fuel in a responsible manner.
6. Refer to Chapter Seven and remove the choke solenoid from the engine. Locate the bolts that retain the intake manifold to the cylinder head. Refer to Chapter Eight and remove the intake manifold mounting bolts. Carefully pull the intake manifold away from the cylinder head.
7. Use a blunt gasket scraper and carefully scrape all gasket material from the mounting location on the intake manifold. Carefully remove all gasket material from the spacer plate and the carburetor mounting surface.
8. Refer to *Carburetor Repair* in this chapter and repair the carburetor(s) as required.
9. Install these components in the reverse order of removal while doing the following:
   a. Install *new* gaskets in all locations.
   b. Make sure all gaskets and are positioned as noted prior to removal.
   c. Refer to Chapter Eight for procedures and attach the intake manifold to the cylinder head.
   d. Securely tighten all screws and nuts to the specifications listed in **Table 1**.
   e. Attach all hoses to the locations noted prior to removal.
   f. Inspect all hose clamps and replace if defective.
   g. Refer to Chapter Seven and install the choke solenoid.
10. Refer to Chapter Five and perform all applicable linkage and fuel system adjustments.
11. Install the spark plugs and spark plug leads. Squeeze the primer bulb and check for fuel leakage. Correct fuel leakage at once. Clean the battery terminals then connect the cables to the battery, if so equipped.

Silencer Cover and Carburetor Removal/Installation (Models BF75A and BF90A)

1. Refer to **Figure 27** during the removal and installation procedure. Remove the spark plugs and connect the spark plug leads to an engine ground. Disconnect both battery cables from the battery on electric start models only.
2. Make notes or drawings indicating all hose routing and connection points prior to removal.
3. Loosen and remove the two bolts, sleeves and grommets that retain the intake duct. Note the position of the intake duct to the silencer cover and remove the duct and gasket from the silencer cover.
4. Mark or note the silencer cover bolt locations *prior to* removing them. Note the hose routing and pull the crankcase breather hose from the top fitting on the silencer cover. Remove the upper and lower bolts and washers, then carefully pull the silencer/cover from the front carburetor mounting plate.
5. Remove *both* drain hoses from their mounting location in the lower engine cover (**Figure 30**). Connect a length of

fuel hose to the top carburetor drain fitting (**Figure 32**). Direct the hose into a container for capturing fuel. Locate and loosen the float bowl drain screw (**Figure 31**). Drain all fuel from the carburetor, then tighten the drain screw and remove the section of fuel hose. Repeat this procedure for the remaining two carburetors. Dispose of the fuel in a responsible manner.

6. Locate the fuel hose connecting the fuel pump to the T fitting near the carburetors. Remove the fuel hose clamp then carefully pull the fuel hose connecting the fuel pump to the carburetor from the carburetor hose fitting. Drain all fuel from the hose into the container. Dispose of the fuel in a responsible manner.

7. Refer to Chapter Seven and remove the choke solenoid from the engine. Locate the bolts that retain the intake manifold to the cylinder head. Refer to Chapter Eight and remove the intake manifold mounting bolts. Carefully pull the intake manifold away from the cylinder head.

8. Use a blunt gasket scraper and carefully scrape all gasket material from the mounting location on the intake manifold. Carefully remove all gasket material from the spacer plate and the carburetor mounting surface.

9. Refer to *Carburetor Repair* in this chapter and repair the carburetor(s) as required.

10. Install these components in the reverse order of removal while doing the following:
    a. Install *new* gaskets in all locations.
    b. Make sure all gaskets are positioned as noted prior to removal. Position the triangle mark on the intake duct to the silencer gasket *toward the silencer cover.*
    c. Refer to Chapter Eight for procedures and attach the intake manifold to the cylinder head.
    d. Securely tighten all screws and nuts to the specifications listed in **Table 1**.
    e. Attach all hoses to the locations noted prior to removal.
    f. Inspect all hose clamps and replace if defective.
    g. Refer to Chapter Seven and install the choke solenoid.

11. Refer to Chapter Five and perform all applicable linkage and fuel system adjustments.

12. Install the spark plugs and spark plug leads. Squeeze the primer bulb and check for fuel leakage. Correct any fuel leakage at once. Clean the battery terminals, then connect the cables to the battery, if so equipped.

Silencer Cover and Throttle Body Removal/Installation (Model BF115A and BF130A)

1. Refer to **Figure 28** during the removal and installation procedures. Remove the spark plugs and connect the

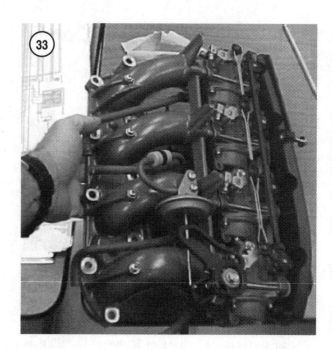

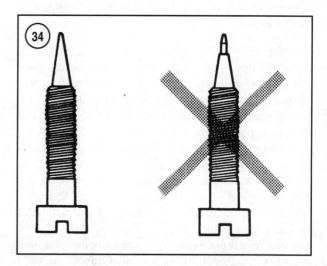

spark plug leads to an engine ground. Disconnect both cables from the battery on electric start models only.

2. Make notes or drawings indicating all hose routing and connection points prior to removal.

3. Disconnect the hose from the fitting on the bottom of the silencer cover. Pull the breather hose from its connection on the silencer cover. Loosen and remove the three bolts that retain the silencer cover to the front of the base engine.

4. Loosen the large hose clamp connecting the large rubber tube to the throttle body. Carefully pull the silencer cover away from the throttle body. Loosen the single bolt and remove the breather filter housing from the silencer cover. Refer to Chapter Four to service the breather filter.

FUEL SYSTEM REPAIR

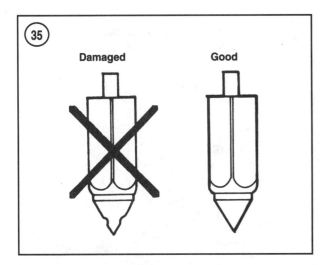

5. Locate and disconnect the throttle position sensor, and air pressure sensor connections from the throttle body. Loosen all adjusting nuts and remove both throttle cables from the throttle body.

6. Loosen and remove both retaining nuts from the front and both mounting bolts from the rear of the throttle body. Carefully remove the throttle body from the intake manifold. Remove and discard the throttle body gasket.

7. Use a blunt gasket scraper and carefully scrape all gasket material from the mounting location on the intake manifold. Carefully remove all gasket material from the throttle body and intake manifold mounting surface.

8. Refer to *EFI Components* in this chapter and repair the throttle body(s) as required.

9. Install these components in the reverse order of removal while doing the following:
   a. Install *new* gaskets in all locations.
   b. Make sure all gaskets and are positioned as noted prior to removal. Make sure the large rubber tube is fully seated onto the throttle body and silencer cover.
   c. Securely tighten all screws and nuts to the specifications listed in **Table 1**.
   d. Attach all hoses to the locations noted prior to removal.
   e. Inspect all hose clamps and replace if defective.

10. Refer to Chapter Five and perform all applicable linkage and fuel system adjustments.

11. Install the spark plugs and spark plug leads. Squeeze the primer bulb and check for fuel leakage. Correct any fuel leakage at once. Clean the battery terminals, then connect the cables to the battery, if so equipped.

CARBURETOR REPAIR

To ensure success when repairing carburetors, always work in a clean environment. Mark all hose connections before removal and refer to the illustrations to ensure correct hose routing. On multiple-carburetor engines (**Figure 33**), repair *one* carburetor at a time. Some models have fuel and air jet sizes calibrated to the cylinder in which they supply fuel.

Arrange all components on a clean surface as they are removed from the carburetor. Place them in the same location after they have been cleaned.

Using a suitable solvent, clean all deposits from the carburetor passages, fuel jets, orifices and fuel bowl. Use compressed air and blow through the passages to remove contaminants. Be very careful when removing fuel jets from the carburetor if the carburetor has significant amounts of corrosion or other deposits. Fuel jets are easily damaged when excessive force is required for removal. Clean the carburetor without removing the fuel jets if the jets cannot be easily removed from the carburetor.

Inspect pilot jet adjusting screws for worn or damaged surfaces (**Figure 34**) and replace as required.

Use a ruler to check and correct the float level prior to installing the float. Set the float *exactly* as specified to ensure proper fuel delivery. Float specifications are provided in **Table 2**. Replace the float if it does not move freely on the pivot pin.

Inspect the fuel valve needle for damaged sealing surfaces (**Figure 35**). Inspect the valve seat for pitting, worn or irregular surfaces. Replace worn or damaged components.

Refer to **Figure 36** (BF20 and BF2A models), **Figure 37** (BF50, BF5A, BF75, BF8A and BF100 models), **Figure 38** (BF9.9A and BF15A) and **Figure 39** (all other models except BF115A and BF130A).

CAUTION
Make certain all fuel jets are installed into the correct location in the carburetor. Improper fuel calibration can result if fuel jets are incorrectly installed. Severe engine damage can occur from improper fuel calibration.

CAUTION
Never use stiff steel wire to clean carburetor passages. Material can be removed from the inner diameter of the orifice disturbing the fuel calibration. Carburetor replacement may be required if passages are damaged during the cleaning process.

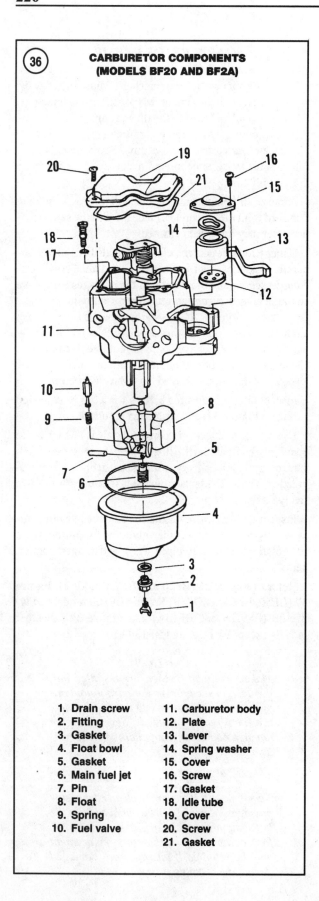

CARBURETOR COMPONENTS (MODELS BF20 AND BF2A)

1. Drain screw
2. Fitting
3. Gasket
4. Float bowl
5. Gasket
6. Main fuel jet
7. Pin
8. Float
9. Spring
10. Fuel valve
11. Carburetor body
12. Plate
13. Lever
14. Spring washer
15. Cover
16. Screw
17. Gasket
18. Idle tube
19. Cover
20. Screw
21. Gasket

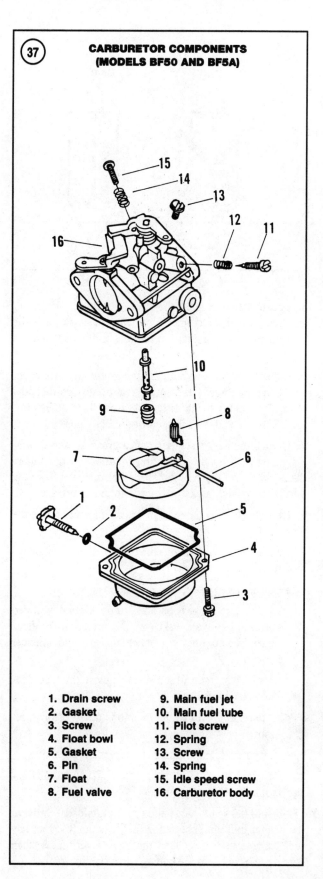

CARBURETOR COMPONENTS (MODELS BF50 AND BF5A)

1. Drain screw
2. Gasket
3. Screw
4. Float bowl
5. Gasket
6. Pin
7. Float
8. Fuel valve
9. Main fuel jet
10. Main fuel tube
11. Pilot screw
12. Spring
13. Screw
14. Spring
15. Idle speed screw
16. Carburetor body

FUEL SYSTEM REPAIR

38 CARBURETOR COMPONENTS (MODELS BF9.9A AND BF15A)

1. Drain screw
2. Gasket
3. Screw
4. Float bowl
5. Gasket
6. Pin
7. Float
8. Fuel valve
9. Plug
10. Main fuel tube
11. Idle speed screw
12. Main fuel jet
13. Gasket
14. Pilot screw
15. Carburetor

NOTE
Never compromise the cleaning process for the carburetor(s). Residual debris or deposits in the carburetor may break free at a later time and block passages. Use compressed air and blow through all passages to ensure they are completely clear.

Disassembly/Assembly (BF20 and BF2A Models)

Refer to **Figure 36** during the disassembly/assembly procedures. Mark all components prior to removal from the carburetor.

1. Position the carburetor drain side down over a container suitable for capturing fuel. Loosen and remove the drain screw from the bottom of the float bowl. Drain the fuel from the carburetor.

2. Remove the large nut from the bottom of the float bowl and carefully remove the float bowl from the carburetor. Discard the gasket from the float bowl retaining nut and the float bowl to the carburetor mating surface.

3. With the float resting on the needle valve, measure the float height as shown in **Figure 40**. Compare the measurement with the specification listed in **Table 2**. Replace the float and needle valve if an incorrect measurement is noted.

4. Remove the float pin, float, needle valve spring and needle valve (**Figure 36**).

5. Carefully remove the main fuel jet and the main fuel tube (**Figure 36**) from the carburetor.

6. Remove the four screws and the top cover from the carburetor. Discard the top cover gasket. Count the number or turns as you remove the pilot jet adjusting screw from the side of the carburetor.

7. Remove the two screws and the fuel cock lever cover. Pull the spring washer and lever from the carburetor. Discard the gasket under the lever.

8. Install in the reverse order of disassembly while noting the following:

   a. Clean all passages completely.
   b. Inspect all components for cracked or worn areas and replace as required.
   c. Inspect the float for cracks or any indication of leakage and replace as required. Replace the float bowl, top cover and drain screw gaskets.
   d. Install the pilot jet adjusting screw. Thread the screw into the carburetor body the same number of turns noted during removal

9. Refer to *Silencer Cover and Carburetor/Throttle Body* in this chapter and install the carburetor on the engine.

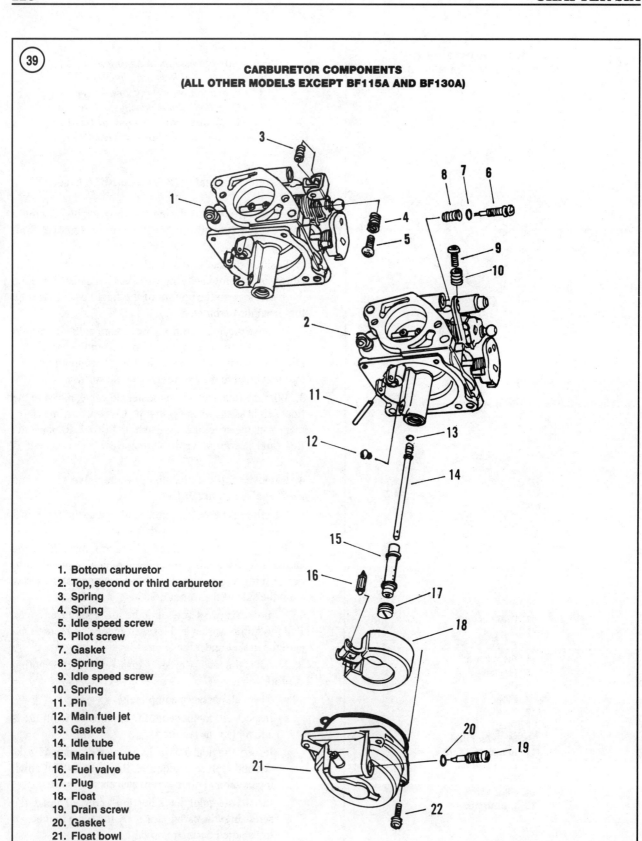

FUEL SYSTEM REPAIR

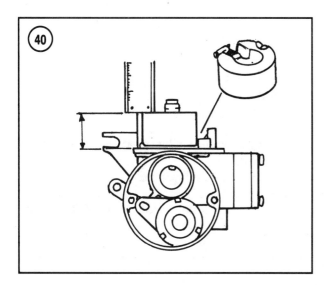

Disassembly/Assembly (Models BF50, BF5A, BF75, BF8A and BF100)

Refer to **Figure 37** during the disassembly/assembly procedure. Mark all components prior to removal from carburetor.

1. Position the carburetor drain side down over a container suitable for capturing fuel. Loosen and remove the drain screw from the side of the float bowl. Drain the fuel from the carburetor. Remove and discard the drain screw gasket.
2. Remove the four screws from the float bowl and carefully remove the float bowl from the carburetor. Remove and discard the gasket from the float bowl to the carburetor mating surface.
3. Remove the float pin, float, needle valve spring and needle valve.
4. Carefully remove the main fuel jet and the main fuel tube from the carburetor.
5. Remove the pilot jet adjusting screw from the side of the carburetor.
6. Install in the reverse order of disassembly while noting the following:
    a. Check and/or adjust the float height as described in Step 7.
    b. Clean all passages completely.
    c. Inspect all components for cracked or worn areas and replace as required.
    d. Inspect the float for cracks or any indication of leakage and replace as required.
    e. Replace the float bowl and drain screw gaskets.
    f. Securely tighten all screws.

7. With the float resting on the needle valve measure the float height (A, **Figure 40**). Compare the measurement with the specification listed in **Table 2**. Remove the float and carefully bend the tab up or down until the correct measurement is obtained.
8. Refer to *Silencer Cover and Carburetor/Throttle Body* in this chapter and install the carburetor to the engine.

Disassembly/Assembly (Models BF9.9A and BF15A)

Refer to **Figure 38** during the disassembly/assembly procedure. Mark all components prior to removal from the carburetor.

1. Position the carburetor drain side down over a container suitable for capturing fuel. Loosen and remove the drain screw from the side of the float bowl. Drain all fuel from the carburetor. Remove and discard the drain screw gasket.
2. Remove the four screws from the float bowl and carefully remove the float bowl from the carburetor. Remove and discard the gasket from the float bowl to the carburetor mating surface.
3. With the float resting on the needle valve measure the float height as shown in **Figure 40**. Compare the measurement with the specification listed in **Table 2**. Replace the float and needle valve if an incorrect measurement is noted.
4. Remove the float pin, float, needle valve spring and needle valve.
5. Carefully remove the fuel tube plug and main fuel tube from the carburetor.
6. Carefully remove the main fuel jet from the side of the carburetor fuel tube casting. Remove the pilot jet adjusting screw and idle speed screw from the side of the carburetor. Record the number of turns necessary to remove each screw for reference during assembly.
7. Install in the reverse order of disassembly while noting the following:
    a. Clean all passages completely.
    b. Inspect all components for cracked or worn areas and replace as required.
    c. Inspect the float for cracks or any indication of leakage and replace as required.
    d. Replace the float bowl and drain screw gaskets.
    e. Securely tighten all screws.
    f. Install the pilot jet adjusting screw and idle speed screw into the carburetor the same number of turns as noted prior to removal.
8. Install the carburetors as described in this chapter.

Disassembly/Assembly All Other Models

Refer to **Figure 39** during the disassembly/assembly procedure. Internal components may vary from one carburetor to the next. Disassemble and repair one carburetor at a time to prevent mixing of the components. Mark each carburetor mounting location (top, middle, bottom) on the carburetor casting prior to removing them from the intake manifold. Mark all components prior to removal from the carburetor.

1. Loosen and remove the two screws, then carefully remove the dashpot from the intake manifold.
2. Carefully pry the throttle linkage and choke linkage from the carburetors.
3. Mark all fuel hose connections, then remove all hoses from the carburetors.
4. Fully loosen, but do not remove, all mounting bolts from the silencer cover/carburetor mounting plate. Carefully remove the silencer cover/carburetor mounting plate and carburetors from the intake manifold.
5. Remove all spacers, mounting gaskets and alignment pins. Discard the mounting gaskets.
6. Remove all mounting bolts and carefully remove the carburetors from the silencer cover/carburetor mounting plate. Remove the gasket and spacers. Discard the gasket. Clean all gasket material from all components.
7. Position the carburetor drain side down over a container for capturing fuel. Loosen and remove the drain screw from the float bowl. Drain all fuel from the carburetor. Remove and discard the drain screw gasket.
8. Mark the float bowl to carburetor position then remove the four screws from the float bowl. Carefully remove the float bowl from the carburetor. Remove and discard the float bowl gasket.
9. Remove the float pin, float, needle valve spring and needle valve.
10. Carefully remove the fuel tube plug, main fuel tube and idle tube from the fuel tube casting.
11. Remove the main fuel jet from the carburetor. Remove the pilot jet adjusting screw and carburetor calibration screws from the carburetor. Count the number of turns required to remove the pilot jet adjusting screw and carburetor calibration screw for reference during assembly.
12. Install in the reverse order of disassembly while nothing the following:
    a. Clean all passages completely.
    b. Inspect all components for cracked or worn areas and replace as required.
    c. Inspect the float for cracks or any indication of leakage and replace as required.
    d. Install the pilot jet adjusting screw and carburetor calibration screw into the carburetor the same number of turns as noted on removal.
    e. Check and/or adjust the float height as indicated in Step 13.
    f. Install the UP marking on the throttle linkage facing up.
    g. Adjust the dashpot following the procedure listed in Chapter Five.
13. With the float resting on the needle valve, measure the float height (A, **Figure 40**). Compare the measurement with the specification listed in **Table 2**. Remove the float and carefully bend the tab up or down until the correct measurement is obtained.
14. Refer to Chapter Eight and install the intake manifold.
15. Install the carburetors as described in this chapter.

EFI COMPONENTS

WARNING
High fuel pressure is generated by the fuel injection system. Always wear eye protection when working with the system. Never smoke or work around sparks or any source of ignition. Correct any fuel leaks before operating the engine.

This section provides removal, repair and installation procedures for all fuel injection components.

Minute particles of dirt can adversely effect the operation of the fuel injection system. Plug all disconnected hoses to prevent contamination while repairing fuel injection components. Always work in a clean environment. Take all necessary precautions to prevent any contaminants from entering the system.

High fuel pressure is required for the fuel injection system to operate correctly. To avoid dangerous fuel leakage never reuse any O-ring, gasket or sealing washer if they are removed or disturbed.

Check the condition of all hoses and clamps following the procedures listed under *Fuel Hoses and Clamps* in this chapter.

Refer to *Fuel Rail Pressure Test* in Chapter Three and bleed all pressure from the fuel system *prior* to removing any fuel system components. To assist with EFI component location and hose connections, refer to **Figure 28** and **Figure 41**.

CAUTION
Mark all hose connections to ensure they are installed correctly. Incorrect hose con-

FUEL SYSTEM REPAIR

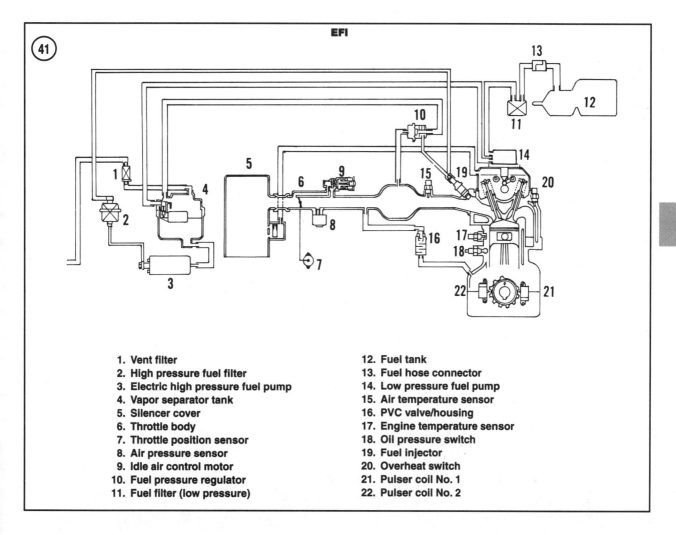

EFI

1. Vent filter
2. High pressure fuel filter
3. Electric high pressure fuel pump
4. Vapor separator tank
5. Silencer cover
6. Throttle body
7. Throttle position sensor
8. Air pressure sensor
9. Idle air control motor
10. Fuel pressure regulator
11. Fuel filter (low pressure)
12. Fuel tank
13. Fuel hose connector
14. Low pressure fuel pump
15. Air temperature sensor
16. PVC valve/housing
17. Engine temperature sensor
18. Oil pressure switch
19. Fuel injector
20. Overheat switch
21. Pulser coil No. 1
22. Pulser coil No. 2

nections can result in a fuel leak or water entry into the fuel system.

Vapor Separator Tank

This section provides removal, repair and installation procedures for the vapor separator tank. Prior to removal, mark all hose connections on the vapor separator tank (**Figure 42**). Have a shop towel and a container nearby when removing hoses and components; residual fuel may spill from the disconnected hoses and components. Clean up all spilled fuel at once.

CAUTION
Considerable effort may be required when removing the screws from the top cover. Avoid using an impact driver as the top cover or tank may be damaged. Drill out and replace the screws if necessary.

CAUTION
Never attempt to assemble the vapor separator tank without new O-rings and sealing washers. Dangerous fuel leakage can occur by reusing these components.

1. Disconnect both battery cables from the battery on electric start models. Remove the spark plugs and connect the spark plug leads to an engine ground.
2. Bleed all fuel pressure from the system before removing any components as described in Chapter Three.
3. Note the alignment of the fuel hose and triangle mark on top of the high pressure fuel filter, then carefully disconnect the high pressure fuel hose fitting. Mark all hose connection points, then remove all hose clamps and hoses connecting the engine to the vapor separator tank. *Do not remove the hose connecting the tank to the electric pump at this time.*
4. Locate and disconnect the high-pressure electric fuel pump electrical connector from the engine harness.

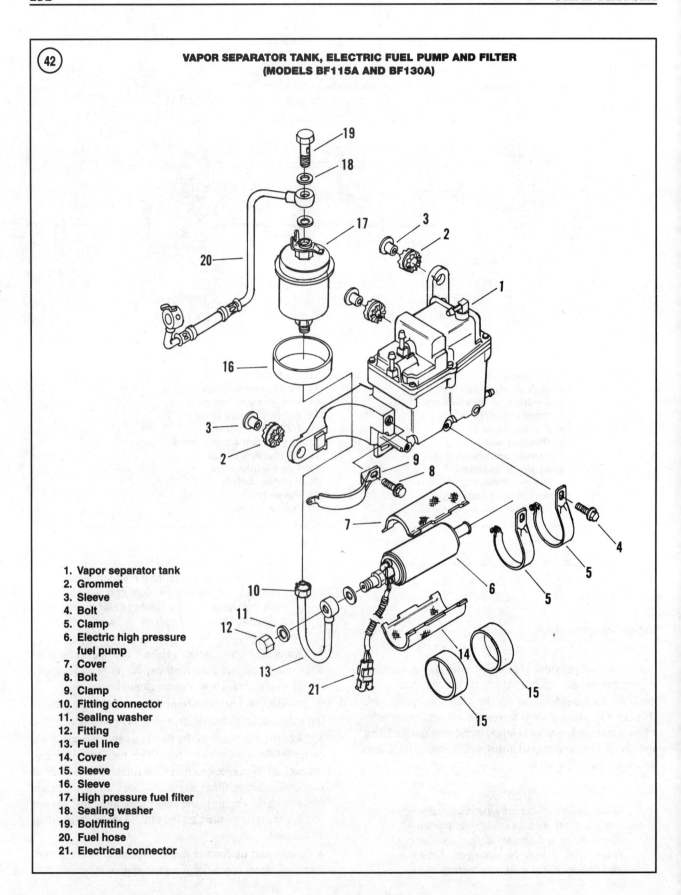

FUEL SYSTEM REPAIR

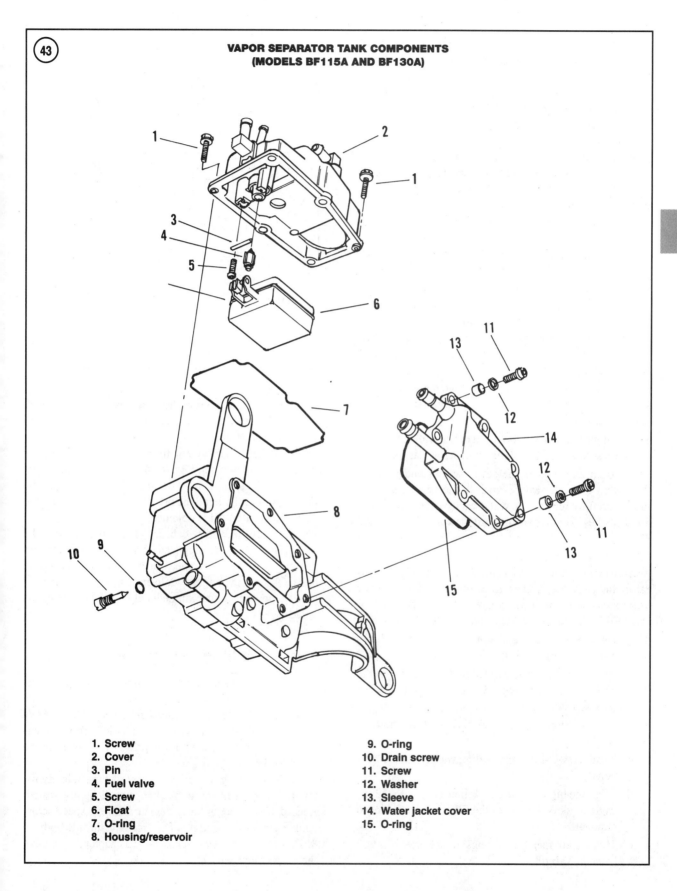

43 VAPOR SEPARATOR TANK COMPONENTS (MODELS BF115A AND BF130A)

1. Screw
2. Cover
3. Pin
4. Fuel valve
5. Screw
6. Float
7. O-ring
8. Housing/reservoir
9. O-ring
10. Drain screw
11. Screw
12. Washer
13. Sleeve
14. Water jacket cover
15. O-ring

5. Loosen and remove the three bolts holding the vapor separator tank to the base engine. Place the vapor separator tank on a clean work surface.

6. Place a suitable container under the vapor separator tank, then loosen and remove the drain screw on the vapor separator tank. Drain the fuel from the tank through the hose fitting. While holding the vapor separator tank over a container, carefully squeeze the hose clamp ends and remove the clamps and hose that connects the vapor separator tank to the high pressure electric fuel pump. Drain the fuel from the hose and fuel pump.

7. While holding the tank over the container loosen the flare nut fuel line connection at the bottom of the high-pressure fuel filter. Drain the fuel from the high-pressure fuel filter and fuel line.

8. Remove the bolt and clamp that retains the high pressure fuel filter to the vapor separator tank. Remove the filter. Mark the insulating sleeve position, then remove the two bolts and clamps that retain the high pressure fuel pump to the vapor separator tank. Remove the fuel pump and insulating sleeves.

9. Remove the six screws that retain the top cover to the vapor separator tank. Remove the top cover. Remove and discard the O-ring.

10. Remove the float pin, float and needle valve. Remove the drain screw and discard the drain screw gasket.

11. Loosen and remove the seven screws and washers that retain the water cavity cover to the vapor separator tank. Carefully remove the water cavity cover and alignment sleeves. Remove and discard the water cavity cover O-ring.

12. Clean all components in a suitable solvent. Use compressed air and blow debris from all hoses and vapor separator tank passages. Inspect all components for cracks or worn areas and replace as required. Inspect the float for cracks or indication of leakage and replace as required.

13. Assemble the vapor separator by reversing the disassembly steps, noting the following:

   a. Install the high-pressure electric fuel pump with the positive terminal facing UP or toward the vapor separator tank.
   b. Refer to Step 15 and check and/or adjust the float height.
   c. Install new O-rings and sealing washers in all locations.
   d. Align the high-pressure fuel filter hose with the triangle mark on the top of the filter as noted prior to removal.
   e. Tighten all fuel line fittings to the specification listed in **Table 1**.

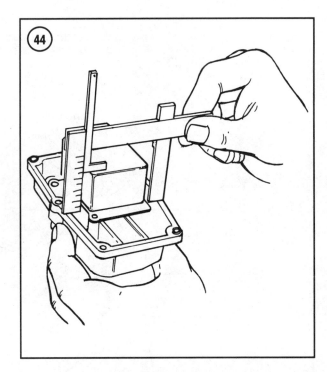

   f. Align the notches in the insulating sleeves with the high pressure fuel pump retaining clamps as noted prior to removal.

14. With the float resting on the needle valve measure the float height as shown in **Figure 44**. Compare the measurement with the specification listed in **Table 2**. Remove the float and carefully bend the brass tab up or down until the correct measurement is obtained.

15. Connect the battery cables to the battery. Install the spark plugs and spark plug leads. Squeeze the primer bulb and check for fuel leakage. Correct any fuel leakage at once. Observe the engine while an assistant starts the engine. Stop the engine immediately, if fuel leakage is noted.

Throttle Body Disassembly and Assembly

Refer to **Figure 45** during the disassembly and assembly procedures.

1. Refer to *Silencer Cover and Carburetor/Throttle Body* in this chapter and remove the throttle body from the engine. *Do not* remove the throttle position sensor from the throttle body.

2. While counting the *exact* number of turns, slowly rotate the idle speed screw clockwise until lightly seated. Record the number of turns, then turn the idle speed screw counterclockwise until it is free from the throttle body.

3. Refer to *Air Pressure Sensor* in this chapter and remove the air pressure sensor.

FUEL SYSTEM REPAIR

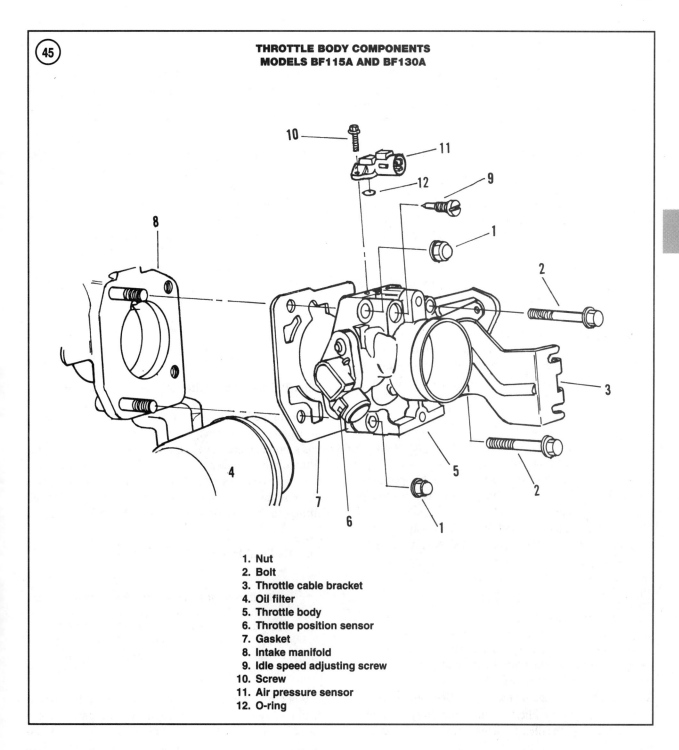

**THROTTLE BODY COMPONENTS
MODELS BF115A AND BF130A**

1. Nut
2. Bolt
3. Throttle cable bracket
4. Oil filter
5. Throttle body
6. Throttle position sensor
7. Gasket
8. Intake manifold
9. Idle speed adjusting screw
10. Screw
11. Air pressure sensor
12. O-ring

4. Avoid allowing any cleaner to contact the throttle position sender. Use spray carburetor cleaner and carefully clean the throttle body passages and throttle plate. Blow any debris or contaminants from the passages and surfaces with compressed air.

5. Install the idle speed screw into its correct location. Slowly turn the idle speed screw clockwise until lightly seated. Turn the screw counterclockwise the exact number of turns recorded in Step 2.

6. Refer to *Air Pressure Sensor* in this chapter and install the air pressure sensor.

7. Refer to *Silencer Cover and Carburetor/Throttle Body* in this chapter and install the throttle body onto the engine.

High-pressure Electric Fuel Pump

Refer to **Figure 42** to assist with component location and position.

1. Refer to *Vapor Separator Tank* in this section. Follow the steps necessary to remove the high-pressure fuel pump (6, **Figure 42**) from the vapor separator tank.
2. Position the high-pressure fuel pump over a container to capture fuel.
3. Mark the fuel line position to the wire connectors.
4. While supporting the high-pressure fuel pump, loosen the fuel hose connecting nut (12, **Figure 42**) from the end of the fuel pump. Remove the fuel line and discard the sealing washers. Blow all debris from the fuel line with compressed air.
5. Note the wire color and wire terminal markings, then remove the wire terminals from the high pressure fuel pump.
6. Securely connect the wires to the correct terminals on the high-pressure fuel pump as noted prior to removal.
7. Position a new sealing washer onto the high pressure end of the high-pressure fuel pump. Position the fuel line, another new sealing washer, then the fuel hose nut. Hand tighten at this time.
8. Refer to *Vapor Separator Tank* in this section and follow all steps necessary to install the high-pressure fuel pump to the vapor separator tank.
9. Tighten the fuel hose connecting nut to the specification listed in **Table 1** after connecting the fuel line to the high pressure filter.
10. Observe all fuel hoses and connections as an assistant starts the engine. Stop the engine immediately if fuel leakage is detected. Correct all fuel leaks before operating the engine.

Low-Pressure Fuel Filter

1. Disconnect both battery cables from the battery on electric start models. Remove the spark plugs and connect the spark plug leads to an engine ground.
2. Locate the fuel filter on the engine. See **Figure 15**.
3. Carefully pull the filter retaining clip away from the fuel filter and lift the filter from the recess in the lower engine cover.
4. Squeeze the ends of spring type hose clamps to remove them from the fuel filter fitting. Replace corroded or weak hose clamps. Note the arrow on the fuel hose fitting prior to removing the hoses from the fuel filter.
5. Place a container under the fuel filter. Carefully twist or pull the hoses to remove them from the filter. Discard the fuel filter.
6. Inspect the fuel hoses and fuel clamps as described in this chapter.
7. Install the fuel filter with its arrow facing toward the vapor separator tank. Push the fuel hoses fully onto each filter fitting.
8. Install the spring type hose clamps onto each hose connection. Make sure all connections are secure and neither the filter nor fuel hoses will interfere with any components on the engine. Squeeze the primer bulb as you inspect all hoses and connections for fuel leakage. Correct all fuel leaks at once.
9. Carefully lower the fuel filter into the recess as you hold the retaining clip away from the fuel filter. Release the retaining clip and check it to ensure correct clip position on the fuel filter as indicated.
10. Install the spark plugs and spark plug leads. Clean the terminals and connect the cables to the battery on electric start models. Check for fuel leakage as soon as the engine is started. Stop the engine immediately if leakage is detected. Correct any fuel leakage at once.

High-Pressure Fuel Filter Removal/Installation

Locate the high pressure fuel filter (17, **Figure 42**) on the vapor separator tank. Refer to *Vapor Separator Tank* in this section and remove and install the high-pressure fuel filter to the vapor separator tank. Clean all hoses and fittings with compressed air. Install new sealing washers in all locations when lines or hoses are disturbed. Tighten all fittings to the specifications listed in **Table 1**.

Fuel Rail and Injectors Removal/Installation

CAUTION
Use care when installing the injectors into the intake manifold and when installing the fuel rail onto the injector connection. Never force the fuel rail into position. The O-ring(s) may become damaged and result in a fuel leak.

Work in a clean environment and make sure that no contaminants enter the fuel system. Minute particles can cause a serious malfunction with the fuel injection system. Some fuel leakage may occur during removal. Have a container for holding fuel and shop towels nearby. Clean up any spilled fuel at once.

1. Disconnect both battery cables from the battery on electric start models. Remove all spark plugs and connect the spark plug leads to an engine ground.
2. Refer to *Fuel Rail Pressure Test* in Chapter Three and bleed all fuel pressure from the system before removing

FUEL SYSTEM REPAIR

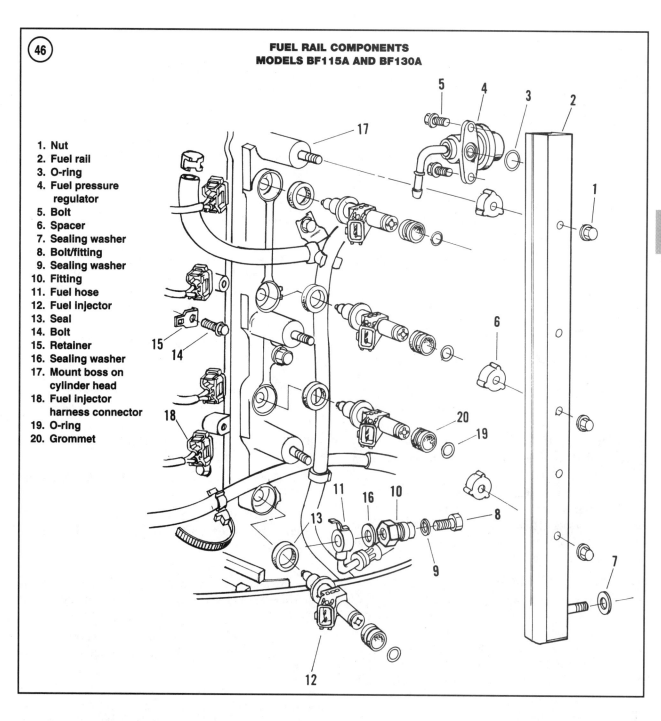

FUEL RAIL COMPONENTS MODELS BF115A AND BF130A

1. Nut
2. Fuel rail
3. O-ring
4. Fuel pressure regulator
5. Bolt
6. Spacer
7. Sealing washer
8. Bolt/fitting
9. Sealing washer
10. Fitting
11. Fuel hose
12. Fuel injector
13. Seal
14. Bolt
15. Retainer
16. Sealing washer
17. Mount boss on cylinder head
18. Fuel injector harness connector
19. O-ring
20. Grommet

any components. Refer to **Figure 46** to assist with identification and location for the fuel rail components.

3. Remove the fuel pressure test fitting from the bottom of the fuel rail. Discard the sealing washer. Carefully pull the vacuum hose from the fitting on the fuel pressure regulator. Slide the clamp away from the fitting, then pull the fuel return hose from the fitting on the fuel pressure regulator. Drain any fuel in the hose into a suitable container.

4. Note the connection points of each fuel injector and wire harness connector. Carefully remove the wire harness connector from each fuel injector.

5. Remove the three nuts (1, **Figure 46**) that retain the fuel rail to the intake manifold. Carefully pull the fuel rail from the intake manifold.

6. Remove the fuel injectors from either the fuel rail or the intake manifold. Handle the injectors carefully and lay them on their side in a clean and protected area.

7. Remove and discard the O-ring and rubber spacer from the fuel injector-to-fuel rail connection, the rubber sleeves on the fuel rail side of the fuel injectors and the injector seal from the fuel injector or mounting location on the intake manifold.

8. Refer to *Fuel Pressure Regulator* in this section and remove the fuel pressure regulator from the fuel rail.

9. Use compressed air and blow all debris or contaminants from the fuel rail. Inspect the fuel injectors for damage or corroded terminals. Clean dirty terminals. Replace damaged fuel injectors.

10. Refer to *Fuel Hoses and Clamps* in this chapter and inspect the fuel hoses and clamps.

11. Install in the reverse order of assembly while noting the following:
   a. Replace *all* O-rings, seals and spacer sleeves on assembly. Inspect the hoses for damaged areas, brittle or soft conditions and replace as required.
   b. Replace all sealing washers on assembly.
   c. Lubricate all O-rings, seals, and grommets with engine oil. Install them into the correct mounting locations.
   d. Place all fuel injectors into the mounting location on the intake manifold first, then install the fuel rail onto the fuel injectors.
   e. Tighten all fasteners securely or to the specification listed in **Table 1**.

12. Install the spark plugs and spark plug leads. Clean the battery terminals and connect the cables to the battery on electric start models. Check for fuel leakage as soon as the engine is started. Stop the engine immediately if leakage is detected. Correct any fuel leaks at once.

Fuel Pressure Regulator Removal/Installation

1. Disconnect both battery cables from the battery on electric start models. Remove the spark plugs and connect the spark plug leads to an engine ground.

2. Refer to *Fuel Rail Pressure Test* in Chapter Three and bleed all fuel pressure from the system before removing any components.

3. Locate the fuel pressure regulator on the fuel rail. Note all hose connections and routing. Remove the hose clamp, then remove the fuel return hose from the fuel pressure regulator. Drain any fuel from the hose.

4. Note the fuel pressure regulator position on the fuel rail (4, **Figure 46**). Loosen the two bolts that retain the fuel pressure regulator to the fuel rail (5, **Figure 46**). Remove the fuel pressure regulator from the fuel rail. Remove and discard the O-ring (3, **Figure 46**).

5. Assembly is the reverse of disassembly. Lubricate it with oil and install a new O-ring onto the fuel pressure regulator. Install all hoses and hose clamps into position. Securely tighten all fasteners and clamps.

6. Install all spark plugs and spark plug leads. Clean the battery terminals and connect the cables to the battery on electric start models. Check for fuel leakage as soon as the engine is started. Stop the engine immediately if leakage is detected.

Throttle Position Sender Replacement

Removal and replacement of the throttle position sender is not recommended on Honda outboards. Replacement of the throttle body is required if a faulty throttle position sensor is indicated.

Refer to *Throttle Body and Silencer Cover* in this chapter for the replacement procedure.

Air Pressure Sensor Removal/Installation

1. Disconnect both battery cables from the battery on electric start models. Remove the spark plugs and connect the spark plug leads to an engine ground.

2. Locate the air pressure sensor (20, **Figure 28**) on the engine.

3. Locate and disconnect the air pressure sensor from the engine harness connector (18, **Figure 28**). Clean the terminals on both connectors.

4. Note the position of the air pressure sensor on the throttle body. Remove both screws and remove the air pressure sensor and O-ring from the throttle body. Discard the O-ring.

5. Inspect the passage directly below the air pressure sensor mounting location. Use compressed air and blow any debris from the passage.

6. Lubricate with oil and install a new O-ring onto the air pressure sensor. Position the air pressure sensor onto the throttle body. Install and securely tighten the retaining screws.

7. Clean the terminals, then connect the air pressure sensor to the harness connector.

8. Install all spark plugs and spark plug leads. Clean the battery terminals and connect the cables to the battery on electric start models. Check for fuel leakage as soon as the engine is started. Stop the engine immediately if leakage is detected. Correct any fuel leaks at once.

FUEL SYSTEM REPAIR

Idle Air Control Motor Removal/Installation

1. Disconnect both battery cables from the battery. Remove the spark plugs and connect the spark plug leads to an engine ground.
2. Locate the idle air control motor (23, **Figure 28**) on the engine.
3. Locate and disconnect the idle air control motor from the engine harness connector. Clean the terminals on both connectors.
4. Note the position of the idle air control motor on the intake manifold. Remove both retaining bolts and remove the idle air control motor, filter and O-ring from the intake manifold. Discard the O-ring.
5. Inspect the passage directly below the idle air control motor mounting location. Use compressed air and blow any debris from the passage. Clean or replace the idle air control motor filter.
6. Install a new O-ring onto the idle air control motor. Position the idle air control motor onto the intake manifold. Install and securely tighten the retaining bolts.
7. Inspect and clean the harness terminals, then connect the engine harness connector to the idle air control motor.
8. Install the spark plugs and spark plug leads. Clean the battery terminals and connect the cables to the battery on electric start models.
9. Check for fuel leakage as soon as the engine is started. Stop the engine immediately if leakage is detected.

Air Temperature Sensor Removal/Installation

1. Disconnect both battery cables from the battery. Remove the spark plugs and connect the spark plug leads to a suitable engine ground, such as a clean cylinder head or cylinder block bolts.
2. Locate the air temperature sensor (39, **Figure 28**) on the engine.
3. Locate and disconnect the air temperature sensor from the engine harness connector. Clean the terminals on both connectors.
4. Note the position of the air temperature sensor on the intake manifold. Using a suitable wrench carefully turn the sensor counterclockwise and remove the sensor and O-ring from the intake manifold. Discard the O-ring.
5. Inspect the passage at the air temperature sensor mounting location. Use compressed air and blow any debris from the passage. Clean any debris from the threaded opening.
6. Install a new O-ring onto the air temperature sensor. Thread the air temperature sensor into the opening by hand, then tighten the sensor to the specification listed in **Table 1**.
7. Inspect and clean the harness terminals, then connect the engine harness connector to the air temperature sensor.
8. Install all spark plugs and spark plug leads. Clean the battery terminals and connect the battery cables to the battery. Check for fuel leakage as soon as the engine is started. Stop the engine immediately if leakage is detected. Correct any fuel leaks at once.

Engine Temperature Sensor Removal/Installation

1. Disconnect both battery cables from the battery. Remove the spark plugs and connect the spark plug leads to an engine ground.
2. Locate the engine temperature sensor (20, **Figure 15**) on the engine.
3. Locate and disconnect the engine temperature sensor from the engine harness connector. Clean the terminals on both connectors.
4. Note the position of the engine temperature sensor on the base engine. Using a wrench, carefully turn the sensor counterclockwise and remove the sensor and O-ring from the base engine. Discard the O-ring.
5. Inspect the passage at the engine temperature sensor mounting location. Use compressed air and blow any debris from the passage. Clean any debris from the threaded opening.
6. Lubricate with oil and install a new O-ring onto the engine temperature sensor. Thread the engine temperature sensor into the opening by hand, then tighten the sensor to the specification listed in **Table 1**.
7. Inspect and clean the harness terminals and connect the engine harness connector to the engine temperature sensor.
8. Install all spark plugs and spark plug leads. Clean the battery terminals and connect the cables to the battery. Check for fuel leakage as soon as the engine is started. Stop the engine immediately if leakage is detected. Correct any fuel leaks at once.

PCV Valve/Housing Removal/Installation

1. Disconnect both battery cables from the battery. Remove the spark plugs and connect the spark plug leads to a suitable engine ground, such as a clean cylinder head or cylinder block bolts.
2. Locate the PVC valve and housing (16, **Figure 15**) on the engine. Slide the hose clamp at the bottom of the housing away from the fitting, then carefully pull the lower hose from the housing.

3. Carefully pull the PCV valve and grommet from the housing. Remove the six bolts that attach the housing to the base engine then carefully pull the housing from the base engine.

4. Clean the PCV valve and the housing in a suitable solvent and dry with compressed air. Replace the housing if it is cracked, damaged or distorted.

5. Shake the PCV valve to check for a stuck valve. Replace the PCV valve if dirt or other contaminants are present after cleaning or if the valve cannot be heard when it is shaken. Replace the grommet if it has torn, worn or damaged surfaces.

6. Installation is the reverse of removal. Securely tighten all bolts and clamps. Make sure all hoses are properly routed and connected.

7. Install the spark plugs and spark plug leads. Clean the battery terminals and connect the battery to the battery. Check for fuel leakage as soon as the engine is started. Stop the engine immediately if leakage is detected. Correct any fuel leaks at once.

Vent Hose Filter Removal/Installation

Locate the vent hose filter (1, **Figure 15**). Visually inspect the filter for contaminants. If contamination is noted replace the filter.

1. Disconnect both battery cables from the battery. Remove the spark plugs and connect the spark plug leads to an engine ground.
2. Carefully slide the vent hose filter down and out of the filter retainer.
3. Note the direction the arrow on the filter body is facing. Mark the hose connection points and routing then, remove the hoses from the vent hose filter.
4. Install the replacement vent hose filter with the arrow facing the direction noted during removal. The large diameter end of the filter must face down. Make sure both hoses are fully installed on the hose fittings on the filter.
5. Carefully slide the filter up and into the filter retainer.
6. Install all spark plugs and spark plug leads. Clean the battery terminals and connect the cables to the battery. Check for fuel leakage as soon as the engine is started. Stop the engine immediately if leakage is detected. Correct any fuel leaks at once.

FUEL SYSTEM REPAIR

TABLE 1 TIGHTENING TORQUE

Fastener	Torque
Fuel pump-mounting bolt/screw	
BF50, BF5A	Use standard tightening torque per bolt size
BF75, BF8A, BF100	Use standard tightening torque per bolt size
BF9.9A, BF15A	5 N•m (44 in.-lb.)
BF20A, BF25A, BF30A	10 N•m (89 in.-lb.)
BF35A, BF40A, BF45A, BF50A	10 N•m (89 in.-lb.)
BF75A, BF90A	9 N•m (80 in.-lb.)
BF115A, BF130A	Use standard tightening torque per bolt size
Electric fuel pump-to-fuel filter hose sealing bolt	
BF115A, BF130A	22.0 N•m (16 ft.-lb.)
Fuel filter flare type nut fitting	
BF115A, BF130A	
Lower fitting	33 N•m (24 ft.-lb.)
Upper fitting	37 N•m (27 ft.-lb.)
Fuel pressure test/high pressure fuel hose at fuel rail	
BF115A, BF130A	
Small fitting	12 N•m (106 in.-lb.)
Large fitting	22 N•m (16 ft.-lb.)
Air temperature sensor	
BF115A, BF130A	18 N•m (13 ft.-lb.)
Engine temperature sensor	
BF115A, BF130A	18 N•m (13 ft.-lb.)

TABLE 2 FLOAT SPECIFICATIONS

Model	Float height
BF20, BF2A	10.5-13.5 mm (0.413-0.531 in.)
BF50, BF5A	9.0-11.0 mm (0.354-0.433 in.)
BF75, BF8A, BF100	9.85-10.15 mm (0.388-0.400 in.)
BF9.9A, BF15A	13.0-15.0 mm (0.511-0.591 in.)
BF20A, BF25A and BF30A	14.0 mm (0.551) in.)
BF35A, BF40A, BF45A and BF50A	14.0 mm (0.551 in.)
BF75A and BF90A	11.50 mm (0.453 in.)
BF115A and BF130A	29.0-34.0 mm (1.142-1.339 in.)

Chapter Seven

Electrical and Ignition

This chapter provides removal, inspection and installation procedures for the starting, charging, warning and ignition systems. Battery maintenance and testing are also provided. Torque specifications and electrical specifications are provided in **Tables 1-5**, located at the end of this chapter.

STARTING SYSTEM

This section provides removal, inspection and installation for the starting system components. Repair procedures are also provided for the starter motor.

Starter Relay

Starter relay mounting locations vary by model. Refer to the provided illustrations and information to locate the starter relay.

On models BF9.9A, BF15A, BF20A, BF25A and BF30A, the starter relay mounts directly to the side of the electric starter motor (**Figure 1**).

On models BF35A, BF40A, BF45A and BF50A, the starter relay is mounted below the electric starter motor, near the silencer cover (**Figure 2**).

On models BF75A, BF90A, BF115A and BF130A, the starter relay is mounted to a bracket positioned above the electric starter motor (**Figure 3**). On these models, a starter solenoid is mounted to the electric starter motor. Refer to *Electric Starter Motor Repair* in this chapter if replacing the starter solenoid is required.

Removal/Installation (models BF9.9A, BF15A, BF20A, BF25A and BF30A)

Refer to **Figure 1** during the removal and installation.

1. Disconnect both battery cables from the battery. Remove the spark plugs and connect the spark plug leads to an engine ground.

2. Note the terminal connection points to ensure correct installation. Disconnect the two small connectors and wires from the relay. Clean the wire connectors of all corrosion or contamination.

3. Note the position of the large wire terminal prior to loosening the wire terminal nuts.

4. Remove the wire terminal cover, nuts and large wire connectors from the starter relay. Clean all corrosion or contamination from the connectors.

5. Loosen and remove the starter relay attaching screw and spacer. Remove the relay from the electric starter motor.

6. Installation is the reverse of removal while noting the following:
   a. Ensure that the large wire terminal is positioned correctly on the starter relay as noted prior to removing the wire.
   b. Securely tighten all fasteners.
   c. Route all wires in a manner that prevents interference with other engine components.

7. Clean and connect the battery cables to the proper terminal. Install the electrical component cover if removed. Check for proper starter relay operation.

ELECTRICAL AND IGNITION

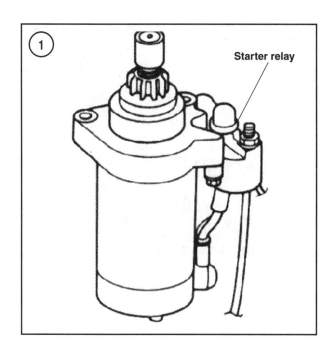

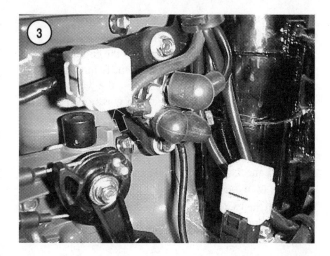

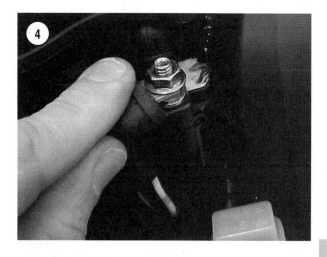

Removal/Installation (models BF35A, BF40A, BF45A and BF50A)

Refer to **Figure 2** during the removal and installation.

1. Disconnect both battery cables from the battery. Remove the spark plugs and connect the spark plug leads to an engine ground.

2. Note the terminal connections to ensure correct connection. Disconnect the small plug connector and wire from the relay. Clean the wire connector of all corrosion or contamination.

3. Note the position of the large wire terminal (**Figure 4**) prior to loosening the wire terminal nuts. Note the wire connection points and wire routing, then remove the terminal nuts and all wires.

4. Loosen and remove the small bolt and ground wire from the solenoid. Pull the large wire and grommet from the notch on the starter relay-mounting bracket.

5. Carefully pull the fuse holder up to remove it from the starter relay-mounting bracket. Pull the cable retainer from the hole in the mounting bracket.

6. Remove the second mounting bolt and lift the starter relay from the engine. Clean all corrosion or contamination from the mounting location and mount bolt bosses.

7. Install in the reverse order of removal while noting the following:

   a. Make sure that all wires are routed and connected as noted prior to removal.

   b. Route all wires to prevent interference with other engine components.

   c. Securely tighten all terminal nuts and mounting fasteners.

   d. Properly position all wire terminal covers to prevent electrical arcing.

8. Clean and connect the battery cables to the proper terminal. Install the electrical component cover if removed. Check for proper starter relay operation.

Removal/Installation (models BF75A, BF90A, BF115A and BF130A)

Refer to **Figure 3** during the removal and installation.
1. Disconnect both battery cables from the battery. Remove the spark plugs and connect the spark plug lead to an engine ground..
2. Note the terminal connections to ensure correct installation.
3. Release the wire retainer, then disconnect the plug connector and wire from the relay. Clean all corrosion and contamination from the wire connector.
4. Pull the terminal covers away from the terminals. Note the orientation of the large wire terminal (**Figure 5**) prior to loosening the wire terminal nuts. Note the wire connection points and routing then remove the terminal nuts and all wires.
5. Carefully pull the fuse holder from the starter relay-mounting bracket.
6. Remove the mounting bolts, washers, grommets and sleeves from the starter relay. Carefully pull the starter relay from the engine. Clean all corrosion or contamination from the mounting location and mount bolt bosses.
7. Installation is the reverse of removal. Note the following:
   a. Ensure that all wires are routed and connected as noted prior to removal.
   b. Route all wires to prevent interference with other engine components.
   c. Tighten all terminal nuts and mounting fasteners securely.
   d. Properly position all wire terminal covers to prevent electrical arcing.
8. Clean and connect the battery cables to the proper terminal. Check for proper starter relay operation.

Key Switch Removal/Installation (Remote Control Models)

Follow Steps 1-8 for models with the *key switch located in the remote control*.
Follow Steps 3-5 for models with *dash-mounted key switch*.
1. Disconnect both battery cables from the battery terminals. Refer to Chapter Fourteen to remove the remote control from its mounting location.

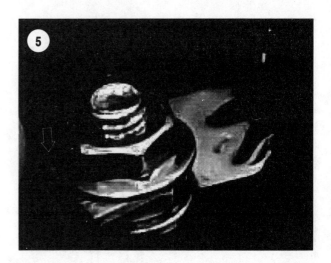

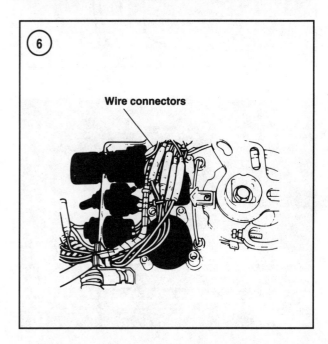

2. Disassemble the remote control to the point the key switch leads and retainer are accessible.
3. Use the wiring diagrams located at the end of the manual to locate the key switch wires. Identify the wire colors and trace them to the key switch. Note the wire attaching locations. Disconnect the key switch wires from the wire harness (**Figure 6**).
4. Loosen and remove the key switch-retaining nut. Remove the key switch.
5. Install the key switch to its mounting location. Securely tighten the retaining nut.
6. Attach the key switch wires to the correct harness connector. Ensure that the wire does not interfere with other components.

ELECTRICAL AND IGNITION

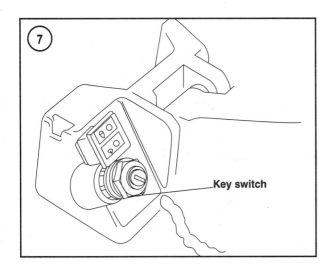

points. Carefully disconnect each key switch wire from the tiller control wire harness.

3. Support the key switch as you carefully loosen and remove the large nut that retains the key switch. Remove the key switch from the tiller bracket.

4. Clean any corrosion or contamination from the surfaces and screw threads of the access panel.

5. Installation is the reverse of removal, noting the following:
   a. Ensure that the key switch wires are routed to prevent interference with other components.
   b. All connector terminals are free of debris and/or corrosion.
   c. The large nut that retains the starter button is tightened securely.
   d. Securely tighten the access panel screws.

6. Install the spark plugs and spark plug leads. Clean the battery terminals and connect the cables to the battery.

Start Button Removal/Installation

This component is located on the starboard side of the carry handle near the shift selector (**Figure 8**). Access the start button wires and fasteners through the opening at the bottom of the carry handle.

1. Disconnect both battery cables from the battery terminals. Remove the spark plugs and connect the spark plug leads to a suitable engine ground, such as a clean cylinder head or cylinder block bolt.

2. Refer to the wiring diagrams located at the end of the manual to identify and locate the start button wires. Trace the wires to the connections at the main engine wire harness. Note the wire connection points and wire routing, then disconnect the start button wires from the main engine wire harness.

3. Hold the start button in position as you remove the large nut in the carry handle opening. Carefully pull the start button from the carry handle as you guide the wires and connections through the carry handle opening.

4. Installation is the reverse of removal. Note the following:
   a. Ensure that the start button wires are routed to prevent interference with other components.
   b. Be certain all connector terminals are free of debris, corrosion or contamination.
   c. Make sure the large nut that retains the starter button is securely tightened.

5. Install the spark plugs and spark plug leads. Clean the battery terminals, then connect the cables to the battery.

7. Refer to Chapter Fourteen and assemble then install the control to its mounting location.

8. Install the spark plugs and spark plug leads. Clean the battery terminals and connect the cables to the battery.

Key Switch Removal/Installation
(Tiller control models)

The switch is mounted to the tiller control bracket (**Figure 7**). Access the key switch and its wire connectors through the access panel located at the bottom of the bracket.

1. Disconnect both battery cables from the battery terminals. Remove the spark plugs and connect the spark plug leads to an engine ground.

2. Remove the six screws and the access panel from the bottom of the tiller bracket. Locate the key switch and its wire connectors. Note all wire routing and connection

Neutral Switch Removal/Installation (Models BF75, BF8A and BF100)

1. Disconnect both battery cables from the battery terminals. Remove the spark plugs and connect the spark plug leads to an engine ground.
2. Refer to the wiring diagrams located at the end of the manual to identify and locate the neutral switch wires. Disconnect the start button wires from the main engine wire harness.
3. Disconnect the blue and black/white wires from the neutral switch. Loosen the retaining screw and lift the neutral switch from the engine.
4. Position the replacement neutral switch onto its mounting location. Install the retaining screw but do not tighten it at this time.
5. Place the shift selector into neutral gear. Slide the neutral switch until the mark on the plate (**Figure 9**) aligns with the end of the neutral switch. Securely tighten the retaining screw.
6. Inspect the position of the detent roller. Refer to Chapter Five and adjust the shift system if the detent roller does not align with the neutral notch. Repeat Step 5 after performing adjustment.
7. Install the spark plugs and spark plug leads. Clean the battery terminals and connect the cables to the battery.

Neutral Switch Removal/Installation (All Other Models)

1. Disconnect both battery cables from the battery terminals. Remove the spark plugs and connect the spark plug leads to an engine ground.
2. Refer to the wiring diagrams located at the end of the manual to identify and locate the neutral switch wires. Disconnect the start button wires from the main engine wire harness.
3. Position the shift selector in neutral. Remove the retaining screw(s) and pull the neutral switch from the engine.
4. Position the replacement neutral switch onto the engine and install the retaining screw. DO NOT tighten the screw at this time.
5. Align the center of the switch plunger with the center actuator tip as shown in **Figure 10**. Hold the switch in this position and securely tighten the retaining screw(s). If you are unable to correctly align the neutral switch with the center of the actuator tip, refer to Chapter Five, adjust the shift system and repeat this step.
6. Operate the shift selector then check the neutral switch alignment as described in Step 5.

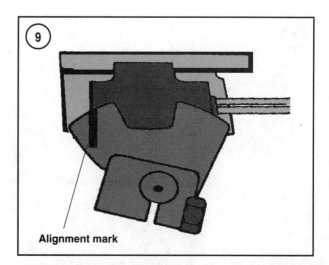

Alignment mark

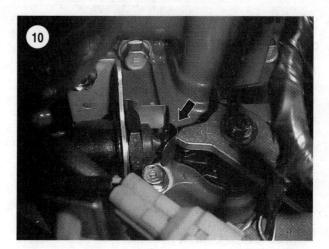

7. Install the spark plugs and spark plug leads. Clean the battery terminals and connect the cables to the battery.

Choke Solenoid Removal/Installation

1. Disconnect both battery cables from the battery. Remove the spark plugs and connect the spark plug leads to an engine ground.
2. Locate the choke solenoid on the engine. Note the wire connection points and routing, then disconnect the choke solenoid wires from the main engine wire harness.
3. Loosen the bolt on the choke solenoid-mounting bracket (**Figure 11**). Move the choke solenoid forward and away from the choke plunger (**Figure 12**). Pull the choke solenoid from the bracket.
4. Pull the choke lever (on the lower motor cover) to the full choke position. Make sure that the lever remains in this position during adjustments.

ELECTRICAL AND IGNITION

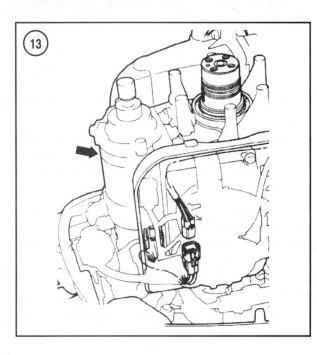

5. Install the replacement choke solenoid into the bracket with the arrow on the component facing UP.
6. Slide the choke solenoid toward the choke plunger until it just bottoms in the choke solenoid housing.
7. Hold the choke solenoid in this position as you tighten the mounting bracket bolt to the specification listed in **Table 1**. Return the choke lever to the normal position by fully pushing it in.
8. Install the spark plugs and spark plug leads. Clean the battery terminals and connect the cables to the battery.

Starter Motor Removal and Installation

1. Disconnect both battery cables from the battery. Locate the electric starter motor on the engine (**Figure 13**).
2. Remove the fasteners and pinion cover, if so equipped.
3. Remove the terminal insulator and the terminal bolt from the starter motor. Clean corrosion or contamination from the cable terminal. Remove the bolts or nuts that retain the starter to the cylinder block. Clean and inspect the mating surfaces for cracks or damage. Replace the housing if defects are noted.
4. Install the electric starter motor and tighten the fasteners securely.
5. Attach the cable terminal to the starter motor and tighten the fastener securely. Install the pinion cover and fasteners if so equipped.
6. Clean and connect battery cables to the correct terminal. Check for proper starter motor operation.

Starter Motor Disassembly

NOTE
Replace all O-rings, seals and gaskets when removed or disturbed. Apply weather-strip adhesive to the mating surfaces of all terminal insulators during assembly.

CAUTION
Never strike the frame of the starter motor with a hard object. If struck, the permanent magnets may crack or break, resulting in starter motor failure.

Electric Starter Motor Disassembly

Refer to **Figures 14-16** for this procedure.
1. Remove the starter as described in this chapter.
2. On models BF75A, BF90A, BF115A and BF130A, remove the two screws and terminal nut from the starter solenoid. Pull the solenoid, spring, and plunger from the electric starter motor.

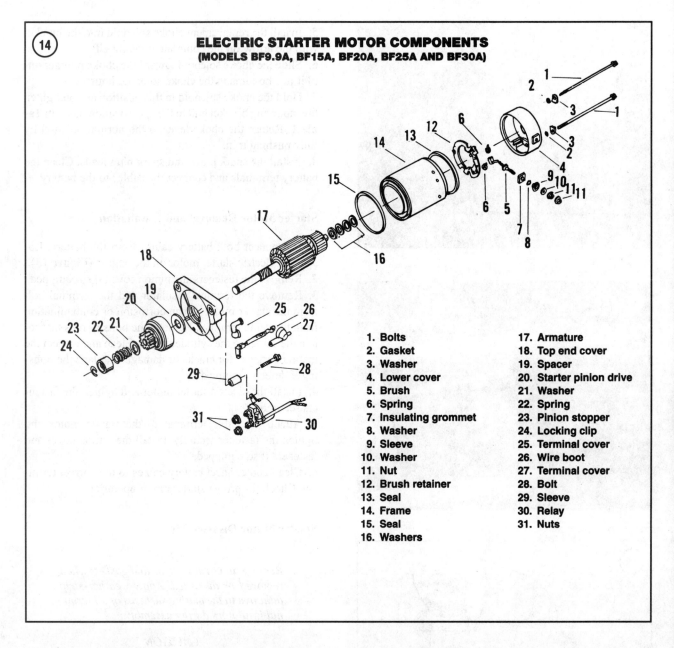

ELECTRIC STARTER MOTOR COMPONENTS
(MODELS BF9.9A, BF15A, BF20A, BF25A AND BF30A)

1. Bolts
2. Gasket
3. Washer
4. Lower cover
5. Brush
6. Spring
7. Insulating grommet
8. Washer
9. Sleeve
10. Washer
11. Nut
12. Brush retainer
13. Seal
14. Frame
15. Seal
16. Washers
17. Armature
18. Top end cover
19. Spacer
20. Starter pinion drive
21. Washer
22. Spring
23. Pinion stopper
24. Locking clip
25. Terminal cover
26. Wire boot
27. Terminal cover
28. Bolt
29. Sleeve
30. Relay
31. Nuts

3. With the starter carefully mounted in a vise, grasp the starter pinion drive (A, **Figure 17**) and stopper and pull it towards the starter to expose the locking clip. Carefully pry the locking clip (B) from the armature shaft. Remove the locking clip and stopper (C).

4. Turn the pinion drive counterclockwise to remove it from the armature shaft.

5. Mark the starter frame and the top and bottom covers for correct alignment during assembly. Support both ends of the starter motor and remove the two throughbolts.

6. Remove the top end cover from the frame assembly. If necessary, lightly tap on the cover with a plastic mallet. Remove and discard the O-ring, if so equipped.

7. On models BF75A, BF90A, BF115A and BF130A, remove the planetary gear assembly, pinion shaft, solenoid lever retainer, solenoid lever and steel ball from the armature and end cover.

8. With the frame assembly placed on its side, lightly tap the exposed end of the armature shaft with a plastic mallet to remove the armature and lower cover from the frame.

9. Note the order of the composite and metal washers on the armature shaft. Wire them together until assembly to ensure they are installed in the same order and position.

10. Carefully pull the lower cover from the armature. Remove and discard the O-ring if so equipped.

ELECTRICAL AND IGNITION

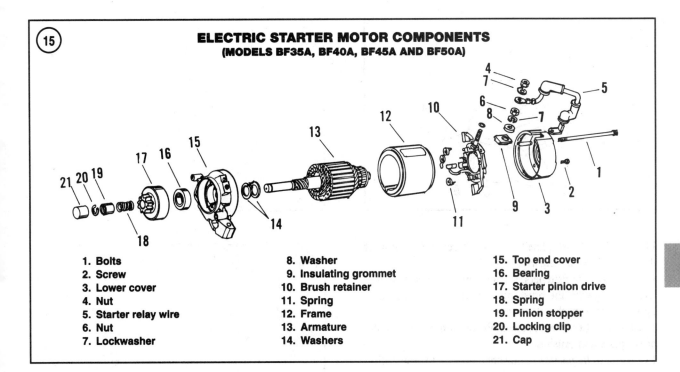

ELECTRIC STARTER MOTOR COMPONENTS
(MODELS BF35A, BF40A, BF45A AND BF50A)

1. Bolts
2. Screw
3. Lower cover
4. Nut
5. Starter relay wire
6. Nut
7. Lockwasher
8. Washer
9. Insulating grommet
10. Brush retainer
11. Spring
12. Frame
13. Armature
14. Washers
15. Top end cover
16. Bearing
17. Starter pinion drive
18. Spring
19. Pinion stopper
20. Locking clip
21. Cap

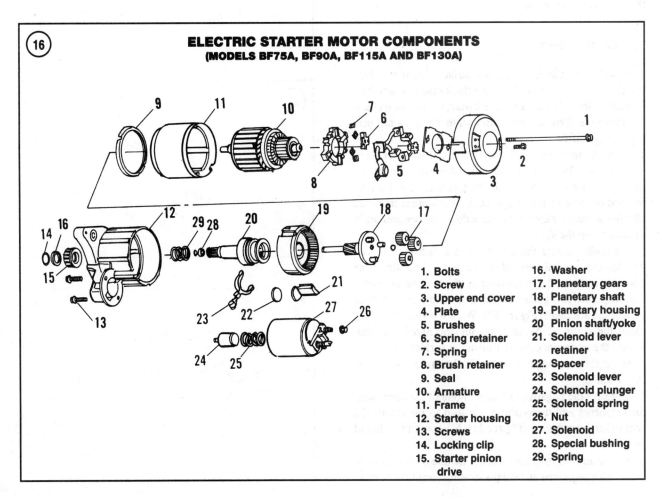

ELECTRIC STARTER MOTOR COMPONENTS
(MODELS BF75A, BF90A, BF115A AND BF130A)

1. Bolts
2. Screw
3. Upper end cover
4. Plate
5. Brushes
6. Spring retainer
7. Spring
8. Brush retainer
9. Seal
10. Armature
11. Frame
12. Starter housing
13. Screws
14. Locking clip
15. Starter pinion drive
16. Washer
17. Planetary gears
18. Planetary shaft
19. Planetary housing
20. Pinion shaft/yoke
21. Solenoid lever retainer
22. Spacer
23. Solenoid lever
24. Solenoid plunger
25. Solenoid spring
26. Nut
27. Solenoid
28. Special bushing
29. Spring

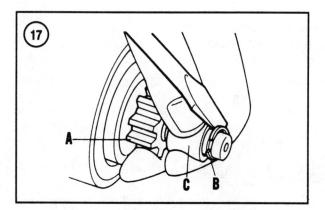

11. Mark the brush plate to ensure correct orientation of the lower cover during assembly.
12. Remove the fasteners, starter terminal nuts and insulators along with the brush plate. Use compressed air to blow debris from the components.
13. Use a mild solvent to clean all components except the brush plate and brushes.
14. Refer to *Inspection* in this chapter prior to assembling the electric starter motor.

Starter Motor Inspection

1. Place the pinion drive on a flat surface. Attempt to turn the pinion clockwise and counterclockwise (**Figure 18**). The drive should turn freely clockwise, but not turn counterclockwise. Replace the pinion drive if it does not perform as specified.
2. Inspect the pinion drive for chipped, cracked or worn teeth (**Figure 19**). Replace the pinion drive if you note any of these conditions. Inspect the helical splines at the pinion end of the armature. Replace the armature if there are chipped areas or if the pinion drive does not turn smoothly up and down the shaft.
3. Carefully secure the armature in a soft-jawed vise. Tighten the vise only enough to secure the Armature. Use 600 grit carburundum (abrasive cloth) to remove corrosion deposits and glazed surfaces from the commutator area of the armature (**Figure 20**). Work the area enough to clean the surfaces. Avoid removing too much material. Rotate the armature often to polish the surfaces evenly.
4. Select the ohm function on a volt/ohm meter. Select the R × 1 scale.
5. Connect the negative test lead to one of the commutator segments and the positive test lead to the laminated section of the armature (**Figure 21**). No continuity should be noted.
   a. Connect the negative test lead to one of the commutator segments and the positive test lead to the arma-

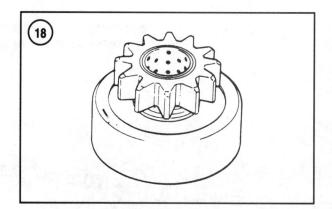

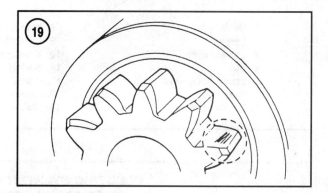

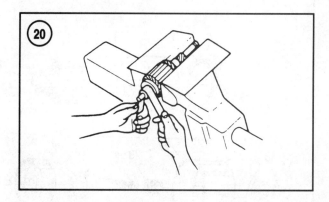

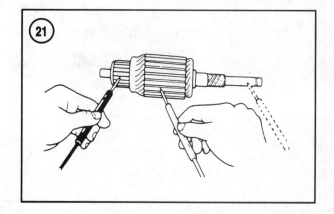

ELECTRICAL AND IGNITION

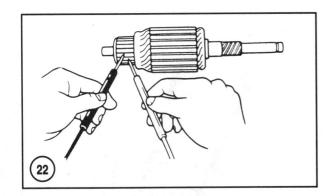

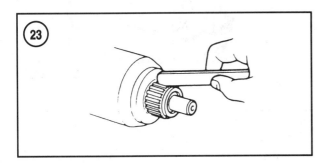

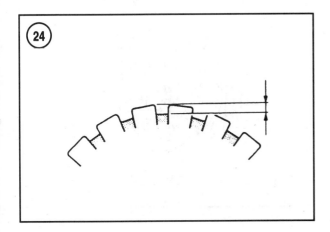

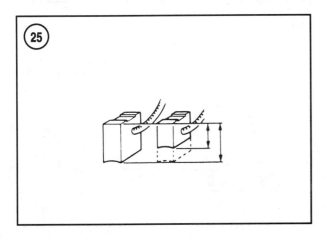

ture shaft (**Figure 21**). No continuity should be noted.

b. Connect the negative test lead to one of the commutator segments and the positive test lead to each of the remaining commutator segments (**Figure 22**). Continuity must be present between each segment.

c. Replace the armature if any incorrect meter readings are noted.

6. Use a disposable nail file or a small file (**Figure 23**) to remove the metal and mica particles from the area between and below the commutator segments (undercut).

7. Blow away any particles with compressed air and use a depth micrometer to measure the depth of the undercut between the segments (**Figure 24**). Compare the measurement with the specification listed in **Table 2**. Replace the armature if the undercut is less than the specification.

8. Measure the brush length as shown in **Figure 25**. Compare the brush length with the specification listed in **Table 2**. Replace all brushes if any of them are less than the specification. Replace all brushes if corrosion or contamination is present, or any chipping or irregular surfaces are noted.

9. Inspect the magnets in the frame assembly for corrosion or other contamination and clean as required. Inspect the frame assemble for cracked or loose magnets. Replace the frame assembly if it cannot be adequately cleaned or damaged magnets are noted.

10. Inspect the bearing surfaces on the armature and the bushings for discoloration and excessive or uneven wear. Replace any questionable bearings/bushings using a suitable pulling tool and driver. Replace the armature if rough or uneven surfaces are present on bearing surfaces.

11. On models BF75A, BF90A, BF115A and BF130A, refer to *Starter Solenoid Testing* in this section, then test the solenoid.

Starter Solenoid Testing (Models BF75A, BF90A, BF115A and BF130A)

Use a volt/ohm meter to test the circuits within the starter solenoid.

1. Remove the starter solenoid (**Figure 26**) from the starter motor.

2. Select the ohm function on a volt/ohm meter. Select the R × 1 scale on the meter.

3. Connect the positive test lead to the small terminal (A, **Figure 26**). Connect the negative test lead to an unpainted surface of the starter solenoid. Continuity should be present.

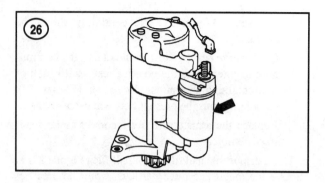

4. Connect the positive test lead to the small terminal (**Figure 26**). Connect the negative test lead to the large terminal (**Figure 26**). Continuity should be present.

5. Replace the starter solenoid if it does not perform as specified.

Starter Motor Assembly

1. Align the marks made previously and install the brush plate on the lower starter cover. Tighten all fasteners securely.

2. Fabricate a brush-retaining tool to assist with the armature installation. Bend a stiff piece of thin rod into a U shape and position it between the brushes (**Figure 27**). Install the armature and carefully remove the tool. If possible, manually hold the brushes away and carefully slide the armature into position. Release the brushes and inspect for damage before proceeding (**Figure 28**).

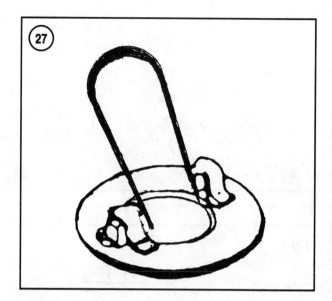

3. Wipe a small amount of water-resistant grease on the bottom cover bushing. Install the washer over the lower end of the armature shaft.

4. Install a new O-ring (if so equipped) onto the lower cover. While holding the armature firmly in position in the lower cover, install the frame assembly over the armature. Align the match marks and anti-rotation structures (**Figure 29**). Install the stack of washers over the upper end of the armature shaft in the same position as removed.

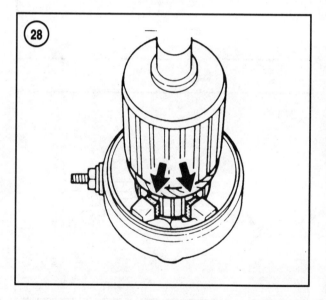

5. On models BF75A, BF90A, BF115A and BF130A, install the pinion shaft, solenoid lever and retainer, planetary and steel ball into the end cover. Apply water-resistant grease to the planetary gears. Lubricate with grease and attach the plunger to the yoke. Install the spring and starter solenoid to the electric starter motor. Securely tighten the mounting screws.

6. Install a new O-ring or sealing ring onto the upper cover. Wipe a small amount of a water-resistant grease onto the bearing surface in the upper cover. Align the reference marks and install the upper cover over the armature. Install the throughbolts and tighten securely.

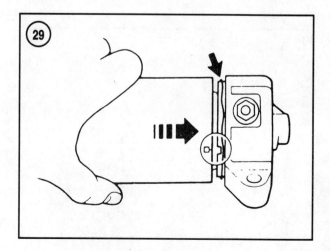

ELECTRICAL AND IGNITION

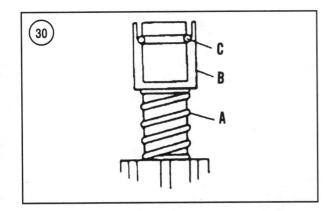

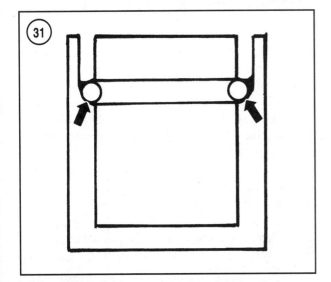

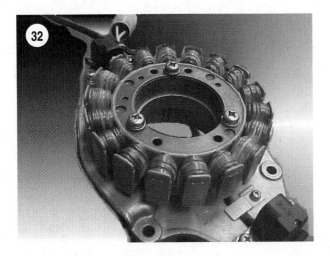

7. Thread the pinion drive onto the armature shaft. Install the spring (A, **Figure 30**) and pinion stopper (B, **Figure 30**) onto the shaft. Push the pinion stopper toward the starter and position the locking clip (C, **Figure 30**) into

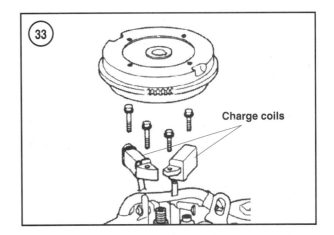

the groove on the armature shaft (**Figure 31**). Use pliers to re-form the locking clip if distorted during removal.

8. Follow Steps 4-6 under *Starter Motor Removal and Installation* and install the electric starter motor. Check for proper starter motor operation.

CHARGING SYSTEM

This section provides removal and installation instructions for the battery charging/lighting coil, voltage regulator/rectifier and belt-driven alternator.

CAUTION
It may be necessary to use an impact driver to remove the battery charge/lighting coil or the ignition charge coil mounting screws. Work carefully and avoid the use of excessive force. The cylinder block can be damaged if excessive force is used.

Battery Charge/Lighting Coil Removal/Installation

Models BF20, BF2A, BF115A and BF130A are not equipped with a battery charge/lighting coil.

On models BF75A and BF90A, the battery charge/lighting coil in mounted under the starter pulley and alternator rotor at the top of the engine (**Figure 32**).

On all other models, the battery charge/lighting coil is fastened to a mounting base alongside the ignition charge coils (**Figure 33**).

Flywheel, starter pulley and/or rotor removal is required to access the battery charge/lighting coil on all models. Refer to Chapter Eight for removal and installation of these components.

Prior to component removal, make a drawing or take a photograph of the wire routing. This important step helps ensure proper routing during assembly.

Note the size and location of plastic locking tie clamps that must be removed and replace them with new clamps on assembly.

1. Disconnect both battery leads from the battery terminal on electric start models. Remove the spark plugs and connect the spark plug leads to an engine ground. Refer to Chapter Eleven and remove the rewind starter, if so equipped. Refer to Chapter Eight and remove the flywheel, starter pulley, and/or rotor.

2. Refer to the wiring diagrams located at the end of the manual to identify the wire colors for the battery charge/lighting coil.

3. Note the wire routing and connection points. Disconnect the battery charge/lighting coil wires from the rectifier/regulator, rectifier or terminal block.

4. Note the screw locations prior to removal. Remove all screws (**Figure 32** or **Figure 33**) that retain the battery charge/lighting coil to the mounting base.

5. Mark the position of the battery charge/lighting coil relative to its mounting location and remove it from the engine. Carefully guide the wires during removal. Clean the battery charge/lighting coil mounting location of corrosion and debris. If necessary, inspect, clean and repair the threads for the mounting screws.

6. Carefully route the coil wires and place the battery charge/lighting coil on the mounting location. Make certain that the battery charge/lighting coil is fully seated on its mounting base. Install the screws, spacers and washers in their original locations and tighten them securely.

7. Clean and inspect all terminals. Connect the battery charge/lighting coil wires to the proper terminals. Install the flywheel and rewind starter (if so equipped) following the procedures listed in chapter eight and chapter eleven.

8. Install the spark plugs and spark plug leads. Clean the battery terminals and connect the cables to the battery on electric start models. Check for proper charging and ignition system operation.

Voltage Rectifier/Regulator Removal/Installation

1. Disconnect both battery leads from the battery terminal on electric start models. Remove all spark plugs and connect the spark plug leads to an engine ground.

2. Use the wiring diagrams located at the end of the manual to identify the wire colors used for the rectifier/regulator. Trace the wires to the component on the engine (**Figure 34**).

3. Mark the wire connections to the rectifier/regulator to ensure proper connections during assembly. Disconnect the wires.

4. Remove the screws that retain the rectifier/regulator unit to its mounting location (**Figure 34**). Carefully route the disconnected wires and remove the component from the engine.

5. If necessary, clean, inspect and repair the threads in the mounting location. Clean all corrosion or contamination from the mounting location.

6. Carefully route the rectifier/regulator unit leads and install the component to its mounting location. Tighten the retaining screws securely.

7. Install the spark plugs and spark plug leads. Clean the battery terminals and connect the cables to the battery on electric start models. Check for proper charging and ignition system operation.

Belt-Driven Alternator Removal/Installation

Have the alternator repaired at a reputable alternator and starter motor repair shop. Proper testing requires the use of equipment that simulates actual running conditions. This type of alternator is used on numerous other applications and internal components are readily available. Contact a Honda dealership if the selected repair shop is unable to locate required components.

1. Disconnect both battery leads at the battery.

2. Locate the output terminal (A, **Figure 35**) and harness connector (B, **Figure 35**) on the alternator. Note the wire connection points and wire routing, then disconnect all wires from the alternator.

3. Loosen the adjusting bolt located near the lower starboard side of the alternator. Loosen the alternator pivot nut and bolt (**Figure 36**), then carefully push the alternator toward the large pulley to release the belt tension. Slip the drive belt from the alternator pulley.

ELECTRICAL AND IGNITION

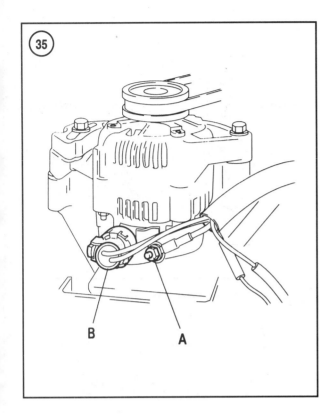

5. To install the alternator, position it onto the mounting location. Install the bolts, washers, spacers and nuts that retain the alternator to the mounting bracket. Tighten them by hand.

6. Place the drive belt onto the large pulley and the alternator pulley. Ensure that the grooves in the belt align with the grooves in both pulleys.

7. Install the adjusting bolt into the bracket. Tighten the adjusting bolt until the drive belt deflects 8.0-9.0 mm (0.32-0.35 in.) when 98.0 N (22.0 lb.) of force is applied to the belt at a midway point (**Figure 36**).

8. Tighten the mounting bolt and nut to the specification listed in **Table 1**. Connect the wire harness connection and output wire to the locations noted during removal. Ensure that all wires and connections will not interfere with other engine components.

9. Install the spark plugs and spark plug leads. Clean the battery terminals and connect the cables to the battery. Operate the engine for 10 minutes or more to allow the belt tension to stabilize then check the belt tension as indicated in Step 7.

IGNITION SYSTEM

This section provides removal, inspection and installation procedures for the ignition charge coil, pulser coil, CDI unit, engine control unit, breaker points and the ignition coil.

Models BF20, BF2A, BF50 and BF5A

Removing the flywheel is not required to replace the ignition charge coil on these models. A feeler gauge is required to properly position the component on the base engine.

1. Remove the spark plug and connect the spark plug lead to an engine ground.

2. Refer to Chapter Eleven and remove the rewind starter from the engine. On models BF20 and BF2A, refer to Chapter Eight and remove the fan cover from the engine.

3. Locate the ignition charge coil on the engine. Disconnect the stop circuit wire and spark plug lead from the engine harness or engine. Remove the screws that retain the ignition charge coil to the engine (**Figure 37**).

4. Carefully route the disconnected wires and remove the coil from the engine.

5. If necessary, clean, inspect and repair the threads in the mounting location. Clean all corrosion or contamination from the mounting location. Carefully route the ignition charge coil leads, then install the component to its mount-

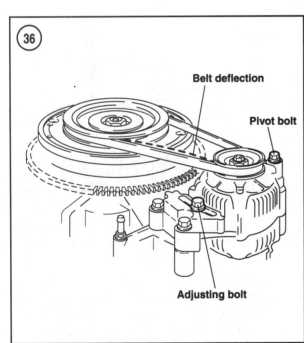

4. Remove the retaining bolts and nuts that retain the alternator. Lift the alternator from the engine. Remove the adjusting bolt from the mounting bracket.

ing location. *Do not* tighten the mounting screws at this time.

6. Rotate the magnet portion of the flywheel until it is *away* from the ignition charge coil. Using a feeler gauge, position the ignition charge coil the specified distance (both coil ends) from the flywheel (**Figure 37**). Refer to **Table 3** for specifications. Securely tighten the retaining screws. Clean the terminals then connect the stop circuit wire to the harness.

7. On models BF20, BF2A, install the fan cover. On all models, install the rewind starter.

8. Install the spark plug and spark plug lead. Check for proper operation.

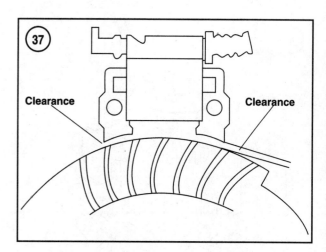

Ignition Charge Coil (Models BF75A, BF90A, BF115A and BF130A)

These models use a battery powered ignition system that does not incorporate an ignition charge coil.

NOTE

The battery charge and ignition charge coils appear almost identical on most models. Use the wire colors and illustrations to identify the components.

Ignition Charge Coil Removal/Installation (All Other Models)

Removal of the flywheel is required to access the ignition charge coil. To assist with component identification, refer to the wiring diagrams located at the back of this manual. Avoid removing the wrong component. Always trace the wire color used to the ignition charge coil on the engine.

1. Disconnect both battery cables from the battery terminal on electric start models. Remove all spark plugs and connect the spark plug leads to an engine ground. Refer to Chapter Eleven for procedures and remove the rewind starter, if so equipped. Refer to Chapter Eight for procedures and remove the flywheel, starter pulley, and/or rotor.

2. Note the wire routing and connection points. Disconnect the ignition charge coil wires from the CDI Unit, main engine harness, stop circuit and/or terminal block.

3. Note the screw locations prior to removal. Remove the screws (**Figure 38**) that retain the ignition charge coil to the mounting base.

4. Note the position of the ignition charge coil relative to its mounting location and remove the component from the engine. Carefully guide the wires during removal. Re-

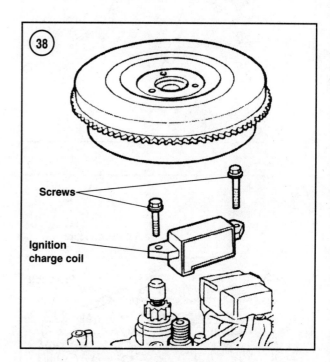

move any corrosion or debris from the ignition charge coil mounting location. If necessary, inspect, clean and repair the threads of the mounting screws.

5. Carefully route the wires and install the ignition charge coil. Make certain the ignition charge coil is fully seated on the mounting base. Install the screws, spacers and washers in their original locations and tighten them securely.

6. Clean and inspect all terminals. Connect the ignition charge coil wires to the proper terminals. Install the flywheel and rewind starter (if so equipped).

7. Install the spark plugs and spark plug leads. Clean the battery terminals and connect the cables to the battery on

ELECTRICAL AND IGNITION

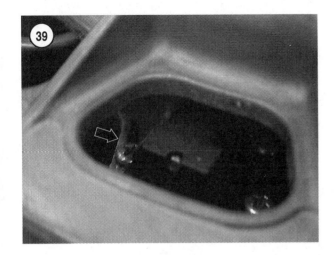

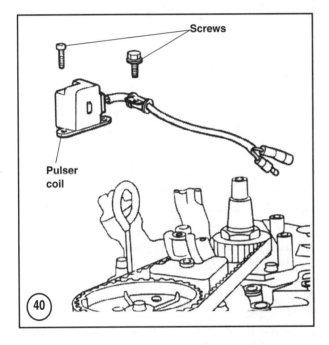

3. Refer to Chapter Eight and remove the camshaft pulley. Inspect the advance mechanism in the camshaft pulley for free movements. Clean all debris from the mechanism.

4. Refer to the illustrations and wire colors to identify the pulser coil (**Figure 39**). Note the pulser coil position, wire routing and connection points. Disconnect the wires from the CDI unit and/or wire harness.

5. Remove the two screws, washers and sleeves that retain the pulser coil to the engine remove the wire retaining clip and lift the pulser coil from the engine.

6. Clean all corrosion and debris from the mounting location and screw openings.

7. Installation is the reverse of removal. Note the following:
   a. Route all wires to prevent interference with other components.
   b. Position the pulser coil and its fasteners as noted prior to removal.
   c. Securely tighten all fasteners.

8. Refer to Chapter Eight for procedures, then install the camshaft pulley. Refer to Chapter Eleven and install the rewind starter, if so equipped.

9. Install the spark plugs and spark plug leads. Clean the battery terminals and connect the cables to the battery, if so equipped.

Pulser Coil Removal/Installation (Models BF9.9A and BF15A)

Refer to **Figure 40** during the removal and installation procedure.

1. Disconnect both battery cables from the battery. Remove the spark plugs and connect the spark plug leads to an engine ground.

2. Refer to the illustrations and wire colors to identify the pulser coil (**Figure 40**). Note the pulser coil position, wire routing and connection points. Remove the wire clip for the pulser coil wires located near the pulser coil. Disconnect the pulser coil wire connectors from the engine wire harness.

3. Remove the two screws that retain the pulser coil to the cylinder head. Carefully guide the wires as you lift the pulser coil from the engine.

4. Clean all corrosion and debris from the mounting location and screw openings.

5. Installation is the reverse of removal. Note the following:
   a. Route all wires as noted prior to removal and in a manner that prevents interference with other components.

electric start models. Check for proper charging and ignition system operation.

Pulser Coil Removal/Installation (Models BF75, BF8A and BF100)

Refer to **Figure 39** during the removal and installation procedure.

1. Disconnect both battery cables from the battery. Remove the spark plugs and connect the spark plug leads to an engine ground.

2. Refer to Chapter Eleven and remove the rewind starter, if so equipped.

b. Position the pulser coil and its fasteners as noted prior to removal.
c. Securely tighten all fasteners.

6. Install the spark plugs and spark plug leads. Clean the battery terminals and connect the cables to the battery, if so equipped.

Pulser Coil Removal/Installation (Models BF20A, BF25A, BF30A, BF35A, BF40A and BF50A)

To assist with component location and identification, refer to **Figure 41** during the removal and installation procedures.

1. Disconnect both battery cables from the battery. Remove the spark plugs and connect the spark plug leads to a suitable engine ground such as a clean cylinder head or cylinder block bolt.
2. Refer to Chapter Eleven and remove the rewind starter, if so equipped.
3. Refer to Chapter Eight and remove the camshaft pulley.
4. Refer to the illustrations and wire colors to identify the pulser coil (**Figure 41**). Note the pulser coil position, wire routing and connection points. Disconnect the wires from the engine wire harness at the four terminal connectors.
5. Remove the three screws that retain the pulser coil to the engine. Guide the wires as you lift the pulser coil from the engine.
6. Clean all corrosion and debris from the mounting location and screw openings.
7. Installation is the reverse of removal. Note the following:
    a. Route all wires in a manner that prevents interference with other components.
    b. Position the pulser coil and its fasteners as noted prior to removal.
    c. Securely tighten all fasteners.
8. Refer to Chapter Eight and install the camshaft pulley. Refer to Chapter Eleven and install the rewind starter.
9. Install the spark plugs and spark plug leads. Clean the battery terminals and connect the battery cables to the battery, if so equipped.

Pulser Coil Removal/Installation (Models BF75A and BF90A)

On these models, replace both pulser coils as a unit. Use a feeler gauge to properly position the pulser coil to the rotor. Refer to **Figure 42** during the removal and installation procedures.

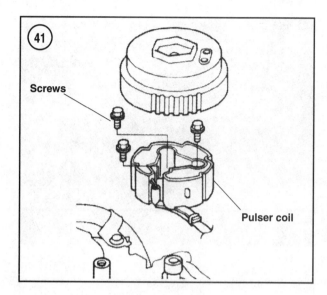

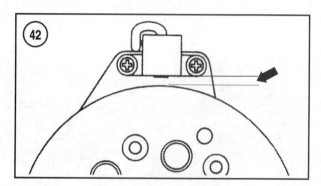

1. Disconnect both battery cables from the battery. Remove the spark plugs and connect the spark plug leads to an engine ground.
2. Refer to Chapter Eight and remove the starter pulley from the base engine.
3. Refer to the illustrations and wire colors to identify the pulser coil (**Figure 42**). Note the pulser coil position, wire colors, wire routing and connection points. Disconnect the pulser coil wires from the main engine harness.
4. Remove the two screws that retain each pulser coil to the engine. Remove the wire retaining plates located near the pulser coils. Guide the wires as you lift the pulser coil from the engine.
5. Clean all corrosion and debris from the mounting location and screw openings.
6. Installation is the reverse of removal. Note the following:
    a. Route all wires in a manner that prevents interference with other components.
    b. Position the pulser coils and fasteners as noted prior to removal.

ELECTRICAL AND IGNITION

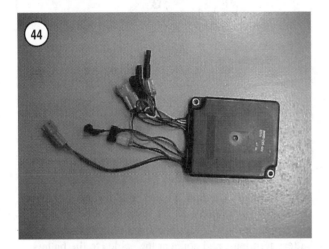

1. Disconnect both battery cables from the battery. Remove the spark plugs and connect the spark plug leads to an engine ground.
2. Refer to the illustration and wire colors to identify the pulser coils (**Figure 43**). Note the pulser coil position, wire colors, wire routing and connection points then disconnect the pulser coil wire connector from the main engine harness.
3. Remove the two screws that retain each pulser coil to the engine. Remove the wire retaining clamps located on each pulser coil wire. Guide the wires as you lift the pulser coils from the engine.
4. Clean all corrosion or debris from the mounting location and screw openings.
5. Installation is the reverse of removal. Note the following:
    a. Route all wires in a manner that prevents interference with other components.
    b. Position the pulser coils and fasteners as noted prior to removal.
    c. Securely tighten all fasteners.
6. Install the spark plugs and spark plug leads. Clean the battery terminals and connect the cables to the battery.

CDI Unit Removal/Installation

CDI unit (**Figure 44**) appearance and mounting location varies by model. Refer to the wiring diagrams located at the end of the manual to identify the wire colors leading to the CDI unit. Trace the wires to the component on the engine.

1. Disconnect the battery cables from the battery terminals. Remove the electrical component cover (on models so equipped) to access the CDI unit and terminals.
2. Note all wire attaching points and routing to ensure proper connections during assembly. Disconnect all wires connected to the CDI unit. Inspect and clean all terminal connections within the wire harness connector.
3. Locate and remove the screws that retain the CDI unit to its attaching point. Make note of any ground wires connected at these points. Make sure they are properly connected during assembly.
4. Remove the CDI unit. Clean any corrosion or contamination from the CDI mounting location. If necessary, clean, inspect and repair the mounting fastener threads.
5. Install the CDI unit and tighten all fasteners securely. Check all ground wires for proper connection. Use care when routing all wires. They must not interfere with other components.
6. Clean, inspect and attach all wires to the correct terminal connections.

   c. Securely tighten all fasteners.
   d. Adjust the pulser coil-to-rotor clearance as described in Step 7.
   e. Ensure that the pulser coil wires are routed under the wire-retaining plate, as noted prior to removal.

7. Refer to **Table 3** for the specification. Locate the pulser coil the indicated distance from the flywheel (**Figure 42**). Securely tighten the retaining screws after adjustment.
8. Install the spark plugs and spark plug leads. Clean the battery terminals, then connect the cables to the battery.

Pulser Coil Removal/Installation (Models BF115A and BF130A)

On these models, replace both pulser coils as a unit. Refer to **Figure 43** during the removal and installation procedure.

7. Install the electrical component cover if removed. Install the spark plugs and spark plug leads. Clean the battery terminals and connect the cables to the battery, if so equipped.

Engine Control Unit Removal/Installation

Removal and installation of the engine control unit is similar to the CDI unit. Refer to the procedure for the CDI unit to remove and install the engine control unit.

Breaker Points Removal/Installation (Models So Equipped)

Refer to **Figure 45** during the removal and installation procedure.
1. Disconnect both battery cables from the battery. Remove the spark plugs and connect the spark plug leads to an engine ground.
2. Refer to Chapter Eleven and remove the rewind starter, if so equipped.
3. Refer to Chapter Eight and remove the camshaft pulley. Inspect the advance mechanism in the camshaft pulley for free movement. Clean all debris from the mechanism.
4. Locate the breaker points (**Figure 45**). Measure and record the breaker point gap. Make notes or drawings of wire routing and connection points. Note the mounting location and position of the condenser and breaker points. Disconnect the wires from the breaker points and condenser.
5. Remove the two screws and washers that retain the breaker points to the engine. Remove the wire retaining clip and lift the breaker points from the engine. Do not rotate the camshaft pulley.
6. Remove its screw and lift the condenser from the engine.
7. Clean all corrosion or debris from the mounting location and screw holes.
8. Installation is the reverse of removal. Note the following:
   a. Route all wires in a manner that prevents interference with other components.
   b. Securely tighten all fasteners.
   c. Adjust the breaker points as described in Step 9.
9. Loosen the mounting screws and move the breaker points until the gap is equal to the gap noted in Step 4. Securely tighten the breaker points mounting screws.
10. Refer to Chapter Eight and install the camshaft pulley. Adjust the ignition timing as described in Chapter Four. Refer to Chapter Eleven and install the rewind starter, if so equipped.
11. Install the spark plugs and spark plug leads. Clean the battery terminals and connect the cables to the battery, if so equipped.

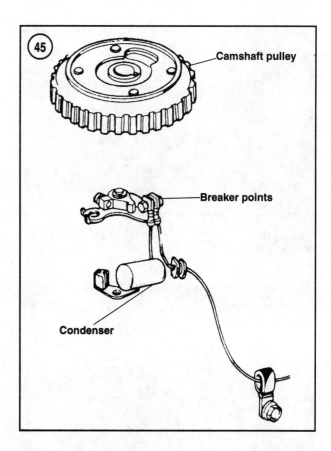

Ignition Coil Removal/Installation

Refer to **Figure 46**.
1. Disconnect both battery cables from the battery. Remove the spark plugs and connect the spark plug leads to a suitable engine ground, such as a clean cylinder head or cylinder block bolt.
2. Note the ignition coil wires prior to disconnecting them. Disconnect the ignition coil wires from the engine wire harness and the spark plug leads from the spark plugs.
3. Remove the mounting hardware and the ignition coil. Clean and inspect the wire connections, fastener threads and the mounting locations.
4. Install the coil and mounting hardware. Tighten the fasteners securely.
5. Install the spark plugs and spark plug leads. Clean the battery terminals and connect the cables to the battery, if so equipped.

ELECTRICAL AND IGNITION

WARNING SYSTEM COMPONENTS

This section provides identification and removal and installation procedures for the overheat switch, warning horn, throttle switch and warning light panel.

Overheat Switch Removal/Installation

Refer to the wiring diagrams located at the end of the manual to identify the wire color for the overheat switch. Disconnect the switch wires from the main harness. Remove the overheat switch from its threaded mounting boss with a suitable wrench. Clean all corrosion and debris from the threads in the mounting boss. Refer to *Overheat Switch Testing* in Chapter Three for additional information.

Low Oil Pressure Switch Removal/Installation

Refer to *Checking Oil Pressure* in Chapter Three to remove and install the oil pressure switch.

Warning Horn Removal/Installation

On applications with the key switch mounted into the remote control, the warning horn is mounted inside the control. Refer to Chapter Fourteen and disassemble the control enough to access the warning horn.

On applications with a dash mounted key switch, the warning horn is mounted under the dash and near the key switch.

Regardless of the mounting location the replacement procedures are similar. Disconnect the terminals and clean them. Remove any fasteners for the horn. Install the replacement horn and connect the wire terminals. Make sure that all wires and terminals will not interfere with other components.

Throttle Switch Removal/Installation

The throttle switch is located within the remote control assembly. Refer to Chapter Fourteen for the disassembly procedures to access the throttle switch. Disassemble the remote control to the point necessary to remove the throttle switch.

Warning Light Panel Removal/Installation

On remote control models, refer to Chapter Fourteen to disassemble the remote control enough to access the panel retainer and wire connection. On tiller control models, the panel retainer and leads are easily accessible at the lower front motor cover. Regardless of the mounting location the replacement procedures are similar. Note all wire terminal connection points and wire routing. Disconnect the terminals and clean them. Remove the retainer for the panel. Install the panel and attach the retainer. Connect the wire terminals at the locations noted prior to removal. Ensure that all wires and terminals will not interfere with other components on assembly.

Engine Mounted Oil Pressure Indicator Light Removal/Installation

Locate the component on the front of the lower engine cover. Note the wire terminal connection points and wire routing and disconnect the wires from the engine wire harness. Note the mounting position of the light then loosen and remove the retaining nut from the lower engine cover. Install the light into the cover and position it as noted prior to removal. Securely tighten the retaining nut. Connect the wires and route the wire as noted prior to disconnecting them. Ensure that the wires will not interfere with any components on the engine.

BATTERY MAINTENANCE AND TESTING

Battery Requirements

Batteries used in marine applications are subjected to far more vibration and pounding action than automotive applications. Always use a battery that is designated for marine use (**Figure 47**). These batteries are constructed with thicker cases and plates than typical automotive batteries. This allows them to better handle the marine environment.

Use a battery that meets or exceeds the amperage requirements for the engine. Refer to **Table 4** for the battery requirements. Some marine batteries list *marine/deep cycle* on the label. Deep cycle batteries are constructed to allow repeated discharge and charge cycles. These batteries are designed to power accessories such as trolling motors. Always charge deep cycle batteries at a low amperage rate. They are generally not designed for charging or discharging at rapid rates. **Table 4** provides the usage hours, or capacity, for both 80- and 105-amp-hour batteries. Approximate recharge times are listed as well. Compare the amperage draw of the accessory with the information provided in **Table 4**. Deep cycle batteries can be used as the starting battery providing they meet the cold cranking amperage requirements for the engine.

Cable Connections

Insufficient or dirty cable connections cause many problems in marine applications. Use cable connectors that are securely crimped or molded to the cable. Avoid the use of temporary or emergency clamps for normal usage. They are prone to corrosion and do not meet the coast guard requirements for terminal connections.

Use a cover on the positive terminal post (**Figure 48**). They are available at marine dealerships.

Battery Mounting Requirements

Make sure the battery is securely mounted in the boat to avoid acid spills or electrical arcing that can cause a fire. The most common types of battery mounting include the bracket mounted to the floor of the boat and the support across the top of the battery (**Figure 48**). Another type is the battery case and cover that encloses the battery and secures it to the boat structure (**Figure 49**). When properly installed, either of these provide secure mounting and protection for the terminals.

Mount the battery in a location that allows easy access for maintenance. Ensure that the battery terminals are not able to contact any component in the mounting area.

WARNING
When mounting a battery in a boat constructed of aluminum, take extra precaution to ensure that the battery is securely mounted to eliminate the possibility of the battery contacting metal components. Elec-

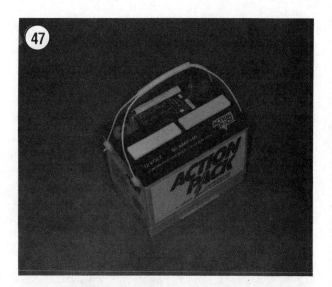

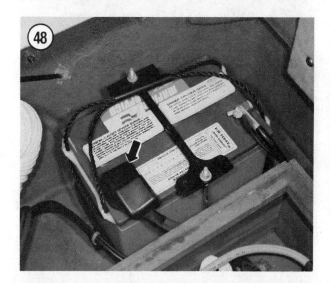

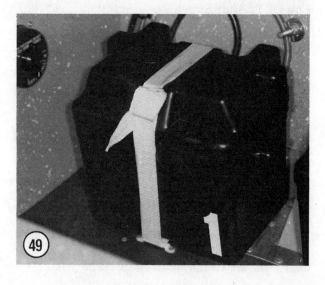

ELECTRICAL AND IGNITION

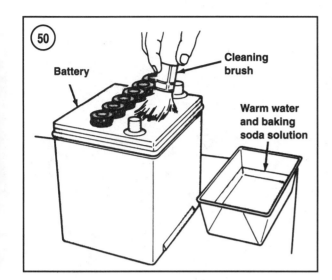

50
Battery — Cleaning brush — Warm water and baking soda solution

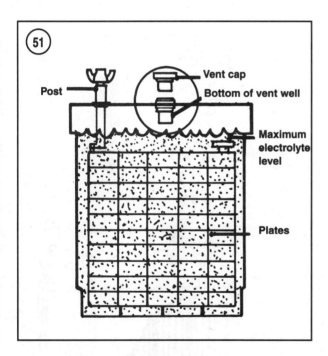

51
Post — Vent cap — Bottom of vent well — Maximum electrolyte level — Plates

trical arcing can result in fire or explosion if a fuel source is present. Bodily injury, death or damage to property can occur. Batteries produce explosive gasses that can ignite when arcing is present.

Battery Case Inspection and Maintenance

WARNING
Always wear gloves and protective eyewear when working with batteries. Batteries contain a corrosive and dangerous acid solution. Never smoke or allow any source of ignition to be near a battery. Batteries produce explosive gases that can ignite and result in battery explosion when a source of ignition is present.

CAUTION
Never allow the water and baking soda solution to enter the battery cells through the vent caps. The baking soda will neutralize the electrolyte and cause permanent damage to the battery.

Inspect the battery case for cracks, leakage, abrasion points and other damage when the battery is removed for charging. Replace the battery if any questionable condition exists. During normal usage a corrosive deposit forms on the top of the battery. This deposit may allow the battery to discharge at a rapid rate, as current can travel through the deposits from one post to the other.

Make sure the battery caps are properly installed. Remove the battery from the boat and carefully wash loose material from the top of the battery with clean water. Use a solution of warm water and baking soda along with a soft bristle brush to clean the deposits from the battery (**Figure 50**). Wash the battery with clean water to remove all of the baking soda solution from the battery case.

WARNING
Use care when lifting or transporting the battery. With age the carry strap can become weak and break. If the battery is dropped the case may break. Use other suitable means to lift and transport the battery.

NOTE
Never overfill the battery. The electrolyte may expand with the heat created from charging and overflow from the battery.

Check the battery electrolyte level on a regular basis. Heavy usage or usage in warm climates increases the frequency for adding water to the battery. Carefully remove the vent caps (**Figure 51**) and inspect the electrolyte level in each cell. The electrolyte level should be 3/16 in. (5 mm) above the plates, yet below the bottom of the vent well (**Figure 51**). Use distilled water to fill the cells to the proper level. Never use battery acid to correct the electrolyte level; the overly acidic solution will damage the plates.

Cleaning the Terminals

Clean the battery terminals at regular intervals and anytime the battery cable is removed. Use a battery cleaning

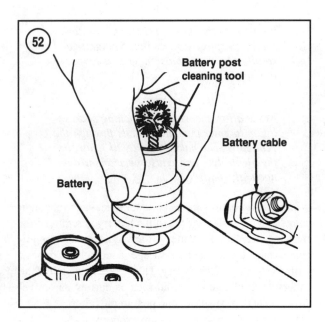

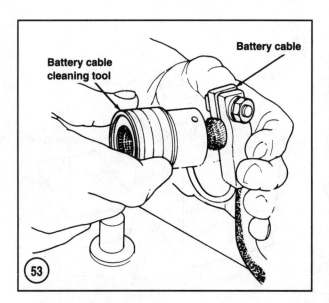

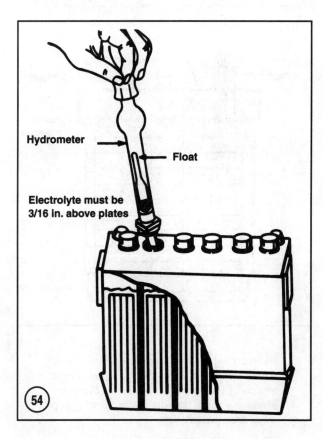

tool available at most automotive part stores. Remove the cable and clean the post as indicated (**Figure 52**). Avoid removing too much material from the post or the cable may not attach properly. Rotate the tool on the post until the post is cleaned of corrosion.

Use the other end of the tool to clean the cable end terminal (**Figure 53**). Clean spade type connectors and the attaching nuts with the wire brush end of the tool.

Attaching the Terminals

Apply a coating of petroleum gel (Vaseline) or other corrosion prevention compound on the battery post and cable terminal. Tighten the fasteners securely. Avoid using excessive force when tightening the terminals.

Battery Testing

NOTE
Inaccurate readings will result if the specific gravity is checked immediately after adding water to the battery. To ensure accuracy, charge the battery for 15-20 minutes before testing the specific gravity.

Two methods are commonly used to test batteries. A load tester or carbon pile is used to check the battery voltage when a load is applied across the terminals. A hydrometer is used to check the specific gravity of the battery electrolyte. This gives an accurate reading of the charge level of the battery. The use of a hydrometer is the most practical method for checking battery condition. Hydrometers are available at most automotive part stores. Select one that has number graduation that spans 1.100-1.300 readings.

To use the hydrometer, insert the tip into the vent opening and use the ball to draw some of the electrolyte into the hydrometer (**Figure 54**). Read the specific gravity in

ELECTRICAL AND IGNITION

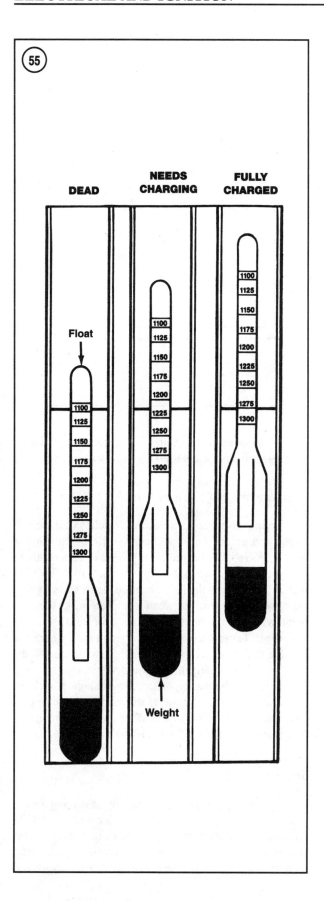

Figure 55

all cells. When using a temperature compensating hydrometer, take several readings in each cell to allow the hydrometer to adjust to the electrolyte temperature. Always return the electrolyte to the cell from which it was drawn. With the hydrometer in a vertical position, determine the specific gravity by reading level of the float (**Figure 55**). A specific gravity reading of 1.260 or higher indicates a fully charged battery. Compare the hydrometer readings with the information provided in **Table 5** to determine the level of charge. Always charge the battery when the specific gravity varies more that .050 from one cell to another.

NOTE
Add 0.004 to the reading for every 10°
above 25° C (77° F) when the hydrometer is
not a temperature compensating model.
Subtract 0.004 from the reading for every
10° below 25° (77° F).

Voltage While Cranking Test

Measuring the voltage at the battery terminals while cranking the engine can check the battery condition. Select the voltage function of a volt/ohm meter. Select the 20-volt scale. Connect the positive test lead to the positive battery terminal. Connect the negative test lead to an engine ground. Measure the voltage while cranking the engine (**Figure 56**). Charge the battery if the voltage drops below 9.6 volts while cranking. Test the cranking voltage again. Replace the battery if it is not capable of maintaining a minimum of 9.6 volts under cranking load.

Battery Storage

Batteries lose some of the charge during storage. The rate of discharge increases in a warm environment. Store the battery in a cool dry location to minimize discharge. Check the specific gravity every 30 days and charge the battery as required. Perform the maintenance on the battery case and terminals as described in this chapter. Refer to *Battery Charging* for battery charging times.

WARNING
Batteries produce explosive hydrogen gas, especially while charging. Charge the battery in a well-ventilated area. Wear protective eyewear and suitable gloves when working around batteries. Never smoke or allow any source of ignition in the area where batteries are stored or charged. Never allow any non-insulated components to contact the battery terminals. The battery

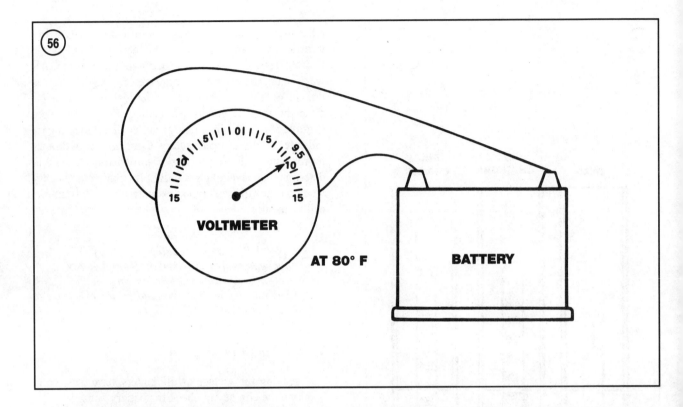

can explode resulting in serious bodily injury, death or damage to property.

Battery Charging

Remove the battery from the boat when charging. Batteries create explosive hydrogen gas. Because most boats provide limited ventilation, this explosive gas may remain in the area for a fair amount of time. In addition to the hazards of explosion, the gas may cause accelerated corrosion of components in the battery compartment. Removing the battery allows you to inspect the case for damage and cleaning and maintenance on the battery terminals.

WARNING
Use extreme caution when connecting any wires to the battery terminals. Avoid making the last connection at the battery terminal. Explosive hydrogen gas in and around the battery may ignite and lead to an explosion.

Connecting the charger

Make the connections to the battery *before* plugging the charger in or switching the charger ON to avoid arcing at the terminals. Connect the battery charger cables to the proper terminals on the battery. Plug the charger into a power supply and select the 12-volt battery setting.

Charging rate and charging times

Charging the battery at a slow rate results in a more sufficient charge and helps prolong the life of the battery. With a severely discharged battery, it may be necessary to charge the battery at a higher amperage rate for a few minutes before starting the lower rate charge. A severely discharged battery will not allow the charging process to begin without first (boost) charging at the high rate.

Refer to **Table 4** for battery charging times. Check the specific gravity often and halt the charging process if the battery is fully charged. A severely discharged battery may require as long as eight hours to recharge. Check the temperature of the electrolyte during the charging process. Stop the charging process if the electrolyte temperature reaches or exceeds 53° C (127° F).

Jump Starting

Jump starting provides the capability of starting the engine with a discharged battery connected to a fully charged battery. Jump starting can be dangerous if the correct procedure is not followed. Never attempt to jump start an engine with a frozen battery. Always check and

ELECTRICAL AND IGNITION

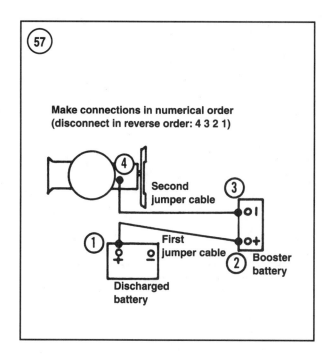

Make connections in numerical order (disconnect in reverse order: 4 3 2 1)

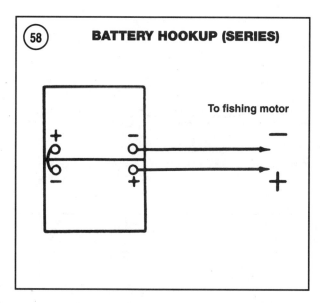

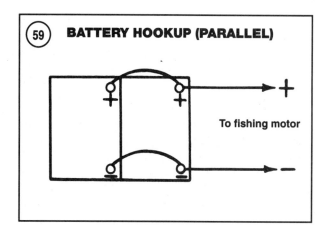

metallic or conductive material. Never allow the clamps to contact other clamps.

1. Connect the jumper cable clamp to the positive terminal of the discharged battery (1, **Figure 57**).
2. Connect the same jumper cable clamp to the positive terminal of the fully charged battery (2, **Figure 57**).
3. Connect the second jumper cable clamp to the negative terminal of the fully charged battery (3, **Figure 57**).
4. Make the final connection to a good engine ground on the outboard with the discharged battery (4, **Figure 57**).
5. Make sure the cables and clamps are positioned so that they will not interfere with moving components.
6. Start the engine and remove the cables in the reverse of the connection.

Wiring for 12- and 24-Volt Electric Trolling Motors

Many fishing boats are provided with an electric trolling motor that requires 24 volts to operate. Two or more batteries are necessary with these applications. A series battery hookup (**Figure 58**) provides 24 volts for the trolling motor.

A series connection provides the approximate total of the two batteries, which equals 24 volts. The amperage provided is the approximate average of the two batteries.

Connect the trolling motor batteries in a parallel arrangement (**Figure 59**) if the trolling motor requires 12 volts to operate.

The voltage provided is the approximate average of the two batteries, which equals 12 volts. The amperage provided is the approximate total of the two batteries.

correct the electrolyte level in each battery before making any connection. A significant risk of explosion exists if the electrolyte level is at or below the top of the plates. Always use a good pair of jumper cables with clean connector clamps. Keep all clamps totally separate from any

TABLE 1 TIGHTENING TORQUE

Fastener	Torque
Oil pressure switch	
BF50, BF5A	7-10 N•m kg/cm (62-89 in.-lb.)
All other models	9 N•m (80 in.-lb.)
Choke solinoid mounting bracket	
BF35A, BF40A, BF45A, BF50A	9 N•m (80 in.-lb.)
Alternator mounting fasteners	
8 mm nut	24 N•m (18 ft.-lb.)
10 mm bolt	44 N•m (33 ft.-lb.)

TABLE 2 STARTER MOTOR SPECIFICATIONS

Model	Brush length mm (in.)	Mica depth mm (in.)
BF9.9A, BF15A, BF20A, BF25A, BF30A	8.5-12.5 (0.335-0.492)	0.15 (0.006)
BF35A, BF40A, BF45A, BF50A	12.0-16.0 (0.472-0.630)	0.2-0.5 (0.008-0.020)
BF75A, BF90A, BF115A, BF130A	7.0-12.3 (0.276-0.484)	0.2-0.5 (0.008-0.020)

TABLE 3 IGNTION COIL/PULSER COIL TO FLYWHEEL CLEARANCE

Ignition coil	
BF20, BF2A	0.20-0.60 mm (0.0079-0.0236 in.)
BF50, BF5A	0.20-0.60 mm (0.0079-0.0236 in.)
Pulser coil	
BF75A, BF90A	0.70-0.80 mm (0.0276-0.0315 in.)

TABLE 4 BATTERY CAPACITY (HOURS OF USE)

Amperage Draw	Hours of usage	Recharge Time (Approximate)
With 80 amp-hour battery:		
5 amps	13.5 hours	16 hours
15 amps	3.5 hours	13 hours
25 amps	1.8 hours	12 hours
With 105 amp-hour battery:		
5 amps	15.8 hours	16 hours
15 amps	4.2 hours	13 hours
25 amps	2.4 hours	12 hours

TABLE 5 BATTERY STATE OF CHARGE (SPECIFIC GRAVITY)

Specific gravity	Percentage of charge remaining
1.120-1.140	0
1.135-1.155	10
1.150-1.170	20
1.160-1.180	30
1.175-1.195	40
1.190-1.210	50
1.205-1.225	60
1.215-1.235	70
1.230-1.250	80
1.245-1.265	90
1.260-1.280	100

Chapter Eight

Base Engine

This chapter provides complete base engine rebuild procedures.

When replacing external or easily accessible components, complete base engine disassembly is not required. Follow the step by step disassembly procedures until the required component is accessible. Reverse the disassembly steps to install the required component(s).

Significant variations in the repair procedures exist from one model to the next. The procedures are tailored to the unique requirements of each model.

Virtually all engine-mounted components must be removed to perform a complete rebuild. References are made to other chapters in this manual for component removal and installation instructions. When performing a minor repair or replacing external mounted engine components, remove only the components necessary to access the faulty component(s). Refer to the illustrations to determine which components must be removed to access the component and its fasteners.

Tables 1-12 are at the end of this chapter. **Table 1** provides tightening torque specification for engine fasteners and standard torque specifications. Refer to the standard torque specifications in **Table 1** if a specific torque value is not listed for a component. **Tables 2-12** provide component tolerances and dimensions.

Base engine overhaul or rebuild requires special service tools and equipment, accurate measuring devices, a calibrated torque wrench and a considerable amount of mechanical skill. A reputable marine dealership should perform the engine repair if any of these requirements are lacking. A large part of the cost for repair is due to engine removal, disassembly and cleaning of the components. A considerable amount of expense can be saved by performing these operations yourself. Another advantage is saving time and inconvenience to transport and store your boat at the dealership. Many marine dealerships have a backlog during the boating season. Performing the labor-intensive removal, disassembly and cleaning process yourself will likely hasten the repair process.

If performing the entire repair, contact your local Honda dealership to purchase the required parts and special service tools. Secure all special tools before attempting any repair. The use of makeshift tools may result in damaged base engine components. Many times the damage caused by using makeshift tools far exceeds the cost of the special service tool. Use a reputable machine shop for cylinder honing and measurements as required.

BASE ENGINE REMOVAL AND INSTALLATION

Preparation for Removal and Installation

Visually inspect the engine to locate the fuel supply hose and battery connections. Most hoses and wire connections must be removed when performing a complete disassembly. Many of the hoses are much more accessible after the engine is removed. Disconnect only the hoses and wires necessary to remove the base engine. The other wires and hoses can be removed afterward.

BASE ENGINE

271

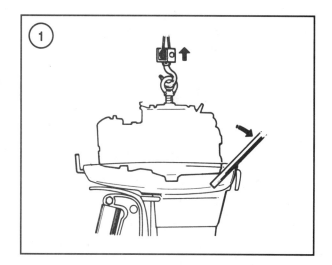

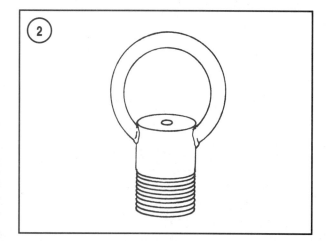

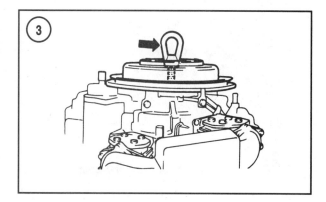

Diagrams of the fuel and electrical systems are listed throughout this manual. Use them to assist with hose and wire routing. To speed up the installation of the base engine and ensure correct connection, *always* take pictures or make a drawing of all wire and hose connections *before* beginning the base engine removal process.

Secure the proper lifting equipment (**Figure 1**) before attempting to remove the engine. It is not difficult to manually lift a 15 hp and smaller engine if you have some assistance. Larger engines require an overhead hoist. A complete engine may weigh 300 lb. (136 kg) or more. Use assistance when lifting or moving any engine. Use the lifting hook (**Figure 2**) or special adapter that threads into the flywheel/rotor (**Figure 3**). The part number for these special adapters is listed in the procedures.

CAUTION
Use care when lifting the base engine from the midsection. Corrosion may form at the engine-to-midsection mating surface and prevent easy removal. To help prevent damage to the machined surfaces, avoid using any sharp object to pry the components apart.

WARNING
Avoid serious bodily injury or death. The base engine may abruptly separate from the midsection during removal. Avoid using excessive force when lifting the base engine with an overhead hoist. Use pry bars to carefully separate the base engine from its mount before lifting with a hoist.

Engine Removal (Models BF20 AND BF2A)

1. Refer to Chapter Nine and remove the gearcase from the engine.

2. Refer to Chapter Eleven and remove the rewind starter.

3. Refer to Chapter Six and remove the fuel tank.

4. Remove the four screws (5, **Figure 4**) and pull the lower exhaust tube cover (4, **Figure 4**) from the base engine. Remove all three bolts (2, **Figure 4**) then lift the lower cover/housing (1, **Figure 4**) from the base engine.

5. Remove both bolts and washers (2 and 3, **Figure 5**) from the upper exhaust tube cover (1, **Figure 5**). Remove both nuts (4, **Figure 5**) from the exhaust tube mounting studs.

6. Provide support for the base engine (6, **Figure 5**) during removal of the mount bolts (7, **Figure 5**). Carefully lift the base engine from the midsection and place it on a clean work surface.

7. Remove and discard the base engine-mounting gasket (10, **Figure 5**). Inspect the alignment pins (9, **Figure 5**) for damaged or worn surfaces. Place them in their respective location on the midsection mating surface. Remove both bolts (12, **Figure 5**) and pull the exhaust tube (5, **Fig-**

BASE ENGINE

ure 5) from the midsection. Remove and discard both exhaust tube mounting gaskets (11, **Figure 5**).

8. Clean all mating surfaces and inspect them for corroded or damaged surfaces. Replace any damaged components.

Engine Installation (Models BF20 and BF2A)

1. Install new exhaust tube gaskets (11, **Figure 5**). Position the exhaust tube over the mounting studs. Thread the nuts (4, **Figure 5**) onto the studs and hand-tighten them.
2. Place a new gasket onto the midsection-to-base engine mating surface. Slowly lower the base engine onto the midsection.
3. Align the exhaust tube to midsection bolt holes with the holes in the gasket. Install the bolts (12, **Figure 5**) and hand-tighten them.
4. Install the three base engine mounting bolts (7, **Figure 5**) and tighten them to the specification listed in **Table 1**.
5. Tighten the exhaust tube bolts and nut (4 and 12, **Figure 5**) to the specification listed in **Table 1**.
6. Install the bolts and washer (2 and 3, **Figure 5**) and the upper exhaust tube cover (1, **Figure 5**) onto the midsection (8, **Figure 5**). Tighten the bolts to the specification listed in **Table 1**.
7. Position the lower cover/housing (1, **Figure 4**) onto the base engine. Install all three bolts (2, **Figure 4**) and tighten them to the specification listed in **Table 1**.
8. Position the lower exhaust tube cover (4, **Figure 4**) onto the engine. Install the four screws (5, **Figure 4**) and tighten them securely.
9. Refer to Chapter Six and install the fuel tank.
10. Refer to Chapter Eleven and install the rewind starter.
11. Refer to Chapter Nine and install the gearcase.
12. Perform all applicable adjustments following the procedures listed in Chapter Five. Refer to Chapter Four and fill the crankcase or oil pan with the proper oil.

Engine Removal (Models BF50 and BF5A)

1. Refer to Chapter Nine and remove the gearcase from the engine.
2. Note the lead connections and remove the wires going to the stop switch and the oil pressure indicator light from the main harness.
3. Disconnect the control cables from throttle and shift linkages. Route the cables away from the base engine to avoid damaging them during engine removal and installation.

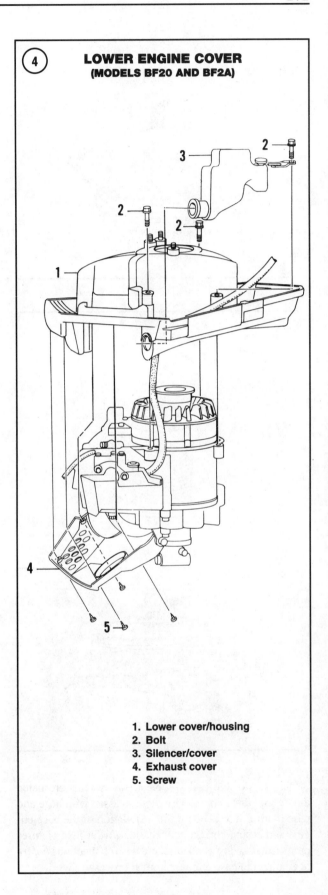

LOWER ENGINE COVER (MODELS BF20 AND BF2A)

1. Lower cover/housing
2. Bolt
3. Silencer/cover
4. Exhaust cover
5. Screw

BASE ENGINE

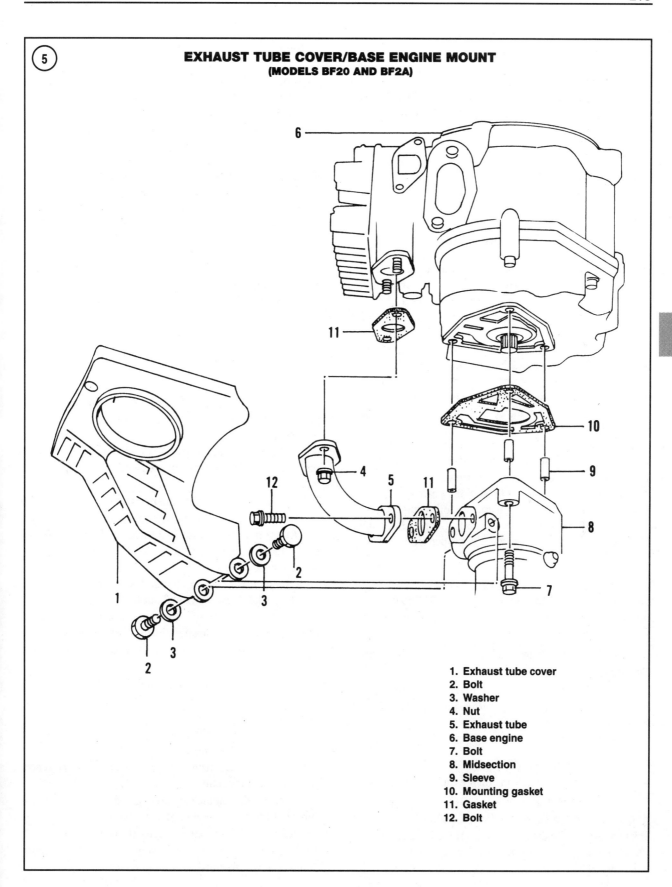

4. Loosen and remove the mounting bolts then carefully lift the base engine from its mount. Remove and discard the mounting gasket (**Figure 6**).

5. Remove the bolt, washer and nuts (1-3, **Figure 7**) then lift the lower motor cover (5, **Figure 7**) from the drive shaft housing (4, **Figure 7**).

6. Clean the base engine-to-drive shaft housing mating surfaces. Replace the components if there are corroded or damaged surfaces.

Engine Installation (Models BF50 and BF5A)

1. Position the lower engine cover onto the drive shaft housing. Install the bolts, washers and nuts (**Figure 7**) and tighten them to the specification listed in **Table 1**.

2. Place a new gasket onto the midsection-to-base engine mating surface. Slowly lower the base engine (**Figure 6**) onto the midsection. Ensure that all bolt holes are properly aligned and the gasket is not damaged during installation.

3. Install the nine base engine mounting bolts (**Figure 6**) and tighten them to the specification listed in **Table 1**.

4. Refer to Chapter Six and connect the fuel hose to the fuel pump.

5. Refer to Chapter Eleven and install the rewind starter.

6. Connect the engine stop switch and oil pressure indicator light wires to the engine wire harness.

7. Refer to Chapter Nine and install the gearcase.

8. Perform all applicable adjustments following the procedures listed in Chapter Five. Refer to Chapter Four and fill the crankcase or oil pan with the proper oil.

Engine Removal (Models BF75, BF8A, BF9.9A, BF100 and BF15A)

1. Refer to Chapter Nine and remove the gearcase from the engine.

2. Refer to Chapter Thirteen and remove both lower mount covers, mounts and the drive shaft housing from the engine.

3. Refer to Chapter Six and remove the fuel tank-to-fuel pump hose from the fuel pump.

4. Remove the stop switch and oil pressure indicator light wires from the main harness.

5. Disconnect the control cables from throttle and shift linkages. Route the cables away from the base engine to avoid damaging them during base engine removal and installation.

6. Refer to Chapter Eleven and remove the rewind starter from the base engine.

7. Loosen and remove the mounting bolts (1, **Figure 8**), then carefully lift the base engine (2, **Figure 8**) from its mount. Remove and discard the mounting gasket (3, **Figure 8**).

8. Note the drive shaft seal (4, **Figure 8**) position with markings on the UP side. Carefully pry up and remove the drive shaft seal (4, **Figure 8**). Discard the seal.

9. Clean the base engine-to-drive shaft housing mating surfaces. Inspect them for corroded or damaged surfaces. Replace the component(s) if defective.

Engine Installation (Models BF75, BF8A, BF9.9A, BF100 and BF15A)

CAUTION
Use extreme care to ensure that the crankshaft or other components do not damage the drive shaft seal.

1. Clean all debris from the drive shaft seal bore. Use a piece of tubing or a socket that is slightly smaller in diameter than the seal to carefully push the new seal into its bore. Make sure that the seal is installed as noted prior to removal. Apply a light coat of grease to the seal lip to ease installation.

2. Place a new gasket onto the midsection (3, **Figure 8**).

3. Be certain that the oil pickup tube and screen (6, **Figure 8**) are not pinched or dislocated while lowering the base engine.

4. Slowly lower the base engine (2, **Figure 8**) onto the midsection. Ensure that all bolt holes are properly aligned and the gasket is not damaged during installation.

5. Install the base engine mounting bolts (1, **Figure 8**) and tighten them to the specification listed in **Table 1**.

6. Refer to Chapter Six then connect the fuel hose to the fuel pump.

7. Clean the engine-to-drive shaft housing mating surfaces. Replace the components if there are corroded or damaged surfaces.

8. Refer to Chapter Eleven and install the rewind starter.

9. Install any disconnected wires, cables or hoses. Make sure they are routed in a manner that prevents interference with other components.

10. Connect the engine stop switch and oil pressure indicator light wires to the engine wire harness.

11. Refer to Chapter Nine and install the gearcase.

12. Refer to Chapter Thirteen and install the drive shaft housing, lower mounts and mount covers.

BASE ENGINE

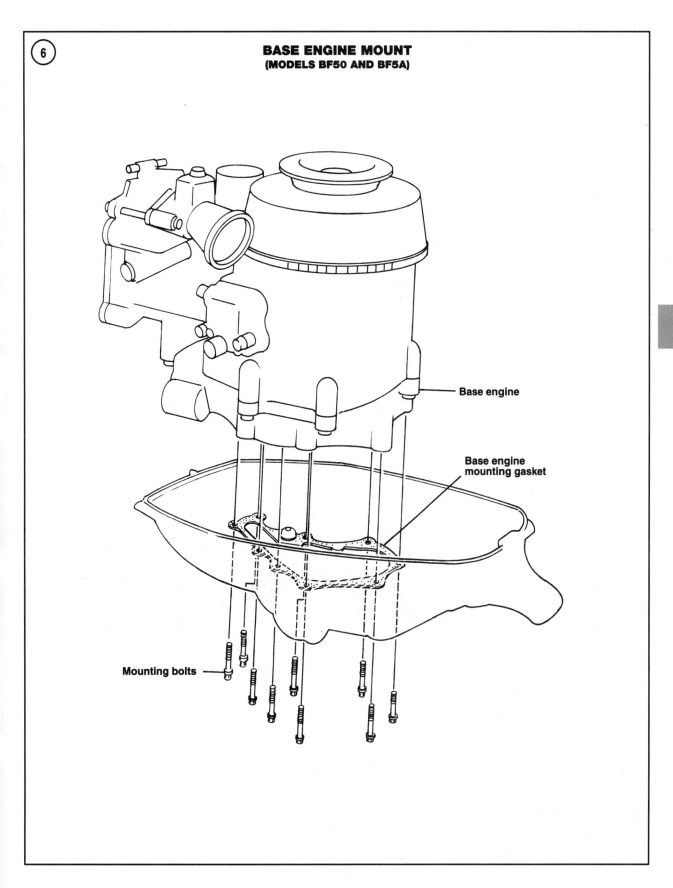

⑥ **BASE ENGINE MOUNT**
(MODELS BF50 AND BF5A)

- Base engine
- Base engine mounting gasket
- Mounting bolts

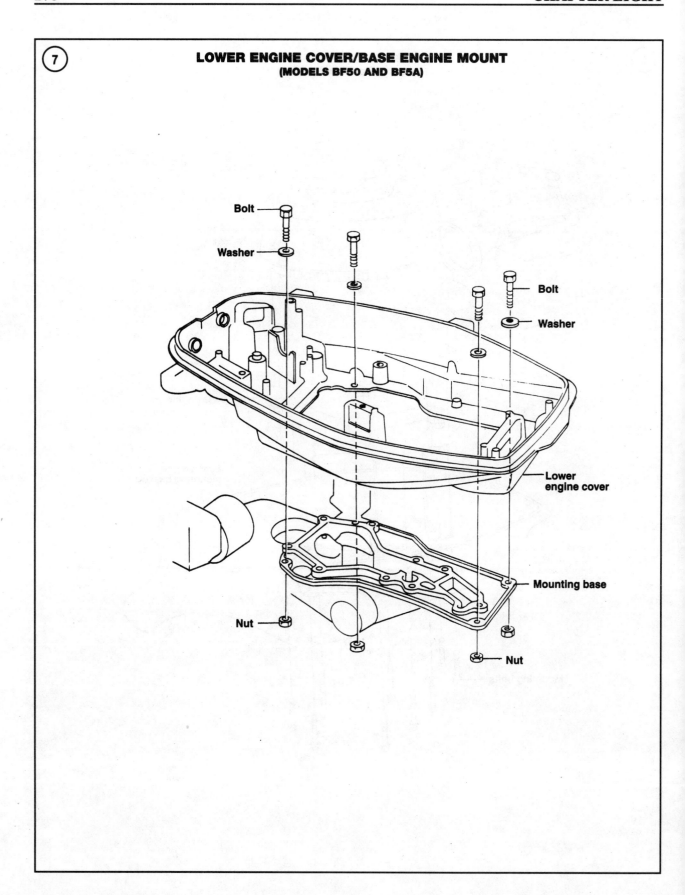

BASE ENGINE 277

⑧ ENGINE LOWER MOUNT
(BF75, BF8A, BF9.9A, BF100 AND BF15A)

1. Bolt
2. Base engine
3. Base engine mounting gasket
4. Seal
5. Lower motor cover
6. Oil pickup/screen
7. Crankshaft

13. Perform all applicable adjustments following the procedures listed in Chapter Five. Refer to Chapter Four and fill the crankcase or oil pan with the proper oil.

Engine Removal (Models BF20A, BF25A and BF30A)

CAUTION
Lift the base engine slowly. Maintain support to ensure that the base engine is lifted straight off the midsection. The drive shaft and other components may be damaged if the base engine is lifted or lowered at an angle.

1. Refer to Chapter Nine and remove the gearcase from the engine.
2. Disconnect the control cables from throttle and shift linkages. Route the cables away from the base engine to avoid damaging them during base engine removal and installation. Activate the tilt/lock lever and tilt the engine enough to remove the drive shaft housing (4, **Figure 9**).
3. Refer to Chapter Thirteen and remove the lower engine mount covers and mounts (1 and 2, **Figure 9**).
4. Support the drive shaft housing (4, **Figure 9**) and remove the bolts and washers (3 and 5, **Figure 9**). Carefully lower the drive shaft housing from the engine.
5. Position the engine vertically. Place a suitable container under the oil pan (2, **Figure 10**). Remove the oil drain plug (3, **Figure 10**) and drain the oil from the pan.
6. Remove the bolts (5, **Figure 10**) and remove the exhaust tube (1, **Figure 10**). Discard the exhaust tube gasket.
7. Carefully pull the water tube and grommet (13 and 14, **Figure 10**) from the oil pan.
8. Remove the bolts and washers (7 and 8, **Figure 10**), then carefully lower the oil pan (2, **Figure 10**) from the mounting bracket. Thoroughly clean the oil pan. Check for corroded or damaged surfaces.
9. Remove the bolts (9, **Figure 10**) then lower the oil pickup tube and screen (10, **Figure 10**) from the engine. Remove and discard the mounting gasket (11, **Figure 10**). Remove the dipstick (6, **Figure 10**).
10. Thoroughly inspect the engine for any remaining hoses, linkage or wires that are connected to the base engine assembly. Note their routing and connection points and remove them.
11. Attach a suitable cable or chain, lifting hook and hoist to the base engine mounted lifting hook (1, **Figure 11**). Lift the hoist just enough to remove any slack in the cable or chain.
12. Locate and remove the mounting bolts and washers (2 and 3, **Figure 11**). Carefully lift the base engine from the mounting bracket and place it on a clean work surface.
13. Remove and discard the mounting gasket (5, **Figure 11**). Clean the base engine-to-drive shaft housing mating surfaces. Clean the oil pan-to-mounting bracket and exhaust tube-to-mounting bracket mating surfaces. Replace the component(s) if they are corroded or damaged.
14. Inspect the alignment pins (7, **Figure 11**) for damaged or worn surfaces. Place them in their respective location on the mounting bracket-to-base engine mating surface.

Engine Installation (Models BF20A, BF25A and BF30A)

1. Make sure that all debris and contamination are removed from the engine mounting surfaces. Apply a light coating of liquid gasket compound, such as Perma-Gasket No. 2, to the mating surfaces of the base engine and mounting bracket. Place all locating pins (7, **Figure 11**) into their correct locations in the mounting bracket.
2. Place the new engine mounting gasket (5, **Figure 11**) onto the mounting bracket (6, **Figure 11**). Using a hoist, hook and chain or cable, carefully lower the base engine into position on the mounting bracket. Ensure that the locating pins enter their bores as the base engine is lowered.
3. Install the bolts and washers (2 and 3, **Figure 11**) and tighten them in a circular pattern or sequence to the specification listed in **Table 1**.
4. Place a new oil pan mounting gasket (11, **Figure 10**) onto the mounting bracket. Install the oil pickup/screen (10, **Figure 10**). Install the bolts (9, **Figure 10**) and tighten them to the specification listed in **Table 1**.
5. Install the oil pan (2, **Figure 10**) to the mounting bracket. Install the bolts and washers (7 and 8, **Figure 10**) and tighten them to the specifications listed in **Table 1**. Refer to Chapter Four and install the oil drain plug and washer.
6. Place a new gasket (12, **Figure 10**) onto the exhaust tube (1, **Figure 10**). Install the tube and three bolts (5, **Figure 10**). Tighten them to the specification listed in **Table 1**.
7. Apply water-resistant grease to the water tube grommet (14, **Figure 10**). Install the water tube (13, **Figure 10**) into the larger diameter side of the grommet. Push the wa-

BASE ENGINE 279

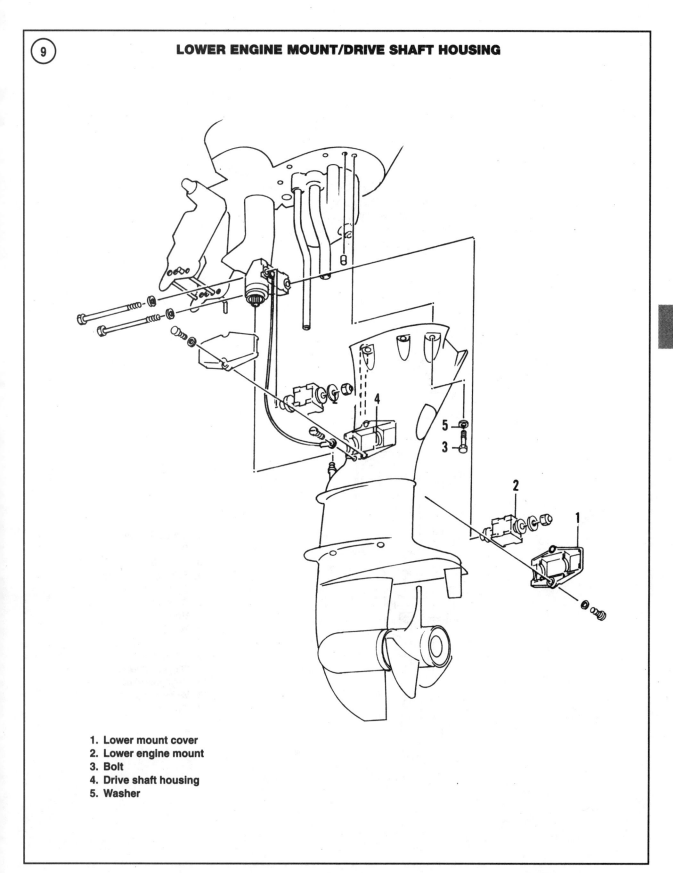

LOWER ENGINE MOUNT/DRIVE SHAFT HOUSING

1. Lower mount cover
2. Lower engine mount
3. Bolt
4. Drive shaft housing
5. Washer

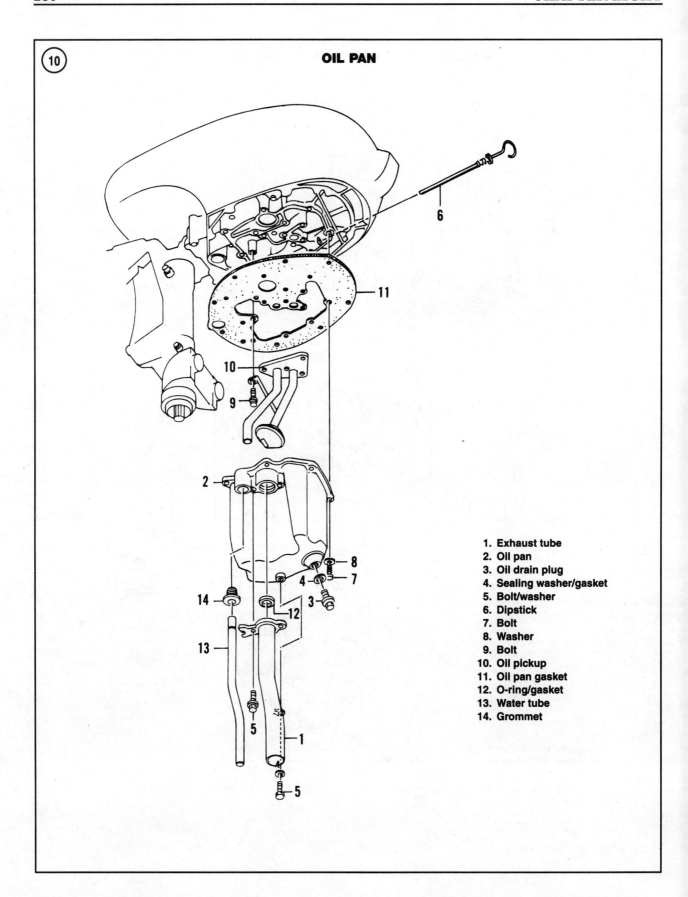

BASE ENGINE

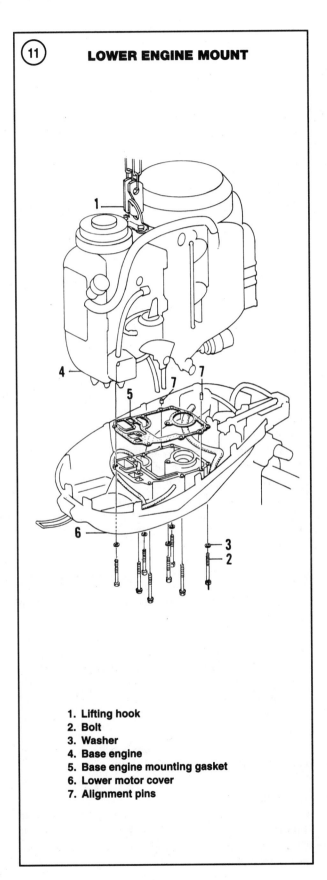

11. LOWER ENGINE MOUNT

1. Lifting hook
2. Bolt
3. Washer
4. Base engine
5. Base engine mounting gasket
6. Lower motor cover
7. Alignment pins

ter tube and grommet into the water tube opening on the oil pan. Install the dipstick.

8. Refer to Chapter Thirteen and install the drive shaft housing (4, **Figure 9**) and mounts to the mounting bracket.

9. Refer to Chapter Nine and install the gearcase to the engine.

10. Attach all cables, hoses or wires. Make sure they are routed in a manner that prevents them from interfering with other components.

11. Perform all applicable adjustments following the procedures listed in Chapter Five. Refer to Chapter Four and fill the crankcase or oil pan with the proper oil.

Engine Removal (Models BF35A, BF40A, BF45A and BF50A)

1. Refer to Chapter Nine and remove the gearcase from the engine.

2. Disconnect the control cables from throttle and shift linkages. Route the cables away from the engine to avoid damaging them during base engine removal and installation. Activate the manual relief valve (Chapter Twelve) and tilt the engine enough to allow removal of the drive shaft housing (9, **Figure 12**).

3. Refer to Chapter Thirteen, then remove the lower engine mount covers and mounts (1 and 2, **Figure 12**).

4. Remove the screws retaining the lower motor skirt (8, **Figure 12**) to the mounting bracket. Remove the bolt, washer and spacer (3 and 4, **Figure 12**) as you support the lower motor skirt.

5. Support the drive shaft housing (9, **Figure 12**) and remove the bolts and washers (10 and 11, **Figure 12**). Carefully lower the drive shaft housing and lower motor skirt (8, **Figure 12**) from the engine.

6. Position the engine vertically. Place a container under the oil pan (2, **Figure 10**). Remove the oil drain plug (3, **Figure 10**) and drain the oil from the pan.

7. Remove the bolts (5, **Figure 10**) then remove the exhaust tube (1, **Figure 10**). Discard the exhaust tube gasket.

8. Carefully pull the water tube and grommet (13 and 14, **Figure 10**) from the oil pan.

9. Remove the bolts (7, **Figure 10**) and carefully lower the oil pan (2, **Figure 10**) from the mounting bracket. Thoroughly clean the oil pan. Check for corroded or damaged surfaces. Replace the oil pan if defective.

10. Remove both bolts (9, **Figure 10**) and lower the oil pickup tube and screen (10, **Figure 10**) from the engine.

Remove and discard the O-ring from the upper end of the tube (11, **Figure 10**). Remove the dipstick (6, **Figure 10**).

11. Thoroughly inspect the engine for any remaining hoses, linkage or wires that are connected to the base engine. Note their routing and connection points and remove them.

12. Attach a suitable cable or chain, lifting hook and hoist to the base engine mounted lifting hook (1, **Figure 11**). Lift the hoist just enough to remove any slack in the cable or chain.

13. Locate and remove all mounting bolts and washers (2 and 3, **Figure 11**). Carefully lift the base engine from the mounting bracket. Place the base engine on a clean work surface.

14. Remove and discard the mounting gasket (5, **Figure 11**). Clean the engine mounting surfaces. Clean the oil pan-to-mounting bracket and exhaust tube-to-mounting bracket mating surfaces. Replace the components if there are corroded or damaged surfaces.

15. Inspect the locating pins (7, **Figure 11**) for damaged or worn surfaces. Place them in their respective locations in the primary gear housing.

16. Refer to *Primary Gear Housing* in this chapter for repair information on the primary gear housing.

Engine Installation (Models BF35A, BF40A, BF45A and BF50A)

CAUTION
Use extreme caution when lowering the base engine onto the primary gear housing. Make sure the crankshaft gear and primary gear housing gear mesh properly. Use a wooden dowel or other soft object to rotate the gear while lowering the base engine.

1. Make sure that all debris and contamination are removed from the base engine-mating surface. Apply a light coat of liquid gasket compound such as Permatex No. 2, to the mating surfaces of the base engine and primary gear housing. Place all locating pins (7, **Figure 11**) into their correct location in the primary gear housing.

2. Place the new engine mounting gasket (5, **Figure 11**) onto the mounting bracket. Using a suitable lifting hoist, hook and chain or cable, carefully lower the base engine into position on the mounting bracket. Make sure the locating pins enter their bores and the gear teeth mesh as the engine is lowered.

3. Install the bolts and washers (2 and 3, **Figure 11**) and tighten them in a circular pattern to the specification listed in **Table 1**.

4. Place a new oil pan mounting gasket (11, **Figure 10**) onto the mounting bracket. Install the oil pickup/screen (10, **Figure 10**). Install the bolts (9, **Figure 10**) and tighten them to the specification listed in **Table 1**.

5. Install the oil pan (2, **Figure 10**) to the mounting bracket. Install the retaining bolts and washers (7 and 8, **Figure 10**) and tighten them to the specifications listed in **Table 1**. Refer to Chapter Four and install the oil drain plug and washer.

6. Place a new gasket (12, **Figure 10**) onto the exhaust tube (1, **Figure 10**). Install the tube and the mounting bolts (5, **Figure 10**) to the oil pan. Tighten to the specification listed in **Table 1**.

7. Apply water-resistant grease to the water tube grommet (14, **Figure 10**). Install the water tube (13, **Figure 10**) into the larger diameter side of the grommet. Push the water tube and grommet into the water tube opening on the oil pan. Install the dipstick.

8. Refer to Chapter Thirteen and install the drive shaft housing (4, **Figure 9**) and mounts on the mounting bracket.

9. Install the lower motor skirt (8, **Figure 12**) and tighten its fasteners securely.

10. Refer to Chapter Nine and install the gearcase on the engine.

11. Attach all disconnected cable hoses or wires. Ensure they are routed in a manner that prevents them from interfering with other components.

12. Perform all applicable adjustments following the procedures listed in Chapter Five. Refer to Chapter Four and fill the crankcase or oil pan with the proper oil.

Engine Removal (Models BF75A and BF90A)

1. Refer to Chapter Nine and remove the gearcase from the engine.

2. Disconnect the control cables from throttle and shift linkages. Route the cables away from the base engine to avoid damaging them during engine removal and installation.

3. Activate the manual relief valve (Chapter Twelve) and tilt the engine enough to allow removal of the drive shaft housing (9, **Figure 12**).

4. Refer to Chapter Seven and remove the electric starter motor from the base engine.

5. Refer to Chapter Thirteen and remove the lower engine mount covers and mounts.

6. Remove the screws that retain the lower motor skirt (**Figure 12**) to the mounting bracket. Remove the bolt, washer and spacer (3 and 4, **Figure 12**) as you support the lower motor skirt.

BASE ENGINE

LOWER ENGINE MOUNT/DRIVE SHAFT HOUSING

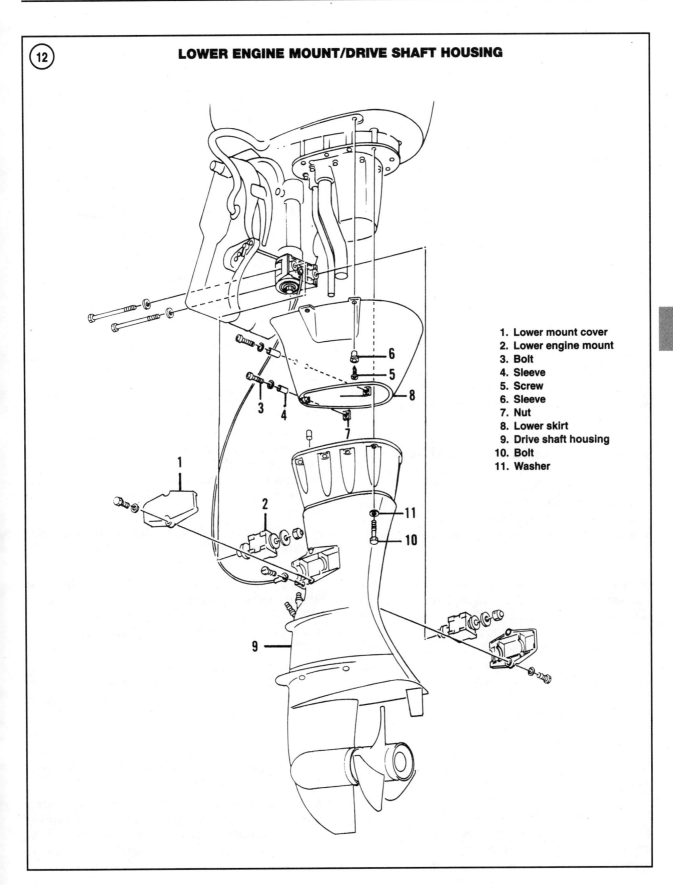

1. Lower mount cover
2. Lower engine mount
3. Bolt
4. Sleeve
5. Screw
6. Sleeve
7. Nut
8. Lower skirt
9. Drive shaft housing
10. Bolt
11. Washer

7. Support the drive shaft housing (9, **Figure 12**) and remove the bolts and washers (10 and 11, **Figure 12**). Carefully lower the drive shaft housing and lower motor skirt (8, **Figure 12**) from the engine.

8. Position the engine vertically. Place a container under the oil pan (2, **Figure 10**). Remove the oil drain plug (3, **Figure 10**) and drain the oil from the pan.

9. Remove the bolts and washers (5, **Figure 10**), then remove the exhaust tube (1, **Figure 10**). Discard the exhaust tube gasket.

10. Carefully pull the water tube and grommet (13 and 14, **Figure 10**) from the oil pan.

11. Remove the bolts (7, **Figure 10**) then carefully lower the oil pan (2, **Figure 10**) from the mounting bracket. Thoroughly clean the oil pan. Check for corroded or damaged surfaces. Replace the oil pan if defective.

12. Refer to Chapter Four and remove the timing belt cover from the engine.

13. Thread a lifting hook (Honda part No. 07SPZ-ZW0010Z or Mercury part no. 91-90455) *fully* into the rotor/starter pulley as shown in **Figure 13**.

14. Remove the mounting bolt and nut then lower the oil pickup tube and screen (10, **Figure 10**) from the engine. Remove the dipstick (6, **Figure 10**).

15. Thoroughly inspect the engine for any remaining hoses, linkage or wires that are connected to the base engine. Note their routing and connection points and remove them.

16. Attach a suitable cable or chain to the lifting hook and hoist to the engine lifting hook (1, **Figure 11**). Lift the hoist just enough to remove any slack from the cable or chain.

17. Locate and remove all mounting bolts and washers (**Figure 14**). Make sure the base engine remains level as you carefully lift it from the mounting bracket. Place the base engine on a clean work surface. Avoid supporting the base engine on the mounting studs (5, **Figure 14**).

18. Remove and discard the mounting gasket (6, **Figure 14**). Clean the engine mounting surfaces. Clean the oil pan mating surfaces. Replace the components if there are corroded or damaged surfaces.

19. Inspect the locating pins (7, **Figure 14**) for damaged or worn surfaces. Place them in their respective bores in the mounting bracket.

Engine Installation (Models BF75A and BF90A)

1. Make sure that all debris and contaminants are removed from the base engine to the mounting bracket mating surface. Apply a light coating of liquid gasket compound, such as Permatex No. 2, to the mating surfaces

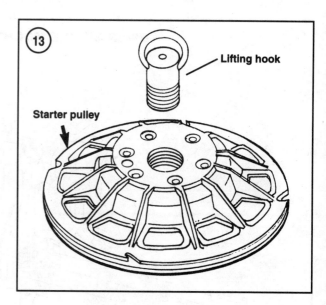

of the base engine and mounting bracket. Place all locating pins (7, **Figure 11**) into their correct locations in the mounting bracket.

2. Ensure that the marks on the shift shaft gears are aligned as shown in **Figure 15**.

3. Place the new base engine mounting gasket (6, **Figure 14**) onto the mounting bracket. Using a suitable lifting hoist, hook and chain or cable, carefully lower the base engine into position on the mounting bracket. Ensure that the locating pins enter their bores as the base engine is lowered.

4. Install the bolts and washers (**Figure 14**) and tighten them in a circular pattern to the specification listed in **Table 1**.

5. Place a new oil pan mounting gasket (11, **Figure 10**) onto the mounting bracket. Install the oil pickup/screen (10, **Figure 10**) on the bracket. Install its mounting bolt and nut and tighten them to the specification listed in **Table 1**.

6. Install the oil pan (2, **Figure 10**) to the mounting bracket. Install the retaining bolts and washers (7 and 8, **Figure 10**) and tighten them to the specifications listed in **Table 1**. Install the oil drain plug and washer.

7. Place a new gasket (12, **Figure 10**) onto the exhaust tube (1, **Figure 10**). Install the tube and the three mounting bolts (5, **Figure 10**) on the oil pan. Tighten to the specifications listed in **Table 1**.

8. Apply water-resistant grease to the water tube grommet (14, **Figure 10**). Install the water tube (13, **Figure 10**) into the larger diameter side of the grommet. Push the water tube and grommet into the water tube opening on the oil pan. Install the dipstick.

BASE ENGINE

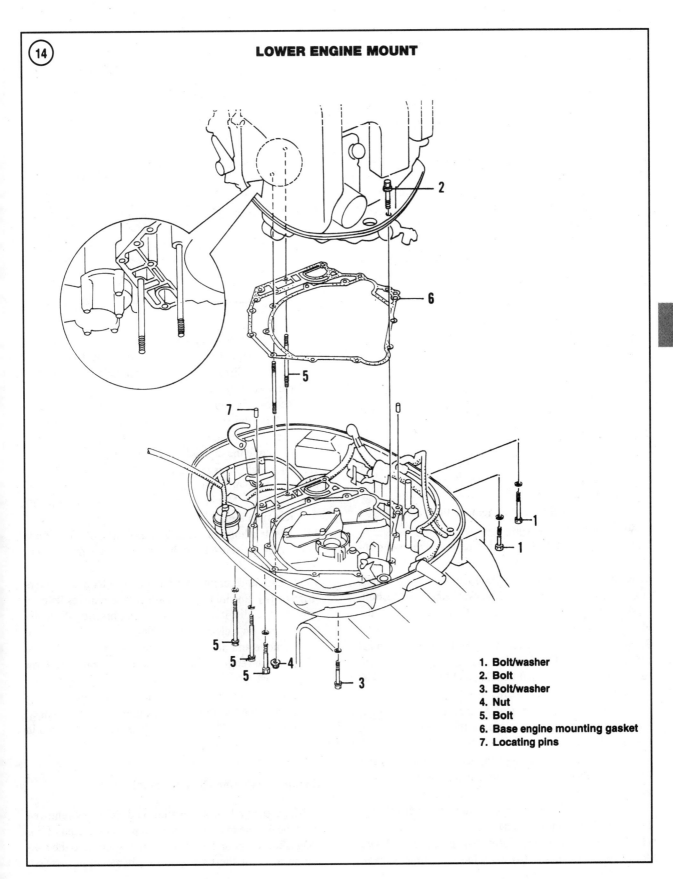

LOWER ENGINE MOUNT

1. Bolt/washer
2. Bolt
3. Bolt/washer
4. Nut
5. Bolt
6. Base engine mounting gasket
7. Locating pins

9. Refer to Chapter Thirteen and install the drive shaft housing (4, **Figure 9**) and mounts to the mounting bracket.

10. Install the lower motor skirt (8, **Figure 12**) and securely tighten its fasteners.

11. Refer to Chapter Nine and install the gearcase on the engine.

12. Refer to Chapter Seven and install the electric starter motor.

13. Attach any disconnected cable hose or wire harness connection as noted prior to removal. Make sure they are routed in a manner that will prevent them from interfering with other components.

14. Perform all applicable adjustments following the procedures listed in Chapter Five. Refer to Chapter Four and fill the crankcase or oil pan with the proper oil.

Engine Removal (Models BF115A and BF130A)

1. Refer to Chapter Nine and remove the gearcase from the engine.

2. Disconnect the control cables from throttle and shift linkages. Route the cables away from the base engine to avoid damaging them during base engine removal and installation.

3. Activate the manual relief valve (Chapter Twelve) and tilt the engine enough to allow removal of the drive shaft housing (9, **Figure 12**).

4. Refer to Chapter Seven and remove the electric starter motor from the base engine.

5. Refer to Chapter Thirteen and remove the lower engine mount covers and mounts.

6. Remove the screws that retain the lower motor skirt (**Figure 12**) to the mounting bracket. Remove the bolt, washer and spacer (3 and 4, **Figure 12**) as you support the lower motor skirt.

7. Support the drive shaft housing (9, **Figure 12**) and remove the bolts and washers (10 and 11, **Figure 12**). Carefully lower the drive shaft housing and lower motor skirt (8, **Figure 12**) from the engine.

8. Position the engine vertically. Place a container under the oil pan (2, **Figure 10**). Remove the oil drain plug (3, **Figure 10**) and drain the oil from the pan.

9. Remove the three bolts and washers (5, **Figure 10**) and remove the exhaust tube (1, **Figure 10**). Discard the exhaust tube gasket.

10. Carefully pull the water tube and grommet (13 and 14, **Figure 10**) from the oil pan.

11. Remove the bolts (7, **Figure 10**) and carefully lower the oil pan (2, **Figure 10**) from the mounting bracket.

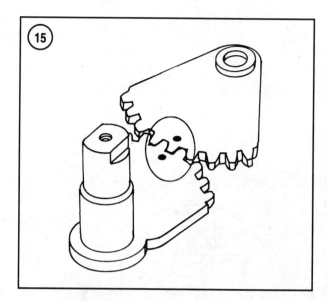

Thoroughly clean the oil pan. Check for corroded or damaged surfaces and replace the oil pan if defective.

12. Refer to Chapter Four and remove the timing belt cover from the engine.

13. Remove the mounting bolt and nut, then lower the oil pickup tube and screen (10, **Figure 10**) from the engine. Remove and discard the O-ring from the upper end of the tube. Remove the dipstick (6, **Figure 10**).

14. Thoroughly inspect the engine for any remaining hoses, linkage or wires that are connected to the base engine assembly. Note their routing and connection points then remove them.

15. Attach a hoist to the engine lifting hook (1, **Figure 11**). Lift the hoist just enough to remove slack from the cable or chain.

16. Locate and remove all mounting bolts and washers (**Figure 14**). Ensure that the base engine remains level as you carefully lift it from the mounting bracket. Place the base engine on a clean work surface.

17. Remove and discard the mounting gasket (6, **Figure 14**). Clean the engine mounting surfaces. Clean the oil pan and exhaust tube mating surfaces. Replace the components if there are corroded or damaged surfaces.

18. Inspect the locating pins (7, **Figure 14**) for damaged or worn surfaces. Place them in their respective bores in the mounting bracket.

Engine Installation (BF115A and BF130A)

1. Make sure all contamination and debris is removed from the engine mating surface. Apply a light coat of liquid gasket compound, such as Permatex No. 2, to the mating surfaces of the base engine and mounting bracket.

BASE ENGINE

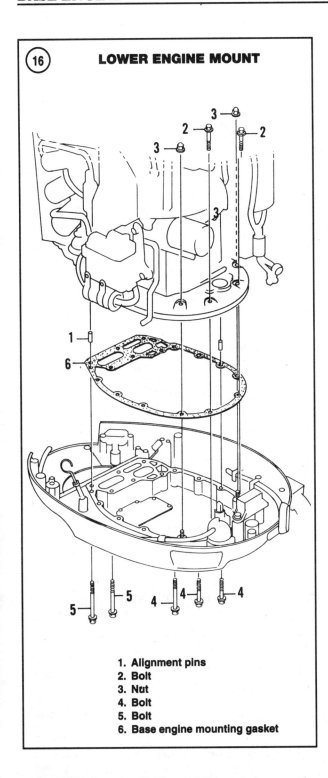

16 LOWER ENGINE MOUNT

1. Alignment pins
2. Bolt
3. Nut
4. Bolt
5. Bolt
6. Base engine mounting gasket

Place all locating pins (1, **Figure 16**) into their correct locations in the mounting bracket.

2. Be certain that the marks on the shift shaft gears are aligned as shown in **Figure 15**.

3. Place the new engine mounting gasket (6, **Figure 16**) onto the mounting bracket. Using a suitable lifting hoist, hook and chain or cable, carefully lower the base engine into position on the mounting bracket. Ensure that the locating pins enter their bore as the base engine is lowered.

4. Install all bolts and washers (**Figure 16**) and tighten them in a circular pattern to the specification listed in **Table 1**.

5. Place a new oil pan mounting gasket (11, **Figure 10**) onto the mounting bracket. With a new O-ring at the upper end, install the oil pickup/screen (10, **Figure 10**) on the bracket. Install its mounting bolt and nut and tighten them to the specification listed in **Table 1**.

6. Install the oil pan (2, **Figure 10**) to the mounting bracket. Install the retaining bolts and washers (7 and 8, **Figure 10**) and tighten them to the specifications listed in **Table 1**. Install the oil drain plug and washer.

7. Place a new gasket (12, **Figure 10**) onto the exhaust tube (1, **Figure 10**). Install the tube and the mounting bolts (5, **Figure 10**) to the oil pan. Tighten them to the specification listed in **Table 1**.

8. Apply water-resistant grease to the water tube grommet (14, **Figure 10**). Install the water tube (13, **Figure 10**) into the larger diameter side of the grommet. Push the water tube and grommet into the water tube opening on the oil pan. Install the dipstick.

9. Refer to Chapter Thirteen then install the drive shaft housing (9, **Figure 12**) and mounts on the mounting bracket.

10. Install the lower motor skirt (8, **Figure 12**) and securely tighten its fasteners.

11. Refer to Chapter Nine and install the gearcase on the engine.

12. Refer to Chapter Seven and install the electric starter motor on the base engine.

13. Attach all cables, hoses or wires. Ensure they are routed in a manner that will prevent them from interfering with other components.

14. Perform all applicable adjustments following the procedures listed in Chapter Five. Refer to Chapter Four and fill the crankcase or oil pan with the proper oil.

FLYWHEEL

CAUTION
Use only the appropriate tools and procedures to remove the flywheel. Never strike the flywheel with a hard object. The magnets may break and result in poor ignition system performance or potential damage to other engine components.

WARNING
Wear safety glasses when removing or installing the flywheel or other components of the engine. Never use a hammer or other tools without using safety glasses.

Ensure that the base engine is securely held *before* attempting to remove the flywheel or pulleys. A flywheel holder and a flywheel-removing tool are required to remove the flywheel and pulleys. Obtain a commercially available strap wrench (or Honda part No. 07KGB-001010A) to hold the flywheel during fastener removal.

Flywheel Removal/Installation (Models BF20 and BF2A)

NOTE
All flywheel-attaching nuts are standard or right-hand threads. Turn counter-clockwise to loosen and clockwise to tighten them.

1. Remove the spark plug and connect the spark plug lead to an engine ground.
2. Refer to Chapter Eleven and remove the rewind starter from the base engine.
3. Refer to *Base Engine Removal and Installation* and remove the lower motor cover from the base engine.
4. Use a strap wrench to hold the flywheel as you remove the flywheel nut. Lift the starter pulley and the fan from the flywheel (**Figure 17**).
5. Obtain a two-jaw puller from an automotive or tool supply store. Position the jaws on the flywheel on an area away from the magnets (**Figure 18**). Turn the puller bolt until it becomes tight.
6. Provide support for the flywheel and lightly tap the puller bolt. Tighten the bolt and tap it again if the flywheel does not dislodge from the crankshaft. Repeat this step if necessary.
7. Lift the flywheel from the base engine. Remove the two-jaw puller. Remove the woodruff key from the slot in the crankshaft taper. Retrieve the woodruff key from the ignition coils or flywheel magnets if not found in the slot. Use compressed air to remove contamination or debris from the flywheel magnets and other surfaces. Inspect the flywheel for cracked or damaged magnets.
8. Inspect the woodruff key for corrosion, bent or marked surfaces and replace if it is not in excellent condition.
9. Installation is the reverse of removal. Note the following:
    a. Ensure that the locating tabs on the fan align with the location holes in the flywheel.

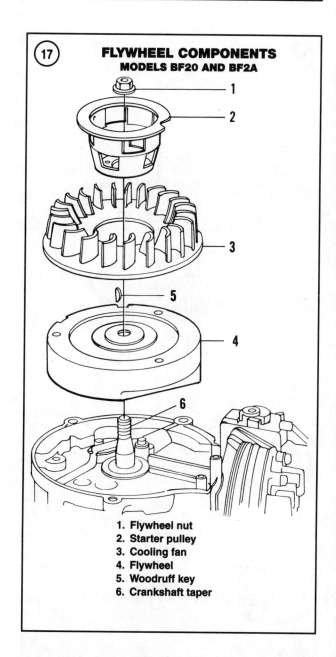

FLYWHEEL COMPONENTS
MODELS BF20 AND BF2A
1. Flywheel nut
2. Starter pulley
3. Cooling fan
4. Flywheel
5. Woodruff key
6. Crankshaft taper

b. Remove all debris and contamination from the crankshaft taper, flywheel, fan and starter pulley.
c. Install the woodruff key in the flywheel and crankshaft slot on assembly.
d. Tighten the flywheel nut to the specification listed in **Table 1**.

10. Refer to Chapter Seven for the correct the ignition coil to flywheel clearance. Refer to *Base Engine Removal and Installation* and install the lower motor cover.

11. Refer to Chapter Eleven and install the rewind starter to the base engine.

BASE ENGINE

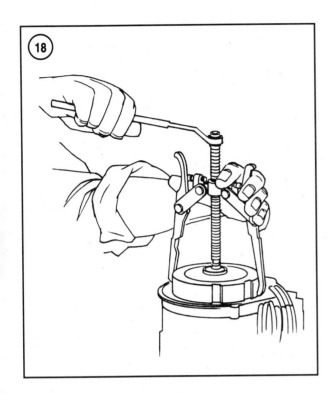

12. Perform applicable adjustments following the procedures listed in Chapter Five. Install the spark plug and spark plug lead.

Flywheel Removal/Installation (Models BF50 and BF5A)

1. Disconnect both battery cables from the battery, if so equipped. Remove the spark plug and connect the spark plug lead to an engine ground.

2. Refer to Chapter Eleven and remove the rewind starter from the base engine.

3. Use a strap wrench to hold the flywheel then remove the flywheel nut. Lift the starter pulley from the flywheel (**Figure 17**).

4. Use Honda flywheel puller part No. 07935-805003 or other suitable puller to remove the flywheel from the crankshaft. Position the puller on the flywheel as shown in **Figure 19**. Ensure that the puller bolts are adequately engaged in the threaded holes and the puller surface is paral-

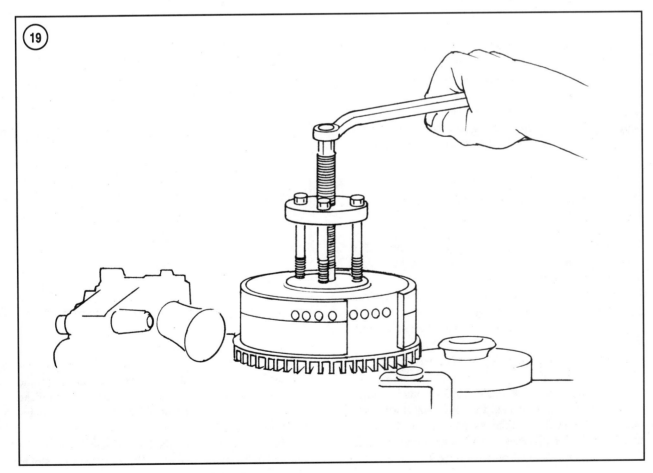

lel to the flywheel surface. Turn the puller bolt until it becomes tight.

5. Provide support for the flywheel and lightly tap the puller bolt. Tighten the bolt and tap it again if the flywheel did not dislodge from the crankshaft. Repeat this step if necessary.

6. Lift the flywheel from the base engine. Remove the bolts and puller. Remove the woodruff key from the slot in the crankshaft taper. Retrieve the woodruff key from the ignition coils or flywheel magnets if not found in the slot. Inspect the woodruff key for corrosion, bent or marked surfaces and replace if not in excellent condition.

7. Use compressed air to remove contamination or debris from the flywheel magnets and other surfaces. Replace the flywheel if there are cracked or damaged magnets or other surfaces.

8. Installation is the reverse of removal. Note the following:
   a. Ensure that the locating tabs on the fan align with the location holes in the flywheel.
   b. Remove all debris and contamination from the crankshaft taper, flywheel and starter pulley.
   c. Install the woodruff key in the crankshaft slot.
   d. Tighten the flywheel nut to the specification listed in **Table 1**.

9. Refer to Chapter Seven and check the ignition coil-to-flywheel clearance.

10. Refer to Chapter Eleven and install the rewind starter to the base engine.

11. Perform all applicable adjustments following the procedures listed in Chapter Five. Install the spark plug and spark plug lead. Clean the battery terminals, then connect the cables to the battery.

Flywheel Removal/Installation (Models BF75, BF8A, BF9.9A and BF15A)

1. Disconnect both battery cables from the battery, if so equipped. Remove the spark plugs and connect the spark plug leads to an engine ground.

2. Refer to Chapter Eleven and remove the rewind starter (1, **Figure 20**) from the base engine.

3. Remove the bolts (3, **Figure 20**) and lift the starter pulley (4, **Figure 20**) from the flywheel (5, **Figure 20**).

4. Use a strap wrench to hold the flywheel then remove the flywheel nut.

5. Use Honda part No. 07935-805003 or other suitable puller to remove the flywheel from the crankshaft. Position the puller on the flywheel as indicated in **Figure 19**. Ensure the both puller bolts are adequately engaged into the threaded holes and the puller surface is parallel to the

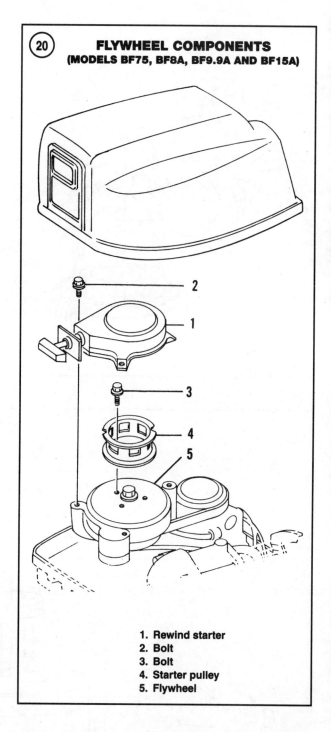

FLYWHEEL COMPONENTS (MODELS BF75, BF8A, BF9.9A AND BF15A)

1. Rewind starter
2. Bolt
3. Bolt
4. Starter pulley
5. Flywheel

flywheel surface. Turn the puller bolt until it becomes tight.

6. Provide support for the flywheel and lightly tap the puller bolt. Tighten the bolt and tap the bolt again if the flywheel will not pop free from the crankshaft. Repeat this step if necessary.

7. Lift the flywheel from the base engine. Remove the bolts and puller. Remove the woodruff key from the slot in

BASE ENGINE

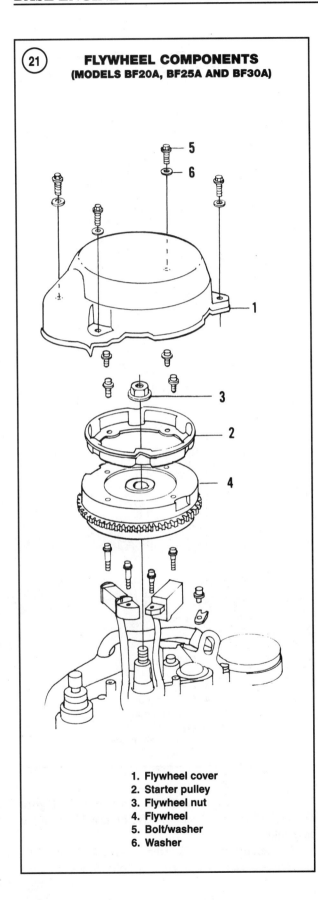

㉑ FLYWHEEL COMPONENTS (MODELS BF20A, BF25A AND BF30A)

1. Flywheel cover
2. Starter pulley
3. Flywheel nut
4. Flywheel
5. Bolt/washer
6. Washer

the crankshaft taper or from the ignition coils or flywheel magnets if not found in the slot. Inspect the woodruff key for corrosion, bent or marked surfaces and replace it if it is not in excellent condition.

8. Use compressed air to remove debris from the flywheel magnets and other surfaces. Replace the flywheel if there are cracked or damaged magnets or other surfaces.

9. Installation is the reverse of removal. Note the following:

    a. Ensure that the starter pulley bolt holes are properly aligned prior to assembly.
    b. Make sure all debris and contamination is removed from the crankshaft taper, flywheel and starter pulley.
    c. Install the woodruff key in the crankshaft slot.
    d. Tighten the flywheel nut to the specifications listed in **Table 1**.

10. On manual start models, refer to Chapter Eleven to install the rewind starter to the base engine. On electric start models, install the flywheel cover and securely tighten the mounting bolts and washers.

11. Perform all applicable adjustments following the procedures listed in Chapter Five. Install the spark plugs and spark plug leads. Clean the battery terminals and connect the cables to the battery.

Flywheel Removal/Installation (Models BF20A, BF25A and BF30A)

1. Disconnect both battery cables from the battery. Remove the spark plugs and connect the spark plug leads to an engine ground.

2. On manual start models, refer to Chapter Eleven and remove the rewind starter from the base engine.

3. On electric start models, remove the bolts and washers (5 and 6, **Figure 21**) and lift the flywheel cover (1, **Figure 21**) from the base engine.

4. Remove the bolts and starter pulley (2, **Figure 21**) from the flywheel (4, **Figure 21**).

5. Use a strap wrench to hold the flywheel and remove the flywheel nut (3, **Figure 21**). Lift the starter pulley (2, **Figure 17**) and the fan (3, **Figure 17**) from the flywheel (4, **Figure 21**).

6. Obtain a large three-jaw puller from an automotive or tool supply store. Position the jaws on the flywheel on an area away from the magnets as shown in **Figure 22**. Turn the puller bolt until it is tight.

7. Provide support for the flywheel and lightly tap the puller bolt. Tighten the bolt and tap the bolt again if the

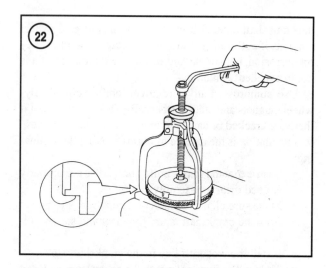

flywheel does not dislodge from the crankshaft. Repeat this step if necessary.

8. Lift the flywheel from the base engine. Remove the three-jaw puller. Remove the woodruff key from the slot in the crankshaft taper. Retrieve the woodruff key from the ignition coils or flywheel magnets if not found in the slot. Use compressed air to remove contamination or debris from the flywheel magnets and other surfaces. Replace the flywheel if there are cracked or damaged magnets or other surfaces.

9. Inspect the woodruff key for corrosion, bent or marked surfaces and replace it if it is not in excellent condition.

10. Installation is the reverse of removal. Note the following:
    a. Remove all debris and contamination from the crankshaft taper, flywheel, fan and starter pulley.
    b. Properly position the woodruff key in the crankshaft slot.
    c. Tighten the flywheel nut to the specification listed in **Table 1**.

11. Refer to Chapter Seven and check the ignition coil to flywheel clearance. Refer to *Base Engine Removal and Installation* and install the lower motor cover.

12. Refer to Chapter Eleven and install the rewind starter to the base engine. Perform all applicable adjustments following the procedures listed in Chapter Five. Install the spark plugs and spark plug leads. Connect the battery cables to the battery.

Flywheel Removal/Installation (Models BF35A, BF40A, BF45A and BF50A)

1. Disconnect both battery cables from the battery. Remove the spark plugs and connect the spark plug leads to an engine ground..

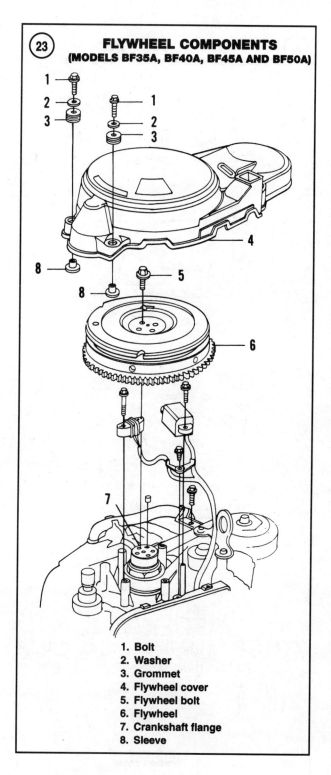

2. Remove the bolt, washer and grommet (1-3, **Figure 23**) then lift the flywheel cover (4, **Figure 23**) from the base engine.

3. Use a strap wrench to hold the flywheel (6, **Figure 23**), then remove the flywheel retaining bolts (5, **Figure 23**).

BASE ENGINE

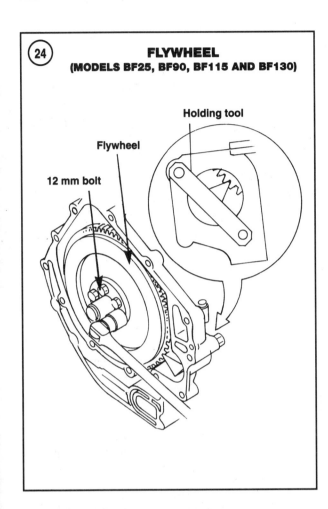

Figure 24 FLYWHEEL (MODELS BF25, BF90, BF115 AND BF130)

4. Carefully lift the flywheel from its mounting flange on the crankshaft (7, **Figure 23**).

5. Use compressed air to remove debris from the flywheel magnets and other surfaces. Replace the flywheel if there are cracked or damaged magnets or other worn or defective surfaces.

6. Installation is the reverse of removal. Note the following:
   a. Remove all debris and contamination from the crankshaft surface and flywheel.
   b. Install the locating pin in the respective hole in the flywheel.
   c. Tighten the flywheel mounting bolts to the specification listed in **Table 1**.

7. Perform all applicable adjustments following the procedures listed in Chapter Five.

8. Install the flywheel cover (4, **Figure 23**) then the grommets and collars (3 and 8, **Figure 23**). Install the washers and bolts (1 and 2, **Figure 23**). Securely tighten the bolts. Install the spark plugs and spark plug leads. Clean the battery terminals and connect the cables to the battery.

Flywheel Removal/Installation (Models BF75A and BF90A)

The flywheel is mounted to the bottom of the base engine on these models. Use Honda flywheel holder part No. 07SPB-ZW10100 or equivalent to prevent flywheel rotation during the removal procedure.

1. Refer to *Base Engine Removal and Installation* in this chapter and remove the base engine.

2. Install the flywheel holding tool to the electric starter mounting boss as shown in **Figure 24**. Securely tighten the tool mounting bolts.

3. Remove the bolts (1, **Figure 25**) and the oil pump housing (2, **Figure 25**) from the base engine. Refer to base engine repair for oil pump housing repair if required.

4. Remove the oil pump gasket (3, **Figure 25**) and residual material from the engine and oil pump housing. *Do not allow any debris to enter the passages on the mating surfaces.*

5. Remove the mounting bolts (6, **Figure 25**) and the coupler (5, **Figure 25**) from the flywheel. Remove the flywheel (7, **Figure 25**) from the crankshaft flange (8, **Figure 25**). Remove the holding tool from the electric starter motor mounting boss.

6. Use compressed air to remove debris from the flywheel and crankshaft surface. Replace the flywheel if you note any cracked or damaged starter gear teeth or other worn or defective surfaces.

7. Refer to *Base Engine Removal and Installation* in this chapter and install the base engine.

Flywheel Removal/Installation (Models BF115A and BF130A)

The flywheel is mounted to the bottom of the base engine on these models. Use Honda flywheel holder part No. 07SPB-ZW50100 or equivalent to prevent flywheel rotation during the removal procedure.

1. Refer to *Base Engine Removal and Installation* in this chapter, then remove the base engine.

2. Install the flywheel holding tool on the electric starter mounting boss as shown in **Figure 24**. Securely tighten the tool mounting bolts.

3. Remove the six flywheel mounting bolts then remove the flywheel from the crankshaft. Remove the holding tool from the electric starter motor mounting boss.

4. Use compressed air to remove debris from the flywheel and crankshaft surface. Replace the flywheel if you note cracked or damaged starter gear teeth or other worn or defective surfaces.

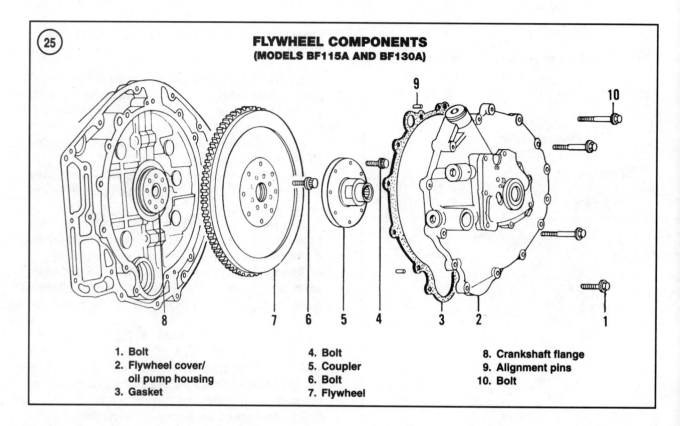

1. Bolt
2. Flywheel cover/oil pump housing
3. Gasket
4. Bolt
5. Coupler
6. Bolt
7. Flywheel
8. Crankshaft flange
9. Alignment pins
10. Bolt

5. Install the flywheel in the reverse order of removal, plus the following:
   a. Remove all debris removed from the flywheel and crankshaft surfaces.
   b. Use the Honda flywheel holder (part No. 07SPB-ZW50100) to prevent flywheel rotation during installation.
   c. Tighten the flywheel mounting bolts to the specification in **Table 1**.
   d. Make sure the oil pump mating surfaces are clean and install a new pump mounting gasket.
   e. Apply water-resistant grease to the seal lips in the oil pump housing.
   f. Tighten the oil pump housing bolts to the specification in **Table 1**.
   g. Install the engine as described in this chapter.

TIMING BELT

Never pry the timing belt from the pulleys with a screwdriver or other object. Use only your fingers to remove the belt. Replace the timing belt if it is contaminated by grease or oil. Replace the timing belt if it is worn, cracked or damaged or otherwise defective. Clean all debris from the pulleys and dry with compressed air. Replace the pulleys if they are worn, cracked or damaged or otherwise defective.

CAUTION
To avoid damage to the valve train and other base engine components, do not allow the flywheel or camshaft to rotate unless the timing belt is correctly installed.

Removal/Installation (Models BF75, BF8A, BF100, 9.9A and BF15A)

1. Disconnect both battery terminals from the battery, if so equipped. Remove the spark plugs and connect the spark plug leads to an engine ground.
2. Refer to *Valve Adjustment* in Chapter Four and position the timing marks at the TDC firing position for the No. 1 cylinder.
3. Should the timing marks not align, refer to *Valve Adjustment* in Chapter Four and locate the valve adjusting screws (**Figure 26**). Loosen each adjusting screw to the maximum amount. Remove the timing belt and align each timing mark individually if required.
4. Refer to *Flywheel Removal and Installation* in this chapter and remove the flywheel from the engine. Make sure the timing mark on the camshaft pulley is aligned

BASE ENGINE

with the mark on the rewind starter-mounting bracket. Install the flywheel and realign the marks if necessary.

5. Using only your fingers, carefully move the timing belt up (**Figure 27**) on the camshaft pulley to remove it from the camshaft pulley. Do not use a screwdriver as you may damage the timing belt.

6. Remove the belt from the crankshaft pulley. Clean all debris from the pulleys and the top of the engine. Use compressed air or a degreasing solvent.

7. Replace the camshaft pulley and crankshaft pulley if there are worn or damaged teeth.

8. Without moving either pulley, install the timing belt over the crankshaft pulley. Using only your fingers, slowly work the timing belt fully onto the camshaft pulley.

9. Refer to *Flywheel Removal and Installation* in this chapter and install the flywheel.

10. Refer to *Valve Adjustment* in Chapter Four and adjust the valves. Install the spark plugs and spark plug leads. Clean the battery terminals and connect the cables if so equipped.

Removal/Installation (Models BF20A, BF25A, BF30A BF35A, BF40A, BF45A and BF50A)

1. Disconnect both battery terminals from the battery, if so equipped. Remove the spark plugs and connect the spark plug leads to an engine ground.

2. Refer to *Valve Adjustment* in chapter four and align the timing marks at the TDC firing position for the No. 1 cylinder.

3. Should the timing marks not align, refer to *Valve Adjustment* in Chapter Four and locate the valve adjusting screws (**Figure 26**). Loosen each adjusting screw to the maximum amount. Remove the timing belt and align each timing mark individually if required.

4. Refer to *Flywheel Removal and Installation* in this chapter and remove the flywheel from the engine. Check to ensure the timing mark on the camshaft pulley is aligned with the mark on the timing belt lower cover. Replace the flywheel and realign the marks if necessary.

5. Refer to *Pulley Removal and Installation* in this chapter and remove the upper guide plate from the crankshaft pulley.

6. Refer to Chapter Seven then remove the ignition charge and battery charging coil from the engine.

7. Using long-nose locking pliers, carefully remove the tensioner spring (**Figure 28**) from the post on the cylinder block. Pivot the timing belt tensioner away from the timing belt (**Figure 28**).

8. Using only your fingers, carefully remove the timing belt from the camshaft and crankshaft pulleys. Do not use a screwdriver as you may damage the timing belt.

9. Remove the timing belt from the crankshaft pulley. Clean all debris from the pulleys and the top of the engine. Use compressed air or a suitable degreasing solvent.

10. Replace the camshaft pulley and crankshaft pulley if there are worn or damaged teeth.

11. Without moving either pulley, install the timing belt over the crankshaft pulley. Using only your fingers, slowly work the timing belt fully onto the camshaft pulley.

12. Ensure that the timing marks are aligned as shown in **Figure 28**.

13. Pivot the timing belt tensioner toward the timing belt. Using long nose locking pliers install the end of the tensioner spring onto the post on the cylinder block.

14. Refer to *Pulley Removal and Installation* in this chapter and install the upper guide plate on the crankshaft pulley. Refer to Chapter Seven and install the ignition charge coil and battery-charging coil.

15. Refer to *Flywheel Removal and Installation* in this chapter and install the flywheel.

16. Refer to *Valve Adjustment* in Chapter Four and adjust the valves.

17. Install the spark plugs and spark plug leads. Clean the battery terminals and connect the cables, if so equipped.

Removal/Installation (Models BF75A and BF90A)

1. Disconnect both battery terminals from the battery. Remove the spark plugs and connect the spark plug leads to an engine ground.

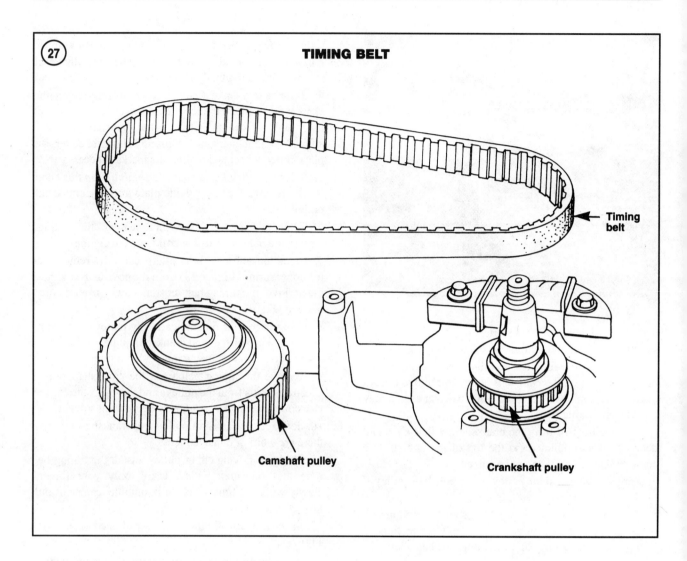

TIMING BELT

2. Refer to *Valve Adjustment* in Chapter Four and position the timing marks at the TDC firing position for the No. 1 cylinder.

3. Should the timing marks not align, refer to *Valve Adjustment* in Chapter Four and locate the valve adjusting screws (**Figure 26**). Loosen each adjusting screw to the maximum amount. Remove the timing belt and align each timing mark individually if required.

4. Refer to *Flywheel Removal and Installation* in this chapter and install the flywheel holding tool (**Figure 24**) on the flywheel.

5. Refer to *Pulley Removal and Installation* in this chapter and remove the starter pulley (1, **Figure 29**) and rotor (2, **Figure 29**) from the base engine.

6. Refer to Chapter Seven and remove the battery charging coil (3, **Figure 29**) and pulser coils (4, **Figure 29**) from the mounting base (5, **Figure 29**).

7. Note the location of all mounting bolts, spacers and wire retaining clamps then remove the mounting base (5, **Figure 29**) from the engine.

8. Using long-nose locking pliers, carefully remove the tensioner spring (**Figure 28**) from the post on the cylinder block. Pivot the timing belt tensioner away from the timing belt (**Figure 28**).

9. Using only your fingers, carefully remove the timing belt from the camshaft and crankshaft pulleys. Do not use a screwdriver as you may damage the timing belt. Do not disturb the crankshaft pulley upper guide plate.

10. Remove the timing belt from the crankshaft pulley. Clean all debris from the pulleys and the top of the engine. Use compressed air or a suitable degreasing solvent.

11. Replace the camshaft pulley and crankshaft pulley if they have worn or damaged teeth.

12. Without moving either pulley, install the timing belt over the crankshaft pulley. Using only your fingers, slowly work the timing belt fully onto the camshaft and

BASE ENGINE

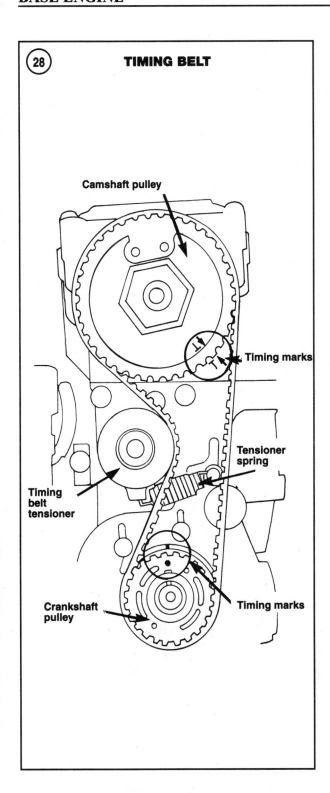

28   **TIMING BELT**

Camshaft pulley

Timing marks

Tensioner spring

Timing belt tensioner

Crankshaft pulley

Timing marks

crankshaft pulleys. Ensure that the upper crankshaft pulley guide plate is properly positioned on the pulley.

13. Pivot the timing belt tensioner toward the timing belt. Using long-nose locking pliers, install the end of the tensioner spring onto the post on the cylinder block.

14. Install the mounting base (5, **Figure 29**) onto the engine. Tighten the fasteners to the specification listed in **Table 1**.

15. Refer to Chapter Seven and install the battery charging and pulser coils (3 and 4, **Figure 29**) to the mounting base (5, **Figure 29**).

16. Refer to *Pulley Removal and Installation* and install the rotor and starter pulley (1 and 2, **Figure 29**) to the crankshaft.

17. Refer to *Flywheel Removal and Installation* then remove the flywheel holding tool from the base engine.

18. Refer to *Valve Adjustment* in Chapter Four and adjust the valves.

19. Install the spark plugs and spark plug leads. Clean the battery terminals and connect the battery cables.

Removal/Installation (Models BF115A and BF130A)

1. Disconnect both battery terminals from the battery. Remove the spark plugs and connect the spark plug leads to an engine ground.

2. Refer to *Valve Adjustment* in Chapter Four and align the timing marks to the TDC firing position for the No. 1 cylinder.

3. Should the timing marks not align, refer to *Valve Adjustment* in Chapter Four and locate the valve adjusting screws (**Figure 26**). Loosen each adjusting screw to the maximum amount. Remove the timing belt and align each timing mark individually if required.

4. Refer to *Flywheel Removal and Installation* in this chapter and install the flywheel holding tool (**Figure 24**) on the flywheel.

5. Refer to Chapter Seven and remove the alternator and drive belt (**Figure 30**) from the engine.

6. Refer to *Pulley Removal and Installation* in this chapter and remove the cooling fan and crankshaft pulley (**Figure 30**).

7. Refer to *Balancer Belt Removal and Installation* in this section and remove the balancer pulley and balancer belt (**Figure 30**).

8. Using long-nose locking pliers, carefully remove the tensioner spring (**Figure 28**) from the post on the cylinder block. Pivot the timing belt tensioner away from the timing belt (**Figure 28**).

9. Using only your fingers, carefully remove the timing belt from the camshaft and crankshaft pulleys. Do not use a screwdriver as you may damage the timing belt.

10. Remove the timing belt from the crankshaft pulley. Clean all debris from the pulleys and the top of the engine. Use compressed air or a suitable degreasing solvent.

11. Replace the camshaft pulley and crankshaft pulley if the teeth are worn or damaged.

12. Without moving either pulley, install the timing belt over the crankshaft pulley. Using only your fingers, slowly work the timing belt fully onto the camshaft and crankshaft pulleys.

13. Pivot the timing belt tensioner toward the timing belt. Using long-nose locking pliers, install the end of the tensioner spring onto the post on the cylinder block.

14. Refer to *Balancer Belt Removal and Installation* in this section and install the balancer pulley and balancer belt (**Figure 30**).

15. Refer to *Pulley Removal and Installation* in this chapter, then install the cooling fan and crankshaft pulley (**Figure 30**).

16. Repeat Step 2 to verify the timing marks as correctly aligned.

17. Refer to Chapter Seven and install the alternator and its drive belt (**Figure 30**) to the base engine.

18. Remove the flywheel holding tool from the base engine.

19. Refer to *Valve Adjustment* in Chapter Four and adjust the valves.

20. Install the spark plugs and spark plug leads. Clean the battery terminals and connect the battery cables.

Balancer Belt Removal and Installation (Models BF115A and BF130A)

1. Disconnect both battery terminals from the battery. Remove all spark plugs and connect the spark plug leads to an engine ground.

2. Refer to *Valve Adjustment* in Chapter Four and align the timing marks to the TDC firing position for the No. 1 cylinder.

3. Should the timing marks not align, refer to *Valve Adjustment* in Chapter Four and locate the valve adjusting screws (**Figure 26**). Loosen each adjusting screw to the maximum amount. Remove the timing belt and align each timing mark individually as required.

4. Refer to *Flywheel Removal and Installation* in this chapter and install the flywheel holding tool (**Figure 24**) on the flywheel.

5. Refer to *Pulley Removal and Installation* in this chapter and remove the cooling fan and crankshaft pulley (3 and 4, **Figure 30**).

6. Using long-nose locking pliers, carefully remove the tensioner spring from the post on the engine (**Figure 31**).

7. Using only your fingers, carefully remove the balancer belt (**Figure 32**) from the starboard side balancer pulley, port side balancer pulley and drive pulley (**Figure 32**).

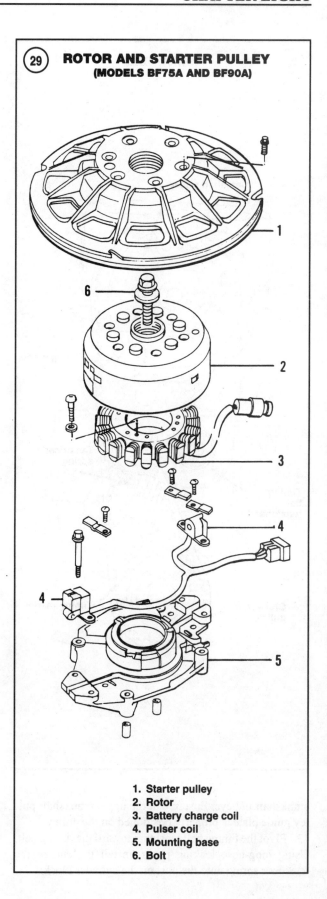

29 ROTOR AND STARTER PULLEY (MODELS BF75A AND BF90A)

1. Starter pulley
2. Rotor
3. Battery charge coil
4. Pulser coil
5. Mounting base
6. Bolt

BASE ENGINE

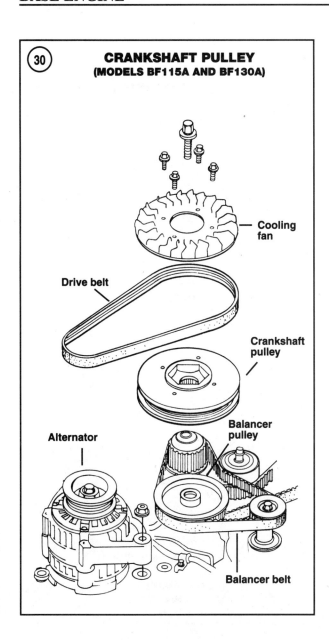

Figure 30 CRANKSHAFT PULLEY (MODELS BF115A AND BF130A)

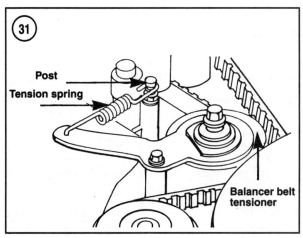

Figure 31

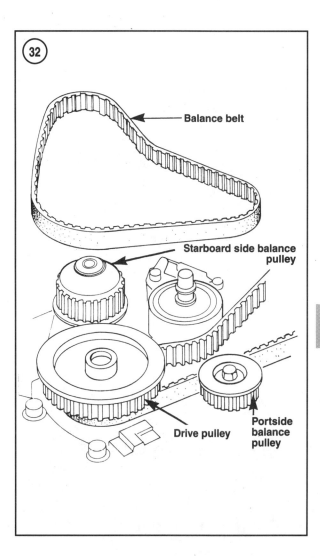

Figure 32

8. Confirm that the timing marks are still aligned.

9. Make sure that the mark on the drive pulley aligns with the mark on the cylinder block. If the marks are not aligned, remove the flywheel holding tool, then remove and re-install the timing belt following the procedures listed in this chapter.

10. Rotate the starboard side balancer pulley until the mark on the pulley aligns with the arrow on the lower belt cover (**Figure 33**).

11. Rotate the port side balancer pulley until the mark on the pulley aligns with the raised mark on the lower belt cover (**Figure 34**).

12. Without disturbing the pulleys, carefully install the balancer belt (**Figure 32**) onto all three pulleys.

13. Pivot the balancer belt tensioner toward the balancer belt. Using long-nose locking pliers install the end of the tensioner spring onto the post on the cylinder block.

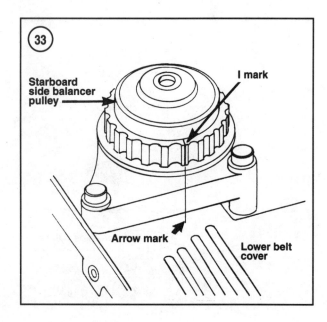

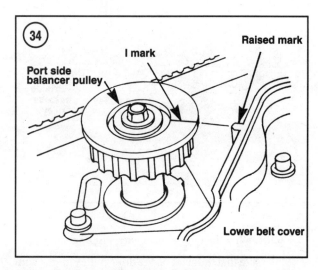

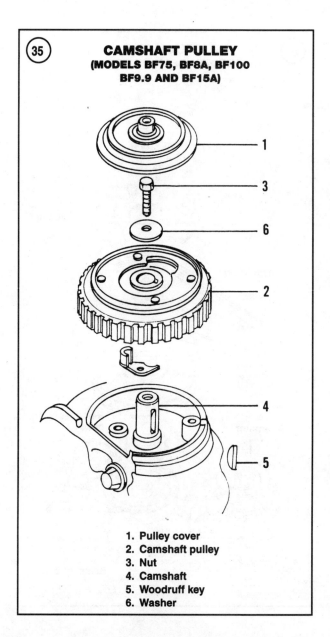

14. Check the alignment of the port and starboard balancer pulleys as indicated in Steps 10 and 11. Repeat Steps 9-12 if the marks do not align.

15. Refer to *Pulley Removal and Installation* in this chapter and install the cooling fan and crankshaft pulley (**Figure 30**).

16. Install the spark plugs and spark plug leads. Clean the battery terminals and install the cables to the battery.

Camshaft Pulley Removal/Installation (Models BF75, BF8A, BF100, BF9.9A and BF15A)

1. Disconnect both battery cables from the battery if so equipped. Remove all spark plugs and connect the spark plug leads to an engine ground.

2. Carefully pry the camshaft pulley cover (1, **Figure 35**) from the camshaft pulley (2, **Figure 35**).

3. Loosen but do not remove the camshaft pulley retaining nut and washer (3 and 6, **Figure 35**).

4. Refer to *Timing Belt Removal and Installation* in this chapter and remove the timing belt. Ensure that the timing marks remain aligned.

5. Without moving the camshaft pulley, remove the camshaft pulley retaining bolt and washer (3 and 6, **Figure 35**).

6. Pull the camshaft pulley from the camshaft using a suitable puller.

BASE ENGINE

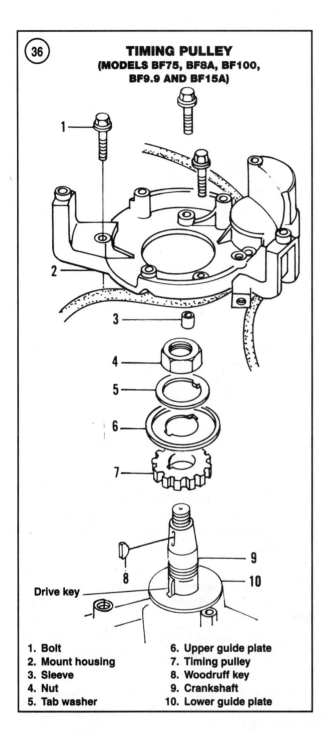

TIMING PULLEY
(MODELS BF75, BF8A, BF100, BF9.9 AND BF15A)

1. Bolt
2. Mount housing
3. Sleeve
4. Nut
5. Tab washer
6. Upper guide plate
7. Timing pulley
8. Woodruff key
9. Crankshaft
10. Lower guide plate

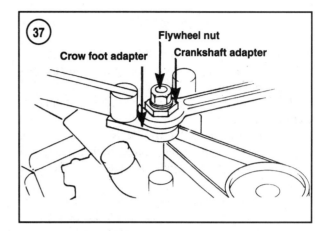

7. Remove the woodruff key (5, **Figure 35**) from the slot in the camshaft taper (4, **Figure 35**). Retrieve the woodruff key from the pulser coil, breaker points or pulley mounted magnets if not found in the slot. Replace the woodruff key if you note corrosion, bent or marked surfaces.
8. Use compressed air to remove debris from the pulley, pulser coil, magnets and other surfaces. Replace the camshaft pulley if there are cracked or damaged magnets or other surfaces. Replace the advance mechanism if you observe damaged springs or levers.
9. Place the woodruff key (5, **Figure 35**) in the slot of the camshaft taper (4, **Figure 35**).
10. Without rotating the camshaft, install the camshaft pulley onto the camshaft with the woodruff key slot aligned with the woodruff key.
11. Without rotating the camshaft pulley, install the camshaft pulley-retaining bolt and washer and hand tighten only.
12. Refer to *Timing Belt Removal and Installation* and install the timing belt.
13. Tighten the camshaft pulley retaining bolt and washer (3, **Figure 35**) to the specification listed in **Table 1**.
14. Carefully press the camshaft pulley cover into the recess in the camshaft pulley.
15. Refer to Chapter Eleven and install the rewind starter to the base engine.
16. Install the spark plugs and spark plug leads. Clean the battery terminals and connect the cables to the battery, if so equipped.

Timing Pulley Removal/Installation (Models BF75, BF8A, BF100, BF9.9 and BF15A)

Removal of the timing pulley requires using a crankshaft adapter Honda part No. 07923-ZA00000. Purchase this from your Honda dealership.
1. Refer to *Timing Belt Removal and Installation* in this chapter and remove the flywheel and timing belt.
2. Remove the bolts (1, **Figure 36**) then lift the mount housing and sleeve (2 and 3, **Figure 36**) from the base engine.
3. Install the crankshaft adapter (**Figure 37**) onto the crankshaft taper (9, **Figure 36**) with the tool slot aligned with the woodruff key slot. Without rotating the crank-

shaft, install the flywheel nut and hand tighten to retain adapter on the crankshaft.

4. Hold the crankshaft adapter (**Figure 37**) stationary as you loosen the timing pulley retaining nut using a crowfoot adapter (**Figure 37**).

5. Remove the crankshaft adapter. Without rotating the crankshaft, remove the timing pulley retaining nut and tabbed washer (4 and 5, **Figure 36**). Note their position, then remove the upper pulley guide, timing pulley and lower pulley guide (6,7 and 10, **Figure 36**) from the crankshaft.

6. Remove the timing pulley drive key from its slot in the crankshaft. Inspect the woodruff key and timing pulley drive key for corrosion, bent or marked surfaces and replace if not in excellent condition.

7. Use compressed air and a degreasing solvent to remove debris from the crankshaft, timing pulley and other surfaces. Replace the timing pulley if you note any cracked, worn or damaged surfaces.

8. Install the pulley in the reverse order of removal, note the following:
   a. Do not allow the crankshaft to turn during pulley installation.
   b. Make sure the woodruff and timing pulley drive keys are properly positioned in their slots.
   c. Install the timing pulley upper and lower guides with their tapered edges facing the timing pulley.
   d. Use the flywheel nut to retain the crankshaft adapter to the crankshaft while tightening the timing pulley nut.
   e. Tighten the timing pulley to the specification in **Table 1**.

9. Install the flywheel and timing belt as described in this chapter.

Camshaft Pulley Removal/Installation (Models BF9.9A and BF15A)

1. Disconnect both battery cables from the battery, if so equipped. Remove all spark plugs and connect the spark plug leads to an engine ground.

2. Loosen but do not remove the camshaft pulley retaining bolt and washer (1 and 2, **Figure 38**).

3. Refer to *Timing Belt Removal and Installation* in this chapter and remove the timing belt. Ensure that the timing marks remain aligned.

4. Without moving the camshaft pulley, remove the camshaft pulley retaining bolt and washer (1 and 2, **Figure 38**).

5. Pull the camshaft pulley from the camshaft using a suitable puller.

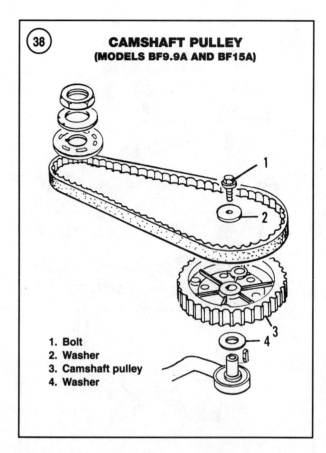

38 CAMSHAFT PULLEY (MODELS BF9.9A AND BF15A)
1. Bolt
2. Washer
3. Camshaft pulley
4. Washer

6. Remove the lower washer (4, **Figure 38**) from the camshaft. Remove the woodruff key (5, **Figure 38**) from the slot in the camshaft. Inspect the woodruff key for corrosion, bent or marked surfaces and replace it if it is not in excellent condition.

7. Use compressed air to remove debris from the camshaft pulley and other surfaces. Inspect the camshaft pulley for cracked or damaged magnets and replace if any defects are noted.

8. Place the lower washer (4, **Figure 38**) onto the camshaft. Place the woodruff key (5, **Figure 38**) in the camshaft key slot.

9. Without rotating the camshaft, position the camshaft pulley onto the camshaft with the woodruff key slot aligned with the woodruff key.

10. Without rotating the camshaft pulley, install the camshaft pulley-retaining bolt and washer hand tight.

11. Refer to *Timing Belt Removal and Installation* and install the timing belt and other components.

12. Tighten the camshaft pulley retaining bolt and washer (1 and 2, **Figure 38**) to the specification listed in **Table 1**.

13. Refer to Chapter Eleven and install the rewind starter.

BASE ENGINE

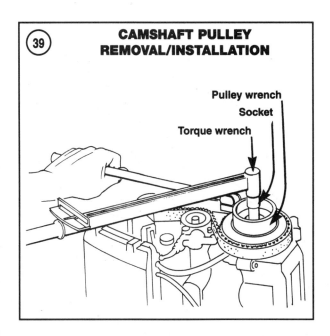

39 CAMSHAFT PULLEY REMOVAL/INSTALLATION

Pulley wrench
Socket
Torque wrench

Figure 39. Tighten the bolt to the specification listed in **Table 1**.

10. Install the spark plugs and spark plug leads. Clean the battery terminals and connect the cables to the battery, if so equipped.

Timing Pulley Removal/Installation (Models BF20A, BF25A and BF30A)

1. Refer to *Timing Belt Removal and Installation* in this chapter and remove the flywheel and timing belt. Ensure the timing marks on the camshaft pulley and base engine are aligned.
2. Install the crankshaft adapter (**Figure 37**) onto the crankshaft taper (**Figure 36**) with the tool slot aligned with the woodruff key slot. Without rotating the crankshaft, install the flywheel nut and hand tighten to retain the adapter to the crankshaft.
3. Hold the crankshaft adapter (**Figure 37**) stationary as you loosen the timing pulley retaining nut using a 1-$^{13}/_{16}$ in. crowfoot adapter (**Figure 37**).
4. Remove the crankshaft adapter. Without rotating the crankshaft, remove the timing pulley retaining nut (4, **Figure 36**). Remove the upper pulley guide (6, **Figure 36**), timing pulley (7) and lower pulley guide (10) from the crankshaft.
5. Remove the timing pulley drive key from its slot in the crankshaft. Inspect the woodruff key and timing pulley drive key for corrosion, bent or marked surfaces. Replace the keys if not in excellent condition.
6. Use compressed air and a degreasing solvent to remove debris from the crankshaft, timing pulley and other surfaces. Replace the timing pulley if you note cracked, worn, or damaged surfaces.
7. Installation is the reverse of removal. Note the following:
   a. Make sure the crankshaft does not rotate during assembly.
   b. Correctly position the woodruff key and timing pulley drive key in their respective slots in the crankshaft.
   c. Install the timing pulley upper and lower guides so their edges face the timing pulley.
   d. Use the flywheel nut to retain the crankshaft adapter to the crankshaft while tightening the timing pulley nut.
   e. Tighten the timing pulley nut to the specification in **Table 1**.
8. Refer to *Timing Belt Removal/Installation* in this chapter and install the flywheel and timing belt.

14. Install the spark plugs and spark plug leads. Clean the battery terminals and connect the cables to the battery, if so equipped.

Camshaft Pulley Removal/Installation (Models BF20A, BF25A and BF30A)

1. Disconnect both battery cables from the battery, if so equipped. Remove the spark plugs and connect the spark plug leads to an engine ground.
2. Refer to *Timing Belt Removal and Installation* in this chapter and remove the timing belt. Ensure that the timing marks remain aligned.
3. Without moving the camshaft pulley, hold the camshaft pulley stationary with a 1-$^{13}/_{16}$ in. wrench and loosen the 8 mm camshaft pulley bolt as shown in **Figure 39**. Remove the bolt from the camshaft pulley.
4. Pull the camshaft pulley from the camshaft using a suitable puller.
5. Use compressed air to remove debris from the camshaft pulley and other surfaces. Replace the camshaft pulley if you note cracked or damaged magnets.
6. Without rotating the camshaft, position the camshaft pulley onto the camshaft with the pin on the camshaft pulley aligned with the slot in the camshaft.
7. Without rotating the camshaft pulley, install the camshaft pulley-retaining bolt. Hand-tighten only.
8. Refer to *Timing Belt Removal and Installation* and install the timing belt and other components.
9. Hold the camshaft pulley stationary then tighten the camshaft pulley retaining bolt using the tools shown in

Camshaft Pulley Removal/Installation (Models BF35A, BF40A, BF45A and BF50A)

Camshaft pulley removal and installation requires a 56.0 mm crowfoot wrench or Honda pulley wrench part No. 07LPA-ZV30200, Honda crankshaft holding tool part No. 07926-VA2000A (or equivalent) and Honda pulley wrench part No. 07LPA-30200 (or equivalent).

1. Disconnect both battery cables from the battery (if so equipped). Remove all spark plugs and connect the spark plug lead to a suitable ground, such as a clean cylinder head or cylinder block bolts.
2. Refer to *Timing Belt Removal and Installation* in this chapter and remove the timing belt. Ensure that the timing marks remain aligned.
3. Without moving the camshaft pulley, hold the camshaft pulley stationary with a pulley wrench and loosen the 8 mm camshaft pulley bolt as shown in **Figure 40**. Remove the bolt from the camshaft pulley.
4. Pull the camshaft pulley from the camshaft.
5. Use compressed air to remove contamination or debris from the camshaft pulley and other surfaces. Inspect the camshaft pulley for cracked or damaged magnets or other surfaces and replace if any defects are noted.
6. Without rotating the camshaft position the camshaft pulley onto the camshaft with the pin on camshaft pulley aligned with the slot in the camshaft.
7. Without rotating the camshaft pulley, install the camshaft pulley-retaining bolt. Hand-tighten only.
8. Refer to *Timing Belt Removal/Installation* and install the timing belt and other components.
9. Hold the camshaft pulley stationary. Using the pulley wrench, tighten the camshaft pulley bolt (**Figure 40**) to the specification listed in **Table 1**.
10. Install the spark plugs and spark plug leads. Clean the battery terminals then connect the cables to the battery, if so equipped.

Timing Pulley Removal/Installation (Models BF35A, BF40A, BF45A and BF50A)

Use a crankshaft adapter (**Figure 41**) to hold the crankshaft stationary during the entire removal and installation procedures.

1. Refer to *Timing Belt Removal and Installation* in this chapter and remove the flywheel and timing belt. Ensure that the timing marks on the camshaft pulley and engine are aligned.
2. Without rotating the flywheel, attach the pulley wrench or 56 mm crowfoot adapter to the timing pulley retaining nut (1, **Figure 42**).

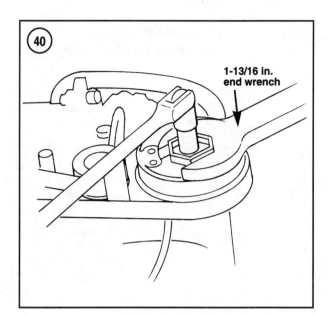

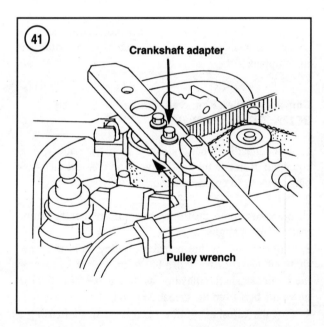

3. Using two of the removed flywheel retaining bolts, attach the crankshaft adapter to the crankshaft as shown in **Figure 41**. Do not allow the crankshaft to rotate.

4. Hold the crankshaft adapter (**Figure 41**) stationary as you loosen the timing pulley retaining nut (1, **Figure 42**).

5. Remove the crankshaft adapter. Without rotating the crankshaft, remove the timing pulley retaining nut. Remove the upper pulley guide (3, **Figure 42**), timing pulley (4) and lower pulley guide (5) from the crankshaft.

6. Remove the timing pulley drive key (6, **Figure 42**) from its slot in the crankshaft. Inspect the timing pulley

BASE ENGINE

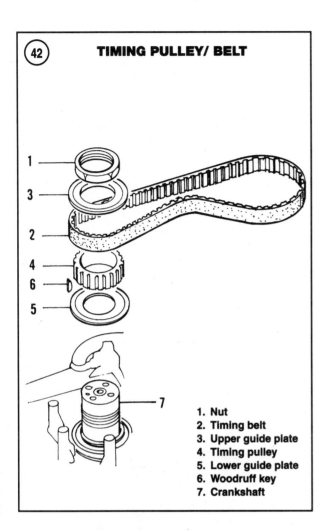

42 TIMING PULLEY/ BELT

1. Nut
2. Timing belt
3. Upper guide plate
4. Timing pulley
5. Lower guide plate
6. Woodruff key
7. Crankshaft

Camshaft Pulley Removal/Installation (Models BF75A and BF90A)

Camshaft pulley removal and installation is virtually identical to models BF35A, BF40A, BF45A and BF50A using the same removal tools.

Starter pulley, rotor and timing pulley removal requires a flywheel holding tool, Honda part No. 07SPB-ZW10100, to prevent crankshaft rotation.

1. Disconnect both battery cables from the battery. Remove the spark plugs and connect the spark plug leads to an engine ground.
2. Refer to *Flywheel Removal and Installation* in this chapter and install the flywheel holding tool.
3. Loosen and remove the retaining bolts (1, **Figure 43**) then remove the starter pulley (2) from the rotor (4).
4. Remove the retaining bolt and washer (3, **Figure 43**), then pull the rotor from the crankshaft.
5. Refer to Chapter Seven and remove the battery charging coil (6, **Figure 43**) and pulser coils (7) from the mounting bracket (9).
6. Note the position of the bracket then remove the mounting bolts and the mounting bracket (9, **Figure 43**).
7. Refer to *Timing Belt Removal and Installation* in this chapter and remove the timing belt (11, **Figure 43**).
8. Remove the upper pulley guide (10, **Figure 43**), timing pulley (13) and lower pulley guide (14) from the crankshaft.
9. Remove the timing pulley drive key (12, **Figure 43**) from its slot in the crankshaft. Inspect the timing pulley drive key for corrosion, bent or marked surfaces. Replace the keys if they are not in excellent condition.
10. Use compressed air and a degreasing solvent to remove debris from the crankshaft, timing pulley and other surfaces. Replace the timing pulley if you observe cracked, worn or damaged surfaces.
11. Install in the reverse order of removal, while noting the following:
    a. Make sure the crankshaft does not turn during installation.
    b. Make sure the timing pulley drive key is installed correctly in the slot in the crankshaft.
    c. Install the timing pulley upper and lower guides with their tapered edge facing the timing pulley.
    d. Install the battery charging coil and pulser coils as described in Chapter Seven.
    e. Tighten the rotor and starter pulley retaining bolts to the standard torque specification in **Table 1**, then an additional 90°.
12. Refer to *Timing Belt Removal and Installation* and install the timing belt, flywheel and other components.

drive key for corrosion, bent or marked surfaces. Replace the key if it is not in excellent condition.

7. Use compressed air and a degreasing solvent to remove debris from the crankshaft, timing pulley and other surfaces. Replace the timing pulley if you observe cracked, worn or damaged surfaces.
8. Install in the reverse order of removal while noting the following:
    a. Make sure the crankshaft does not turn during assembly.
    b. Make sure the woodruff and timing pulley drive keys are correctly installed in their respective slots.
    c. Install the timing pulley upper and lower guides with their tapered edges facing the timing pulley.
    d. Attach the crankshaft adapter to the crankshaft using two flywheel bolts and tighten the pulley nut to the specification in **Table 1**.
9. Refer to *Timing Belt Removal/Installation* in this chapter and install the timing belt and flywheel.

13. Refer to *Flywheel Removal and Installation* and remove the flywheel holding tool.
14. Install the spark plugs and spark plug leads. Clean the battery terminals and connect the cables to the battery.

Camshaft Pulley Removal/Installation (Models BF115A and BF130A)

The camshaft pulley removal and installation procedure is virtually identical to the procedure for models BF35A, BF40A, BF45A and BF50A. The same removal tools are used.

The flywheel holding tool (Honda part No. 07SPB-ZW50100) is required when removing and installing the crankshaft, drive and timing pulleys.

Crankshaft and Drive Pulleys Removal/Installation (Models BF115A and BF130A)

1. Disconnect both battery terminals from the battery. Remove all spark plugs and connect the spark plug leads to an engine ground.
2. Refer to *Valve Adjustment* in Chapter Four and position the No. 1 cylinder at TDC of the compression stroke. Make sure the timing marks are aligned as described under *Valve Adjustment*.
3. If the timing marks do not align properly, refer to *Timing Belt Removal/Installation* in this chapter and align the timing marks.
4. Refer to *Flywheel Removal and Installation* in this chapter and install the flywheel holding tool on the engine.
5. Remove the bolts (3, **Figure 44**), then the cooling fan (2) from the crankshaft pulley (4).
6. Refer to *Balancer Belt Removal and Installation* in this chapter and remove the balancer belt from the base engine.
7. Remove the crankshaft pulley retaining bolt (1, **Figure 44**). Remove the crankshaft pulley (4, **Figure 44**) from the crankshaft. Use the same puller as used for flywheel removal on models BF9.9A and BF15A. Refer to *Flywheel Removal and Installation* in this chapter for additional information.
8. Carefully lift the drive pulley (7, **Figure 44**) from the crankshaft.
9. Remove the bolts (10, **Figure 44**) then the lifting hook (11, **Figure 44**) from the base engine.
10. Install the balancer belt as described in this chapter.
11. Complete the remaining assembly by reversing the order of disassembly.

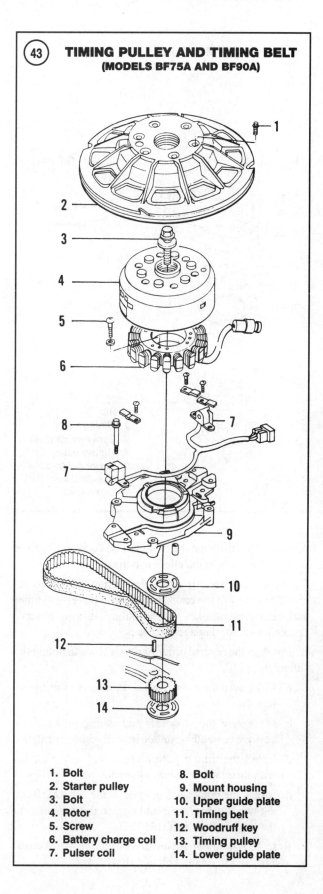

43 TIMING PULLEY AND TIMING BELT (MODELS BF75A AND BF90A)

1. Bolt
2. Starter pulley
3. Bolt
4. Rotor
5. Screw
6. Battery charge coil
7. Pulser coil
8. Bolt
9. Mount housing
10. Upper guide plate
11. Timing belt
12. Woodruff key
13. Timing pulley
14. Lower guide plate

BASE ENGINE

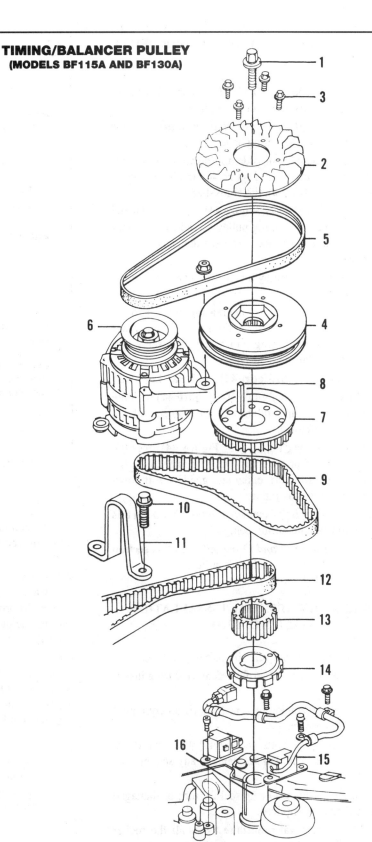

TIMING/BALANCER PULLEY
(MODELS BF115A AND BF130A)

1. Bolt
2. Cooling fan
3. Bolt
4. Crankshaft pulley
5. Alternator belt
6. Alternator
7. Balancer pulley
8. Woodruff key
9. Balancer drive belt
10. Bolt
11. Lifting hook
12. Timing belt
13. Timing pulley
14. Lower guide plate
15. Pulser coil
16. Crankshaft

Timing Pulley Removal/Installation (Models BF115A and BF130A)

1. Refer to *Crankshaft and Drive Pulley* in this chapter and remove the crankshaft and drive pulleys.

2. Refer to *Timing Belt Removal and Installation* in this chapter and remove the timing belt.

3. Note the orientation (up side and down side) and remove the timing pulley (13, **Figure 44**) and lower pulley guide (14, **Figure 44**) from the crankshaft.

4. Remove the drive key (8, **Figure 44**) from its slot in the crankshaft. Inspect the timing pulley drive key for corrosion, bent or marked surfaces. Replace the keys if not in excellent condition.

5. Replace the timing pulley if there are worn, cracked or damaged surfaces.

6. Use compressed air and a degreasing solvent to remove debris from the crankshaft, timing pulley and other surfaces. Replace the timing pulley if you observe any cracked, worn or damaged surfaces.

7. Place the drive key (8, **Figure 44**) crankshaft key slot.

8. Install the lower pulley guide (14, **Figure 44**) with the fingers facing the engine and the key slot aligned with the drive key (8, **Figure 44**).

9. Position the timing pulley (13, **Figure 44**) over the crankshaft as noted prior to removal. Carefully slide the timing pulley over the drive key and gently tap it down against the lower pulley guide.

10. Refer to *Timing Belt Removal and Installation* in this chapter and install the timing belt.

11. Refer to *Crankshaft and Drive pulley* in this section and install the drive and crankshaft pulleys.

ROCKER ARM REMOVAL/INSTALLATION (ALL MODELS)

1. Place the engine in the full tilt position.

2. Mark the rocker arm cover for reference during installation.

3. Disconnect the crankcase vent hose (if so equipped) from the rocker arm cover.

4. Remove the cover bolts and carefully pry the cover from the cylinder head. Do not damage any sealing surfaces.

5. Inspect the gasket or O-ring seal for torn or damaged areas and replace if required.

6. Reverse the removal procedure to install the rocker arm cover. Tighten the cover bolts to the standard torque specification in **Table 1**.

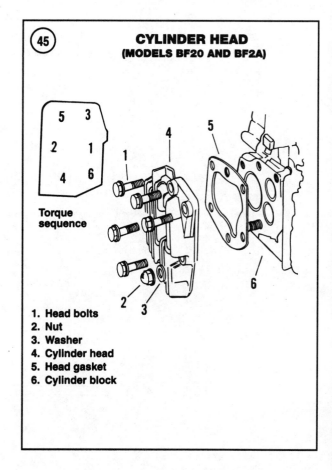

45 CYLINDER HEAD (MODELS BF20 AND BF2A)

Torque sequence

1. Head bolts
2. Nut
3. Washer
4. Cylinder head
5. Head gasket
6. Cylinder block

CYLINDER HEAD

This section provides cylinder head removal and installation procedures. Always loosen the cylinder head bolts in the reverse of the tightening sequence. Tightening sequences are indicated in **Figures 45-51**.

Always install a new cylinder head gasket when removed. Thoroughly clean the gasket surfaces before installing the gasket and cylinder head.

Coat the threads of the cylinder head bolts with engine oil prior to installation. Install all head bolts and hand-tighten. Check the alignment of the mating surfaces. Refer to **Figures 45-51** for the proper torque sequence. Torque the head bolts in three steps to the torque specification listed in Table 1.

CAUTION
To prevent damaged valves or other internal engine components, loosen all valve adjusting screws the maximum amount prior to removing or installing the cylinder head.

NOTE
Always torque cylinder head bolts and nuts in three steps. Tighten the bolts and nuts in

BASE ENGINE

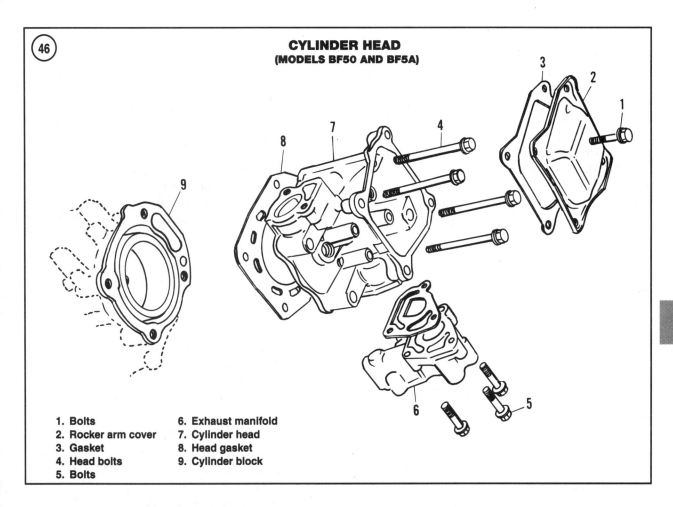

CYLINDER HEAD (MODELS BF50 AND BF5A)

1. Bolts
2. Rocker arm cover
3. Gasket
4. Head bolts
5. Bolts
6. Exhaust manifold
7. Cylinder head
8. Head gasket
9. Cylinder block

sequence to one-third of the final torque. Repeat the sequence and tighten them to two-thirds, then to the full torque specification listed in **Table 1**.

Removal/Installation (Models BF20 and BF2A)

1. Remove the rocker arm cover as described in this chapter.
2. Note the location of all bolts (1, **Figure 45**) prior to removal to ensure correct bolt installation.
3. Loosen each bolt in reverse of the tightening sequence one-quarter turn at a time until they are free from the cylinder head.
4. Lightly tap the cylinder head with a plastic mallet to free it from the cylinder block.
5. Remove and discard the head gasket (5, **Figure 45**). Refer to *Cleaning the Cylinder Head* in this chapter and clean the cylinder head and combustion chamber.
6. Inspect the cylinder head for deep scratches, cracks, pitting or other damaged surfaces. Replace the cylinder head if defects are noted.

7. Replace the cylinder block if at the cylinder head mating surfaces there are deep scratches, cracks, pitting or other damage.
8. Using a thread tap, clean all debris from the cylinder head bolt holes.
9. Align the new head gasket with the bolt holes in the cylinder head. Wipe a light coat of engine oil to the threaded portion of the head bolts and nut.
10. Place the head gasket and cylinder head onto the cylinder block and thread the head bolts in finger-tight. Tighten the head bolts in sequence to the specification listed in **Table 1**.
11. Refer to *Valve Adjustment* in Chapter Four to adjust the valves.

Removal/Installation (Models BF50 and BF5A)

1. Remove the rocker arm cover as described in this chapter.
2. Note the location of the bolts (4 and 5, **Figure 46**) prior to removal to ensure correct bolt installation.

3. Remove the exhaust manifold retaining bolts (5, **Figure 46**) and carefully tap the exhaust manifold (6, **Figure 46**) loose from the cylinder head (7, **Figure 46**). Discard the manifold gasket. Clean all gasket material from the mating surfaces.

4. Loosen each bolt (4, **Figure 46**) in reverse sequence ¼ turn at a time until they are free from the cylinder head. Lightly tap the cylinder head with a plastic mallet to free it from the cylinder block.

5. Remove and discard the head gasket (8, **Figure 46**).

6. Inspect the cylinder head as described in this chapter.

7. Replace the cylinder block if at the cylinder head mating surfaces there are deep scratches, cracks, pitting or other damage.

8. Using a thread tap, clean all debris from the cylinder head bolt holes.

9. Align the new head gasket with the bolt holes in the cylinder head. Wipe a light coat of engine oil on the threaded portion of the head bolts and nut.

10. Place the head gasket and cylinder head onto the cylinder block and thread the head bolts in finger-tight. Tighten the head bolts in sequence to the specification listed in **Table 1**. Install the exhaust manifold with a new gasket to the cylinder head. Tighten the bolts to the standard torque specification listed in **Table 1**.

11. Refer to *Valve Adjustment* in Chapter Four and adjust the valves. Complete the remaining assembly by reversing the disassembly steps.

Removal/Installation (Models BF75, BF8A and BF100)

1. Remove the rocker arm cover as described in this chapter.

2. Refer to *Pulley Removal and Installation* in this chapter and remove the timing cam pulley from the cylinder head. Refer to Chapter Six and remove the carburetor from the engine.

3. Refer to *Intake Manifold Removal and Installation* in this chapter and remove the intake manifold from the cylinder head.

4. Note the location of the bolts (1, **Figure 47**) prior to removal to ensure correct bolt installation.

5. Loosen each bolt (1, **Figure 47**) in reverse of the tightening sequence one-quarter turn at a time until they are free from the cylinder head. Lightly tap the cylinder head with a plastic mallet to free it from the cylinder block.

6. Remove and discard the head gasket (4, **Figure 47**). Ensure the alignment dowels are placed within their recess in the cylinder block (5, **Figure 47**).

7. Refer to *Oil Pump Removal and Installation* in this chapter and remove the oil pump from the cylinder head.

8. Refer to *Cylinder Head Inspection* in this chapter to inspect the cylinder head as required.

9. Replace the cylinder block if at the cylinder head mating surfaces there are deep scratches, cracks, pitting or other damage.

10. Using a thread tap, clean all debris from the cylinder head bolt holes.

11. Refer to *Oil Pump Removal and Installation* in this chapter and install the oil pump on the cylinder head.

12. Align the new head gasket with the bolt holes in the cylinder head. Wipe a light coating of engine oil on the threaded portion of the head bolts and nut.

13. Place the head gasket and cylinder head onto the cylinder block and thread the head bolts in finger-tight. Tighten the head bolts in sequence to the specification listed in **Table 1**.

14. Refer to *Pulley Removal and Installation* in this chapter and install the camshaft pulley.

15. Refer to *Intake Manifold Removal and Installation* and install the intake manifold.

16. Refer to Chapter Six and install the carburetor to the engine.

17. Adjust the valves as described in Chapter Four.

Removal/Installation (Models BF9.9A and BF15A)

1. Remove the base engine as described in this chapter.

2. Remove the rocker arm cover as described in this chapter.

3. Refer to *Pulley Removal and Installation* in this chapter and remove the timing cam pulley from the cylinder head. Refer to Chapter Six and remove the carburetor from the engine.

4. Refer to *Intake Manifold Removal and Installation* in this chapter and remove the intake manifold from the cylinder head.

5. Note the location of the bolts (1, **Figure 48**) prior to removal to ensure correct bolt installation.

6. Loosen each bolt (1, **Figure 48**) in reverse of the tightening sequence one-quarter turn at a time until they are free from the cylinder head. Lightly tap the cylinder head with a plastic mallet to free it from the cylinder block.

7. Remove and discard the head gasket (3, **Figure 48**). Refer to *Oil Pump Removal and Installation* in this chapter and remove the oil pump from the cylinder head.

8. Note the exhaust tube position. Remove all four nuts and carefully tap the exhaust tube from the cylinder head. Remove and discard the exhaust tube mounting gasket. Scrape all gasket material from the mounting surfaces.

BASE ENGINE 311

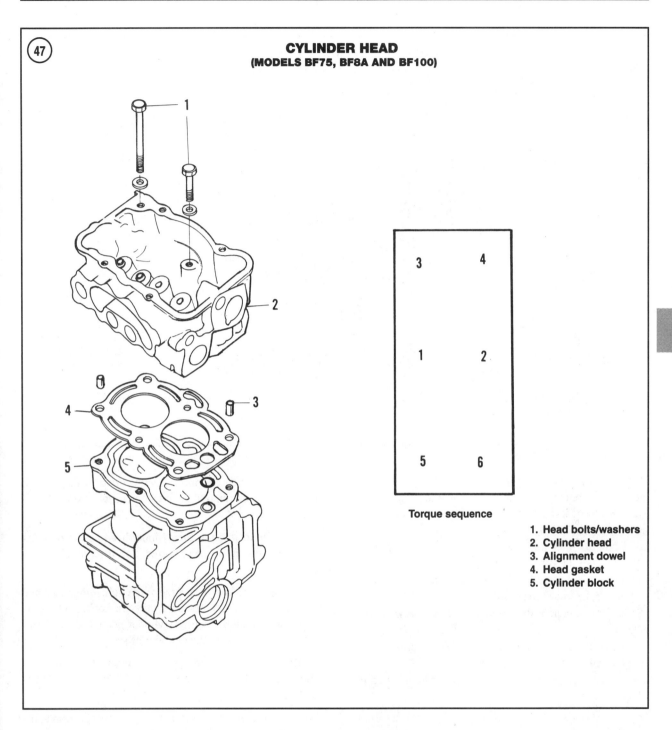

CYLINDER HEAD
(MODELS BF75, BF8A AND BF100)

Torque sequence

1. Head bolts/washers
2. Cylinder head
3. Alignment dowel
4. Head gasket
5. Cylinder block

9. Refer to *Cylinder Head Inspection* in this section to inspect and repair the cylinder head as required.

10. Replace the cylinder block if at the cylinder head mating surfaces there are deep scratches, cracks, pitting or other damage.

11. Using a thread tap, clean all debris from the cylinder head bolt holes.

12. Refer to *Oil Pump Removal and Installation* in this chapter and install the oil pump to the cylinder head.

13. Install a new gasket then install the exhaust tube to the cylinder head. Securely tighten the mounting nuts. Make sure the tube is mounted as noted prior to removal.

14. Align the new head gasket with the bolt holes in the cylinder head. Wipe a light coating of engine oil on the threaded portion of the head bolts and nut.

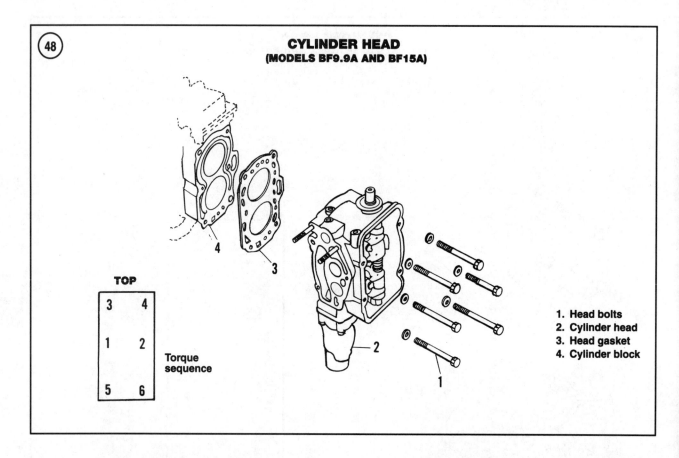

15. Place the head gasket and cylinder head onto the cylinder block and thread the head bolts in finger-tight. Tighten the head bolts in sequence to the specification listed in **Table 1**.
16. Refer to *Pulley Removal and Installation* in this chapter and install the camshaft pulley.
17. Refer to *Intake Manifold Removal and Installation* and install the intake manifold.
18. Refer to Chapter Six and install the carburetor to the engine.
19. Refer to *Base Engine Removal and Installation* in this chapter and install the base engine.
20. Adjust the valves following the procedures listed in Chapter Four.

Removal/Installation (Models BF20A, BF25A, BF35A, BF40A, BF45A, BF50A and BF30A)

1. Remove the rocker arm cover as described in this chapter.
2. Refer to *Pulley Removal and Installation* in this chapter and remove the timing cam pulley from the cylinder head. Refer to Chapter Six and remove the carburetor from the engine.
3. Refer to *Intake Manifold Removal and Installation* in this chapter and remove the intake manifold from the cylinder head.
4. Note the location of the cylinder head mounting bolts prior to removal to ensure correct bolt installation on assembly.
5. Loosen each bolt in reverse of the tightening sequence one-quarter turn at a time until they are free from the cylinder head. Lightly tap the cylinder head with a plastic mallet to free it from the cylinder block.
6. Remove and discard the head gasket (2, **Figure 49**). Refer to *Oil Pump Removal and Installation* in this chapter and remove the oil pump from the cylinder head.
7. Refer to *Cylinder Head Inspection* in this section to inspect the cylinder head as required.
8. Replace the cylinder block if at the cylinder head mating surfaces there are deep scratches, cracks, pitting or other damage.
9. Using a thread tap, clean all debris from the cylinder head bolt holes.
10. Refer to *Oil Pump Removal and Installation* in this chapter and install the oil pump.

BASE ENGINE

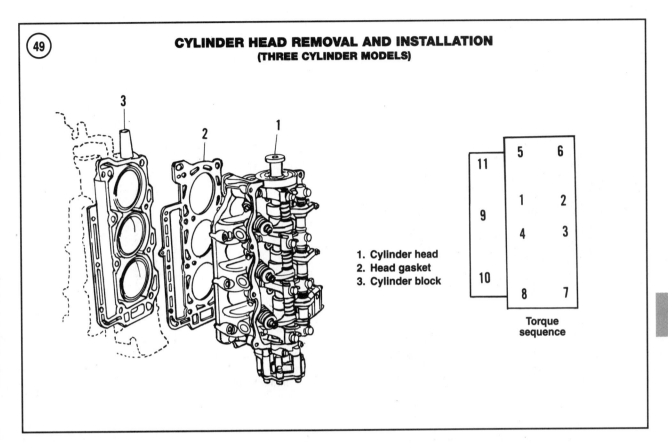

49 CYLINDER HEAD REMOVAL AND INSTALLATION
(THREE CYLINDER MODELS)

1. Cylinder head
2. Head gasket
3. Cylinder block

Torque sequence

11. Align the new head gasket with the bolt holes in the cylinder head. Wipe a light coating of engine oil on the threaded portion of the head bolts and nut.

12. Place the head gasket and cylinder head onto the cylinder block and thread the head bolts in finger-tight. Tighten the head bolts in sequence to the specification listed in **Table 1**.

13. Refer to *Pulley Removal and Installation* in this chapter and install the camshaft pulley.

14. Refer to *Intake Manifold Removal and Installation* and install the intake manifold.

15. Refer to Chapter Six and install the carburetor to the engine.

16. Adjust the valves following the procedures listed in Chapter Four.

17. Complete the remaining assembly by reversing the disassembly steps.

Removal/Installation (Models BF75A and BF90A)

1. Remove the rocker arm cover as described in this chapter.

2. Refer to *Pulley Removal and Installation* in this chapter and remove the timing cam pulley from the cylinder head.

3. Refer to Chapter Six and remove the carburetor from the engine. Refer to *Intake Manifold Removal and Installation* in this chapter then remove the intake manifold from the cylinder head.

4. Note the location of all cylinder head mounting bolts prior to removal to ensure correct bolt installation on assembly.

5. Loosen each bolt in reverse of the tightening sequence one-quarter turn at a time until they are free from the cylinder head. Lightly tap the cylinder head with a plastic mallet to free it from the cylinder block.

6. Remove and discard the head gasket (2, **Figure 50**). Refer to *Oil Pump Removal and Installation* in this chapter and remove the oil pump from the cylinder head.

7. Refer to *Cylinder Head Inspection* in this section to inspect the cylinder head as required.

8. Carefully thread a 6 mm—1.0 pitch bolt into the oil passage fitting (4, **Figure 50**). Carefully pull the fitting and O-ring (6, **Figure 50**) from the oil passage at the mating surface. Discard the O-ring. Ensure the alightment pins (3, **Figure 5**) are positioned within their bores in the cylinder block mating surface.

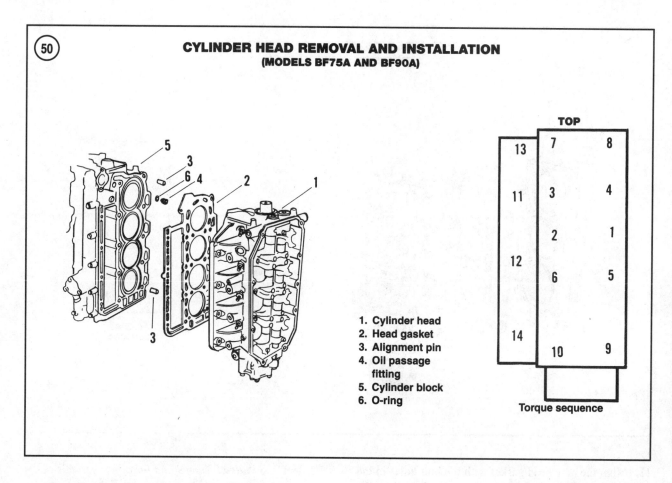

50. CYLINDER HEAD REMOVAL AND INSTALLATION (MODELS BF75A AND BF90A)

1. Cylinder head
2. Head gasket
3. Alignment pin
4. Oil passage fitting
5. Cylinder block
6. O-ring

Torque sequence

---

9. Replace the cylinder block if at the cylinder head mating surfaces there are deep scratches, cracks, pitting or other damage.

10. Using a thread tap, clean all debris from the cylinder head bolt holes. Clean any debris or contamination from the oil passage fitting and its mounting bore.

11. Coat the oil passage fitting with engine oil and place a new O-ring on the fitting. Use the same bolt used for removal and carefully push it into the oil passage bore. Make sure the fitting is firmly seated within the bore.

12. Refer to *Oil Pump Removal and Installation* in this chapter and install the oil pump.

13. Align the new head gasket with the bolt holes in the cylinder head. Wipe a light coating of engine oil on the threaded portion of the head bolts and nut.

14. Place the head gasket and cylinder head onto the cylinder block and thread the head bolts in finger-tight. Tighten the head bolts in sequence to the specification listed in **Table 1**.

15. Refer to *Pulley Removal and Installation* in this chapter and install the camshaft pulley.

16. Refer to *Intake Manifold Removal and Installation* and install the intake manifold.

17. Refer to Chapter Six and install the carburetor to the engine.

18. Adjust the valves following the procedures listed in Chapter Four.

Removal/Installation (Models BF115A and BF130A)

1. Remove the flywheel cover and rocker arm cover.

2. Refer to *Pulley Removal and Installation* in this chapter and remove the camshaft pulley from the cylinder head. Refer to Chapter Six and remove the fuel rail from the engine.

3. Refer to *Intake Manifold Removal and Installation* in this chapter and remove the intake manifold from the cylinder head.

4. Note the location of all cylinder head mounting bolts prior to removal to ensure correct bolt installation on assembly.

5. Loosen each bolt in reverse of the tightening sequence one-quarter turn at a time until they are free from the cylinder head. Lightly tap the cylinder head with a plastic mallet to free it from the cylinder block.

6. Remove and discard the head gasket (2, **Figure 51**).

BASE ENGINE

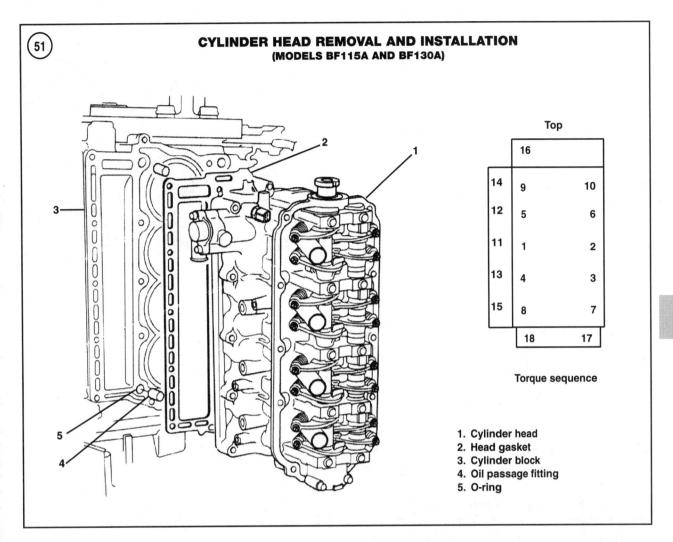

CYLINDER HEAD REMOVAL AND INSTALLATION (MODELS BF115A AND BF130A)

Torque sequence

1. Cylinder head
2. Head gasket
3. Cylinder block
4. Oil passage fitting
5. O-ring

7. Refer to *Cylinder Head Inspection* in this section to Inspect the cylinder head as required.

8. Carefully thread a 6 mm 1.0 pitch bolt into the oil passage fitting (4, **Figure 51**). Carefully pull the fitting and O-ring (5, **Figure 51**) from the oil passage at the mating surface. Discard the O-ring. Ensure the alignment pins are positioned within their bore in the cylinder block mating surface.

9. Replace the cylinder block if at the cylinder head mating surfaces there are deep scratches, cracks, pitting or other damage.

10. Using a thread tap, clean all debris from the cylinder head bolt holes. Clean any debris or contamination from the oil passage fitting and its mounting bore.

11. Place a new O-ring on the fitting. Use the same bolt used for removal and carefully push it into the oil passage bore. Ensure the fitting is firmly seated within the bore.

12. Refer to *Oil Pump Removal and Installation* in this chapter and install the oil pump to the cylinder head.

13. Align the new head gasket with the bolt holes in the cylinder head. Wipe a light coating of engine oil on the threaded portion of the head bolts and nut.

14. Place the head gasket and cylinder head onto the cylinder block and thread the head bolts in finger-tight. Tighten the head bolts in sequence to the specification listed in **Table 1**.

15. Refer to *Pulley Removal and Installation* in this chapter and install the camshaft pulley.

16. Refer to *Intake Manifold Removal and Installation* and install the intake manifold.

17. Refer to Chapter Six and install the fuel rail to the engine.

18. Adjust the valves as described in Chapter Four.

19. Complete the remaining assembly by reversing the disassembly steps.

Cylinder Head Disassembly and Assembly

As components are removed from the cylinder head, arrange them so they can be installed in their original location and position.

If possible, remove the rocker arm shaft(s) (**Figure 52**) as an assembly. This will help prevent missing or mixed components. Use a suitable valve spring compressor (**Figure 53**) to remove the valve components from the cylinder head. During assembly, lubricate all shafts, seals, spacers and pivot points with engine oil or lubriplate moly lube.

Models BF50 and BF5A

1. Refer to *Cylinder Head Removal and Installation* in this section and remove the cylinder head from the base engine.
2. Remove the locknut (8, **Figure 54**) from each rocker arm stud (11, **Figure 54**). Remove each adjusting nut and rocker arm (9 and 10, **Figure 54**) from the rocker arm stud.
3. Carefully pull each push rod (13, **Figure 54**) from the guide plate (12, **Figure 54**).
4. Using a deep socket, loosen and remove each rocker arm stud (11, **Figure 54**) from the cylinder head (3, **Figure 54**). Remove the valve rotator from the stem of the exhaust valve (2, **Figure 54**).
5. Position the valve spring compressor onto the valve spring as shown in **Figure 53**. Tighten the compressor enough to allow removal of the valve keepers (7, **Figure 55**) from the intake valve stem (1, **Figure 54**). Slowly loosen the compressor to release the valve spring cap, valve spring, valve spring base and valve.
6. Compress the spring and slide the valve spring cap sideways to release the cap from the exhaust valve stem (2, **Figure 54**).
7. Refer to *Cylinder Head Inspection* in this section and inspect and measure all components.
8. Assemble the cylinder by reversing the order of disassembly, plus the following:
   a. Make sure all components are installed in their original locations and position.
   b. Make sure the valve keepers are fully seated after installation.
   c. Make sure the valve spring caps are centered on the valve springs.
   d. Tighten the rocker arm studs to 30 N·m (22 ft.-lb.).
9. Install the cylinder head as described in this chapter.

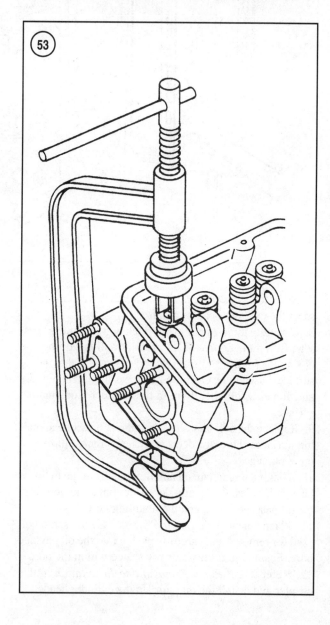

BASE ENGINE

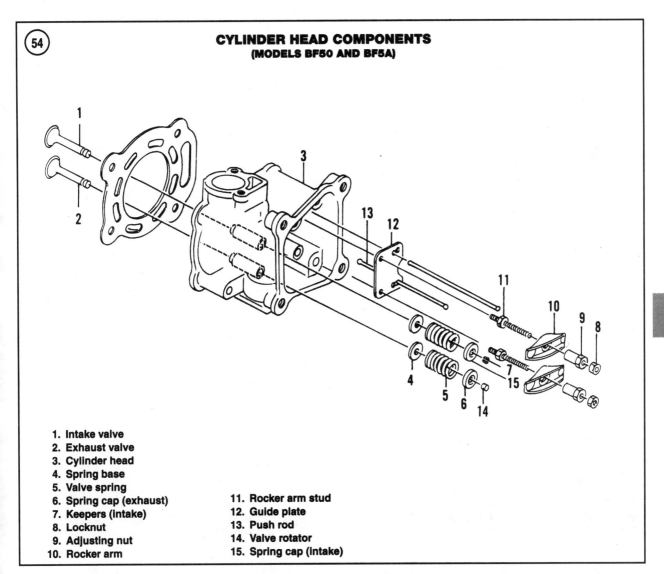

54 CYLINDER HEAD COMPONENTS
(MODELS BF50 AND BF5A)

1. Intake valve
2. Exhaust valve
3. Cylinder head
4. Spring base
5. Valve spring
6. Spring cap (exhaust)
7. Keepers (intake)
8. Locknut
9. Adjusting nut
10. Rocker arm
11. Rocker arm stud
12. Guide plate
13. Push rod
14. Valve rotator
15. Spring cap (intake)

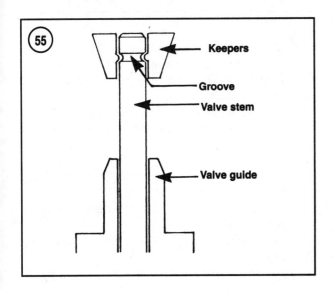

55 Keepers — Groove — Valve stem — Valve guide

Models BF75, BF8A and BF100

1. Refer to *Cylinder Head Removal and Installation* in this section and remove the cylinder head from the base engine.

2. Loosen the locknut (16, **Figure 56**) and rotate each adjusting screw (17, **Figure 56**) counterclockwise until it engages only two to three threads of each rocker arm (3, **Figure 56**).

3. Slowly slide the rocker arm shaft (15, **Figure 56**) from the cylinder head. Remove the rocker arms (3, **Figure 56**), springs (1), spacers (2) and collars (4) as the rocker arm shaft passes through them. Keep them in order.

4. Carefully slide the camshaft (6, **Figure 56**) and thrust washers (5) from the cylinder head.

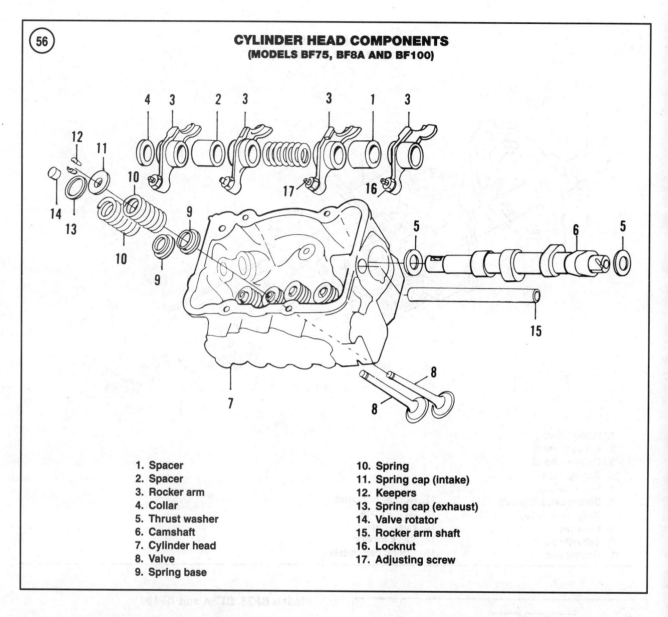

CYLINDER HEAD COMPONENTS (MODELS BF75, BF8A AND BF100)

1. Spacer
2. Spacer
3. Rocker arm
4. Collar
5. Thrust washer
6. Camshaft
7. Cylinder head
8. Valve
9. Spring base
10. Spring
11. Spring cap (intake)
12. Keepers
13. Spring cap (exhaust)
14. Valve rotator
15. Rocker arm shaft
16. Locknut
17. Adjusting screw

5. Remove the valve rotator (14, **Figure 56**) from the stem of both exhaust valves (8, **Figure 56**).

6. Position the valve spring compressor onto the valve spring as shown in **Figure 53**. Tighten the compressor enough to allow removal of the valve keepers (12, **Figure 56**) from intake valve stem. Slowly loosen the compressor to release the valve spring cap (11, **Figure 56**), valve spring (10), valve spring base (9) and valve.

7. Compress the spring and slide the valve spring cap sideways to release the cap from the exhaust valve stem (13, **Figure 56**).

8. Refer to *Cylinder Head Component Inspection* in this section and inspect and measure all components.

9. Assemble the cylinder head by reversing the order of disassembly.

   a. Make sure all components are installed in their original locations and orientation.
   b. Lubricate all shafts and pivot points with engine oil during assembly.
   c. Position the thrust washers (5, **Figure 56**) at the ends of the camshaft-to-cylinder head mating surface.
   d. Install all spacers, springs, collars and rocker arms on the rocker arm shaft as the shaft is installed into the cylinder head.
   e. After installation, make sure the valve keepers are fully seated.
   f. Make sure the exhaust valve spring cap is centered on the valve spring.

10. Install the cylinder head as described in this chapter.

BASE ENGINE

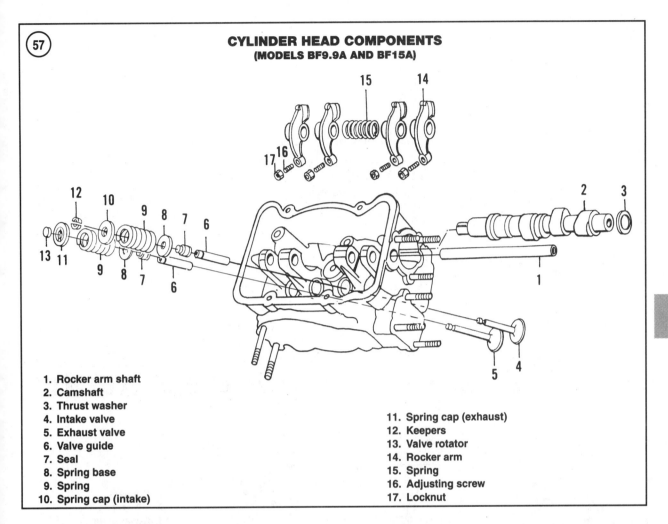

57 CYLINDER HEAD COMPONENTS (MODELS BF9.9A AND BF15A)

1. Rocker arm shaft
2. Camshaft
3. Thrust washer
4. Intake valve
5. Exhaust valve
6. Valve guide
7. Seal
8. Spring base
9. Spring
10. Spring cap (intake)
11. Spring cap (exhaust)
12. Keepers
13. Valve rotator
14. Rocker arm
15. Spring
16. Adjusting screw
17. Locknut

Models BF9.9A and BF15A

1. Refer to *Cylinder Head Removal and Installation* in this section and remove the cylinder head from the base engine.

2. Loosen the locknut (17, **Figure 57**) and rotate each adjusting screw (16, **Figure 57**) counterclockwise until it engages only two to three threads of each rocker arm (14, **Figure 57**).

3. Thread a bolt into the threaded opening of the rocker arm shaft. Using the bolt, slowly slide the rocker arm shaft (1, **Figure 57**) from the cylinder head. Remove the rocker arms (14, **Figure 57**) and springs (15) as the rocker arm shaft passes through them. Keep them in order.

4. Carefully slide the camshaft (2, **Figure 57**) and thrust washer (3) from the cylinder head.

5. Remove the valve rotator (13, **Figure 57**) from the stem of both exhaust valves (5, **Figure 57**).

6. Position the valve spring compressor on the valve spring as shown in **Figure 53**. Tighten the compressor just enough to allow removal of the valve keepers (12, **Figure 55**) from the intake valve stem (4, **Figure 57**). Slowly loosen the compressor and release the valve spring cap (10, **Figure 57**), valve spring (9), valve spring base (8) and valve (4).

7. Compress the spring and slide the valve spring cap (11, **Figure 57**) sideways to release the cap from the exhaust valve stem (5, **Figure 57**).

8. Refer to *Cylinder Head Component Inspection* in this section and inspect and measure all components.

9. Assemble the cylinder by reversing the disassembly procedure.

   a. Make sure all components are installed in their original locations and positions.

   b. Lubricate all shafts and pivot points with engine oil during assembly.

   c. Position the thrust washer (3, **Figure 57**) at the end of the camshaft.

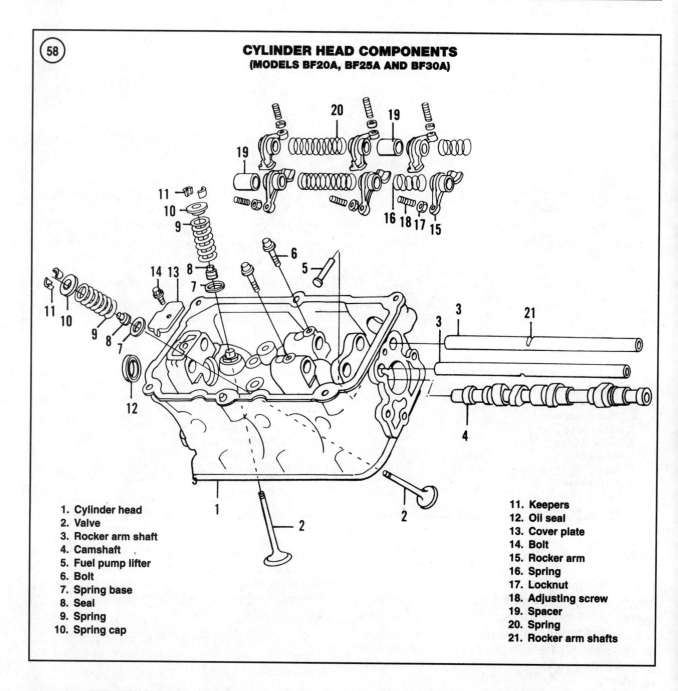

CYLINDER HEAD COMPONENTS (MODELS BF20A, BF25A AND BF30A)

1. Cylinder head
2. Valve
3. Rocker arm shaft
4. Camshaft
5. Fuel pump lifter
6. Bolt
7. Spring base
8. Seal
9. Spring
10. Spring cap
11. Keepers
12. Oil seal
13. Cover plate
14. Bolt
15. Rocker arm
16. Spring
17. Locknut
18. Adjusting screw
19. Spacer
20. Spring
21. Rocker arm shafts

d. Install all spacers, springs, collars and rocker arms on the rocker arm shaft as the shaft is installed into the cylinder head.

e. Make sure the keepers (12, **Figure 57**) for the intake valve are fully seated in the tapered recess in the valve spring cap and in the grooves in the valve stem.

f. Make sure the exhaust valve spring cap is centered on the valve spring.

10. Install the cylinder head as described in this chapter.

Models BF20A, BF25A and BF30A

1. Refer to *Cylinder Head Removal and Installation* in this section and remove the cylinder head from the base engine.

2. Loosen the locknut (17, **Figure 58**) and rotate each adjusting screw (18, **Figure 58**) counterclockwise until it engages only two to three threads of each rocker arm (15, **Figure 58**).

3. Remove both rocker arm retaining bolts (6, **Figure 58**) from the cylinder head.

BASE ENGINE

4. Slowly slide the rocker arm shafts (3, **Figure 58**) from the cylinder head. Remove the rocker arms (15, **Figure 58**) and springs (16) as the rocker arm shaft passes through them. Keep them in order.
5. Carefully slide the camshaft (4, **Figure 58**) from the cylinder head.
6. Remove the fuel pump push rod (5, **Figure 58**) from its bore in the cylinder head.
7. Position the valve spring compressor onto the valve spring as shown in **Figure 53**. Tighten the compressor enough to allow removal of the valve keepers (11, **Figure 58**) from each valve stem (2, **Figure 58**). Slowly loosen the compressor to release the valve spring cap (10, **Figure 58**), valve spring (9), valve spring base and valve (2).
8. Using care to avoid damaging the seal bore, carefully pry the camshaft seal (12, **Figure 58**) from the cylinder head. Discard the seal. Remove the screw (14, **Figure 58**) then lift the cover (13, **Figure 58**) from the cylinder head.
9. Using needle nose pliers, remove the oil seals (8, **Figure 58**) from the valve guides.
10. Refer to *Cylinder Head Component Inspection* in this section and inspect and measure all components.
11. Assemble the cylinder head by reversing the disassembly procedure. Note the following:
   a. Position the new seal (12, **Figure 58**) with its lip facing the cylinder head. Use a suitable driver to carefully push the seal into its bore in the cylinder head.
   b. Use your thumbs to press the new seals (8, **Figure 58**) onto the cylinder head (**Figure 62**).
   c. Install all components in their original locations and positions.
   d. Lubricate all components with engine oil or Lubriplate during assembly.
   e. Install the rocker arm shafts (3, **Figure 58**) with their notches (21, **Figure 58**) facing apart.
   f. Make sure the valve keepers are fully seated after installation.
12. Install the cylinder head as described in this chapter.

Models BF35A, BF40A, BF45A and BF50A

1. Refer to *Cylinder Head Removal and Installation* in this section and remove the cylinder head from the base engine.
2. Loosen the locknut (20, **Figure 59**) and rotate each adjusting screw (19, **Figure 59**) counterclockwise until it engages only two to three threads of the each rocker arm (16, **Figure 59**).
3. Remove the bolts (14, **Figure 59**) and rocker arm retaining brackets from the cylinder head. Ensure the alignment sleeves (21, **Figure 59**) are positioned in the cylinder head mounting location.
4. Note the location of the oil holes in the rocker arm shafts *prior* to removing them from the bracket. Slowly slide the rocker arm shafts (9, **Figure 59**) from the brackets (12 and 13, **Figure 59**). Remove the rocker arms and springs as the rocker arm shaft passes through them. Keep them in order.
5. Carefully slide the camshaft (10, **Figure 59**) from the cylinder head.
6. Remove the fuel pump push rod (22, **Figure 59**) from its bore in the cylinder head.
7. Position the valve spring compressor onto the valve spring as shown in **Figure 53**. Tighten the compressor enough to allow removal of the valve keepers (4, **Figure 59**) from each valve stem. Slowly loosen the compressor to release the valve spring cap (5, **Figure 59**), valve spring (6), valve and spring base (7).
8. Using care to avoid damaging the seal bore, carefully pry the camshaft seal (11, **Figure 59**) from the cylinder head. Discard the seal.
9. Using needle nose pliers, remove the oil seal (8, **Figure 59**) from the valve guide.
10. Refer to *Cylinder Head Component Inspection* in this section and inspect and measure all components.
11. Assemble the cylinder head by reversing the disassembly procedure. Note the following:
   a. Position the new seal (11, **Figure 59**) with its lip facing the cylinder head. Push the seal into its bore using a suitable driver.
   b. Press the new valve stem seals (8, **Figure 59**) onto the valve guides using your thumbs.
   c. Install all components in their original locations and position.
   d. Lubricate all shafts and pivot points with engine oil or Lubriplate during assembly.
   e. Install the starboard side rocker arm shaft with the notches facing the intake side of the cylinder. Install the port side rocker arm shaft with the holes facing away from the cylinder head.
   f. After assembly, make sure the valve keepers are fully seated.
   g. Install the cylinder head as described in this chapter.

Models BF75A and BF90A

1. Refer to *Cylinder Head Removal and Installation* in this section and remove the cylinder head from the base engine.
2. Loosen the locknut (20, **Figure 60**) and rotate each adjusting screw (19, **Figure 60**) counterclockwise until it

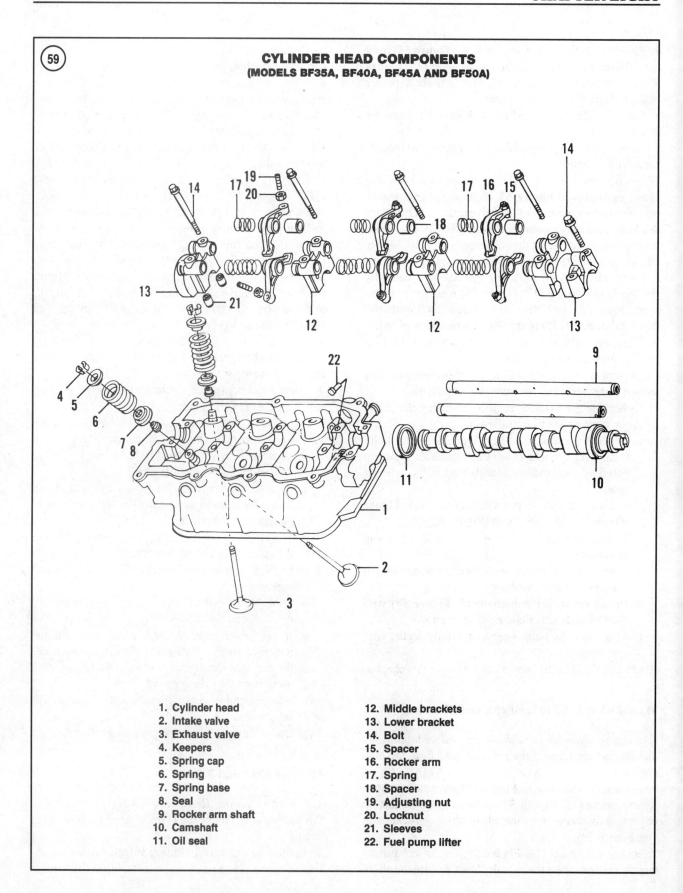

BASE ENGINE

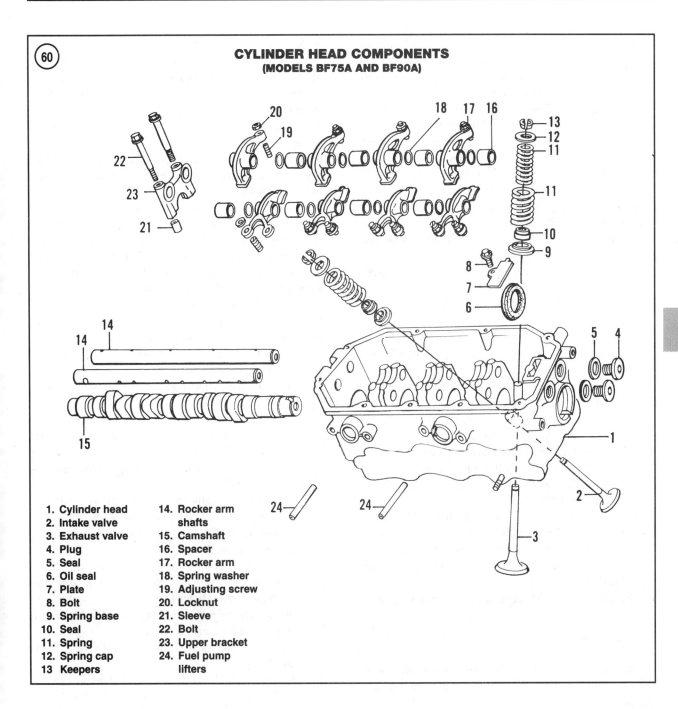

CYLINDER HEAD COMPONENTS (MODELS BF75A AND BF90A)

1. Cylinder head
2. Intake valve
3. Exhaust valve
4. Plug
5. Seal
6. Oil seal
7. Plate
8. Bolt
9. Spring base
10. Seal
11. Spring
12. Spring cap
13. Keepers
14. Rocker arm shafts
15. Camshaft
16. Spacer
17. Rocker arm
18. Spring washer
19. Adjusting screw
20. Locknut
21. Sleeve
22. Bolt
23. Upper bracket
24. Fuel pump lifters

engages only two to three threads of the each rocker arm (17, **Figure 60**).

3. Remove the bolts and rocker arm retaining brackets (23, **Figure 60**) from the cylinder head. Ensure the alignment sleeves (21, **Figure 60**) are positioned in the cylinder head mounting location.

4. Remove both plugs (4, **Figure 60**) and washers (5) from the cylinder head. Note the location of the oil holes in the rocker arm shaft *prior* to removing them from the brackets. Thread a bolt with a 12 mm x 1.25 mm thread pitch into the threaded opening of the rocker arm shafts. Slowly slide the rocker arm shafts (14, **Figure 60**) from the cylinder head.

5. Remove the rocker arms (17, **Figure 60**), spacers (16) and spring washers (18) as the rocker arm shaft passes through them. Keep them in order.

6. Carefully slide the camshaft (15, **Figure 60**) from the cylinder head. Remove the bolt (8, **Figure 59**) and lift the cover (7, **Figure 59**) from the cylinder head.

7. Remove both fuel pump lifters (24, **Figure 59**) from the cylinder head. Using care to avoid damaging the seal bore, carefully pry the camshaft seal (6, **Figure 60**) from the cylinder head. Discard the seal.

8. Position the valve spring compressor onto the valve spring as shown in **Figure 53**. Tighten the compressor enough to allow removal of the valve keepers (13, **Figure 60**) from each valve stem (2 and 3, **Figure 60**). Slowly loosen the compressor to release the valve spring cap (12, **Figure 60**), valve spring base (9) and springs (11).

9. Using needle nose pliers, remove the oil seal (10, **Figure 60**) from the valve guide.

10. Refer to *Cylinder Head Inspection* in this section and inspect and measure all components.

11. Assemble the cylinder head by reversing the disassembly procedure. Note the following:
   a. Position the new seal (6, **Figure 60**) with its lip facing inward. Using a suitable driver, carefully push the seal into its bore.
   b. Press the new valve stem seals (10, **Figure 60**) onto the valve guides (**Figure 62**) using your thumbs.
   c. Install all components in their original locations and positions.
   d. Lubricate all shafts and pivot points with engine oil or Lubriplate during assembly.
   e. Install the starboard rocker arm shaft with the seven oil holes facing UP. Install the port rocker arm shaft with the four oil holes facing away from the starboard rocker arm shaft.
   f. Make sure the bracket mounting bolts (22, **Figure 60**) align with the notches in the rocker arm shaft.
   g. Tighten the bracket bolts (22, **Figure 60**) securely.
   h. Make sure the valve keepers are fully seated after installation.

12. Install the cylinder head as described in this chapter.

Models BF115A and BF130A

1. Refer to *Cylinder Head Removal and Installation* in this section and remove the cylinder head from the base engine.

2. Loosen the locknut (14, **Figure 61**) and rotate each adjusting screw (13, **Figure 61**) counterclockwise until it engages only two to three threads of the each rocker arm (15, **Figure 61**).

3. Remove the bolts (21, **Figure 61**) and rocker arm retaining brackets from the cylinder head. Carefully lift the rocker arm shaft (19, **Figure 61**) and brackets (20) and all other components as an assembly from the cylinder head. Ensure the alignment pins (12, **Figure 61**) are installed into their recess in the cylinder head.

4. Note the location of the oil holes in the rocker arm shaft *prior* to removing them from the brackets. Remove all rocker arms (15, **Figure 61**), spacers (16) and spring washers (17) from the Rocker Arm Shafts (19). Keep them in order.

5. Carefully lift the camshaft (10, **Figure 61**) from the cylinder head.

6. Using care to avoid damaging the seal bore, carefully pry the camshaft seals (11, **Figure 61**) from the cylinder head. Discard the seal.

7. Position the valve spring compressor onto the valve spring as shown in **Figure 53**. Tighten the compressor enough to allow removal of the valve keepers (8, **Figure 61**) from each valve stem (1 and 2, **Figure 61**). Slowly loosen the compressor to release the valve spring cap (7, **Figure 61**), valve spring base (4) and springs (6). Remove them from the valve stem.

8. Using needle nose pliers, remove the oil seal (5, **Figure 61**) from the valve guide (3, **Figure 61**).

9. Refer to *Cylinder Head Inspection* in this section and inspect and measure all components.

10. Assemble the cylinder head by reversing the disassembly procedure. Note the following:
   a. Position the new seal (11, **Figure 61**) with its lip facing IN. Carefully push the seal into its bore using a suitable driver.
   b. Install all components in their original locations and orientation.
   c. Press the new valve stem seals (5, **Figure 61**) onto the valve guides (**Figure 62**) using your thumbs.
   d. Lubricate all shafts and pivot points with engine oil and Lubriplate during assembly.
   e. Install the starboard rocker arm shaft with the oil holes facing UP. Install the port rocker arm shaft with the four oil holes facing UP.
   f. Make sure the rocker arm brackets (20, **Figure 61**) align with the locating pins (12).
   g. Make sure the valve keepers are fully seated after assembly.

11. Install the cylinder head as described in this chapter.

Cylinder Head Inspection

1. Remove the carbon after removing the valves from the cylinder head. Use a blunt scraper to remove carbon deposits from the combustion chamber (**Figure 63**). Avoid scraping aluminum material from the cylinder head. Thoroughly clean the components and perform all applicable measurements.

2. Check for surface warpage by placing a straightedge at various points (**Figure 64**) on the cylinder head mating

BASE ENGINE

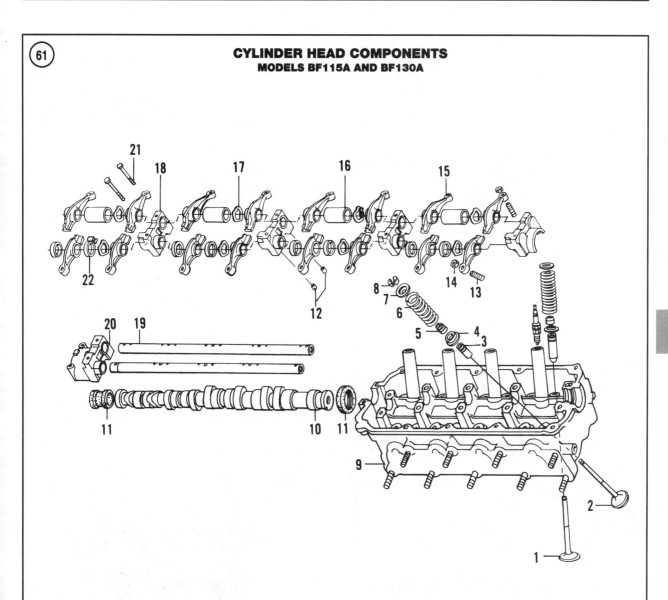

CYLINDER HEAD COMPONENTS
MODELS BF115A AND BF130A

1. Intake valve
2. Exhaust valve
3. Valve guide
4. Spring base
5. Seal
6. Spring
7. Spring cap
8. Keepers
9. Cylinder head
10. Camshaft
11. Oil seal
12. Alignment pins
13. Adjusting screw
14. Locknut
15. Rocker arm
16. Spacer
17. Spring washer
18. Middle bracket
19. Rocker arm shafts
20. Upper bracket
21. Bolt
22. Spacer

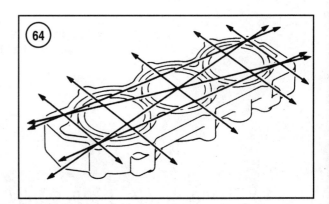

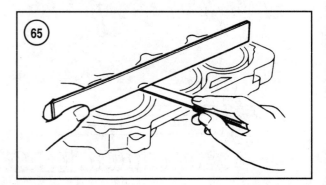

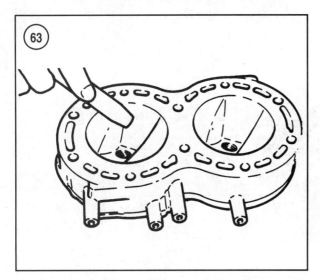

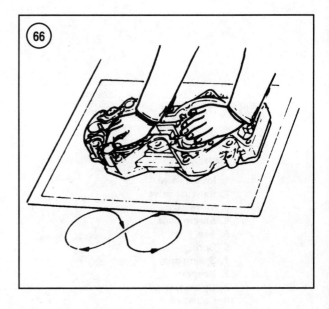

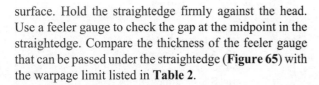

surface. Hold the straightedge firmly against the head. Use a feeler gauge to check the gap at the midpoint in the straightedge. Compare the thickness of the feeler gauge that can be passed under the straightedge (**Figure 65**) with the warpage limit listed in **Table 2**.

3. Placing a sheet of 600-grit abrasive paper on a surfacing plate can true minor warpage. Use slight downward pressure and move the cylinder head in a figure eight motion as shown in **Figure 66**.

4. Stop periodically and check the amount of warpage. Remove only the material necessary to remove the excess warpage.

5. Thoroughly clean the cylinder head with hot soapy water and dry with compressed air when finished.

6. Have a reputable machine shop perform this operation for you if you do not have access to a surfacing plate.

Valve Inspection

1. Inspect the valve stem for wear, cracked or damaged surfaces.

2. Using a micrometer, measure each valve stem at the valve stem contact areas (**Figure 67**). Record the intake and exhaust valve measurements for each cylinder. Com-

BASE ENGINE

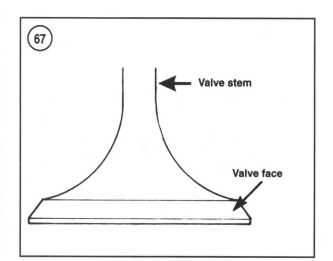

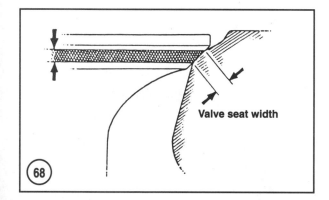

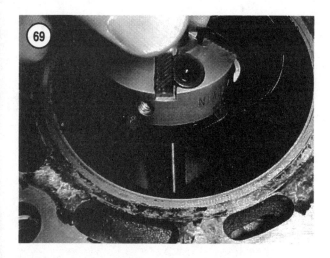

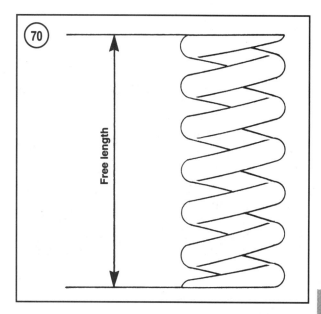

pare your measurements to the specification listed in **Table 3**.

3. Replace the valve if it is damaged or excessively worn.

4. Inspect the valve seats for cracked, pitted or damaged surfaces.

5. Using a vernier caliper or other measuring device, measure and record the width of the valve seat between the points indicated in **Figure 68**. Compare the measurements with the specification listed in **Table 2**.

6. Have the valve seat reconditioned (**Figure 69**) at a reputable machine shop if it is defective or an incorrect valve seat width is indicated. The valve seats on all Honda outboards are cut to a 45° angle.

7. Inspect each valve spring for worn, damaged or cracked surfaces. Never switch the intake and exhaust valve springs as their respective tension may differ. Damage to the valve and other components can occur when valve springs are installed onto the wrong valve.

8. Perform valve spring measurements with the valve spring removed from the cylinder head and all other components removed from the valve spring (free length). Measure the free length of each spring at the points indicated in (**Figure 70**).

9. Compare your measurements with the specifications listed in **Table 3**. Replace any valve spring when incorrect valve spring free length is indicated.

10. Replace the valve if there are chipped, cracked, pitted or worn valve face areas (**Figure 67**).

11. Use a black felt tip marker to coat the valve face with ink. Assemble the valve, valve spring and its hardware to the cylinder head.

12. Use a soft-faced hammer and carefully tap the valve stem enough to open the valve. Tap the valve open several times.

13. Carefully remove the valve from the cylinder head. Inspect the valve face and note the valve seating marks (**Figure 71**) from the valve contact with the valve seat.

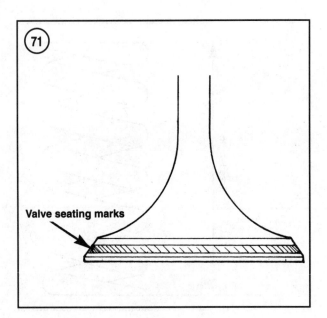

14. Correct valve seating causes a consistent contact area to be visible on the valve face. The marks should be centered on the valve face and should be about half as wide or more as the valve face (**Figure 71**).

15. Have the seats reconditioned if the marks are not centered on the valve face, are too narrow or are not consistent around the valve face. Have the seats reconditioned at a reputable machine shop. Take the valves with the cylinder head so the machinist can lap the valves to the seats and ensure a good fit of the valves to the seat.

Rocker Arm and Rocker Arm Shaft Insapection

1. Inspect each rocker arm for worn or damaged surfaces.

2. Using an inside micrometer, measure and record the bore diameter (**Figure 72**).

3. Compare your measurements with the specification listed in **Table 4**. Replace any rocker arm if it is excessively worn or damaged.

4. Inspect each rocker arm shaft for worn, corroded or discolored areas.

5. Using an outside micrometer, measure and record the shaft diameter at the areas of contact with the rocker arms (**Figure 73**).

6. Patterns that form on the surfaces of the rocker arm shaft indicate the points to measure.

7. Compare your measurements with the specification listed in **Table 4**. Replace the rocker arm shaft if damaged or excessively worn.

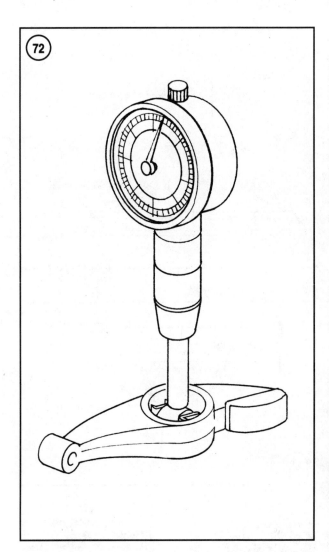

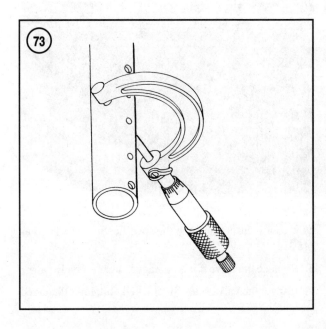

BASE ENGINE

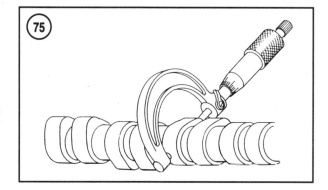

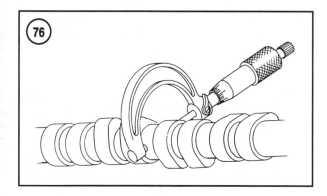

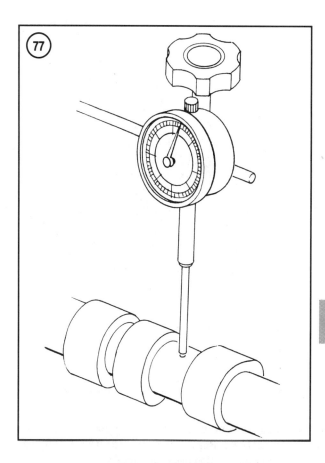

Camshaft, Pushrods and Tappets

Measure the camshaft lobes and bearing surfaces as applicable to the selected model. Disassemble the cylinder block to access the camshaft on models BF20, BF2A, BF50 and BF5A. Replace the camshaft if the surfaces are worn, cracked or corroded (**Figure 74**). Replace the pushrods and tappets (models BF20, BF2A, BF50 and BF5A) if there are worn or damaged surfaces.

1. Use an outside micrometer to measure the height of the camshaft lobes as indicated in **Figure 75**.
2. Record the measurement for each lobe.
3. Compare your measurements with the specifications listed in **Table 5**.
4. Replace the camshaft if the lobe height is less than the minimum specification.
5. Measure the camshaft (**Figure 76**) at the bearing journals (contact surfaces with the cylinder block or cylinder head).
6. Compare your measurements with the specifications listed in **Table 5**. Replace the camshaft if the diameter of any journal is less than the specification listed in **Table 5**.
7. Place the camshaft on V-blocks located under the top and bottom journals (**Figure 77**). The blocks must allow rotation of the camshaft.
8. Securely mount a dial indicator in a manner that positions the tip or plunger directly over and contacting one of the middle camshaft journals.
9. Observe the dial indicator as you slowly rotate the camshaft. Record the measurement.
10. Repeat the measurement on all journals. The amount of needle movement on the dial indicator indicates the camshaft runout.

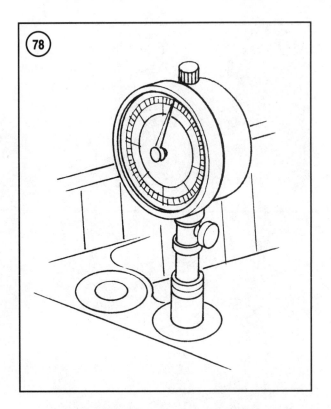

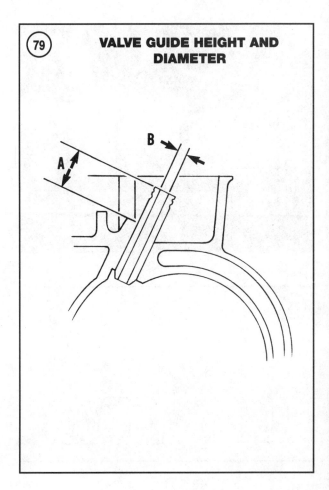

11. Compare your measurements with the specifications listed in **Table 5**. Replace the camshaft if the runout exceeds the specification listed in **Table 5**.

Valve Guide Inspection and Measurement

CAUTION
Make sure that the replacement valve guides are installed to the proper depth and are not damaged during installation. Improper installation can lead to poor valve sealing, increased valve wear and base engine failure.

Valve guide measurement requires using precision measuring instruments. Have a reputable machine shop perform these measurements if you do not have access to the required equipment or are not familiar with its use. Use an accurate inside micrometer (**Figure 78**) to measure the valve guide stem bore. Use a depth micrometer to measure the valve guide depth.

1. Using a suitable inside micrometer, measure the diameter of the valve guide bore (B, **Figure 79**). Take measurements at several locations in the length of the bore.

2. Rotate the micrometer 90° and repeat the measurements at several locations in the length of the bore.

3. Compare your measurements with the specification listed in **Table 2**. Have a reputable machine shop replace

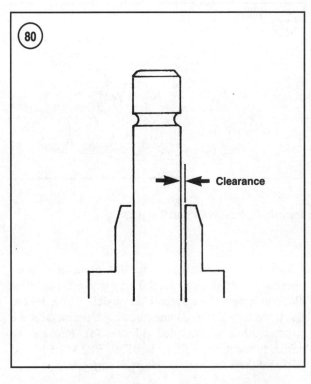

BASE ENGINE

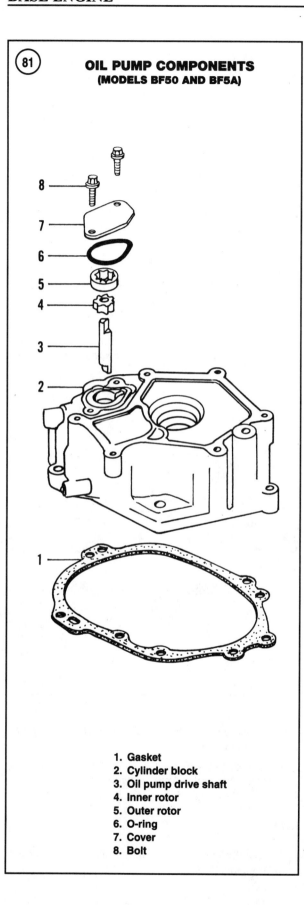

81

**OIL PUMP COMPONENTS
(MODELS BF50 AND BF5A)**

1. Gasket
2. Cylinder block
3. Oil pump drive shaft
4. Inner rotor
5. Outer rotor
6. O-ring
7. Cover
8. Bolt

the valve guides if any measurement is greater than the specification.

4. Ensure that the valve guides are installed to the depth (A, **Figure 79**) listed in **Table 2**.

5. Subtract the valve stem diameter from the valve guide bore diameter to determine the valve guide clearance (**Figure 80**).

6. Compare your calculation with the specification listed in **Table 3**. Replace the valve or valve guide to correct the valve guide clearance.

Oil Pump Removal, Inspection and Installation

Oil Pump mounting location and components used vary by model. Refer to this section for the selected model to locate the oil pump. To assist with component identification and position, refer to **Figures 81-83** during removal, inspection and installation of the oil pump

Models BF20 and BF2A

Models BF20 and BF2A utilize a connecting rod-mounted paddle to move oil within the base engine instead of an oil pump. Removal, inspection and installation of the paddle is listed in the base engine repair section of this chapter.

Models BF50 and BF5A

Models BF50 and BF5A utilize a rotary type oil pump (**Figure 81**) mounted to the top of the cylinder block. It is driven by a drive shaft (3, **Figure 81**) connected to the camshaft within the crankcase.

Models BF115A and BF130A

Models BF115A and BF130A utilize a rotary type oil pump (**Figure 82**) mounted within the lower flywheel cover. It is driven by a direct connection to the flywheel coupler.

All other models

All other models utilize a rotary type oil pump mounted to the lower end of the cylinder head (**Figure 83**). It is driven by a direct connection to the camshaft.

OIL PUMP

On models BF50 and BF5A, remove the flywheel to access the oil pump components. Refer to *Flywheel Re-*

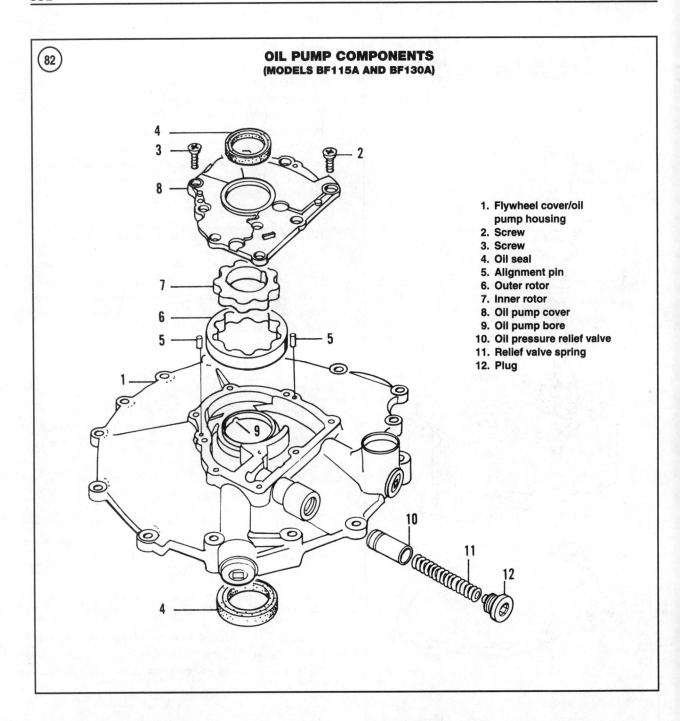

82 OIL PUMP COMPONENTS
(MODELS BF115A AND BF130A)

1. Flywheel cover/oil pump housing
2. Screw
3. Screw
4. Oil seal
5. Alignment pin
6. Outer rotor
7. Inner rotor
8. Oil pump cover
9. Oil pump bore
10. Oil pressure relief valve
11. Relief valve spring
12. Plug

moval and Installation in this chapter for the removal procedure.

On models BF115A and BF130A, remove the flywheel lower cover/oil pump housing to access the oil pump components. Refer to *Flywheel Removal and Installation* in this chapter for the removal procedure.

On all other models, removing the cylinder head may be required to access the oil pump mounting bolt/screws. When necessary, refer to *Cylinder Head Removal and Installation* in this chapter.

Apply engine oil to all shafts, O-rings and mounting surfaces on assembly. Apply a water-resistant grease to the lips of all oil seals during installation.

Removal

1. Record the location of all mounting bolts and screws *prior to removing them*.

BASE ENGINE

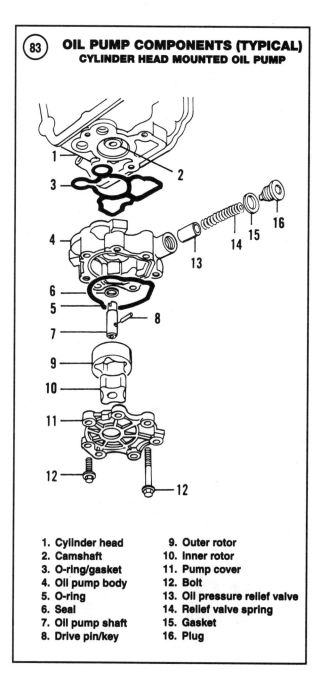

83. OIL PUMP COMPONENTS (TYPICAL) CYLINDER HEAD MOUNTED OIL PUMP

1. Cylinder head
2. Camshaft
3. O-ring/gasket
4. Oil pump body
5. O-ring
6. Seal
7. Oil pump shaft
8. Drive pin/key
9. Outer rotor
10. Inner rotor
11. Pump cover
12. Bolt
13. Oil pressure relief valve
14. Relief valve spring
15. Gasket
16. Plug

Disassembly

1. Remove and discard any mounting gasket, seal or O-ring if disturbed. Replace them with new components during installation.

2. Remove the bolts or screws then carefully pry the oil pump cover from the oil pump. Note the up and down orientation of the inner and outer rotor, then carefully lift them from the pump body.

3. Note the seal lip direction on models BF115A and BF130A. Carefully drive them from the oil pump housing and oil pump cover.

4. Pull the oil pump drive shaft and thrust washer, if so equipped, from the oil pump body.

5. Use a small punch and carefully push the rotor drive pin, if so equipped, from the oil pump drive shaft.

6. Refer to *Inspection* in this section then inspect and measure all applicable components.

Assembly

1. On models BF115A and BF130A, position the new oil seals with the lips facing the direction noted prior to removing them. Use a properly sized socket or section of tubing to carefully drive the new oil seals into the oil pump housing and oil pump cover. Apply a water-resistant grease to the lips of both seals.

2. Apply engine oil to all internal components prior to assembly. Install the drive pin into the oil pump drive shaft. Ensure the pin protrudes an even amount on each side.

3. On models BF50 and BF5A, rotate the oil pump drive shaft as you install it into the shaft bore in the cylinder block. When aligned with the camshaft, the oil pump drive shaft drops into position.

4. Install the thrust washer and oil pump drive shaft (if so equipped) into the oil pump body.

5. Install the inner rotor into the pump body. Ensure the rotor aligns with the drive pin or drive surface on the oil pump drive shaft. Place the outer rotor over the inner rotor and carefully rotate it until it slips into the oil pump housing. Make sure the UP orientation is facing as noted prior to removal.

6. Install a new O-ring to the oil pump cover and install the cover to the oil pump.

7. Install the cover bolts or screws and tighten them in a crossing pattern to the specification listed in **Table 1**.

2A. On models BF50 and BF5A do not remove the oil pump as the pump body is integral with the cylinder block.

2B. On models BF115A and BF130A, remove the flywheel cover/oil pump housing as indicated.

2C. On all other models, support the oil pump as you remove the mounting screws (12, **Figure 83**) from the oil pump and cylinder head. Carefully pull the oil pump from the cylinder head. Remove and discard any O-ring or gasket (3, **Figure 83**) from the oil pump mounting surface.

Installation

1A. On models BF115A and BF130A, refer to *Flywheel Removal and Installation* in this chapter and install the oil pump housing/flywheel cover on the engine.

1B. On all other models, follow Steps 2-7 to install the oil pump to the cylinder head.

2. Place a new O-ring or gasket on the mating surface.

3. Carefully position the oil pump shaft against the lower end of the camshaft.

4. Slowly rotate the oil pump body until the oil pump drive shaft aligns with the drive surfaces at the lower end of the camshaft.

5. Lightly hold the oil pump against the cylinder head as the shafts align.

6. Lower the oil pump enough to prevent the o-ring or gasket from contacting the mating surfaces.

7. Rotate the oil pump body until the mounting bolts align with their respective holes in the cylinder head. Thread the bolts in hand tight.

8. Tighten the mounting bolts in a crossing pattern to the specification listed in **Table 1**.

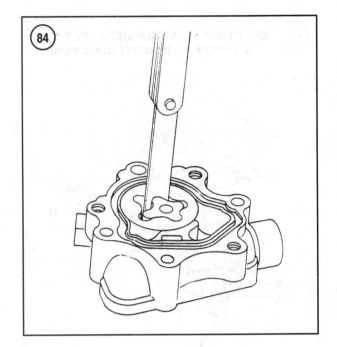

Inspection

1. Clean all components using a suitable solvent and dry them with compressed air. Make sure that all debris is removed prior to measurement.

2. Replace the oil pump if any you observe worn, cracked, corroded or discolored areas.

3. Place the inner and outer rotor into the oil pump body. Using feeler gauges, measure the clearance between the inner and outer rotor as shown in **Figure 84**. Select the feeler gauge that passes between the rotors with a slight drag. Compare your measurement with the specification listed in **Table 6**. Replace the inner and outer rotor if the clearance is greater than the specification.

4. Place the outer rotor into the pump body.

5. Using a narrow feeler gauge, measure the rotor-to-pump body clearance as shown in **Figure 85**. Select the gauge that passes between the rotor and pump body with a slight drag.

6. Compare the clearance to the specification in **Table 6**.

7. If the clearance exceeds the specification, measure the pump body diameter as follows:
   a. Using an inside micrometer or vernier caliper, measure the diameter of the pump as shown in **Figure 86**.
   b. Compare the diameter to the specification in **Table 6**.

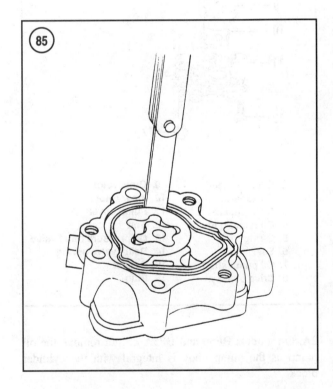

   c. If the pump body diameter is within specification, replace the pump rotor. If the body diameter exceeds specification, replace the oil pump assembly.

8. Measure the oil pump body depth as shown in **Figure 87** using a depth micrometer. Replace the oil pump if the depth exceeds the specification in **Table 6**.

BASE ENGINE

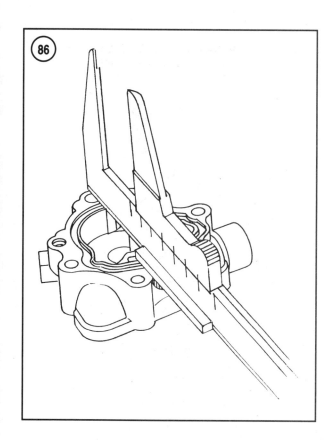

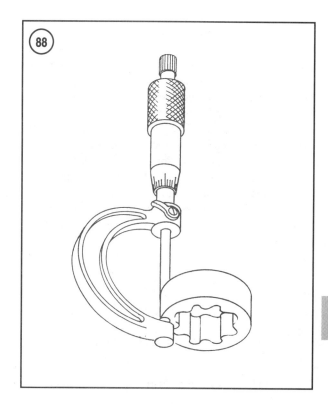

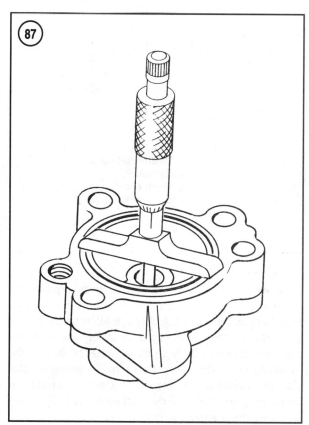

9. Measure the height of the outer pump rotor as shown in **Figure 88**. Replace the outer rotor is its height is less than the specification in **Table 6**.

BASE ENGINE DISASSEMBLY

Always make notes, drawings and photographs of all externally mounted engine components *before* beginning disassembly. Although illustrations are provided throughout this manual, not all hose and wire routing/connections are identical. The time used to make notes, drawings and photographs will save a great deal of time during the assembly process. Correct hose and wire routing is important for proper engine operation. An incorrectly routed hose or wire may interfere with linkage movement, resulting in a lack of throttle control. Hoses or wires may chafe and short or leak if allowed to contact sharp or moving parts. Other components such as fuel pumps can be mounted in two or more positions. If possible, remove a cluster of components that share common wires or hoses. This reduces the time required to disassemble/assemble the engine and reduces the chance of improper connections during assembly.

Bearings and some other internal engine components can be removed and reused during assembly if they are in good condition. The component inspection section of this chapter indicates which components must be replaced. It is a good practice to replace all insert type bearings, piston rings, piston pin lock rings, seals, gaskets and connecting rod bolts/nuts during assembly. If bearings must be reused, make certain that they remain in the same location from which they were removed. Piston rings must be replaced and cylinder bores honed if the piston is removed. The cost of these components is small compared to the damage caused to other components should they fail.

Use muffin tins or egg cartons to organize the fasteners as they are removed. Tag the fasteners to mark their correct location on the base engine.

Never use corroded or damaged fasteners. Replace locking type nuts if they are not in excellent condition. Connecting rod bolts must be replaced during engine assembly.

WARNING
Always use assistance when lifting or moving the base engine. Make sure that the base engine is securely resting or clamped to the work surface before beginning work.

External Component Removal

1. Place the engine on a suitable work surface. Securely clamp or fasten the base engine down to the work surface with bolts and/or nuts.
2. Remove the timing belt following the procedure listed in this chapter. Do not allow the crankshaft or camshaft to rotate after removing the timing belt.
3. Remove the timing belt tensioner, all pulleys and lower timing belt covers on models so equipped, following the procedures listed in this chapter.
4. Refer to Chapter Seven and remove all applicable electrical and ignition components from the base engine.
5. Refer to Chapter Six and remove all applicable fuel system components from the base engine.
6. Make notes, photographs or drawings of the mounting location and orientation and remove any remaining clamps or brackets from the base engine.
7. Refer to *Cylinder Head Removal/Installation* in this chapter and remove the cylinder head from the cylinder block.
8. Refer to *Crankcase Disassembly* in this chapter for additional disassembly procedures.

Water Jackets and Thermostats

Refer to **Figures 89-96**. When removing water jacket covers or crankshaft covers, always loosen the bolts and/or nuts in the reverse of the tightening sequence. Loosen each bolt or nut one-quarter turn at a time in reverse sequence until they turn freely. Always replace gaskets during assembly. Clean all debris from the water passages and mating surfaces. Replace all surfaces if they have cracks, pitting or damaged areas. Replace any components with excessively corroded surfaces. Inspect the anodes in the water jackets for excessive corrosion. Replace them along with their mounting bolt to protect them from corrosion. Be sure to clean all debris from the anode mounting surfaces prior to installation.

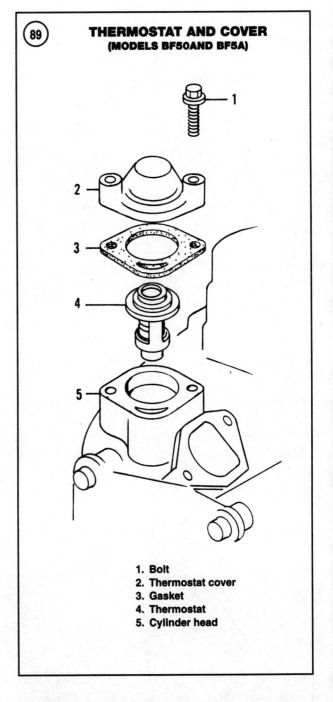

THERMOSTAT AND COVER
(MODELS BF50 AND BF5A)

1. Bolt
2. Thermostat cover
3. Gasket
4. Thermostat
5. Cylinder head

BASE ENGINE

⑨⓪ THERMOSTAT AND COVER
(MODELS BF75, BF8A AND BF100)

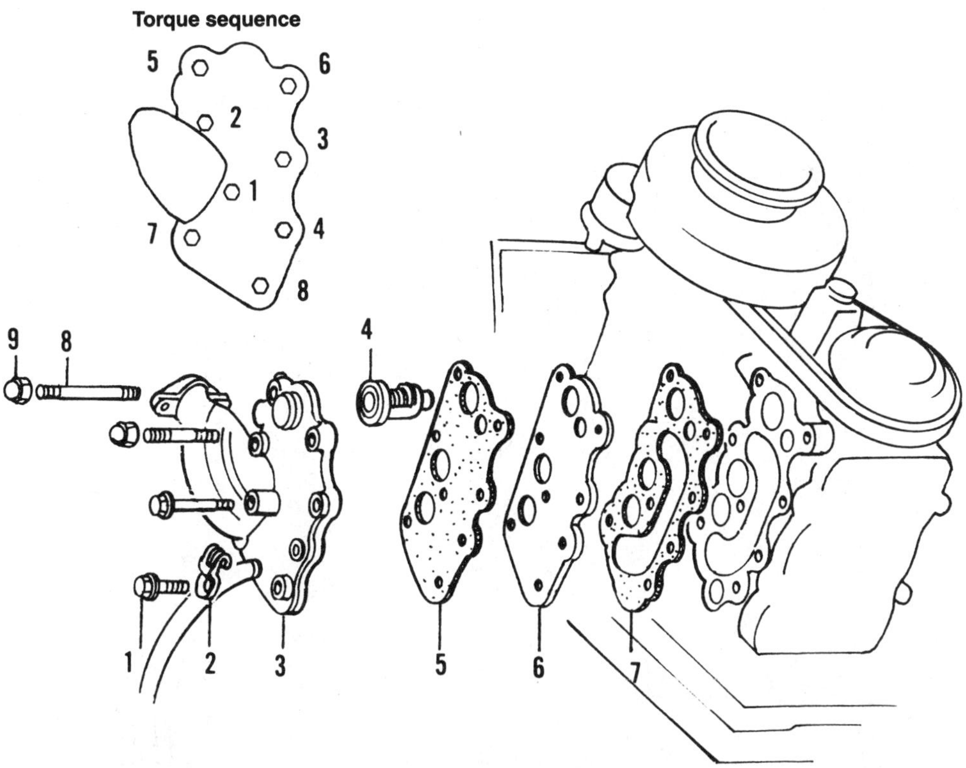

Torque sequence

1. Bolt
2. Clamp
3. Intake manifold
4. Thermostat
5. Gasket
6. Plate
7. Gasket
8. Stud
9. Nut

Removal

Outboard engines are exposed to a more corrosive environment than other types of engines. Corroded fasteners can be quite difficult to remove. Corrosion will be more prevalent if the engine is operated in saltwater. Avoid using excessive force when a fastener appears to be seized. Much time and expense is wasted removing the remnant of a broken fastener. Use patience and refer to Chapter Two in this manual for useful tips on removing stubborn fasteners.

1. Loosen water jacket, thermostat cover, water pressure valve or exhaust cover bolts gradually in reverse sequence to help prevent plate warpage. Refer to **Figures 89-96** for torque sequences. Use caution when it is necessary to pry a component loose. Avoid using any sharp object that may damage the mating surfaces of the components. Castings or contact areas are usually present that allow you to pry the components apart without risking damage to mating surfaces.

2. Locate and remove the thermostat housing, if so equipped, from the base engine. Note the side of the ther-

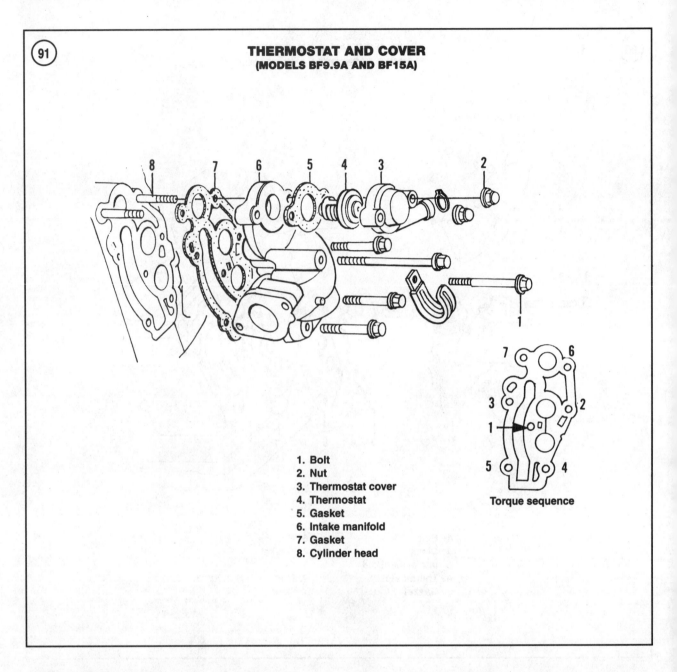

91 THERMOSTAT AND COVER (MODELS BF9.9A AND BF15A)

1. Bolt
2. Nut
3. Thermostat cover
4. Thermostat
5. Gasket
6. Intake manifold
7. Gasket
8. Cylinder head

Torque sequence

mostat that faces toward the cylinder block. Use pliers to pull the thermostat from its seat.
3. Remove and discard the housing gasket.
4. Inspect the thermostat for corrosion deposits. Refer to Chapter Three and test the thermostat.
5. Locate and remove the water pressure valve cover, if so equipped, along with the gasket and spring. Discard the gasket, seals or O-rings.
6. Inspect the plunger and spring for worn, damaged or corroded surfaces. Replace any defective components.
7. Inspect all bolts and bolt holes for damaged or corroded threads. Clean all threads with the correct thread tap. Repair any damaged or corroded threads using thread inserts. Replace any corroded bolts.

Installation

Installation of water jackets and thermostats is the reverse of removal. Install new gaskets, seals and O-rings at all locations. Gasket sealer is not required on the gaskets, seals or O-rings. Tighten all covers and jackets in three steps following the torque sequence listed in **Figures**

BASE ENGINE

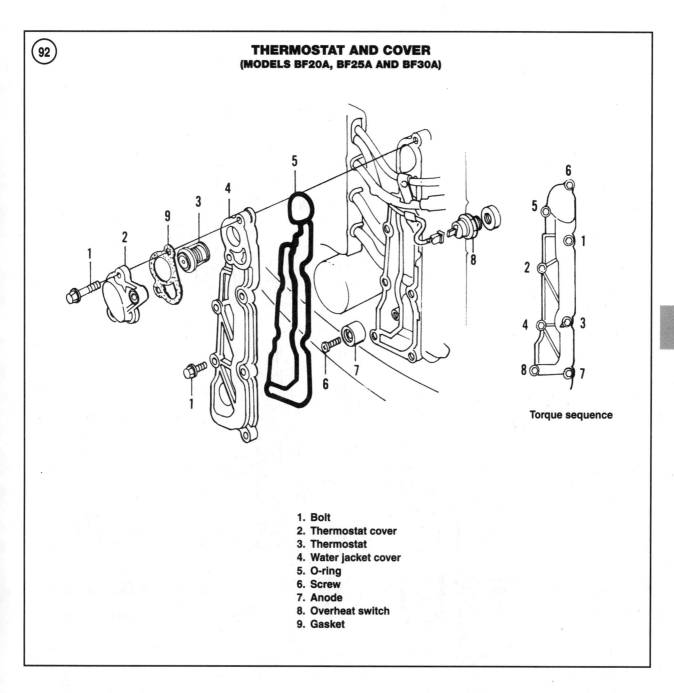

92 THERMOSTAT AND COVER
(MODELS BF20A, BF25A AND BF30A)

Torque sequence

1. Bolt
2. Thermostat cover
3. Thermostat
4. Water jacket cover
5. O-ring
6. Screw
7. Anode
8. Overheat switch
9. Gasket

89-96. Check for and correct any leakage immediately after starting the engine.

Crankcase Disassembly

Refer to **Figures 97-104**.

1. Loosen each fastener one-quarter turn at a time, in reverse sequence, until all fasteners are loose. Remove all fasteners by hand when they turn easily.

2. On models BF9.9A and BF15A, remove the top cover (2, **Figure 100**) and the breather/vent housing (10, **Figure 100**) from the cylinder block.

3. Make sure that all fasteners are removed. Locate suitable pry points (**Figure 105**) and carefully pry the crankcase cover loose from the cylinder block.

4. Hold the crankshaft into the cylinder block and pull the crankcase cover from the cylinder block (**Figure 106**).

5. On models BF20, BF2A, BF50 and BF5A, carefully pull the camshaft and lifters from the crankcase.

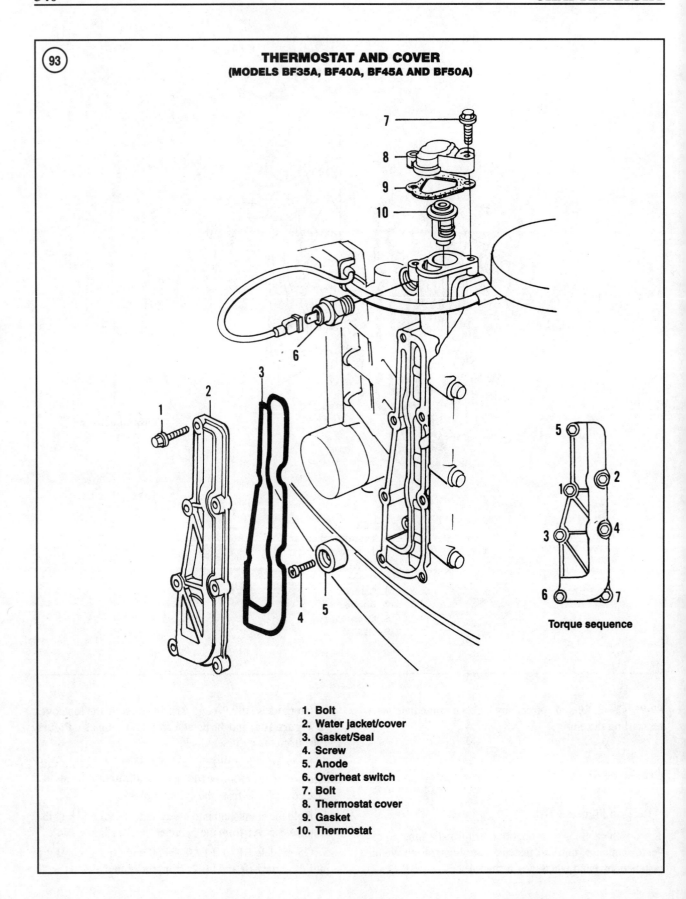

BASE ENGINE

341

⑨④ THERMOSTAT, WATER PRESSURE RELIEF VALVE AND COVER
(MODELS BF75A AND BF90A)

Torque sequence

1. Bolt
2. Water pressure valve cover
3. O-ring
4. Grommet
5. Fitting/cover
6. O-ring
7. Valve/plunger
8. Spring
9. Bolt
10. Screw
11. Anode
12. Gasket/seal
13. Water jacket/cover
14. Thermostat
15. Gasket
16. Thermostat cover
17. Bolt
18. Cylinder block
19. Bolt
20. Flush valve cover
21. O-ring
22. Grommet
23. Housing
24. O-ring
25. Valve/plunger
26. Spring

6. On models BF20 and BF2A, carefully remove the lubrication wheel, thrust washer and shaft from the cylinder block.

7. On models BF50 and BF5A, remove the oil pickup tube/screen and pressure relief valve/spring from the crankcase cover.

8. Refer to *Piston and Connecting Rod Removal and Installation* in this chapter and remove each connecting rod and piston from the cylinder block.

9. Remove the seals from the ends of the crankshaft (**Figure 107**). Refer to *Crankshaft Removal and Installation* in this section and remove the crankshaft from the cylinder block.

10. Refer to *Balancer Shaft Removal and Installation* in this chapter and remove both balancer shafts from the cylinder block.

11. Note their location and seal lip direction and carefully pry any remaining seals from the cylinder block. Work

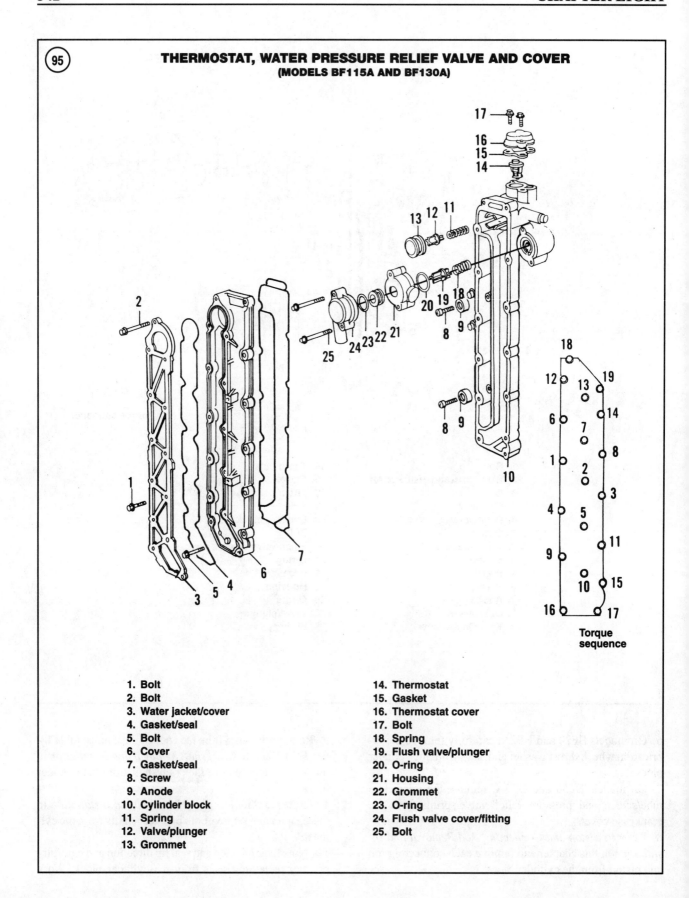

BASE ENGINE

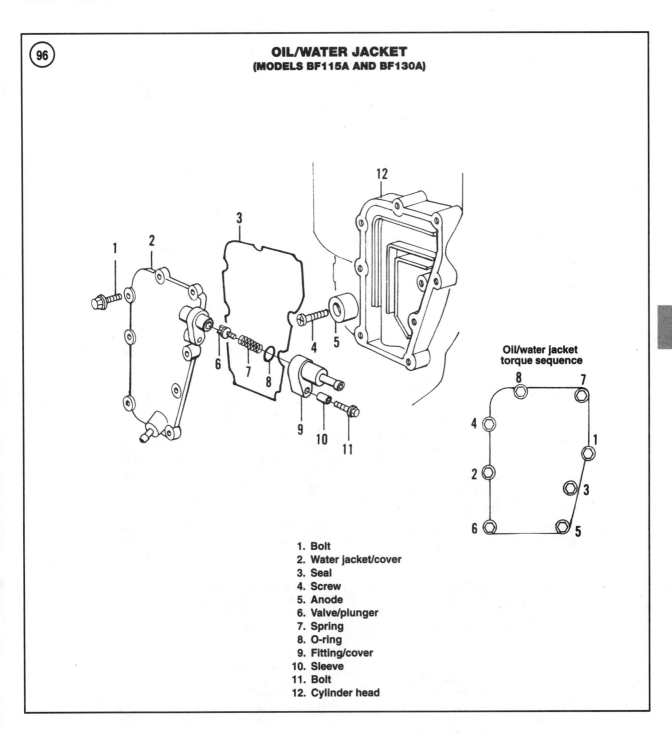

96 OIL/WATER JACKET (MODELS BF115A AND BF130A)

1. Bolt
2. Water jacket/cover
3. Seal
4. Screw
5. Anode
6. Valve/plunger
7. Spring
8. O-ring
9. Fitting/cover
10. Sleeve
11. Bolt
12. Cylinder head

Oil/water jacket torque sequence

carefully to avoid damaging the seal bore or other surfaces.

Piston and Connecting Rods

Always keep components organized when removed. The piston, connecting rod and related components must be installed into the same cylinder as removed unless the component is replaced. Mark the cylinder number on pistons and rods on a non-contact area as they are removed. Use an ink marker that can withstand solvent cleaning or a scratch awl to mark the components. On inline engines, the No. 1 cylinder is the top cylinder.

The connecting rod cap is matched to the connecting rod. Install the cap onto the rod in the proper position *im-*

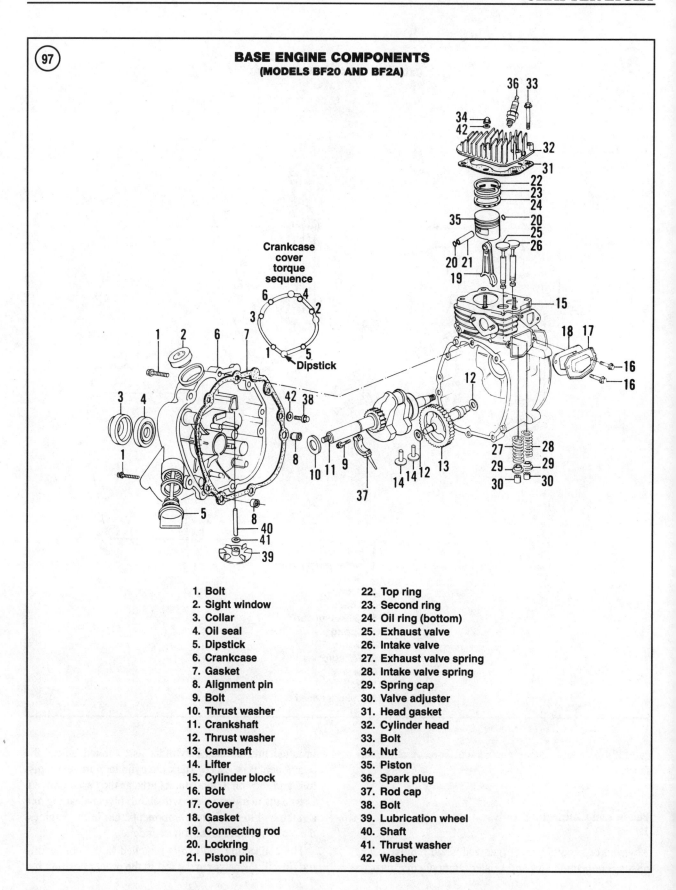

BASE ENGINE

345

BASE ENGINE COMPONENTS
(MODELS BF50 AND BF5A)

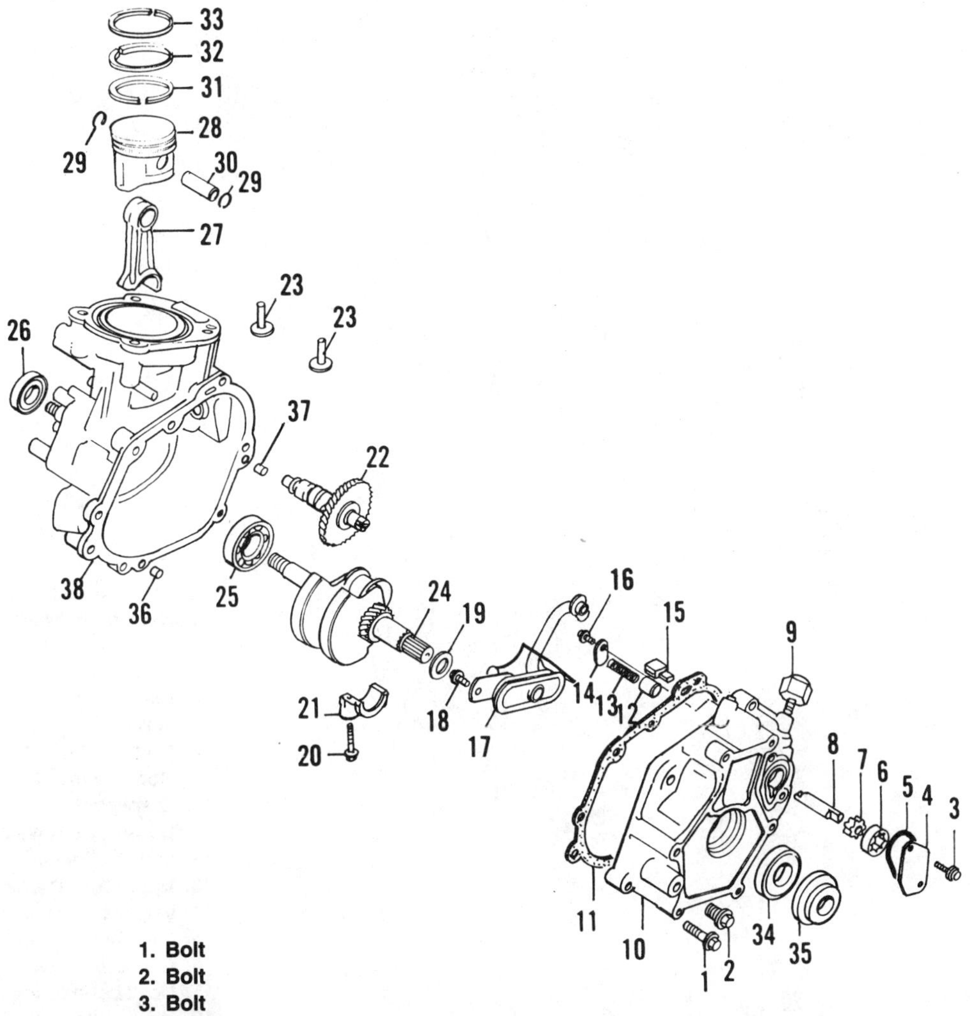

1. Bolt
2. Bolt
3. Bolt
4. Pump cover
5. O-ring
6. Outer rotor
7. Inner rotor
8. Oil pump shaft
9. Oil pressure switch
10. Crankcase
11. Gasket
12. Oil pressure relief valve
13. Relief valve spring
14. Retainer
15. Coupler
16. Screw
17. Oil pickup/screen
18. Bolt
19. Thrust washer
20. Rod bolt
21. Rod cap
22. Camshaft
23. Lifter
24. Crankshaft
25. Ball bearing
26. Oil seal
27. Connecting rod
28. Piston
29. Lockring
30. Piston pin
31. Oil ring (bottom)
32. Second ring
33. Top ring
34. Oil seal
35. Collar
36. Alignment dowel
37. Alignment dowel
38. Crankcase

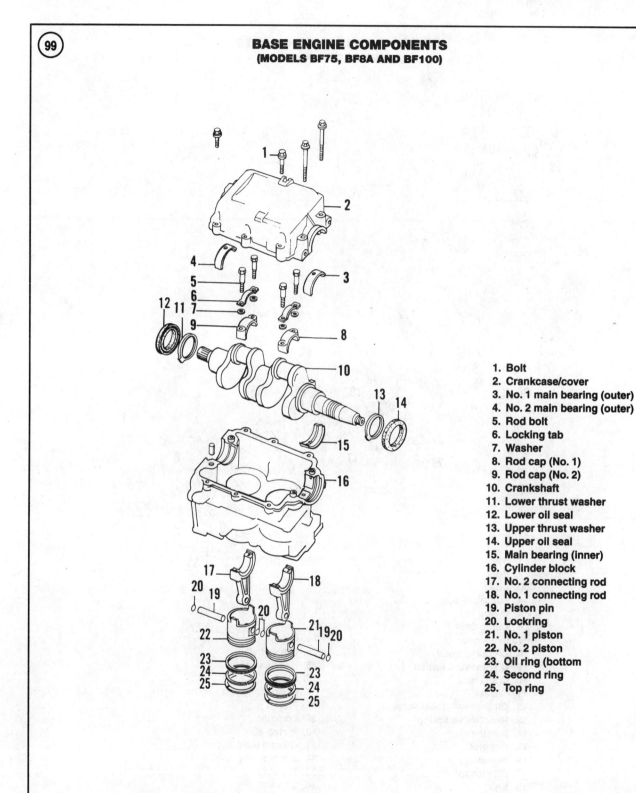

BASE ENGINE

347

BASE ENGINE COMPONENTS
(MODELS BF9.9A AND BF15A)

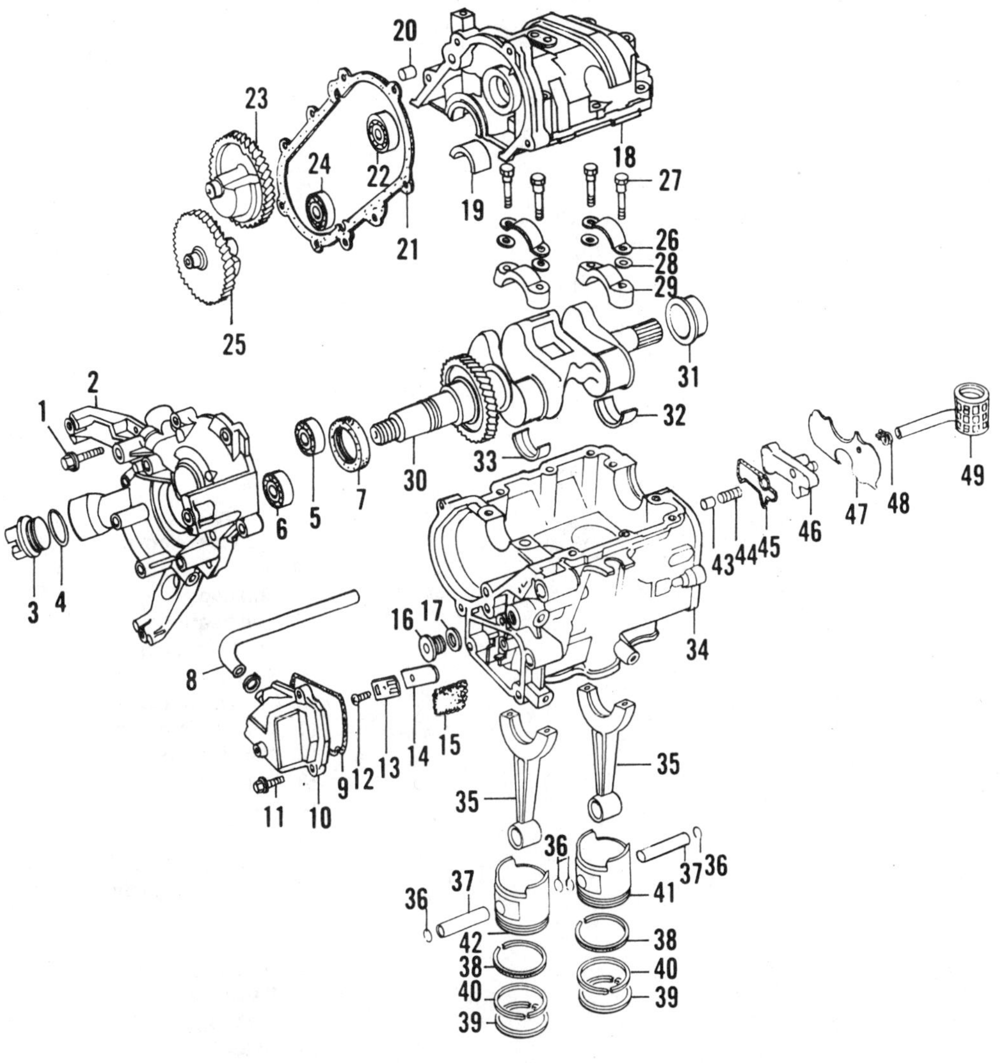

1. Bolt
2. Top cover
3. Oil fill cap
4. O-ring
5. Ball bearing (upper)
6. Ball bearing (upper)
7. Oil seal
8. Breather tube
9. Gasket
10. Breather housing
11. Bolt
12. Screw
13. Retainer
14. Plate
15. Filter
16. Plug
17. Gasket
18. Crankcase/cover
19. Main bearing (outer)
20. Alignment pin
21. Gasket
22. Ball bearing (lower)
23. Balancer shaft
24. Ball bearing (lower)
25. Balancer shaft
26. Locking tab
27. Bolt
28. Washer
29. Rod cap
30. Crankshaft
31. Oil seal
32. No. 2 connecting rod bearing
33. No. 1 connecting rod bearing
34. Cylinder block
35. Connecting rod
36. Lockring
37. Piston pin
38. Oil ring (lower)
39. Top ring
40. Second ring
41. No. 2 piston
42. No. 1 piston
43. Oil pressure relief valve
44. Relief valve spring
45. O-ring
46. Cover
47. Mount gasket
48. Clamp
49. Oil pickup/screen

CHAPTER EIGHT

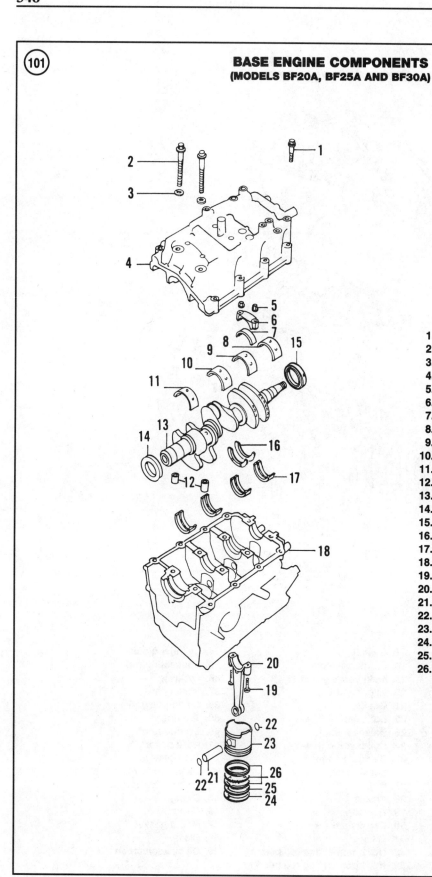

BASE ENGINE COMPONENTS (MODELS BF20A, BF25A AND BF30A)

1. Bolt
2. Bolt
3. Washer
4. Crankcase/cover
5. Nut
6. Rod cap
7. Rod bearing
8. No. 1 main bearing
9. No. 2 main bearing
10. No. 3 main bearing
11. No. 4 main bearing
12. Alignment dowel
13. Crankshaft
14. Oil seal
15. Oil seal
16. Thrust spacers
17. Main bearings (inner)
18. Cylinder block
19. Rod bolt
20. Connecting rod
21. Piston pin
22. Lockring
23. Piston
24. Top ring
25. Second ring
26. Oil ring (bottom)

BASE ENGINE

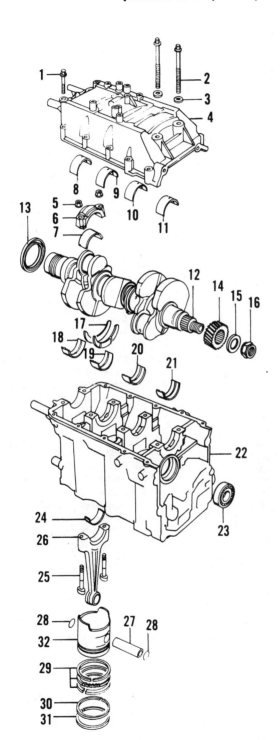

BASE ENGINE COMPONENTS
(MODELS BF35A, BF40A, BF45A AND BF50A)

1. Bolt
2. Bolt
3. Washer
4. Crankcase/cover
5. Nut
6. Rod cap
7. Rod bearing
8. No. 1 main bearing (inner)
9. No. 2 main bearing (inner)
10. No. 3 main bearing (inner)
11. No. 4 main bearing (inner)
12. Crankshaft
13. Oil seal
14. Gear
15. Washer
16. Locknut
17. Thrust spacers
18. No. 1 main bearing (outer)
19. No. 2 main bearing (outer)
20. No. 3 main bearing (outer)
21. No. 4 main bearing (outer)
22. Cylinder block
23. Ball bearing (primary gear)
24. Rod bearing
25. Rod bolt
26. Connecting rod
27. Piston pin
28. Lockring
29. Oil ring (bottom)
30. Second ring
31. Top ring
32. Piston

CHAPTER EIGHT

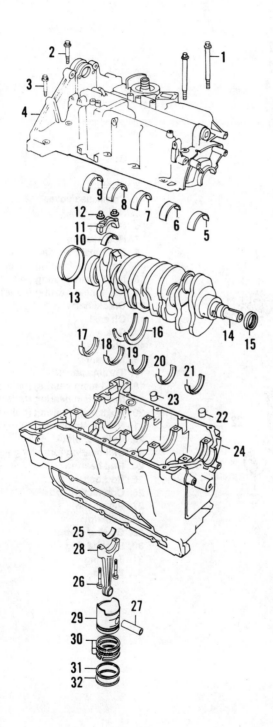

103 BASE ENGINE COMPONENTS (MODELS BF75A AND BF90A)

1. Bolt
2. Bolt
3. Bolt
4. Crankcase/cover
5. No. 1 main bearing (outer)
6. No. 2 main bearing (outer)
7. No. 3 main bearing (outer)
8. No. 4 main bearing (outer)
9. No. 5 main bearing (outer)
10. Rod bearing
11. Rod cap
12. Nut
13. Lower oil seal
14. Crankshaft
15. Upper oil seal
16. Thrust spacers
17. No. 5 main bearing (inner)
18. No. 4 main bearing (inner)
19. No. 3 main bearing (inner)
20. No. 2 main bearing (inner)
21. No. 1 main bearing (inner)
22. Aligning dowel (small)
23. Aligning dowel (large)
24. Cylinder block
25. Rod bearing
26. Rod bolt
27. Piston pin
28. Connecting rod
29. Piston
30. Oil ring (bottom)
31. Second ring
32. Top ring

BASE ENGINE

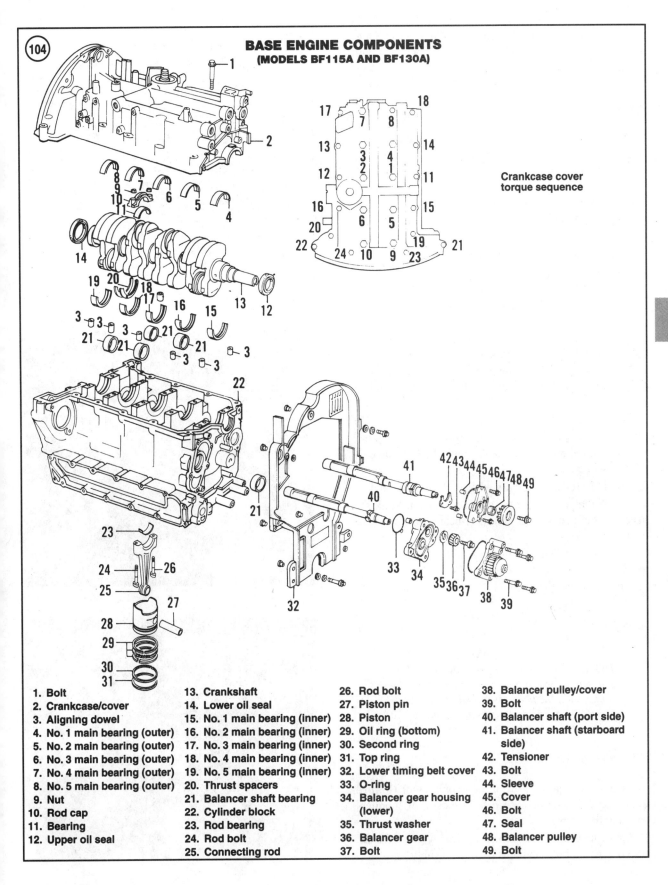

mediately after removing the piston/rod from the cylinder block. Do not allow the rod cap to become switched with another rod.

Removal

1. Alternately loosen each connecting rod bolt or nut (**Figure 108**) in one-quarter turn increments until they turn easily. Support the piston.
2. Remove the two bolts and nuts for the rod cap. Gently tap the rod cap to loosen the cap.
3. Mark the flywheel side of the rod cap, then remove the cap.
4. Mark the top side of the bearings if they must be reused.
5. Remove the insert type bearings (**Figure 109**) from the crankshaft and place them into their location in the rod cap.
6. Use a large wooden dowel or hammer handle to push the piston and rod assembly (4 and 5, **Figure 110**) out of the cylinder head side of the block. Provide continuous support of the piston (5, **Figure 110**) during the removal process.
7. Note the UP marking on the piston dome (**Figure 111**) relative to the crankshaft when removed.
8. Position the rod cap on the rod with the UP side correctly positioned.
9. Install the rod bolts and thread in until hand tight only.
10. Mark the piston with the cylinder number. Mark the inside of the piston skirt and the I-beam portion of the connecting rod.
11. Repeat Steps 2-10 for the remaining cylinders. Refer to *Piston/Connecting Rod Disassembly and Assembly* for piston ring removal.

Installation

> **CAUTION**
> *DO NOT force the piston into the bore. Piston rings and other components will be damaged if the piston is forced into the bore if any interference is present. Remove the piston and check the ring gap alignment and ring compressor fit if the piston will not slide into the bore.*

Installation requires a piston ring compressor (**Figure 112**). These can be purchased from most tool suppliers and automotive parts stores.

1. Lubricate the cylinder bore and piston with engine oil. Install new rod bolts and nuts during assembly.

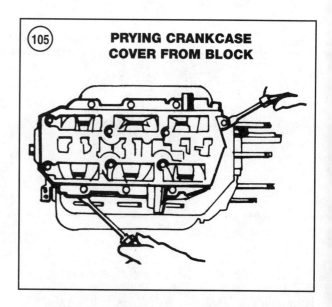
105 PRYING CRANKCASE COVER FROM BLOCK

BASE ENGINE

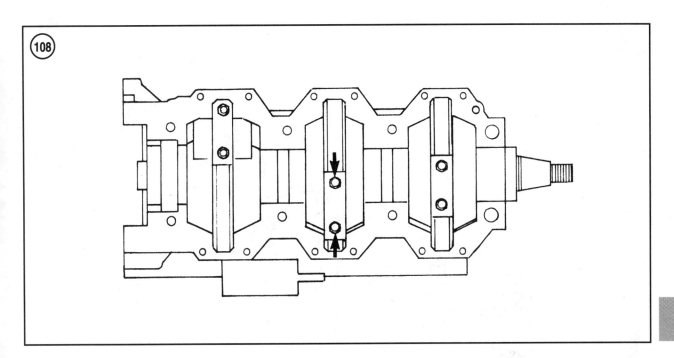

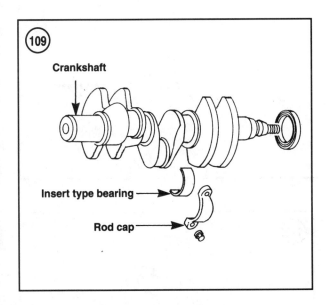

2. Without disturbing the piston ring alignment, install the piston ring compressor over the piston.

3. Tighten the piston ring compressor just enough to compress the rings into the ring grooves. Do not overtighten the compressor. The piston must be able to slide through the ring compressor (**Figure 112**).

4. Rotate the crankshaft until the connecting rod journal for the selected cylinder is at the bottom of its stroke.

5. Noting the UP mark (**Figure 113**) on the piston, place the piston skirt into the correct cylinder. Make sure the piston marking is positioned correctly.

6. Using a wooden dowel or hammer handle, carefully tap the piston into the bore (**Figure 112**) until the piston top is slightly above the cylinder head mating surface.

7. Provide support for the piston and carefully rotate the cylinder block to access the connecting rod.

8. Place the bearing into the connecting rod so the tab (**Figure 114**) engages the notch in the connecting rod. Apply engine oil to the bearing surface. Gently tap the piston into the bore as you guide the bearing to the crankshaft.

9. Place the bearing into the rod cap with the tab engaging the notch in the rod cap. Apply oil to the bearing surface.

10. Ensure that the cap is correctly positioned and place the cap onto the connecting rod. Hand-tighten the new rod bolts and nuts (**Figure 108**).

   a. On models BF20 and BF2A, the paddle on the rod cap must face the camshaft.

11. Check the alignment of the rod cap and connecting rod (**Figure 115**) by passing a sharpened pencil tip across the mating surfaces. Replace the connecting rod if uneven surfaces are detected with the pencil tip.

12. Tighten the rod cap bolts or nuts in alternating steps to the specification listed in **Table 1**.

   a. On models BF75, BF8A and BF15A, bend the locking tabs against the flat portion of the rod bolts after tightening the rod bolts. Rotate the crankshaft to check for smooth operation. Remove the piston and connecting rod and check for proper installation if any binding, roughness or unusual noise is detected. Repeat all steps for the remaining cylinders.

354 CHAPTER EIGHT

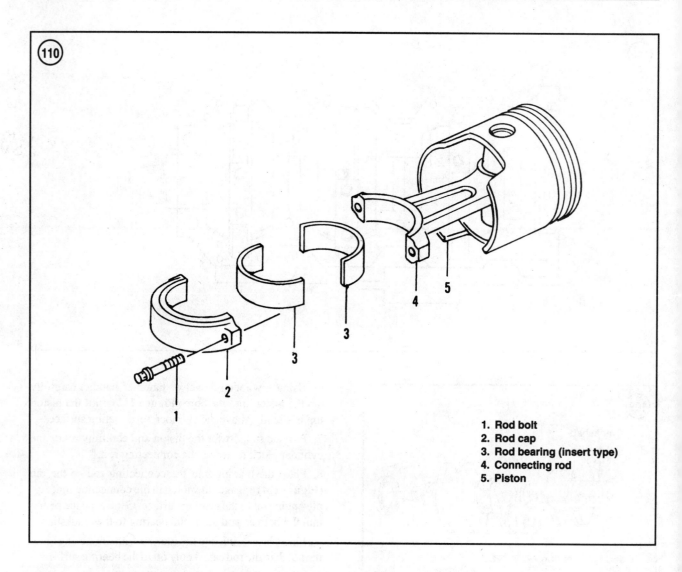

1. Rod bolt
2. Rod cap
3. Rod bearing (insert type)
4. Connecting rod
5. Piston

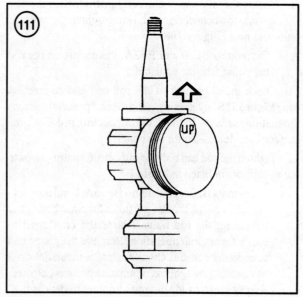

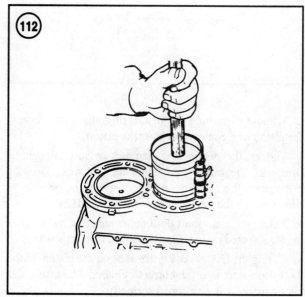

BASE ENGINE

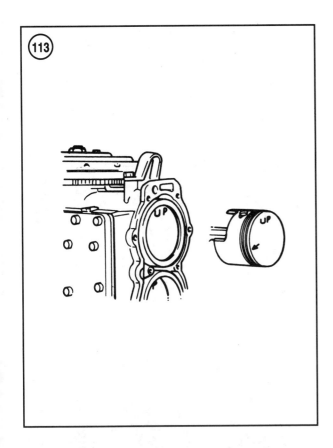

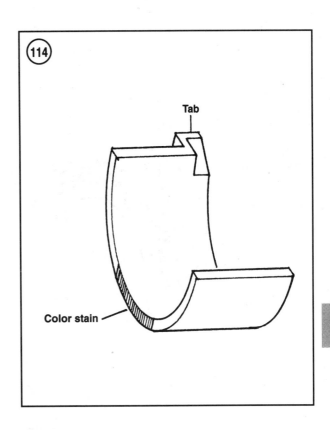

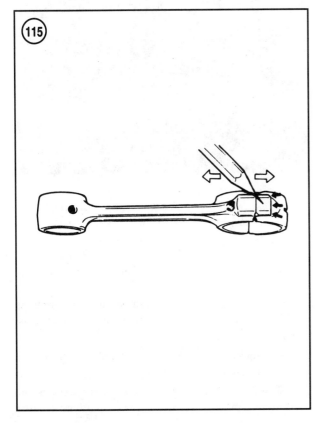

Piston, Connecting Rod

WARNING
Wear safety glasses when working with the base engine. Piston pin retaining rings and other components may spring free and result in serious bodily injury.

NOTE
Heat the piston if necessary to remove the piston pin. Use only enough heat to attain a temperature of approximately 140°. Use heavy gloves on your hand to support the piston and carefully drive the pin from the piston.

Special tools are required when removing or installing the piston pin on press fit models. Have a reputable machine shop or Honda dealership perform this operation. Refer to **Figures 97-104** to determine the components used.

Disassembly

1. Carefully remove each piston ring from the piston using a piston ring expanding tool (**Figure 116**) or gloved hands. Keep all rings arranged in a manner to identify the top, second and bottom rings.

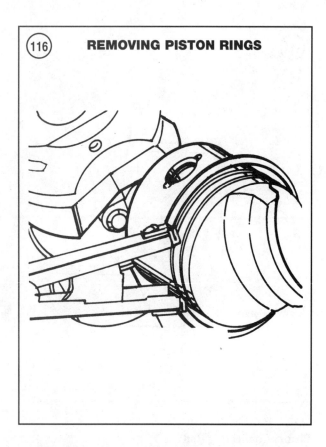

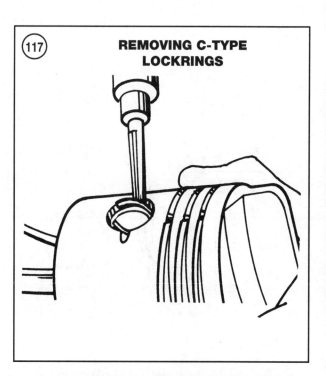

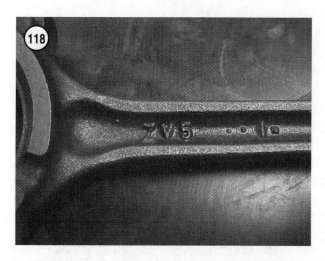

2. Use a sharp pick, needle nose pliers (**Figure 117**) or a small screwdriver to remove both lockrings from the piston(s). Place a shop towel over the lockring and hold a finger or thumb against the lockring opening during removal to prevent the ring from springing free upon removal. Work carefully to avoid damaging the lockring groove. Discard the removed lockrings.

3. Note the up marking on the piston relative to the ZV or other marks on the connecting rod (**Figure 118**).

4. Use a socket to push the piston pin from the piston. The tool used must be slightly smaller than the piston pin. Refer to **Table 8** for piston pin diameters.

5. Pull the piston from the rod when the pin has cleared the rod.

6. Note their location and up or down position and using a small screwdriver carefully pry the bearings from the rod cap and connecting rod.

7. Refer to *Inspection* in this chapter and perform all applicable inspection and measurements.

Assembly

CAUTION
Use care when spreading the rings for installation onto the piston. Spread the gap ends only enough to allow the rings to slide over the piston. The ring will break or crack if spread too much on installation.

1. Position the connecting rod within the piston pin bore area at the bottom of the piston. Ensure that the markings on the connecting rod face the same direction as the up marking on the piston or the direction noted prior to disassembly.

2. Use a socket to push the piston pin into the piston pin bore in the piston and connecting rod.

3. Use needle nose pliers to install the new lockrings into their groove in each end of the piston pin bore (**Figure**

BASE ENGINE

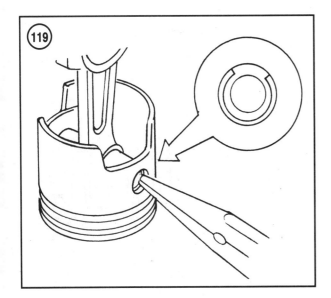

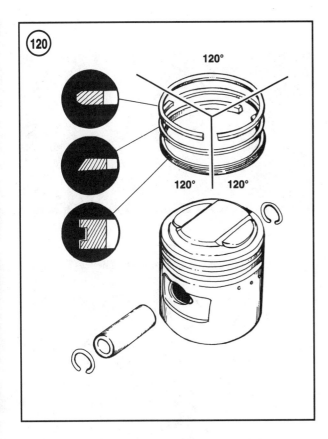

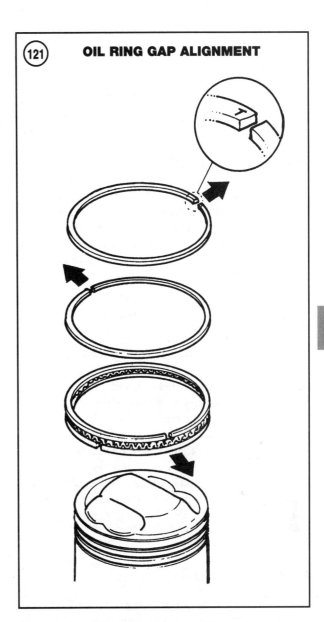

5. Use a ring expanding tool (**Figure 116**) to expand the rings just enough to clear the piston and carefully slide them into position.

6. Rotate the rings to position the ring gaps 120° apart from each other (**Figure 120**). Position the oil ring rails (thin rings) approximately 12° offset from the gap in the spacer (thick portion) (**Figure 121**).

119). Rotate the lockrings to position the gap down or toward the crankshaft. Ensure the lockrings are fully seated in their grooves.

4. Refer to the instructions supplied with the new rings to properly locate the rings on the piston. Marks on the rings face up and the chrome rings indicate the top.

Crankshaft Removal (All Models)

CAUTION
Avoid using excessive force when removing the crankshaft from the cylinder block. The use of excessive force may dislodge or dam-

age the main bearings or cause irreparable damage to the cylinder block and other components.

On models BF20, BF2A, BF50 and BF5A, slide the crankshaft (**Figure 97** and **Figure 98**) from the cylinder block after removing the piston and connecting rod. Note its position (crankshaft side) then remove the thrust washer from the crankshaft.

On all other models, carefully remove the insert type main bearings from the crankshaft. Provide padding to prevent damage to the mating surfaces. Use pry bars to carefully pry the crankshaft from the cylinder block (**Figure 122**). Record their mounting location and remove the inner main bearings and thrust spacers (**Figure 123**) from the cylinder block.

Crankshaft and camshaft installation (models BF20, BF2A, BF50, BF5A)

1. Apply engine oil to the ball bearing of the crankshaft.
2. Apply a small amount of water-resistant grease to the lips of the crankcase mounted seals and the thrust washer. Slide the thrust washer over the end of the crankshaft.
3. Position it against the thrust surface on the crankshaft as noted prior to removal.
4. Carefully slide the crankshaft into the cylinder block. Place the valve lifters into the cylinder block.
5. Apply oil to all contact surfaces of the camshaft. Align the timing marks on the camshaft and crankshaft as shown in **Figure 124**, then install the camshaft into the cylinder block.

Crankshaft installation (All models except BF20, BF2A, BF50 and BF5A)

Check the main bearing clearances using Plastigage (**Figure 125**) prior to assembling the cylinder block. Bearing clearance specifications are in **Table 10**.
1. Make sure all surfaces are clean and dry. Place the main bearings onto their mounting location in the cylinder block.
2. Carefully lower the crankshaft onto the bearings.
3. Place a section of plastigage across the bearing surface as shown in **Figure 126**. Do not rotate the crankshaft.
4. Install the outer main bearings at their respective location on the crankshaft.
5. Refer to *Crankcase Assembly* in this section and install the crankcase on the cylinder block.
6. Refer to *Crankcase Disassembly* in this section and remove the crankcase from the cylinder block.
7. Carefully remove each outer main bearing from the crankshaft.

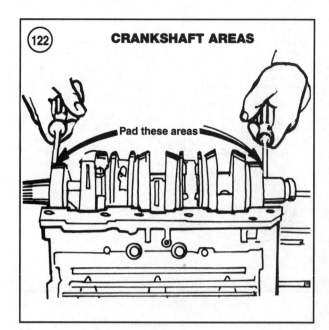

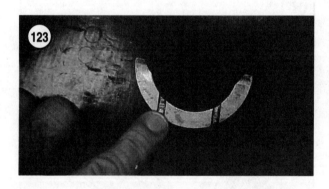

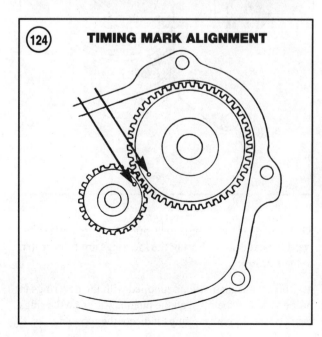

BASE ENGINE

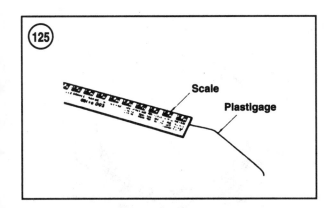

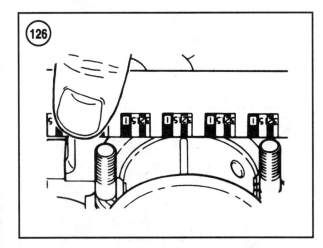

8. Gauge the main bearing clearance by comparing the flattened Plastigage with the marks on the Plastigage envelope (**Figure 126**).

9. Compare the clearance with the specifications listed in **Table 10**. Refer to *Bearing Selection* and replace the bearing if incorrect clearances are noted. Check the clearance after bearing replacement.

10. Refer to *Inspection* in this chapter if incorrect clearances are found.

11. Apply engine oil to the bearing surfaces and install the selected main bearings in the correct location.

12. Install the thrust spacers (**Figure 123**) into the cylinder block with the grooved sides facing the crankshaft surface. Continue the assembly of the cylinder block.

BASE ENGINE INSPECTION AND MEASUREMENT

This section provides instruction for cleaning, inspecting and measuring internal base engine components. Crankshaft gear and bearing removal/installation procedures are also included.

Use compressed air to blow any loose debris from the components. Using clean solvent, wash all components, except the cylinder block, one at a time and make sure the markings are present after washing. Mark the cylinder number on the component again if needed. Allow the solvent to drain for a few minutes and use compressed air to remove any remaining solvent. Cover the components with shop towels to protect them from dust contamination.

CAUTION
Never allow bearings to spin while blowing them dry with compressed air. The bearing will be damaged within a few seconds. Hold the bearing still while drying.

Cleaning

1. Use a scraper to remove deposits and remaining gasket material from the exhaust plates, covers, and the mating surfaces of the cylinder block. Work carefully and avoid scratching or damaging mating surfaces. Use hot soapy water to clean the cylinder block, exhaust covers and cylinder heads. Clean the block with pressurized water.

2. Dry the cylinder block, covers and cylinder heads with compressed air.

3. Apply engine oil to the cylinder walls immediately after the walls are dry to prevent corrosion.

4. Aluminum deposits will be present on the cylinder walls if piston failure has occurred. Use a blunt tip of a screwdriver to carefully pry the aluminum particles from the cylinder walls. Minor deposits will likely disappear during the honing process.

CAUTION
Never use a wire brush to remove carbon from the piston. Small particles of steel may become imbedded into the piston surface. These small particles glow when hot and cause preignition or detonation damage to the piston.

WARNING
Use heavy gloves and extreme caution when cleaning the ring grooves. Used piston rings are very sharp.

5. Use a dull chisel or blunt screwdriver to remove carbon deposits from the top of the piston. Use very light force to help prevent gouging or scratching of the piston. Use a Scotchbrite pad and mild solvent to remove remaining carbon deposits from the piston.

6. Use a broken piece of the piston ring from the ring groove that is being cleaned to remove carbon from the

ring grooves (**Figure 127**). Use a top ring for the top ring groove and bottom ring for the bottom ring groove. Using the wrong type of piston ring can cause damage to the ring groove. Use enough force to remove the carbon only. Never allow the ring to scrape aluminum material from the groove. Use a brush and solvent to remove remaining carbon deposits.

Inspection

1. Inspect the cylinder bores for cracks or deep grooves. Deep grooves or cracks in the cylinder bores usually cannot be cleaned by honing the cylinder. Replace the cylinder block or have a sleeve installed if the damage is excessive. Contact a reputable marine dealership or machine shop to locate a source for block sleeving.
2. Inspect the mating surfaces of the engine, exhaust cover, water jacket and crankcase covers for cracks, excessive corrosion, scratches or other damage.
3. White powder-like deposits in the combustion chamber usually means that water is entering the combustion chamber. Inspect the cylinder walls and cylinder head thoroughly for cracks if this type of deposit is noted. Inspect the cylinder head gasket for discolored areas indicating leakage. Replace any defective or suspect components.
4. Inspect all bolt holes for cracks, corrosion or damaged threads. Use a thread tap to clean the threads of corrosion or sealant. Pay particular attention to the cylinder head bolt holes.
5. Clean and inspect all bolts, nuts and washers for the engine. Replace any fasteners with damaged threads or a stretched appearance. The price of the bolt and/or nut is far less than the cost of repairing the damage that results if it fails.
6. Replace the locating pins or dowels (**Figure 128**) if damaged.
7. Use compressed air to blow any debris from all passages in the cylinder block.

NOTE
The cylinder block and crankcase cover are a matched assembly. Replace the entire assembly if either portion requires replacement.

Pistons and connecting rods

1. Inspect the pistons for eroded surfaces at the edge of the dome, cracks near the ring grooves, cracks or missing portions in the piston dome.

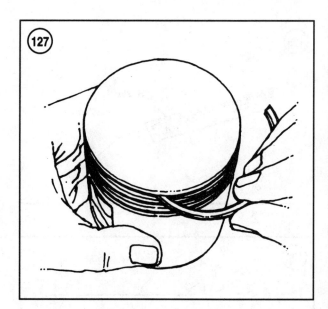

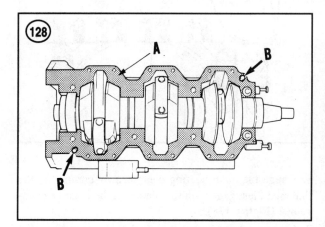

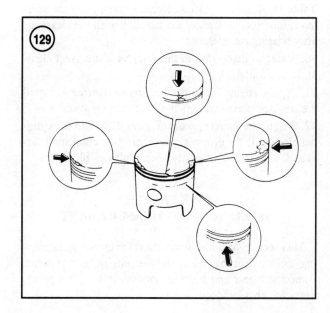

BASE ENGINE 361

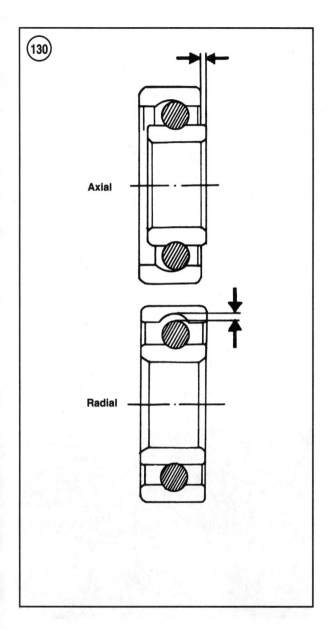

130

Axial

Radial

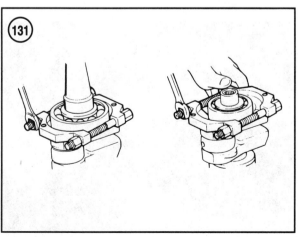

131

2. Inspect for erosion in the ring groove and scoring or scuffing on the piston skirt (**Figure 129**).

3. Inspect the piston pin for worn or damaged areas. Inspect the lockring groove for damaged areas. Replace the piston if any of these are noted.

4. Replace the connecting rod(s) if bent or has discolored, excessively worn or damaged bearing surfaces.

Thrust Bearing

Replace the thrust bearing (**Figure 123**) if there are worn, discolored or rough surfaces.

Crankshaft

NOTE
Some minor surface corrosion, glaze-like deposits or minor scratches can be cleaned with crocus cloth or 320-grit carburundum. Polish the surfaces enough to remove the deposits. Excessive use can remove a considerable amount of material from the connecting rod and crankshaft surfaces.

1. Inspect the crankshaft bearing surfaces for cracks, corrosion etching, bluing or discolored appearance. Also check for rough or irregular surfaces or transferred bearing material.

2. Replace the crankshaft if any of these defects are noted. Grinding the crankshaft and installing undersize bearings is not recommended.

3. Use compressed air and blow any debris from any passages in the crankshaft.

4. On models so equipped, remove the ball bearings from the crankshaft only if excessive play or rough operation is noted. The removal process will damage the bearing. Replace the bearing if it is removed.

5. Grasp the bearing and move it to check for axial and radial play (**Figure 130**). Rotate it while applying axial and radial load. Replace the bearing if play or rough operation is noted.

Crankcase ball bearing removal and installation

1. Use a universal bearing separator and a press to remove the bearing from the crankshaft or balancer shaft.

2. Install the separator over the ball bearing and snug the clamping nuts (**Figure 131**). Use a block to protect the crankshaft end.

3. Place the separator on a press. Support the crankshaft as you press the bearing from the crankshaft (**Figure 132**).

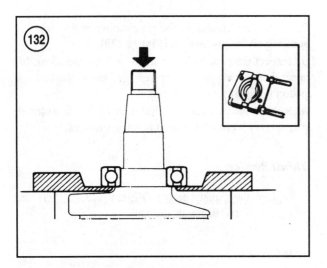

4. Use a section of pipe or tubing to press the new bearing onto the crankshaft. The tubing selected must contact only the inner surfaces of the bearing (**Figure 133**).
5. Support the crankshaft and press the bearing onto the crankshaft until fully seated.

Crankshaft gear removal and installation

Remove the gear from the crankshaft (**Figure 134**) only if it needs to be replaced. Replace the gear if there are worn, damaged or missing teeth. . Refer to *Gear Selection* in this section.

1. Refer to *Pulley Removal and Installation* in this chapter for information on the crankshaft holding tool.
2. Install the tool on the flywheel mounting surface as indicated.
3. Carefully bend the staked portion of the nut away from the notch on the crankshaft (**Figure 135**). Remove the nut and pull the gear from the crankshaft with a suitable puller. Discard the nut.
4. Refer to *Gear Selection* in this chapter and select the proper gear for the cylinder block.
5. Carefully align the gear splines with the splines on the crankshaft. Tap the gear into position.
6. Install a new nut and tighten it to the specifications listed in **Table 1**.
7. Using a center punch, stake the nut into the notch of the crankshaft as shown in **Figure 135**.

Gear selection

1. Locate the numbers stamped into the cylinder block near the mounting surface (**Figure 136**). The last digit of the number identifies the gear that must be used with this particular cylinder block.

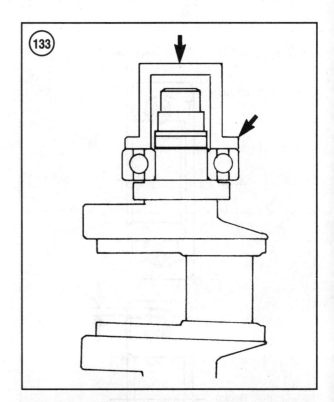

BASE ENGINE

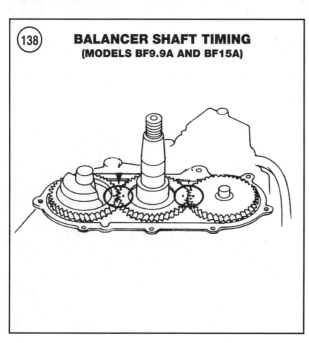

BALANCER SHAFT TIMING
(MODELS BF9.9A AND BF15A)

2. Locate the color spot on the gear (**Figure 137**). Install a gear with the part number and color spot indicated.
    a. If the cylinder block code is 1, install a gear with a yellow spot (part No. 23413-ZV5-000).
    b. If the cylinder block code is 2, install a gear with a blue spot (part No. 23412-ZV5-000).
    c. If the cylinder block code is 3, install a gear with a white spot (part No. 23411ZV5-000).

Balancer Shaft Removal, Inspection and Installation (Models BF9.9A and BF15A)

Crankshaft driven balancer shafts (**Figure 100**) are used on models BF9.9A and BF15A. Remove them after removing the top cover (**Figure 100**). Replace the balancer shaft if there are cracked, worn or missing gear teeth. Refer to *Crankshaft* in this chapter for information on inspection, removal and installation of the ball bearing. Use a slide hammer to remove the ball bearings from the cylinder block or top cover and replace if required. Install the bearings by carefully tapping them into their respective bores. Install the balancer shafts after the crankcase is installed. Align the timing marks on the balancer shafts with the marks on the crankshaft as shown in **Figure 138**.

Balancer Shaft Removal, Inspection and Installation (Models BF115A and BF130A)

Belt-driven balancer shafts (**Figure 104**) are used on models BF115A and BF130A. They are supported with bearings pressed into their respective bores in the cylinder block. Removal and installation of these bearings require special tools and equipment. Have a reputable machine shop remove and install these bearing if required.

1. Remove the balancer shaft covers from the top of the cylinder block (**Figure 104**).
2. Carefully pull the balancer shafts from the cylinder block. Remove and discard any O-ring or gasket.
3. Mark gear relationship to the pulley and remove the gear and thrust washers from the balancer shaft housing.
4. Replace any components if there are worn, cracked or damaged areas.
5. Replace the bearings in the balancer shaft bore if they are worn, rough or damaged.
6. Lubricate both balancer shafts with engine oil. Install new O-rings and gaskets as required and carefully slide the balancer shafts into the cylinder block.
7. Install the gear and thrust washer into the balancer shaft housing. Ensure it is timed to the pulley using the marks made prior to removal.

364

8. Mate the balancer shaft covers, housings and gears to the cylinder block. Install the mounting bolts and securely tighten them.
9. Refer to *Timing Belt Removal and Installation* in this chapter to install the balancer drive belt.

Intake Manifold

Refer to **Figure 139** for this procedure.
1. Loosen the mounting bolts, nuts and washers and carefully remove the intake manifold from the engine.
2. Remove and discard all gaskets and O-rings.
3. Clean any debris or contamination from the mating surfaces.
4. Install new gaskets, O-rings and seals as required.
5. Mount the intake manifold on the base engine. Starting with the center fasteners and working outward, securely tighten the mounting bolts, nuts and washers to the specification listed in **Table 1**.

Camshaft

Refer to *Cylinder Head Component Inspection and Measurement* in this chapter for procedures to inspect and measure the camshaft on all models.

On models BF50 and BF5A, inspect the compression relief mechanism (**Figure 140**) for worn or damaged springs and weights and replace as needed.

Measuring the Components

Specialized measuring equipment is used to perform these measurements. Have a reputable marine repair shop or machine shop perform the measurements, if you do not have the proper equipment or are unfamiliar with them.

All components must be clean and dry before measuring.

Crankshaft rod journal clearance

1. Using an outside micrometer, measure the diameter of the crankshaft connecting rod journal (**Figure 141**) at the No. 1 cylinder connecting rod contact surface. Record your measurements.
2. Measure the crankshaft connecting rod journal diameters for all remaining cylinders. Compare your measurements with the specifications listed in **Table 10**.
3. Replace the crankshaft if any of the measurements are less than the listed specifications.
4. Using an outside micrometer, measure the diameter of the main journals (**Figure 142**).

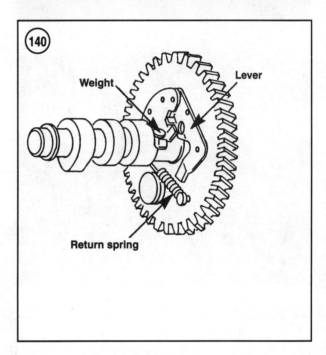

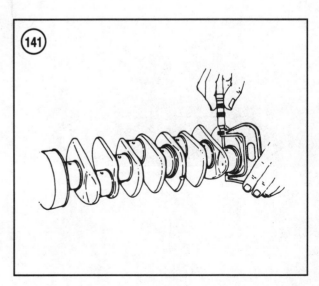

BASE ENGINE

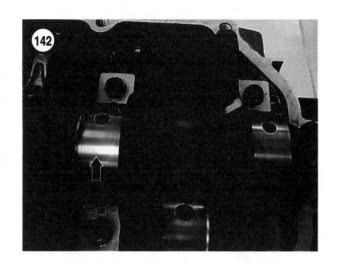

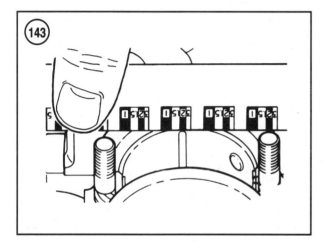

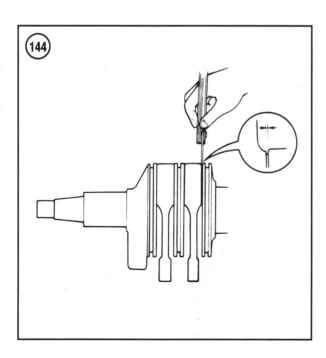

5. Compare your measurements with the specifications listed in **Table 10**. Replace the crankshaft if any measurement is less than the listed specification.

Connecting rod bearing clearance

1. Secure the crankshaft into a vise using soft jaws.

2. Install the selected bearings into the dry and clean surfaces of the connecting rod and rod cap for No. 1 cylinder.

3. Place the connecting rod onto the No. 1 crankshaft connecting rod journal. Make sure the marks on the connecting rod face the same direction as noted prior to removal.

4. Place a section of Plastigage on the crankshaft connecting rod journal surface as indicated (**Figure 143**). Install the rod cap in the position as noted prior to removal.

5. Without rotating the connecting rod on the crankshaft, tighten the connecting rod, bolts or nuts to the specifications listed in **Table 1**.

6. Loosen the fasteners and carefully remove the rod cap from the connecting rod.

7. Use the marking on the Plastigage envelope to measure the width of the flattened Plastigage. The width indicates the connecting rod bearing clearance. Record the measured clearance for each connecting rod.

8. Refer to *Connecting Rod Side Clearance* in this section and perform the measurements as applicable.

9. Remove the connecting rod from the crankshaft. Repeat these steps for all remaining connecting rods.

10. Compare your measurements with the specifications listed in **Table 10**. Refer to *Bearing Selection* in this chapter if any of the clearances are not within the listed specification. Perform these measurements after selecting different bearings.

Connecting rod side clearance

1. Use feeler gauges to measure the distance from the side of the connecting rod to the thrust surface on the crankshaft at the points indicated in **Figure 144**.

2. Record the thickness of the feeler gauge that passes between the components with a slight drag.

3. Compare your measurements with the specification listed in **Table 10**.

4. Replace the connecting rod if the measurements are not within the specification and measure again. Replace the crankshaft if the measurements are still beyond the listed specification.

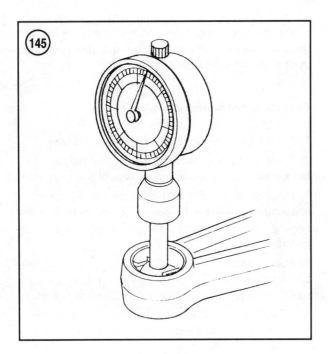

Pistons and connecting rods

1. Using an inside micrometer measure the diameter of the piston pin bore (**Figure 145**) in the connecting rod. Record the measurement and repeat for all remaining connecting rods.

2. Compare your measurements with the specification listed in **Table 9**. Replace any connecting rod with measurements greater than the listed specification.

3. Using an outside micrometer, measure the diameter of the piston at a point 90° from the piston pin bore and 10.0 mm (0.40 in.) from the bottom of the skirt (**Figure 146**).

4. Compare the measurement to the specification listed in **Table 8**.

5. Use an inside micrometer to measure the piston pin bore diameter at both sides of the piston as shown in **Figure 147**. Compare the measurements with the specification listed in **Table 8**. Record your measurements and repeat the measurements for the remaining pistons.

6. Replace the piston and piston pin if your measurements are beyond the listed specification.

7. Measure the piston pin diameter at the piston and rod contact areas as shown in **Figure 148**.

8. Compare the measurement with the specifications listed in **Table 8**. Measure and record the measurements for all piston pins in the engine.

9. Replace the piston and piston pin if the respective piston pin measurements are beyond the listed specifications.

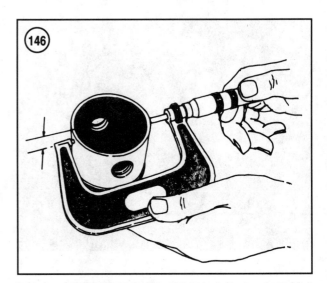

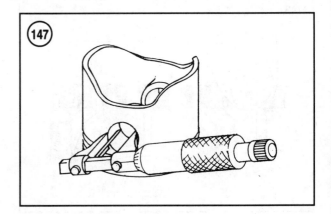

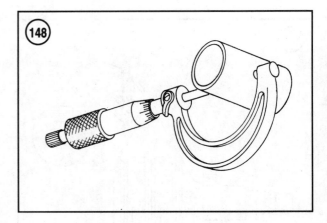

Piston ring side clearance

Refer to *Piston and Connecting Rod Disassembly and Assembly* in this chapter to install and remove the piston rings.

1. Carefully spread and install new rings onto the piston.

BASE ENGINE

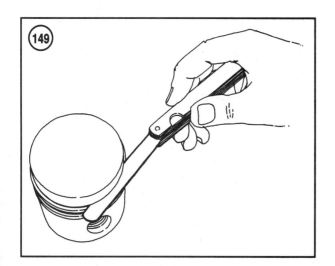

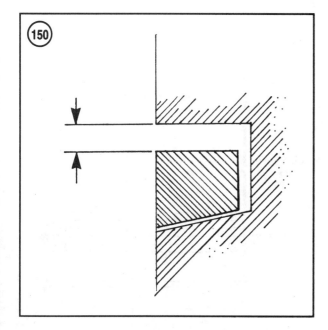

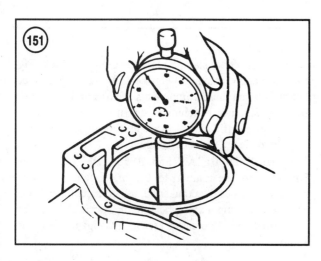

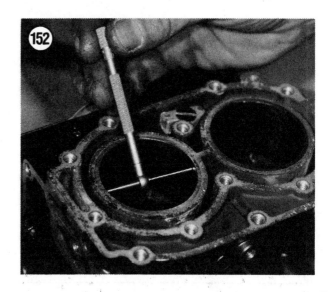

2. Using feeler gauges, measure the piston ring side clearance as shown in **Figure 149**.

3. Measure and record the clearance of the top, middle and bottom piston rings. Insert the feeler gauge at the square side of the ring (**Figure 150**) for accurate measurement.

4. Remove the piston rings from the pistons.

5. Compare the measurements with the specifications listed in **Table 8**.

6. If incorrect measurements are noted, use an outside micrometer to measure the thickness of the rings. Compare your measurements with the specification listed in **Table 8**.

7. Replace the rings if your measurements are not within the listed specification.

8. Replace the piston if the clearance is not within the listed specification but the ring thickness is correct.

Cylinder Bore

1. Have the cylinder bore lightly honed at a qualified marine repair or machine shop before taking any measurements. Additional honing may be required if the cylinders are glazed or aluminum deposits are present. Clean the cylinder block as described in this chapter.

2. Use either a dial type cylinder bore gauge (**Figure 151**) or spring-type cylinder bore gauge (**Figure 152**) to measure the cylinder bore. Take the measurements near the top, bottom and middle of the cylinder bore (**Figure 153**) and then at 90° apart at all three depths as shown in **Figure 153**. Record all measurements.

3. Compare the measurements with the specification listed in **Table 7**. Replace the cylinder block or have the

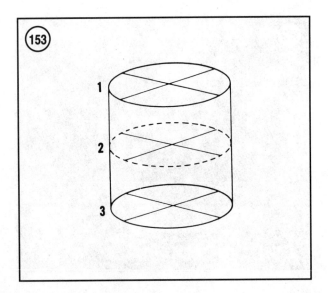

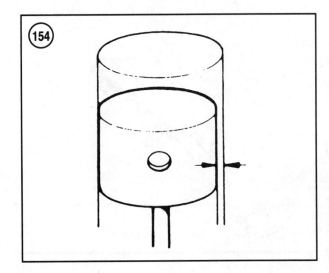

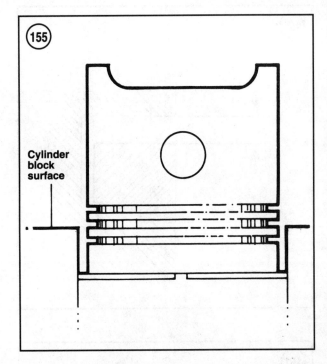

block sleeved if any of your measurements exceed the specification listed in **Table 7**.

4. Subtract the piston diameter from the smallest bore diameter for a given cylinder. The calculation indicates the piston clearance (**Figure 154**). Compare the clearance with the specification listed in **Table 7**.

Piston Ring End Gap

1. Measure the ring gap for all rings and cylinders after the cylinder bore and piston diameters are correct.
2. Carefully compress and install the ring into the top of the bore.
3. Use a piston (without rings) and slowly push the *new* ring (**Figure 155**) to the depth of approximately 20.0 mm (0.79 in.) below the top of the bore.
4. Use a feeler gauge to measure the ring end gap when the ring is installed into the cylinder bore (**Figure 156**).
5. Compare the measurement with the specification listed in **Table 8**. For some models a normal ring gap is listed along with a limit. Try a different (new) ring if the measurements are not within the specification.
6. Repeat the cylinder bore measurements and/or verify that the correct rings are being used if the measurements are still incorrect.
7. Make certain the rings are tagged or marked to ensure they are installed onto the correct piston and into the proper cylinder bore on assembly.

Bearing Selection

Bearing selection is required when replacing the insert-type bearings for the crankshaft or cylinder block.

Numbers or letters stamped into the cylinder block (**Figure 157**) and crankshaft (**Figure 158**) are used to select bearings when these components are assembled. Correct bearing clearance is achieved, assuming all components are within specification. Always use Plastigage during assembly to ensure proper clearances.

Models BF20, BF2A, BF50, BF50A, BF75, BF8A and BF100 do not use numbers for bearing selection. On these models, measure the crankshaft and connecting rods and replace any component(s) beyond the specifications. Verify correct bearing clearances with Plastigage during assembly.

BASE ENGINE

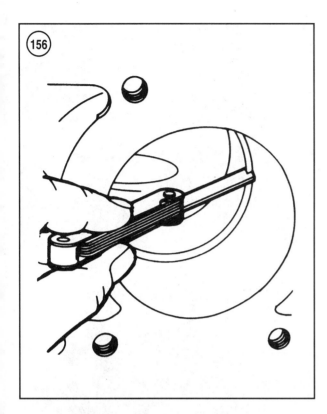

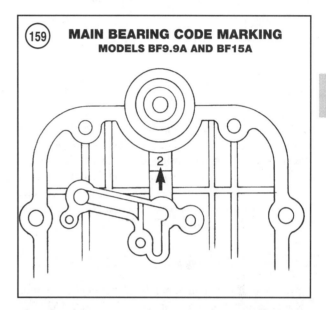

Models BF9.9A and BF15A use numbers stamped into the cylinder block (**Figure 159**) and crankshaft (**Figure 160**) to allow selection of the main bearings for the crankshaft. Numbers are not listed for selecting bearings for the connecting rod bearings. On these models, measure the crankshaft and connecting rods and replace any component(s) that exceed the specification. Verify correct bearing clearance with Plastigage during assembly.

Using the numbers or letters, refer to **Table 11** to determine the bearings to use. Bearings are identified by a color stained on the side surface. Order replacement bearings by color code from a Honda dealership.

Crankshaft main bearings

On models BF9.9A and BF15A, record the number on the cylinder block (**Figure 159**) and the number on the crankshaft (**Figure 160**). Using the recorded numbers, refer to **Table 11** to determine the color code of the bearings to use for each journal.

On all other models, record the first number, letter or color spot on the crankshaft (**Figure 161**). This indicates the crankshaft main bearing code for the No. 1 or top main bearing journal. The second number, letter or color spot indicates the No. 2 main bearing journal and so on. Record the number, letter or color spot for each journal on the crankshaft.

Note the first number or letter stamped into the cylinder block near the mounting surface (**Figure 162**). This indi-

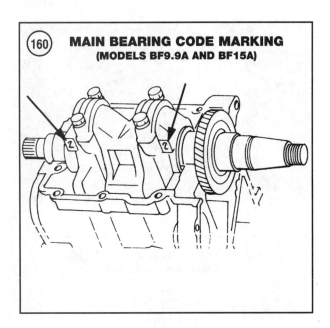

cates the cylinder block main bearing code for the No. 1 or top main bearing journal. The second number or letter indicates the No. 2 main bearing journal and so on. Record the number or letter for each journal on the crankshaft.

Using the recorded numbers, letters or color spots, refer to **Table 11** to determine the color code of the bearing to use for each individual journal.

Connecting rod bearings

Note and record the first number, letter or color spot on the crankshaft at the point indicated in **Figure 163**. This indicates the crankshaft rod bearing code for the No. 1 or top connecting rod. The second number, letter or color spot indicates crankshaft rod bearing code for the No. 2 connecting rod and so on. Record the number, letter or color spot for each connecting rod surface.

Note and record the number stamped into the side of the connecting rod (**Figure 164**). This number indicates the connecting rod bearing code for the selected connecting rod. Record the number for each connecting rod and its journal number.

Using the recorded numbers, letters or color spots, refer to **Table 12** to determine the color code of the bearing to use for each individual connecting rod.

Cylinder Block Assembly

Clean the cylinder block thoroughly after the honing process to remove any contamination. Use hot, soapy water under pressure. Do not use solvent. Use compressed air to dry the cylinder block. Wipe the cylinder bores with a

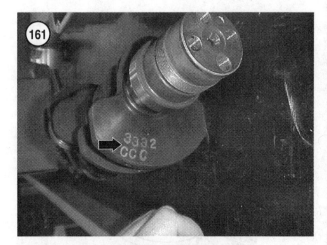

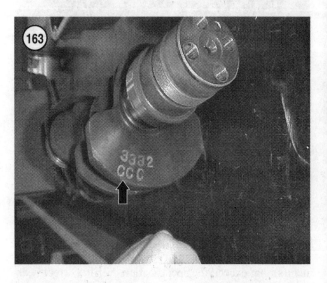

white shop towel. The cleaning process is complete when the towel is clean after wiping the cylinder bores. To prevent corrosion, thoroughly coat the cylinder bores with

BASE ENGINE

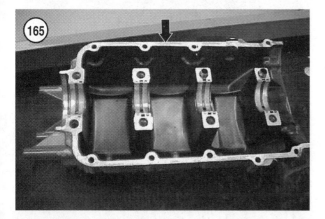

engine oil or its equivalent immediately after the cleaning process.

Ensure that all crankcase-to-cylinder block alignment pins are in position. Clean all debris from the cylinder block to crankcase mating surfaces (**Figure 165**). Install all removed seals (**Figure 166**) with the seal lips facing in or as noted prior to removing them. Use a section of tub-

ing to carefully push seals in position. Coat all seal lips with water-resistant grease prior to installing them.

Refer to **Figures 97-104** during assembly to assist with component location and orientation. Lubricate all internal components with engine oil on assembly.

1. Refer to *Crankshaft Removal and Installation* in this chapter and install the crankshaft into the cylinder block.
2. On models so equipped, refer to *Balancer Shaft Removal and Installation* in this chapter and install the balancer shafts.
3. Refer to *Piston and Connecting Rod Removal and Installation* in this chapter and install each piston and rod into the cylinder block.
4. Refer to *Crankcase/Crankcase Cover Installation* in this chapter and install the crankcase/cover to the cylinder block.
5. On models BF20 and BF2A, refer to *Valve Components Removal and Installation* in this chapter and install the valves and springs into the cylinder block.
6. Refer to *Water Jackets and Thermostats* in this chapter and install all water jackets and thermostats onto the cylinder block.
7. Refer to Chapter Four and install the oil filter, if so equipped. Fill the engine with the proper oil after installing the engine.
8. Refer to *Cylinder Head Removal, Repair And Installation* in this chapter and install the cylinder head on the cylinder block.
9. Install the timing belt tensioner, all pulleys and lower timing belt covers on models so equipped following the procedures listed in this chapter.
10. Refer to Chapter Seven and install all applicable electrical and ignition components onto the engine.
11. Refer to Chapter Six and install all applicable fuel system components from the engine.
12. Install any remaining clamps, hoses, switches or brackets onto the engine.

Crankcase Cover Installation

1. On models BF20 and BF2A, carefully install the lubrication wheel, thrust washer and shaft into their bore in the crankcase.
2. On models BF50 and BF5A, lubricate the pressure relief valve and slide it into its bore in the cylinder block. Install the spring and cover for the valve. Install the oil pickup tube/screen and securely tighten the fastener.
3. Make sure all thrust bearings or spacers are installed in the position noted prior to removing them.
4. On models BF20, BF2A, BF50 and BF5A, install a new gasket on the cylinder block-to-crankcase mating

surface. On all other models, apply a *very light* coat of liquid gasket compound (Three Bond No. 1141C) to the areas of the crankcase/crankcase cover that directly contact the cylinder block (**Figure 167**). Do not allow the liquid gasket to contact any other surfaces.

5. Carefully install the crankcase cover on the cylinder block. Install the bolts, washers and nuts at the locations noted prior to removing them. Tighten them in sequence hand tight only.

6. Rotate the crankshaft to ensure smooth movement of the internal components. Remove the crankcase cover and check for improperly installed components if any binding or rough rotation is noted. Do not complete the assembly until the cause of the binding or rough rotation is corrected.

7. Torque the crankcase cover bolts/washer and nuts in three steps to the specification listed in **Table 1**. Be sure to follow the torque sequence listed in **Figures 97-104.**

8. On models BF9.9A and BF15A, install a new gasket and install the top cover (2, **Figure 100**) onto the cylinder block. Make sure the balancer shafts enter the bearings in the top cover. Install the fasteners and tighten them in sequence to the specification listed in **Table 1**. Install the breather/vent housing (10, **Figure 100**) with a new gasket on the cylinder block. Securely tighten the mounting bolts.

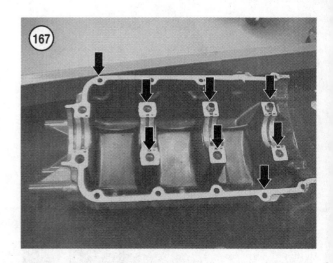

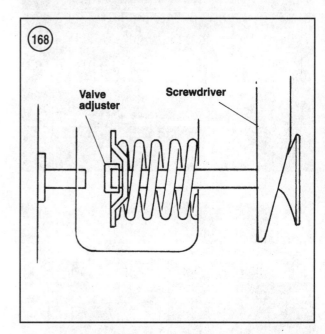

Valve Components Removal and Installation (Models BF20 and BF2A)

This section has valve removal and installation procedures for models BF20 and BF2A. Refer to *Cylinder Head Removal, Repair and Installation* in this chapter for valve removal and installation on all other models.

1. Refer to *Valve Adjustment* in Chapter Four and remove the lifter cover from the cylinder block.
2. Refer to *Cylinder Head Removal and Installation* in this chapter and remove the cylinder head.
3. Rotate the crankshaft until one of the valves is fully open. Use a blunt screwdriver to hold the valve open (**Figure 168**) and rotate the crankshaft 180° clockwise (as viewed from the flywheel). Carefully pry the valve adjuster (**Figure 168**) from the valve stem.
4. Install a valve spring compressor (1, **Figure 169**) or modified C-clamp to contact the valve spring cap (5, **Figure 169**).
5. Ensure the clamp contacts the center of the valve, then slowly tighten the valve spring compressor or clamp until the valve spring (4, **Figure 169**) is collapsed.
6. Using needle nose pliers, carefully remove the valve spring cap (5, **Figure 169**) from the valve spring.

7. Release the tension on the valve spring compressor or clamp. Carefully remove the valve and spring from the cylinder block.

8. Refer to *Cylinder Head Removal and Installation* in this chapter and inspect, repair or replace any worn or defective components.

9. Installation is the reverse of removal noting:

   a. Install components in the location noted prior to removal.

   b. Ensure that the valve spring cap in centered onto the valve spring and valve stem groove on assembly (**Figure 170**).

10. Refer to Chapter Four and adjust the valve clearance.

BASE ENGINE

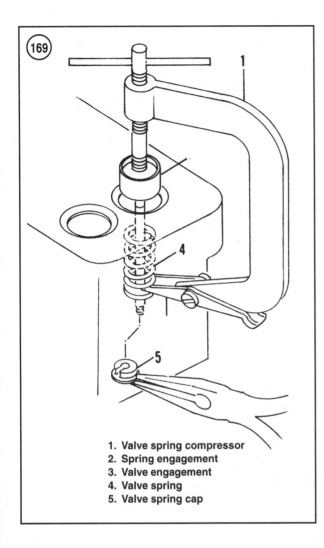

1. Valve spring compressor
2. Spring engagement
3. Valve engagement
4. Valve spring
5. Valve spring cap

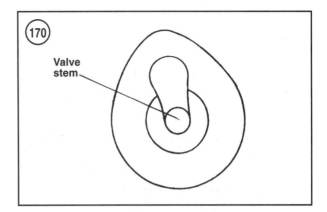

11. Refer to *Cylinder Head Removal and Installation* in this chapter and install the cylinder head to the cylinder block.

PRIMARY GEARCASE REPAIR

Primary gearcase repair is only required on models BF35A, BF40A, BF45A and BF50A. The major components of the primary gearcase (**Figure 171**) include the gearcase/mounting bracket, drive shaft seals, gear and ball bearing. Repairs involve replacing the gear, bearing or seals and cleaning debris from the gearcase/mounting bracket. Remove the engine to access the components.

1. Mark the up side of the gear. Pull the gear from the gearcase/mounting bracket ball bearing. Replace the gear if it has worn, cracked, or missing teeth.
2. Inspect the ball bearing. Do not remove the ball bearing unless it needs to be replaced. Remove the ball bearing from the housing with a slide hammer.
3. Clean all debris from the housing. Dry all components with compressed air.
4. If replacement is required, record the seal depth and seal lip direction then, carefully drive the seals from their location below the ball bearing.
5. Position the seals in their bore with the seal lips facing the direction noted prior to removing them. Use a section of tubing to carefully push the new seals into their bores. Make sure the seals reach the depth noted prior to removing them.
6. Use a section of tubing to carefully tap the new ball bearing fully into its bore in the gearcase/mounting bracket. The tubing must contact only the outer race of the ball bearing.
7. Carefully slide the gear into the ball bearing with the up side facing up, as noted prior to removal.

BREAK-IN PROCEDURE

During the first few hours of running, many of the components of the engine need to avoid full load until wear patterns are established. To ensure a reliable and durable repair, perform the break-in procedures anytime internal components of the base engine are replaced.

Full break-in is achieved in approximately 10 hours of running time. Increased oil consumption can be expected during this period. Refer to Chapter Four and check the oil level frequently during break-in. Check the tightness of all external fasteners after completing the break-in procedure.

Follow the break-in procedure as indicated:

Allow the engine to run at idle speed for the first 15 minutes of running.

For the next 45 minutes of running, do not allow the engine to exceed 2,500 rpm or one-quarter throttle. Avoid running the engine for extended periods of time in neutral gear during the first hour.

During the second hour of running, advance the throttle to a maximum of three-quarter throttle to get the boat on plane. Immediately reduce the throttle to two-third or less. During this second hour, run the engine at varying throttle openings. Occasionally advance the throttle to wide open for one minute or less. Do not operate the engine for extended periods of time at full throttle.

During the next eight hours of operation the throttle can be advanced to wide open for up to five minutes. Run the engine at three-quarter throttle or less for a few minutes after reaching full speed to allow the engine to cool.

Table 1 TIGHTENING TORQUE

Flywheel nut	
BF20, BF2A	45-55 N•m (33-41 ft.-lb.)
BF50, BF5A	70-80 N•m (52-59 ft.-lb.)
BF75, BF8A, BF100	65 N•m (48 ft.-lb.)
BF9.9A, BF15A	25 N•m (18 ft.-lb.)
BF20A, BF25, BF30	115 N•m (85 ft.-lb.)
BF35A, BF40A,	66 N•m (49 ft.-lb.)
BF45A, BF50A, BF75A, BF90A	103 N•m (76 ft.-lb.)
BF115A, BF130A	
12 mm bolt	118 N•m (87 ft.-lb.)
8 mm bolt	32 N•m (24 ft.-lb.)
Connecting rod bolt/nut	
BF20, BF2A	4-6 N•m (35-53 in.-lb.)
BF50, BF5A	11-13 N•m (97-115 in.-lb.)
BF75, BF8A, BF100	10 N•m (89 in.-lb.)
BF9.9A, BF15A	12 N•m (106 in.-lb.)
BF20A, BF25A, BF30A	24 N•m (17 ft.-lb.)
BF35A, BF40A, BF45A, BF50A	28 N•m (21 ft.-lb.)
BF75A, BF90A	31 N•m (23 ft.-lb.)
BF115A, BF130A	20 N•m (15 ft.-lb.)*
Timing pulley nut	
BF75, BF8A, BF100	23.0 N•m (16.0 ft.-lb.)
(7.5, 8, 9.9 models)	

(continued)

BASE ENGINE

Table 1 TIGHTENING TORQUE (continued)

Cam shaft pulley bolt	
BF75, BF8A, BF100	10 N•m (89 in.-lb.)
(7.5, 8, 9.9 hp models)	
BF9.9A, BF15A	25 N•m (18 ft.-lb.)
BF20A, BF25, BF30A	65 N•m (48 ft.-lb.)
BF35A, BF40A, BF45, BF50A	130 N•m (96 ft.-lb.)
BF75A, BF90A	56 N•m (41 ft.-lb.)
(75, 90 hp models)	
Crankshaft pulley bolt	
BF115A, BF130A	245 N•m (181 ft.-lb.)
Oil pump to cylinder block/cylinder head	
BF75, BF8A, BF100	9 N•m (80 in.-lb.)
BF20, BF25, BF30A	13.0 N•m (115 in.-lb.)
BF35A, BF40A, BF45, BF50A	13.0 N•m (115 in.-lb.)
BF75A and BF90A	
6 mm bolt	12 N•m (106 in.-lb.)
8 mm bolt	26 N•m (19 ft.-lb.)
Oil pump cover to flywheel cover/oil pump housing	
BF115A, BF130A	7 N•m (62 in.-lb.)
Base engine-to-drive shaft housing	
BF20, BF2A	11 N•m (97 in.-lb.)
BF50, BF5A	11 N•m (97 in.-lb.)
BF75, BF8A, BF100	10 N•m (89 in.-lb.)
All other models	39 N•m (29 ft.-lb.)
Drive gear (on lower end of crankshaft)	
BF35A, BF40A, BF45A, BF50A	92 N•m (68 ft.-lb.)
Tensioner adjusting nut	
All models	44 N•m (32 ft.-lb.)
Cylinder head-to-cylinder block	
BF20, BF2A	8-12 N•m (71-106 in.-lb.)
BF50, BF5A	22-28 N•m (16-21 ft.-lb.)
BF75, BF8A, BF100	22 N•m (16 ft.-lb.)
BF9.9A, BF15A	26 N•m (19 ft.-lb.)
BF20A, BF25A, BF30A	29 N•m (21 ft.-lb.)*
BF35A, BF40A, BF45, BF50A	
8 mm bolts	27 N•m (20 ft.-lb.)
10 mm bolts	38 N•m (28 ft.-lb.)*
BF75A, BF90A	
8 mm bolts	26 N•m (19 ft.-lb.)
10 mm bolts	69 N•m (51 ft.-lb.)
BF115A and BF130A	44 N•m (32 ft.-lb.)**
Crankcase to cylinder block fasteners	
BF20, BF2A	9-12 N•m (80-106 in.-lb.)
BF50, BF5A	22-28 N•m (16-21 ft.-lb.)
BF75, BF8A, BF100	
6 mm bolt	11 N•m (97 in.-lb.)
8 mm bolt	23 N•m (17 ft.-lb.)
BF9.9A, BF15A	
6 mm bolt	11 N•m (97 in.-lb.)
8 mm bolt	22 N•m (16 ft.-lb.)
BF20A, BF25A and BF30A	
6 mm bolt	12 N•m (106 in.-lb.)
8 mm bolt	29 N•m (21 ft.-lb.)*
(continued)	

Table 1 TIGHTENING TORQUE (continued)

Crankcase to cylinder block fasteners (continued)	
BF35A, BF40A, BF45A and BF50A	
6 mm bolt	11 N•m (97 in.-lb.)
8 mm bolt	28 N•m (21 in.-lb.)*
BF75A and BF90A	
8 mm bolt	26 N•m (19 ft.-lb.)
10 mm bolt	25 N•m (18 ft.-lb.)*
BF115A and BF130A	
131 mm length bolt	51 N•m (38 ft.-lb.)
40 mm length bolt	47 N•m (35 ft.-lb.)
55 mm length bolt	39 N•m (29 ft.-lb.)
Balancer shaft covers-to-cylinder block	
BF115A and BF130A	
Port side shaft cover	25 N•m (18 ft.-lb.)
Balancer shaft covers-to-cylinder block	
Starboard side shaft cover	25 N•m (18 ft.-lb.)
Water jacket/cover and thermostat cover	
All models	12 N•m (106 in.-lb.)
Intake manifold	
BF20A, BF25A, BF30A	12 N•m (106 in.-lb.)
BF35A, BF40A, BF45A, BF50A	12 N•m (106 in.-lb.)
BF 75A, BF90A	26 N•m (19 ft.-lb.)
BF115A, BF130A	
Bolt	29 N•m (21 ft.-lb.)
Nut	39 N•m (29 ft.-lb.)
Standard torque	
5mm bolt/nut	4-7 N•m (35-62 in.-lbs)
6mm bolt/nut	8-12 N•m (70-106 in.-lbs.)
8mm bolt/nut	20-28 N•m (15-21 ft.-lbs,)
10 mm bolt/nut	35-40 N•m (26-30 ft.-lbs.)

*Tighten to specification, then tighten an additional 90 degrees.
**Tighten to specification, then tighten an additional 180 degrees.

Table 2 CYLINDER HEAD SPECIFICATIONS

Model	Standard diameter mm (in.)	Wear limit mm (in.)
Maximum allowable warpage		
All models	–	0.100 mm (0.0394 in.)
Valve guide bore diameter		
BF20, BF2A	5.500 mm (0.2165 in.)	5.560mm (0.2188 in.)
BF50, BF5A		
Intake valve	5.500 mm (0.2165 in.)	5.540 mm) (0.2181 in.)
Exhaust valve	5.500 mm (0.2165 in.)	5.570 mm (0.2192 in.)
BF75, BF8A, BF100	5.500-5.512 mm (0.2165-0.2170 in.)	5.40mm (0.2181 in.)

(continued)

Table 2 CYLINDER HEAD SPECIFICATIONS (continued)

Model	Standard diameter mm (in.)	Wear limit mm (in.)
Valve guide bore diameter (continued)		
9.9A and BF15A		
Intake	5.500 mm (0.2165 in.)	5.540 mm (0.2181 in.)
Exhaust	5.500 mm (0.2165 in.)	5.570 mm (0.2192 in.)
BF20A, BF25A, BF30A		
Intake	5.500-5.512 mm (0.2165-0.2170 in.)	5.540 mm (0.2181 in.)
Exhaust	5.500-5.512 mm (0.2165-0.2170 in.)	5.540 mm (0.2181 in.)
BF35A, BF40A, BF45A, BF50A		
Intake	5.500-5.512 mm (0.2165-0.2170 in.)	5.530 mm (0.2177 in.)
Exhaust	5.500-5.512 mm (0.2165-0.2170 in.)	5.530 mm (0.2177 in.)
BF75A, BF90A		
Intake	5.500-5.512 mm (0.2165-0.2170 in.)	5.540 mm (0.2181 in.)
Exhaust	6.600-6.615 mm (0.2598-0.2604 in.)	6.640 mm (0.2614 in.)
BF115A and BF130A		
Intake	5.515-5.530 mm (0.2171-0.2177 in.)	5.550 mm (0.2185 in.)
Exhaust	5.515-5.530 mm (0.2171-0.2177 in.)	5.550 mm (0.2185 in.)
Valve guide depth		
BF20, BF2A		
Intake and exhaust	18.00 mm (0.7087 in.)	–
BF50, BF5A		
Intake	1.00 mm (0.0394 in.)	–
Exhaust	1.00 mm (0.0394 in.)	–
BF75, BF8A, BF100		
Intake	15.00 mm (0.5906 in.)	–
Exhaust	13.00 mm (0.5118 in.)	–
BF9.9A, BF15A		
Intake and exhaust	7.00 mm (0.2756 in.)	–
BF20A, BF25A, BF30A		
Intake and exhaust	7.00 mm (0.2756 in.)	–
BF35A, BF40A, BF45, BF50A		
Intake and exhaust	13.00 mm (0.5118 in.)	–
BF75A, BF90A		
Intake	17.50 mm (0.6890 in.)	–
Exhaust	15.50 mm (0.6102 in.)	–
BF115A, BF130A		
Intake	21.20 mm (0.8346 in.)	–
Exhaust	20.63 mm (0.8122 in.)	–
Valve seat width		
BF20, BF2A	0.700 mm (0.0276 in.)	1.000 mm (0.0394 in.)
BF50, BF5A	0.800 mm (0.0300 in.)	1.800 mm (0.0709 in.)
BF75, BF8A, BF100	0.700 mm (0.0276 in.)	2.000 mm (0.0787 in.)
(continued)		

Table 2 CYLINDER HEAD SPECIFICIATIONS (continued)

Model	Standard diameter mm (in.)	Wear limit mm (in.)
Valve seat width (continued)		
BF9.9, BF15	1.000 mm (0.0394 in.)	2.000 mm (0.0787 in.)
BF20A, BF25A, BF30A	0.900-1.100 mm (0.0354-0.0433 in.)	2.000 mm (0.0787 in.)
BF35A, BF40A, BF45A, BF50A	1.250 mm (0.0492 in.)	1.250 mm (0.0492 in.)
BF75A, BF90A	1.250-1.550 mm (0.0492-0.0610 in.)	2.000 mm (0.0787 in.)
BF115A and BF130A	1.250-1.550 mm (0.0492-0.0610 in.)	2.000 mm (0.0787 in.)

Table 3 VALVE SPECIFICATIONS

Model	Standard mm (in.)	Wear limit mm (in.)
Valve stem diameter		
BF20, BF2A		
Intake	5.490 mm (0.2161 in.)	5.450 mm (0.2146 in.)
Exhaust	5.445 mm (0.2144 in.)	5.400 mm (0.2126 in.)
BF50, BF5A		
Intake	5.480 mm (0.2157 in.)	5.450 mm (0.2146 in.)
Exhaust	5.440 mm (0.2142 in.)	5.410 mm (0.2130 in.)
BF75, BF8A, BF100		
Intake	5.468-5.480 mm (0.2153-0.2157 in.)	5.080 mm (0.2000 in.)
BF75, BF8A, BF100		
Exhaust	5.435-5.450 mm (0.2140-0.2146 in.)	4.750 mm (0.1870 in.)
BF 9.9A, BF15A		
Intake	5.490 mm (0.2161 in.)	5.470 mm (0.2154 in.)
Exhaust	5.470 mm (0.2154 in.)	5.450 mm (0.2146 in.)
BF20A, BF25A, BF30A		
Intake	5.475-5.490 mm (0.2156-0.2161 in.)	5.450 mm (0.2146 in.)
Exhaust	5.455-5.470 mm (0.2148-0.2154 in.)	5.430 mm (0.2138 in.)
BF35A, BF40A, BF45A, BF50A		
Intake	5.480-5.490 mm (0.2157-0.2161 in.)	5.450 mm (0.2146 in.)
Exhaust	5.460-5.470 mm (0.2150-0.2154 in.)	5.420 mm (0.2134 in.)
BF75A, BF90A		
Intake	5.475-5.490 mm (0.2156-0.2161 in.)	5.450 mm (0.2146 in.)
Exhaust	6.555-6.570 mm (0.2581-0.2587 in.)	6.530 mm (0.2571 in.)
BF115A, BF130A		
Intake	5.485-5495mm (0.2159-0.2163 in.)	5.455 mm (0.2148 in.)

(continued)

Table 3 VALVE SPECIFICATIONS (continued)

Model	Standard mm (in.)	Wear limit mm (in.)
Valve stem diameter (continued)		
BF115A, BF130A (continued)		
Exhaust	5.450-5.460 mm (0.2146-0.2150 in.)	5.420 mm (0.2134 in.)
Valve guide-to-valve stem clearance		
BF50, BF5A		
Intake	0.020-0.044 mm (0.0008-0.0017 in.)	0.070 mm (0.0028 in.)
Exhaust	0.060-0.087 mm (0.0024-0.0034 in.)	0.150 mm (0.0060 in.)
BF75, BF8A, BF100		
Intake and exhaust	0.060-0.100 mm (0.0024-0.0394 in.)	–
BF9.9A, BF15A		
Intake	0.010-0.037 mm (0.00039-0.00146 in.)	0.070 mm (0.00276 in.)
Exhaust	0.030-0.057 mm (0.00118-0.00224 in.)	0.120 mm (0.00472 in.)
BF20A, BF25A, BF30A		
Intake	0.010-0.037 mm (0.00039-0.00146 in.)	0.070 mm (0.00276 in.)
Exhaust	0.030-0.057 mm (0.00118-0.00224 in.)	0.120 mm (0.00472 in.)
BF35A, BF40A, BF45A, BF50A		
Intake	0.010-0.032 mm (0.00039-0.00126 in.)	0.060 mm (0.00236 in.)
Exhaust	0.030-0.052 mm (0.00118-0.0020 in.)	0.100 mm (0.0039 in.)
BF75A, BF90A		
Intake	0.010-0.037 mm (0.00039-0.00146 in.)	0.070 mm (0.00276 in.)
Exhaust	0.030-0.060 mm (0.00118-0.00236 in.)	0.120 mm (0.00472 in.)
BF115A, BF130A		
Intake	0.020-0.045 mm (0.00078-0.00177 in.)	0.080 mm (0.00314 in.)
Exhaust	0.055-0.080 mm (0.00217-0.00315 in.)	0.120 mm (0.00472 in.)
Valve spring free length		
BF20, BF2A	27.100 mm (1.0669 in.)	25.000 mm (0.9843 in.)
BF50, BF5A	29.600 mm (1.1654 in.)	*
BF75, BF8A, BF100	28.900 mm (1.1378 in.)	27.400 mm (1.0787 in.)
BF9.9A, BF15A	36.800 mm (1.4488 in.)	36.300 mm (1.4291 in.)
BF20A, BF25A, BF30A	36.800 mm (1.4488 in.)	35.300 mm (1.3898 in.)
BF35A, BF40A, BF45A, BF50A, BF75A, BF90A	36.900 mm (1.4528 in.)	34.500 mm (1.3583 in.)
Intake	46.000 mm (1.8110 in.)	*
Inner exhaust	41.700 mm (1.6417 in.)	*
Outer exhaust	44.100 mm (1.7362 in.)	*

(continued)

Table 3 VALVE SPECIFICATIONS (continued)

Model	Standard mm (in.)	Wear limit mm (in.)
Valve spring free length (continued)		
BF115A, BF130A		
Intake	53.660 mm (2.1260 in.)	*
Exhaust	55.580 mm (2.1882 in.)	*

* Minimum length limits are not provided for this model. Replace the spring when measurements are less than the standard length.

Table 4 ROCKER ARM/SHAFT SPECIFICATIONS

	Standard mm (in.)	Wear limit mm (in.)
Rocker arm bore diameter		
BF75, BF8A, BF100	13.0-13.030 mm (0.5118-0.5130 in.)	13.060 mm (0.5142 in.)
BF9.9A, BF15A	13.0 mm (0.5118 in.)	13.040 mm (0.5134 in.)
BF20A, BF25A, BF30A	13.0-13.018 mm (0.5118-0.5125 in.)	13.040 mm (0.5134 in.)
BF35A, BF40A	14.010-14.028 mm (0.5516-0.5523 in.)	14.050 mm (0.5531 in.)
BF45A, BF50A, BF75A, BF90A	17.000-17.018 mm (0.6693-0.6700 in.)	17.040 mm (0.6708 in.)
BF115A, BF130A		
Intake	20.012-20.030 mm (0.7878-0.7885 in.)	*
Exhaust	18.012-18.030 mm (0.7091-0.7098 in.)	*
Rocker arm shaft diameter		
BF75, BF8A, BF100	12.947-12.968 mm (0.510-0.511 in.)	12.920 mm (0.5087 in.)
BF9.9, BF15	12.968 mm (0.5106 in.)	12.930 mm (0.5091 in.)
Rocker arm shaft diameter		
BF20A, BF25A, BF30A	12.962-12.980 mm (0.5103-0.5110 in.)	12.920 mm (0.5087 in.)
BF35A, BF40A, BF45A, BF50A	13.976-13.994 mm (0.5502-0.5509 in.)	13.950 mm (0.5492 in.)
BF75A, BF90A	16.962-16.980 mm (0.6678-0.6685 in.)	16.920 mm (0.6661 in.)
BF115A, BF130A		
Intake	19.972-19.993 mm (0.7863-0.7872 in.)	*
Exhaust	17.976-17.994 mm (0.7077-0.7084 in.)	*

*Wear limit specification not available. Replace the rocker arm or rocker arm shaft if the diameter exceeds the specification.

BASE ENGINE

Table 5 CAMSHAFT SPECIFICATIONS

	Intake lobe mm (in.)	Exhaust lobe mm (in.)
Lobe height		
BF20, BF2A	20.470-20.820 mm (0.8059-0.8197 in.)	20.470-20.820 mm (0.8059-0.8197 in.)
BF50, BF5A	27.450-27.710 mm (1.0807-1.0909 in.)	27.500-27.747 mm (1.0827-1.0924 in.)
BF75 (breaker point ignition)	22.750-23.000 mm (0.8957-0.9055 in.)	22.750-23.000 mm (0.8957-0.9055 in.)
BF75, BF8A (electronic ignition)	26.250-26.500 mm (1.0335-1.0433 in.)	22.950-23.200 mm (0.9035-0.9134 in.)
BF100 (breaker point ignition)	24.750-25.000 mm (0.9744-0.9843 in.)	24.750-25.000 mm (0.9744-0.9843 in.)
BF100 (electronic ignition)	24.950-25.200 mm (0.9823-0.9921 in.)	24.960-25.200 mm (0.9827-0.9921 in.)
BF9.9A	23.640-23.890 mm (0.9307-0.9406 in.)	23.690-23.940 mm (0.9327-0.9425 in.)
BF15A	24.210-24.470 mm (0.9531-0.9634 in.)	24.270-24.520 mm (0.9555-0.9654 in.)
BF20A, BF25A	23.843-24.313 mm (0.9387-0.9572 in.)	23.905-24.345 mm (0.9411-0.9586 in.)
BF30A	23.995-24.465 mm (0.9447-0.9632 in.)	24.056-24.496 mm (0.9471-0.9644 in.)
BF35A, BF40A, BF45A, BF50A	34.708-35.248 mm (1.3665-1.3877 in.)	34.753-35.293 mm (1.3682-1.3895 in.)
BF75A, BF90A	39.808-40.248 mm (1.5673-1.5846 in.)	39.657-40.097 (1.5613-1.5786 in.)
BF115A, BF130A	38.274-38.359 mm (1.5069-1.5102 in.)	37.651-37.756 mm (1.4823-1.4865 in.)
Camshaft journal diameter		
BF20, BF2A	12.184 mm (0.4797 in.)	12.150 mm (0.4783 in.)
BF50, BF5A		
Oil pump end	13.984 mm (0.5506 in.)	13.950 mm (0.5492 in.)
Cam gear end	20.000 mm (0.7874 in.)	19.680 mm (0.7750 in.)
BF75, BF8A, BF100	15.866-15.984 mm (0.6246-0.6293 in.)	15.916 mm (0.6266 in.)
BF9.9A, BF15A		
Oil pump end	15.984 mm (0.6293 in.)	15.950 mm (0.6280 in.)
Cam gear end	17.984 mm (0.7080 in.)	17.950 mm (0.7067 in.)
BF20A, BF25A, BF30A		
No. 1 journal	19.959-19.980 mm (0.7858-0.7866 in.)	19.930 mm (0.7846 in.)
No. 2 journal	29.939-29.960 mm (1.1787-1.1795 in.)	29.900 mm (1.1772 in.)
No. 3 journal	17.966-17.984 mm (0.7073-0.7080 in.)	17.940 mm (0.7063 in.)

(continued)

Table 5 CAMSHAFT SPECIFICATIONS (continued)

	Intake lobe mm (in.)	Exhaust lobe mm (in.)
Camshaft journal diameter (continued)		
BF35A, BF40A, BF45A, BF50A, BF75A, BF90A	22.959-22.980 mm (0.9039-0.9047 in.)	22.930 mm (0.9028 in.)
No. 1 journal	31.950-31.975 mm (1.2579-1.2589 in.)	31.930 mm (1.2571 in.)
No. 2 journal	47.930-47.955 mm (1.8870-1.8880 in.)	47.900 mm (1.8858 in.)
No. 3 journal	48.430-48.455 mm (1.9067-1.9077 in.)	48.400 mm (1.9055 in.)
No. 4 journal	48.930-48.955 mm (1.9264-1.9274 in.)	48.900 mm (1.9252 in.)
No. 5 journal	35.950-35.975 mm (1.4154-1.4163 in.)	35.930 mm (1.4146 in.)
BF115A and BF130A		
No. 1 - No. 5 journal	27.935-27.950 mm (1.0998-1.1004 in.)	*
BF20, BF2A	12.200 mm (0.4803 in.)	12.25 mm (0.4823 in.)
BF50, BF5A	14.000 mm (0.5512 in.)	14.04 mm (0.5528 in.)
BF75, BF8A, BF100	56.000 mm (2.2047 in.)	56.165 mm (2.2112 in.)
BF9.9A, BF15A	58.000 mm (2.2835 in.)	58.055 mm (2.2856 in.)
BF20A, BF25A and BF30A		
No. 1 journal	20.000-20.021 mm (0.7874-0.7882 in.)	20.050 mm (0.7894 in.)
No. 2 journal	30.000-30.025 mm (1.1811-1.1821 in.)	30.060 mm (1.1834 in.)
No. 3 journal	18.000-18.027 mm (0.7087-0.7097 in.)	18.060 mm (0.7110 in.)
BF35A, BF40A, BF45A, BF50A, BF75A, BF90A	23.000-23.021 mm (0.9055-0.9063 in.)	23.050 mm (0.9075 in.)
No. 1 journal	32.000-32.025 mm (1.2598-1.2608 in.)	32.060 mm (1.2622 in.)
No. 2 journal	48.000-48.025 mm (1.8898-1.8907 in.)	48.060 mm (1.8921 in.)
No. 3 journal	48.500-48.525 mm (1.9095-1.9104 in.)	48.560 mm (1.9118 in.)
No. 4 journal	49.000-49.025 mm (1.9291-1.9301 in.)	49.060 mm (1.9315 in.)
No. 5 journal	36.000-36.025 mm (1.4173-1.4183 in.)	36.060 mm (1.4197 in.)
BF115A, BF130A	28.000-28.024 mm (1.10236-1.1033 in.)	*
Camshaft oil clearance		
BF20, BF25A, BF30A		
No. 1 journal	0.020-0.062 mm (0.0008-0.0024 in.)	0.080 mm (0.0032 in.)
No. 2 journal	0.040-0.086 mm (0.0016-0.0034 in.)	0.110 mm (0.0043 in.)
No. 3 journal	0.016-0.061 mm (0.0006-0.0024 in.)	0.080 mm (0.0032 in.)
(continued)		

BASE ENGINE

Table 5 CAMSHAFT SPECIFICATIONS (continued)

	Intake lobe mm (in.)	Exhaust lobe mm (in.)
Camshaft oil clearance (continued)		
BF35A, BF40A, BF45A, BF50A, BF75A, BF90A	0.016-0.052 mm (0.0006-0.0020 in.)	0.070 mm (0.0028 in.)
No. 1 & 5 journals	0.025-0.075 mm (0.0010-0.0030 in.)	0.100 mm (0.0039 in.)
No. 2-4 journals	0.045-0.095 mm (0.0018-0.0037 in.)	0.120 mm (0.0047 in.)
BF115A and BF130A	0.050-0.089 mm (0.0020-0.0035 in.)	0.150 mm (0.0059 in.)
Camshaft runout		
BF20A, BF25A, BF30A	0.030 mm (0.0012 in.)	0.050 mm (0.0020 in.)
BF75A, BF90A	0.030 mm (0.0012 in.)	0.050 mm (0.0020 in.)
BF115A, BF130A	0.030 mm (0.0012 in.)	0.040 mm (0.0016 in.)

*Wear limit specifications not available. Replace the camshaft/cylinder head if the measurement exceeds specification.

Table 6 OIL PUMP SPECIFICATIONS

	Standard mm (in.)	Wear limit mm (in.)
Rotor-to-rotor clearance		
BF50, BF5A	0.150 mm (0.006 in.)	0.200 mm (0.008 in.)
BF75, BF8A, BF100	0.150 mm (0.006 in.)	0.200 mm (0.008 in.)
BF9.9A, BF15A	0.150 mm (0.006 in.)	0.200 mm (0.008 in.)
BF20A, BF25A, BF30A	0.150 mm (0.006 in.)	0.200 mm (0.008 in.)
BF35A, BF40A, BF45A, BF50A, BF75A,	0.150 mm (0.006 in.)	0.200 mm (0.008 in.)
BF75A, BF90A	0.020-0.160 mm (0.0008-0.0063 in.)	0.200 mm (0.008 in.)
BF115A, BF130A	0.040-0.160 mm (0.0016-0.0063 in.)	0.200 mm (0.008 in.)
Rotor-to-pump body clearance		
BF50, BF5A	0.150-0.210 mm (0.006-0.008 in.)	0.260 mm (0.010 in.)
BF75, BF8A, BF100	0.150 mm (0.006 in.)	0.260 mm (0.010 in.)
BF9.9A, BF15A	0.100-0.210 mm (0.004-0.008 in.)	0.260 mm (0.010 in.)
BF20A, BF25A, BF30A	0.150-0.210 mm (0.006-0.008 in.)	0.260 mm (0.010 in.)
BF35A, BF40A, BF45A, BF50A, BF75A,	0.150-0.220 mm (0.006-0.009 in.)	0.260 mm (0.010 in.)
BF75A, BF90A	0.100-0.190 mm (0.004-0.007 in.)	0.230 mm (0.009 in.)
BF115A, BF130A	0.100-0.190 mm (0.004-0.007 in.)	0.200 mm (0.008 in.)
Pump body diameter		
BF50, BF5A	23.150 (0.9114 in.)	23.200 mm (0.9134 in.)
BF75, BF8A, BF100	23.150-23.180 mm (0.9114-0.9126 in.)	23.230 mm (0.9146 in.)
BF9.9A, BF15A	29.100 mm (1.1457 in.)	29.300 mm (1.1535 in.)
BF20A, BF25A, BF30A	40.710-40.740 mm (1.6028-1.6039 in.)	40.760 mm (1.6047 in.)

(continued)

Table 6 OIL PUMP SPECIFICATIONS (continued)

	Standard mm (in.)	Wear limit mm (in.)
Pump body diameter (continued)		
BF35A, BF40A	50.150-50.180 mm (1.9744-1.9756 in.)	50.200 mm (1.9764 in.)
BF45A and BF50A, BF75A, BF90A	80.000-80.040 mm (3.1496-3.1512 in.)	80.060 mm (3.1520 in.)
BF115A, BF130A	84.000-84.030 mm (3.3071-3.3085 in.)	n/a
Pump body depth		
BF50, F5A	12.00 mm (0.4724 in.)	12.06 mm (0.4748 in.)
BF9.9A, BF15A	13.02 mm (0.5126 in.)	13.08 mm (0.5150 in.)
BF20A, BF25A, BF30A	15.020-15.050 mm (0.5913-0.5925 in)	15.090 mm (0.5940 in.)
BF35A, BF40A	17.020-17.050 mm (0.6701-0.6713 in.)	17.090 mm (0.6728 in.)
BF45A, BF50A, BF75A, BF90A	18.020-18.050 mm (0.7095-0.7106 in.)	18.090 mm (0.7122 in.)
BF115A, BF30A	12.520-12.550 mm (0.4929-0.4941 in.)	n/a
Outer rotor height		
BF50, BF5A	11.980 mm (0.4717 in.)	11.950 mm (0.4705 in.)
BF9.9, BF15	13.000 mm (0.5118 in.)	12.950 mm (0.5098 in.)
BF20A, BF25A, BF30A	14.980-15.000 mm (0.5898-0.5906 in.)	14.960 mm (0.5890 in.)
BF35A, BF40A, BF45A, BF50A	16.980-17.000 mm (0.6685-0.6693 in.)	16.930 mm (0.6665 in.)
BF75A, BF90A	17.980-18.000 mm (0.7079-0.7087 in.)	17.960 mm (0.7071 in.)
BF115A, BF130A	12.480-12.500 (0.4913-0.4921 in.)	n/a

Table 7 CYLINDER BORE SPECIFICATIONS

	Standard mm (in.)	Wear limit mm (in.)
Cylinder diameter		
BF20, BF2A	46.000 mm (1.8110 in.)	46.050 mm (1.8130 in.)
BF50, BF5A	60.000 mm (2.3622 in.)	60.070 mm (2.3650 in.)
BF75, BF8A, BF100	56.000-56.015 mm (2.2047-2.2053 in.)	56.165 mm (2.2112 in.)
BF9.9A, BF15A	58.000 mm (2.2835 in.)	58.055 mm (2.2856 in.)
BF20A, BF25A, BF30A	58.000-58.015 mm (2.2835-2.2841 in.)	58.055 mm (2.2856 in.)
BF35A, BF40A, BRF45A, BF50A	70.000-70.015 mm (2.7559-2.7565 in.)	70.060 mm (2.7583 in.)
BF75A, BF90A	75.000-75.015 mm (2.9528-2.9534 in.)	75.055 mm (2.9549 in.)
BF115A, BF130A	86.000-86.015 mm (3.3858-3.3864 in.)	86.070 mm (3.3886 in.)

(continued)

BASE ENGINE

Table 7 CYLINDER BORE SPECIFICATIONS (continued)

	Standard mm (in.)	Wear limit mm (in.)
Piston clearance		
BF20, BF2A	0.000-0.030 mm (0.0000-0.0012 in.)	0.130 mm (0.0051 in.)
BF50, BF5A	0.015-0.050 mm (0.0006-0.0020 in.)	0.100 mm (0.0039 in.)
BF75, BF8A, BF100	0.010-0.055 mm (0.0004-0.0022 in.)	0.120 mm (0.0047 in.)
BF9.9A, BF15A	0.015-0.050 mm (0.0006-0.0020 in)	0.100 mm (0.0039 in.)
BF20A, BF25A, BF30A	0.010-0.045 mm (0.0004-0.0018 in.)	0.100 mm (0.0039 in.)
BF35A, BF40A, BF45A, BF50A	0.010-0.045 mm (0.0004-0.0018 in.)	0.090 mm (0.0035 in.)
BF75A, BF90A	0.010-0.035 mm (0.0004-0.0014 in.)	0.100 mm (0.0039 in.)
BF115A, BF130A	0.020-0.045 mm (0.0008-0.0018 in.)	0.050 mm (0.0020 in.)

Table 8 PISTON/RING SPECIFICATIONS

	Standard mm (in.)	Wear limit mm (in.)
Piston diameter		
BF20, BF2A	45.995 mm (1.8108 in.)	45.920 mm (1.8079 in.)
BF50, BF5A	59.985 mm (2.3616 in.)	59.920 mm (2.3591 in.)
BF75, BF8A, BF100	55.960-55.990 mm (2.203-2.204 in.)	55.880 mm (2.2000 in.)
BF9.9A, BF15A	57.985 mm (2.2829 in.)	57.920 mm (2.2803 in.)
BF20A, BF25A, BF30A	57.970-57.990 mm (2.2823-2.2831 in.)	57.920 mm (2.2803 in.)
BF35A, BF40A	69.970-69.990 mm (2.7547-2.7555 in.)	69.910 mm (2.7524 in.)
BF45A, BF50A, BF75A, BF90A	74.980-74.990 mm (2.9520-2.9524 in.)	74.920 mm (2.9496 in.)
BF115A, BF130A	85.970-85.980 mm (3.3846-3.3850 in.)	85.960 mm (3.3843 in.)
Piston pin bore		
BF 20, BF2A	10.002 mm (0.3938 in.)	10.050 mm (0.3957 in.)
BF50, BF5A	18.002 mm (0.7087 in.)	18.020 mm (0.7095 in.)
BF75, BF8A, BF100	14.002-14.008 mm (0.5513-0.5515 in.)	14.048 mm (0.5531 in.)
BF9.9A, BF15A	14.002 mm (0.5513 in.)	14.020 mm (0.5520 in.)
BF20A, BF25A, BF30A	14.002-14.008 mm (0.5513-0.5515 in.)	14.020 mm (0.5520 in.) 14.020 mm (0.5520 in.)
BF35A, BF40A, BF45A, BF50A	18.002-18.008 mm (0.7087-0.7090 in.)	18.012 mm (0.7091 in.)
BF75, BF90	19.010-19.016 mm (0.7485-0.7487 in.)	n/a

(continued)

Table 8 PISTON/RING SPECIFICATIONS (continued)

	Standard mm (in.)	Wear limit mm (in.)
Piston pin bore (continued)		
BF115A, BF130A	21.960-21.963 mm (0.8646-0.8647 in.)	n/a
Piston pin diameter		
BF20, BF2A	10.000 mm (0.3937 in.)	9.995 mm (0.3935 in.)
BF50, BF5A	18.000 mm (0.7087 in.)	17.970 mm (0.7074 in.)
BF75, BF8A, BF100	13.994-14.000 mm (0.5509-0.5512 in.)	13.954 mm (0.5494 in.)
BF9.9A, BF15A	14.000 mm (0.5512 in.)	13.970 mm (0.5500 in.)
BF20A, BF25A, BF30A	13.994-14.000 mm (0.5509-0.5512 in.)	13.970 mm (0.5500 in.)
BF35A, BF40A, BF45A BF50A	17.994-18.000 mm (0.7084-0.7087 in.)	17.954 mm (0.7069 in.)
BF75A, BF90A	18.996-19.000 mm (0.7479-0.7480 in.)	18.970 mm (0.7469 in.)
BF115A, BF130A	21.961-21.965 mm (0.8646-0.8648 in.)	n/a
Piston ring end gap		
BF20, BF2A		
Top and second	0.150-0.350 mm (0.0059-0.0138 in.)	1.000 mm (0.0394 in.)
Oil ring	0.200-0.800 mm (0.0079-0.0315 in.)	1.000 mm (0.0394 in.)
BF50, BF5A		
Top, second, oil	0.150-0.350 mm (0.00591-0.01378 in.)	0.500 mm (0.01969 in.)
BF75, BF8A, BF100	0.150-0.350 mm (0.00591-0.01378 in.)	1.000 mm (0.03937 in.)
BF9.9A, BF15A		
Top	0.150-0.300 mm (0.00591-0.01181 in.)	0.500 mm (0.01969 in.)
Second	0.350-0.500 mm (0.01378-0.01969 in.)	0.700 mm (0.02756 in.)
Oil	0.200-0.800 mm (0.00787-0.03150 in.)	1.000 mm (0.03937 in.)
BF20A, BF25A and BF30A		
Top	0.150-0.300 mm (0.00591-0.01181 in.)	0.500 mm (0.01969 in.)
Second	0.350-0.500 mm (0.01378-0.01969 in.)	0.700 mm (0.02756 in.)
Oil	0.200-0.800 mm (0.00787-0.03150 in.)	1.000 mm (0.03937in.)
BF35A, BF40A, BF45A, BF50A		
Top	0.150-0.300 mm (0.00591-0.01181 in.)	0.800 mm (0.03150 in.)
Second	0.300-0.450 mm (0.01181-0.01772 in.)	0.950 mm (0.03740 in.)
Oil	0.200-0.700 mm (0.00787-0.02756 in.)	1.000 mm (0.03937 in.)

(continued)

BASE ENGINE

Table 8 PISTON/RING SPECIFICATIONS (continued)

	Standard mm (in.)	Wear limit mm (in.)
Piston ring end gap (continued)		
BF75A and BF90A		
Top, second	0.150-0.300 mm (0.00591-0.01181 in.)	0.600 mm (0.02362 in.)
Oil	0.200-0.800 mm (0.00785-0.03150 in.)	0.900 mm (0.03543 in.)
BF115A and BF130A		
Top	0.200-0.350 mm (0.00785-.013780 in.)	0.600 mm (0.02362 in.)
Second	0.400-0.550 mm (0.01575-0.02165 in.)	0.700 mm (0.02756 in.)
Oil	0.200-0.700 mm (0.00789-0.02756 in.)	0.800 mm (0.03150 in.)
Piston ring side clearance		
BF20, BF2A		
Top ring	0.055-0.090 mm (0.0022-0.0035 in.)	0.150 mm (0.0059 in.)
Second ring	0.055-0.085 mm (0.0022-0.0033 in.)	0.150 mm (0.0059 in.)
BF50, BF5A		
Top, second, oil	0.015-0.045 mm (0.0006-0.0018 in.)	0.100 mm (0.0039 in.)
BF75, BF8A, BF100		
Top ring	0.025 mm (0.0010 in.)	0.100 mm (0.0039 in.)
Second ring	0.025 mm (0.0010 in.)	0.100 mm (0.0039 in.)
Oil ring	0.015 mm (0.0006 in.)	0.100 mm (0.0039 in.)
BF9.9A, BF15A		
Top, second	0.0250-0.055 mm (0.00098-0.00217 in.)	0.100 mm (0.0039 in.)
Oil ring	0.0550-0.140 mm (0.00217-0.00551 in.)	0.200 mm (0.0079 in.)
BF20A, BF25A, BF30A		
Top	0.025-0.055 mm (0.00098-0.00217 in.)	0.100 mm (0.0039 in.)
Second	0.025-0.055 mm (0.00098-0.00217 in.)	0.100 mm (0.0039 in.)
Oil	0.055-0.140 mm (0.00217-0.00551 in.)	0.200 mm (0.0078 in.)
BF35A, BF40A, BF45A, BF50A		
Top	0.040-0.065 mm (0.0016-0.0026 in.)	0.100 mm (0.0039 in)
Second	0.015-0.045 mm (0.0006-0.0018 in.)	0.100 mm (0.0039 in.)
Oil	0.055-0.140 mm (0.0022-0.0055 in.)	0.150 mm (0.0059 in.)
BF75A, BF90A		
Top	0.030-0.060 mm (0.0012-0.0024 in.)	0.100 mm (0.0039 in.)
Second	0.030-0.055 mm (0.0012-0.0022 in.)	0.100 mm (0.0039 in.)

(continued)

Table 8 PISTON/RING SPECIFICATIONS (continued)

	Standard mm (in.)	Wear limit mm (in.)
Piston ring side clearance (continued)		
BF75A, BF90A (continued)		
Oil	0.045-0.145 mm (0.0018-0.0057 in.)	0.200 mm (0.0079 in.)
BF115A, BF130A		
Top	0.035-0.060 mm (0.0014-0.0024 in.)	0.130 mm (0.0051 in.)
Second	0.030-0.055 mm (0.0012-0.0022 in.)	0.130 mm (0.0051 in.)
Piston ring width		
BF20, BF2A		
Top and second ring	1.500 mm (0.0591 in.)	1.370 mm (0.0539 in.)
BF75, BF8A, BF100		
Top ring	1.460-1.475 mm (0.0575-0.0581 in.)	1.360 mm (0.0535 in.)
Second ring	1.475-1.490 mm (0.0581-0.0587 in.)	1.370 mm (0.0539 in.)
Oil ring	2.475-2.490 mm (0.0974-0.0980 in.)	2.370 mm (0.0933 in.)
BF9.9A, BF15A		
Top and second ring	1.200 mm (0.0472 in.)	1.080 mm (0.0425 in.)
BF20A, BF25A, BF30A		
Top and second ring	1.175-1.190 mm (0.0463-0.0469 in.)	1.080 mm (0.0425 in.)
BF35A, BF40A, BF45A, BF50A		
Top	0.990-1.025 mm (0.0390-0.0404 in.)	0.960 mm (0.0378 in.)
Second	1.190-1.225 mm (0.0469-0.0482 in.)	1.160 mm (0.0457 in.)
BF75A, BF90A		
Top	1.170-1.190 mm (0.0461-0.0469 in.)	1.080 mm (0.0425 in.)
Second	1.475-1.490 mm (0.0581-0.0587 in.)	1.380 mm (0.0543 in.)
BF115A, BF130A		
Top	1.170-1.185 mm (0.0461-0.0467 in.)	n/a
Second	1.175-1.190 mm (0.0463-0.0469 in.)	n/a

Table 9 CONNECTING ROD SPECIFICATIONS

	Standard diameter mm (in.)	Maximum bore diameter mm (in.)
Piston pin bore		
BF20, BF2A	10.006 mm (0.3939 in.)	10.050 mm (0.3957 in.)
BF50, BF5A	18.005 mm (0.7089 in.)	18.040 mm (0.7102 in.)
BF75, BF8A, BF100	14.005-14.020 mm (0.5514-0.5520 in.)	14.070 mm (0.5539 in.)

(continued)

BASE ENGINE

Table 9 CONNECTING ROD SPECIFICATIONS (continued)

	Standard diameter mm (in.)	Maximum bore diameter mm (in.)
Piston pin bore (continued)		
BF9.9A, BF15A	14.005 mm (0.5514 in.)	14.040 mm (0.5528 in.)
BF20A, BF25A, BF30A	14.010-14.022 mm (0.5516-0.5520 in.)	14.050 mm (0.5531 in.)
BF35A, BF40A, BF45A, BF50A	18.016-18.034 mm (0.7093-0.7100 in.)	18.050 mm (0.7106 in.)
BF75A, BF90A	18.960-18.980 mm (0.7465-0.7472 in.)	n/a
BF115A, BF130A	21.970-21.976 mm (0.8650-0.8652 in.)	n/a
Crankshaft lower end bearing (bore diameter)		
BF50, BF5A	30.020 mm (1.1819 in.)	30.050 mm (1.1831 in.)

Table 10 CRANKSHAFT SPECIFICATIONS

	Standard	Wear limit
Connecting rod bearing clearance		
BF20, BF2A	0.016-0.038 mm (0.0006-0.0015 in.)	0.100 mm (0.0039 in.)
BF50, BF5A	0.040-0.063 mm (0.0016-0.0025 in.)	0.080 mm (0.0032 in.)
BF75, BF8A, BF100	0.040-0.068 mm (0.0016-0.0027 in.)	0.083 mm (0.0033 in.)
BF9.9A, BF15A	0.040-0.066 mm (0.0016-0.0026 in.)	0.080 mm (0.0032 in.)
BF20A, BF25, BF30A	0.018-0.042 mm (0.0007-0.0017 in.)	0.080 mm (0.0032 in.)
BF35, BF45, BF45A, BF50A	0.016-0.040 mm (0.0006-0.0016 in.)	0.050 mm (0.0020 in.)
BF75A, BF90A	0.020-0.038 mm (0.0008-0.0015 in.)	0.050 mm (0.0020 in.)
BF115A, BF130A	0.026-0.044 mm (0.0010-0.0017 in.)	n/a
Crankshaft rod bearing journal diameter		
BF20, BF2A	17.984 mm (0.7080 in.)	17.940 mm (0.7063 in.)
BF50, BF5A	28.980 mm (1.1409 in.)	29.950 mm (1.1791 in.)
BF75, BF8A, BF100	27.967-27.980 mm (1.1011-1.1015 in.)	27.952 mm (1.1005 in.)
BF9.9A, BF15A	29.980 mm (1.1803 in.)	29.950 mm (1.1791 in.)
BF20A, BF25A, BF30A	31.987-32.011 mm (1.2593-1.2603 in.)	31.960 mm (1.2583 in.)
(continued)		

Table 10 CRANKSHAFT SPECIFICATIONS (continued)

	Standard mm (in.)	Wear limit mm (in.)
Crankshaft rod bearing journal diameter (continued)		
BF35A, BF40A, BF45A, BF50A	37.976-38.000 mm (1.4951-1.4961 in.)	37.940 mm (1.4937 in.)
BF75A, BF90A	44.976-45.000 mm (1.7707-1.7717 in.)	44.960 mm (1.7701 in.)
BF115A, BF130A	44.976-45.000 mm (1.7707-1.7717 in.)	44.960 mm (1.7701 in.)
Connecting rod side clearance		
BF20, BF2A	0.200-0.900 mm (0.0079-0.0354 in.)	1.100 mm (0.0433 in.)
BF50, BF5A	0.100-0.700 mm (0.0039-0.0276 in.)	1.000 mm (0.0393 in.)
BF75, BF8A, BF100	0.600 mm (0.0236 in.)	1.300 mm (0.0512 in.)
BF9.9A, BF15A	0.150-0.350 mm (0.0059-0.0138 in.)	0.700 mm (0.0276 in.)
BF20A, BF25A, BF30A	0.120-0.270 mm (0.0047-0.0106 in.)	0.400 mm (0.0157 in.)
BF35A, BF40A, BF45A, BF50A	0.050-0.200 mm (0.0020-0.0079 in.)	0.300 mm (0.0118 in.)
BF75A, BF90A	0.150-0.300 mm (0.0015-0.0118 in.)	0.400 mm (0.0157 in.)
BF115A, BF130A	0.150-0.300 mm (0.0059-0.0118 in.)	0.400 mm (0.0157 in.)
Main journal diameter		
BF50, BF5A	24.993 mm (0.9840 in.)	
BF75, BF8A, BF100	44.976-45.000 mm (1.7707-1.7715 in.)	44.960 mm (1.7701 in.)
BF9.9, BF15	33.000 mm (1.2992 in.)	32.980 (1.2984 in.)
BF20A, BF25A, BF30A	35.986-36.002 mm (1.4168-1.4174 in.)	35.960 mm (1.4157 in.)
BF35A, BF40A, BF45A, BF50A	39.982-40.006 mm (1.5741-1.5750 in.)	39.949 mm (1.5728 in.)
BF75A, BF90A	54.976-55.000 mm (2.1644-2.1654 in.)	54.960 mm (2.1638 in.)
BF115A, BF130A		
No. 1 journal	54.980-55.004 mm (2.1646-2.1655 in.)	n/a
No. 2 journal	54.980-55.004 mm (2.1646-2.1655 in.)	n/a
No. 3 journal	54.976-55.000 mm (2.1644-2.1654 in.)	n/a
No. 4 journal	54.980-55.004 mm (2.1646-2.1655 in.)	n/a
No. 5 journal	54.992-55.016 mm (2.1650-2.1660 in.)	n/a

(continued)

BASE ENGINE

Table 10 CRANKSHAFT SPECIFICATIONS (continued)

	Standard mm (in.)	Wear limit mm (in.)
Lower main bearing diameter (oil pan mounted)		
BF50, BF5A	25.013 mm (0.9848 in.)	25.040 mm (0.9858 in.)
Main bearing clearance		
BF50, BF5A	0.020-0.046 mm (0.0008-0.0018 in.)	0.070 mm (0.0028 in.)
BF75, BF8A, BF100	0.020-0.065 mm (0.0008-0.0026 in.)	0.080 mm (0.0031 in.)
BF9.9A, BF15A	0.021-0.040 mm (0.0008-0.0016 in.)	0.050 mm (0.0020 in.)
BF20A, BF25A, BF30A	0.020-0.044 mm (0.0008-0.0017 in.)	0.060 mm (0.0024 in.)
BF35, BF45, BF45A, BF50A	0.020-0.038 mm (0.0008-0.0015 in.)	0.050 mm (0.0020 in.)
BF75A, BF90A	0.025-0.043 mm (0.0010-0.0017 in.)	n/a
BF115A, BF130A		
Journal No. 1	0.027-0.045 mm (0.0011-0.0018 in.)	0.050 mm (0.0020 in.)
Journal No. 2	0.027-0.045 mm (0.0011-0.0018 in.)	0.050 mm (0.0020 in.)
Journal No. 3	0.031-0.049 mm (0.0012-0.0019 in.)	0.030 mm (0.0012 in.)
Journal No. 4	0.027-0.045 mm (0.0011-0.0018 in.)	0.050 mm (0.0020 in.)
Journal No. 5	0.017-0.035 mm (0.0007-0.0014 in.)	0.040 mm (0.0016 in.)
Crankshaft side clearance		
BF35A, BF40A, BF45A, BF50A	0.050-0.300 mm (0.0020-0.0118 in.)	0.450 mm (0.0177 in.)
BF75A, BF90A	0.100-0.350 mm (0.0039-0.0138 in.)	0.450 mm (0.0177 in.)
BF115A, BF130A	0.100-0.350 mm (0.0039-0.0138 in.)	0.450 mm (0.0177 in.)

Table 11 MAIN BEARING SELECTION

Model	Crankshaft code	Cylinder block code	Bearing color used
Crankshaft main bearing			
BF9.9A, BF15A	1	1	Red
	1	2	Yellow
	1	3	Green
	2	1	Yellow
	2	2	Green
	2	3	Brown
	3	1	Green
	3	2	Brown
	3	3	Black
(continued)			

Table 11 MAIN BEARING SELECTION

Model	Crankshaft code	Cylinder block code	Bearing color used
Crankshaft main bearing (continued)			
BF20A, BF25A, BF30A	1	A	Red
	1	B	Pink
	1	C	Yellow
	2	A	Pink
	2	B	Yellow
	2	C	Green
BF35A, BF40A, BF45A, BF50A, BF75A, BF90A	1	A	Red
	1	B	Pink
	1	C	Yellow
	1	D	Green
	2	A	Pink
	2	B	Yellow
	2	C	Green
	2	D	Brown
	3	A	Yellow
	3	B	Green
	3	C	Brown
	3	D	Black
	4	A	Green
	4	B	Brown
	4	C	Black
	4	D	Blue
BF115A, BF130A			
Journals 1-4	1 or I	1, A or I	Yellow
	1 or I	2, B or II	Yellow/Green
	1 or I	3, C or III	Green
	1 or I	4, D or IIII	Green/Brown
	2 or II	1, A or I	Yellow/Green
	2 or II	2, B or II	Green
	2 or II	3, C or III	Green/Brown
	2 or II	4, D or IIII	Brown
	3 or IIII	1, A or I	Green
	3 or IIII	2, B or II	Green/Brown
	3 or IIII	3, C or III	Brown
	3 or IIII	4, D or IIII	Brown/Black
	4 or IIII	1, A or I	Green/Brown
	4 or IIII	2, B or II	Brown
	4 or IIII	3, C or III	Brown/Black
	4 or IIII	4, D or IIII	Black
	5 or IIIII	1, A or I	Brown
	5 or IIIII	2, B or II	Brown/Black
	5 or IIIII	3, C or III	Black
	5 or IIIII	4, D or IIII	Black/Blue
	6 or IIIIII	1, A or I	Brown/Black
	6 or IIIIII	2, B or II	Black
	6 or IIIIII	3, C or III	Black/Blue
	6 or IIIIII	4, D or IIII	Blue
Journal No. 5	1 or I	1, A or I	Pink
	1 or I	2, B or II	Pink/Yellow
	1 or I	3, C or III	Yellow

(continued)

BASE ENGINE

Table 11 MAIN BEARING SELECTION (continued)

Model	Crankshaft code	Cylinder block code	Bearing color used
Crankshaft main bearing (continued) BF115A, BF130A (continued) Journal No. 5 (continued)			
	1 or I	4, D or IIII	Yellow/Green
	2 or II	1, A or I	Pink/Yellow
	2 or II	2, B or II	Yellow
	2 or II	3, C or III	Yellow/Green
	2 or II	4, D or IIII	Green
	3 or IIII	1, A or I	Yellow
	3 or IIII	2, B or II	Yellow/Green
	3 or IIII	3, C or III	Green
	3 or IIII	4, D or IIII	Green/Brown
	4 or IIII	1, A or I	Yellow/Green
	4 or IIII	2, B or II	Green
	4 or IIII	3, C or III	Green/Brown
	4 or IIII	4, D or IIII	Brown
	5 or IIIII	1, A or I	Green
	5 or IIIII	2, B or II	Green/Brown
	5 or IIIII	3, C or III	Brown
	5 or IIIII	4, D or IIII	Brown Black
	6 or IIIIII	1, A or I	Green/Brown
	6 or IIIIII	2, B or II	Brown
	6 or IIIIII	3, C or III	Brown/Black
	6 or IIIIII	4, D or IIII	Black

Table 12 CRANKPIN BEARING SELECTION

Model	Connecting rod code	Crankshaft code	Bearing used
BF20A, BF25A, BF30A	1	A	Red
	1	B	Yellow
	1	C	Green
	2	A	Yellow
	2	B	Green
	2	C	Brown
	3	A	Green
	3	B	Brown
	3	C	Black
BF35A, BF40A, BF45A, BF50A, BF75A, BF90A	1	A	Red
	1	B	Pink
	1	C	Yellow
	1	D	Green
	2	A	Pink
	2	B	Yellow
	2	C	Green
	2	D	Brown
	3	A	Yellow
	3	B	Green
	3	C	Brown
	3	D	Black
	4	A	Green
(continued)			

Table 12 CRANKPIN BEARING SELECTION (continued)

	Connecting rod code	Crankshaft code	Bearing used
BF75, BF90 (continued)	4	B	Brown
	4	C	Black
	4	D	Blue
BF115A, BF130A	1 or I	A or I	Red
	1 or I	B or II	Pink
	1 or I	C or III	Yellow
	1 or I	D or IIII	Green
	2 or II	A or I	Pink
	2 or II	B or II	Yellow
	2 or II	C or III	Green
	2 or II	D or IIII	Brown
	3 or III	A or I	Yellow
	3 or III	B or II	Green
	3 or III	C or III	Brown
	3 or III	D or IIII	Black
	4 or IIII	A or I	Green
	4 or IIII	B or II	Brown
	4 or IIII	C or III	Black
	4 or IIII	D or IIII	Blue

Chapter Nine

Gearcase Repair

This chapter provides gearcase removal, installation, disassembly, inspection and assembly procedures.

Special tools and special measuring devices are required to repair many components in the gearcase. Contact a Honda dealership to purchase the required tools.

Use only the required tools. The use of makeshift tools may result in damage to the housing or internal components of the gearcase.

Table 1 and **Table 2** provide tightening torque specifications and gear backlash specifications. **Table 1** and **Table 2** are located at the end of this chapter.

The drive and driven gears (**Figure 1**) are precisely aligned to provide durability and quiet operation. Variations occur when manufacturing gears, bearings, shafts and housings. Shims are used to compensate for these manufacturing variances. The shims are typically located next to the bearings that support the gears and shafts. Shimming operations involve using special tools to measure and determine the shim thickness required to properly position the gears. Never compromise this important step. The durability of the gearcase is substantially reduced if the gears are improperly positioned. Shimming procedures must be performed if replacing gears, bearings, shafts or housings. Refer to the *Shim Selection* in this chapter for instructions.

Repair or maintenance involving the gearcase can be as simple as servicing the water pump or as complicated as a complete gearcase rebuild. Gearcase failure is usually the result of impact with an underwater object or lack of sufficient gearcase maintenance. Gearcase maintenance is provided in Chapter Four.

A reputable marine repair shop should perform the repairs if the required tools and/or mechanical skill is wanting. Improper repair can result in extensive and expensive damage to the gearcase.

GEARCASE OPERATION

The gearcase provides a means to transfer the rotation of the drive (vertical) shaft (A, **Figure 1**) to the propeller (horizontal) shaft (B, **Figure 1**). Gears (**Figure 2**) attached to each shaft are used to transfer to the rotational force to the propeller shaft.

Models BF20 and BF2A do not have shifting capability. All other models use a propeller shaft mounted sliding clutch (**Figure 3**) to provide neutral, forward and reverse gears. The remote control, tiller handle or engine mounted gear selector is used for gear selection. Shafts, linkage or cables move the clutch.

Non-Shifting Units

The drive and driven gears rotate anytime the engine is running. On models BF20 and BF2A, the propeller shaft maintains a constant connection to the driven gear. This provides continuous clockwise rotation of the propeller shaft when the engine is running. These are essentially start in gear engines. To provide reverse thrust, the entire

engine is pivoted so that the propeller thrust is directed under the boat. If neutral thrust is desired, the engine is simply switched OFF.

NOTE
Models with an L in the model designation are equipped with a left-hand rotation gearcase. The gearcase provides forward thrust when the propeller shaft is rotated counterclockwise (as viewed from the rear). A left-hand propeller must be used on this gearcase.

Shifting Units (Standard Rotation)

Neutral, forward and reverse operations are provided on all models, except BF20 and BF2A. The drive and both driven gears rotate anytime the engine is running. A propeller shaft mounted sliding clutch engages the propeller shaft to either the front or rear mounted gear.

When neutral gear is desired, (**Figure 4**) the propeller shaft is allowed to remain stationary as the gears rotate. No propeller thrust is delivered.

When forward gear is desired, (**Figure 4**) the sliding clutch is moved with the shift mechanism to the front mounted gear. The propeller shaft rotates in the direction of the front mounted gear as the clutch dogs engage with the dogs on the front mounted gear. This provides the propeller shaft rotational direction necessary for forward thrust.

When reverse thrust is desired, (**Figure 4**) the sliding clutch is moved with the shift mechanism to the rear mounted driven gear. The propeller shaft will rotate in the direction of the rear-mounted gear as the clutch dogs engage the dogs on the rear mounted gear. This provides the propeller shaft rotational direction necessary for reverse thrust.

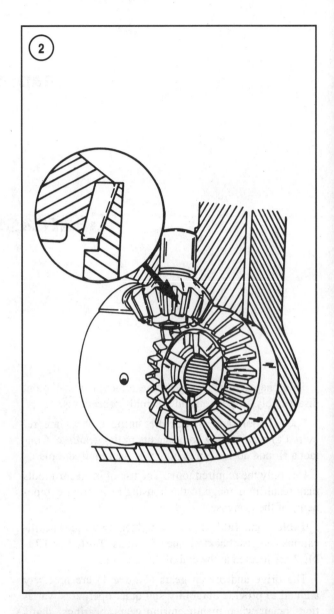

GEARCASE REPAIR

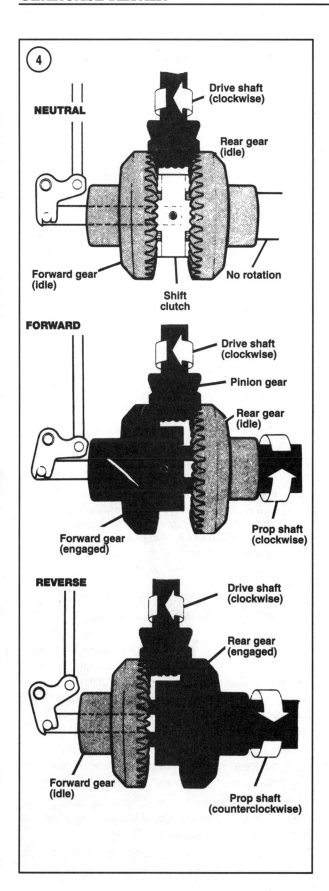

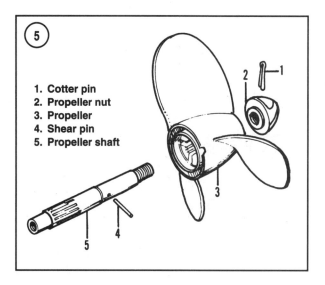

Left Rotation Gearcase Shifting Units

Left propeller shaft rotation is used for forward thrust on models with an *L* in the model designation. Left models are used alongside a right or standard rotation model on most dual engine applications. The use of the left-hand unit allows for balanced propeller torque from the two engines. Changes to internal gearcase components cause the opposite gear to engage as the gears are selected. If forward gear is selected, the rear-mounted gear drives the propeller shaft. If reverse thrust is selected, the front-mounted gear drives the propeller shaft.

CAUTION
Never use a left-hand rotation gearcase with a right hand propeller. Also never use a right-hand gearcase with a left-hand propeller. Gearcase component failure may result from continued operation in the wrong direction for forward thrust.

PROPELLER

Two methods are used for absorbing shock and mounting of the propeller. A shear pin design is used on models BF20, BF2A, BF50, BF5A, BF75, BF8A and BF100. A thrust hub design is used on all other models.

With the shear pin design, the propeller is held to the propeller shaft with the propeller nut (2, **Figure 5**) and cotter pin (1). A shear pin (4, **Figure 5**) is positioned in its hole in the propeller shaft (5, **Figure 5**). The shear pin engages a slot in and drives the propeller. The shear pin is designed to break in the event of underwater impact and provides some protection for gearcase components.

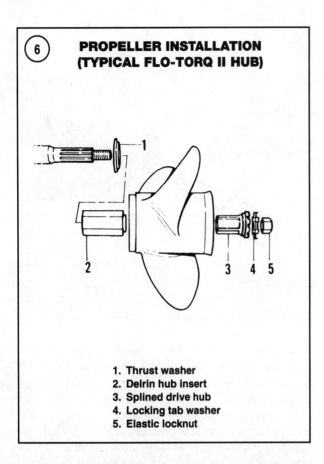

6 PROPELLER INSTALLATION (TYPICAL FLO-TORQ II HUB)

1. Thrust washer
2. Delrin hub insert
3. Splined drive hub
4. Locking tab washer
5. Elastic locknut

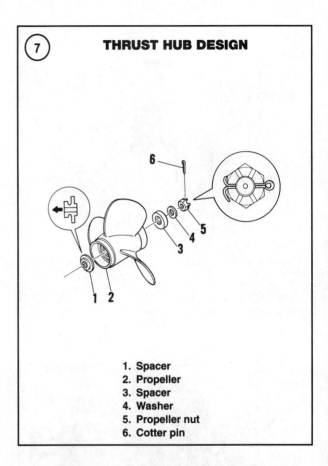

7 THRUST HUB DESIGN

1. Spacer
2. Propeller
3. Spacer
4. Washer
5. Propeller nut
6. Cotter pin

With the thrust hub design the propeller is driven by a splined connection of the propeller shaft to the rubber or plastic drive hub. The rubber thrust hub is pressed into a bore in the propeller and provides a cushion effect when shifting. It also provides some protection for the gearcase components in the event of underwater impact. Some models BF75A, BF90A, BF115A and BF130A have a plastic drive hub (**Figure 6**). On models BF75A, BF90A, BF115A and BF130A, the propeller is held to the propeller shaft with a locking tab washer and propeller nut (**Figure 6**). On all other models, a propeller nut (5, **Figure 7**) and cotter pin (6) retain the propeller to the propeller shaft. A forward-mounted spacer (1, **Figure 7**) directs the propeller thrust to a tapered area of the propeller shaft.

Your outboard may be equipped with a Honda supplied propeller or one offered by various aftermarket manufacturers. Because of this, the attaching hardware and drive hub design may differ from the illustrations provided for Honda propellers. Contact a propeller repair shop or marine dealership for parts and information for other brands of propellers.

CAUTION
Use light force if necessary to remove the propeller from the propeller shaft. Excessive force can result in damage to the propeller, propeller shaft and internal components of the gearcase. Have a reputable marine repair shop or propeller repair shop remove the propeller if you are unable to remove the propeller by normal means.

Removal/Installation (Shear Pin Design)

Always replace the cotter pin and shear pin when removed. Purchase the replacement pins at a marine dealership and ensure that the proper size and material are selected. The cotter pin is made of stainless steel. Use a shear pin designated for the correct model to ensure it will shear at the required load.

1. Disconnect both battery cables from the battery, if so equipped. Remove the spark plugs and connect the spark plug leads to an engine ground.

2. Use pliers to straighten and remove the cotter pin. To prevent propeller rotation, place a block of wood between the propeller and the gearcase.

3. Use the correct size socket and turn the propeller nut counterclockwise to loosen and remove the propeller nut.

GEARCASE REPAIR

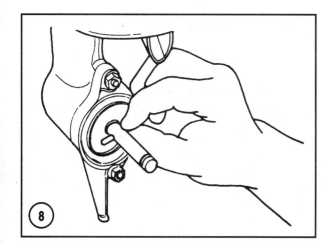

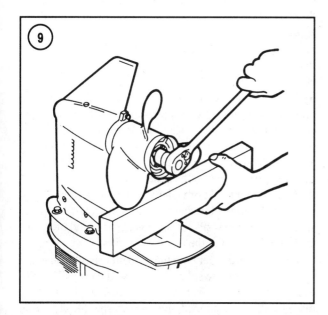

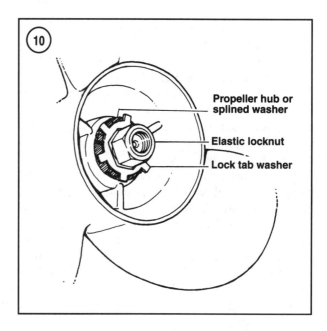

8. Position a new shear pin into the shear pin hole (**Figure 8**). Use a small hammer and gently drive the pin into the propeller shaft until the same amount of the pin protrudes from each side of the propeller shaft.

9. Apply a light coat of water-resistant grease to the shear pin and propeller shaft threads. Apply grease to the propeller shaft and the splined bore in the propeller. Slide the propeller onto the propeller shaft. Rotate the propeller while pushing Forward until the shear pin engages the slot in the propeller.

10. Install the propeller nut until hand tight. Position a block of wood between the propeller and housing to prevent rotation (**Figure 9**). Tighten the propeller nut to the specification listed in **Table 1**. Loosen the propeller nut just enough to align the hole in the propeller nut with the hole in the threaded section of the propeller shaft. Install a new cotter pin and bend the ends over. Check for a snug fit of the propeller on the propeller shaft. Install the spark plug and spark plug leads. Clean the battery terminals and connect the cables, if so equipped, to the battery.

Removal/Installation (Models BF75A, BF90A, BF115A and BF130A)

1. Disconnect both battery cables from the battery, if so equipped. Remove the spark plugs and connect the spark plug leads to an engine ground.

2. Place a block of wood between the propeller and the gearcase (**Figure 9**).

3. Carefully bend the tabs up and clear from the splined spacer (**Figure 10**).

4. Pull the propeller from the propeller shaft. Use a block of wood for a cushion and carefully drive the propeller rearward, if necessary. Replace or repair the propeller if it has damaged or worn surfaces.

5. Gently drive the shear pin until it is flush on one side of the propeller shaft. Use pliers to carefully remove the shear pin from the propeller shaft.

6. Inspect the shear pin hole for burrs or elongation of the hole. Dress burrs with a file. Place a new shear pin in the shear pin hole. The correct fit is fairly snug. Propeller shaft replacement is required if a new shear pin wobbles or is excessively loose in its hole.

7. Clean all surfaces of the propeller shaft and propeller bore for the shaft. Inspect the shear pin engagement slot in the propeller for damage or wear. Replace the propeller if excessive wear is noted in these areas.

4. Remove the propeller nut and splined spacer from the propeller shaft (**Figure 6**).

5. Pull the propeller from the propeller shaft. Use a block of wood as a cushion and carefully drive the propeller from the shaft if necessary. Use light force only to avoid damaging the propeller or gearcase components.

6. Note the position and remove the inner spacer (1, **Figure 6**) from the propeller shaft. Tap the spacer lightly if it is seized to the propeller shaft.

7. Slide the drive hub (2, **Figure 6**) from its bore in the propeller. Clean all debris from the propeller shaft.

8. Inspect the propeller shaft for twisted splines or excessively worn areas. Rotate the propeller shaft while observing for shaft deflection. Remove and replace the propeller shaft if excessively worn areas, twisted splines or a bent shaft is noted. Refer to gearcase disassembly in this chapter.

9. Apply a light coat of water-resistant grease to all surfaces of the propeller shaft.

10. Clean and install the inner spacer. The tapered side of the inner spacer and propeller shaft must contact at the tapered surfaces.

11. Slide the small tapered end of the drive hub into the propeller bore.

12. Install the propeller onto the propeller shaft. Make sure the propeller seats fully against the inner spacer.

13. Rotate the splined spacer to align its splines with the propeller shaft splines. Install the splined spacer (3, **Figure 6**) and tab washer (4) onto the propeller shaft.

14. Place a block of wood between the propeller and housing (**Figure 9**) to prevent propeller rotation. Install the tab washer and propeller nut with the elastic side of the nut facing out. Tighten the propeller nut to the specification listed in **Table 1**.

15. If necessary, tighten the propeller nut to align one or more of the tabs on the tab washer with the notches in the splined spacer. Bend the tabs down into the slots in the splined spacer (**Figure 10**).

16. Install all spark plugs and spark plug leads. Clean the battery terminals then connect the cables to the battery.

Removal/Installation (Rubber Thrust Hub Design)

Always install a new cotter pin (6, **Figure 7**) anytime the propeller is removed. Purchase the cotter pin at a reputable marine dealership. Make sure the pin is of the correct size and material.

Inspect the propeller for black rubber material in the drive hub area. Have the hub inspected at a propeller repair facility if this material is noted. It normally indicates that the propeller hub has spun in the propeller bore. Satisfactory performance is not possible with a spun propeller hub.

1. Disconnect both battery cables from the battery, if so equipped. Remove the spark plugs and connect the spark plug leads to an engine ground.

2. Use pliers to straighten and remove the cotter pin (6, **Figure 7**) from the propeller nut.

3. Position a block of wood between the propeller and the housing to prevent propeller rotation (**Figure 9**). Use the correct sized socket to loosen and remove the propeller nut. Note the position and remove the plain washer, if so equipped, and the splined washer (3, **Figure 7**) from the propeller shaft.

4. Pull the propeller from the propeller shaft. Use a block of wood to cushion and carefully drive the propeller from the shaft if necessary. Use light force only to avoid damaging the propeller or gearcase components.

5. Note the position and remove the inner spacer (1, **Figure 7**) from the propeller shaft. Tap the spacer lightly if it is seized to the propeller shaft.

6. Clean all debris from the propeller shaft. Inspect the propeller shaft for twisted splines or excessively worn areas. Rotate the propeller shaft while examining for shaft deflection. Replace the propeller shaft if excessively worn areas, twisted splines or a bent shaft is noted. Refer to gearcase disassembly in this chapter.

7. Apply a light coat of water-resistant grease to all surfaces of the propeller shaft. Clean and install the inner spacer. The tapered side of the inner spacer and propeller shaft must contact at the tapered surfaces.

8. Install the propeller onto the propeller shaft. Rotate the propeller to align the splines and slide the propeller fully against the inner spacer. Install the splined washer (3, **Figure 7**) and, if so equipped, the plain washer (4, **Figure 7**) onto the propeller shaft.

9. Place a wooden block between the propeller and housing to prevent propeller rotation. Install the propeller nut with the cotter pins facing out. Tighten the propeller nut to the specification listed in **Table 1**. Align the cotter pin hole in the propeller shaft with one of the slots in the propeller nut. Install a new cotter pin and use pliers to bend the ends over.

10. Install the spark plugs and spark plug leads. Clean the battery terminals and connect the cables to the battery, if so equipped.

GEARCASE REMOVAL AND INSTALLATION

Always remove the propeller prior to removing the gearcase. Refer to *Propeller Removal/Installation* in this chapter.

GEARCASE REPAIR

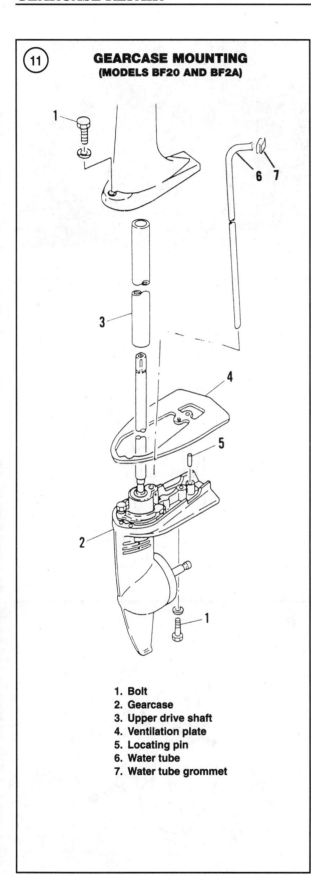

① GEARCASE MOUNTING (MODELS BF20 AND BF2A)

1. Bolt
2. Gearcase
3. Upper drive shaft
4. Ventilation plate
5. Locating pin
6. Water tube
7. Water tube grommet

Always remove the spark plugs and disconnect both battery cables, if so equipped, from the battery prior to removing the gearcase.

Drain the gearcase lubricant prior to removal if the gearcase requires disassembly. Refill the gearcase after installation. Refer to Chapter Four for gearcase draining and filling instructions.

Clean any debris or contamination from the drive shaft, shift shafts and gearcase. Inspect the grommet that connects the water tube to the water pump for damage or deteriorated condition. Replace as required. Apply grease to the grommet. Make sure the dowels or locating pins are properly positioned in the gearcase during assembly.

NOTE
Use caution if using a pry bar to separate the housings. Always make sure all fasteners are removed before attempting to pry the gearcase from the drive shaft housing. Use a blunt pry bar and locate a pry point near the front and rear mating surfaces. Apply moderate heat to the gearcase-to-drive shaft housing mating surfaces if corrosion prevents easy removal.

CAUTION
Never apply grease to the top of the drive shaft or fill the connection at the crankshaft. The grease may create a hydraulic lock on the shaft that can cause failure of the engine, gearcase or both. Use a light coat of water-resistant grease to the sides or splined section of the drive shaft prior to installation.

CAUTION
Work carefully when installing the upper end of the drive shaft into the crankshaft. The lower seal on the crankshaft may be dislodged or become damaged by the drive shaft. Never force the drive shaft into position. Rotate the drive shaft clockwise and attempt to install the gearcase again if difficulty is noted.

Removal/Installation (Models BF20 and BF2A)

1. Disconnect the spark plug lead. Remove the bolt and washer above the propeller shaft (1, **Figure 11**).

2. Support the gearcase (2, **Figure 11**) as you remove the bolt and washer (1, **Figure 11**) located in the drive shaft housing.

3. Carefully remove the gearcase from the drive shaft housing. Remove the lower plate (4, **Figure 11**) and upper

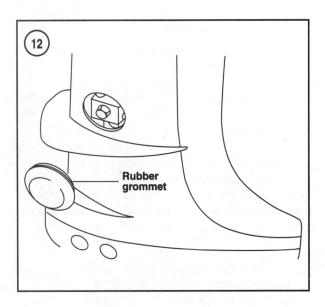

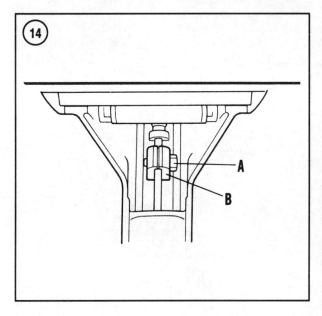

drive shaft (3, **Figure 11**) from the gearcase and/or drive shaft housing.

4. Reposition the water tube (6, **Figure 11**) into the grommet (7) if it comes out with the gearcase. The grommet is located near the engine mounting surface.

5. Retrieve the locating pin (5, **Figure 11**). Install the pin in the hole provided in the gearcase. Clean all debris from upper end of the drive shaft.

6. Apply a very light coat of water-resistant grease to the locating pin and upper end of the lower drive shaft. Position the plate (4, **Figure 11**) over the locating pin and onto the gearcase-to-drive shaft housing mating surfaces.

7. Install the upper drive shaft over the lower drive shaft and carefully guide the drive shaft into the drive shaft housing. Make sure that the water tube (6, **Figure 11**) is aligned with the grommet on the water pump.

8. Install the gearcase to the driveshaft housing while rotating the drive shaft clockwise until the drive shaft square connection engages with the crankshaft. When properly aligned, the housing contacts the drive shaft housing and slips into position. Align the water tube with the grommet during installation. Make sure the locating pin is positioned into its hole in the drive shaft housing.

9. With the gearcase held in position, install both bolts and washers. Tighten the bolts to the specification listed in **Table 1**. Attach the spark plug leads. Run the engine and check for correct cooling system operation.

Removal/Installation (Models BF50 and BF5A)

1. Disconnect both battery cables from the battery, if so equipped. Remove the spark plugs and connect the spark plug leads to an engine ground.

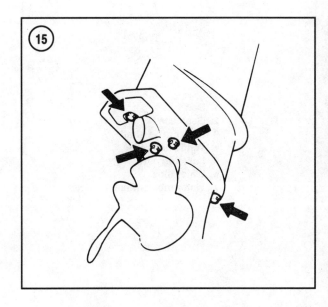

GEARCASE REPAIR

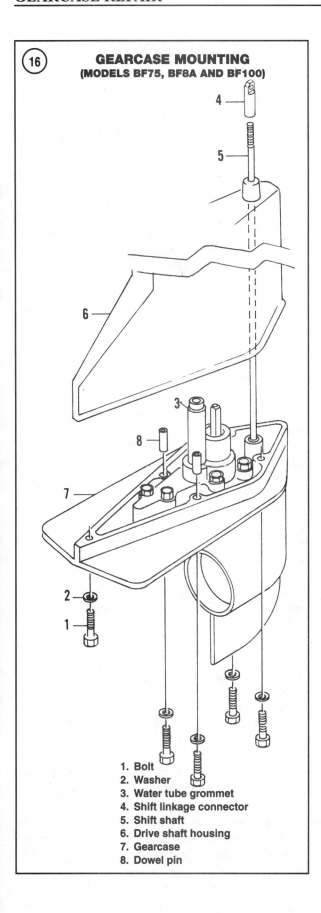

GEARCASE MOUNTING (MODELS BF75, BF8A AND BF100)

1. Bolt
2. Washer
3. Water tube grommet
4. Shift linkage connector
5. Shift shaft
6. Drive shaft housing
7. Gearcase
8. Dowel pin

2. Shift the engine into forward gear.

3. Remove the rubber grommet (**Figure 12**) from the lower port side of the drive shaft housing to access the shift shaft connector (**Figure 13**).

4. Locate the shift shaft connector (B, **Figure 14**). Scribe or mark the connector position on the upper and lower shift shafts. This step saves a great deal of time when performing shift linkage adjustments.

5. Remove the bolt (A, **Figure 14**) and remove the shift shaft connector from the upper and lower shift shafts.

6. Support the gearcase and remove the four bolts (**Figure 15**) that secure the gearcase to the drive shaft housing. (**Figure 16**).

7. Remove the gearcase from the drive shaft housing. Reposition the water tube and sealing grommet if they are dislodged during removal of the gearcase.

8. Apply water-resistant grease to all gearcase mating surfaces. Apply a light coat of grease to the sides of the drive shaft connection points.

9. Carefully insert the drive shaft into the drive shaft housing. Guide the water tube into the grommet on the water pump while installing the gearcase. If difficult installation occurs, lower the gearcase and slightly rotate the drive shaft clockwise to align the drive shaft with the crankshaft. Repeat this step until the drive shaft enters the crankshaft and the gearcase mates to the drive shaft housing.

10. Make sure the shift shafts align with the shift shaft connector. Install the mounting bolts (**Figure 15**); tighten them to the specification listed in **Table 1**.

11. Position the shift shaft connector onto the shift shaft and align it with the marks made prior to removal. Rotate the propeller to ensure that the gearcase is in the same gear as the shift selector. Tighten the shift shaft connector bolt. Install the grommet into the port side of the drive shaft housing.

12. Refer to Chapter Five and adjust the shift linkage. Install the spark plugs and spark plug leads. Clean the battery terminals and connect the cables to the battery, if so equipped. Check for proper shift and cooling system operation before returning the engine to service.

Removal/Installation (Models BF75, BF8A and BF100)

CAUTION
Never rotate the propeller shaft counterclockwise to align the drive shaft with the crankshaft. The water pump impeller can suffer damage that leads to overheating of the engine.

1. Disconnect both battery cables from the battery, if so equipped. Remove the spark plugs and connect the plug leads an engine ground. Shift the engine into neutral.
2. Locate the shift shaft linkage connector in the engine cover on the lower front portion. Remove the locking pin to disconnect the shift shaft from the shift linkage.
3. Count the turns as you remove the shift linkage connector from the upper end of the shift shaft (4, **Figure 16**).
4. Support the gearcase as you loosen the five bolts (1, **Figure 16**) from the gearcase. Remove the gearcase from the drive shaft housing. Pry at the points located near the front and rear of the gearcase. Install the water tube into position in the drive shaft housing if dislodged during removal of the gearcase.
5. Apply water-resistant grease to the splined area of the drive shaft and to the water tube grommet in the water pump housing. Make sure that the dowel pin (8, **Figure 16**) is properly positioned in the gearcase.
6. Place the shift selector into reverse. Make sure that the shift shaft enters the proper opening. Guide the water tube into the water pump grommet (3, **Figure 16**) and insert the drive shaft into the splined crankshaft. Lower the gearcase and slightly rotate the drive shaft clockwise if the gearcase and drive shaft housing do not mate. Repeat this step until the splined connections align and the housings mate. Ensure that the water tube enters the water pump grommet.
7. Secure the gearcase in position and install the fasteners. Tighten the fasteners to the specification provided in **Table 1**.
8. Align the upper and lower shift shafts. Thread the upper shift shaft linkage connector (4, **Figure 16**) onto the lower shift shaft with the number of turns recorded during removal. Make sure the nut makes several turns of engagement onto the lower shift shaft.
9. Refer to Chapter Five and adjust the shift linkage and or cables. Install the spark plugs and spark plug leads. Clean the battery terminals and connect the cables to the battery. Run the engine to check for proper shift and cooling system operation before putting the engine into service.

Removal/Installation (Models BF9.9A and BF15A)

1. Disconnect both battery cables from the battery, if so equipped. Remove the spark plugs and connect the battery cables to an engine ground. Shift the engine into reverse.
2. Locate the shift shaft connector at the lower forward side of the drive shaft housing (**Figure 17**). Loosen the lower jam nut. Count the number of turns as you thread the upper connector from the lower shift shaft. Record the number of turns for reference during installation.

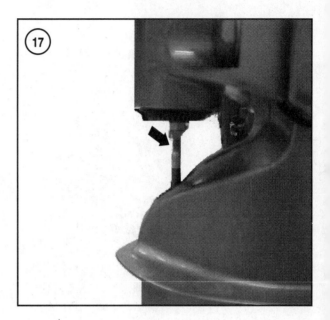

3. Support the gearcase and remove the bolts (1, **Figure 18**) and washers from the gearcase (3) and drive shaft housing (9).
4. Carefully remove the gearcase from the drive shaft housing. Pry at the points located near the front and rear of the gearcase. Carefully lower the gearcase from the drive shaft housing when it becomes free. Retain the aligning dowels (4, **Figure 18**) from the gearcase or drive shaft housing upon removal.
5. If it becomes dislodged during removal, install the water tube and sealing grommet (6, **Figure 18**) into position in the drive shaft housing. Remove the upper drive shaft (8, **Figure 18**) from the lower drive shaft or crankshaft.
6. Apply a light coat of water-resistant grease to the splined and square portion of the drive shaft, water tube grommet and alignment dowels. Position the shift selector into reverse gear.
7. Guide the water tube into the water pump discharge hole while inserting the drive shaft into the crankshaft. Lower the gearcase and slightly rotate the drive shaft clockwise if the drive shaft does not engage the crankshaft. Repeat this step until the shafts align and the gearcase and drive shaft housing mate. Never force the gearcase into position. Damage to the shift shafts and drive shaft seal could result.
8. Support the gearcase as you install the mounting bolts and washers. Tighten them to the specification listed in **Table 1**.
9. Thread the shift shaft upper nut or connector onto the lower shift shaft the same number of turns noted during removal. Refer to Chapter Five and adjust the shift linkage.

GEARCASE REPAIR

GEARCASE MOUNTING
(MODELS BF9.9A AND BF15A)

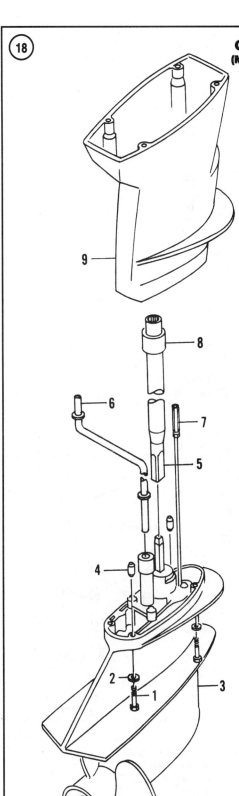

1. Bolt
2. Washer
3. Gearcase
4. Alignment pin/dowel
5. Square end of upper drive shaft
6. Water tube
7. Shift shaft
8. Coupling seal end of upper drive shaft *
9. Drive shaft housing

* later models use a male splined connection.

10. Install the spark plugs and spark plug leads. Clean the battery terminals and connect the cables to the battery.

Removal/Installation (Models BF20A, BF25A and BF30A)

1. Disconnect both battery cables from the battery, if so equipped. Remove the spark plugs and connect the plug leads to an engine ground. Shift the engine into reverse gear.

2. Locate the shift shaft connector at the lower forward side of the drive shaft housing (**Figure 17**). Loosen the lower jam nut. Count the number of turns as you remove the upper connector from the lower shift shaft. Record the number of turns for reference during installation.

3. Support the gearcase as you remove the bolts (6, **Figure 19**) and washers that retain the gearcase (7, **Figure 19**) to the drive shaft housing.

4. Remove the gearcase from the drive shaft housing. Pry at the points located near the front and rear of the gearcase. Carefully lower the gearcase from the drive shaft housing when it becomes free. Retain the aligning dowels (3, **Figure 19**) upon removal.

5. If it becomes dislodged during removal, install the water tube into the sealing grommet at the upper end of the drive shaft housing.

6. Apply a light coat of water-resistant grease to the splined portion of the drive shaft (4, **Figure 19**), water tube grommet and alignment dowels (3, **Figure 19**). Position the shift selector into reverse gear.

7. Guide the water tube into the water pump discharge hole while inserting the drive shaft into the crankshaft connection. Lower the gearcase and slightly rotate the drive shaft clockwise. Repeat this step until the shafts align and the gearcase and drive shaft housing mate. Never force the gearcase into position. Damage to the shift shafts and drive shaft seal may result.

8. Provide support for the gearcase as you install the mounting bolts and washers. Tighten them to the specification listed in **Table 1**.

9. Thread the shift shaft upper nut or connector onto the lower shift shaft the number of turns noted during removal. Refer to Chapter Five and adjust the shift linkage.

10. Install the spark plugs and spark plug leads. Clean the battery terminals and connect the cables to the battery.

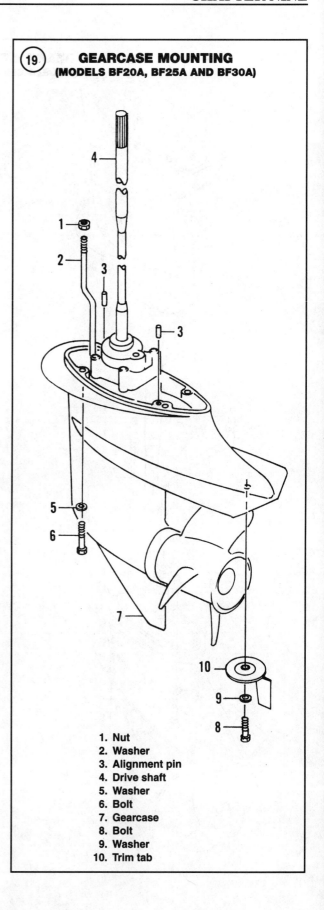

19 GEARCASE MOUNTING (MODELS BF20A, BF25A AND BF30A)

1. Nut
2. Washer
3. Alignment pin
4. Drive shaft
5. Washer
6. Bolt
7. Gearcase
8. Bolt
9. Washer
10. Trim tab

GEARCASE REPAIR

GEARCASE MOUNTING
MODELS BF35A, BF40A, BF45A AND BF50A

1. Drive shaft
2. Shift shaft locknut
3. Shift shaft
4. Locating pin or dowel
5. Washer
6. Bolt
7. Gearcase
8. Washer
9. Long bolt
10. Trim tab
11. Washer
12. Bolt
13. Speedometer hose coupling/fitting
14. Locating pin or dowel
15. Drive shaft housing
16. Water tube grommet

Removal/Installation (Models BF35A, BF40A, BF45A and BF50A)

1. Disconnect both battery cables from the battery. Remove the spark plugs and connect the plug leads to an engine ground. Shift the engine into reverse gear.

2. Locate the shift shaft connector at the lower forward side of the drive shaft housing (**Figure 17**). Loosen the lower jam nut. Count the number of turns as you remove the upper connector from the lower shift shaft. Record the number of turns for reference during installation.

3. Note the location and position of the mounting bolts (6, **Figure 20**) and washers (5).

4. Use a black marker to mark the trim tab position relative to the gearcase (**Figure 21**) Remove the bolt (12, **Figure 20**) and washer then lightly tap the trim tab (10, **Figure 20**) with a plastic mallet to remove it from the gearcase.

5. Cut the speedometer tube as close as possible to the fitting.

6. Remove the bolt (9, **Figure 20**) and washer (8) that are located above the trim tab. The trim tab must be removed to access the bolt.

7. Support the gearcase as you remove the bolts and washers from the gearcase and drive shaft housing.

8. Remove the gearcase from the drive shaft housing. Pry at the points located near the front and rear of the gearcase. Carefully lower the gearcase from the drive shaft housing when it becomes free.

9. Retain the aligning dowels (14, **Figure 20**) upon removal.

10. If it becomes dislodged during removal, install the water tube into position in the drive shaft housing (16, **Figure 20**).

11. Apply a light coat of water-resistant grease to the splined portion (1, **Figure 20**) of the drive shaft, the water tube grommet (16, **Figure 20**) and alignment dowels. Position the shift selector in reverse gear.

12. Guide the water tube into the water pump discharge hole while inserting the drive shaft into the crankshaft connection. Lower the gearcase and slightly rotate the drive shaft clockwise. Repeat this step until the shafts align and the gearcase and drive shaft housing mate. Never force the gearcase into position. Damage to the shift shafts and drive shaft seal could result.

13. Support the gearcase as you install the mounting bolts and washers. Tighten them to the specification listed in **Table 1**.

14. Thread the shift shaft upper nut or connector onto the lower shift shaft the number of turns noted during removal.

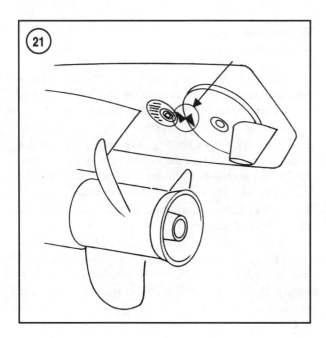

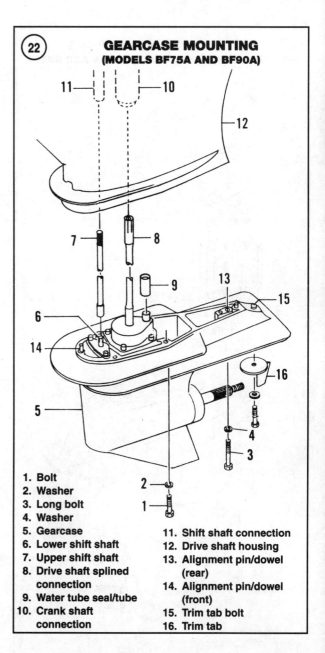

GEARCASE MOUNTING (MODELS BF75A AND BF90A)

1. Bolt
2. Washer
3. Long bolt
4. Washer
5. Gearcase
6. Lower shift shaft
7. Upper shift shaft
8. Drive shaft splined connection
9. Water tube seal/tube
10. Crank shaft connection
11. Shift shaft connection
12. Drive shaft housing
13. Alignment pin/dowel (rear)
14. Alignment pin/dowel (front)
15. Trim tab bolt
16. Trim tab

15. Slightly heat the cut end of the speedometer tube and carefully slide it into position onto the fitting (13, **Figure 20**). Allow the tube to cool before tugging on it.

16. Clean the surfaces then install the trim tab, bolt and washer. Align the marks made prior to removal and securely tighten the trim tab bolt.

17. Refer to Chapter Five and adjust the shift linkage.

18. Install the spark plugs and spark plug leads. Clean the battery terminals and connect the battery cables to the battery.

Removal/Installation (Models BF75A and BF90)

NOTE
Some 1999 BF75A and BF90A models are equipped with the same gearcase as BF115A and BF130A models. Inspect the water pump to identify the gearcase design. Models prior to 1999 are equipped with a stainless steel water pump body. BF75A and BF90A models equipped with a plastic water pump body use the 1999 gearcase. On models so equipped, refer to the illustrations and procedures for BF115A and BF130A models.

Removal and installation procedures for both standard and left hand gearcases are virtually identical. On multiple engine applications, always mark the propeller and gearcase to ensure they are installed to the proper engine on assembly.

1. Disconnect both battery cables from the battery. Remove the spark plugs and connect the plug leads to an engine ground. Shift the engine into neutral gear.

2. Use a black marker to mark the trim tab position relative to the gearcase (**Figure 21**).

3. Note the location and position of the mounting bolts and washers (1-4, **Figure 22**).

4. Cut the speedometer tube as close as possible to the fitting.

5. Support the gearcase and remove the bolts and washers from the gearcase (5, **Figure 22**) and drive shaft housing (12).

GEARCASE REPAIR

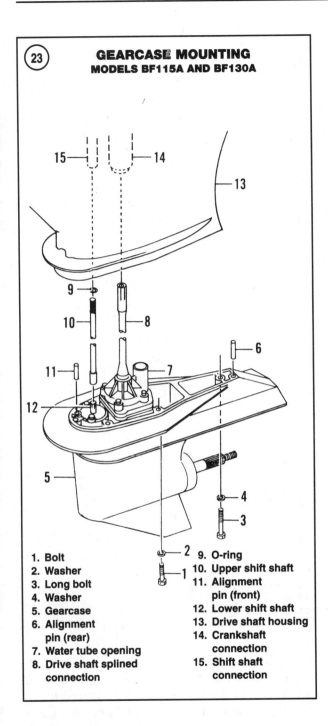

**23. GEARCASE MOUNTING
MODELS BF115A AND BF130A**

1. Bolt
2. Washer
3. Long bolt
4. Washer
5. Gearcase
6. Alignment pin (rear)
7. Water tube opening
8. Drive shaft splined connection
9. O-ring
10. Upper shift shaft
11. Alignment pin (front)
12. Lower shift shaft
13. Drive shaft housing
14. Crankshaft connection
15. Shift shaft connection

9. If they become dislodged during removal, install the water tube and upper shift shaft (7, **Figure 22**) into position in the drive shaft housing.

10. Apply a light coat of water-resistant grease to the splined portion (8, **Figure 22**) of the drive shaft, the water tube guide (9, **Figure 22**), shift shaft splines (6, **Figure 22**) and alignment dowels (13 and 14, **Figure 22**). Position the shift selector in neutral gear.

11. Rotate the drive shaft clockwise to verify the gearcase is in neutral. Rotate the shift shaft as you rotate the drive shaft clockwise until neutral is indicated.

12. The one missing spline on the lower shift shaft must face forward. Guide the lower shift shaft (7, **Figure 22**) into the upper shift shaft and the water tube into the water tube guide (9, **Figure 22**) while inserting the drive shaft into the crankshaft (10, **Figure 22**). Lower the gearcase and slightly rotate the drive shaft clockwise. Repeat this step until the shafts align and the gearcase and drive shaft housing mate. Never force the gearcase into position. Damage to the shift shafts and drive shaft seal may result.

13. Provide support for the gearcase as you install the mounting bolts and washers. Tighten them to the specification listed in **Table 1**.

14. Slightly heat the cut end of the speedometer tube and carefully slide it into position onto the fitting. Allow the tube to cool before tugging on it.

15. Clean the mounting/mating surfaces and install the trim tab and bolt (15, **Figure 22**) to the gearcase. Align the marks made prior to removal and securely tighten the trim tab bolt.

16. Refer to Chapter Five and adjust the shift linkage.

17. Install the spark plugs and spark plug leads. Clean the terminals and connect the cables to the battery. Check for proper shift operation and make necessary corrections prior to operating the engine.

Removal/Installation (Models BF115A and BF130A)

1. Disconnect both battery cables from the battery. Remove the spark plugs and connect the plug leads to an engine ground. Shift the engine into neutral gear.

2. Use a black marker to mark the trim tab adjustment relative to the gearcase (**Figure 21**).

3. Note the location and position of the mounting bolts and washers (1-4, **Figure 23**).

4. Cut the speedometer tube as close as possible to the fitting.

5. Support the gearcase and remove the bolts and washers from the gearcase (5, **Figure 23**) and drive shaft housing (13).

6. Remove the bolt (15, **Figure 22**) and lightly tap the trim tab to remove it from the gearcase.

7. Remove the gearcase from the drive shaft housing. Pry at the points located near the front and rear of the gearcase. Carefully lower the gearcase from the drive shaft housing when it becomes free.

8. Retain the aligning dowels (13 and 14, **Figure 22**) from the gearcase or drive shaft housing upon removal.

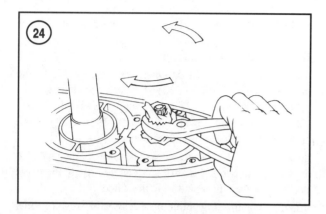

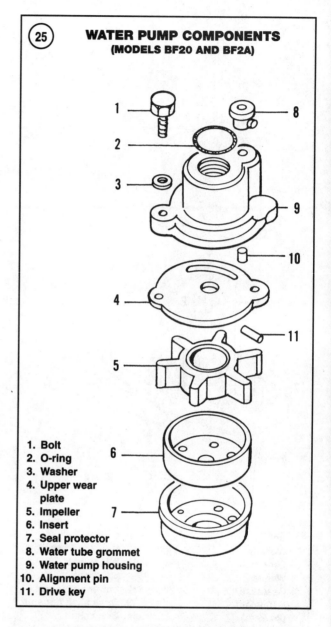

WATER PUMP COMPONENTS (MODELS BF20 AND BF2A)

1. Bolt
2. O-ring
3. Washer
4. Upper wear plate
5. Impeller
6. Insert
7. Seal protector
8. Water tube grommet
9. Water pump housing
10. Alignment pin
11. Drive key

6. Remove the bolt (15, **Figure 22**) and lightly tap the trim tab to remove it from the gearcase.

7. Remove the gearcase from the drive shaft housing. Pry at the points located near the front and rear of the gearcase. Carefully lower the gearcase from the drive shaft housing when it becomes free.

8. Retain the aligning dowels (6 and 11, **Figure 23**) from the gearcase or drive shaft housing upon removal.

9. If they become dislodged during removal, install the water tube and upper shift shaft into position in the drive shaft housing.

10. Apply a light coat of water-resistant grease to the splined portion (8, **Figure 23**) of the drive shaft, the water tube guide (7, **Figure 23**), shift shaft splines (12, **Figure 23**) and alignment dowels (6 and 11, **Figure 23**). Position the shift selector in neutral.

11. Rotate the drive shaft clockwise to verify the gearcase is in neutral. Rotate the shift shaft (**Figure 24**) as you rotate the drive shaft clockwise until neutral is indicated. The one missing spline on the lower shift shaft must face forward.

12. Guide the lower shift shaft (12, **Figure 23**) into the upper shift shaft and the water tube into the water pump opening (7, **Figure 23**) while inserting the drive shaft into the crankshaft (14, **Figure 23**). Slightly rotate the drive shaft clockwise if the drive shaft does not engage the crankshaft. Repeat this step until the shafts align and the gearcase and drive shaft housing mate. Never force the gearcase into position. Damage to the shift shafts and drive shaft seal could result.

13. Support the gearcase as you install the mounting bolts and washers. Tighten them to the specification listed in **Table 1**.

14. Slightly heat the cut end of the speedometer tube and carefully slide it into position onto the fitting. Allow the tube to cool before tugging on it.

15. Clean the mounting/mating surfaces then install the trim tab and bolt to the gearcase. Align the marks made prior to removal and securely tighten the trim tab bolt.

16. Refer to Chapter Five and adjust the shift linkage.

17. Install the spark plugs and spark plug leads. Clean the battery terminals and connect the battery cables to the battery. Check for proper shift operation. Make necessary corrections prior to operating the engine.

WATER PUMP

This section provides water pump disassembly, inspection and assembly instructions.

GEARCASE REPAIR

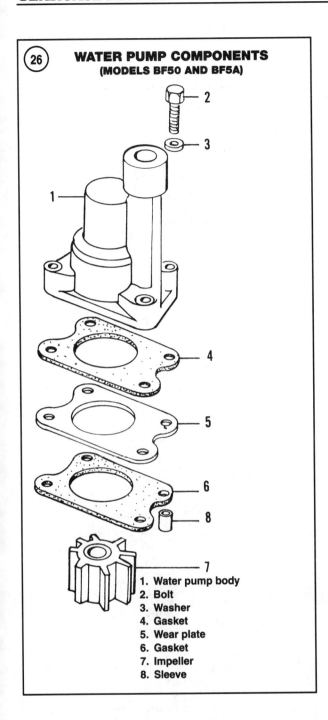

26 WATER PUMP COMPONENTS (MODELS BF50 AND BF5A)

1. Water pump body
2. Bolt
3. Washer
4. Gasket
5. Wear plate
6. Gasket
7. Impeller
8. Sleeve

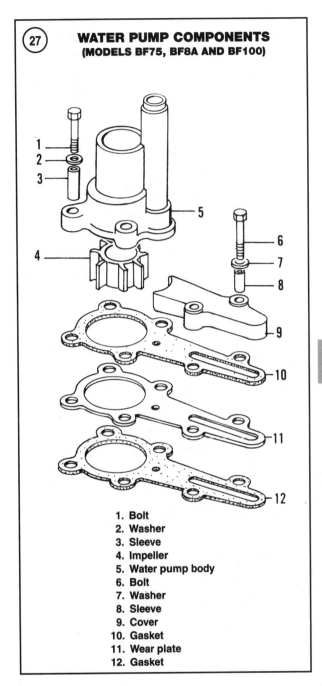

27 WATER PUMP COMPONENTS (MODELS BF75, BF8A AND BF100)

1. Bolt
2. Washer
3. Sleeve
4. Impeller
5. Water pump body
6. Bolt
7. Washer
8. Sleeve
9. Cover
10. Gasket
11. Wear plate
12. Gasket

Replace the impeller, seals, O-rings and all gaskets anytime the water pump is serviced. Never use questionable parts. Doing so may compromise the reliability of this vital component. Water pump components are inexpensive compared to the damage that can happen if the pump fails.

Water Pump Disassembly

Four water pump designs are used; however the disassembly and assembly procedures are similar on all models. Refer to **Figures 25-31**. The actual components may differ slightly from the illustration.

1. Refer to *Gearcase Removal* in this chapter and remove the gearcase from the engine.

2. Remove all fasteners that retain the water pump cover/body to the water pump base.

3. Remove the water tube seals, drive shaft seals and rear covers.

CHAPTER NINE

28 WATER PUMP COMPONENTS
(MODELS BF9.9A AND BF15A)

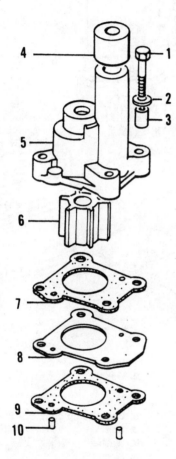

1. Bolt
2. Washer
3. Sleeve
4. Water tube seal/grommet
5. Water pump body
6. Impeller
7. Gasket
8. Wear plate
9. Gasket
10. Alignment pin/dowel

29 WATER PUMP COMPONENTS
(MODELS BF20A, BF25A, BF30A, BF35A, BF40A, BF45A AND BF50A)

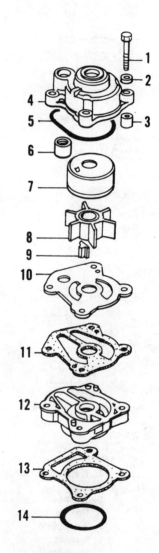

1. Bolt
2. Washer
3. Sleeve
4. Water pump body
5. O-ring
6. Water tube seal/grommet
7. Insert
8. Impeller
9. Drive key
10. Wear plate
11. Gasket
12. Water pump base
13. Gasket
14. O-ring

GEARCASE REPAIR

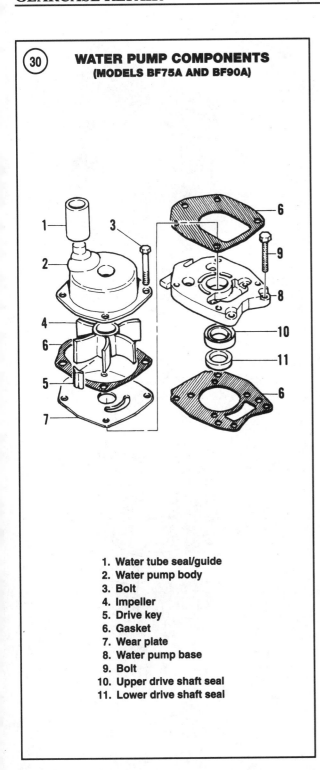

30 WATER PUMP COMPONENTS (MODELS BF75A AND BF90A)

1. Water tube seal/guide
2. Water pump body
3. Bolt
4. Impeller
5. Drive key
6. Gasket
7. Wear plate
8. Water pump base
9. Bolt
10. Upper drive shaft seal
11. Lower drive shaft seal

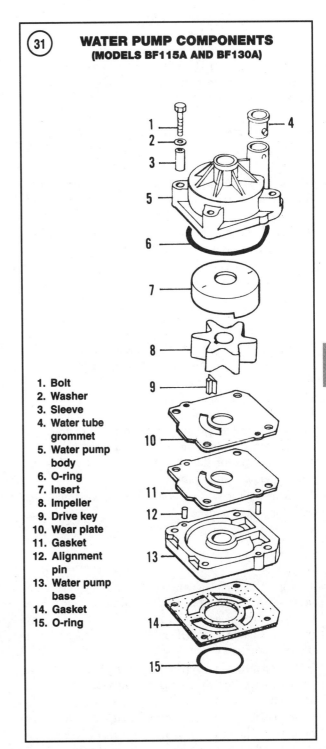

31 WATER PUMP COMPONENTS (MODELS BF115A AND BF130A)

1. Bolt
2. Washer
3. Sleeve
4. Water tube grommet
5. Water pump body
6. O-ring
7. Insert
8. Impeller
9. Drive key
10. Wear plate
11. Gasket
12. Alignment pin
13. Water pump base
14. Gasket
15. O-ring

4A. On models BF20 and BF2A, remove the O-ring (2, **Figure 25**) and the water tube sealing grommet (8, **Figure 25**) from the drive shaft.

4B. On models BF50 and BF5A, remove the water tube grommet from the water pump body.

4C. On models BF75, BF8A and BF100, remove the bolts (6, **Figure 27**), washers (7), sleeves (8) and cover plate (9) from the gearcase.

4D. On models BF9.9A and BF15A, remove the water tube grommet (4, **Figure 28**) from the water pump body.

4E. On models BF75A and BF90A, remove the water tube guide (1, **Figure 30**) from the water pump body.

4F. On models BF115A and BF130A, pry the tip from the body then remove the water tube grommet (4, **Figure 31**) from the water pump body.

5. Carefully pry the cover or water pump body from the water pump base or gearcase mounting location. Remove and discard the sealing O-ring or gasket that seals the water pump cover to the water pump base.

6. Mark the up side of the impeller if it must be reused. Remove the water pump impeller from the water pump cover or base.

7. Remove the impeller if it remained on the drive shaft when the cover was removed. Use a chisel and carefully break the inner hub of the impeller if it is seized to the drive shaft. Do not allow the chisel to contact the drive shaft.

8. Remove and retain the drive key from the impeller or slot on the drive shaft.

9A. On models BF20 and BF2A, use a small screwdriver to carefully pry the insert cartridge (6, **Figure 33**) from the gearcase.

9B. On all other models, mark the forward and up direction and remove the wear plate from the water pump mounting location. Do not remove the water pump base unless access to drive shaft seals is required. Refer to *Gearcase Repair* in this chapter for water pump base removal and installation procedures.

10. Scrape all gasket material from the wear plate and water pump body/cover.

Water Pump Inspection

1. Inspect the impeller (**Figure 32**) for brittle, missing or burnt vanes. Squeeze the vanes toward the hub and release the vanes. The vanes should spring back to the extended position. Replace the impeller if there are damaged, burnt, brittle or stiff vanes.

2. Inspect the water pump insert for burned, worn or damaged surfaces. Replace the insert if there are any defects are noted.

3. Inspect the water pump cover for melted plastic or indications of impeller material on the insert. Replace the cover and the water pump base if you note either defect.

4. Replace the water tube grommet if you observe a burned appearance, cracked surface or brittle material.

5. Replace the wear plate if there are warped surfaces, worn grooves, melted plastic or other damaged areas.

6. Clean all debris or contamination from the drive shaft. The impeller must slide freely onto the drive shaft.

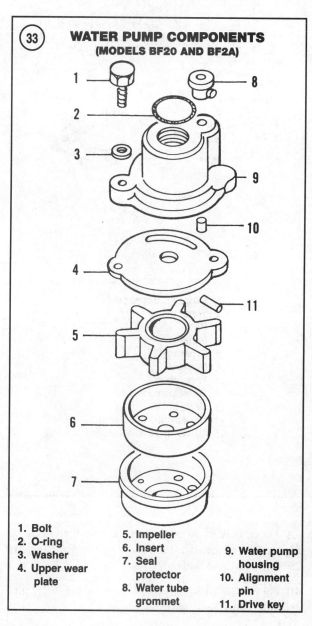

GEARCASE REPAIR

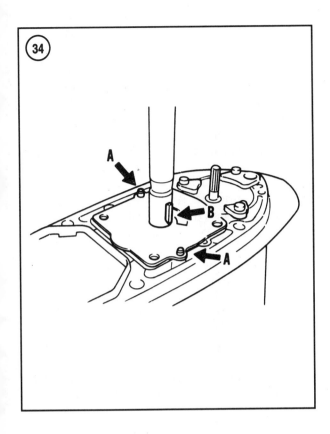

34

Water Pump Assembly

1. Refer to *Gearcase Disassembly* and install the water pump base assembly if it is removed.

2. On models BF20 and BF2A, install the insert cartridge (6, **Figure 33**) into the gearcase. Ensure that the tab on the insert slides into the hole in the seal protector (7, **Figure 33**).

3. Install a new gasket onto the water pump base or gearcase.

4. Position the wear plate onto the water pump base or gearcase mounting location. Make sure the alignment holes in the wear plate fit over the alignment pins (A, **Figure 34**).

5. Install a new gasket to the upper side of the wear plate. Ensure that all bolt and alignment pin holes align with the wear plate and gaskets.

6. Apply a light coat of water-resistant grease to the impeller drive key, drive shaft bore in the impeller and drive shaft key slot. Install the drive key into the slot on the drive shaft (B, **Figure 34**).

7. On models BF20 and BF2A, apply a light coat of water-resistant grease into the drive shaft key slot. Install the impeller drive key into the drive key slot. Apply a light coat of water-resistant grease to the drive shaft and water pump impeller bore in the insert.

8. On models BF20 and BF2A, slide the new impeller over the drive shaft until it contacts the insert. Rotate the drive shaft clockwise as you lightly push down on the impeller. Rotate the drive shaft until the impeller has completely entered the insert.

9. On all models, except BF20 and BF2A, slide the impeller over the drive shaft then position it onto the drive key. Apply water-resistant grease to the surfaces of the insert in the water pump cover. Install a new gasket or O-ring onto the water pump cover. Use a very light coat of 3M weather-strip adhesive to hold the gasket or O-ring in position.

10. On all models, except BF20 and BF2A, slide the cover over the drive shaft and allow it to rest on the impeller vanes. Rotate the drive shaft clockwise (**Figure 35**) while lightly pressing down on the water pump cover. Continue to rotate the drive shaft while pressing down on the cover until the impeller enters the water pump body and fully seats to the wear plate.

11. On models BF20 and BF2A, apply grease to the impeller contact surfaces. Install the top wear plate over the drive shaft and onto the insert. Install the water pump cover into position.

12. For all models, install all sleeves, washers, nuts and bolts. Tighten them to the standard tightening torque specifications listed in **Table 1**. Use a crossing pattern and torque in two or more steps. Apply grease and install the water tube sealing grommet into position in the water pump cover.

13. On models BF115A and BF130A, ensure that the tip on the insert enters the locating hole in the water pump cover.

14. On models BF75, BF8A and BF100, position the rear cover (9, **Figure 27**) onto the water pump gaskets. Install the sleeve, washer and bolt into the rear cover. Securely tighten the bolt.

15. Refer to *Gearcase Installation* in this chapter and install the gearcase. Run the engine and check for proper operation of the cooling system.

GEARCASE REPAIR

This section covers complete disassembly, inspection and assembly procedures for the gearcase. Repairs to the gearcase may not require complete gearcase disassembly. If complete disassembly is not required, follow the procedure until the required component is accessible. Reverse the disassembly steps to assemble and install these components.

When replacing the propeller shaft seals, refer to the *Gearcase Cap/Bearing Carrier*.

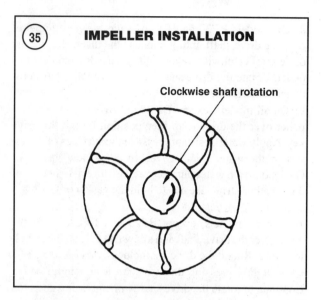

35 IMPELLER INSTALLATION
Clockwise shaft rotation

When replacing the seals on the drive shaft, refer to *Water Pump Base*. Drive shaft removal may be required with some models. Refer to *Gearcase Disassembly* for procedures when required.

If the repair involves the replacement of gears, bearings, drive shaft or housing, the entire repair and shimming procedures must be followed.

NOTE
Some 1999 BF75A and BF90A models are equipped with the same gearcase as BF115A and BF130A models. Inspect the water pump to identify the gearcase design. Models prior to 1999 are equipped with a stainless steel water pump body. BF75A and BF90A models equipped with a plastic water pump body use the 1999 gearcase. On models so equipped, refer to the illustrations and procedures for BF115A and BF130A models.

NOTE
Refer to the serial number tag for the type of gearcase used on the engine. Models with an L in the model designation use a left-hand or counter rotation gearcase. Other models use the standard or right-hand gearcase.

Gearcase Disassembly

Refer to **Figures 36-44** as applicable during gearcase disassembly. Remove the gearcase from the engine and remove the water pump assembly before beginning the disassembly process. Refer to *Gearcase Removal and Installation* and *Water Pump Servicing* in this chapter.

Mount the gearcase in a holding fixture or a sturdy vise. Use padded jaws or wooden blocks to protect the surfaces of the gearcase. Clamp the gearcase on the skeg (lower fin) when using a vise.

Note the location and thickness of all shims in the gearcase (**Figure 45**) as they are removed. Use a micrometer to measure and record each shim thickness at each location. Make sure that all shims are removed before cleaning the gear case. Wire the shims together or place them in an envelope. Always note the shim location in the gearcase.

Use pressurized water to thoroughly clean all debris from the external surfaces of the gearcase prior to disassembly. Pay particular attention to the bearing carrier area as debris can easily become trapped in hidden recesses. This step helps prevent debris from contaminating the bearings during the disassembly process.

1. Refer to Chapter Four and drain all gear lubricant from the gearcase.
2. Refer to *Gearcase Removal and Installation* in this chapter and remove the gearcase from the engine.
3. Refer to *Water Pump* in this chapter and remove the water pump.
4. Refer to *Gearcase Cap/Bearing Carrier* in this chapter and remove the gearcase cap/bearing carrier from the gearcase.
5. Refer to *Water Pump Base/Drive Shaft Seals* in this chapter and remove the water pump base and drive shaft seals from the gearcase.
6. Refer to *Pinion Gear and Drive Shaft* in this chapter and remove the pinion gear, drive shaft and drive shaft bearings from the gearcase housing.
7. Refer to *Lower Shift Shaft/Retainer* in this chapter and remove the shift shaft retainer and lower shift shaft.
8. Refer to *Propeller Shaft* in this chapter and remove the propeller shaft from the gearcase housing.
9. Refer to *Front Mounted Gear* in this chapter and remove the front mounted gear and bearing from the gearcase or propeller shaft.
10. Refer to *Bearing Race* in this chapter and remove all remaining bearing races and other components from the gearcase.
11. Refer to *Anodes and other Gearcase Components* in this chapter and remove all remaining components from the gearcase.

CAUTION
When using heat to assist with the removal of a component, make sure to keep the flame away from the seals or O-rings. Never heat

GEARCASE REPAIR

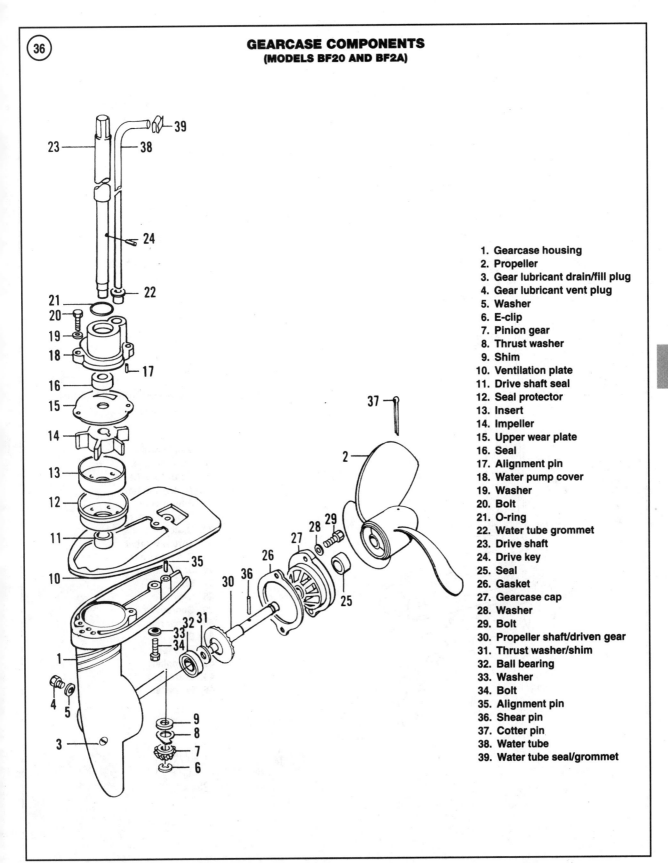

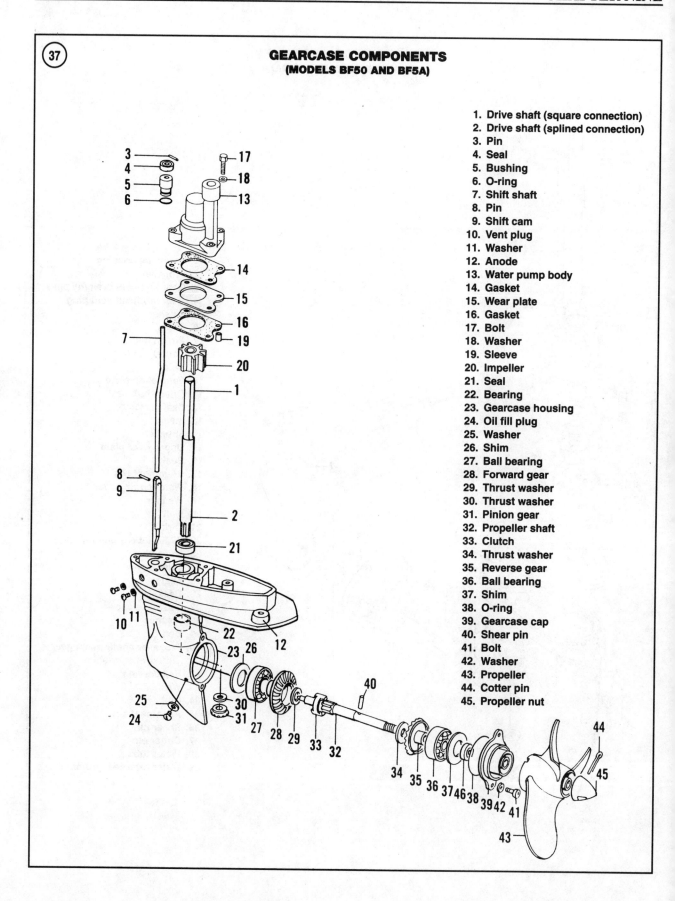

GEARCASE REPAIR

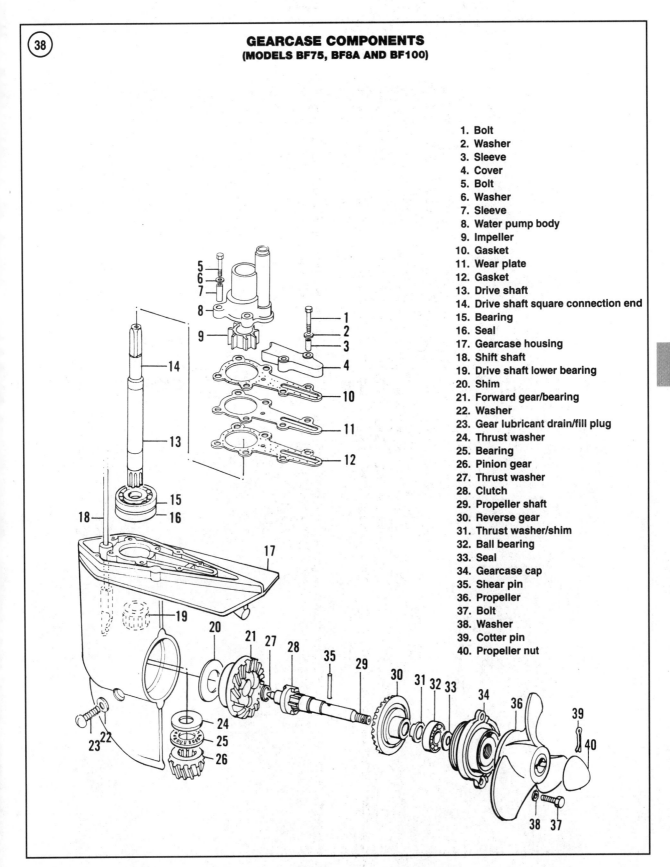

**GEARCASE COMPONENTS
(MODELS BF75, BF8A AND BF100)**

1. Bolt
2. Washer
3. Sleeve
4. Cover
5. Bolt
6. Washer
7. Sleeve
8. Water pump body
9. Impeller
10. Gasket
11. Wear plate
12. Gasket
13. Drive shaft
14. Drive shaft square connection end
15. Bearing
16. Seal
17. Gearcase housing
18. Shift shaft
19. Drive shaft lower bearing
20. Shim
21. Forward gear/bearing
22. Washer
23. Gear lubricant drain/fill plug
24. Thrust washer
25. Bearing
26. Pinion gear
27. Thrust washer
28. Clutch
29. Propeller shaft
30. Reverse gear
31. Thrust washer/shim
32. Ball bearing
33. Seal
34. Gearcase cap
35. Shear pin
36. Propeller
37. Bolt
38. Washer
39. Cotter pin
40. Propeller nut

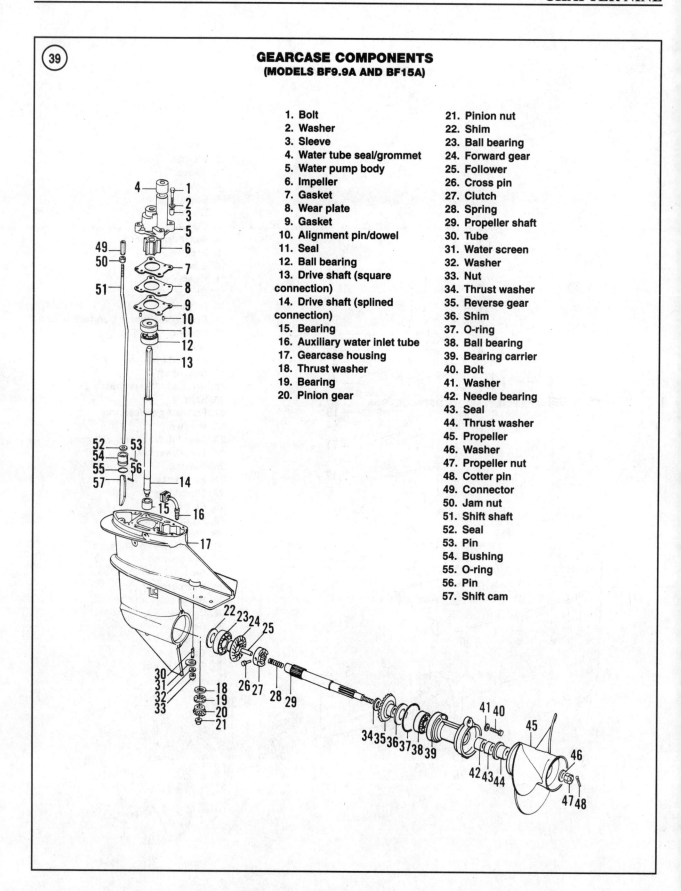

GEARCASE COMPONENTS
(MODELS BF9.9A AND BF15A)

1. Bolt
2. Washer
3. Sleeve
4. Water tube seal/grommet
5. Water pump body
6. Impeller
7. Gasket
8. Wear plate
9. Gasket
10. Alignment pin/dowel
11. Seal
12. Ball bearing
13. Drive shaft (square connection)
14. Drive shaft (splined connection)
15. Bearing
16. Auxiliary water inlet tube
17. Gearcase housing
18. Thrust washer
19. Bearing
20. Pinion gear
21. Pinion nut
22. Shim
23. Ball bearing
24. Forward gear
25. Follower
26. Cross pin
27. Clutch
28. Spring
29. Propeller shaft
30. Tube
31. Water screen
32. Washer
33. Nut
34. Thrust washer
35. Reverse gear
36. Shim
37. O-ring
38. Ball bearing
39. Bearing carrier
40. Bolt
41. Washer
42. Needle bearing
43. Seal
44. Thrust washer
45. Propeller
46. Washer
47. Propeller nut
48. Cotter pin
49. Connector
50. Jam nut
51. Shift shaft
52. Seal
53. Pin
54. Bushing
55. O-ring
56. Pin
57. Shift cam

GEARCASE REPAIR

GEARCASE COMPONENTS
(MODELS BF20A, BF25A AND BF30A)

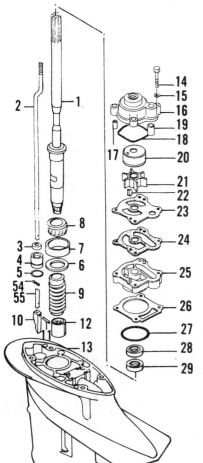

1. Drive shaft
2. Shift shaft
3. Seal
4. Bushing
5. O-ring
6. Shim
7. Bearing race
8. Roller bearing
9. Lubrication sleeve
10. Shift cam
11. Pin
12. Roller bearing
13. Gearcase housing
14. Bolt
15. Washer
16. Water pump body
17. Sleeve
18. O-ring
19. Water tube seal/grommet
20. Insert
21. Impeller
22. Drive key
23. Wear plate
24. Gasket
25. Water pump base
26. Gasket
27. O-ring
28. Upper drive shaft seal
29. Lower drive shaft seal
30. Follower
31. Bearing
32. Clutch spring
33. Cross pin
34. Clutch
35. Connector
36. Spring
37. Propeller shaft
38. Pinion gear
39. Pinion nut
40. Shim
41. Bearing race
42. Roller bearing
43. Forward gear
44. Thrush washer
45. Reverse gear
46. O-ring
47. Ball bearing
48. Shim
49. Shim
50. Bearing carrier
51. Needle bearing
52. Inner propeller shaft seal
53. Outer propeller shaft seal
54. Retaining pin
55. Shaft

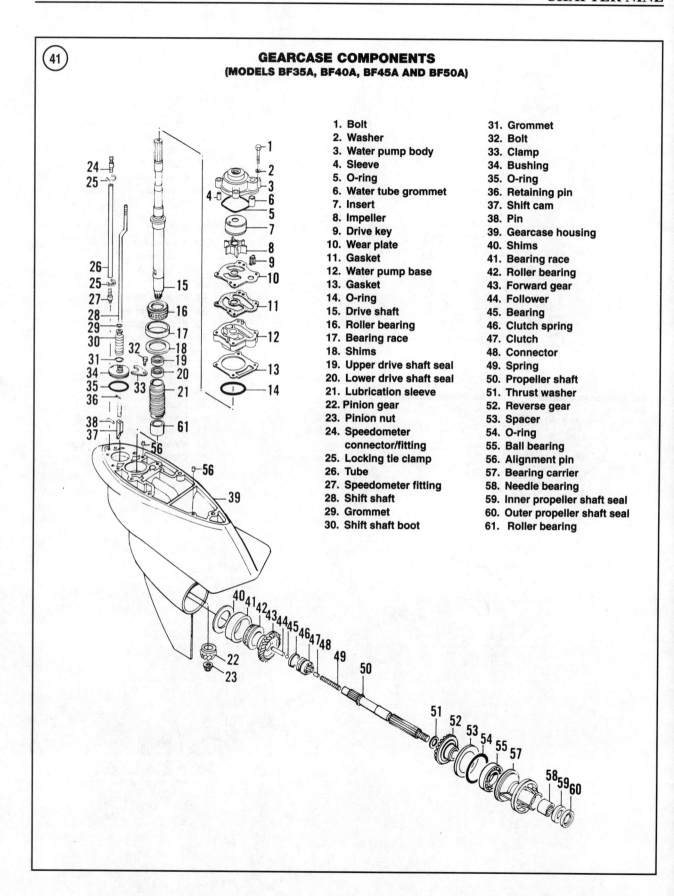

GEARCASE REPAIR

GEARCASE COMPONENTS
(MODELS BF75A AND BF90A)

(42)

1. Water tube seal/guide
2. Bolt
3. Washer
4. Sleeve
5. Water pump body
6. Impeller
7. Drive key
8. Gasket
9. Wear plate
10. Gasket
11. Bolt
12. Washer
13. Water pump base
14. Upper drive shaft seal
15. Lower drive shaft seal
16. Gasket
17. Roller bearing
18. Bearing sleeve
19. Lubrication sleeve
20. Drive shaft sleeve
21. O-ring
22. Drive shaft
23. Shift shaft adapter *
24. Bolt
25. Seal
26. Bushing
27. O-ring
28. Shift shaft
29. E-clip
30. Shims
31. Bearing race
32. Roller bearing
33. Gearcase housing
34. Gasket
35. Gear lubricant vent/plug
36. Gear lubricant vent/plug
37. Gear lubricant drain/fill plug
38. Pinion nut
39. Pinion gear
40. Shift cam
41. Shim
42. Bearing race
43. Roller bearing
44. Needle bearing
45. Forward gear
46. Follow
47. Connector
48. Bearings (3)
49. Spring
50. Clutch
51. Cross pin
52. Clutch spring
53. Propeller shaft
54. Reverse gear
55. O-ring
56. Thrust bearing
57. Bearing race
58. Roller bearing
59. Bearing carrier
60. Washer
61. Nut
62. Needle bearing
63. Inner propeller shaft seal
64. Outer propeller shaft seal
65. Thrust washer
66. Propeller
67. Tab washer
68. Propeller nut

*not used on all models

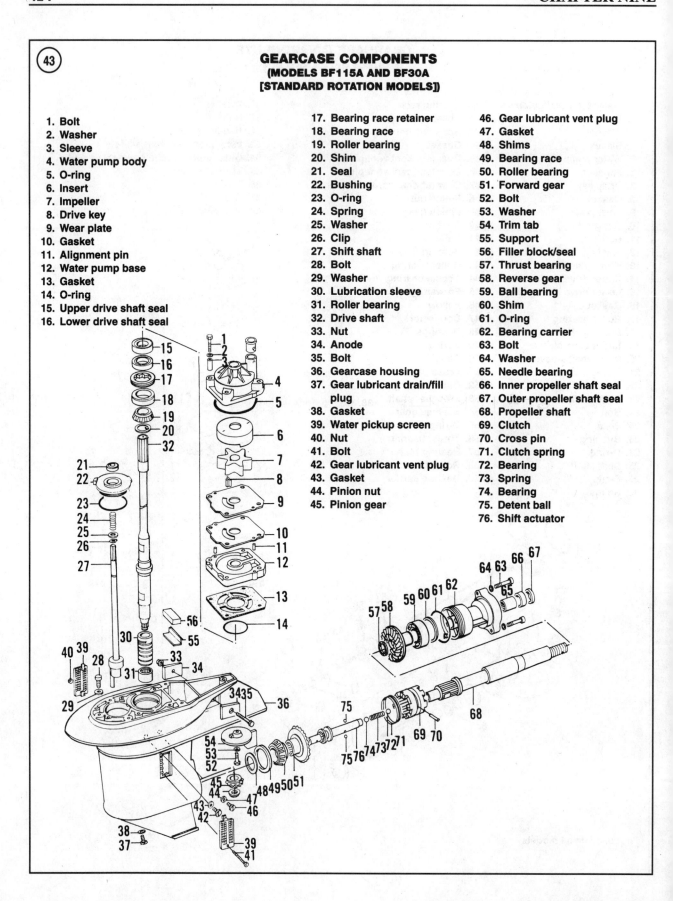

GEARCASE REPAIR

GEARCASE COMPONENTS
(MODELS BF115A AND BF130A [LEFT ROTATION MODELS])

1. Bolt
2. Washer
3. Sleeve
4. Water pump body
5. O-ring
6. Insert
7. Impeller
8. Drive key
9. Wear plate
10. Gasket
11. Alignment pin
12. Water pump base
13. Gasket
14. O-ring
15. Upper drive shaft seal
16. Lower drive shaft seal
17. Bearing race retainer
18. Bearing race
19. Roller bearing
20. Shim
21. Drive shaft
22. Nut
23. Anode
24. Filler block/seal
25. Support
26. Lubrication sleeve
27. Roller bearing
28. Seal
29. Bushing
30. O-ring
31. Spring
32. Washer
33. Clip
34. Shift shaft
35. Bolt
36. Water screen
37. Nut
38. Gear lubricant fill/vent plug
39. Washer
40. Gear lubricant fill/vent plug
41. Washer
42. Pinion gear
43. Pinion nut
44. Shims
45. Ball bearing
46. Reverse gear
47. Bolt
48. Bolt
49. Washer
50. Trim tab
51. Forward gear
52. Gear retainer
53. Shims
54. Bearing race
55. Roller bearing
56. Thrust bearing
57. Thrust washer
58. Spacer
59. O-ring
60. Bearing carrier
61. Washer
62. Bolt
63. Needle bearing
64. Inner propeller shaft seal
65. Outer propeller shaft seal
66. Propeller shaft
67. Clutch
68. Cross pin
69. Clutch spring
70. Bearing
71. Spring
72. Bearing
73. Detent ball
74. Shift actuator
75. Gearcase housing

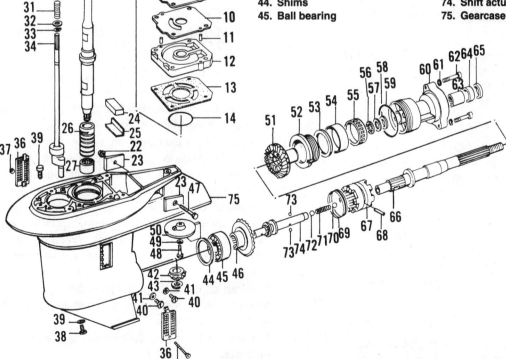

Gearcase Cap/Bearing Carrier Removal/Installation

CAUTION
Some gearcase cap and bearing carriers incorporate a step or ledge within the bore for the propeller shaft support bearing. Installing from the wrong end of the bore prevents proper installation of the bearing into the assembly. Install the bearings into the cap or carrier using the bore entrance that allows bearing installation without interference from the step.

NOTE
Remove the gearcase cap or bearing carrier using a torch to apply heat to the gearcase near the gearcase-to-cap mating surface. Continually move the flame to apply even heat.

the housing to the point that the finish is burned. Continually move the flame around the mating surface to apply heat evenly. Excessive use of heat can distort or melt the gearcase.

NOTE
Apply heat to assist with removing the cover nut, on models so equipped. If corrosion prevents rotation and removal of the cover nut, drill two holes approximately 25 mm (1 in.) apart into the surface of the cover nut. Drill the holes to the depth of the cover nut thickness. Use a chisel to break a small section from the cover nut at the drilled holes. Remove the cover nut with the cover nut tool as indicated.

WARNING
Always wear safety glasses anytime you are striking any object with a hammer. When using a hammer, anyone in the area must wear safety glasses.

Models BF35A, BF40A, BF45A and BF50A may require a special bearing carrier removal tool and cover nut tool, part No. 07LPC-ZV30200 and 07LPA-ZV30100. Purchase these tools from a local Honda dealership.

On most models, use a two-jaw puller to remove the gearcase cap/bearing carrier. These are available from most tool suppliers.

Removal/Installation (Models BF20A, BF2A, BF50, BF5A, BF75, BF8A and BF100)

1. Mark the locations of the gearcase cap mounting bolts. Mark the up position relative to the gearcase to ensure proper installation. Remove both bolts and washers from the gearcase cap (**Figure 46**).
2. Carefully pry the case from the housing. Remove and discard the O-ring or gasket at the gearcase. Inspect the surfaces for corroded, worn or damaged surfaces and replace the gearcase cap if defects are noted.
3. Clean all corrosion or contamination from the gearcase cap mounting bolts and bolt holes. Inspect the bolts for damaged threads or other defects. Repair any damaged threads in the housing. Replace the mounting bolts if defective.
4. Clean all debris from the propeller shaft surfaces to prevent contamination of the gearcase during installation of the gearcase cap.
5. Clean all debris from the gearcase to gearcase cap mating surface.
6. Install a new O-ring or gasket to the gearcase cap. Coat the O-ring with gearcase lubricant.

GEARCASE REPAIR

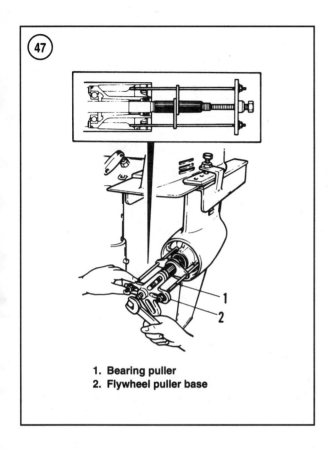

1. Bearing puller
2. Flywheel puller base

1. Use pressurized water to wash the bearing carrier prior to removal. This helps prevent contamination of the gearcase during removal procedures.

2. Mark the locations of the bearing carrier mounting bolts. Mark the UP position relative to the gearcase to ensure proper installation. Remove both bolts and washers from the bearing carrier (**Figure 46**).

3. Use a bearing puller tool to loosen the bearing carrier (**Figure 47**). Pull the bearing carrier from the gearcase (**Figure 48**). Remove and discard the O-ring from the bearing carrier upon removal. Inspect all surfaces for corroded, worn or damaged areas. Replace the bearing carrier when defects are noted.

4. Clean all corrosion and contamination from the bearing carrier mounting bolts and bolt holes. Inspect the bolts for damaged threads or other defects. Repair any damaged threads in the housing. Replace the mounting bolts if defective.

5. Clean all debris from the propeller shaft surfaces.

6. Clean all debris from the gearcase-to-bearing carrier mating surface.

7. Install a new O-ring onto the bearing carrier. Coat the O-ring with gearcase lubricant. Apply water-resistant grease to the bearing carrier surfaces that directly contact the gearcase housing.

8. Apply water-resistant grease to the propeller shaft seal lips in the bearing carrier. Rotate the drive shaft clockwise as you carefully slide the bearing carrier over the propeller shaft and into position.

9. Slowly rotate the bearing carrier to align the UP side (as noted prior to removal) with the bolt holes. Lightly tap the bearing carrier into position in the gearcase. Rotate the drive shaft clockwise to ensure correct gear mesh. Install the washers and bolts into the threaded holes.

10. Tighten the bolts to the specification listed in **Table 1**.

7. Apply a liberal amount of water-resistant grease to the propeller shaft seal lips in the bearing carrier. Rotate the drive shaft clockwise as you carefully slide the bearing carrier over the propeller shaft and into position.

8. Slowly rotate the gearcase cap to align the UP side (as noted prior to removal) with the bolt holes. Lightly tap the gearcase cap into position on the gearcase. Install the washers and bolts into the gearcase. Rotate the drive shaft clockwise to ensure correct gear mesh.

9. Tighten the bolts to the specification listed in **Table 1**.

Removal/installation (models BF9.9A, BF15A, BF20A, BF25A, BF30A, BF75A, BF90A, BF115A and BF130A)

CAUTION
On models BF75A and BF90A, serious damage to internal gearcase components can occur if the thrust bearing slips from the bearing carrier during installation. Be certain the large thrust bearing remains in position during installation of the bearing carrier into the gearcase. Do not force the carrier into position until you verify all components are in position.

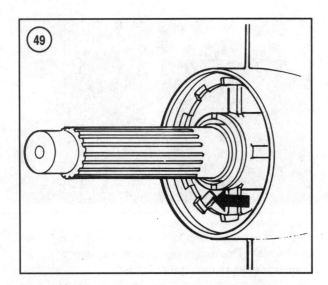

Removal/installation (models BF35A, BF40A, BF45A and BF50A)

1. Use pressurized water to wash the bearing carrier prior to removal. This helps prevent contamination of the gearcase during the removal procedures.
2. Bend the tabs on the tab washer away from the cover nut notches (**Figure 49**).
3. Use the cover nut tool (part No. 07LPA-ZV30100) to loosen and remove the cover nut (**Figure 50**).
4. Carefully pry the tab washer away from the top of the gearcase opening. Pull the tab at the bottom of the tab washer from the hole at the bottom of the gearcase opening and pull the tab washer away. Discard the tab washer.
5. Mark the UP direction on the bearing carrier relative to the gearcase to ensure correct installation.
6. Use a bearing puller tool to loosen and pull the bearing carrier from the gearcase (**Figure 47**). Discard the O-ring from the bearing carrier.
7. Inspect all surfaces for corroded, worn or damaged areas and replace the bearing carrier if necessary.
8. Clean all corrosion or contamination from the cover nut and cover nut threads in the gearcase housing. Inspect the cover nut for damaged threads or other defects. Repair any damaged threads in the housing. Replace the cover nut if damaged.
9. Clean all debris from the propeller shaft surfaces to prevent contamination of the gearcase during installation of the gearcase cap.
10. Clean all debris from the gearcase-to-bearing carrier mating surface.
11. Install a new O-ring onto the bearing carrier. Coat the O-ring with gearcase lubricant. Apply water-resistant grease to the bearing carrier surfaces that directly contact the gearcase housing and the cover nut threads.

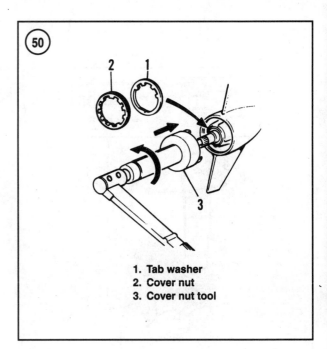

1. Tab washer
2. Cover nut
3. Cover nut tool

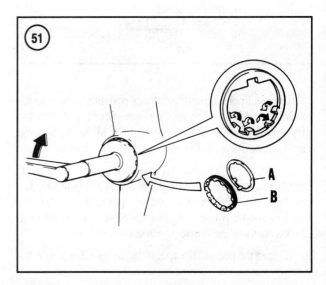

12. Apply water-resistant grease to the propeller shaft seal lips in the bearing carrier. Rotate the drive shaft clockwise as you carefully slide the bearing carrier over the propeller shaft and into position.

13. Slowly rotate the bearing carrier to align the UP side, as noted prior to removal. Lightly tap the bearing carrier until fully seated in the gearcase. Rotate the drive shaft clockwise to ensure correct gear mesh.

14. Install the new tab washer into the gearcase with the lower tab inserted into the hole in the gearcase opening. Ensure the tab washer aligns with the recess in the bearing

GEARCASE REPAIR

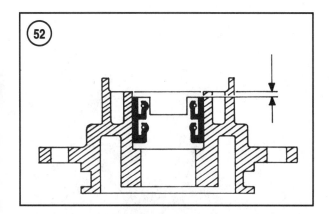

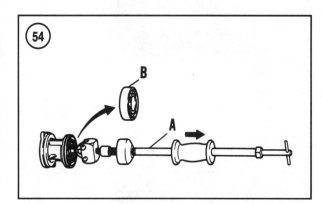

carrier. Thread the cover nut into the gearcase by hand until it contacts the tab washer.

15. Use the cover nut tool to tighten the cover nut to the specification listed in **Table 1**.

16. Check the alignment of the tabs on the tab washer and the notches on the cover nut (**Figure 51**). Tighten the cover nut slightly if necessary to ensure that one or more tabs can be bent into the notches in the cover nut. Bend all remaining tabs away from the cover nut.

Gearcase Cap/Bearing Carrier Disassembly/Assembly

Models BF20 and BF2A

1. Use a depth micrometer to measure the depth of the propeller shaft seal (**Figure 52**) in the seal bore prior to removal.
2. Using care to avoid damaging the seal bore, pry the seal from the gearcase cap. Discard the seal.
3. Clean all debris or contamination from the seal bore.
4. Position the new seal in the seal bore with the number or lettered side facing out. Use a driver (part No. 07749-0010000 and 07746-0041000) or other suitable tool to drive the seal into the bore until it reaches the depth recorded in Step 1.
5. Apply water-resistant grease to the seal lip(s).

Models BF50, BF5A, BF75, BF8A and BF100

NOTE
Remove the ball bearing and needle bearings from the gearcase cap only if replacement is required. Removal damages the bearings.

1. Secure the gearcase cap in a vise with soft jaws. Pull the reverse gear (rear mounted gear) from the gearcase cap. Use two screwdrivers to carefully pry the gear (**Figure 53**) from the ball bearing if it cannot be removed by hand.
2. Use a slide hammer (A, **Figure 54**) to remove the ball bearing (B, **Figure 54**) from the gearcase cap. Discard the bearing.
3. Pull the shim(s) or thrust washer from the gearcase cap.
4. Use a depth micrometer to measure the depth of the propeller shaft seal (**Figure 52**) in the seal bore prior to removal.
5. Using care to avoid damaging the seal bore, pry the seal from the gearcase cap with a small screwdriver. Discard the seal. Clean all debris from the seal bore.
6. Position the new seal in the seal bore with the number or lettered side facing out the propeller side.
7. Use a driver (part No. 07749-0010000 and 07746-0010100) or other suitable tool to drive the seal in the bore (**Figure 55**) until it reaches the depth recorded in Step 1 or it bottoms in the gearcase cap.
8. Refer to *Inspection* in this chapter to determine if components must be replaced.
9. Apply gear lubricant to all surfaces of the ball bearing and the bore in the gearcase cap. Install the shim or thrust

430 CHAPTER NINE

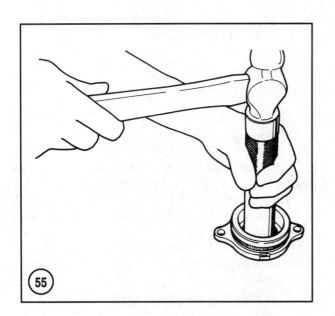

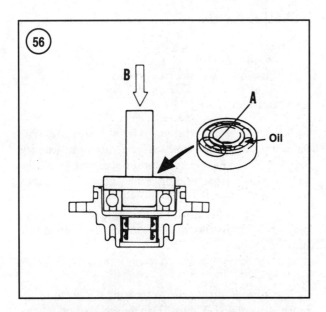

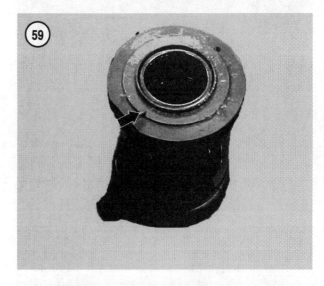

GEARCASE REPAIR

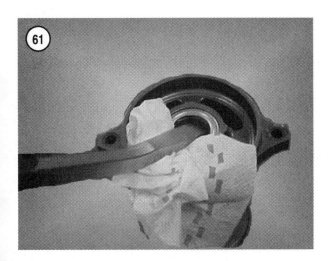

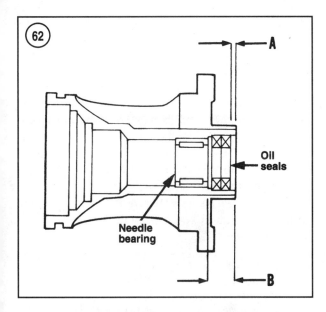

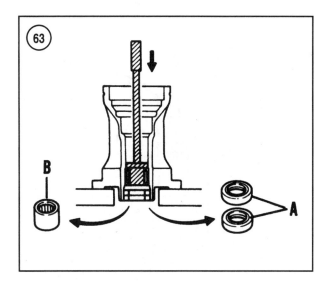

washer into position within the gearcase cap. Position the new ball bearing into its bore with its number or letters facing away from the propeller side.

10. Use a bearing driver (Honda part No. 07749-0010300) to carefully press or lightly tap (B, **Figure 56**) the ball bearing (A, **Figure 56**) into the bearing cap until fully seated.

11. Use a wooden block or other material to cushion the gear and press the gear into the ball bearing until fully seated.

12. Apply water-resistant grease to the seal lip(s).

Models BF75A and BF90A

1. Secure the bearing carrier in a vise with soft jaws. Pull the reverse gear from the carrier (**Figure 57**). Remove the thrust bearing (**Figure 58**) and bearing spacer (**Figure 59**) from the bearing carrier.

2. Use a slide hammer (**Figure 60**) to remove the roller bearing from the bearing carrier. Discard the bearing.

3. Skip this step if needle bearing replacement is required. To prevent damage, place a shop towel against any contacted surfaces of the bearing carrier. Using care to avoid damaging the seal bore, pry the seal from the bearing carrier with a pry bar (**Figure 61**). Discard the seal. Clean all debris from the seal bore.

4. Using a depth micrometer, measure the depth of the needle bearing in the bearing carrier (B, **Figure 62**. Record this measurement for use during assembly.

5. Use bearing driver (part No. 07949-371001) or other suitable tool (**Figure 63**) to press the seals and needle bearing (A, B, **Figure 63**) from the bearing carrier.

6. Clean all debris from the bearing carrier. Refer to *Inspection* in this chapter to determine if components must be replaced.

7. Place the new needle bearing into the bore with the numbered or lettered side facing the propeller side. Use a bearing driver (part No. 07746-0040700) and carefully press the new bearing into the bearing carrier (**Figure 64**) until it contacts the step in the bore or reaches the depth noted prior to removal.

8. Apply Loctite 271 (red) to the outer diameter of the inner seals prior to installation. Position a new inner seal into the seal bore with the lip facing the reverse gear side. Use a seal driver (part No. 07SPD-ZW0040Z) or other suitable tool to press the inner seal (**Figure 65**) in until its surface is just below the seal bore opening.

9. Apply Loctite 271 (red) to the outer diameter of the outer seals prior to installation. Place the outer seal onto the inner seal with the lip facing the propeller side. Place

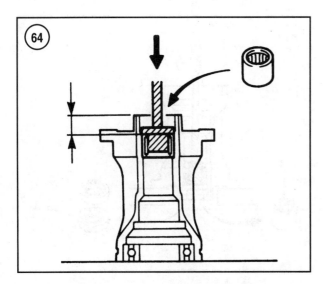

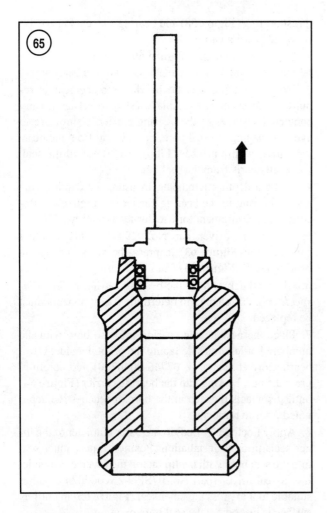

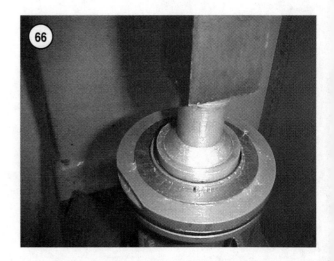

10. Apply gear lubricant to all surfaces of the roller bearing and its bore in the bearing carrier. Place the bearing into the bore opening with the numbered or lettered side facing toward the reverse gear side.

11. Use bearing driver (Honda part No. 07SPD-ZW0030Z) or other suitable tool to press the bearing (**Figure 66**) into the bearing carrier until it just contacts the step or bottom of its bore.

12. Place the thrust bearing and bearing spacer (**Figure 59** and **Figure 60**) onto the bearing carrier. Apply gear lubricant to the thrust bearing.

13. Place the reverse gear (**Figure 57**) into the bearing carrier. Ensure it fully seats against the thrust bearings.

14. Apply water-resistant grease to the seal lip(s).

CAUTION
On models BF75A and BF90A, damage to the internal gearcase components can occur if the thrust bearing slips from the bearing carrier during installation. Ensure the large thrust bearing remains in position during installation of the bearing carrier into the gearcase. Do not force the carrier into position until you verify all components are in position.

Models BF115A and BF130A (left hand rotation)

1. Use bolts to secure the bearing carrier to a fixture (**Figure 67**). Use the spanner tool (part No. 07WPA-ZW50100 to loosen and remove the forward gear retainer along with the forward gear from the bearing carrier.

2. Remove the thrust bearing (56, **Figure 44**), bearing race (54) and shim (53) from the bearing carrier. Mark the components so they can be installed facing the same direction from which they were removed.

the seal driver tool into the seal with the short step side facing the seal. Press the outer seal (**Figure 65**) into the carrier until the seal driver contacts the bearing carrier.

GEARCASE REPAIR

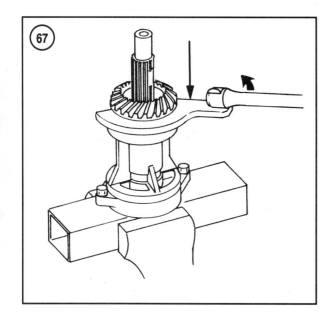

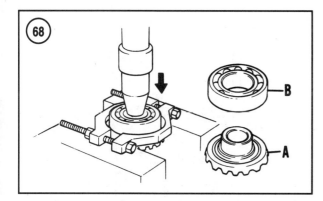

8. Clean all debris from the bearing carrier. Refer to *Inspection* in this chapter to determine which components require replacement.

9. Place the new needle bearing into the bore with the numbered or lettered side facing the propeller side. Use a bearing driver (part No. 07746-0010200) and carefully press (**Figure 64**) the new bearing into the bearing carrier until it contacts the step in the bore or reaches the depth noted prior to removal.

10. Apply Loctite 271 to the outer diameter of the inner seal. Position the new inner seal into the seal bore with the lip facing the reverse gear side.

11. Use a seal driver (part No. 07947-SB00100) or other suitable tool to press the inner seal (**Figure 65**) in until its surface is just below the seal bore opening.

12. Apply Loctite 271 to the outer diameter of the outer seal. Place the outer seal onto the inner seal with the lip facing the propeller side. Press the outer seal along with the inner seal (**Figure 65**) into the carrier until the outer seal just reaches the depth noted prior to removal.

13. Place the shims into the gear retainer. Place the smaller diameter opening of the race down into the bore. Using a suitable driver, press the bearing race into the retainer until it is fully seated against the shims.

14. Set the forward gear on a press platform with the gear teeth facing down. Place the gear retainer over the forward gear with the threaded side facing UP. Place the tapered roller bearing onto the shaft of the gear with the taper facing down. Using a suitable driver, press the tapered roller bearing onto the shaft of the gear until fully seated.

15. Place the thrust shim into the bearing carrier in the direction noted prior to removal. Place the bearing race onto the thrust shim with the rounded edge facing the thrust shim. Place the thrust bearing onto the bearing race in the direction noted prior to removal.

16. Install the bearing carrier. Carefully thread the gear retainer into the threaded section of the bearing carrier. Use the spanner (part No. 07WPA-ZW50100) to tighten (**Figure 67**) the gear retainer to 103.0 N·m (76.0 ft. lbs.).

17. Apply water-resistant grease to the seal lip(s).

All other models

1. Secure the bearing carrier in a vise with soft jaws. Pull the reverse gear (rear mounted gear) from the gearcase cap.

2. Use a slide hammer (**Figure 69**) to remove the reverse gear along with the ball bearing from the bearing carrier. Use a slide hammer (**Figure 70**) to remove the ball bearing if it remains in the bearing carrier.

3. Use a universal bearing separator to contact the forward gear (A, **Figure 68**) during bearing removal. Support the gear as you press the gear from the gear retainer/bearing (B, **Figure 68**).

4. Do not remove the bearing race unless replacement of the race or gear retainer is required. Do not reuse the retainer and race after they have been disassembled.

5. Place a shop towel against the bearing carrier. Using care to avoid damaging the seal bore, pry the seal from the bearing carrier with a pry bar or screwdriver (**Figure 61**). Discard the seal. Clean all debris from the seal bore.

6. Using a depth micrometer, measure the depth of the needle bearing in the bearing carrier (B, **Figure 62**). Record this measurement for use during assembly.

7. Use an appropriately sized section of pipe or rod to press the needle bearing (B, **Figure 63**) and propeller shaft seals (A) from the bearing carrier (**Figure 63**).

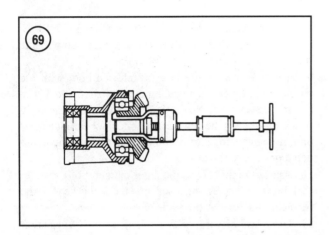

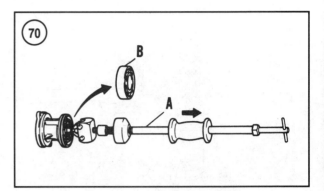

3. Remove any spacers and/or shims from the bearing carrier.

4. Use a bearing separator to contact the reverse gear as shown in **Figure 68**. Select an appropriately sized section of tubing that will contact only the shaft of the gear. Support the gear as you press it from the ball bearing.

5. Note the location and remove any spacers or shims from between the reverse gear and ball bearing.

6. Use a depth micrometer to measure the depth of the propeller shaft seal (**Figure 71**) in the seal bore prior to removal.

7. Using care to avoid damaging the seal bore, pry the seal from the bearing carrier with a pry bar (**Figure 61**). Discard the seal. Clean all debris from the seal bore.

8. For models BF9.9A, BF15A, BF115A and BF130A, pull the needle bearing from the bearing carrier with a slide hammer.

9. Use a bearing driver or other suitable tool to (**Figure 63**) to press or drive the seals (A, **Figure 63**) and needle bearing (B) from the bearing carrier.
    a. For models BF20A, BF25A and BF30A, use Honda driver (No. 07946-KM40701).
    b. For models BF35A, BF40A, BF45A and BF50A, use Honda driver (No. 07749-0010000).

10. Clean all debris from the bearing carrier. Refer to *Inspection* in this chapter to determine which components require replacement.

11. Place the new needle bearing into the bore with the numbered or lettered side facing the propeller side. Use the specified bearing driver and carefully press (**Figure 64**) the new bearing into the bearing carrier until it contacts the step in the bore or just reaches the depth noted prior to removal.
    a. On models BF9.9A and BF15A, use Honda driver part No. 07746-0010700.
    b. On models BF20A, BF25A and BF30A, use Honda driver part No. 07746-0010000.

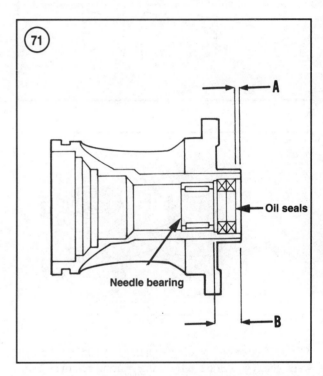

    c. On models BF35A, BF40A, BF45A and BF50A, use Honda driver part No. 07749-0010000.
    d. On models BF115A and BF130 (standard rotation), use Honda driver part No. 07746-0010200.

12. Apply Loctite 271 (red) to the outer diameter of both seals prior to installation. Use the same tool specified in Step 11 or other suitable tool to install the seals. Press the inner seal (**Figure 65**) into its bore until its surface is just below the seal bore opening.

13. Place the outer seal onto the inner seal with the lip facing the propeller side. Press the outer seal along with the inner seal until it just reaches the depth recorded in Step 6.

14. Apply gear lubricant to all surfaces of the ball bearing and its bore in the bearing carrier. Install the spacer, shim or thrust washer onto the shaft of the reverse gear in the di-

GEARCASE REPAIR

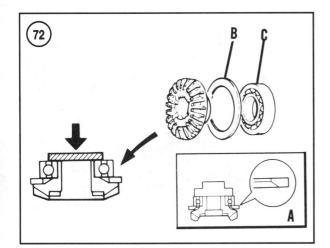

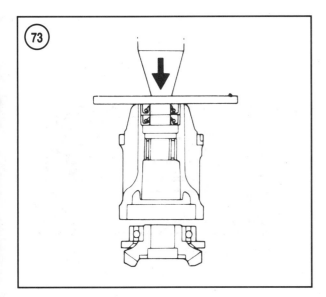

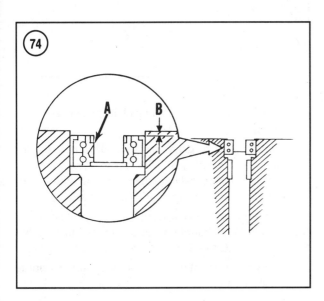

rection and position noted prior to removal. Install the new ball bearing onto the shaft of the gear with any number or letters facing up or away from the gear.

15. Locate a section of tubing or other suitable driver that is slightly larger than the diameter of the reverse gear shaft. Carefully press (**Figure 72**) the ball bearing fully onto the reverse gear.

16. On models BF20A, BF25A and BF30A, place the shims into the ball bearing bore of the bearing carrier. On all models, lubricate the ball bearing surfaces and its bearing carrier bore with gear lubricant. Place the ball bearing/gear assembly into the ball bearing bore of the bearing carrier.

17. Use a block of solid wood or other material to cushion the gear and press the bearing carrier fully onto the ball bearing and reverse gear (**Figure 73**).

18. Apply water-resistant grease to the seal lip(s).

Drive Shaft Seals

On models BF20, BF2A, BF50, BF5A, BF75, BF8A, BF100, BF9.9A and BF15A, the drive shaft seals are mounted in the gearcase. Removal of the drive shaft is required for seal removal and installation.

On all other models, the drive shaft seals are mounted in the water pump base. Removal of the water pump base is required prior to seal removal and installation.

Drive Shaft Seals Removal/Installation (Gearcase-Mounted Seals)

1. Refer to *Water Pump* in this chapter and remove all water pump components. Discard any removed or disturbed gaskets or O-rings.
2. Refer to *Gearcase Cap/Bearing Carrier* in this chapter and remove the gearcase cap or bearing carrier from the gearcase.
3. Refer to *Propeller Shaft* in this chapter and remove the propeller shaft from the gearcase.
4. Refer to *Pinion Gear and Drive Shaft* in this chapter and remove the drive shaft from the gearcase.
5. On models BF20 and BF2A, remove the seal protector (12, **Figure 36**) from the gearcase.
6. Using a depth micrometer, measure the depth of the upper seal (B, **Figure 74**) relative to the top surface of the gearcase. Record this measurement for reference during installation.
7. Note the seal lip direction (A, **Figure 74**), then carefully pry the upper seal from the seal bore with a small pry bar. Record the seal lip direction. Repeat this step for the lower seal. Discard the seals.

8. Clean all debris from the seal bore. Apply Loctite 271 to the outer diameter of both seals during installation.

9. Select an appropriately sized section of pipe or other suitable driver to use as an installation tool. Place the new lower seal into the seal bore with its seal lip facing the direction noted prior to removal.

10. Carefully push or drive the lower new seal into the bore until its surface is just below the seal bore opening. Place the new upper seal onto the lower seal with its seal lip facing the direction noted prior to removal.

11. Carefully push or drive the upper and lower seals into the bore until they bottom out or the top seal just reaches the depth recorded in Step 5. Apply water-resistant grease to the seal lips prior to drive shaft installation.

12. Refer to *Pinion Gear and Drive Shaft* in this chapter and install the drive shaft into the gearcase.

13. Refer to *Propeller Shaft* in this chapter and install the propeller shaft into the gearcase.

14. Refer to *Gearcase Cap/Bearing Carrier* in this chapter and install the gearcase cap or bearing carrier into the gearcase.

15. Refer to *Water Pump Servicing* in this chapter and install all water pump components. Replace any removed gaskets or O-rings with new ones.

Drive Shaft Seals Removal/Installation (Water Pump Base Mounted Seals)

1. Refer to *Water Pump* in this chapter and remove all water pump components. Discard any removed or disturbed gaskets or O-rings.

2. On models BF75A and BF90A, remove the bolt and washers (11 and 12, **Figure 42**) that retain the water pump base to the gearcase.

3. Protect the gearcase surfaces while carefully prying the water pump base (**Figure 75**) from the gearcase. Note the mounting position. Remove and discard the water pump base gaskets from the base and wear plate.

4. Using a depth micrometer, measure the depth of the upper seal (**Figure 76**) relative to the surface of the water pump base. Record this measurement for use during installation.

5. Note the seal lip direction (B, **Figure 76**) and carefully pry the upper seal from the seal bore with a small pry bar. Record the seal lip direction. Repeat this step for the remaining seal. Discard the seals.

6. Clean all debris from the seal bore. Apply Loctite 271 to the outer diameter of both seals during installation.

7. Select an appropriately sized section of pipe or other suitable driver for use as an installation tool. Place the

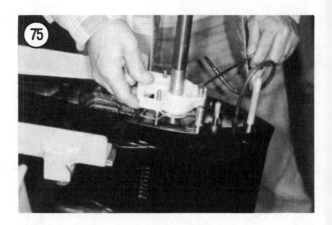

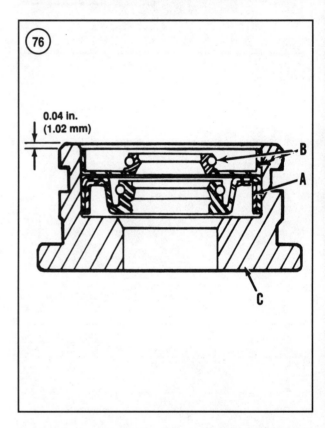

new lower seal into the seal bore with its seal lip facing the direction noted prior to removal.

8. Carefully push or drive the lower new seal into the bore until its surface is just below the seal bore opening. Place the new upper seal onto the lower seal with its seal lip facing the direction noted prior to removal.

9. Carefully push or drive the upper and lower seals into the bore until they bottom out or the top seal just reaches the depth recorded in Step 4.

10. Apply water-resistant grease to the seal lips prior to drive shaft installation.

GEARCASE REPAIR

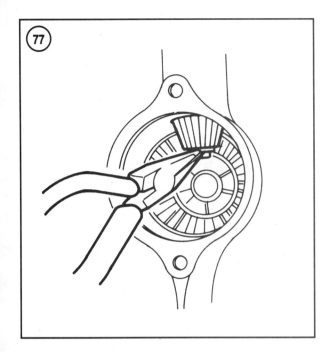

5. Support the pinion gear as you pull up on the drive shaft. Pull the pinion gear, shims and thrust washer from the gearcase.
6. Clean all debris from the drive shaft, pinion gear, bearings and gearcase surfaces.
7. Refer to *Inspection* in this chapter and inspect all components. Replace any worn or defective components.
8. Install the seal protector into the drive shaft bore. Place the shims, thrust washer and pinion gear into position in the gearcase. Mesh the pinion gear teeth with the driven gear teeth.
9. Rotate the drive shaft as you carefully slide it into its bore. Rotate the drive shaft until it engages the splined section of the pinion gear and drops into position.
10. Use needlenose pliers to install a new E-clip (**Figure 77**) into the drive shaft groove below the pinion gear.
11. Complete the remaining assembly by reversing the disassembly steps.

Drive Shaft and Pinion Gear Bearings Removal/Installation

Models BF50, BF5A, BF75, BF8A, BF100, BF9.9A and BF15A

1. Refer to *Gearcase Cap/Bearing Carrier* in this chapter and remove the gearcase cap from the gearcase.
2. Refer to *Water Pump* in this chapter and remove the water pump components from the gearcase.
3. Refer to *Water Pump Base/Drive Shaft Seals* in this chapter and remove the drive shaft seals.
4A. Refer to *Propeller Shaft* in this chapter and remove the propeller shaft from the gearcase.
4B. On models BF9.9A and BF15A, use a suitable socket to loosen and remove the pinion nut from the drive shaft.
5. Support the pinion gear as you pull up on the drive shaft. Pull the drive shaft from the gearcase.
6. Remove the pinion gear from the gearcase. Note their respective position and location. Remove the thrust washer and bearing (if so equipped) from the gearcase.
7. Do not remove the lower drive shaft bearing unless replacement is required. Remove the lubrication sleeve (if so equipped) from the gearcase prior to removal of the bearing.
8. Use a depth gauge to measure the distance from the top or mating surface of the gearcase to the top of the needle bearing (C, **Figure 78**). Record the measurement.
9A. Record the position, either facing up or down, of the numbered side of the bearing. On models BF75, BF8A and BF100, remove the bearing from the drive shaft bore with a slide hammer.

11. Install new gaskets and/or O-rings onto the water pump to gearcase mating surfaces. Carefully slide the water pump base over the drive shaft and into position on the gearcase. Install new gaskets then install the wear plate to the water pump base. On models BF75A and BF90A, install the water pump base mounting bolts and washers. Securely tighten the bolts.
12. Refer to *Water Pump* in this chapter and install all remaining water pump components.

Drive Shaft and Pinion Gear Bearings Removal/Installation

> *NOTE*
> *The drive shaft bearing must be installed to the proper depth within the bearing and seal housing to ensure that the bearing contacts the drive shaft at the proper location. The housing does not provide a step or shoulder for the bearing. Slowly tap the bearing into position. Check the depth frequently during installation.*

1. Refer to *Gearcase Cap/Bearing Carrier* in this chapter and remove the gearcase cap from the gearcase.
2. Refer to *Water Pump Servicing* in this chapter and remove the water pump components from the gearcase.
3. Remove the seal protector from the drive shaft bore.
4. Use a pair of needlenose pliers to remove the E-clip from its groove on the drive shaft (**Figure 77**).

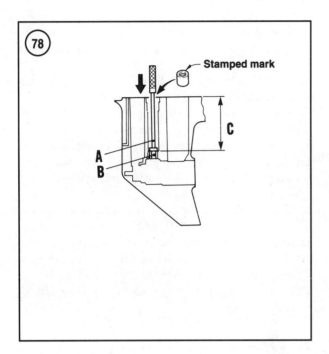

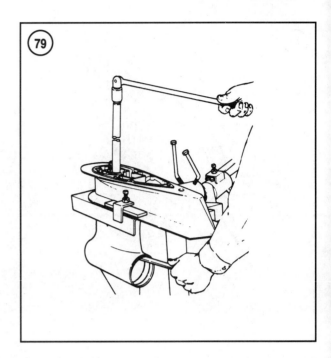

9B. On other models, select an appropriately sized socket, section of pipe or rod to drive the bearings from the bore. The removal tool used must be large enough to contact the bearing yet not large enough to contact the gearcase. Apply heat to the outside surface of the gearcase (near the bearing) to aid in removal.

10. Clean all debris from the drive shaft, pinion gear, bearings and drive shaft bore. Apply gear lubricant to all surfaces of the new drive shaft bearing. Place the new bearing into the top side of the bore with the numbers facing UP.

11. Select an appropriately sized socket (B, **Figure 78**) and extension or pipe (A, **Figure 78**) and carefully drive the bearing into the bore until it just reaches the depth noted in Step 8.

12. Refer to *Drive Shaft Seals* in this chapter and install the drive shaft seals.

13. Lubricate the thrust washer and bearing (if so equipped) with gear lubricant and install them into the gearcase in the location and direction noted during removal.

   a. On models BF9.9A and BF15A, apply Loctite 271 to the threads and install a new pinion nut onto the drive shaft.
   b. Use an appropriate socket that engages the drive shaft, and tighten the pinion nut to the specification listed in **Table 1**.

14. Complete the remaining installation by reversing the removal steps.

Models BF75A and BF90A

1. Special tools are required for removal and installation of the drive shaft and pinion bearings. Tools required include:
   a. Drive shaft adapter (part No. 07SPB-ZW10200)
   b. Bearing race adapter (part No. 07SPC-ZW0021Z)
   c. Driver rod (part No. 07SPC-13779)
   d. Guide (part No.07SPD-ZW0072A)
   e. Threaded adapter (part No.07SPD-ZW0071A)
   f. Threaded and nut (part No. 07SPD-31229)
   g. Drive shaft preload tool (part No. 07SPJ-ZW0011A)
   h. Pinion gear shimming tool (part No. 07SPJ-ZW0023A)

   Purchase these tools from a Honda dealership.

2. Refer to *Gearcase Cap/Bearing Carrier* in this chapter and remove the bearing carrier from the gearcase.

3. Refer to *Water Pump* in this chapter and remove the water pump components from the gearcase.

4. Refer to *Drive Shaft Seals* in this chapter and remove the drive shaft seals.

5. Refer to *Propeller Shaft* in this chapter and remove the propeller shaft from the gearcase.

6. Engage a socket and breaker bar onto the pinion nut (**Figure 79**). Place the drive shaft adapter onto the end of the drive shaft (**Figure 80**). Use an appropriately sized socket or wrench to turn the drive shaft adapter. Rotate the drive shaft counterclockwise to loosen and remove the pinion nut.

GEARCASE REPAIR

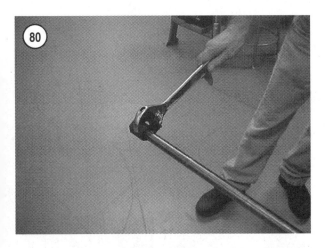

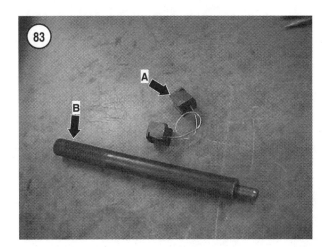

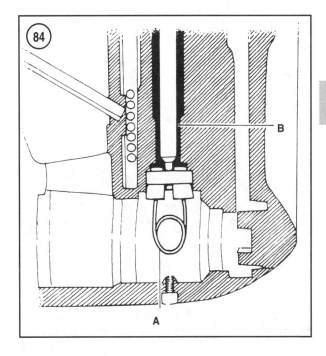

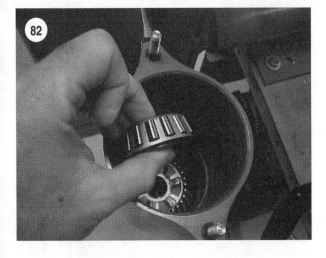

7. Pull the drive shaft from the gearcase. Remove the pinion gear from the gearcase (**Figure 81**). Remove the pinion bearing from it location above the pinion gear (**Figure 82**).

8. Install the race adapter (A, **Figure 83**) onto the pinion bearing race (**Figure 84**). Place the driver rod (B, **Figure 84**) into the race adapter (A, **Figure 84**). Tap the top of the driver rod to remove the pinion bearing race and shims from the gearcase.

9. Use a bearing puller to remove the needle bearing from the drive shaft bore (**Figure 85**).

10. Clean all debris or contamination from the drive shaft, pinion gear, bearings and drive shaft bore. Refer to *Inspection* in this chapter.

11. Apply gear lubricant to all surfaces of the new drive shaft bearing. Place the drive shaft needle bearing into the drive shaft bore with the numbered side facing UP. Position the guide onto the bearing and carefully tap the top of

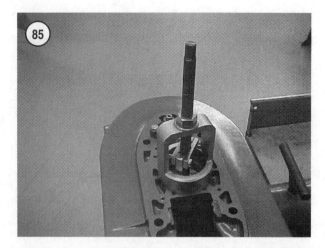

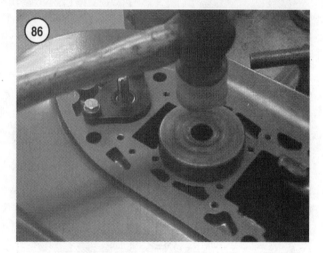

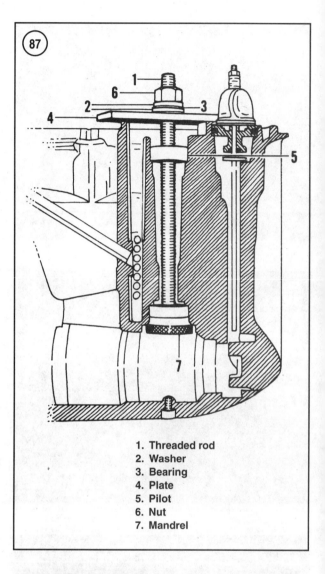

1. Threaded rod
2. Washer
3. Bearing
4. Plate
5. Pilot
6. Nut
7. Mandrel

the guide (**Figure 86**) until it contacts the gearcase. Leave the guide on the gearcase for Step 12.

12. Place the bearing race onto the threaded adapter (7, **Figure 87**). Place the shims onto the top of the bearing race. Install the threaded rod through the guide and drive shaft bore, then fully thread it into the threaded adapter (**Figure 87**).

13. Tighten the nut (**Figure 87**) on the threaded rod until the pinion bearing is fully seated. Refer to *Forward Gear* in this chapter and install the forward gear and bearing assembly into the gearcase. Remove the threaded rod, adapter and guide.

14. Install the lower drive shaft bearing on the drive shaft and seat it against the lower race. Position the pinion gear into the gearcase and align it with the drive shaft bore. Make sure the pinion gear teeth mesh with the forward gear teeth.

15. Lubricate the drive shaft bearing surfaces with gearcase lubricant and carefully slide the drive shaft into the drive shaft bore and into the lower bearing. Slowly ro-

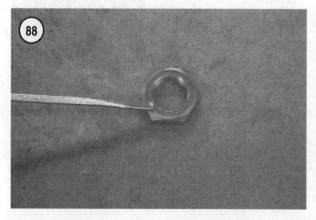

tate the drive shaft to align its splined section with the pinion gear splines. The drive shaft drops into position when the splines are aligned.

GEARCASE REPAIR

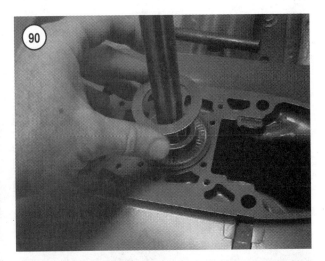

16. Thread the original pinion nut onto the drive shaft (**Figure 88**) with its recessed side facing the pinion gear. Place a socket and breaker bar on the pinion nut (**Figure 79**). Place the drive shaft adapter onto the end of the drive shaft (**Figure 80**). Tighten the pinion nut to the specification in **Table 1**.

17. Place the lower portion and bearing of the drive shaft preload tool over the drive shaft and onto the gearcase as shown in **Figure 89**. Place the thrust washer onto the bearing (**Figure 90**). Install the spring and the remaining parts of the tool onto the drive shaft as shown in **Figure 91**.

18. Tighten both set screws (**Figure 92**) to secure the tool to the drive shaft. Turn the large nut down (**Figure 92**) enough to preload the drive shaft in the UP direction. Rotate the drive shaft several times to seat the bearings.

19. Select the disc portion of the shimming tool with the No. 3 stamped into the surface (**Figure 93**). Align the No. 8 gauging surface of the tool (**Figure 94**) with the opening on the disc (**Figure 95**). Carefully install the shimming tool into the gearcase (**Figure 96**). Make sure the tool engages the needle bearing in the forward gear for alignment.

20. Slowly rotate the tool to align the gauging surface with the pinion gear teeth (**Figure 97**). The gauging surface must be parallel with the pinion gear teeth. Use feeler gauges to measure the clearance between the gauging surface and the pinion gear teeth (**Figure 98**). The clearance should be 0.64 mm (0.025 in.).

21. Follow all applicable steps to remove the pinion bearing race if incorrect clearance is indicated. Change the total thickness of the shims (above the race) until a correct

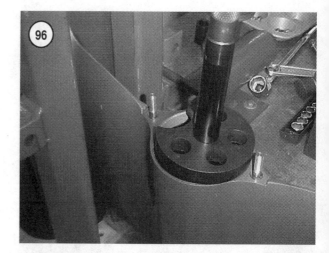

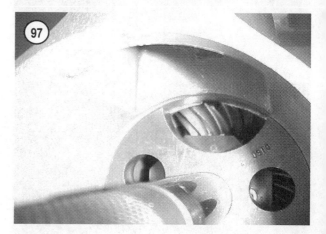

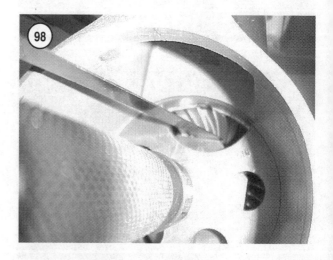

clearance is obtained. Several changes may be required to correct the clearance measurements. Shims in varying thickness can be purchased through a Honda dealership.

22. Remove the pinion gear shimming tool and preload tool. Apply Loctite Type 271 to the threads of the new pinion nut. Install the pinion nut as indicated in Step 16.

23. Complete the remaining assembly by reversing the disassembly steps.

Models BF115A and BF130A

A drive shaft adapter (part No. 07SPB-ZW10200) and retaining nut wrench (part No. 07916-MB00002) are required for drive shaft, pinion gear and bearing removal.

Refer to **Figure 43** or **Figure 44** during the removal and installation procedure.

1. Refer to *Gearcase Cap/Bearing Carrier* in this chapter and remove the bearing carrier from the gearcase.

GEARCASE REPAIR

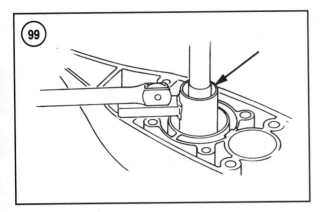

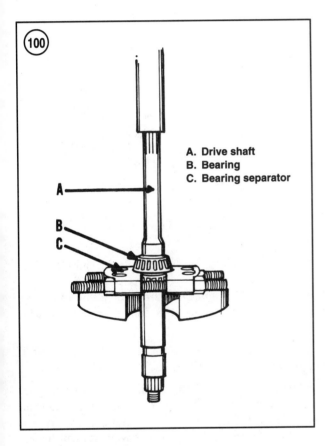

A. Drive shaft
B. Bearing
C. Bearing separator

drive shaft counterclockwise to loosen and remove the pinion nut.

6. Position the retainer nut wrench over the drive shaft and engage the drive shaft bearing retainer (**Figure 99**). Loosen and remove the drive shaft bearing retainer.

7. Support the pinion gear as you lift the drive shaft and bearing race from the gearcase. Remove the shims from the drive shaft bore and retain them for assembly. Remove the pinion gear from the gearcase.

8. Do not remove the lower drive shaft bearing unless replacement is required. Refer to *Inspection* to determine if replacement is required. Remove the lubrication sleeve, if so equipped, from the gearcase prior to removal of the bearing.

9. Use a depth gauge to measure the distance from the mating surface of the gearcase to the top of the needle bearing (C, **Figure 78**). Record the measurement.

10. Record the position of the numbered side of the bearing. Select an appropriate sized socket, section of pipe or rod to drive the bearings from the bore. The removal tool used must be large enough to contact the bearing yet not large enough to contact the gearcase. Apply heat to the outside surface of the gearcase near the bearing to aid in removal of the bearing.

11. Remove the bearing from the drive shaft only if replacement of the shaft or bearing is required. Use a bearing separator (C, **Figure 100**) to support the bearing. Press the drive shaft (A, **Figure 100**) from the bearing (B, **Figure 100**).

12. Refer to *Inspection* in this chapter to determine if components require replacement.

13. Clean all debris from the drive shaft, pinion gear, bearings and drive shaft bore. Apply gear lubricant to all surfaces of the new drive shaft bearing. Place the new bearing into the top side of the bore with the numbers facing UP.

14. Select an appropriately sized socket (B, **Figure 78**) and extension or pipe (A, **Figure 78**) and carefully drive the bearing into the bore until it just reaches the depth noted in Step 9. Install the lubrication sleeve into the drive shaft bore.

15. Position the bearing onto the drive shaft in the position noted during removal. Use a section of pipe or tubing (A, **Figure 101**) and a bearing separator to press the bearing (C, **Figure 101**) fully onto the drive shaft (B, **Figure 101**).

16. Position the pinion gear into the gearcase. Make sure it meshes with the forward gear teeth. Rotate the drive shaft as you carefully slide it into the lower drive shaft bearing. When the splined section of the drive shaft aligns with the pinion gear splines, the drive shaft will drop into position.

2. Refer to *Water Pump* in this chapter and remove the water pump components from the gearcase.

3. Refer to *Drive Shaft Seals* in this chapter and remove the drive shaft seals.

4. Refer to *Propeller Shaft* in this chapter and remove the propeller shaft from the gearcase.

5. Engage a socket and breaker bar onto the pinion nut (**Figure 79**). Place the drive shaft adapter onto the end of the drive shaft (**Figure 80**). Use an appropriately sized socket or wrench to turn the drive shaft adapter. Rotate the

17. Install the shims into the drive shaft bore. Position them onto the step or ledge in the bore.
18. Install the bearing race over the drive shaft and onto the drive shaft bearing. Place the bearing retainer onto the bearing race. Using the retaining nut wrench, tighten the retaining nut to 123.0 N·m (91 ft. lbs.).
19. Apply Loctite 271 to the threaded portion and install the pinion nut onto the drive shaft threads finger-tight. Refer to Step 5 for information. Using the drive shaft adapter and a breaker bar and socket, tighten the pinion nut to the specification listed in **Table 1**.
20. Complete the remaining assembly by reversing the disassembly steps.

Models BF20A and BF50A

1. Refer to *Gearcase Cap/Bearing Carrier* in this chapter and remove the bearing carrier from the gearcase.
2. Refer to *Water Pump* in this chapter and remove the water pump components from the gearcase.
3. Refer to *Drive Shaft Seals* in this chapter and remove the drive shaft seals.
4. Refer to *Propeller Shaft* in this chapter and remove the propeller shaft from the gearcase.
5. Engage a socket and breaker bar onto the pinion nut (**Figure 79**). Place the drive shaft adapter onto the end of the drive shaft (**Figure 80**). Use the correct size socket or wrench to turn the drive shaft adapter. Rotate the drive shaft counterclockwise to loosen and remove the pinion nut.
6. Pull the drive shaft from the gearcase. Remove the pinion gear from the gearcase (**Figure 81**).
7. Use a slide hammer (A, **Figure 102**) to remove the drive shaft bearing race and shims (B, **Figure 102**) from the drive shaft bore. Retain the shims for use during assembly.
8. Remove the lubrication sleeve from the drive shaft bore.
9. Do not remove the lower drive shaft bearing unless replacement is required. Refer to *Inspection* to determine if replacement is required. Remove the lubrication sleeve (if so equipped) from the gearcase prior to removal of the bearing.
10. Use a depth gauge and measure the distance from the top surface of the gearcase to the top of the drive shaft lower bearing (C, **Figure 78**). Record the measurement.
11. Select an appropriate sized socket, section of pipe or rod to drive the lower bearing from the bore. The removal tool used must be large enough to contact the bearing yet not large enough to contact the gearcase. Apply heat to the outside surface of the gearcase near the bearing to aid in removal of the bearing. Drive the bearing from the gearcase.

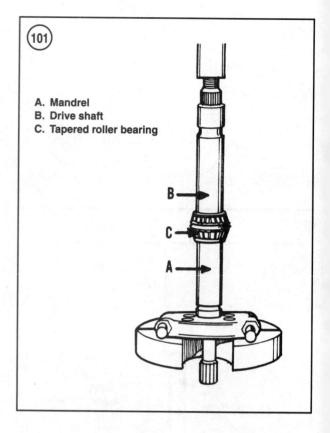

A. Mandrel
B. Drive shaft
C. Tapered roller bearing

12. Remove the bearing from the drive shaft only if replacement of the shaft or bearing is required. Use a bearing separator (C, **Figure 100**) to support the bearing. Press the drive shaft (A, **Figure 100**) from the bearing (B, **Figure 100**).
13. Refer to *Inspection* in this chapter to determine if components must be replaced.
14. Clean all debris from the drive shaft, pinion gear, bearings and drive shaft bore. Apply gear lubricant to all surfaces of the new drive shaft bearing. Place the new bearing into the top side of the bore with the numbers facing up.
15. Select an appropriately sized socket (B, **Figure 78**) and extension or pipe (A, **Figure 78**) and carefully drive the bearing into the bore until it just reaches the depth noted in Step 10. Install the lubrication sleeve into the drive shaft bore.
16. Position the bearing onto the drive shaft in the direction noted during removal. Use a section of pipe or tubing (A, **Figure 101**) and a bearing separator to press the bearing (C, **Figure 101**) fully onto the drive shaft (B, **Figure 101**).

GEARCASE REPAIR

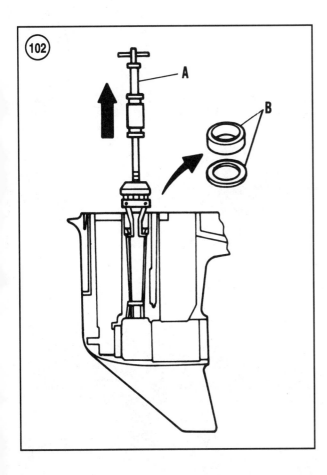

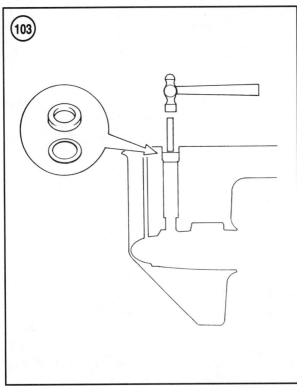

17. Place the shims into the drive shaft bore. Position them onto the step or ledge in the bore. Place the bearing race into the drive shaft bore with the larger diameter side facing up. Use a section of pipe or other suitable driver to drive the bearing race down until fully seated in the bore (**Figure 103**). The driver used must contact only the flat portions of the bearing race and be slightly smaller than the race diameter.

18. Install the pinion gear into the gearcase. Make sure the pinion gear teeth mesh with the forward gear teeth. Rotate the drive shaft as you lower it into its bore. It will drop into position when the splined section engages the pinion gear.

19. Apply Loctite 271 to the threaded portion and install the pinion nut onto the drive shaft threads (finger tight). Using the drive shaft adapter and a breaker bar and socket, tighten the pinion nut to the specification listed in **Table 1**.

20. Complete the remaining assembly by reversing the disassembly steps.

Lower Shift Shaft Removal/Installation

Models BF50, BF5A, BF75, BF8A, BF100, BF9.9A, BF15A, BF20A, BF25A and BF30A

1. Refer to *Gearcase Cap/Bearing Carrier* in this chapter and remove the bearing cap or bearing carrier from the gearcase.
2. Refer to *Propeller Shaft* in this chapter and remove the propeller shaft from the gearcase.
3. Remove the retaining pin (3, **Figure 37**), if so equipped, using needlenose pliers or a small punch.
4. Remove the locknut (50, **Figure 39**), if so equipped, from the shift shaft.
5. Carefully pry the shift shaft bushing (5, **Figure 37**) from the gearcase with a small screwdriver.
6. Pull the entire shift shaft from the gearcase.
7. Remove and discard the O-ring (6, **Figure 37**) from the shift shaft bushing.
8. Mark the mating surfaces of the shift shaft and shift cam (7, 9, **Figure 37**) to ensure correct assembly.
9. Use a small punch to drive the pin (8, **Figure 37**) from the shift shaft and shift cam (9, **Figure 37**). Slide the shift shaft bushing from the shift shaft.
10. Note the seal lip direction, then carefully pry the seal (4, **Figure 37**) from its bore in the shift shaft bushing. Discard the seal.
11. Refer to *Inspection* in this chapter to determine which components must be replaced.
12. Installation is the reverse of removal. Note:

a. Use a suitable driver to install the new seal into the shift shaft bushing in the direction noted prior to removal. Apply water-resistant grease to the seal lip.
b. Lubricate it with gear lubricant and install a new O-ring into position and slide the shift shaft bushing onto the shift shaft.
c. Align the marks on the shift cam and shift shaft prior to installing the pin.
d. Install the shift shaft with the tapered side of the cam facing the propeller end of the gearcase.
e. Make sure the shift shaft bushing is fully seated into the gearcase.
f. Refer to the applicable section to install all remaining components.

Models B35A, BF40A, BF45A and BF50A

1. Refer to *Gearcase Cap/Bearing Carrier* in this chapter and remove the bearing carrier from the gearcase.
2. Refer to *Propeller Shaft* in this chapter and remove the propeller shaft from the gearcase.
3. Mark the shift shaft bushing-to-gearcase mating surface to ensure correct position on assembly.
4. Remove the bolt (32, **Figure 41**) and clamp (33) from the gearcase. Carefully pry the shift shaft bushing (34. **Figure 41**) from the gearcase. Lift the entire shift shaft assembly from the gearcase.
5. Mark the mating surfaces of the shift shaft (28, **Figure 41**) and shift cam (37) to ensure correct assembly. Carefully drive the pin (38, **Figure 41**) from the shift cam (37) and shift shaft (28). Remove the shift cam from the shift shaft.
6. Remove both grommets (29 and 31, **Figure 41**) from the shift shaft boot (30, **Figure 41**) and pull the shift shaft boot away from the shift shaft bushing. Discard the grommets.
7. Remove the retaining pin (36, **Figure 41**) from the shift shaft then slide the shift shaft bushing (34, **Figure 41**) from the shift shaft. Discard the O-ring (35, **Figure 41**) from the shift shaft bushing.
8. Refer to *Inspection* in this chapter to determine which components must be replaced.
9. Installation is the reverse of removal. Note:
a. Lubricate the new O-ring with gear lubricant. Install it into position and slide the shift shaft bushing onto the shift shaft.
b. Install new grommets onto the shift shaft and shift shaft bushing. Install the retainer into the shift shaft after installing the shift shaft bushing.
c. Align the marks on the shift cam and shift shaft prior to installing the pin.

d. Install the shift shaft with the tapered side of the cam facing the propeller end of the gearcase.
e. Make sure the shift shaft bushing is fully seated into the gearcase. Align the marks made prior to removal then securely tighten the bolt and clamp.

10. Refer to the applicable section to install all remaining components.

Models BF75A and BF90A

1. Refer to *Gearcase Cap/Bearing Carrier* in this chapter and remove the bearing carrier from the gearcase.
2. Refer to *Propeller Shaft* in this chapter and remove the propeller shaft from the gearcase.
3. Remove the bolts (24, **Figure 42**) and carefully pry and lift the shift shaft bushing (**Figure 104**) from the gearcase. Discard the O-ring from the shift shaft bushing.
4. Pull the shift shaft from the gearcase (**Figure 105**) and remove the E-clip from the shift shaft.

GEARCASE REPAIR

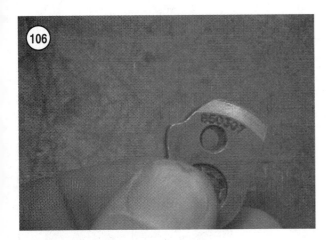

c. Apply water-resistant grease to the shift shaft seal lip.
d. Lubricate it with gear lubricant then install a new o-ring onto the shift shaft bushing.
e. Install the shift shaft and bushing into the gearcase.

Models BF115A and BF130A

Refer to **Figure 43** or **Figure 44** to assist with component identification and position.

1. Refer to *Gearcase Cap/Bearing Carrier* in this chapter and remove the bearing carrier from the gearcase.
2. Shift the gearcase into neutral while turning the drive shaft clockwise.
3. Locate the shift shaft bushing and attaching bolt and washer (**Figure 107**). Mark the mating surfaces of the shift shaft bushing and gearcase to ensure correct assembly.
4. Carefully pry and lift the shift shaft bushing (**Figure 104**) and the shift shaft from the gearcase. Discard the O-ring from the shift shaft bushing.
5. Note the respective location and position of all shift shaft components and remove the E-clip from the shift shaft. Slide the spring, washer and shift shaft bushing from the shift shaft.
6. Note the seal lip direction and use a small screwdriver to carefully pry the shift shaft seal from the shift shaft bushing. Discard the seal.
7. Refer to *Inspection* in this chapter to determine which components must be replaced.
8. Installation is the reverse of disassembly. Note:
   a. Apply Loctite 271 to the inner diameter of the seal bore and use an appropriately sized socket or section of tubing and install the new seal into the shift shaft bushing. Ensure the lip is facing up.
   b. Apply water-resistant grease to the shift shaft seal lip.
   c. Lubricate a new O-ring with gear lubricant and install it onto the shift shaft bushing.
   d. Install the propeller shaft prior to installing the shift shaft.
   e. On standard rotation models, install the shift shaft into the bore with lower tip or lever positioned toward the starboard side of the gearcase.
   f. On left-hand rotation models, install the shift shaft into the bore with the lower tip or lever positioned toward the port side of the gearcase.
9. Slightly rotate (clockwise and counterclockwise) the shift shaft during installation to ensure it engages the shift actuator (76, **Figure 43**).

5. Use needlenose pliers to reach into the gearcase and remove the shift cam (**Figure 106**) from its mounting boss, which is directly under the shift shaft bore. Note the marks on the shift cam. The marks must face down when installed in the gearcase.

6. Mark the UP side of each component and slide the shift shaft bushing from the shift shaft.

7. Note the seal lip direction and carefully pry the shift shaft seal (25, **Figure 42**) from the shift shaft bushing. Discard the seal.

8. Refer to *Inspection* in this chapter to determine which components must be replaced.

9. Assembly is the reverse of installation. Note:
   a. Make sure the marks on the shift cam face down when installed in the gearcase.
   b. Apply Loctite 271 to the inner diameter of the seal bore and use an appropriately sized socket or section of tubing to drive the new seal into the shift shaft bushing. Ensure the lip is facing up or away from the gearcase.

Propeller Shaft Removal/Installation

CAUTION
Use care to avoid serious damage to the propeller shaft components. After removal, place the propeller shaft assembly on a stable work surface. Make sure the shaft cannot roll off the work surface.

Models BF20 and BF2A

On models BF20 and BF2A, the propeller shaft is an integral part of the driven gear. Simply pull the propeller shaft and shim washer from the gearcase after the drive shaft and the pinion gear are removed. Refer to *Inspection* in this chapter to determine if the propeller shaft must be replaced. Install the shim washer onto the propeller shaft/driven gear. Install the propeller shaft/driven gear into bearing (32, **Figure 36**) located at the front of the gearcase.

Models BF50, BF5A, BF75, BF8A, BF100, BF9.9A and BF15A

On these models, replace the propeller shaft assembly if either the propeller shaft or clutch requires replacement. Note location of the thrust washer(s) on the propeller shaft (32, **Figure 37**) and carefully slide them off. Proper disassembly and assembly of the propeller shaft requires a special tool that is not available in this country. Individual components such as the clutch, pin, spring and follower are available from Honda. Consider having a reputable machine shop remove and install the pin for you using a suitable flaring tool (**Figure 108**). Refer to *Inspection* in this section to determine when components must be replaced.

To remove the propeller shaft, simply pull the shaft from the gearcase (**Figure 109**).

To install the propeller shaft, place all thrust washers (2, **Figure 110**) onto the propeller shaft in the location noted prior to removal. Carefully slide the propeller shaft into the forward gear.

Models BF115A and BF130A

On models BF115A and BF130A, remove the shift shaft before removing the propeller shaft. Refer to **Figure 43** or **Figure 44**.

1. Refer to *Lower Shift Shaft/Retainer* in this chapter and remove the shift shaft from the gearcase. Disassemble the shift shaft as required.

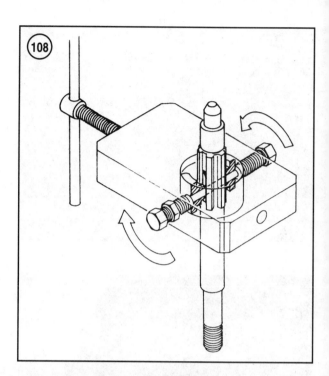

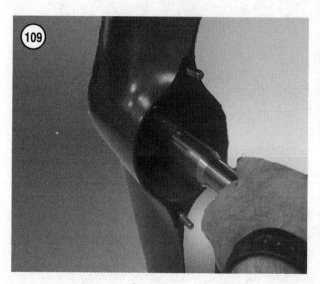

2. On standard rotation models, note the location and position of the thrust bearing (2, **Figure 110**). Carefully slide the thrust bearing from the propeller shaft.

3. Pull the propeller shaft from the gearcase (**Figure 109**).

4. Mark the clutch (4, **Figure 110**) to identify the side that faces the rear mounted gear (1, **Figure 110**).

5. Use a small screwdriver to hook and unwind the spring from the clutch (**Figure 111**).

6. Carefully push the cross pin from the clutch, shift actuator and propeller shaft (**Figure 112**).

GEARCASE REPAIR

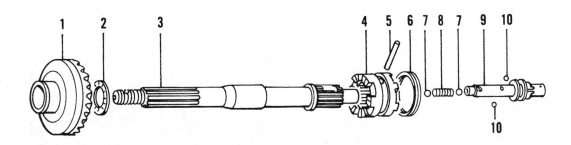

PROPELLER SHAFT COMPONENTS
(MODELS BF115A AND BF130A)

1. Rear mounted gear
2. Thrust bearing/washer
3. Propeller shaft
4. Clutch
5. Cross pin
6. Clutch pin
7. Bearing
8. Spring
9. Shift actuator
10. Detent ball

7. Working over a parts pan or small carton, slide the shift actuator (9, **Figure 110**) from the propeller shaft (3, **Figure 110**). Retain the spring (8, **Figure 110**), detent balls (10), and both bearings (7) for use during assembly.

8. Carefully slide the clutch from the propeller shaft (**Figure 113**). Refer to *Inspection* in this chapter to determine which components require replacement.

9. Place the clutch (4, **Figure 110**) onto the propeller shaft (3, **Figure 111**) with the marked side facing the rear mounted gear (1, **Figure 110**). Ensure the cross pin hole in the clutch aligns with the slot in the propeller shaft.

10. Place the bearing (7, **Figure 110**) into the shift actuator bore in the propeller shaft. Install the spring (8, **Figure 110**) followed by the second bearing (7) into the bore.

11. Apply water-resistant grease to them and place the detent balls (10, **Figure 110**) into their recess on the shift actuator (9, **Figure 110**).

12. Collapse the spring (8, **Figure 110**) as you slide the shift actuator into its bore. Ensure the detent balls remain in place.

13. Rotate the actuator until its cross pin hole aligns with the cross pin hole in the clutch. Slide the cross pin into the clutch and shift actuator. Tug on the actuator to ensure the cross pin passed through the actuator.

14. Being careful to avoid stretching the spring, wind the clutch spring (6, **Figure 110**) onto the clutch. Ensure the springs fits flat against the clutch and at least three loops pass over the cross pin (**Figure 114**).

15. Make sure the shift actuator makes minimal contact with the bearing in the front mounted gear as you carefully slide the propeller shaft into the gearcase.

16. On standard rotation models, place the thrust bearing (2, **Figure 110**) onto the propeller shaft.

17. Refer to *Lower Shift Shaft/Retainer* in this chapter and install the shift shaft into the gearcase.

Models BF20A, BF25A, BF30A, BF35A, BF40A, BF45A and BF50A

Refer to **Figures 40-42** for this procedure.

1. Note the position (reverse gear side) of the thrust washer on the propeller shaft (2, **Figure 115**). Carefully slide the thrust washer or bearing from the propeller shaft.

GEARCASE REPAIR

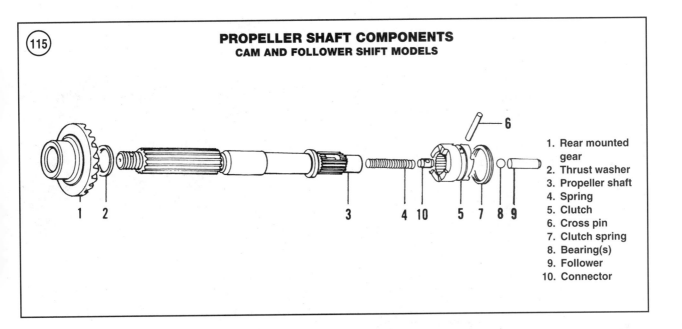

PROPELLER SHAFT COMPONENTS
CAM AND FOLLOWER SHIFT MODELS

1. Rear mounted gear
2. Thrust washer
3. Propeller shaft
4. Spring
5. Clutch
6. Cross pin
7. Clutch spring
8. Bearing(s)
9. Follower
10. Connector

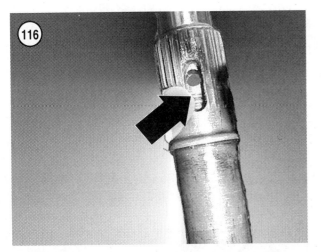

2. Carefully pull the propeller shaft from the gearcase (**Figure 109**). Mark the clutch (5, **Figure 115**) to identify the side that faces the rear mounted gear (1, **Figure 115**).

3. Use a small screwdriver to hook and unwind the clutch spring (7, **Figure 115**) from the clutch (**Figure 111**).

4. Press inward on the cam follower to collapse the spring. Use a small rod or screwdriver to push the cross pin from the clutch (**Figure 112**).

5. Slowly release the tension. Pull the cam follower (9, **Figure 115**) and bearing(s) (8) from the propeller shaft.

6. Tap the propeller shaft on a flat surface to remove the spring (4, **Figure 115**) and connector (10) from the propeller shaft. Mark the side of the connector that faces the spring.

7. Refer to *Inspection* in this chapter to determine which components require replacement.

8. Place the clutch (5, **Figure 115**) onto the propeller shaft (3, **Figure 115**) with the correct side facing the rear mounted gear (1, **Figure 115**). Make sure the cross pin hole in the clutch aligns with the slot in the propeller shaft.

9. Install the spring into the propeller shaft. Slide the connector (10, **Figure 115**) into the propeller shaft with the spring side facing the spring. Align the cross pin hole in the connector with the cross pin hole in the clutch (**Figure 116**).

10. Apply water-resistant grease and place the bearing(s) (8, **Figure 115**) into the propeller shaft and next to the connector. Install the cam follower into the propeller shaft with the pointed side facing out (**Figure 117**).

11. Push in on the cam follower to collapse the spring. Install the cross pin into the clutch and through the hole in the connector (**Figure 118**).

12. Being careful to avoid stretching the spring, wind the clutch spring (7, **Figure 115**) onto the clutch. Ensure the springs fits flat against the clutch and at least three loops pass over the cross pin (**Figure 114**).

13. Place the gearcase in the horizontal position. Keep the propeller shaft in a horizontal position as you slide it into the forward gear.

14. On models so equipped, place the thrust washer (2, **Figure 115**) onto the propeller shaft.

Forward Gear Bearing Replacement

Models BF20 and BF2A

Remove the bearing only if replacement is required. On these models, the ball bearing (1, **Figure 119**) is removed after the propeller shaft (3, **Figure 119**) and shim (2) are removed from the gearcase. Use a slide hammer (A, **Figure 120**) and pull the bearing (B, **Figure 120**) from the housing. Use a bearing driver (part No. 07746-0010100), an appropriately sized section of pipe, a large socket or other suitable tool to drive the bearing into the gearcase (**Figure 121**). The tool selected must be slightly smaller than the diameter of the bearing and it should not contact the housing at any time.

Models BF50, BF5A, BF75, BF8A, BF100, BF9.9A and BF15A

Remove the bearing only if replacement is required. On these models, the bearing can be removed after you pull the forward gear from the gearcase. Use a slide hammer to remove it if it is difficult to remove. Use a slide hammer (**Figure 120**) to pull the bearing from the housing. Retain the shims from below the bearing for use during assembly. Install the shims into the bearing bore prior to installing the new bearing. Use a bearing driver, an appropriately sized section of pipe, large socket or other suitable tool to drive the bearing into the gearcase (**Figure 121**). The tool selected must be slightly smaller than the diameter of the bearing and must not contact the housing at any time. Use the following driver to install the bearing.

1. On models BF50 and BF5A, use driver tool part No. 07746-001030.

2. On models BF75, BF8A and BF100, use driver tool part No. 07746-0040600.

3. On models BF9.9A and BF15A, use driver tool part No. 07746-0040600.

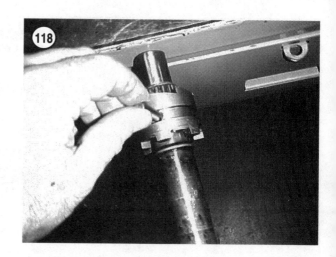

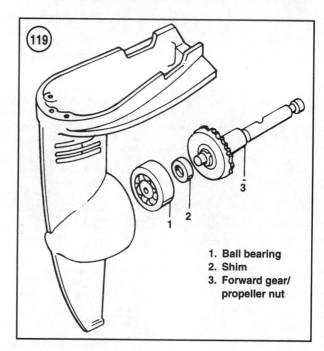

1. Ball bearing
2. Shim
3. Forward gear/propeller nut

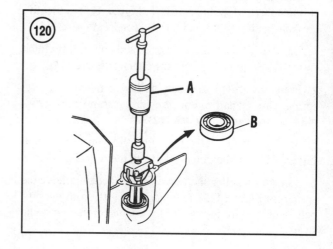

GEARCASE REPAIR

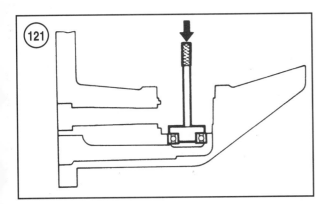

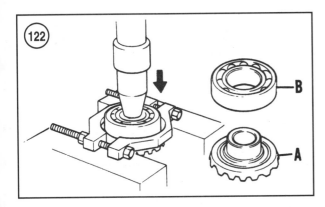

3. Remove the gear from the bearing using an appropriately sized section of pipe, large socket or other suitable tool and a bearing separator. Support the gear as you press the gear from the bearing (A, **Figure 122**). The tool used must be slightly smaller than the diameter of the gear hub.

4. Use an appropriately sized section of pipe, large socket or other suitable tool to press the bearing onto the front mounted gear (**Figure 123**). The tool selected must be slightly larger than the diameter of the propeller shaft bore in the gear and contact only on the inner race of the bearing.

5. Install the shims into the bearing bore prior to installing the bearing and gear.

6. Heat the gearcase with a heat gun to allow for easier installation of the bearing and gear. Use an appropriately sized section of pipe, large socket or other suitable tool to drive the bearing and forward mounted gear into the gearcase (**Figure 121**). The tool selected must be slightly smaller than the diameter of the gear and must not contact the housing at any time. Use a driver of a material that is slightly softer than the gear material to prevent damage to the teeth.

Models BF20A, BF25A, BF30A, BF35A, BF40A, BF45A and BF50A

1. Remove the forward gear after removing the propeller shaft and pinion gear. Simply pull the gear from the gearcase (**Figure 124**). Refer to *Bearing Race and Shims* in this chapter to remove and install the tapered bearing race.

2. Remove the bearing only if replacement is required. Remove the gear from the bearing using an appropriately sized section of pipe, large socket or other suitable tool and a bearing separator. Support the gear as you press the

Models BF115A and BF130A left-hand rotation

1. If replacement is required on these models, the bearing can be removed after you pull the forward gear from the gearcase.

2. Use a slide hammer to remove the gear from the front bearing. Use a slide hammer (**Figure 120**) to pull the bearing from the housing. Retain the shims from below the bearing for use during assembly.

gear from the bearing (A, **Figure 122**). The tool used must be slightly smaller than the diameter of the gear hub.

3. Use an appropriately sized section of pipe, large socket or other suitable tool to press the bearing onto the front mounted gear (**Figure 125**). The tool selected must be slightly larger than the diameter of the propeller shaft bore in the gear and contact only on the inner race of the bearing.

4. Install the bearing and gear assembly into the gearcase with the bearing facing inward. Make sure the bearing seats are properly on the bearing race.

Bearing Race and Shims Removal/Installation

1. Remove the shims or forward gear tapered bearing only if replacing it. Refer to *Inspection* in this chapter to determine if replacement is required.

2. Use a slide hammer and puller assembly (**Figure 126**) and remove the bearing race (A, **Figure 126**) and shims (B, **Figure 126**) from the gearcase. Use a micrometer to measure the individual shim thickness. Record the total shim thickness.

3. Position the gearcase with the gearcase opening facing UP.

4. Inspect the gearcase for the presence of debris and clean as required.

5. Apply gear lubricant to all surfaces of the bearing race.

6. Place the shims (A, **Figure 127**) onto the shoulder or step in the gearcase.

7. Position the race (B, **Figure 127**) into the housing with the tapered side facing outward.

8. Position the indicated driver onto the race with the tapered side down. Use an extension or other suitable rod to carefully drive the race into position.
   a. For models BF20A, BF25A and BF30A, use part No. 07746-0010500.
   b. For models BF35A, BF40A, BF45A and BF50A, use part No. 00746-0010500.
   c. For models BF75A and BF90A, use part No. 07SPD-ZW0010Z.
   d. For models BF115A and BF130A (standard rotation), use part No. 07SPD-ZW0010Z.

Anodes

Refer to the **Figures 36-44**.

Remove the anode if inspection reveals significant deterioration of its surfaces. Note the anode mounting location and position and remove the fasteners. Carefully pry the anode from the gearcase. Use a wire brush or sandpaper to remove all material from the anode mounting sur-

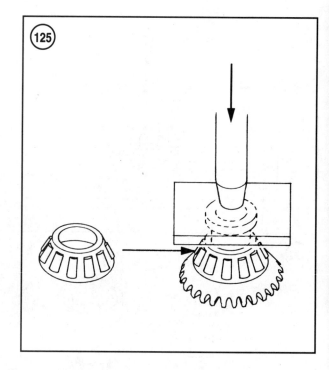

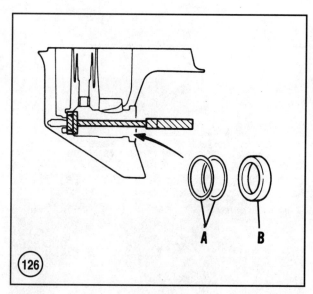

face. Work the surface until only bare aluminum contacts the anode when installed. Never paint or apply any material to the anode. Doing so prevents it from protecting your gearcase from corrosion.

Place the anode on the gearcase. Install the bolts, nuts or other fasteners and securely tighten them.

Water Pickup Screens

Refer to **Figures 36-44**.

GEARCASE REPAIR

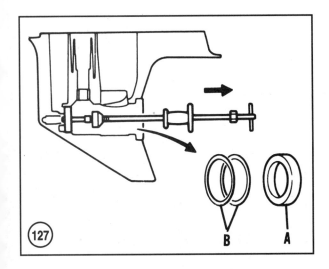

Remove the water pickup screens from the gearcase to remove debris from the water passages. Note the water screen mounting location and position prior to removing them. Locate the fasteners for the screen and remove them. Clean all debris from the water screen and water passages. Inspect all water passage grommets for defects. Replace them if defects are noted.

Install the water screen onto the gearcase and position as noted prior to removal. Install the fasteners and securely tighten them.

Speedometer Fitting

Refer to **Figures 36-44**.

Use a wrench or locking pliers to remove the speedometer fitting from its threaded passage on the gearcase. Apply a *very light coat* of liquid gasket sealer to the threaded portion of the fitting. Install the fitting into the gearcase and securely tighten the fitting.

Gearcase Assembly

This section provides procedures to assemble the gearcase. For assistance with component location and identification, refer to **Figures 36-44**.

Perform the shim selection procedure and backlash measurement if the gears, bearing, housing or the drive shaft have been changed. Shim selection and backlash measurement procedures are provided in this section.

Follow all instructions carefully. Improper assembly can lead to gearcase failure, rapid wear of gears and bearings, sloppy shift operation or noisy operation.

Apply water-resistant grease to the seal lip surfaces during assembly. Apply a light coat of gear lubricant to the surfaces of all needle, roller and ball bearings on assembly. Do not apply any lubricant to the gear surfaces as it can interfere with backlash measurement.

1. Refer to *Bearing Race* in this chapter and install the front mounted bearing race into the gearcase.

2. Refer to *Front Mounted Gear* in this chapter and install the front mounted gear and bearing into the gearcase.

3. Refer to *Pinion Gear and Drive Shaft* in this chapter and install the pinion gear, drive shaft and drive shaft bearings into the gearcase housing.

4. Refer to *Lower Shift Shaft/Retainer* and install the shift shaft retainer and lower shift shaft into the gearcase.

5. Refer to *Propeller Shaft* in this chapter and install the propeller shaft into the gearcase.

6. Refer to *Drive Shaft Seals* in this chapter and install the water pump base and drive shaft seals onto the gearcase.

7. Refer to *Water Pump* in this chapter and install all water pump components.

8. Refer to *Gearcase Cap/Bearing Carrier* in this chapter and install the gearcase cap/bearing carrier to the gearcase.

9. Refer to *Backlash Measurement* in this chapter and check the backlash. Make any required shim changes.

10. Refer to Chapter Three and pressure test the gearcase. Correct any leakage before filling the gearcase with gear lubricant.

11. Refer to *Gearcase Removal and Installation* in this chapter and install the gearcase to the engine.

12. Refer to Chapter Four and fill the gearcase with gear lubricant.

13. Refer to *Anodes and other Gearcase Components* in this section and install all remaining components onto the gearcase.

Component Inspection

This section provides instructions on proper inspection of the gearcase components. Never compromise a proper repair by using damaged or questionable components. If the component fails, it may cause damage that costs far more to repair than the component itself.

Prior to inspection, thoroughly clean all components in a suitable solvent. Use compressed air to dry all components. Never allow bearings to spin while dyring with compressed air.

Use pressurized water to clean the gearcase housing. If cleaning with some components installed is required, clean the gearcase with a suitable solvent instead of water. Use compressed air to thoroughly dry the gearcase.

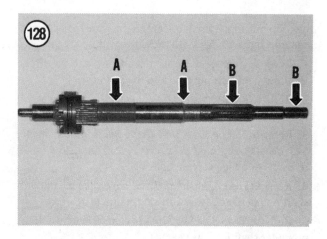

Propeller shaft

Inspect the propeller shaft for bent, damaged or worn conditions. Replace the propeller shaft if defects are noted. Repairing or straightening the propeller shaft is not recommended.

Inspect the propeller shaft surfaces (A, **Figure 128**) for corrosion and damaged or worn areas. Inspect the propeller shaft splines and threaded area (B, **Figure 128**) for twisted splines or damaged propeller nut threads. Inspect the bearing contact areas at the front and midpoint of the propeller shaft. Replace the propeller if discolored areas, rough surfaces, transferred bearing material or other defects are noted.

Inspect the propeller shaft at the seal contact areas. Replace the propeller shaft if deep grooves have worn in the seal contact surfaces.

Place V blocks or suitable support at the points indicated in **Figure 129**. Use a dial indicator to measure the shaft deflection at the rear bearing support area. Securely mount the dial indicator. Observe the dial indicator movement while slowly rotating the propeller shaft. Replace the propeller shaft if the needle movement exceeds 0.2 mm (0.008 in.). Do not attempt to straighten a bent propeller shaft.

Gear and clutch

Inspect both clutch and gear surfaces (B, **Figure 130**) for chipped, damaged, worn or rounded over surfaces. Replace the clutch and gears if any problem is found on either component.

Inspect the gear for worn, broken or damaged teeth (A, **Figure 130**). Note the presence of pitted, rough or excessively worn (highly polished) surfaces. Replace the gear if it is worn or damaged.

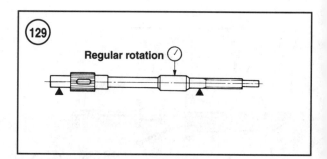

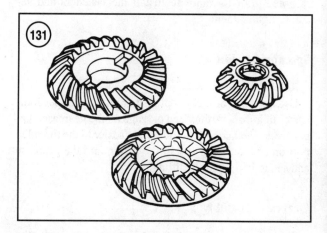

Individual gears are available for some models. Replace all gears (**Figure 131**) when one gear requires replacement to maintain a consistent wear pattern.

Bearing

Clean all bearings thoroughly in solvent and air dry prior to inspection. Replace bearings if the gear lubricant drained from the gearcase is heavily contaminated with metal particles.

GEARCASE REPAIR

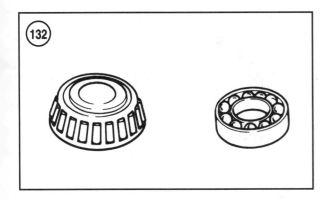

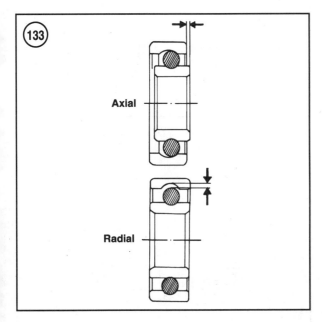

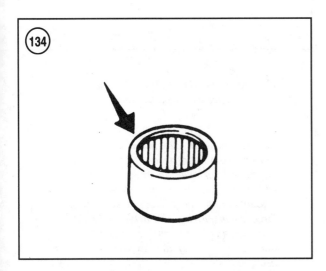

Inspect roller bearing (**Figure 132**) and bearing race surfaces for pitting, rusting, discoloration or rough surfaces. Inspect the bearing race for highly polished or unevenly worn surfaces. Replace the bearing assembly if any of these defects are noted.

Rotate ball bearings and note any rough operation. Move the bearing in the directions shown in **Figure 133**. Note the presence of *axial* or *radial* looseness. Replace the bearing if rough operation or looseness is noted.

Inspect the needle bearings (**Figure 134**) located in the bearing carrier, front driven gear and drive shaft bearing housing. Replace the bearing if flattened rollers, discoloration, rusting, rough surfaces or pitting is noted.

Inspect the propeller shaft and drive shaft at the bearing contact area. Replace the drive shaft and/or propeller shaft along with the needle bearing if discoloration, pitting, transferred bearing material or rough surfaces are noted.

Shift cam/follower and related components

Inspect the bore in the propeller shaft for the presence of debris and damaged or worn areas. Clean debris from the bore.

Inspect the clutch spring for damage, corrosion or weak spring tension and replace if defects are noted.

Inspect the cross pin for damaged, rough or worn surfaces. Replace as required. Inspect the follower or shift actuator spring for damage or corrosion and replace as required.

Inspect the follower or shift actuator for cracked, broken or worn areas. Replace any worn or defective components.

On models BF75A and BF90A, inspect the shift cam for worn, chipped, cracked or corroded surfaces. Replace the shift cam and follower if defects or worn surfaces are noted.

On models BF115A and BF130A, check the detent balls for flat spots, worn areas or pitting and replace as required.

Inspect the shift shaft for worn areas or a bent or twisted condition. Inspect the shift shaft bushing for cracks or a worn shift shaft bore. Replace the housing and/or shift shaft if defects are noted.

Shims, Spacers, Fasteners and Washers

Inspect all shims for bent, rusted or damaged surfaces. Replace any shim that does not appear to be in like-new condition.

Spacers are used in various locations in the gearcase. Some function as thrust bearings or thrust surfaces. Replace them if worn areas are noted or if bent, corroded or damaged. Use only the correct part to replace them. In most cases they are of a certain dimension and made from a specific material.

Replace any locking-type nut unless it is in excellent condition. Replace the pinion nut anytime it is removed from the drive shaft. Install the new nut during final assembly.

Replace any worn or damaged washers located on the pinion gear. These washers are sometimes used as a thrust-loaded surface and are subject to wear.

Shim Selection

Shim selection is only required if replacing major internal components including gears, bearings, drive shaft or the gearcase housing.

On most models, shim selection requires numerous shimming gauges and precise measuring equipment. It is more cost effective to allow a Honda dealership or qualified marine repair shop to perform these measurements for you. Special tools and training are required to determine the proper shims for the gear, bearings, shaft and housing combination.

Shim selection procedures use numbers located in the bearing carrier opening or other areas of the gearcase housing combined with measurements to the gears, shafts and bearings. Make certain that all components of the gearcase are provided to the dealership.

If the use of these tools is not possible, another method of shim selection is possible. Use the same shim thickness as removed from each shim location. Assemble the gearcase and measure *gear backlash*. Gear backlash measurements provide a fairly accurate indication of what shim changes are required. Refer to *Backlash Measurement* in this chapter. Do not rely on the backlash method (except models BF75A and BF90A) for shim selection if the gearcase housing is replaced. Have a Honda dealership gauge your internal components to match the replacement gearcase housing.

On models BF75A and BF90A, backlash measurement is the only means to determine when shim changes are required. Refer to *Backlash Measurement* in this chapter.

Some models are not provided with backlash specifications or procedures. On these models, have the components measured at a local Honda dealership to determine the shims for the various locations.

Backlash Measurement

NOTE
All water pump components must be removed prior to measuring gear backlash.

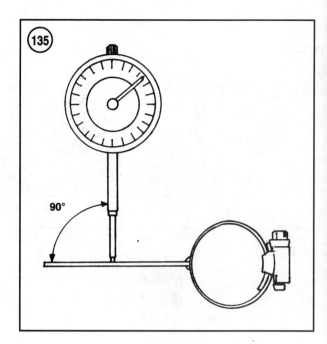

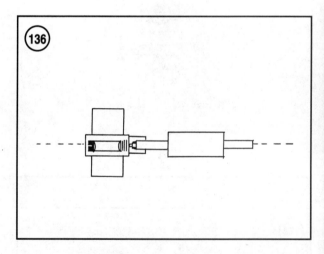

The drag created by the water pump components will prevent accurate measurements.

NOTE
Ensure that all gearcase lubricant is drained from the gearcase prior to measuring gear backlash. An inaccurate reading will result from the cushion effect of the lubricant on the gear teeth. Use very light force when moving the drive shaft during backlash measurements. Inaccurate readings are certain if any excessive force is used.

Backlash measurement gives an indication of the clearance between the pinion and forward or reverse gears.

GEARCASE REPAIR

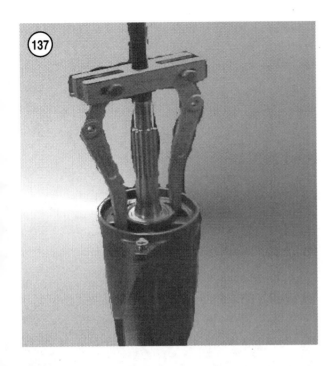

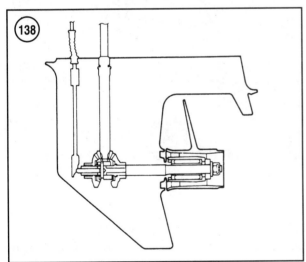

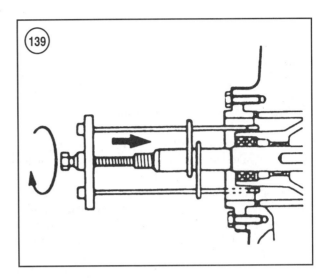

A dial indicator, mount for the dial indicator, bearing puller assembly and backlash indicator tool are required for accurate backlash measurement. Backlash specifications and procedures are not provided for all models. On such models, use the original shims installed in the gearcase.

When attaching the dial indicator and indicator tool, always align the dial indicator at a 90° angle to the indicator arm (**Figure 135**) as viewed from the top. The dial indicator must also be aligned to the same height on the drive shaft and aligned with the backlash indicator as viewed from the side (**Figure 136**). Do not be concerned with the gear (forward, neutral or reverse) during backlash measurement.

Use the specified backlash indicator tool:
1. Models BF20A, BF25A and BF30A use part No. O7MGJ-0010100.
2. Models BF35A, BF40A, BF45A and BF50A use Honda part No. 07LPJ-ZV30200.
3. Models BF75A and BF90A use part No. 07SPK-ZW10100 and 07SPJ-ZW0030Z.
4. Models BF115A and BF130A use part No. 07WPK-ZW50100 and 07SPJ-ZW0030Z.

Apply a load to the propeller shaft using a two-jaw puller as shown in **Figure 137** or install the propeller shaft backward as shown in **Figure 138**. Position the gearcase so the drive shaft is facing UP during all measurements. Turn the drive shaft very gently to take the measurements. *Do not* use enough force to turn the gears. The free movement of the shaft represents the actual gear lash or tooth clearance. Read the amount of free movement on the dial indicator and record the lash for both forward and reverse gears.

Models BF20A, BF25A and BF30A

1. Install a puller as shown in **Figure 139**. Tighten the puller bolt to 5.0 N·m (44.0 in. lbs) to load the propeller in the indicated direction.
2. Install the backlash indicator tool and sleeve (when listed with the part No.) onto the drive shaft as shown in **Figure 140**.
3. Using a suitable mount, attach a dial indicator to the gearcase and align with the backlash indicator tool as shown in **Figure 141**. Ensure the dial indicator tip aligns with the detent on the backlash indicator tool.

4. Push down on the drive shaft with 5.0 kg (11.0 lb.) of force to properly position the drive shaft during backlash measurement.

5. Observe the dial indicator needle movement while gently rotating the drive shaft in both directions. Loosen the backlash indicator tool and rotate the drive shaft 90°. Reposition the dial indicator/backlash indicator tool, then repeat the measurement. Repeat this step until four measurements have been taken. Record the average of the measurements as forward gear backlash.

6. Remove the puller from the propeller shaft. Install the propeller onto the propeller shaft backward (**Figure 142**). Install a washer over the propeller shaft along with the propeller nut. Tighten the nut to 5.0 N·m (44.0 in. lb.).

7. Repeat Step 5. Record the average backlash measurement as reverse gear backlash. Remove the propeller, dial indicator and backlash indicator tool.

8. Refer to *Shim Changes* in this chapter to determine which shim changes are required.

Models BF35A, BF40A, BF45A and BF50A

1. Install a puller as shown in **Figure 139**. Tighten the puller bolt to 5.0 N·m (44.0 in. lbs) to load the propeller in the indicated direction.

2. Install the backlash indicator tool and sleeve (when listed with the part No.) onto the drive shaft as shown in **Figure 140**.

3. Using a suitable mount, attach a dial indicator to the gearcase and align with the backlash indicator tool as shown in **Figure 141**. Ensure the dial indicator tip aligns with the detent on the backlash indicator tool.

4. Push down on the drive shaft with 5.0 kg (11.0 lb.) of force to properly position the drive shaft during backlash measurement.

5. Observe the dial indicator needle movement while gently rotating the drive shaft in both directions. Loosen the backlash indicator tool and rotate the drive shaft 90°. Reposition the dial indicator/backlash indicator tool and repeat the measurement. Repeat this step until four measurements have been taken. Record the average of the measurements as forward gear backlash.

6. Remove the puller from the propeller shaft. Install the propeller onto the propeller shaft in the backward direction (**Figure 142**). Install a washer over the propeller shaft along with the propeller nut. Tighten the nut to 5.0 N·m (44.0 in. lb.).

7. Repeat Step 5. Record the average backlash measurement as reverse gear backlash. Remove the propeller, dial indicator and backlash indicator tool.

8. Refer to *Shim Changes* in this chapter to determine which shim changes are required.

Models BF75A and BF90A

1. Refer to *Pinion Gear and Drive Shaft* in this chapter and install the preload tool onto the gearcase (**Figure 143**). Spin the drive shaft several revolutions to fully seat the drive shaft bearing.

2. Install a puller as shown in **Figure 139**. Tighten the puller bolt to 5.0 N·m (44.0 in. lb.) to load the propeller in the indicated direction.

3. Install the backlash indicator tool and sleeve (when listed with the part No.) onto the drive shaft as shown in **Figure 140**. Clamp the sleeve onto the drive shaft with the backlash indicator tool.

4. Using a suitable mount, attach a dial indicator to the gearcase and align it with the backlash indicator tool as shown in **Figure 141**. Ensure the dial indicator tip is aligned with the mark next to the No. 4 on the backlash indicator tool.

GEARCASE REPAIR

5. Observe the dial indicator needle movement while gently rotating the drive shaft in both directions. Loosen the backlash indicator tool and rotate the drive shaft 90°. Reposition the dial indicator/backlash indicator tool and repeat the measurement. Repeat this step until four measurements have been taken. Record the average of the measurements as forward gear backlash.

6. Remove the puller from the propeller shaft. Remove the dial indicator and backlash indicator tool from the gearcase.

7. Refer to *Pinion Gear and Drive Shaft* in this chapter and remove the preload tool from the gearcase (**Figure 143**).

8. Refer to *Shim Changes* in this chapter to determine which shim changes are required.

Models BF115A and BF130A (right rotation)

1. Refer to *Pinion Gear and Drive Shaft* in this chapter and install the preload tool onto the gearcase (**Figure 143**). Spin the drive shaft several revolutions to fully seat the drive shaft bearing.

2. Install a two-jaw puller as shown in **Figure 139**. Tighten the puller bolt to 5.0 N·m (44.0 in. lb.) to load the propeller in the indicated direction.

3. Install the backlash indicator tool and sleeve (when listed with the part No.) onto the drive shaft as shown in **Figure 140**. Clamp the sleeve onto the drive shaft with the backlash indicator tool.

4. Using a suitable mount, attach a dial indicator to the gearcase and align with the backlash indicator tool as shown in **Figure 141**. Ensure the dial indicator tip is aligned with the mark next to the No. 2 on the backlash indicator tool.

5. Observe the dial indicator needle movement while gently rotating the drive shaft in both directions. Loosen the backlash indicator tool and rotate the drive shaft 90°. Reposition the dial indicator/backlash indicator tool and repeat the measurement. Repeat this step until four measurements have been taken. Record the average of the measurements as forward gear backlash.

6. Remove the puller from the propeller shaft. Install the propeller onto the propeller shaft in the backward direction (**Figure 142**). Install a washer over the propeller shaft along with the propeller nut. Tighten the nut to 5.0 N·m (44.0 in. lb.).

7. Repeat Step 5. Record the average backlash measurement as reverse gear backlash. Remove the propeller, dial indicator and backlash indicator tool.

8. Refer to *Pinion Gear and Drive Shaft* in this chapter and remove the preload tool from the gearcase (**Figure 143**).

9. Refer to *Shim Changes* in this chapter to determine which shim changes are required.

Models BF115A and BF130A (left rotation)

1. Refer to *Bearing Cap/Bearing Carrier* in this chapter and remove the rear mounted gear from the bearing carrier. Install the carrier into the gearcase without the rear mounted gear.

2. Refer to *Pinion Gear and Drive Shaft* in this chapter and install the preload tool onto the gearcase housing (**Figure 143**). Spin the drive shaft several revolutions to fully seat the drive shaft bearing.

3. Install a puller as indicated in **Figure 139**. Tighten the puller bolt to 5.0 N·m (44.0 in. lbs) to load the propeller in the indicated direction.

4. Install the backlash indicator tool and sleeve (when listed with the part No.) onto the drive shaft (**Figure 140**). Clamp the sleeve onto the drive shaft with the backlash indicator tool.

5. Using a suitable mount attach a dial indicator to the gearcase and align with the backlash indicator tool (**Figure 141**). Ensure the dial indicator tip is aligned with the marking next to the No. 2 on the backlash indicator tool.

6. Observe the dial indicator needle movement while gently rotating the drive shaft in both directions. Loosen the backlash indicator tool and rotate the drive shaft 90°. Reposition the dial indicator/backlash indicator tool, then repeat the measurement. Repeat this step until four measurements have been taken. Record the average of the measurements as reverse gear backlash.

7. Remove the puller from the propeller shaft. Refer to *Bearing Cap/Bearing Carrier* in this chapter and install the rear mounted gear into the bearing carrier. Install the carrier into the gearcase.

8. Install the propeller onto the propeller shaft in the backward direction (**Figure 142**). Install a washer over the propeller shaft along with the propeller nut. Tighten the nut to 5.0 N·m (44.0 in. lb.).

9. Repeat Step 5. Record the average backlash measurement as forward gear backlash. Remove the propeller, dial indicator and backlash indicator tool.

10. Refer to *Pinion Gear and Drive Shaft* in this chapter and remove the preload tool from the gearcase (**Figure 143**).

11. Refer to *Shim Changes* in this chapter to determine which shim changes are required.

Shim Changes

Compare the recorded backlash measurements with the specification listed in **Table 2**. No changes are required if both backlash readings are within the listed specifications.

Forward and reverse backlash too high

On all models, except BF75A and BF90A, the pinion gear is likely positioned too high in the gearcase when both readings are above the listed specifications. Shim changes are required to lower the pinion gear closer to both driven gears.

On these models, the shims that set the pinion height are located just below the drive shaft tapered bearing race (A, **Figure 144**). Select a thinner shim or set of shims to position the pinion gear closer to the driven gear(s). This change lowers both backlash readings. Measure the gear backlash to verify lower backlash readings. Further changes may be required if both backlash readings are not within the listed specifications. On models BF75A and BF90A, pinion height is set during the drive shaft installa-

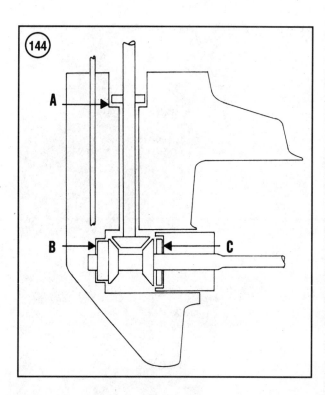

tion. Adjustments to the pinion gear height are not recommended to correct gear backlash.

Forward and reverse backlash too low

On all models, except BF75A and BF90A, the pinion gear is likely positioned too low in the gearcase when both readings are below the listed specification. Shim changes are required to raise the pinion gear away from both driven gears.

On these models, the shims that set the pinion height are located just below the drive shaft tapered bearing race (A, **Figure 144**). Select a thicker shim or set of shims to position the pinion gear further from the driven gear(s). This change increases both backlash readings. Measure the gear backlash to verify increased backlash readings. Further changes may be required if both backlash readings are not within the listed specifications. On models BF75A and BF90A, pinion height is set during the drive shaft installation procedures. On these models, adjustments to the pinion gear height are not recommended to correct gear backlash.

Forward gear backlash too high (right rotation models)

The shims that set the forward gear backlash are located just forward of the front gear bearing (B, **Figure 144**). Se-

GEARCASE REPAIR

lect a thicker shim or set of shims to position the forward gear closer to the pinion gear. This change lowers the forward gear backlash readings without affecting the reverse gear backlash. Measure the gear backlash to verify lower forward gear backlash readings. Further shim changes may be required if both readings are not within the listed specifications.

Forward gear backlash too high (left rotation models)

The shims that set forward gear backlash are located between the *rear* gear and the bearing carrier (C, **Figure 144**). Select a thicker shim or set of shims to position the forward gear closer to the pinion gear. This change lowers the forward gear backlash without affecting the reverse gear backlash. Further shim changes may be required if both readings are not within the listed specifications.

Forward gear backlash too low (right rotation models)

The shims that set forward gear backlash are located just forward of the front gear bearing (B, **Figure 144**). Select a thinner shim or set of shims to position the forward gear further from the pinion gear. This change increases the forward gear backlash without affecting reverse gear backlash. Further shim changes may be required if both readings are not within the specifications.

Forward gear backlash too low (left rotation models)

The shims that set forward gear backlash are located between the *rear* gear and the bearing carrier (C, **Figure 144**). Select a thinner shim or set of shims to position the forward gear further from the pinion gear. This change increases the forward gear backlash reading affecting the reverse gear backlash. Further shim changes may be required if backlash readings are not within the specifications.

Reverse gear backlash too high (right rotation models)

On all models, except BF75A and BF90A, the shims that set reverse gear backlash are located between the reverse gear bearing and the bearing carrier (C, **Figure 144**). Select a thicker shim or set of shims to position the reverse gear closer to the pinion gear. This change lowers the reverse gear backlash without affecting forward gear backlash. Further shim changes may be required if backlash readings are not within the specifications.

Reverse gear backlash too high (left rotation models)

The shims that set the reverse gear backlash are located between the front gear bearing and the step in the housing (B, **Figure 144**). Select a thicker shim or set of shims to position the reverse gear closer to the pinion gear. This change lowers the reverse gear backlash without affecting the forward gear backlash. Further shim changes may be required if backlash readings are not within the specification.

Reverse gear backlash too low (right rotation models)

On all models, except BF75A and BF90A, the shims that set reverse gear backlash are located between the reverse gear bearing and the bearing carrier (C, **Figure 144**). Select a thinner shim or set of shims to position the reverse gear further from the pinion gear. This change increases the reverse gear backlash without affecting the forward gear backlash. Further shim changes may be required if backlash readings are not within the specifications.

Reverse gear backlash too low (left rotation models)

The shims that set reverse gear backlash are located between the front gear bearing and the step in the housing (B, **Figure 144**). Select a thinner shim or set of shims to position the reverse gear further from the pinion gear. This change increases the reverse gear backlash without affecting forward gear backlash. Further changes may be required if backlash readings are not within the specifications.

TABLE 1 TIGHTENING TORQUE

Model	Torque
Gearcase cap/bearing carrier fasteners	
BF20, BF2A	8-12 N•m (71-106 in.-lb.)
BF50, BF5A, BF75, BF8A, BF100	*
BF9.9A, BF15A	8-12 N•m (71-106 in.-lb.)
BF20A, BF25A, BF30A	70.0 N•m (52 ft.-lb.)
BF35A, BF40A, BF45A, BF50A	70.0 N•m (52 ft.-lb.)
BF75A, BF90A	30.0 N•m (22 ft.-lb.)
BF115A, BF130A	35.0 N•m (26 ft.-lb.)
Gearcase-to-drive shaft housing	
BF20. BF2A	8-12 N•m (70.0-104.0 in.-lb.)
BF50, BF5A, BF75, BF8A, BF100	*
BF9.9A, BF15A	*
BF20A, BF25A, BF30A	35.0 N•m (26 ft.-lb.)
BF35A, BF40A, BF45A, BF50A	35.0 N•m (26 ft.-lb.)
BF75A, BF90A	35.0 N•m (26 ft.-lb.)
BF115A, BF130A	35.0 N•m (26 ft.-lb.)
Propeller nut	
BF20, BF2A	Tighten securely and align cotter pin hole
BF50, BF5A	Tighten securely and align cotter pin hole
BF75, BF8A, BF100	Tighten securely and align cotter pin hole
BF9.9A, BF15A	Tighten securely and align cotter pin hole
BF20A, BF25A, BF30A	1.0-35.0 N•m (9 in.-lb. to 26 ft.-lb.)
BF35A, BF40A, BF45A, BF50A	75.0 N•m (55 ft.-lb.)
BF75A, BF90A	75.0 N•m (55 ft.-lb.)
BF115A, BF130A	1.0-44.0 N•m (9.0 in.- lb. to 33.0 ft.-lb.)
Pinion gear nut	
BF9.9A, BF15A	26.0 N•m (19 ft.-lb.)
BF20A, BF25A, BF30A	40.0 N•m (30 ft.-lb.)
BF35A, BF40A, BF45A, BF50A	75.0 N•m (55 ft.-lb.)
BF75A, BF90A	95.0 N•m (70 ft.-lb.)
BF115A, BF130A	132.0 N•m (97 ft.-lb.)
5 mm bolt/nut	4-7 N•m (35-62 in.-lb.)
6 mm bolt/nut	8-12 N•m (71-106 in.-lb.)
8 mm bolt/nut	20.0-28.0 N•m (15-21 ft.-lb.)
10 mm bolt/nut	35.0-40.0 N•m (26-30 ft.-lb.)

* Tighten to the standard torque specification.

TABLE 2 GEAR BACKLASH SPECIFICATIONS

Model	Forward Gear Backlash	Reverse Gear Backlash
BF20A, BF25A, BF30A	0.10-0.29 mm (0.004-0.011 in.)	0.10-0.39 mm (0.004-0.015 in.)
BF35A, BF40A, BF45A, BF50A	0.11-0.34 mm (0.0043-0.0134 in.)	0.11-0.34 mm (0.0043-0.0134 in.)
BF75A, BF90A	0.11-0.34 mm (0.0043-0.0134 in.)	0.11-0.34 mm (0.0043-0.0134 in.)
BF115A, BF130A (standard rotation models)	0.12-0.29 mm (0.005-0.011 in.)	0.12-0.38 mm (0.005-0.015 in.)
BF115A, BF130A (left hand rotation models)	0.12-0.29 mm (0.005-0.011 in.)	0.12-0.38 mm (0.005-0.015 in.)

Chapter Ten

Jet Drives

Jet drives (**Figure 1**) offer significant advantages for shallow water operation. The absence of the propeller and gearcase allows the engine to operate in areas much too shallow for a standard propeller-driven gearcase. This chapter provides repair procedures for the jet drive unit installed on model BF50A.

JET DRIVE OPERATION

Jet Drive Components

The major components of the jet drive include the impeller (1, **Figure 2**), intake opening (2, **Figure 2**), volute tube (3, **Figure 2**) and discharge nozzle (4, **Figure 2**).

Normal installation of a jet drive engine positions the intake opening slightly below the bottom of the boat as shown in **Figure 2**. Overall performance of a jet drive equipped boat is greatly affected by the engine mounting height.

A higher jet mounting height may enhance top speed; however, the pump may ventilate during acceleration or in turns. Ventilation occurs when the pump is unloaded due to air entering the intake instead of water—the engine speed increases yet the boat loses forward thrust.

Mounting the jet pump too low generally results in excessive water spray and speed loss due to the increased drag.

The engine should be mounted just below 6.35 mm (0.25 in.) the height in which ventilation is noted.

Contact the boat manufacturer or a boat dealership that is familiar with jet drive installation for mounting height recommendation.

Thrust Control

The impeller is connected to a shaft supported by bearings on one end and connected into the crankshaft at the other end. Therefore anytime the engine is running, the impeller is turning.

The rotating impeller pulls water through the intake opening and pushes it through the volute tube (3, **Figure 2**). The volute tube directs the water toward the discharge nozzle. The water flowing from the discharge nozzle provides thrust to move the boat. Thrust is increased as the speed of the impeller increases.

Raising a scoop into the water stream flowing from the discharge nozzle provides forward, neutral, and reverse operation. The scoop is moved with a cable-actuated lever that is attached to the scoop lever (**Figure 3**). The cable is moved by direct connection of the control box or tiller shift cable.

Maximum forward thrust is provided when the scoop is positioned away from the water stream exiting the discharge nozzle (**Figure 3**).

Raising the scoop to cover about half of the discharge nozzle opening provides neutral thrust. The scoop directs half of the exiting water in a direction opposite the water exiting the discharge nozzle as shown in **Figure 4**. The thrust is balanced and very little forward or reverse movement occurs.

Reverse thrust is provided by raising the scoop to virtually cover the entire discharge nozzle opening (**Figure 5**). The scoop in the direction opposite the discharge nozzle opening diverts all exiting water. This provides for reverse movement of the boat. The reverse thrust is far less efficient than the forward thrust, resulting in far less power in the reverse direction.

Steering the boat is accomplished as the engine is pivoted port or starboard as with the standard propeller-driven gearcases.

> *CAUTION*
> *The boat may steer in the opposite direction from a propeller driven gearcase when reverse thrust is selected. Practice common maneuvers in reverse while in open water until you are comfortable with the jet drive backing characteristics.*

A disadvantage of jet-drive propulsion is a substantial reduction in efficiency when compared to an equivalent propeller-driven unit. The performance of a jet drive is generally equivalent to 70 % of the same outboard motor equipped with a standard gearcase. As comparison, a model BF50A equipped with a jet drive provides the approximate speed and performance of a 35 hp propeller-driven outboard motor.

Except for the gearcase, a jet drive-equipped model BF50A is identical in all respects to one with a propeller-driven gearcase. For repair or adjustments to components other than the jet drive, refer to the information for model BF50A.

Because jet drive units (**Figure 1**) are installed in place of the standard propeller drive gearcase, the removal and installation procedure is similar to that used for standard

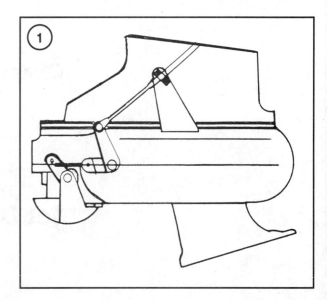

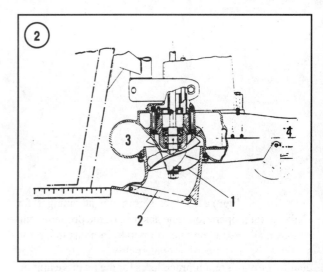

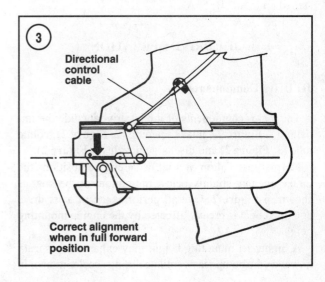

JET DRIVES

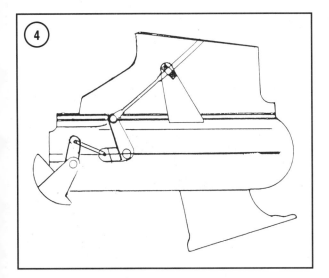

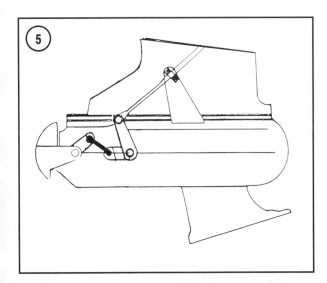

propeller drive gearcase. Refer to *Jet Drive Removal/Installation* in this chapter.

Jet Drive Repair

Since outboards with jet drives can operate in very shallow water, certain components are much more susceptible to wear. Jet drive units ingest a considerable amount of sand, rocks and other debris during normal operation. Components that require frequent inspection include the engine water pump, impeller and intake housing.

Other components that may require repair include the bearing housing, drive shaft bearings and drive shaft.

Engine water pump

The water pump used to cool the powerhead is virtually identical to the pump used on standard propeller drive gearcases.

Refer to the *Water Pump* section in Chapter Nine for water pump inspection and repair procedures. Use the procedure for model BF50A.

Flushing the cooling system

Inspect the engine water pump at regular intervals. The water pump impeller will be damaged within seconds if the engine is started without a supply of water. Use a test tank or a suitable flush adapter to run the engine out of the water.

Sand and other debris quickly wears the water pump components. Frequent inspection is suggested if the engine is run in sand- or silt-laden water. Also, sand and other debris can collect in the powerhead cooling passages. These deposits eventually lead to overheating and increased corrosion. Use the flush adapter to flush debris from the cooling system after running the engine in salt or sand laden water. This important maintenance step can add years to the life of your outboard.

> *CAUTION*
> *Serious engine damage can result from overheating. Constantly monitor the water stream while the engine is running. Stop the engine immediately if the water stream becomes weak or stops.*

1. Disconnect the lubrication hose to access the flush plug (**Figure 6**).
2. Use a large screwdriver to remove the plug on the port side of the jet drive (**Figure 6**). Discard the plug gasket.

3. Thread the flush adapter listed earlier into the threaded opening for the plug. Attach a garden hose to the adapter. Turn the water supply to full open.
4. Start the engine and allow it to run for at least 10 minutes at idle speed.
5. Switch the engine off *then* turn the water supply off.
6. Remove the adapter from the jet drive. Install the plug and new gasket. Tighten the plug securely.

Impeller-to-housing clearance

Worn or damaged surfaces on the impeller or the intake housing allow water to slip past the impeller and result in decreased efficiency. Measure the impeller clearance if increased engine speed is noted along with a loss in top speed or power.

1. Remove the spark plug leads and connect them to an engine ground. Disconnect both battery cables from the battery (electric start models).
2. Locate the intake grate on the bottom of the jet drive. Use long feeler gauges to measure the clearance between the impeller edges and the intake housing as shown in **Figure 7**. Carefully rotate the flywheel and check the clearance in several locations. Determine the *average* clearance measured.
3. The correct average clearance is approximately 0.8 mm (.031 in.). Small variations are acceptable as long as the impeller is not contacting the intake housing and the engine is not exceeding the maximum rated engine speed. Refer to *Impeller Shimming* if excessive clearance is noted or the impeller is contacting the intake housing.
4. Install the spark plugs and spark plug leads. Clean the battery terminals, then connect the cables to the battery.

Jet Drive Removal/Installation

WARNING
Always disconnect the spark plug leads and both battery cables from the battery terminals before working with the jet drive.

Jet drive removal/installation procedures are very similar to propeller-driven gearcase removal and installation.

Disconnect the directional control cable from the scoop lever. Remove the intake housing access to the jet drive mounting bolts. Refer to *Intake Housing* in this chapter. Follow the procedures listed in Chapter Nine for the removal and installation of propeller drive gearcase and remove the jet drive unit from the engine. Disregard the references to the shift shaft when removing or installing a jet drive unit. Install the intake housing if removed to access the mounting bolts. Check and correct the directional

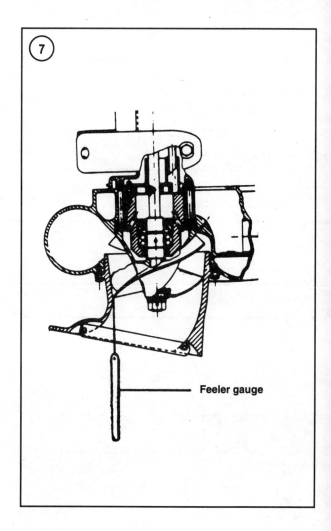

control cable adjustment after installation. Adjust the direction control as described in Chapter Five. Always check for proper cooling system operation after installation.

Intake Housing Removal/Installation

Removal of the intake housing is required when shimming the impeller or when the impeller and housing require inspection for worn or damaged components. Refer to **Figure 8** during disassembly and assembly of the jet drive.

1. Disconnect the spark plug leads. Disconnect both battery cables from the battery terminals.
2. Remove the intake housing mounting bolts (**Figure 8**). Pull the intake housing from the jet drive. Carefully tap the housing loose with a rubber mallet if necessary.
3. Clean and inspect the housing mounting bolts. Replace them if they are corroded or damaged.

JET DRIVES

4. Clean all debris from the intake housing mating surfaces.

5. Inspect the inner surfaces of the intake housing liner for deep scratches, eroded or damaged areas. Replace the liner if these conditions are present and excessive impeller clearance is present. Refer to *Intake Housing Liner*.

6. Install the intake housing onto the jet drive housing with the lower end facing the rear. Apply water-resistant grease to the threads of the bolts. Tighten them to the standard torque specification listed in **Table 1**.

7. Connect all spark plug leads. Clean and connect both battery cables. Run the engine to check for proper operation before putting it back into service.

Intake Housing Liner Replacement

Removing the intake grate may be necessary to access the liner.

1. Refer to *Intake Housing* and remove the intake housing from the jet drive.

2. Locate the bolts on the side of the intake housing that retain the liner to the housing. Note the locations, then remove the bolts.

3. Tap the liner loose with a long punch through the intake grate opening. Place the punch on the edge of the liner and carefully drive it from the housing.

4. Apply a light coat of water-resistant grease to the liner bore in the intake housing. Carefully slide the new liner into position. Align the bolt holes in the liner with the bolt holes in the housing.

5. Apply water-resistant grease to the threads of the bolts. Install them and tighten to the specification listed in **Table 1**. Use a file to remove any burrs or bolt material protruding into the intake housing.

6. Refer to *Intake Housing* and install the intake housing on the jet drive.

Impeller Removal/Installation

Removal of the jet drive is required prior to removing the impeller. Accessing the drive shaft is necessary when removing the impeller nut.

1. Remove the jet drive from the engine.

2. Refer to *Intake Housing* and remove the intake housing from the jet drive.

3. Refer to Chapter Nine for the part number of the drive shaft adapter for model BF50A. Use the adapter to grip the splined end of the drive shaft when removing or installing the impeller.

4. Bend the tabs of the washer (8, **Figure 8**) away from the impeller nut (9, **Figure 8**). Note the location and position of all components prior to removal. Use a socket and adapter to remove the nut, tab washer and lower shims from the drive shaft. Discard the tab washer.

5. Pull the impeller, drive key, sleeve and upper shims from the drive shaft. Use a rubber mallet to carefully tap the impeller loose from the shaft if necessary.

6. Inspect the impeller for worn or damaged areas and replace if defects are noted.

7. Place the sleeve (4, **Figure 8**) and drive key (5) onto the drive shaft. Apply water-resistant grease to the drive key and impeller bore. Slide the upper shims then impeller onto the drive shaft.

8. Place the lower shims, new tab washer (8, **Figure 8**) and an impeller nut onto the drive shaft. Make sure the shims and tab washers are in the proper positions. Use the drive shaft adapter and a suitable socket wrench to tighten the impeller nut securely.

9. Bend the tabs up to secure the impeller nut. Refer to *Intake Housing*, then install the intake housing to the jet drive. Refer to *Impeller-to-Housing Clearance* and measure and correct the clearance. After correct clearance is obtained, install the jet drive.

Impeller Shimming

Shimming the impeller is necessary to ensure proper impeller-to-intake housing clearance. Removal and installation of the intake housing and impeller is required for each shim change. Refer to **Figure 8**.

Refer to *Impeller-to-Intake Housing Clearance* after each shim change for the measurement procedure. Repeat the process until the correct clearance is obtained.

Eight shims are used to position the impeller. All shims are 0.8 mm (.031 in.) thick. Normally shims are located both above and below the impeller.

1. Remove the jet drive from the engine.

2. Remove the intake housing from the jet drive. Refer to *Intake Housing*.

3. Remove the impeller as described in this chapter.

4. If too much impeller to intake housing clearance was measured, remove one shim from below the impeller and place it above the impeller.

5. If too little clearance was measured, remove one shim from above the impeller and place it below the impeller.

6. Install the impeller and intake housing onto the jet drive following the instructions listed in this chapter. Refer to *Impeller-to-Intake Housing Clearance* and measure the clearance. Repeat Steps 1-6 until the correct clearance is obtained.

CHAPTER TEN

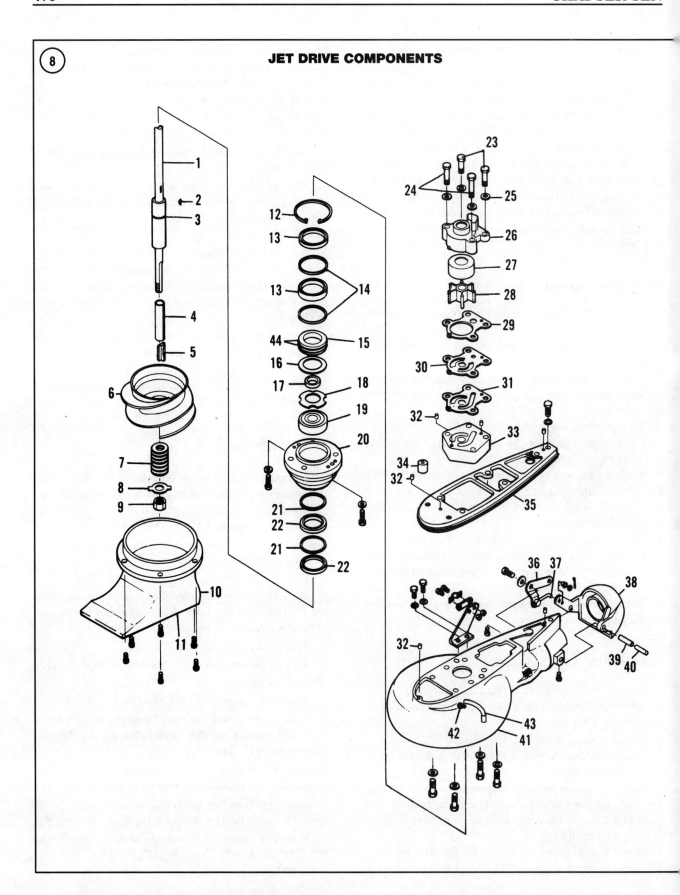

JET DRIVES

1. Drive shaft
2. Woodruff key
3. Thrust ring
4. Nylon sleeve
5. Drive key
6. Impeller
7. Shim
8. Tab washer
9. Nut
10. Intake housing
11. Intake grille
12. Snap ring
13. Seal
14. Retaining ring
15. Upper seal carrier
16. Spacer washer
17. Collar
18. Thrust washer
19. Bearing
20. Bearing housing
21. Retaining ring
22. Seal
23. Bolts (short)
24. Bolts (long)
25. Washers
26. Water pump housing
27. Cartridge insert
28. Impeller
29. Gasket
30. Plate
31. Gasket
32. Dowel pin
33. Spacer plate
34. Rubber sleeve
35. Adapter plate
36. Pivot bracket
37. Linkage rod
38. Thrust gate
39. Nylon sleeve
40. Pivot pin
41. Jet drive pump housing
42. Grease fitting
43. Hose
44. O-rings

Bearing Housing Removal

Drive shaft bearing inspection and/or replacement is required if contamination or a significant amount of water is found when performing routine maintenance to the jet drive. Replace all seals, gaskets and O-rings whenever they are removed. Their cost is far less than the cost to replace damaged components should they fail. Removing the bearing housing is required to access the bearings, shafts, seals and other components.

1. Remove the jet drive from the engine.
2. Refer to *Intake Housing* and remove the intake housing from the jet drive housing.
3. Refer to *Impeller Removal/Installation* and remove the impeller from the drive shaft.
4. Remove the water pump as described in Chapter Nine under BF50A models.
5. Remove the spacer plate (33, **Figure 8**) from the jet drive housing. Locate and remove the bolts and washers securing the bearing housing (**Figure 9**) to the jet drive housing.
6. Pull the bearing housing from the jet drive housing and place it on a clean work surface.

Drive shaft bearing removal and installation

> *WARNING*
> *The components of the bearing housing will become very hot during disassembly and assembly. Take all necessary precautions to protect yourself and others from personal injury.*

> *WARNING*
> *Never use a flame or allow sparks to occur in an area where any combustible material is present. Always have a suitable fire extinguisher nearby when using a flame or other heat-producing device.*

> *CAUTION*
> *Apply only enough heat to allow the bearing housing to expand and slide over the bearing(s). Excessive heat will damage the seals and retainers in the bearing housing. Use a section of appropriately sized pipe and a press (if necessary) to fully seat the bearing(s) in the housing. Press only on the outer bearing race. Use light pressure only. Never drive the bearings into position.*

> *CAUTION*
> *Pay strict attention to the direction the bearings are installed onto the drive shaft. The inner race surfaces must be installed cor-*

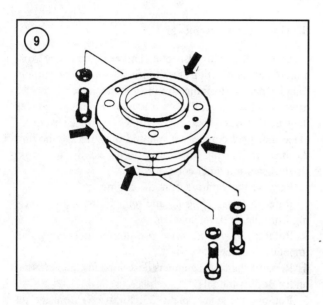

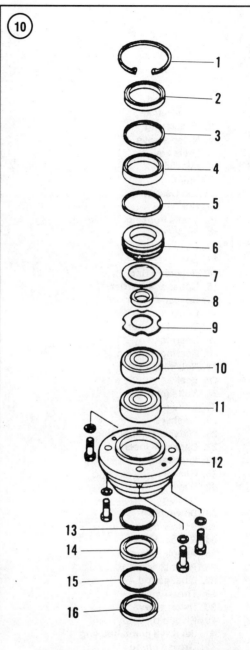

rectly to ensure a durable repair. The inner race thrust surfaces are wider on one side. Refer to the illustrations prior to assembly of the drive shaft.

Refer to **Figure 8** during the disassembly and assembly procedure. Note the location and position of all components prior to removal from the bearing housing. Rotate the drive shaft to check the bearing(s) for rough operation. Replace the bearings if a rough or loose feel is noted.

Do not remove the bearings from the drive shaft unless replacement is required. Removal of the bearings requires that heat be applied to the housing. The seals will likely be damaged and require replacement.

1. Use snap ring pliers to remove the snap ring (1, **Figure 10**) from the housing.

2. Secure the bearing carrier into a soft jaw vise with the impeller end of the drive shaft facing up. Thread the impeller nut onto the shaft to protect the threads. Apply moderate heat to the areas noted with arrows in **Figure 9**. Use a block of wood and hammer to tap on the installed nut end and drive the shaft and bearing(s) from the housing. Gradually increase the amount of heat until the bearing(s) and drive shaft slide from the housing.

3. Remove the seal carrier (6, **Figure 10**) from the drive shaft. Note the position of the seal lips then remove the grease seals (2 and 4, **Figure 10**) and both retaining rings (3 and 5, **Figure 10**) from the seal carrier. Discard the seals. Remove the O-rings from the seal carrier and discard them.

4. Note the location and position, and remove the shim (7, **Figure 10**), collar (8) and thrust washer (9) from the bearing housing.

1. Snap ring
2. Seal
3. Seal retainer
4. Seal
5. Seal retainer
6. Seal carrier
7. Washer
8. Collar
9. Thrust washer
10. Top bearing *
11. Bottom bearing
12. Bearing housing
13. Seal retainer
14. Seal
15. Seal retainer
16. Seal

* A top bearing is not used on all jet drives.

JET DRIVES

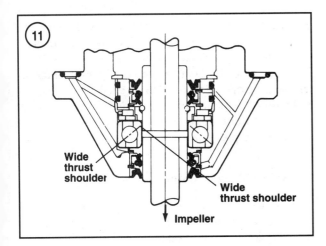

5. Note the seal lip direction prior to removal. Use a screwdriver to remove the retaining rings (13 and 15, **Figure 10**) and seals (14 and 16, **Figure 10**) from the bearing housing. Discard the seals. Press the bearing(s) from the drive shaft.

6. Inspect the drive shaft for damaged surfaces or excessive wear in the seal contact areas. Replace the drive shaft if any defects are noted.

7. Refer to **Figure 11** during the assembly process. Place the thrust washer, if so equipped, onto the drive shaft. Note the position of the bearing thrust surfaces (wide side of the inner race) and slide the bearing(s) onto the shaft as indicated. Use a section of tubing or pipe to press the new bearing(s) onto the drive shaft. The tool used must contact only the inner race of the bearings.

8. Use Loctite Primer T to clean all contamination from the seal bore in the bearing housing. Select a large socket or section of pipe to install the seals into the bearing housing. The tool selected must provide adequate contact for the seal yet not contact the bearing housing during installation.

9. Apply Loctite Primer T to the outer surface of the seal. When dry, apply Loctite 271 to the seal bore and the seal outer surfaces. Place the seal into the housing with the seal lip (open side) facing in the direction noted prior to removal. Press the seal into the bearing housing until seated against the retainer. Wipe the excess Loctite from the seals.

10. Place the retaining ring into the housing groove and the second seal with the lip side (open side) facing the direction noted prior to removal. Apply Loctite 271 to the outer seal surface, then press the second seal in until seated against the first retaining ring. Place the second retaining ring into the housing groove with the notched area aligned with the small hole in the retaining ring groove. Wipe the excess Loctite from the seal area.

11. Apply water-resistant grease to the seal lips and retaining ring prior to installation of the drive shaft and bearings.

12. Place the drive shaft in a vise (soft jaws or pads) with the impeller side up. Set the bearing housing onto the drive shaft. Use a heat lamp or torch to apply heat to the bearing housing in the areas shown in **Figure 9**. Remove the heat and use heavy gloves to push the bearing housing down over the drive shaft bearings. Apply heat gradually until the bearing housing slides fully onto the bearing(s) and the bearing(s) seat in the housing.

13. Install the thrust washer (9, **Figure 10**) onto the shaft with the gray side facing the impeller. Place the collar (8, **Figure 10**) onto the drive shaft. Place the washer (7, **Figure 10**) into the housing in the direction noted prior to removal.

14. Apply Loctite Primer T to the seal bore surfaces in the seal carrier (6, **Figure 10**) and the outer surfaces of the seals (2 and 4, **Figure 10**). Install the first retaining ring into the seal carrier. Apply Loctite 271 to the seal bore and the outer seal surfaces.

15. Place the seal into the seal bore opening with the lip side (open side) facing in the direction noted prior to removal or as indicated in **Figure 11**. Use an appropriately sized socket or section of tubing to push the first seal into the seal carrier until seated against the retainer. The tool selected must provide adequate contact to the seal yet not contact the seal carrier during installation.

16. Place the second retainer into the seal carrier groove and push the second seal into the seal carrier as described in Step 15. Place new O-rings onto the seal carrier. Lubricate the seal lips and all seal carrier surfaces with water-resistant grease. Carefully press the seal carrier into the bearing housing until fully seated.

17. Use snap ring pliers to install the snap ring into the groove in the bearing housing.

Bearing Housing Installation

1. Ensure that the mating surfaces of the bearing housing and jet drive housing are free of debris.

2. Install the housing and shaft into the jet drive housing. Apply water-resistant grease to the threads of the bolts that retain the bearing housing and install them. Tighten the bolts to specifications listed in **Table 1**.

3. Install the aluminum spacer (33, Figure 8) onto the jet drive housing. Refer to *Water Pump Installation* in Chapter Nine for model BF50A, then install the water pump onto the jet drive housing.

4. Refer to *Impeller Removal/Installation* and install the impeller and related components.

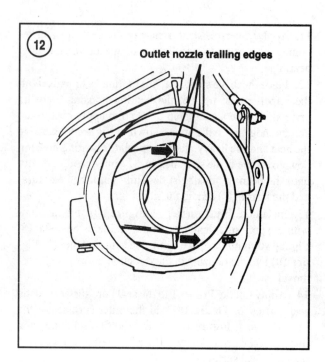

12 Outlet nozzle trailing edges

5. Refer to *Intake Housing* and install the intake housing.
6. Refer to *Impeller to Housing Clearance* and measure the clearance. Correct the clearance as required.
7. Install the jet drive onto the engine. Removal of the intake housing may be required to access the fasteners.
8. Perform the lubrication procedure described in Chapter Four. Perform the direction control adjustments described in Chapter Five.

Correcting Steering Torque

Steering torque causes the boat to steer to the starboard or port side with the engine pointed straight ahead. The tabs (**Figure 12**) in the water discharge opening can be used to correct the steering torque.

Use pliers to bend the trailing end of *both* tabs toward the starboard side of the outlet approximately 1.6 mm (.063 in.) if the boat steers to the starboard direction.

Bend both tabs toward the port side of the outlet if the boat steers toward the port direction.

TABLE 1 STANDARD TIGHTENING TORQUE

Fastener Size	Tightening Torque
5 mm bolt/nut	4-7 N•m (35-62 in.-lb.)
6 mm bolt/nut	8-12 N•m (71-106 in.-lb.)
8 mm bolt/nut	20.0-28.0 N•m (15-21 ft.-lb.)
10 mm bolt/nut	35.0-40.0 N•m (26-30 ft.-lb.)

Chapter Eleven

Rewind Starter

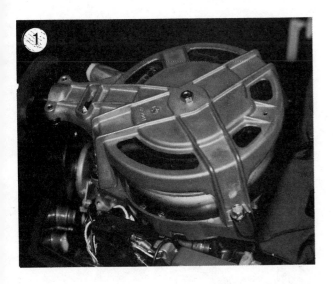

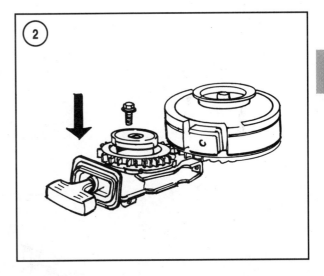

This chapter provides repair procedures for all rewind starter assemblies used on Honda outboards. Follow the step-by-step instructions to perform complete disassembly, inspection and assembly procedures. **Table 1** provides standard tightening torque specifications. **Table 1** is located at the end of this chapter.

All manual start models are equipped with a rewind type starter (**Figure 1**). On models BF20, BF2A, BF50, BF5A, BF75, BF8A and BF100, the rewind starter is the only means for cranking the engine. An electric starting system is available for all other modes.

Rewind Starter Operation (Models BF50 and BF5A)

The rewind assembly on these models is mounted to the upper front side of the base engine and below the flywheel teeth (**Figure 2**).

As the rope (8, **Figure 3**) is pulled, the sheave (7, **Figure 3**) assembly rotates counterclockwise. This causes the helical shaft (portion of the sheave) mounted drive gear (5, **Figure 3**) to move up and engage the teeth on the flywheel. The starter spring winds up within the housing as

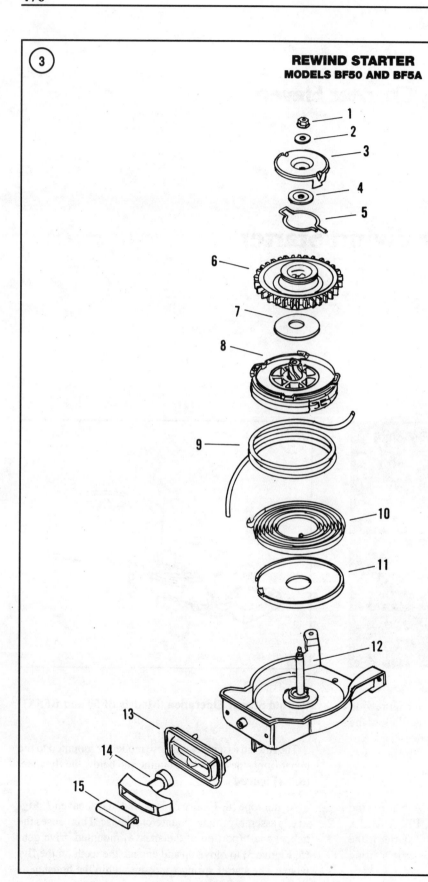

REWIND STARTER

the rope is pulled. Rotation of the starter sheave and drive gear rotates the flywheel.

As the rope is released, the starter spring unwinds causing the sheave to rotate clockwise. This causes the drive gear to move down on the helical shaft disengaging the flywheel teeth. The rope winds around the sheave when released due the action of the starter spring.

Rewind Starter Operation (All Other Models)

On these models, the rewind assembly is mounted to the top of the base engine and directly above the flywheel (**Figure 4**). As the rope (1, **Figure 4**, typical) is pulled, the sheave (2, **Figure 4**, typical) rotates causing the drive pawl (3, **Figure 4**, typical) to pivot from its normal position. This engages the flywheel-mounted starter pulley. This engagement causes the flywheel to rotate with the sheave. As the sheave rotates, the starter spring winds up within the starter housing.

As the rope is released, the starter spring unwinds causing the sheave to rotate counterclockwise direction. Counterclockwise rotation of the sheave causes the drive pawl spring (10, **Figure 4**, typical) to pivot the drive pawl to the normal position thus releasing the starter from the pulley. The rope winds around the sheave when released due to the action of the starter spring.

A rewind starter mounted neutral start mechanism (5, **Figure 4**) is used on models BF9.9A, BF15A, BF20A, BF25A and BF30A to prevent the engine from starting when in gear. This mechanism is cable actuated and prevents the flywheel from rotating when in forward or reverse gear. The gearshift linkage on the engine operates the lockout assembly. Adjustment is required if any components of the mechanism are changed or disturbed. Refer to Chapter Five for adjustment procedures.

Rewind Starter Removal, Repair, Assembly and Installation

CAUTION
When servicing the rewind starter, wear suitable eye protection, gloves and adequate covering over all exposed portions of the body. The starter spring may release from the housing with considerable force. Follow all instructions carefully and wear suitable protection to minimize the risk.

Cleaning and lubrication of the internal components are required when the drive pawl is not engaging properly or the starter is binding when activated.

Use only the correct starter rope. Other types of rope do not withstand the rigorous use and fail in a short amount of time, potentially damaging other components. Contact a Honda dealership to purchase the correct starter rope.

Clean all components, except the rope, in a solvent suitable for composite or plastic components. Use hot soapy water if a suitable solvent is not available. Dry all components with compressed air immediately after cleaning.

Apply water-resistant grease to the bushing, drive pawl, springs and pivot surfaces. In addition, apply grease to the starter spring and housing during assembly.

Use the standard torque specifications listed in **Table 1**.

Refer to **Figures 3-8** to assist with component identification and position.

Removal/Installation (Models BF20 and BF2A)

1. Disconnect both battery cables from the battery, if so equipped. Remove the spark plug(s) and connect the spark plug lead(s) to an engine ground.
2. Lift the upper engine cover to access the fasteners that retain the rewind starter to the base engine. Note the location and position of all fasteners.
3. Remove the nuts (**Figure 9**) and lift the rewind starter assembly along with the engine cover from the base engine. Remove the engine cover along with the rewind starter as the rope handle is removed from the rope during rewind starter disassembly.
4. Remove the washers from the mounting studs.
5. Inspect the starter pulley on the flywheel for worn or damaged surfaces. Refer to Chapter Eight and replace the pulley if any defects are noted.
6. Installation is the reverse of removal, noting the following:
   a. Position all fasteners as noted prior to removal.
   b. Securely tighten all fasteners to the specification listed in **Table 1**.
   c. Check for smooth operation of the rewind starter prior to installation onto the engine.
7. Install the spark plug(s) and spark plug lead(s). Clean the battery terminals and connect the battery cables to the battery, if so equipped.

Removal/Installation (Models BF50 and BF5A)

1. Disconnect both battery cables from the battery, if so equipped. Remove the spark plug(s) and connect the spark plug lead(s) to a suitable engine ground, such as a clean cylinder head or cylinder block bolt.
2. Note the location and orientation of the mounting bolts for the rewind starter prior to removal.

CHAPTER ELEVEN

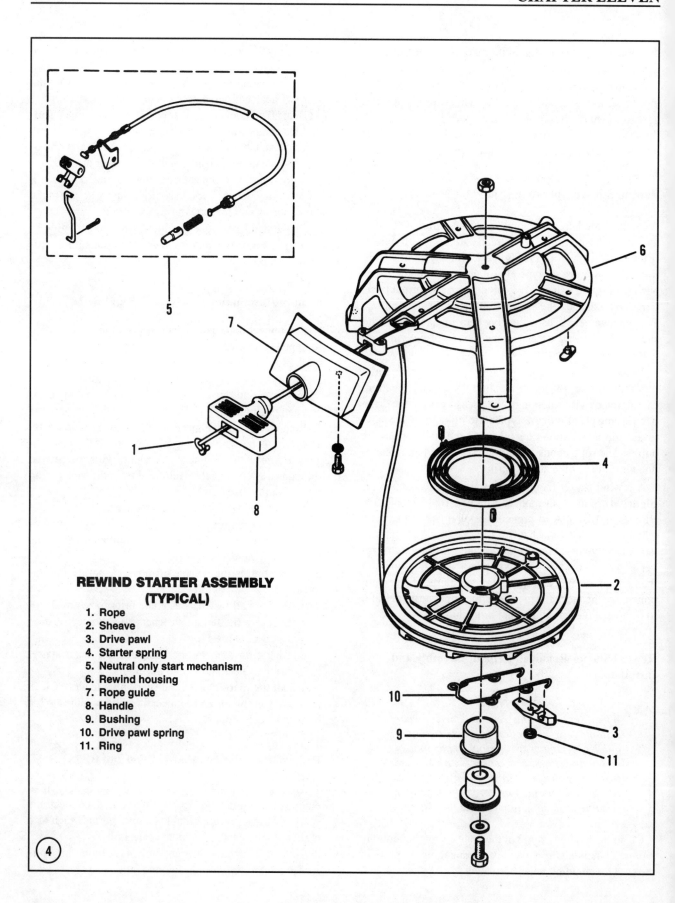

REWIND STARTER ASSEMBLY (TYPICAL)
1. Rope
2. Sheave
3. Drive pawl
4. Starter spring
5. Neutral only start mechanism
6. Rewind housing
7. Rope guide
8. Handle
9. Bushing
10. Drive pawl spring
11. Ring

REWIND STARTER

479

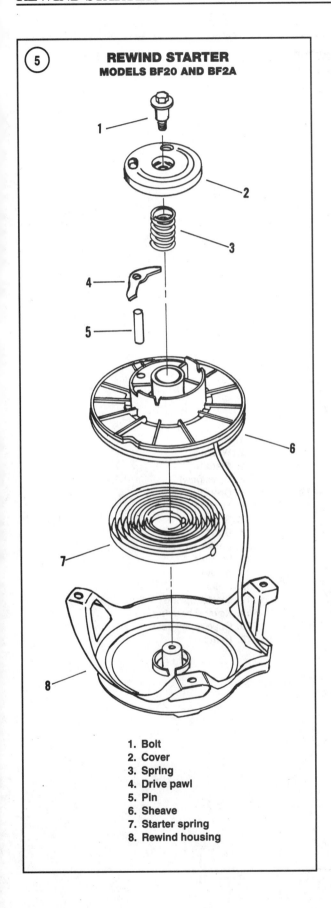

5 REWIND STARTER
MODELS BF20 AND BF2A

1. Bolt
2. Cover
3. Spring
4. Drive pawl
5. Pin
6. Sheave
7. Starter spring
8. Rewind housing

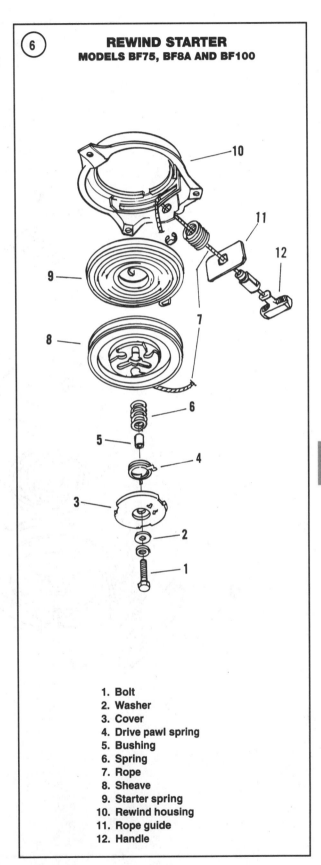

6 REWIND STARTER
MODELS BF75, BF8A AND BF100

1. Bolt
2. Washer
3. Cover
4. Drive pawl spring
5. Bushing
6. Spring
7. Rope
8. Sheave
9. Starter spring
10. Rewind housing
11. Rope guide
12. Handle

11

CHAPTER ELEVEN

⑦ REWIND STARTER
MODELS BF9.9A AND BF15A

1. Bolt
2. Washer
3. Plate
4. Drive pawl
5. Drive pawl spring
6. Friction spring
7. Sheave
8. Bolt
9. Lockwasher
10. Washer
11. Sleeve
12. Roller
13. Starter spring
14. Rewind housing
15. Rope guide seal
16. Handle

REWIND STARTER

REWIND STARTER
MODELS BF20A, BF25A AND BF30A

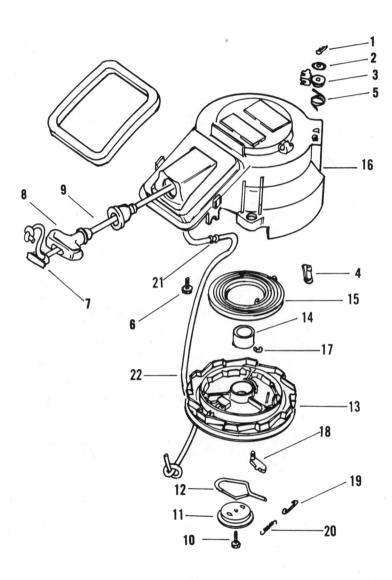

1. Cotter pin
2. Washer
3. Lever
4. Sheave stopper
5. Spring
6. Bolt
7. Plug
8. Handle
9. Rope
10. Bolt
11. Cover
12. Friction spring
13. Sheave
14. Bushing
15. Starter spring
16. Rewind housing
17. E-clip
18. Drive pawl
19. Connector
20. Drive pawl spring
21. Guide
22. Rope

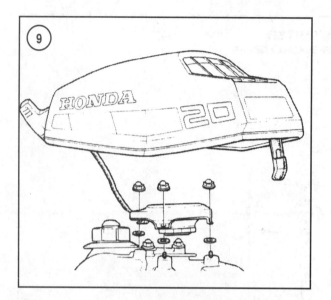

3. Remove all three bolts (**Figure 10**), then lift the rewind starter assembly (**Figure 10**) from the mounting bosses.

4. Inspect the gear teeth on the flywheel for worn or damaged surfaces. Refer to Chapter Eight and replace the flywheel if any defects are noted.

5. Installation is the reverse of removal, noting the following:
   a. Position all fasteners as noted prior to removal.
   b. Securely tighten all fasteners to the specification listed in **Table 1**.
   c. Check for smooth operation of the rewind starter prior to installation onto the engine.

Removal/Installation (Models BF75, BF8A and BF100)

1. Disconnect both battery cables from the battery, if so equipped. Remove the spark plug(s) and connect the spark plug lead(s) to an engine ground.

2. Note the location and position of the mounting bolts for the rewind starter prior to removal.

3. Remove the bolts (**Figure 11**) and lift the rewind starter assembly (**Figure 11**) from the mounting bosses.

4. Inspect the starter pulley (on the flywheel) for worn or damaged surfaces. Refer to Chapter Eight and replace the starter pulley if any defects are noted.

5. Installation is the reverse of removal. Note:
   a. Position all fasteners as noted prior to removal.
   b. Securely tighten all fasteners to the specification listed in **Table 1**.
   c. Check for smooth operation of the rewind starter prior to installation onto the engine.

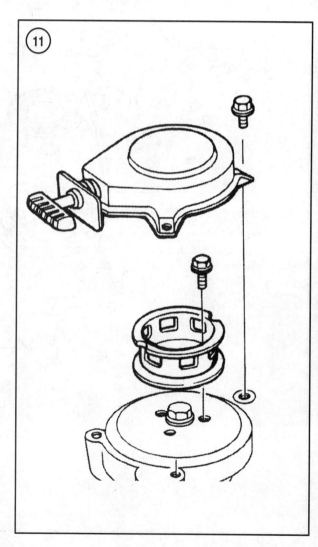

REWIND STARTER

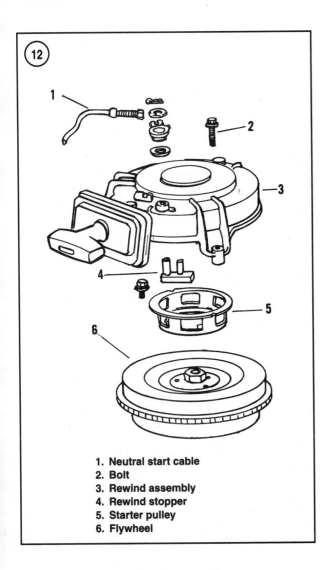

1. Neutral start cable
2. Bolt
3. Rewind assembly
4. Rewind stopper
5. Starter pulley
6. Flywheel

5. Inspect the starter pulley (5, **Figure 12**) for worn or damaged surfaces. Refer to Chapter Eight and replace the starter pulley if any defects are noted.
6. Installation is the reverse of removal, noting the following:
   a. Position all fasteners as noted prior to removal.
   b. Securely Tighten all Fasteners to the specification listed in **Table 1**.
   c. Check for smooth operation of the rewind starter prior to installation onto the engine.
   d. Adjust the neutral start cable following the procedures listed in Chapter Five.
7. Install the spark plug(s) and spark plug lead(s). Clean the battery terminals and connect the battery cables to the battery, if so equipped.

Models BF20A, BF25A and BF30A

1. Disconnect both battery cables from the battery, if so equipped. Remove the spark plug(s) and connect the spark plug lead(s) to an engine ground.
2. Note the location and position of the mounting bolts for the rewind starter prior to removal.
3. Refer to Chapter Five and disconnect the neutral start cable (2, **Figure 13**) from the shift linkage connection.
4. Remove the bolts (1, **Figure 13**), then lift the rewind starter assembly (3, **Figure 13**) from the mounting bosses.
5. Inspect the starter pulley for worn or damaged surfaces. Refer to Chapter Eight and replace the starter pulley if any defects are noted.
6. Installation is the reverse of removal, noting the following:
   a. Position all fasteners as noted prior to removal.
   b. Securely tighten all fasteners to the specification listed in **Table 1**.
   c. Check for smooth operation of the rewind starter prior to installation onto the engine.
   d. Adjust the neutral start cable following the procedures listed in Chapter Five.
7. Install the spark plug(s) and spark plug lead(s). Clean the battery terminals and connect the battery cables to the battery, if so equipped.

6. Install the spark plug(s) and spark plug lead(s). Clean the battery terminals then connect the battery cables to the battery, if so equipped.

Removal/Installation (Models BF9.9A and BF15A)

1. Disconnect both battery cables from the battery, if so equipped. Remove the spark plug(s) and connect the spark plug lead(s) to a suitable engine ground, such as a clean cylinder head or cylinder block bolt.
2. Note the location and orientation of the mounting bolts for the rewind starter prior to removal.
3. Refer to Chapter Five and disconnect the neutral start cable (1, **Figure 12**) from the shift linkage connection.
4. Remove all three bolts (2, **Figure 12**) and lift the rewind starter assembly (3, **Figure 12**) from the mounting bosses.

Rewind Starter Disassembly, Inspection and Assembly

Models BF20 and BF2A

1. Clamp the rope at the rope guide with locking pliers. This prevents the rope from winding into the housing when the handle is removed.

2. Carefully pry the plug and rope from the handle. Untie the knot and pull the handle from the rope. Route the rope through the guide in the top motor cover and remove the rewind starter from the top cover. Place the rewind starter on a clean work surface with the top side down.

3. Hold the rope and rewind starter then release the locking pliers. Allow the rope to slowly wind onto the sheave until the rope is relaxed.

4. Remove the bolt, cover and spring (1-3, **Figure 5**) from the rewind housing. Note the position of the drive pawl spring and cover. Hold down on the sheave (6, **Figure 5**) as you pull the drive pawl (4) and pin (5) from the sheave.

5. Insert a small screwdriver into the hole in the starter sheave (**Figure 14**) and press down to hold the starter spring into the housing. Maintain downward pressure on the spring and lift the sheave and rope from the rewind housing. Carefully route the rope through the hole in the rewind housing. Remove the screwdriver when the sheave clears the housing.

6. Position the housing in a clear area of the floor. Hold the housing down and lightly tap the top of the housing with a mallet until the starter spring (7, **Figure 5**) drops from the housing and completely unwinds.

7. Inspect the cover (2, **Figure 5**) for damaged or worn areas and replace as required. Inspect the drive pawl (4, **Figure 5**) for cracks or worn areas. Replace the pawl if damage or wear is noted.

8. Inspect the bolt (1, **Figure 5**), pin (5) and spring (3) for worn, damaged or corroded surfaces. Replace if any defects are noted.

9. Inspect the entire length of the starter spring (7, **Figure 5**) for cracked, broken or damaged areas. Pay particular attention to the hook at the end of the spring.

10. Inspect the sheave (6, **Figure 5**) for warped, damaged or worn surfaces and replace as required.

11. Inspect the entire length of the rope for cut, worn or frayed areas. Pay particular attention to the length nearest the handle. Replace with the proper type rope if it is not in excellent condition.

12. Inspect the rope guide(s) for damaged or worn areas. Pay particular attention to the area near the rope handle. Replace worn, damaged or corroded components.

13. Measure the length of the starter rope to determine the length for the replacement rope. To prevent the end of the rope from unraveling, carefully melt the cut end of the rope with a small flame. While still molten, use thick gloves and shape the end of the rope into a compact nub. Trim loose pieces from the end when cooled.

14. Wipe the surfaces in the rewind housing where the spring is installed and the shaft with water-resistant grease.

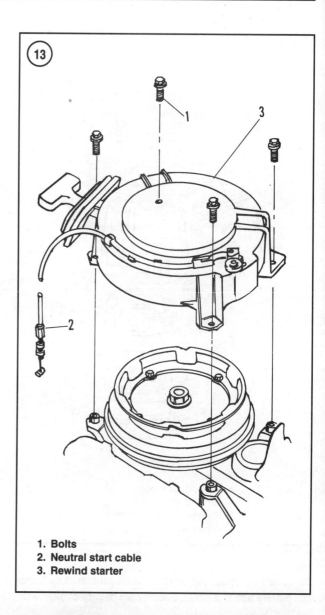

1. Bolts
2. Neutral start cable
3. Rewind starter

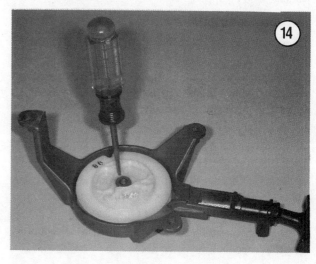

REWIND STARTER

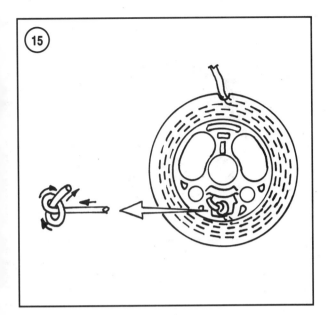

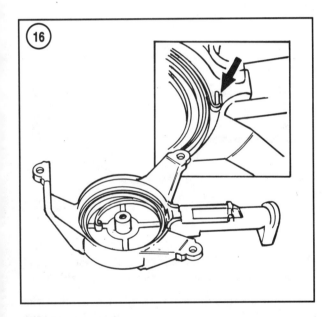

18. Apply a light coat of water-resistant grease to the upper surfaces of the sheave. Install the sheave into the rewind housing. Make sure the hooked end of the rewind spring engages the tab on the sheave. Use a screwdriver and the hole in the sheave to align the hook with the tab, if necessary.

19. While holding the rope in the notch, rotate the sheave two complete turns counterclockwise. Route the rope through the guide opening in the rewind starter housing.

20. Clamp the rope at the rope guide with locking pliers. This prevents the rope from winding into the housing until the handle is installed.

21. Install the pin and drive pawl to the sheave. Apply a light coat of water-resistant grease to these components, then install the spring, cover and bolt in the positions noted prior to removal. Tighten the bolt to the specification listed in **Table 1**.

22. Route the rope through the guide hole in the top motor cover and the handle. Tie a suitable knot in the end of the rope. Remove the locking pliers. Install the plug for the handle and check for smooth operation.

Models BF50 and BF5A

1. Clamp the rope at the rope guide opening in the rewind housing with locking pliers. This prevents the rope from winding into the housing when the handle is removed.

2. Carefully pry the plug and rope from the handle. Untie the knot and pull the handle from the rope. Place the rewind starter on a clean work surface with the top side UP.

3. Hold the rope and rewind starter then release the locking pliers. Allow the rope to slowly wind onto the sheave until the rope is relaxed.

4. Remove the nut and washer (1 and 2, **Figure 3**) from the rewind housing. Note the position of the spring (5, **Figure 3**) and tabs (3) on the cover. The rewind starter will not operate properly if these components are not properly installed. Remove the cover, washer and spring from the rewind starter shaft.

5. Turn the drive gear counterclockwise as you carefully lift it from the rewind starter housing. Remove the rubber washer from the shaft.

6. Insert a small screwdriver into the hole in the starter sheave (**Figure 14**) and press down to hold the starter spring (10, **Figure 3**) into the housing. Maintain downward pressure on the spring and lift the sheave (8, **Figure 3**) and rope (9) from the rewind housing. Carefully route the rope through the hole in the rewind housing. Remove the screwdriver when the sheave clears the housing.

7. Carefully remove the spring housing (11, **Figure 3**) from the rewind housing. While carefully holding the

15. Position one end of the rope through the hole in the sheave and tie a knot as shown in **Figure 15**. Position the knot into the recess in the sheave. Tie a knot in the rope end. Wrap the rope counterclockwise around the sheave.

16. Position the hooked end of the starter spring over the tab in the rewind housing as shown in **Figure 16**. Carefully wind the spring into the housing until all loops are installed and the spring is positioned fully into the housing.

17. Position the sheave with the flywheel end (rope knot is visible) facing up onto the shaft. Route the remaining length of rope into the notch in the sheave as shown.

spring into the housing, slowly unwind and remove the spring.

8. Inspect the cover (3, **Figure 3**) for damaged or worn areas and replace as required. Inspect the drive gear (6, **Figure 3**) for damaged or worn areas. Replace the gear if damage or wear is noted.

9. Inspect the entire length of the starter spring (10, **Figure 3**) for cracked, broken or damaged areas. Pay particular attention to the hook at the end of the spring.

10. Inspect the sheave (8, **Figure 3**) for warped, damaged or worn surfaces and replace as required.

11. Inspect the entire length of the rope for cut, worn or frayed areas. Pay particular attention to the length nearest the handle. Replace with the proper type rope if it is not in excellent condition.

12. Inspect the rope guide(s) for damaged or worn areas. Pay particular attention to the area near the rope handle. Replace worn, damaged or corroded components.

13. Measure the length of the starter rope to determine the length for the replacement rope. To prevent the end of the rope from unraveling, carefully melt the cut end of the rope with a small flame. While still molten, use thick gloves to shape the end of the rope into a compact nub. Trim loose pieces from the end when cooled.

14. Wipe the surfaces in the rewind housing where the spring is installed and the shaft with water-resistant grease.

15. Position one end of the rope through the hole in the sheave and tie a knot as shown in **Figure 15**. Position the knot into the recess in the sheave. Tie a knot in the rope end. Wrap the rope clockwise around the sheave.

16. Position the hooked end of the starter spring over the tab in the starter spring housing as shown in **Figure 17**. Carefully wind the spring into the housing until all loops are installed and the spring is positioned fully into the housing.

17. Position the sheave (rope knot is visible) facing up onto the shaft. Route the remaining length of rope into the notch in the sheave.

18. Apply a light coat of water-resistant grease to the upper surfaces of the sheave. Install the sheave into the rewind housing. Make sure the hooked end of the rewind spring engages the tab on the sheave.

19. While holding the rope in the notch, rotate the sheave two complete turns counterclockwise. Route the rope through the guide opening in the rewind starter housing.

20. Clamp the rope at the rope guide with locking pliers. This prevents the rope from winding into the housing until the handle is installed.

21. Install the rubber washer and drive gear to the sheave. Apply a light coat of water-resistant grease to these components then install the spring, large washer, cover as

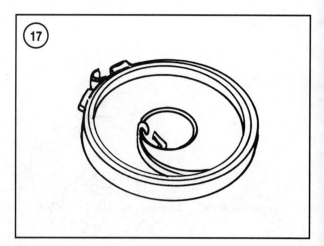

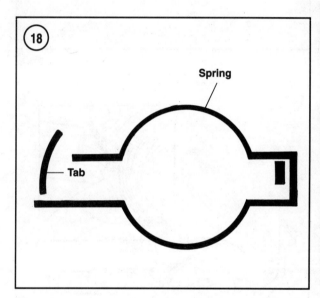

shown in **Figure 18**. Install the small washer and nut. Tighten the nut to the specification listed in **Table 1**.

22. Route the rope through the guide hole in the rewind housing and the handle. Tie a knot in the end of the rope. Remove the locking pliers. Install the plug for the handle, then check for smooth operation.

Models BF75, BF8A and BF100

1. Clamp the rope at the rope guide with locking pliers. This prevents the rope from winding into the housing when the handle is removed.

2. Carefully pry the plug and rope from the handle. Untie the knot and pull the handle from the rope. Place the rewind on a clean work surface with the top side down.

REWIND STARTER

3. Hold the rope and rewind starter then release the locking pliers. Allow the rope to slowly wind onto the sheave until the rope is relaxed.

4. Remove the bolt (1, **Figure 6**), washers (2), cover (3) and drive pawl spring (4) from the rewind housing. Hold down on the sheave (8, **Figure 6**) as you pull the three drive pawls and spring (6, **Figure 6**) from the sheave.

5. Insert a small screwdriver into the hole in the starter sheave (**Figure 14**) and press down to hold the starter spring into the housing. Maintain downward pressure on the spring and lift the sheave and rope from the rewind housing. Carefully route the rope through the hole in the rewind housing. Remove the screwdriver when the sheave has cleared the housing. Remove the bushing (5, **Figure 6**) from the shaft.

6. Position the housing in a clear area of the floor. Hold the housing down and lightly tap the top of the housing with a mallet until the starter spring (9, **Figure 6**) drops from the housing and completely unwinds. Remove the clip and the rope guide from the rewind housing.

7. Inspect the cover (3, **Figure 6**) for damaged or worn areas and replace as required. Inspect the drive pawls for cracks or worn areas. Replace the pawls if damage or wear is noted.

8. Inspect the bolt (1, **Figure 6**), and spring (4) for worn, damaged or corroded surfaces. Replace if any defects are noted.

9. Inspect the entire length of the starter spring (9, **Figure 6**) for cracked, broken or damaged areas. Pay particular attention to the hook at the end of the spring.

10. Inspect the sheave (8, **Figure 6**) for warped, damaged or worn surfaces and replace as required.

11. Inspect the entire length of the rope for cut, worn or frayed areas; pay particular attention to the length nearest the handle. Replace with the proper type rope if it is not in excellent condition.

12. Inspect the rope guide(s) for damaged or worn areas. Pay particular attention to the area near the rope handle. Replace worn, damaged or corroded components.

13. Measure the length of the starter rope to determine the length for the replacement rope. To prevent the end of the rope from unraveling, carefully melt the cut end of the rope with a small flame. While still molten, use thick gloves and shape the end of the rope into a compact nub. Trim loose pieces from the end when cooled.

14. Wipe the surfaces in the rewind housing where the spring is installed and the shaft with water-resistant grease.

15. Position one end of the rope through the hole in the sheave and tie a knot as shown in **Figure 15**. Position the knot into the recess in the sheave. Tie a knot in the rope end. Wrap the rope counterclockwise around the sheave.

16. Position the hooked end of the starter spring over the tab in the rewind housing as shown in **Figure 16**. Carefully wind the spring into the housing until all loops are installed and the spring is positioned fully into the housing.

17. Position the sheave with the flywheel end (rope knot is visible) facing up onto the shaft. Route the remaining length of rope into the notch in the sheave as indicated.

18. Apply a light coat of water-resistant grease to the upper surfaces of the sheave. Install the sheave into the rewind housing. While holding the sheave into the housing, rotate the sheave 120° clockwise.

19. Apply a light coat of water-resistant grease to these components, then install the three drive pawls, bushing, spring and drive pawl spring. Install the cover, washers and bolt. Tighten the bolt to the specification listed in **Table 1**.

20. While holding the rope into the groove, rotate the sheave three and a half turns counterclockwise. Route the rope through the guide opening, guide and rope handle.

21. Clamp the rope at the rope guide with locking pliers. This prevents the rope from winding into the housing until the handle is installed. Install the rope guide and clip.

22. Tie a knot in the end of the rope. Remove the locking pliers. Install the plug for the handle, then check for smooth operation.

Models BF9.9A and BF15A

1. Clamp the rope at the rope guide with locking pliers. This prevents the rope from winding into the housing when the handle is removed.

2. Carefully pry the plug and rope from the handle. Untie the knot and pull the handle from the rope. Place the rewind starter on a clean work surface with the top side down.

3. Hold the rope and rewind starter then release the locking pliers. Allow the rope to slowly wind onto the sheave until the rope is relaxed.

4. Remove the bolt (1, **Figure 7**), washer, cover (3) and spring (6) from the rewind housing. Note the position of the drive pawl (4, **Figure 7**) and drive pawl spring (5). Hold down on the sheave (7, **Figure 7**) as you pull the drive pawl and spring from the sheave.

5. Insert a small screwdriver into the hole in the starter sheave (**Figure 14**) and press down to hold the starter spring into the housing. Maintain downward pressure on the spring and lift the sheave and rope from the rewind housing. Carefully route the rope through the hole in the rewind housing. Remove the screwdriver when the sheave has cleared the housing.

6. Position the housing in a clear area of the floor. Hold the housing down and lightly tap the top of the housing with a mallet until the starter spring (13, **Figure 7**) drops from the housing and completely unwinds.

7. Remove the fasteners and the rope roller from the rewind housing.

8. Inspect the cover (3, **Figure 7**) for damaged or worn areas and replace as required. Inspect the drive pawl for cracks or worn areas. Replace the pawl when damage or wear is noted.

9. Inspect the bolt (1, **Figure 7**), washer (2) and spring (6) for worn, damaged or corroded surfaces. Replace if any defects are noted.

10. Inspect the entire length of the starter spring (13, **Figure 7**) for cracked, broken or damaged areas. Pay particular attention to the hook at the end of the spring.

11. Inspect the sheave (7, **Figure 7**) for warped, damaged or worn surfaces and replace as required.

12. Inspect the entire length of the rope for cut, worn or frayed areas; pay particular attention to the length nearest the handle. Replace with the proper type rope if it is not in excellent condition.

13. Inspect the rope guide(s) for damaged or worn areas. Pay particular attention to the area near the rope handle. Replace worn, damaged or corroded components.

14. Measure the length of the starter rope to determine the length for the replacement rope. To prevent the end of the rope from unraveling, carefully melt the cut end of the rope with a small flame. While still molten, use thick gloves and shape the end of the rope into a compact nub. Trim loose pieces from the end when it has cooled.

15. Wipe the surfaces in the rewind housing where the spring is installed and the shaft with water-resistant grease.

16. Position one end of the rope through the hole in the sheave and tie a knot as shown in **Figure 15**. Position the knot into the recess in the sheave. Tie a knot in the rope end. Wrap the rope counterclockwise around the sheave.

17. Position the hooked end of the starter spring over the tab in the rewind housing as shown in **Figure 16**. Carefully wind the spring into the housing until all loops are installed and the spring is positioned fully into the housing.

18. Position the sheave with the flywheel end (rope knot is visible) facing up onto the shaft. Route the remaining length of rope into the notch in the sheave as indicated.

19. Apply a light coat of water-resistant grease to the upper surfaces of the sheave. Install the sheave into the rewind housing. While holding the sheave in the housing, rotate the sheave in the clockwise direction until spring tension is felt.

20. Apply a light coat of water-resistant grease to these components, then install the drive pawl and drive pawl spring onto the sheave as noted prior to removal. Install the spring, cover, washers and bolt. Tighten the bolt to the specification listed in **Table 1**.

21. While holding the rope into the groove, route the rope through the guide opening and rope handle.

22. Clamp the rope at the rope guide with locking pliers. This prevents the rope from winding into the housing until the handle is installed. Install the rope guide and clip.

23. Tie a knot in the end of the rope. Remove the locking pliers. Install the plug for the handle, then check for smooth operation.

Models BF20A, BF25A and BF30A

1. Clamp the rope at the rope guide with locking pliers. This prevents the rope from winding into the housing when the handle is removed.

2. Carefully pry the plug and rope from the handle. Untie the knot and pull the handle from the rope. Place the rewind starter on a clean work surface with the top side down.

3. Hold the rope and rewind starter then release the locking pliers. Allow the rope to slowly wind onto the sheave until the rope is relaxed.

4. Remove the bolt (10, **Figure 8**), washer cover (11), and spring (12) from the rewind housing.

5. Note the position of the drive pawl (18, **Figure 8**), connector (19) and drive pawl spring (20). Remove the E-clip (17, **Figure 8**). Hold down on the sheave (13, **Figure 8**) as you pull the drive pawl, spring and connector from it.

6. Insert a small screwdriver into the hole in the starter sheave (**Figure 14**) and press down to hold the starter spring into the housing. Maintain downward pressure on the spring and lift the sheave and rope from the rewind housing. Carefully route the rope through the hole in the rewind housing. Remove the screwdriver when the sheave has cleared the housing. Remove the bushing (14, **Figure 8**) from the shaft.

7. Position the housing in a clear area of the floor. Hold the housing down and lightly tap the top of it with a mallet until the starter spring (15, **Figure 8**) drops from the housing and completely unwinds.

8. Remove and discard the cotter pin (1, **Figure 8**), then remove the washer (2), lever (3) and spring (5) from the rewind housing. Note the position, then remove the sheave stopper (4, **Figure 8**) from the rewind housing.

9. Inspect the sheave stopper, lever and related components for worn or damaged components. Replace any defective components.

REWIND STARTER

10. Inspect the cover (11, **Figure 8**) for damaged or worn areas and replace as required. Inspect the drive pawl for cracks or worn areas. Replace the pawl when damage or wear is noted.

11. Inspect the bolt (10, **Figure 8**) and spring (12) for worn, damaged or corroded surfaces. Replace if any defects are noted.

12. Inspect the entire length of the starter spring (15, **Figure 8**) for cracked, broken or damaged areas. Pay particular attention to the hook at the end of the spring.

13. Inspect the sheave (13, **Figure 8**) for warped, damaged or worn surfaces and replace as required.

14. Inspect the entire length of the rope for cut, worn or frayed areas; pay particular attention to the length nearest the handle. Replace with the proper type rope if it is not in excellent condition.

15. Inspect the rope guide(s) for damaged or worn areas. Pay particular attention to the area near the rope handle. Replace worn, damaged or corroded components.

16. Measure the length of the starter rope to determine the length for the replacement rope. To prevent the end of the rope from unraveling, carefully melt the cut end of the rope with a small flame. While still molten, use thick gloves and shape the end of the rope into a compact nub. Trim loose pieces from the end when cooled.

17. Wipe the surfaces in the rewind housing where the spring is installed and the shaft with water-resistant grease.

18. Position one end of the rope through the hole in the sheave and tie a knot as shown in **Figure 15**. Position the knot into the recess in the sheave. Tie a knot in the rope end. Wrap the rope counterclockwise around the sheave.

19. Position the hooked end of the starter spring over the tab in the rewind housing as shown in **Figure 16**. Carefully wind the spring into the housing in the direction indicated until all loops are installed and the spring is positioned fully into the housing.

20. Install the sheave stopper, lever and related components. Install a new cotter pin. Connect the cable to the lever.

21. Position the sheave with the flywheel end (rope knot is visible) facing up onto the shaft. Route the remaining length of rope into the notch in the sheave as indicated.

22. Apply a light coat of water-resistant grease to the upper surfaces of the sheave. Install the sheave into the rewind housing. While holding the sheave into the housing, rotate the sheave five turns counterclockwise. Hold the sheave in this position.

23. Apply a light coat of water-resistant grease to these components and install the drive pawl, drive pawl spring and connector onto the sheave as noted prior to removal. Snap the E-clip onto the pivot point. Install the spring, cover and bolt. Tighten the bolt to the specification listed in **Table 1**.

24. While holding the rope into the groove, route the rope through the guide opening and rope handle.

25. Clamp the rope at the rope guide with locking pliers. This prevents the rope from winding into the housing until the handle is installed. Install the rope guide and clamp.

26. Tie a knot in the end of the rope. Remove the locking pliers. Install the plug for the handle, then check for smooth operation.

Table 1 STANDARD TIGHTENING TORQUE

Fastener size	Tightening torque
5 mm bolt/nut	4-7 N•m (35-62 in.-lb.)
6 mm bolt/nut	8-12 N•m (71-106 in.-lb.)
8 mm bolt/nut	20-28 N•m (15-21 in.-lb.)
10 mm bolt/nut	35-40 N•m (26-30 ft.-lb.)

Chapter Twelve

Power Trim/Tilt Systems

This chapter provides removal, installation and repair procedures for trim and tilt systems. **Table 1** provides tightening torque specifications for trim/tilt system fasteners. **Table 2** provides specifications needed to repair the electric trim motor used on three cylinder systems. **Table 1** and **Table 2** are located at the end of the chapter.

This section provides the procedures to remove and install the trim/tilt system.

Models BF35A, BF40A, BF45A and BF50A are equipped with a gas assisted manual tilt system or the optional single hydraulic cylinder trim/tilt system.

Models BF75A, BF90A, BF115A and BF130A are equipped with a three cylinder trim/tilt system.

WARNING
Never work under any part of the engine without providing suitable support. The engine mounted tilt lock or hydraulic system may collapse and allow the engine to drop. Support the engine with suitable blocks or an overhead cable before working under the engine.

WARNING
The trim/tilt system may contain fluid under high pressure. Always use protective eyewear and gloves when working with the trim/tilt system. Never remove any components or plugs without first bleeding the pressure from the system. Follow the instructions carefully.

CAUTION
Never direct pressurized water (pressure washer) at the seal surfaces when cleaning debris from the trim/tilt system. The water may pass by the seal surface and contaminate the fluid.

Gas-Assisted Manual Tilt System Removal/Installation

Always provide adequate support for the engine prior to working around any trim/tilt system components. To assist with component identification and location, refer to **Figure 1** during the removal and installation procedure.

Fastener location and component appearance vary by model. Mark the location or make note of component location and position prior to removal. Apply water-resistant grease to all bushings and pivot points on assembly.

1. Remove both battery cables from the battery terminals. Remove the spark plugs. Connect the spark plug leads to an engine ground.
2. Activate the tilt lever (**Figure 2**) and pivot the engine in the full *UP* position. Use an overhead hoist or other secure means to support the engine as indicted in **Figure 3**.
3. Use a pair of needlenose pliers to remove and discard the E-clips (1, **Figure 1**) from the upper pivot pin (2, **Figure 1**). Using a small section of tubing or wooden dowel, carefully drive the upper pivot pin (2, **Figure 1**) from its bore in the swivel housing (3, **Figure 1**).

POWER TRIM/TILT SYSTEMS

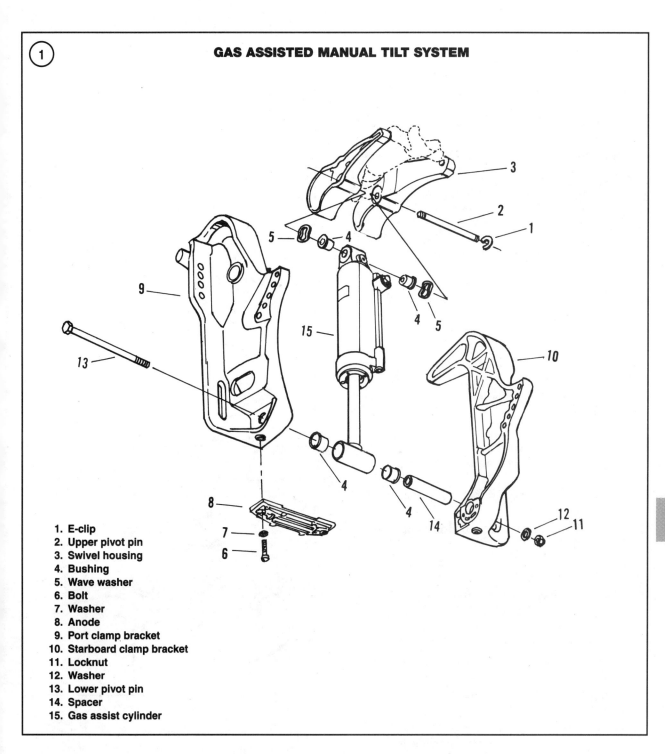

GAS ASSISTED MANUAL TILT SYSTEM

1. E-clip
2. Upper pivot pin
3. Swivel housing
4. Bushing
5. Wave washer
6. Bolt
7. Washer
8. Anode
9. Port clamp bracket
10. Starboard clamp bracket
11. Locknut
12. Washer
13. Lower pivot pin
14. Spacer
15. Gas assist cylinder

4. Loosen the bolt and nut and pull the tilt lever from the gas-assisted manual tilt system.

5. Carefully swing the assist cylinder (15, **Figure 1**) out and away from the swivel housing. Remove both bushings (4, **Figure 1**) and wave washers (5, **Figure 1**) from the cylinder.

6. Remove both bolts and washers (6 and 7, **Figure 1**) from the clamp brackets (10 and 9, **Figure 1**). Carefully pull the anode (8, **Figure 1**) from the clamp brackets.

7. Support the trim/tilt system as you loosen and remove the lower pivot retaining bolt (13, **Figure 1**), nut (11) and washer (12).

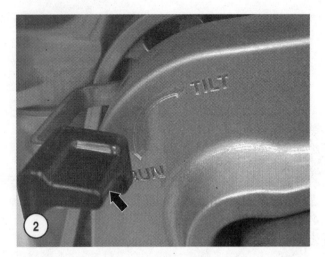

8. Support the trim/tilt system and use a small section of tubing or wooden dowel to carefully drive the lower pivot pin (14, **Figure 1**) from the clamp brackets (9 and 10, **Figure 1**).

9. Spread the clamp brackets (9 and 10, **Figure 1**) and lower the trim/tilt system from the engine. Remove the bushings (4, **Figure 1**) from the trim/tilt system and clamp brackets.

10. Inspect all bushings and pins for damaged or worn surfaces and replace as required.

11. Installation is the reverse of removal, noting the following:
   a. Apply water-resistant grease to all bushings, pivot pins and washers.
   b. Install new E-clips to the grooves on the upper pivot pin during assembly.
   c. Clean all debris from the anode and its mounting surface.
   d. Drive all pivot pins into position with a wooden dowel or section of tubing.
   e. Ensure that all E-clips are properly seated into the groove on the pivot shafts.
   f. Tighten all fasteners to the specification listed in **Table 1**.
   g. Align the marking on the tilt lever with the shaft as noted in **Figure 4**.

12. Install the spark plugs and spark plug leads. Clean the battery terminals and connect the cables to the battery.

Single Hydraulic Cylinder Trim/Tilt Systems Removal/Installation

Make a sketch of the trim wire routing before removal. Apply water-resistant grease to all bushing and pivot points on assembly. Note the size and location of plastic

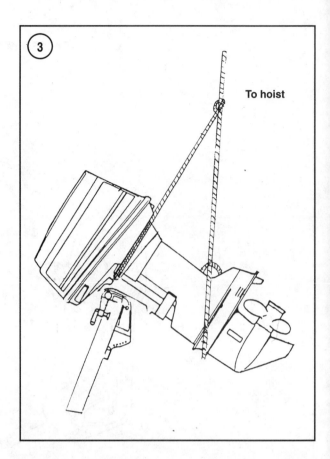

locking tie clamps and replace as required. Refer to **Figure 6** during the removal and installation procedure.

1. Remove both battery cables from the battery terminals. Remove the spark plug leads and connect the spark plug leads to an engine ground.

2. Trace the electric trim/tilt motor wires leading from the trim/tilt system (1, **Figure 6**) to the connections of the main engine harness. Note the wire routing and connection points, then disconnect the wires. Route them out of

POWER TRIM/TILT SYSTEMS

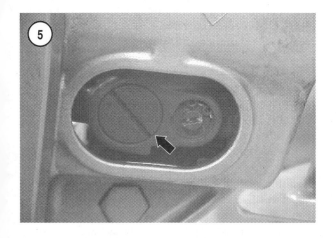

the engine cover and through the clamp bracket mounted wire grommet (18, **Figure 6**). Remove all clamps along with the wires.

3. Locate the manual relief valve access hole (**Figure 5**) on the port clamp bracket. Rotate the valve counterclockwise two to three turns. Carefully tilt the engine to the fully up position. Support the engine with a hoist or other suitable method (**Figure 3**). Securely tighten the manual relief valve.

4. Use a pair of needlenose pliers to remove and discard the E-clips (10, **Figure 6**) from the upper pivot pin (11, **Figure 6**). Using a small section of tubing or wooden

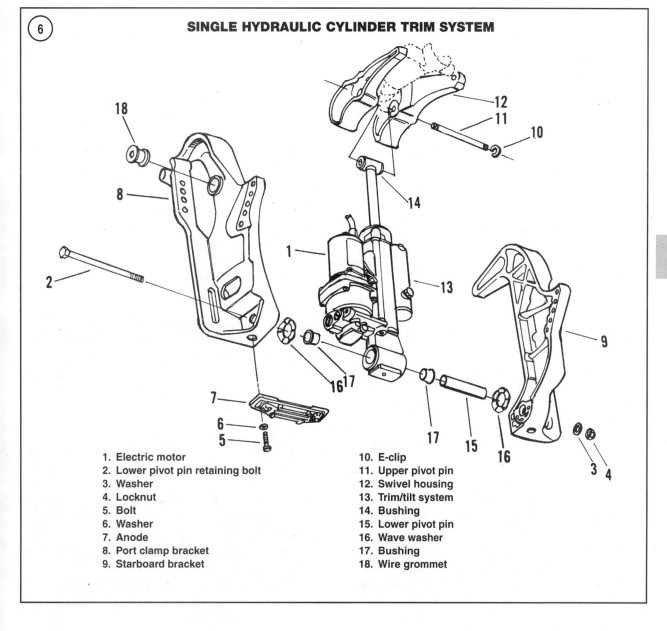

SINGLE HYDRAULIC CYLINDER TRIM SYSTEM

1. Electric motor
2. Lower pivot pin retaining bolt
3. Washer
4. Locknut
5. Bolt
6. Washer
7. Anode
8. Port clamp bracket
9. Starboard bracket
10. E-clip
11. Upper pivot pin
12. Swivel housing
13. Trim/tilt system
14. Bushing
15. Lower pivot pin
16. Wave washer
17. Bushing
18. Wire grommet

dowel, carefully drive the upper pivot pin (11, **Figure 6**) from its bore in the swivel housing (12, **Figure 6**).

5. Carefully swing the trim/tilt system (13, **Figure 6**) out and away from the swivel housing. Remove both bushings (14, **Figure 6**) from the tilt cylinder.

6. Support the trim/tilt system as you remove both bolts and washers (5 and 6, **Figure 6**) from the clamp brackets. Carefully pull the anode (7, **Figure 6**) from the clamp brackets (8 and 9, **Figure 6**).

7. Support the trim/tilt system as you loosen and remove the lower pivot retaining bolt, nut and washer (2-4, **Figure 6**).

8. Support the trim/tilt system and use a small section of tubing or wooden dowel to carefully drive the lower pivot pin (15, **Figure 6**) from the clamp brackets (8 and 9, **Figure 6**) and the trim/tilt system (13, **Figure 6**).

9. Spread the clamp brackets (8 and 9, **Figure 6**) and lower the trim/tilt system from the engine.

10. Remove the wave washers (16, **Figure 6**) and bushings (17, **Figure 6**) from the trim/tilt system and clamp brackets.

11. Inspect all bushings and pins for damaged or worn surfaces and replace as required.

12. Installation is the reverse of removal, noting the following:
   a. Apply water-resistant grease to all bushings, pivot pins and washers.
   b. Route the trim/tilt system wires carefully to avoid interference with other components.
   c. Install new E-clips to the grooves on the upper pivot pin during assembly.
   d. Clean all debris from the anode and its mounting surface.
   e. Drive all pivot pins into position with a wooden dowel or section of tubing.
   f. Ensure that all E-clips are properly seated into the groove on the pivot shafts.
   g. Tighten all fasteners to the specification listed in **Table 1**.

13. Clean the terminals and connect all wires to the main engine harness. Install the spark plugs and spark plug leads. Clean the battery terminals and connect the cables to the battery.

14. Check and correct the fluid level before operating the system. Refer to *Filling and Bleeding Procedure* in this chapter and correct the fluid level. Check for proper operation upon completion.

Three Cylinders Trim/Tilt Systems Removal/Installation

Make a sketch of the trim/tilt system wire routing before disconnecting any wire or wire clamps. Apply water-resistant grease to all bushings and pivot points on assembly. Note the size and location of all plastic locking tie clamps and replace as required.

1. Remove both battery cables from the battery terminals. Remove the spark plugs and connect the spark plug leads to an engine ground. Refer to **Figure 7** during the removal and installation procedure.

2. Trace the electric trim/tilt motor wires leading from the trim/tilt system (1, **Figure 7**) to the connections to the main engine harness. Note the wire routing and connection points, then disconnect the wires. Route them out of the engine cover and through the clamp bracket mounted wire grommet (19, **Figure 7**). Remove all clamps along the wires.

3. Locate the manual relief valve access hole (**Figure 8**) on the port clamp bracket. Rotate the valve counterclockwise two to three turns. Carefully tilt the engine to the fully up position. Support the engine with a hoist or other suitable method (**Figure 3**). Securely tighten the manual relief valve.

4. Use a pair of needlenose pliers to remove and discard the E-clips (10, **Figure 7**) from the upper pivot pin (11, **Figure 7**). Using a small section of tubing or wooden dowel, carefully drive the upper pivot pin (11, **Figure 7**) from its bore in the swivel housing (12, **Figure 7**).

5. Carefully swing the trim/tilt system (13, **Figure 7**) from the clamp bracket. Remove both bushings (14, **Figure 7**) from the tilt cylinder.

6. Support the trim/tilt system as you remove both bolts and washers (5 and 6, **Figure 7**) from the clamp brackets. Carefully pull the anode (7, **Figure 7**) from the clamp brackets (8 and 9, **Figure 7**).

7. Support the trim/tilt system as you loosen and remove the lower pivot retaining bolt, nut and washer (2-4, **Figure 7**).

8. Support the trim/tilt system and use a small section of tubing or wooden dowel to carefully drive the lower pivot pin (15, **Figure 7**) from the clamp brackets (8 and 9, **Figure 7**) and the trim/tilt system (13, **Figure 7**).

9. Spread the clamp brackets (8 and 9, **Figure 7**) and lower the trim/tilt system from the engine.

10. Remove the wave washers (16, **Figure 7**) and bushings (17) from the trim/tilt system and clamp brackets.

11. Inspect all bushings and pins for damaged or worn surfaces and replace them as required.

12. Installation is the reverse of removal, noting the following:

Power Trim/Tilt Systems

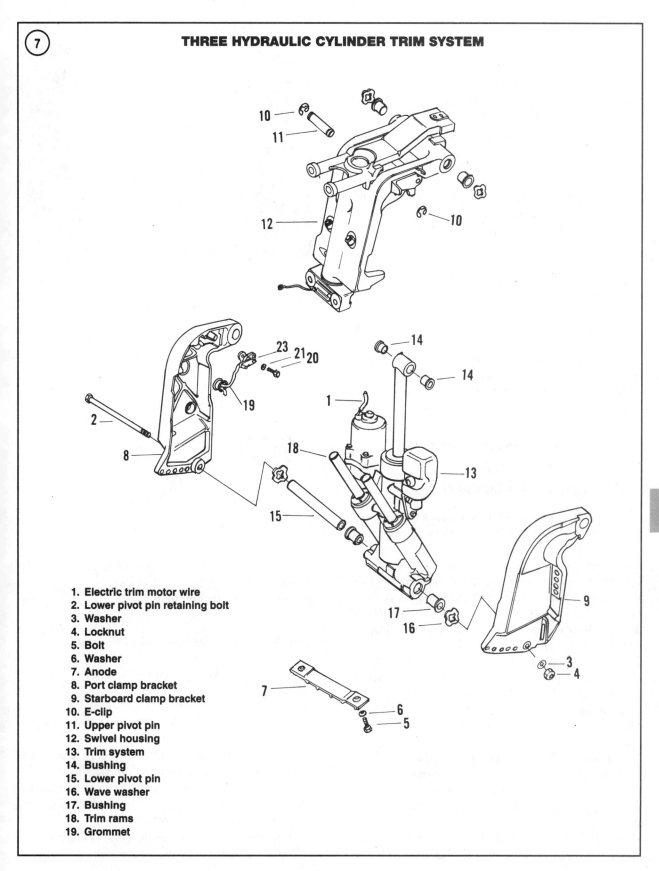

THREE HYDRAULIC CYLINDER TRIM SYSTEM

1. Electric trim motor wire
2. Lower pivot pin retaining bolt
3. Washer
4. Locknut
5. Bolt
6. Washer
7. Anode
8. Port clamp bracket
9. Starboard clamp bracket
10. E-clip
11. Upper pivot pin
12. Swivel housing
13. Trim system
14. Bushing
15. Lower pivot pin
16. Wave washer
17. Bushing
18. Trim rams
19. Grommet

a. Apply water-resistant grease to all bushings, pivot pins and washers.
b. Route the trim/tilt system wires carefully to avoid interference with other components.
c. Install new E-clips to the grooves on the upper pivot pin on assembly.
d. Clean all debris from the anode and its mounting surface.
e. Drive all pivot pins into position with a wooden dowel or a section of tubing.
f. Ensure that all E-clips are properly seated into the groove on the pivot shafts.
g. Tighten all fasteners to the specification listed in **Table 1**.

13. Apply water-resistant grease to the ends of the trim rams (18, **Figure 7**) during assembly. Clean the terminals and connect all wires to the main engine harness.

14. Install the spark plugs and spark plug leads. Clean the battery terminals and connect the battery cables to the battery.

15. Check and correct the fluid level before operating the system. Refer to *Filling and Bleeding Procedure* located in this chapter. Check for proper operation upon completion.

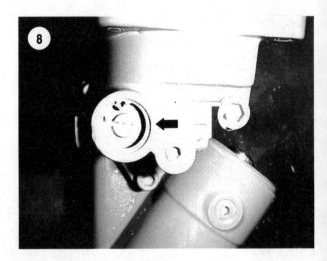

TRIM/TILT SYSTEM COMPONENTS

Trim/Tilt Relay Removal/Installation

All models with power trim and tilt use a trim/tilt relay unit (**Figure 9**). The mounting locations for the relays vary by model. Refer to the wiring diagrams located at the end of this manual to identify the wire colors for the relays. Trace the wires to the component on the engine. Failure of this component can cause either the up, down or both circuits to fail. The entire relay unit must be replaced as a unit. Note the size and location of plastic locking tie clamps and replace them if required.

1. Disconnect both battery cables from the battery. Remove the spark plugs and connect the spark plug leads to an engine ground.
2. Trace the wires to the component on the engine. Mark all wire connection locations and positions before removal.
3. Remove the fasteners for the trim relay. Guide the wires while carefully lifting the relay from the engine. Clean the mounting location and the threaded holes for the mounting fasteners. Clean and inspect all terminal connections.
4. Installation is the reverse of removal. Tighten all fasteners securely. Install the spark plugs and spark plug leads. Clean the battery terminals and connect the cables to the battery.
5. Check for proper operation.

Trim Position Sender Removal/Installation

The trim sender is located on the inside of the port clamp bracket (**Figure 10**). Make a sketch of the sender wire routing and connections prior to removal to ensure proper installation. Note the size and location of plastic locking tie clamps and replace them as required.

1. Disconnect both battery cables from the battery. Remove the spark plugs and connect the spark plug leads to an engine ground. Position the engine to full tilt and engage the tilt lock lever. Support the engine with blocks or a suitable overhead cable (**Figure 3**).
2. Trace the sender wires to the harness connection inside the motor cover and disconnect them. Route the wires out

POWER TRIM/TILT SYSTEMS

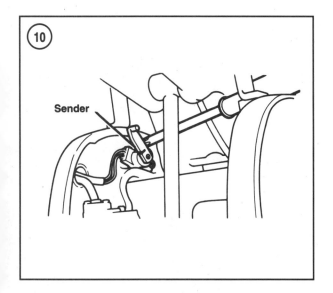

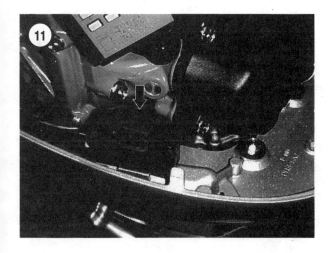

of the motor cover and through the wire grommet (19, **Figure 6** or 18, **Figure 7**) in the port clamp bracket.

3. Remove all clamps prior to trim position sender removal. Inspect the clamps for corrosion or damage and replace as required. To ensure correct installation, use a felt tip marker and trace the sender outline on the mounting location. Remove both fasteners and the sender (**Figure 10**).

4. Clean any corrosion from the mounting location. Clean any corrosion from the threaded holes.

5. Installation is the reverse of removal. Align the sender with the markings and securely tighten the attaching screws.

6. Install the spark plugs and spark plug leads. Clean the battery terminals and connect the cables to the battery. Check for trim gauge and warning system operation.

Trim Control Unit Removal/Installation

Models BF35A, BF40A, BF45A and BF50A with power trim and tilt use a trim control unit. This component is mounted at the rear and port side of the base engine (**Figure 11**). To help locate the unit, refer to the wiring diagrams located at the end of this manual. Identify the wire colors for the trim control unit, then trace the wires to the component on the engine. Note the size and locations of plastic locking tie clamps and replace them if required.

1. Disconnect both battery cables from the battery. Remove the spark plugs and connect the spark plug leads to an engine ground.

2. Trace the wires to the component on the engine. Mark all wire connections before removal.

3. Remove the fasteners for the trim control unit. Carefully guide the wires while sliding the component from the mounting bracket. Clean the mounting location and the threaded holes for the mounting fasteners. Clean and inspect all terminal connections.

4. Installation is the reverse of removal. Securely tighten all fasteners. Install the spark plugs and spark plug leads. Clean the battery terminals and connect the cables to the battery.

5. Check for proper operation.

Electric Trim/Tilt Motor Removal/Installation

The trim/tilt system must operate with clean fluid. A small amount of contamination can prevent proper trim/tilt system operation. Thoroughly clean the trim/tilt system external surfaces with soapy water to remove all debris prior to removing the electric trim/tilt motor. Use compressed air to dry the trim/tilt system.

Work in a clean area and use lint free towels to wipe fluids and debris from components. Cover any openings immediately after removing the trim motor to prevent contamination of the fluid.

> *NOTE*
> *Removal of the port side clamp bracket may be required to access the mounting bolts for the electric trim/tilt motor. Refer to Chapter Thirteen for the clamp bracket removal procedure.*

> *NOTE*
> *To avoid unnecessary disassembly and potential wire interference, always note the position of the electric trim motor and wire harness prior to removing the motor from the system. Use a paint dot or piece of tape*

to mark the location. Never scratch the housing as it promotes corrosion.

1. Disconnect both battery cables from the battery terminals. Remove the spark plugs. Connect the spark plug leads to an engine ground.

2. Locate the manual relief valve. Refer to **Figure 5** for a single-cylinder system and to **Figure 8** for three-cylinder system. Slowly rotate the manual relief valve two to three turns counterclockwise. With an assistant, manually tilt the engine to the fully up position and tighten the manual relief valve to the specification listed in **Table 1**.

3. Engage the tilt lock mechanism and support the engine with an overhead support (**Figure 3**) or suitable blocks. *Slowly* remove the fluid fill/check cap (**Figure 12** or **Figure 13**) to relieve any residual pressure from the system. Trace the electric trim motor wires to the terminal locations on the main engine wire harness. Mark the wire locations to ensure proper connections. Disconnect the electric trim motor wires from the harness connections.

4. Route the wires out of the motor cover area and through the wire grommet on the port clamp bracket (18, **Figure 6** or 19, **Figure 7**). Remove all clamps along the wires. Make a note or sketch of the wire harness routing and trim motor wire position prior to removal. Remove the four mounting bolts (1, **Figure 14** or 1, **Figure 15**) that attach the electric trim/tilt motor to the trim/tilt system. Guide the wires as you carefully lift the electric trim/tilt motor (2, **Figure 14** or 2, **Figure 15**) from the trim/tilt system. If removal is difficult, carefully pry the motor from the system with a flat scraper or dull putty knife. Be careful to avoid damaging the electric motor mounting surface. A fluid or water leak can occur if the surfaces are damaged.

5. Remove and discard the O-ring (3, **Figure 14** and 3, **Figure 15**). On three cylinder systems, note the location and position, then remove the filter (5, **Figure 15**) from the pump assembly. Clean the filter in solvent and air dry. Replace the filter if it is damaged or if debris remains on the filter after cleaning.

6. Note the position of the coupling (4, **Figure 14** or 4, **Figure 15**). Compare the coupling surfaces with the electric motor shaft (**Figure 16**). Determine correct position if the coupling was disturbed during removal of the electric trim motor.

7. Clean and inspect the trim motor to trim/tilt system mating surfaces for corrosion pitting or scratches. *Do not allow any debris to enter the trim fluid.* Replace the component(s) if deep scratches or pitted surfaces are observed. Compete trim/tilt system disassembly, inspection and assembly is required if a considerable amount of de-

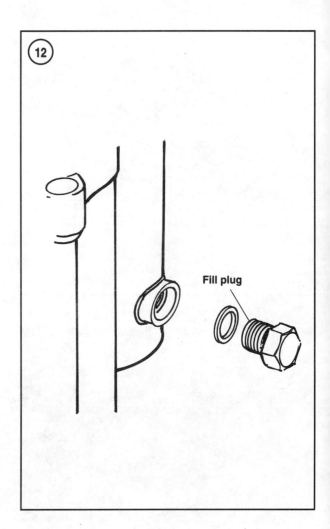

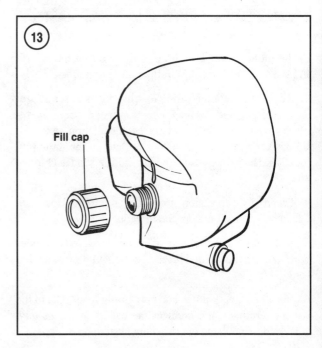

POWER TRIM/TILT SYSTEMS

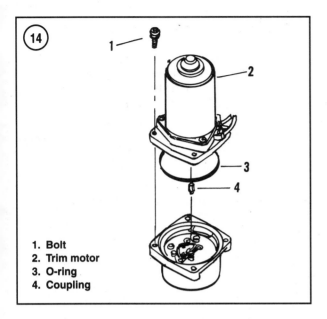

1. Bolt
2. Trim motor
3. O-ring
4. Coupling

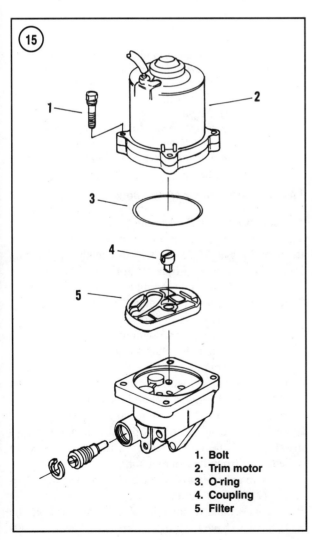

1. Bolt
2. Trim motor
3. O-ring
4. Coupling
5. Filter

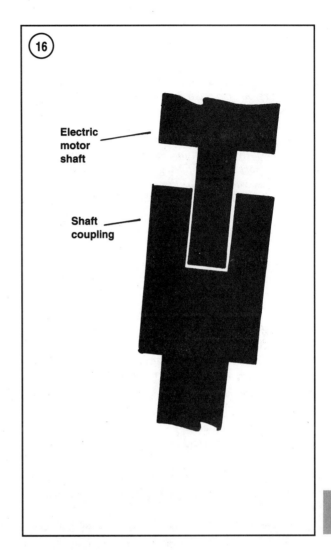

bris is present in the filter. Install the filter onto the pump housing as noted prior to removal.

8. Install a new O-ring onto the electric trim motor to pump sealing surface. Apply water-resistant grease to the coupling mating surfaces during installation. Position the electric motor on the coupling (4, **Figure 14** or 4, **Figure 15**) and rotate the electric trim motor until the coupling shafts aligns (**Figure 16**) and the electric trim motor drops into position.

9. Slowly rotate the electric trim motor to obtain the correct position of the wires and the alignment marks made prior to removal. Install and tighten the mounting bolts in a crossing pattern to the specification listed in **Table 1**. Install the fluid fill/check cap.

10. Install the spark plugs and spark plug leads. Clean the terminals and connect the cables to the battery. Perform the *Filling and Bleeding Procedure* as described in this chapter.

Manual Relief Valve Replacement

WARNING
The trim/tilt system creates very high pressure. Always wear eye and hand protection. Never disconnect any hydraulic lines or remove any fittings without first relieving the pressure from the system. Tilt the engine to the fully up position and provide adequate support against falling. Open the manual relief valve two to three complete turns to relieve the pressure.

Replacing the manual relief valve is simple if the screwdriver slot is intact. If not, heat the tip of a screwdriver, then hold it against the remnants of the valve. The valve material will melt into the shape of the screwdriver tip. Allow the valve to cool, then use the same screwdriver to remove the valve. Never drill the valve out or the seating surface for the O-ring will be damaged.

Inspect the O-rings on the valve even though they will be discarded. Problems may surface if large portions are missing or torn away from the O-rings. The portions usually migrate to a valve or other component within the trim/tilt system and cause the system to malfunction.

1. Disconnect both battery cables from the battery. Remove the spark plugs and connect the spark plug leads to an engine ground.
2. Position the engine in the full tilt position. Engage the tilt lock lever *and* support the engine with an overhead cable (**Figure 3**) or suitable blocks.
3. Locate the manual relief access hole in the clamp bracket. Slowly loosen the valve by rotating it two to three turns in the counterclockwise direction (**Figure 5** or **Figure 8**). Remove the circlip (on models so equipped), then remove the manual relief valve from the opening.
4. Use a suitable light and a small pick to remove any remnants of the valve or O-ring from the opening. Avoid damaging any of the machined surfaces in the opening.
5. Lubricate the new manual relief valve with Dexron II automatic transmission fluid or its equivalent and install *new* O-rings onto the valve. Lubricate the O-rings with Dexron II automatic transmission fluid or its equivalent and install the valve into the opening. Do not tighten the valve at this time.
6. Rotate the valve clockwise until slight resistance can be felt. Rotate the valve one quarter turn clockwise, then one eight turn counterclockwise. Repeat this process until the valve is fully seated. Tighten the manual relief valve to the specification listed in **Table 1**. Refer to *Filling and Bleeding* in this chapter to correct the fluid level and purge air from the system.

Electric Trim/Tilt Motor Repair

This section covers the disassembly, inspection and assembly of the electric trim/tilt motor. Repair procedures are provided for the electric trim/tilt motor used on models BF75A, BF90A, BF15A and BF130A. Replace the electric trim/tilt motor on all other models if it is faulty.

Work in a clean environment to avoid contamination. Use electrical contact cleaner to remove debris from the electric motor components. Electrical contact cleaner is available at most electrical supply sources. It evaporates rapidly and leaves no residue to contaminate the components. Avoid touching the brushes and commutator after cleaning.

CAUTION
Mark the top cover, frame and bottom cover of the electric motor prior to disassembly. Use paint dots or removable tape. Never scratch the components as doing so promotes corrosion of metal components.

NOTE
The magnets in the frame assembly are quite strong. Considerable effort may be required to remove the frame assembly from the armature. Make sure all fasteners are removed and carefully pull the frame and armature apart. Never drop or strike the frame assembly. The magnets might break and damage other components during operation.

Electric trim/tilt motor disassembly

1. Refer to *Trim/Tilt System Electric Motor Replacement* and remove the electric motor from the trim/tilt system. Refer to **Figure 17** during the disassembly procedure. Mark all components (**Figure 18**) prior to disassembly to ensure proper orientation during assembly.
2. Remove the screws (3, **Figure 17**) that attach the frame (14, **Figure 17**) to the bottom cover.
3. Grasp the armature shaft with pliers and a shop towel as shown in **Figure 19**. Pull the armature and bottom cover from the frame assembly.
4. Use two small screwdrivers to carefully collapse the brush springs (9, **Figure 17**) and move the brush away from the commutator. Be careful to avoid damaging the brush or commutator. Carefully pull the armature (5, **Figure 17**) from the bottom cover while the brushes are pulled away from the commutator.
5. Remove the screws (6, **Figure 17**), brushes (8) and retainers (7) from the bottom cover.
6. Disconnect and remove the bi-metal switch from the bottom cover. Note the seal lip direction, then use a suit-

POWER TRIM/TILT SYSTEMS

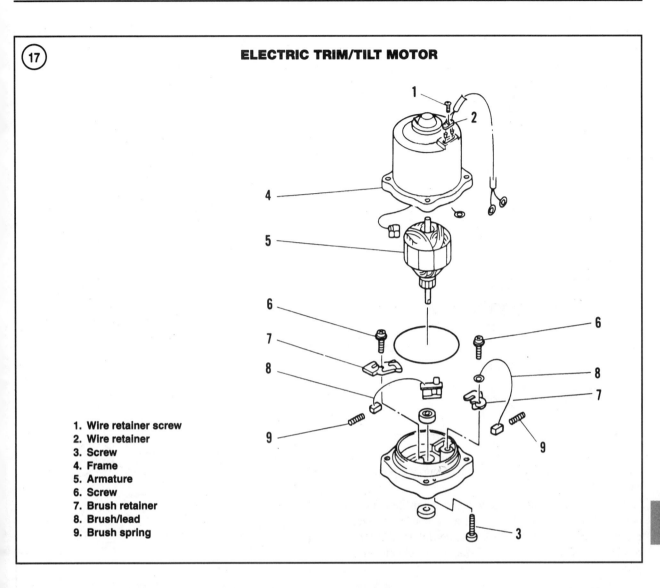

ELECTRIC TRIM/TILT MOTOR

1. Wire retainer screw
2. Wire retainer
3. Screw
4. Frame
5. Armature
6. Screw
7. Brush retainer
8. Brush/lead
9. Brush spring

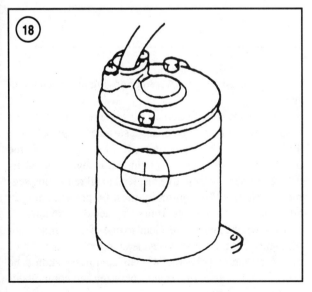

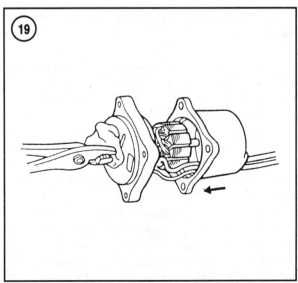

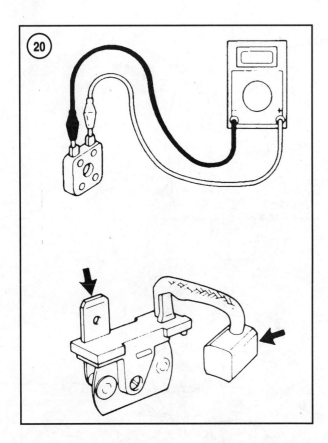

able socket and push the seal from the bottom cover. Discard the seal.

7. Use compressed air to blow debris from the components. Clean contamination from all components with electrical contact cleaner. Refer to *Electric Trim/Tilt Motor Component Inspection and Testing* in this chapter after disassembly.

Electric trim/tilt motor component inspection and testing

Prior to performing any test or measurements, clean debris from all components. Inspect the magnets in the frame assembly for broken or loose magnets and replace the frame assembly if defects are noted.

1. Calibrate an ohmmeter on the R × 1 scale. Connect the positive ohmmeter lead to one of the terminals or brush lead connection at the bi-metal switch (**Figure 20**). Continuity should be noted. Replace the bi-metal switch if continuity is not present.
2. Carefully grip the armature in a vise (**Figure 21**). Use only enough clamping force to retain the armature. Polish the commutator surfaces with 600 grit abrasive paper or carburundum. Polish the surface only. Remove only contamination or glazed surfaces. Periodically rotate the ar-

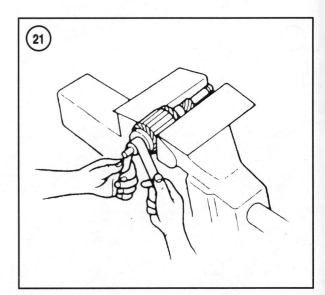

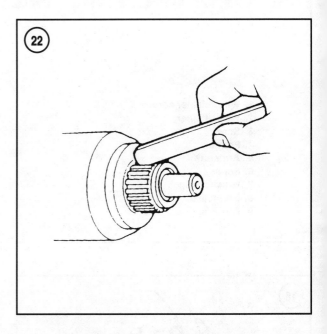

mature to polish evenly. Avoid removing too much material.
3. Use a disposable fingernail file to remove the mica and brush material from the undercut surfaces (**Figure 22**).
4. Calibrate an ohmmeter on the R × 1 scale. Connect the positive test lead to one of commutator segments. Alternately, connect the negative test lead to all remaining segments (**Figure 23**). Continuity must be present between all commutator segments. If not, replace the armature.
5. Connect the positive test lead to one of the commutator segments and the negative test lead to the laminated area of the armature (**Figure 24**). No continuity should be noted. Next, connect the meter between the commutator

Power Trim/Tilt Systems

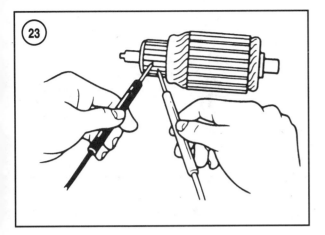

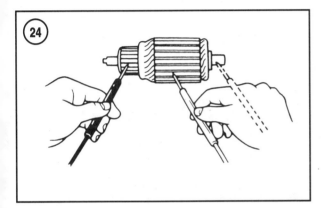

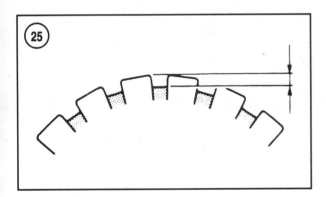

segments and the armature shaft. No continuity should be noted.

6. Inspect the bearing surfaces of the armature for wear or damage and replace as required. Inspect the bushings in the covers and in between the commutator segments. Replace if worn or damaged.

7. Using a depth micrometer measure the depth of the undercut (**Figure 25**). Compare the measurements with the specification listed in **Table 2**. Replace the armature if it is not within the specification.

8. Inspect the brush springs for damage or corrosion. Replace the brush springs if any doubts exist about their condition. Measure the brush length as indicated (A, **Figure 26**). Replace both brushes if either brush is at or below the wear limit in **Table 2**.

Electric trim/tilt motor assembly

1. Clean and dry all components. Apply a light coat of water-resistant grease to the bushing and armature shaft at the bushing contact surface. Do not allow any grease to contact the brushes or commutator surfaces.

2. Refer to **Figure 17** for component orientation. Attach the blue wire terminal to the connection on the bi-metal switch. Install the brush springs, brush retainers, bi-metal switch and brushes into the bottom cover. Tighten the screws securely. Use a suitable socket and push a new seal into the opening in the bottom cover with the seal lip facing down.

3. Use two small screwdrivers to position the brushes fully into the brush holders (the springs are collapsed). Carefully install the commutator end of the armature into the cover and release the brushes. Never force the armature into the cover as the brushes may be damaged.

4. Install a new O-ring onto the bottom cover. Use pliers and a shop towel to maintain the position of the armature and cover (**Figure 19**). Carefully install the armature into the frame. Make sure the armature shaft end enters the bushing inside the frame.

5. Align the marks made prior to disassembly and install the through-bolts or attaching screws. Do not tighten the screws at this time

6. Make sure the O-ring is properly positioned to prevent water leakage. Tighten the through-bolts or screws to the specification listed in **Table 1**.

7. Refer to *Electric Tilt/Trim Motor* and install the motor.

Filling Procedure

Fill the pump housing with fluid during assembly. Use Dexron II automatic transmission fluid in both the single hydraulic cylinder and three cylinder systems.

1. Use the power trim/tilt system or open the manual relief valve (**Figure 5** or **Figure 8**) to position the engine in the fully up position. Engage the tilt lock lever and support the engine with suitable blocks or an overhead cable. Close the manual relief valve.

2. Clean the area around the reservoir fill plug. Slowly loosen and remove the reservoir fill plug. Refer to **Figure 12** for single cylinder systems and to **Figure 13** for three cylinder systems.

3. Fill the unit to the bottom of the opening (**Figure 27**) with the engine in the fully UP position. Install the fill plug. Remove the supports and disengage the tilt lock lever.

4. Cycle the trim to the fully up then down position several times. Check and correct the fluid level as necessary. Tighten the plug to the specification listed in **Table 1**.

Bleeding Procedure

A spongy feel or inability to hold trim under load is a common symptom when air is present in the hydraulic system. The engine usually tucks under when power is applied and tilts out when power is reduced. Minor amounts of air in the system purge into the reservoir during normal operation. If major components have been removed, a significant amount of air can enter the system. Bleeding the air from the system is then required.

1. Operate the trim/tilt system or open the manual relief valve to position the engine fully UP. Correct the fluid level as indicated in Step 3 *Filling procedures*. Install the plug and tighten the manual relief valve.

2. Operate the trim/tilt system until the engine is positioned in the fully DOWN position. Operate the trim to the UP position. Stop the trim immediately if the electric pump motor begins to run faster or it sounds different (pump is ventilating). Open the manual relief valve, position the engine in the fully UP position and support the engine. Check and correct the fluid level. Close the manual relief valve and install the reservoir plug.

3. Continue to repeat Step 2 until the motor reaches full tilt without ventilating the pump. If a large amount of

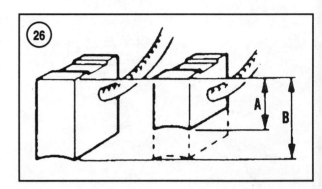

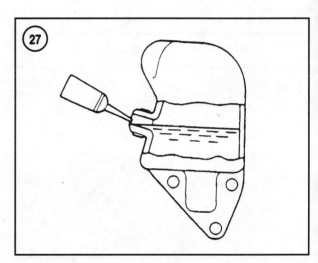

foam is noted in the reservoir, allow the engine to sit for one hour and repeat the process.

4. Cycle the trim fully up and down several times to purge the remaining air from the system. Refer to *Filling Procedures* to make the final fluid level correction.

POWER TRIM/TILT SYSTEMS

TABLE 1 TIGHTENING TORQUE

	Torque N•m (ft.-lb.)
Lower pivot bolt/nut BF35A, BF40A, BF45A, BF50A (Gas assisted manual tilt)	35 N•m (26 ft.-lb.)
Tilt lever bolt/nut BF35A, BF40A, BF45A, BF50A (Gas assisted manual tilt or power trim)	6.5 N•m (58 in.-lb.)
Electric trim motor attaching bolts BF75A, BF90A, BF115A, BF130A	5 N•m (44 in.-lb.)
Manual relief valve BF75A, BF90A, BF115A, BF130A	3.5 N•m (31 in.-lb.)
Fluid reservoir fill/check cap BF75A, BF90A, BF115A, BF130A	2.5 N•m (22 in.-lb.)
Fluid reservoir tank hex bolts BF75A, BF90A, BF115A, BF130A	3.5 N•m (31 in.-lb.)
Trim pump-to-manifold hex bolts BF75A, BF90A, BF115A, BF130A	8.3 N•m (73 in.-lb.)
Trim ram spanner nut BF75A, BF90A, BF115A, BF130A	78.0 N•m (58 ft.-lb.)
Tilt cylinder spanner nut BF75A, BF90A, BF115A, BF130A	162.0 N•m (119 ft.-lb.)
Standard tightening torque 5 mm bolt/nut 6 mm bolt/nut 8 mm bolt/nut 10 mm bolt/nut	4-7 N•m (35-62 in.-lb.) 8-12 N•m (71-106 in.-lb.) 20-28 N•m (15-21 in.-lb.) 35-40 N•m (26-30 ft.-lb.)

TABLE 2 TRIM/TILT ELECTRIC MOTOR SPECIFICATIONS

Brush length BF75A, BF90A, BF115A, BF130A	4.8-9.8 mm (0.189-0.386 in.)
Mica depth BF75A, BF90A, BF115A, BF130A	Greater than 0.5 mm (0.020 in.)

Chapter Thirteen

Midsection

This chapter provides information needed to remove and replace all midsection components, including worn or damaged motor mounts, components damaged from corrosion or impact with underwater objects. Sections are provided that address minor repairs, major repairs and tiller control components. Refer to Chapter Twelve if removal or replacement of trim/tilt system components is required.

Apply water-resistant grease to all bushing, pins and pivot points on assembly. Torque specifications are provided in **Table 1**. **Table 1** is located at the end of this chapter.

> *WARNING*
> *Never work under any part of the engine without providing suitable support. The engine mounted tilt lock or hydraulic system may collapse and allow the engine to drop. Support the engine with suitable blocks or an overhead cable BEFORE working under the engine.*

Minor Repairs

Minor repairs include replacing components that are easily accessible and are not part of major support structures (tilt pin, reverse lock-down mechanism).

1. Tilt the engine to the fully UP position. Provide support for the engine with an overhead cable or other suitable method (**Figure 1** and **Figure 2**).
2. Refer to **Figures 3-9** to locate the faulty component on the engine.
3. Disconnect both battery cables from the battery. Remove the spark plugs and connect the spark plug leads to an engine ground.
4. Note the location and position of the component and all of its fasteners. Remove the fasteners and the component. Install the component in the position noted prior to removal.
5. Replace any corroded or damaged bolts, screws, washers or nuts. Replace E-clips when removed. Replace any worn or damaged bushing or clamps. Lubricate all bush-

MIDSECTION

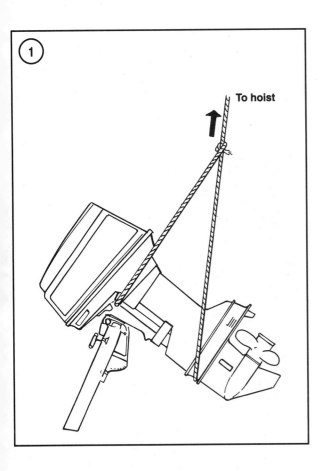

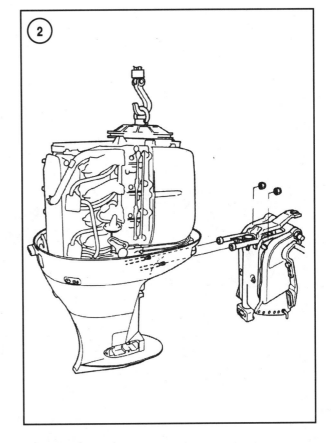

ings and pivot points with water-resistant grease on assembly. Tighten all fasteners to the specifications provided in **Table 1**. Remove the overhead cable or other support (**Figure 1**).

6. Refer to Chapter Five for the adjustment procedure when replacing reverse lock-down mechanism components.
7. Move the engine from the fully UP to fully DOWN position several times. Turn the engine fully starboard to fully port several times. Check for worn, damaged or improperly installed components if any binding, rough operation or looseness is noted.
8. Install the spark plugs and spark plug leads. Clean the battery terminals and connect the cables to the battery.

Major Repairs

NOTE
Replace all locking type or tab washers with new ones when they are removed or disturbed.

NOTE
Note their connection points then disconnect ground wires when necessary to remove other components. Clean all corrosion from the wire contact surface. Ensure all ground wire terminals are securely tightened.

Removal of major midsection components almost always requires removing the gearcase and base engine. Major midsection components can be replaced on smaller engines provided the major components are adequately supported. On larger engines, the engine must be removed from the clamp/swivel bracket to replace major midsection components. Always provide adequate engine support before removing any component. Refer to **Figures 3-9** to determine if removal of the gearcase or base engine is required.

Refer to Chapter Nine for gearcase removal and installation. Refer to Chapter Eight for base engine removal and installation.

Models BF20 and BF2A

Removing the gearcase or the base engine is not required unless replacing drive shaft housing components. Refer to **Figure 3** during disassembly and assembly.

MIDSECTION COMPONENTS
MODELS BF20 AND BF2A

1. Base engine retaining bolt
2. Clamp retaining bolt
3. Base engine gasket
4. Exhaust deflector
5. Sealing block
6. Water tube seal
7. Water tube
8. Mounting sleeves
9. Drive shaft housing
10. Steering friction bolt
11. Spring
12. Tilt tube
13. Tilt bracket
14. Nut
15. Lockwasher
16. Washer
17. Bushing
18. Bolt
19. Nut
20. Washer
21. Tilt pin
22. Transom clamp bolt
23. Port clamp bracket
24. Starboard clamp bracket
25. Pin
26. Lock down spring
27. Bushing
28. Tilt lock lever
29. Thrust block
30. Grease fitting
31. Lower bracket
32. Lower thrust mount
33. Pin

MIDSECTION

509

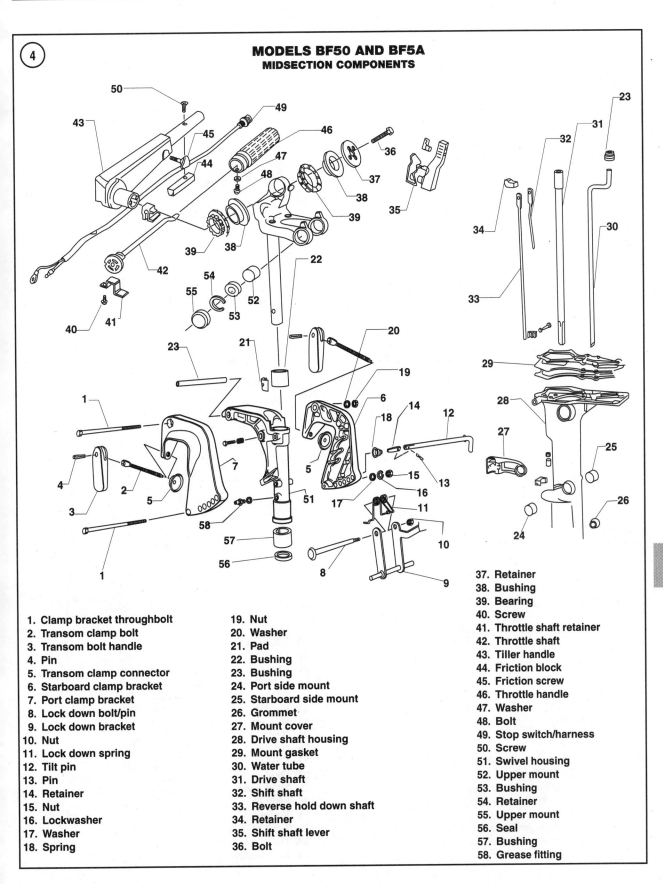

MODELS BF50 AND BF5A MIDSECTION COMPONENTS

1. Clamp bracket throughbolt
2. Transom clamp bolt
3. Transom bolt handle
4. Pin
5. Transom clamp connector
6. Starboard clamp bracket
7. Port clamp bracket
8. Lock down bolt/pin
9. Lock down bracket
10. Nut
11. Lock down spring
12. Tilt pin
13. Pin
14. Retainer
15. Nut
16. Lockwasher
17. Washer
18. Spring
19. Nut
20. Washer
21. Pad
22. Bushing
23. Bushing
24. Port side mount
25. Starboard side mount
26. Grommet
27. Mount cover
28. Drive shaft housing
29. Mount gasket
30. Water tube
31. Drive shaft
32. Shift shaft
33. Reverse hold down shaft
34. Retainer
35. Shift shaft lever
36. Bolt
37. Retainer
38. Bushing
39. Bearing
40. Screw
41. Throttle shaft retainer
42. Throttle shaft
43. Tiller handle
44. Friction block
45. Friction screw
46. Throttle handle
47. Washer
48. Bolt
49. Stop switch/harness
50. Screw
51. Swivel housing
52. Upper mount
53. Bushing
54. Retainer
55. Upper mount
56. Seal
57. Bushing
58. Grease fitting

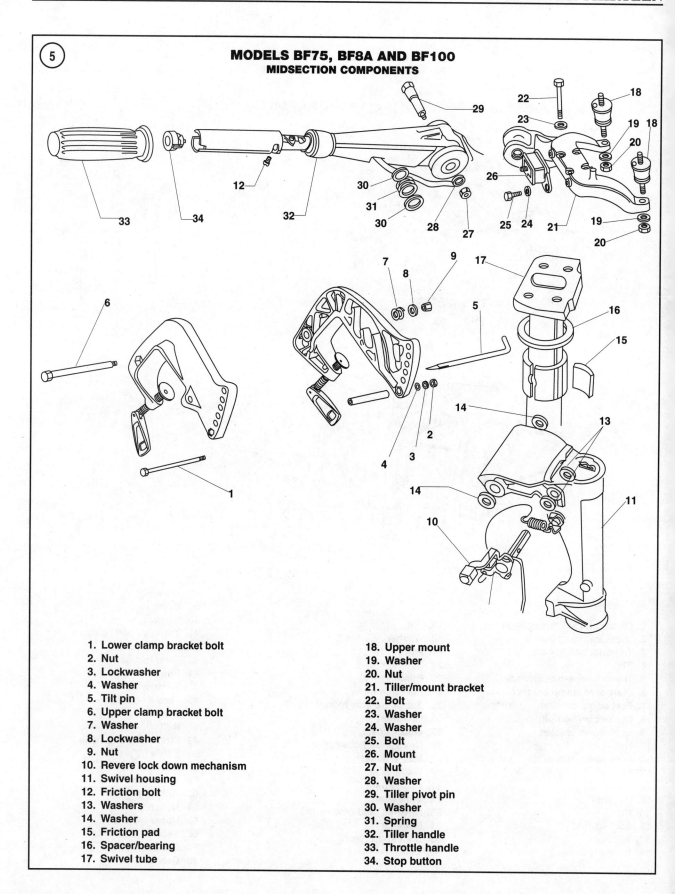

MIDSECTION

1. Remove the spark plug and connect the spark plug lead to an engine ground.
2. Note the location and position of the component and all of its fasteners. Remove the fasteners and the component. Install the component in the position noted prior to removal.
3. Ensure that the hooked end on the tilt lock spring (26, **Figure 3**) clips over the pin (25, **Figure 3**) during assembly.
4. Replace any corroded or damaged bolts, screws, washers or nuts. Replace E-clips if removed. Inspect all bushings, pivot bolts and tubes. Replace any component that is corroded, worn or damaged.
5. Lubricate all bushings and pivot points with water-resistant grease on assembly. Tighten all fasteners to the specifications provided in **Table 1**.
6. Move the engine from the fully UP to fully DOWN position several times. Turn the engine fully starboard to fully port several times. Check for worn, damaged or improperly installed components if any binding, rough operation or looseness is noted.
7. Install the spark plugs and spark plug leads.

Models BF50 and BF5A

Removal of the gearcase or the base engine is not required unless replacing drive shaft housing components. Refer to **Figure 4** during disassembly and assembly.

1. Disconnect both battery cables from the battery, if so equipped. Remove the spark plug and connect the spark plug lead to an engine ground.
2. Note the location and position of the component and all of its fasteners. Remove the fasteners and the component. Install the component in the position noted prior to removal.
3. Measure and record the depth of the bushings (22 and 57, **Figure 4**) in the swivel housing prior to removing them (**Figure 10**).
4. Replace any corroded or damaged bolts, screws, washers or nuts. Replace E-clips when removed. Inspect all bushings, pivot bolts and tubes. Replace any component that is corroded, worn or damaged.
5. Use an appropriately sized section of tubing or socket to carefully drive the upper and lower bushings (22 and 57, **Figure 4**) into the swivel housing. Make sure that they are installed to the proper depth in the swivel housing.
6. Lubricate all bushings and pivot points with water-resistant grease on assembly. Tighten all fasteners to the specifications provided in **Table 1**.
7. Move the engine from the fully UP to fully DOWN position several times. Turn the engine fully starboard to fully port several times. Check for worn, damaged or improperly installed components if any binding, rough operation or looseness is noted.
8. Install the spark plugs and spark plug leads. Clean the battery terminals and connect the cables to the battery.

Models BF75, BF8A and BF100

Removing the gearcase or the base engine is not required unless replacing drive shaft housing components. Refer to Chapter Eight if drive shaft housing removal is required. Refer to **Figure 5** during disassembly and assembly.

1. Disconnect both battery cables from the battery, if so equipped. Remove the spark plugs and connect the spark plug leads to an engine ground.
2. Note the location and position of the component and all of its fasteners. Remove the fasteners and component. Install the component in the position noted prior to removal.
3. Replace any corroded or damaged bolts, screws, washers or nuts. Replace E-clips when removed. Inspect all bushings, pivot bolts and tubes. Replace if worn or damaged areas are noted.
4. Lubricate all bushings and pivot points with water-resistant grease on assembly. Tighten all Fasteners to the specifications provided in **Table 1**.
5. Move the engine from the fully UP to fully DOWN position several times. Turn the engine fully starboard to fully port several times. Check for worn, damaged or improperly installed components if any binding, rough operation or looseness is detected.
6. Install the spark plugs and spark plug leads. Clean the battery terminals and connect the cables to the battery.

Models BF9.9A and BF15A

Removing the gearcase or the base engine is not required unless replacing the drive shaft housing components. Refer to **Figure 6** during disassembly and assembly.

1. Disconnect both battery cables from the battery, if so equipped. Remove the spark plugs and connect the spark plug leads to an engine ground. Disconnect the remote control cables on remote control models.
2. To allow access to the clamp bracket/swivel housing components, provide a suitable overhead lift cable attached to the lifting hook or flywheel hook (**Figure 2**). Lift the engine enough to take the pressure from the clamp brackets. Remove the lower mount cover (46, **Figure 6**), then remove the lower mount bolts at the lower mount bracket (45, **Figure 6**). Remove the upper mount nuts

CHAPTER THIRTEEN

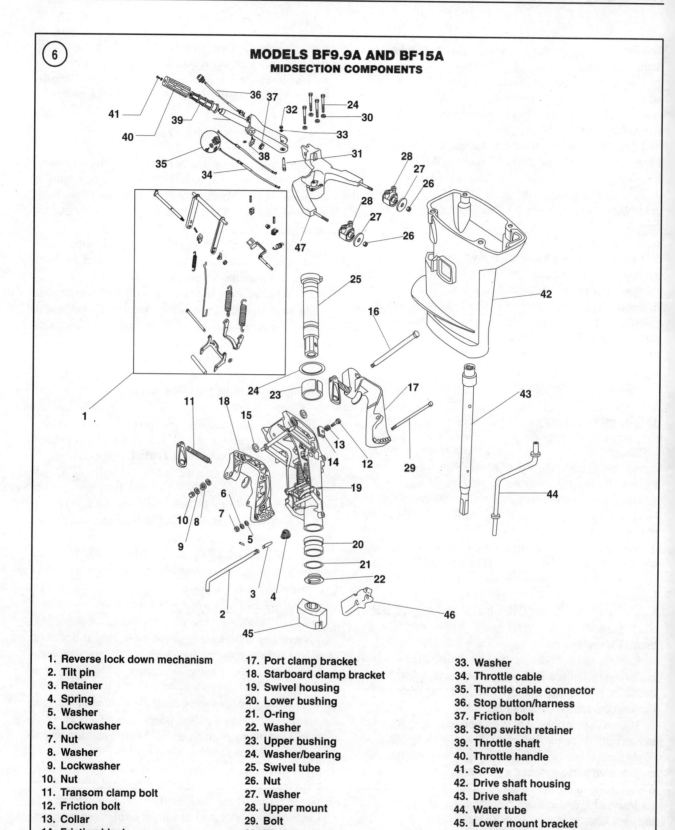

MODELS BF9.9A AND BF15A MIDSECTION COMPONENTS

1. Reverse lock down mechanism
2. Tilt pin
3. Retainer
4. Spring
5. Washer
6. Lockwasher
7. Nut
8. Washer
9. Lockwasher
10. Nut
11. Transom clamp bolt
12. Friction bolt
13. Collar
14. Friction block
15. Washer
16. Clamp bracket bolt
17. Port clamp bracket
18. Starboard clamp bracket
19. Swivel housing
20. Lower bushing
21. O-ring
22. Washer
23. Upper bushing
24. Washer/bearing
25. Swivel tube
26. Nut
27. Washer
28. Upper mount
29. Bolt
30. Washer
31. Tiller arm pivot pin
32. Nut
33. Washer
34. Throttle cable
35. Throttle cable connector
36. Stop button/harness
37. Friction bolt
38. Stop switch retainer
39. Throttle shaft
40. Throttle handle
41. Screw
42. Drive shaft housing
43. Drive shaft
44. Water tube
45. Lower mount bracket
46. Lower mount cover
47. Swivel tube/tiller bracket
48. Lower mount

MIDSECTION

from the mount bracket (47, **Figure 6**). Pull the engine back and move the engine away from the work area.

3. Refer to Chapter Eight and Chapter Nine to remove and install the gearcase and base engine if repairs are necessary to the drive shaft housing components.

4. Note the location and position of the component and fasteners. Remove the fasteners and the component. Install the component in the position noted prior to removal.

5. Measure and record the depth of the bushings (20 and 23, **Figure 6**) in the swivel housing prior to removing them (**Figure 10**).

6. Replace any corroded or damaged bolts, screws, washers or nuts. Replace the E-clips and the circlip from the lower end of the swivel tube when removed. Inspect all bushings, pivot bolts and tubes. Replace if worn or damaged areas are noted.

7. Use an appropriately sized section of tubing or socket to carefully drive the upper and lower bushings (20 and 23, **Figure 6**) into the swivel housing. Ensure that they are installed to the proper depth in the swivel housing.

8. Ensure that the marks on the swivel tube and lower mount bracket align as shown in **Figure 11**.

9. Lubricate all bushings and pivot points with water-resistant grease on assembly. Tighten all fasteners to the specifications provided in **Table 1**.

10. Align the mounts to their respective mounting locations on the clamp bracket and slide the engine into position. After all mount fasteners are securely attached, remove the overhead cable support.

11. Move the engine from the fully up to fully down position several times. Turn the engine fully starboard to fully port several times. Check for worn, damaged or improperly installed components if any binding, rough operation or looseness is noted.

12. Install the spark plugs and spark plug leads. Clean the battery terminals and connect the cables to the battery.

Models BF20A, BF25A and BF30A

Removing the gearcase or the base engine is not required unless replacing drive shaft housing components. Refer to **Figure 7** during disassembly and assembly.

1. Disconnect both battery cables from the battery. Remove the spark plugs and connect the spark plug leads to an engine ground. Disconnect the remote control cables on remote control models.

2. To allow access to the clamp bracket/swivel housing components, provide a suitable overhead lift cable attached to the lifting hook or flywheel hook (**Figure 2**). Lift the engine enough to take the pressure from the clamp brackets. Remove the lower mount cover (15, **Figure 7**). Remove the lower mount nuts and washers (19 and 20, **Figure 7**) from the lower mount bracket (13, **Figure 7**). Remove the plugs and upper mount bolts from within the lower motor cover (24, **Figure 7**). Pull the engine back and move the engine away from the work area.

3. Refer to Chapter Eight and Chapter Nine to remove and install the gearcase and base engine if repairs are necessary to the drive shaft housing components.

4. Note the location and position of the component and all of its fasteners. Remove the fasteners and component. Install the component in the position noted prior to removal.

5. Measure and record the depth of the bushings (5, **Figure 7**) in the swivel housing prior to removing them (**Figure 10**).

6. Replace any corroded or damaged bolts, screws, washers or nuts. Replace the E-clips and the circlip from the lower end of the swivel tube (7, **Figure 7**) if removed. Inspect all bushings, pivot bolts and tubes. Replace if corrosion is present or if worn or damaged areas are noted.

7. Use an appropriately sized section of tubing or socket to carefully drive the upper and lower bushings (5, **Figure 7**) into the swivel housing. Ensure that they are installed to the proper depth in the swivel housing. Install the seal (11, **Figure 7**) into the opening at the lower end of the swivel housing with the lip facing the base engine.

8. Ensure that the marks on the swivel tube and lower mount bracket align as indicated in **Figure 11**.

9. Lubricate all bushings and pivot points with water-resistant grease on assembly. Tighten all fasteners to the specification provided in **Table 1**.

10. Align the mounts to their respective mounting locations on the clamp bracket and slide the engine into position. After all mount fasteners are securely attached, remove the overhead cable support.

11. Move the engine from the fully up to fully down position several times. Turn the engine fully starboard to fully port several times. Check for worn, damaged or improperly installed components if any binding, rough operation or looseness is noted.

12. Attach any disconnected control cables. Refer to Chapter Five for adjustment procedures. Install the spark plugs and spark plug leads. Clean the battery terminals and connect the cables to the battery.

BF35 and BF130A

Removing the gearcase or the base engine is not required unless replacing drive shaft housing components. Refer to **Figure 8** or **Figure 9** during disassembly and assembly.

1. Disconnect both battery cables from the battery. Remove the spark plugs and connect the spark plug leads to

CHAPTER THIRTEEN

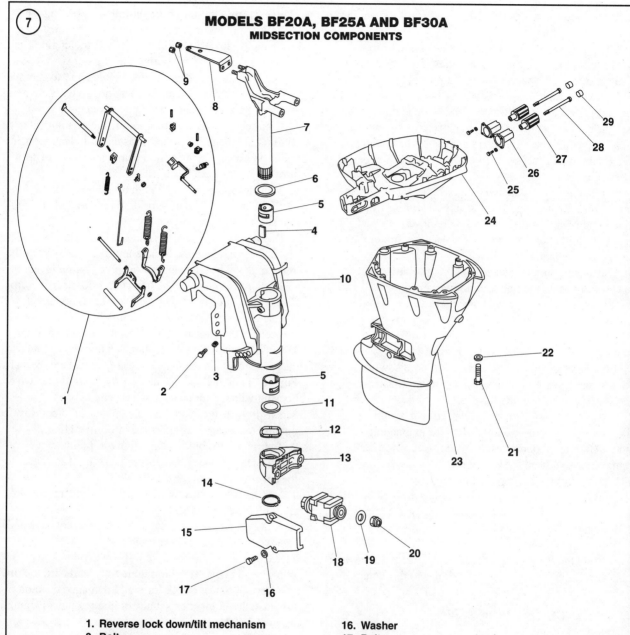

MODELS BF20A, BF25A AND BF30A MIDSECTION COMPONENTS

1. Reverse lock down/tilt mechanism
2. Bolt
3. Spring
4. Friction block
5. Bushing
6. Washer/bearing
7. Swivel tube
8. Remote steering bracket
9. Nuts
10. Swivel housing
11. Seal
12. Wave washer
13. Lower mount bracket
14. Snap ring
15. Lower mount cover
16. Washer
17. Bolt
18. Lower mount
19. Washer
20. Locknut
21. Bolt
22. Washer
23. Drive shaft housing
24. Lower motor cover/mount bracket
25. Bolt
26. Mount retainer
27. Upper mounts
28. Bolt
29. Plugs

MIDSECTION

515

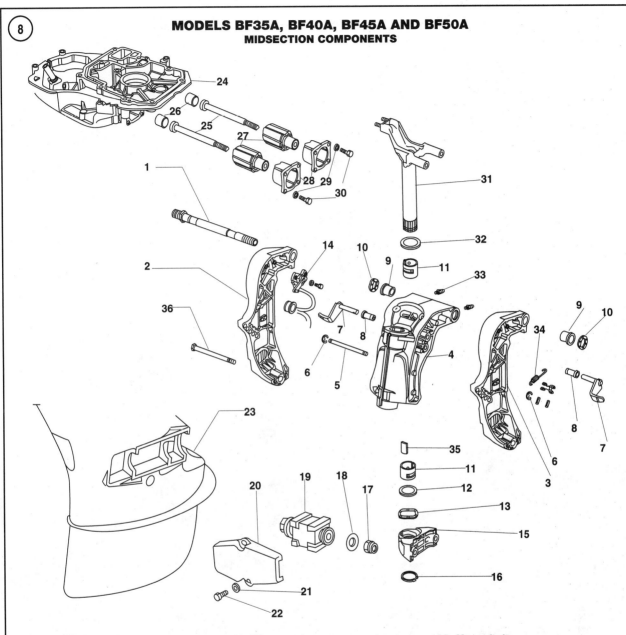

**MODELS BF35A, BF40A, BF45A AND BF50A
MIDSECTION COMPONENTS**

1. Tilt tube
2. Port clamp bracket
3. Starboard clamp bracket
4. Swivel/tilt housing
5. Trim system pivot pin
6. E-clip
7. Tilt lock lever
8. Bushing
9. Bushing
10. Wave washer
11. Bushing
12. Seal
13. Wave washer
14. Trim position sender
15. Lower mount bracket
16. Snap ring
17. Locknut
18. Washer
19. Lower mount
20. Lower mount cover
21. Washer
22. Bolt
23. Drive shaft housing
24. Base engine mount bracket
25. Mount bolts
26. Plugs
27. Upper mount
28. Mount retainer
29. Washer
30. Bolt
31. Swivel tube
32. Washer/bearing
33. Grease fitting
34. Tilt lock spring
35. Friction block
36. Mount bolt

CHAPTER THIRTEEN

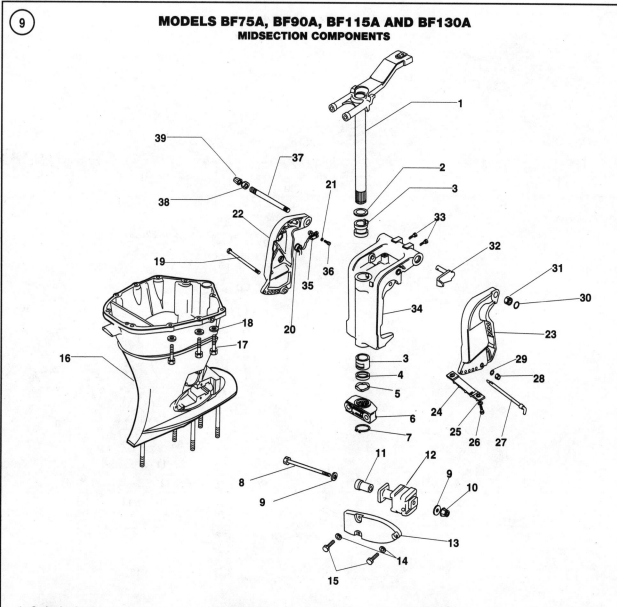

MODELS BF75A, BF90A, BF115A AND BF130A MIDSECTION COMPONENTS

1. Swivel tube
2. Washer/bearing
3. Bushing
4. Seal
5. Wave washer
6. Lower mount bracket
7. Snap ring
8. Mount bolt
9. Washer
10. Locknut
11. Sleeve
12. Lower mount
13. Lower mount cover
14. Washer
15. Bolt
16. Drive shaft housing
17. Bolt
18. Washer
19. Tilt pin
20. Grommet
21. Washer
22. Port clamp bracket
23. Starboard clamp bracket
24. Anode
25. Washer
26. Bolt
27. Tilt pin
28. Locknut
29. Washer
30. O-ring
31. Nut
32. Tilt lock lever
33. Grease fittings
34. Swivel/tilt bracket
35. Trim position sender
36. Screw
37. Tilt tube
38. Nut
39. Cap

MIDSECTION

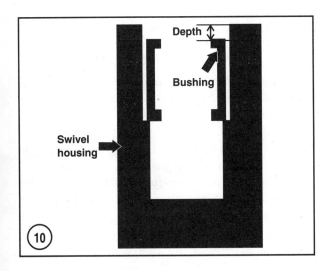

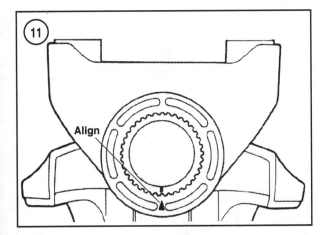

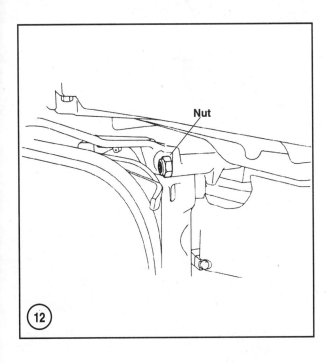

an engine ground. Disconnect the remote control cables on remote control models.

2. To access the clamp bracket/swivel housing components, provide a suitable overhead lift cable attached to the lifting hook or flywheel hook (**Figure 2**). Lift the engine enough to take the pressure from the clamp brackets. Remove the lower mount cover. Remove the lower mount nuts and washers at the lower mount bracket. Loosen and remove the nuts or bolts (**Figure 12**) that retain the upper motor mounts to the swivel tube. Pull the engine back and move the engine away from the work area.

3. Refer to Chapter Eight and Chapter Nine to remove and install the gearcase and base engine if repairs are necessary to the drive shaft housing components.

4. Note the location and position of the component and all of its fasteners. Remove the fasteners and components. Install the components in the position noted prior to removal.

5. Measure and record the depth of the bushings in the swivel housing prior to removing them (**Figure 10**).

6. Replace any corroded or damaged bolts, screws, washers or nuts. Replace E-clips and the circlip from the lower end of the swivel tube if removed. Inspect all bushings, pivot bolts and tubes. Replace if worn or damaged areas are noted.

7. Use an appropriately sized section of tubing or socket to carefully drive the upper and lower bushings into the swivel housing. Ensure that they are installed to the proper depth in the swivel housing. Install the seal into the opening at the lower end of the swivel housing with the lip facing the base engine.

8. Ensure that the marks on the swivel tube and lower mount bracket align as indicated in **Figure 11**.

9. Lubricate all bushings and pivot points with water-resistant grease on assembly. Tighten all fasteners to the specifications provided in **Table 1**.

10. Align the mounts to their respective mounting locations on the clamp bracket and slide the engine into position. After all mount fasteners are securely attached, remove the overhead cable support.

11. Move the engine from the fully up to fully down position several times. Turn the engine fully starboard to fully port several times. Check for worn, damaged or improperly installed components if any binding, rough operation or looseness is noted.

12. Attach any disconnected control cables. Refer to Chapter Five for adjustment procedures. Install the spark plugs and spark plug leads. Clean the battery terminals and connect the cables to the battery.

Tiller Control Components

On all tiller control models (except models BF20 and BF2A), the tiller control houses the throttle cable, stop button and shift linkages/cables. Refer to **Figures 4-6** and **Figures 13-14** during removal and installation of any tiller control components.

For models BF20 and BF2A, refer to Chapter Eight (control is mounted to the base engine).

1. Note the location and position of all components and their fasteners prior to removing them from the tiller control.
2. Most models have throttle and/or shift cables routed through the tiller handle or the tiller control mounting bracket. Use the illustrations to determine which components must be removed for cable access.
3. Replace any cables that have damaged or worn outer jacket surfaces. Push and pull the core wire in the outer jacket. Replace the cable if it does not move smoothly.
4. Refer to Chapter Five for the cable adjustment procedure. Adjust the shift and throttle linkages anytime shift or throttle components are disturbed.
5. Note the wire connection points and wire routing prior to removing the stop button, key switch, warning light panel, trim switch or emergency stop switch. Install all wires and terminals to prevent interference with other components. Install new plastic locking tie clamp when removal is required.
6. Inspect all bushings, pins, wire insulation and cable attaching points. Replace any worn, damaged or corroded components.

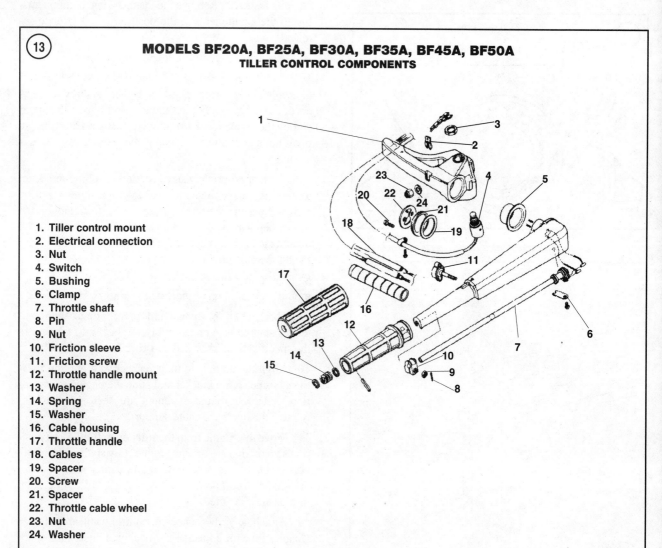

MODELS BF20A, BF25A, BF30A, BF35A, BF45A, BF50A
TILLER CONTROL COMPONENTS

1. Tiller control mount
2. Electrical connection
3. Nut
4. Switch
5. Bushing
6. Clamp
7. Throttle shaft
8. Pin
9. Nut
10. Friction sleeve
11. Friction screw
12. Throttle handle mount
13. Washer
14. Spring
15. Washer
16. Cable housing
17. Throttle handle
18. Cables
19. Spacer
20. Screw
21. Spacer
22. Throttle cable wheel
23. Nut
24. Washer

MIDSECTION

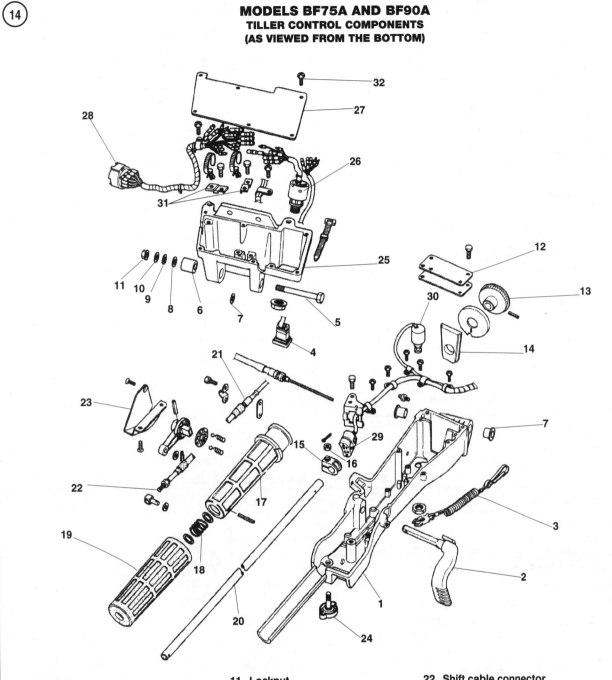

**MODELS BF75A AND BF90A
TILLER CONTROL COMPONENTS
(AS VIEWED FROM THE BOTTOM)**

1. Tiller control housing
2. Shift selector handle
3. Lanyard connector
4. Warning light panel
5. Mounting bolt
6. Bushing
7. Bushing
8. Washer
9. Washer
10. Washer
11. Locknut
12. Throttle shaft retainer
13. Throttle cable wheel
14. Throttle shaft support
15. Friction sleeve
16. Nut
17. Throttle handle mount
18. Spring
19. Throttle handle
20. Throttle shaft
21. Shift cable
22. Shift cable connector
23. Cable connector bracket
24. Friction screw
25. Tiller control bracket
26. Key switch
27. Cover
28. Engine harness connector
29. Trim switch
30. Emergency stop switch
31. Wire retainers
32. Screw

TABLE 1 TIGHTENING TORQUE

	Torque
Upper mount bolts	
BF20, BF2A	20.0-28.0 N•m (14.8-20.7 ft.-lb.)
BF20A, BF25A, BF30A	45.0 N•m (33.2 ft.-lb.)
Upper mount nuts	
BF35A, BF40A, BF45A, BF50A	45.0 N•m (33.2 ft.-lb.)
BF75A, BF90A, BF115A, BF130A	83.0 N•m (61.2 ft.-lb.)
Lower mount nut	
BF20A, BF25A, BF30A	55.0 N•m (40.7 ft.-lb.)
BF35A, BF40A, BF45A, BF50A	55.0 N•m (40.7 ft.-lb.)
BF75A, BF90A, BF115A, BF130A	83.0 N•m (61.2 ft.-lb.)
Lower mount cover bolt	
All models	22.0 N•m (16.2 ft.-lb.)
Lower clamp bracket/trim system throughbolts	
BF50, BF5A	15.0-20.0 N•m (132.8-177.0 in.-lb.)
BF20A, BF25A, BF30A	22.0 N•m (16.2 ft.-lb.)
BF35A, BF40A, BF45A, BF50A	35.0 N•m (25.8 ft.-lb.)
BF75A, BF90A, BF115A, BF130A	35.0 N•m (25.8 ft.-lb.)
Tilt tube nut	
BF20A, BF25A, BF30A	
Port side	17.5 N•m (12.9 ft.-lb.)
Starboard side	32.5 N•m (24.0 ft.-lb.)
BF35A, BF40A, BF45A, BF50A	
Port side	17.5 N•m (12.9 ft.-lb.)
Starboard side	32.5 N•m (24.0 ft.-lb.)
BF75A, BF90A, BF115A, BF130A	17.0 N•m (12.6 ft.-lb.)

Table 2 STANDARD TIGHTENING TORQUE

Fastener size	Tightening torque
5 mm bolt/nut	4-7 N•m (35-62 in.-lb.)
6 mm bolt/nut	8-12 N•m (71-106 in.-lb.)
8 mm bolt/nut	20-28 N•m (15-21 in.-lb.)
10 mm bolt/nut	35-40 N•m (26-30 ft.-lb.)

Chapter Fourteen

Remote Control

The remote control provides a means to control throttle, shifting and other engine operations at a point away from the engine (**Figure 1**). This chapter provides shift cable removal and installation, and remote control disassembly/assembly procedures.

Three common types of controls are used on Honda outboards. Remote control models BF9.9A and BF15A are equipped with a surface-mounted (starboard side of the control station) remote control. This remote control provides throttle, shift and engine stop control. It does not provide a switch for the electric starter motor.

All other remote control models can be equipped with the second type surface mount control (**Figure 1**). This type of control is mounted on the starboard side of the control station. This is the most commonly used remote control on Honda outboards. It provides throttle, shift, ignition switching, emergency stop switch, electric starter motor, and choke solenoid control. Other functions include operation of the throttle switch and tilt/trim system. This control provides the mounting location for the warning light panel.

Models BF75A, BF90A, BF115A and BF130A may be equipped with a panel or binnacle-mounted remote control. With this type of remote control, the ignition switch, choke solenoid switch and warning light panel are all mounted to the dash portion of the control station and are separate from the remote control. The remote control is mounted to the binnacle, starboard or port side of the control station. The throttle/shift handle and outer panel are the only visible components. The remainder of the control is mounted behind the boat structure.

WARNING
A malfunction in the remote control can lead to a lack of shift and throttle control. Never operate an outboard if any malfunction is noted with the remote control. Damage to property, serious bodily injury or death can result if the engine is operated without proper control. Check for proper remote control operation before operating the engine or after performing any service or repair to the remote control.

CAUTION
Always refer to your owner's manual for specific operating instructions for the remote control. Become familiar with all control functions before operating the engine.

Throttle/Shift Cable Removal/Installation

Throttle/shift cable replacement is required if the cable becomes hard to move or excessive play occurs due to cable wear. Mark the cables prior to removal to ensure that the throttle and shift cables are installed to the proper attaching points. Remove and attach one cable at a time to avoid confusion. Refer to **Figures 2-4**.

Refer to **Figure 2** (BF9.9A and BF15A), **Figure 3** (all models with a standard control) and **Figure 4** (BF90A, BF115A and BF130A equipped with a panel mount control).

Models BF9.9A and BF15A

1. Disconnect both battery cables from the battery. Remove the spark plugs and connect the spark plug leads to an engine ground.
2. Remove the screws or bolts attaching the remote control to the boat structure.
3. Carefully remove the attaching screws and back cover from remote control (**Figure 2**).
4. Identify the throttle cable attaching points (A, **Figure 2**). Use a black marker to mark the pin, throttle cable connector and throttle arm in the control to ensure correct assembly.
5. Carefully lift both cables from the rear portion of the control and remove the rear cable support/clamp from the cables.
6. Use a small screwdriver to carefully pry the E-clip from the throttle cable end and attaching point. Discard the E-clip.
7. Remove and discard the cotter pin for the shift cable connector. Carefully lift the shift cable from the remote control.
8. Apply water-resistant grease to the threaded end of the replacement cables. Thread the cable connector onto the threaded end until at least 8.0 mm (0.315 in.) of the threaded end is within the cable connector (**Figure 3**). Tighten the jam nut securely against the cable connector.
9. Apply water-resistant grease to the attaching points of the cables. Position the shift cable connector over the pin on the shift lever (B, **Figure 2**) then install a new cotter pin. Bend both ends of the cotter pin over to ensure a secure connection.
10. Position the throttle cable connector over the pin on the throttle lever (A, **Figure 2**) and install a new E-clip. Ensure the E-clip is properly positioned in the groove on the pin.
11. Position the support/clamp over both cables at the rear portion of the remote control and carefully slip it into its recess in the control housing.
12. Install the back cover and screws (**Figure 2**).
13. Install the control and attaching screws to boat. Refer to Chapter Five and adjust the throttle and shift cables at the engine.
14. Install all spark plugs and spark plug leads. Clean the battery terminals and connect both cables to the battery.

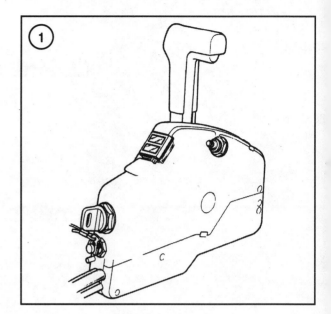

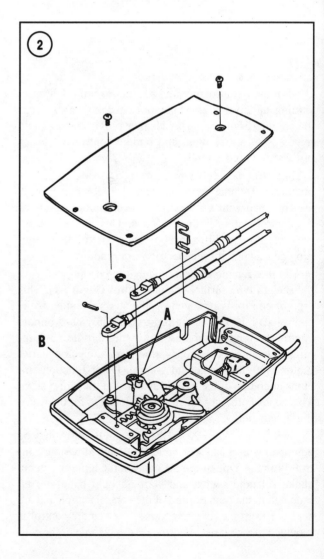

REMOTE CONTROL

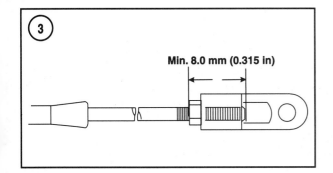

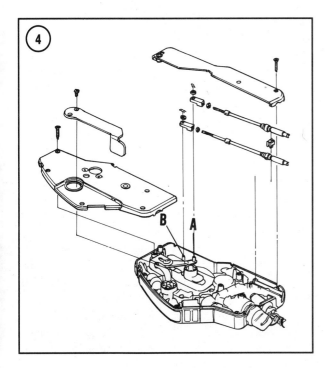

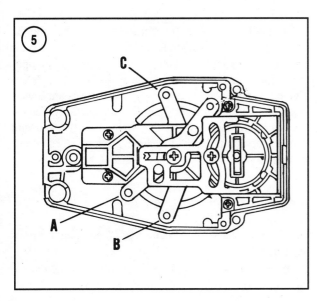

Check for proper shift and throttle operation and correct any problems before operating the engine.

Surface mount remote control for all models (except BF9.9A and BF15A)

1. Disconnect both battery cables from the battery. Remove the spark plugs and connect the spark plug leads to an engine ground.

2. Remove the screws or bolts attaching the remote control to the boat structure.

3. Carefully remove the attaching screws and lower back cover from remote control (**Figure 4**).

4. Identify the cable attaching points (A and B, **Figure 4**). Use a black marker to mark the pin, throttle cable connector and throttle arm in the control to ensure correct assembly.

5. Carefully lift both cables from the rear portion of the control and remove the rear cable support/clamp from between the cables.

6. Remove and discard the cotter pin for the throttle cable connector. Carefully lift the throttle cable from the remote control.

7. Remove and discard the cotter pin for the shift cable connector. Carefully lift the shift cable from the remote control.

8. Apply water-resistant grease to the threaded end of the replacement cables. Thread the cable connector onto the threaded end until at least 8.0 mm (0.314 in.) of the threaded end is within the cable connector (**Figure 3**). Tighten the jam nut securely against the cable connector.

9. Apply water-resistant grease to the attaching points of the cables. Position the shift cable connector over the pin on the shift lever (B, **Figure 4**) then install a new cotter pin. Bend both ends of the cotter pin over to ensure a secure connection.

10. Position the throttle cable connector over the pin on the throttle lever (A, **Figure 3**) and install a new cotter pin. Bend both ends of the cotter pin over to ensure a secure connection.

11. Position the support/clamp over both cables at the rear portion of the remote control and carefully slip it into its recess in the control housing.

12. Install the lower back cover and screws (**Figure 3**).

13. Install the control and attaching screws to boat. Refer to Chapter Five and adjust the throttle and shift cables at the engine.

14. Install all spark plugs and spark plug leads. Clean the battery terminals and connect the cables to the battery. Check for proper shift and throttle operation and correct any problems before operating the engine.

Models BF75A, BF90A, BF115A and BF130A panel or binnacle mount control

NOTE
Apply Loctite 242 to the threads of the remove control handle nut or bolt on assembly.

1. Disconnect both battery cables from the battery. Remove the spark plugs and connect the spark plug leads to an engine ground.
2. Position the shift/throttle control lever into forward gear full throttle. Carefully pry the neutral throttle button from the control handle (inline with the pivot point).
3. Mark the outline of the control handle on the boat structure to ensure the handle is installed correctly on assembly. Remove the bolt in the neutral throttle button bore then carefully pull the handle from the control. Remove both the upper and lower plastic covers from the control panel.
4. Remove the three screws that retain the control to the control panel and carefully route the control away from the mounting structure.
5. Carefully remove the screws and remove the back cover from remote control.
6. Identify the throttle cable attaching points (A, **Figure 4**). Mark the throttle cable attaching points.
7. Identify the shift cable attaching points (B, **Figure 4**). Mark the shift cable attaching points.
8. Note the locations and orientation of the cable retaining grommets at the aft end of the remote control.
9. Remove the screw that retains the throttle cable to the throttle lever (A, **Figure 4**).
10. Remove the screw that retains the shift cable to the shift lever (B, **Figure 4** [standard mount control]) or (C, **Figure 4** [port mounted control]).
11. Carefully lift both cables from the rear portion of the control along with the cable retaining grommets.
12. Place the replacement shift and throttle cables into their respective locations in the remote control. Apply water-resistant grease to the cable pivot points (A, B and C, **Figure 4**).
13. Install the cable end retaining screws and tighten them to the specification listed in **Table 1**.
14. Ensure that the cable retaining grommets are properly positioned into their slots at the aft end of the remote control housing.
15. Install the back cover and securely tighten the retaining screws
16. Position the remote control onto its mounting location on the control panel. Install the remote control mounting screws and securely tighten them. Install the upper and lower plastic covers onto the remote control. Install the plastic sleeve into the recess in the control panel.
17. Ensure that the trim switch is routed to prevent interference with other components. Position the control handle onto the remote control at the location noted prior to removal. Use a deep socket and extension to install the control handle-retaining nut. Tighten the nut to the specification listed in **Table 1**.
18. Refer to Chapter Five and adjust the throttle/shift cable and linkage.
19. Position the control handle in forward gear (full throttle) and carefully push the neutral throttle button into the opening on the control handle-retaining nut.
20. Install the spark plugs and spark plug leads. Clean the battery terminals and connect both cables to the battery. Check for proper shift and throttle operation and correct any problems before operating the engine. Check the operation of the trim/tilt system. Correct any noted problems.

Remote Control Disassembly and Assembly

This section provides procedures for complete disassembly and assembly of the remote controls.

If complete disassembly is not required to access the faulty component(s), perform the disassembly steps until the desired component is accessible. Reverse the disassembly steps to assemble the remote control.

To save a great deal of time on assembly and ensure proper assembly, make notes or drawings prior to removing *any component* from the remote control. Improper assembly can cause internal binding or reversed cable movement.

Clean all components (except electric switches and the warning buzzer) in a suitable solvent. Use compressed air to blow debris from the components. Inspect all components for damaged or worn surfaces. Replace any defective or suspect component. Apply water-resistant grease to all pivot points or sliding surfaces on assembly. Test all electric components when they are removed to ensure proper operation. Refer to Chapter Three for testing procedures for all switches and the warning buzzer.

Models BF9.9A and BF15A

Mark the location and position of *all* components prior to removal.

1. Refer to *Throttle/Shift Cable Removal and Installation* to remove the throttle and shift cables.

REMOTE CONTROL

2. Disconnect the wire harness from the engine then remove the remote control from the boat. Place the control on a clean work surface.

3. Remove the screw (20, **Figure 6**), then carefully lift the throttle lever and washers (17-19, **Figure 6**) from the remote control. Remove the screw and washers (22 and 23, **Figure 6**) then remove the cam gear (24, **Figure 6**) from the remote control.

4. Slide the bushing (26, **Figure 6**) from the control handle shaft. Remove the screw (28, **Figure 6**) then lift the lever (27, **Figure 6**) from the remote control.

5. Pry the cap from the control handle. Remove the retaining screws and lift the control handle from the control. Remove the screw (2, **Figure 6**) to remove the lock bar (3, **Figure 6**), then remove the lock button (4, **Figure 6**) from the handle.

6. Remove any accessible bushings, grommets and retainers at this point. Remove the friction screw and sleeve from its opening at the aft end of the remote control.

7. Make note of all wire connections and routing prior to removal. Disconnect the wires, then remove the emergency stop switch (15, **Figure 6**) and engine stop switch (11, **Figure 6**) from the remote control.

8. Inspect all components for worn, damaged or corroded surfaces and replace them as required.

9. Assembly is the reverse of disassembly. Apply water-resistant grease to all bushings, pivot points and sliding surfaces.

10. Refer to *Throttle/Shift Cable Removal and Installation* and install the cables and the remote control. Check for proper operation before returning the engine into service.

Standard control for all models except BF9.9A and BF15A

Mark the location and position of *all* components prior to removal.

1. Refer to *Throttle/Shift Cable Removal and Installation* and perform Steps 2-7 to remove the throttle and shift cables.

2. Disconnect the wire harness from the engine and remove the remote control from the boat. Place the control on a clean work surface.

3. Remove both retaining screws, then lift the neutral throttle lever from the side of the remote control. Remove the screws, then remove the back cover from the remote control.

4. Remove the wire-retaining clamp to access the wire harness connections. Note all wire connections and routing prior to removal. Disconnect the wires and remove the switches, warning horn and warning light panel from the remote control.

5. Remove the screw and washer (37 and 38, **Figure 7**) along with the E-clip and washers (35, 36 and 47, **Figure 7**) from the remote control. Lift the neutral only throttle cam (39, **Figure 7**) from the control.

6. Remove the E-clip and washers (51 and 52, **Figure 7**). Note their position, then remove the linkage and washer (45 and 46, **Figure 7**) from the remote control. Remove the screw and washer (54 and 53, **Figure 7**), then lift the linkage connector (50, **Figure 7**) from the remote control.

7. Remove the washer (49, **Figure 7**), then lift the plate and collar (33 and 48, **Figure 7**) from the remote control. Inspect the collar for worn or damaged areas. Remove and replace the collar if any defects are noted.

8. Remove the screw (22, **Figure 7**), then carefully remove the plate, spring, pin and washer (19-21, **Figure 7**) from the remote control.

9. Loosen and remove the friction screw (24, **Figure 7**), then lift the friction plate (23, **Figure 7**), nuts and washers from the remote control.

10. Remove the bolt and washer (29 and 28, **Figure 7**) then lift the control actuator wheel (60, **Figure 7**) from the remote control.

11. Loosen the remove the screw and washer (26 and 27, **Figure 7**). Note the position then lift the lever (25, **Figure 7**) from the housing.

12. Remove the throttle/shift handle from the other side of the remote control. Remove both screws (2, **Figure 7**) and the neutral detent block from the remote control.

13. Remove the screw and plate (6 and 7, **Figure 7**) then lift the lock bar and spring (4 and 5, **Figure 7**) from the control handle.

14. Note the wire connection points and routing, then remove the trim switch and grip (8 and 9, **Figure 7**) from the handle. Inspect all components for worn, damaged or corroded surfaces and replace them as required.

15. Assembly is the reverse of disassembly. Apply water-resistant grease to all bushings, pivot points and sliding surfaces. Ensure that the plate (33, **Figure 7**) is installed with the UP mark facing the rear cover on assembly. Ensure that the collar (48, **Figure 7**) is positioned correctly into the opening in the plate on assembly.

16. Refer to *Throttle/Shift Cable Removal and Installation* and install the cables and the remote control. Check for proper operation before returning the engine to service.

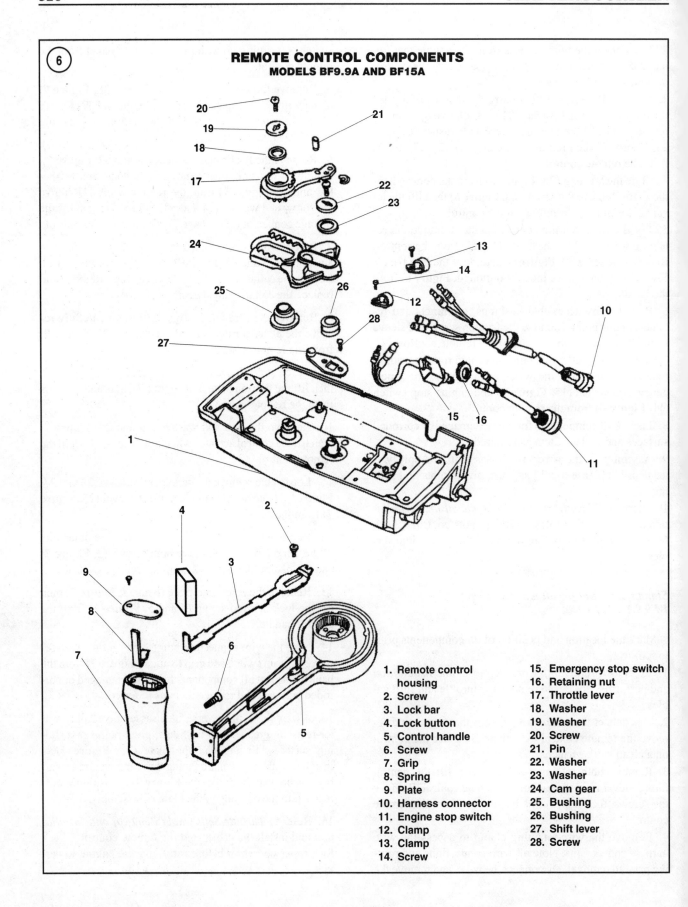

REMOTE CONTROL

SIDE MOUNT STANDARD CONTROL
ALL MODELS (EXCLUDING MODELS BF9.9A AND BF15A)

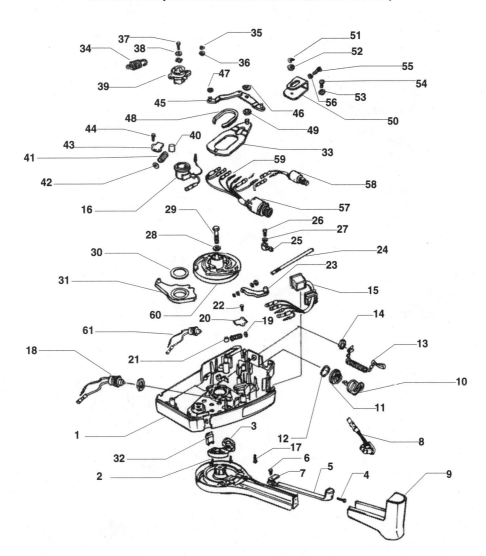

1. Remote control housing
2. Screw
3. Neutral detent block
4. Spring
5. Lock bar
6. Screw
7. Plate
8. Trim/tilt switch
9. Grip
10. Key switch
11. Key switch retaining nut
12. Wave washer
13. Lanyard cord
14. Emergency stop switch retainer
15. Warning light panel
16. Warning horn/buzzer
17. Screw
18. Throttle switch
19. Washer
20. Plate
21. Pin
22. Screw
23. Friction plate
24. Friction screw
25. Lever
26. Screw
27. Washer
28. Washer
29. Bolt
30. Bearing
31. Shift lever
32. Trim/tilt wire grommet
33. Plate
34. Spring
35. E-clip
36. Washer
37. Screw
38. Washer
39. Neutral only throttle cam
40. Pin
41. Spring
42. Washer
43. Plate/retainer
44. Screw
45. Linkage
46. Washer
47. Washer
48. Collar
49. Washer
50. Linkage connector
51. E-clip
52. Washer
53. Washer
54. Screw
55. Screw
56. Washer
57. Key switch
58. Emergency stop switch
59. Electrical harness connector
60. Control actuator wheel
61. Choke solenoid switch

CHAPTER FOURTEEN

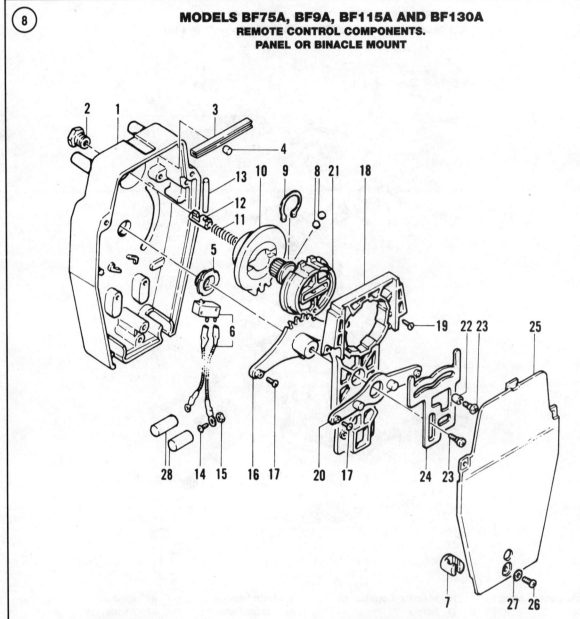

MODELS BF75A, BF9A, BF115A AND BF130A REMOTE CONTROL COMPONENTS. PANEL OR BINACLE MOUNT

1. Remote control housing
2. Handle lock bolt
3. Detent spring
4. Detent roller
5. Bushing
6. Neutral only start switch *
7. Cable grommet
8. Steel balls
9. Snap ring
10. Shift gear
11. Spring
12. Shift lock-out switch
13. Pin
14. Screw
15. Nut
16. Shift arm
17. Screw
18. Support housing
19. Screw
20. Throttle arm
21. Control shaft
22. Throttle plate roller
23. Shoulder screw
24. Throttle plate
25. Rear cover
26. Rear cover
27. Washer
28. Spacer

* not used in all applications

REMOTE CONTROL

Models BF75A, BF90A, BF115A and BF130A panel or binnacle mount control

NOTE
Apply Loctite 242 to the threads of the remote control handle nut or bolt during assembly.

1. Refer to *Throttle/Shift Cable Removal and Installation* to remove the throttle and shift cables.
2. Disconnect the wire harness from the engine then remove the remote control from the boat. Place the control on a clean work surface.
3. Remove the screw (23, **Figure 8**) and lift the throttle plate (24, **Figure 8**) and throttle arm (20).
4. Remove the screws (19, **Figure 8**), then lift the support housing from the remote control.
5. Pull the main control shaft (21, **Figure 8**) from the housing. Remove the snap ring (9, **Figure 8**) from the main control shaft, then pull the shift gear (10, **Figure 8**) from the main control shaft (21, **Figure 8**).
6. Remove the bushing (5, **Figure 8**) from the housing. Remove the spring (3, **Figure 8**) and detent roller (4) from the housing.
7. Inspect all components for worn, damaged or corroded surfaces and replace them as required.
8. Assembly is the reverse of disassembly. Apply water-resistant grease to all bushings, pivot points and sliding surfaces. Ensure that the mark on the shift arm (16, **Figure 8**) and shift gear (10) are aligned as shown in **Figure 9**.

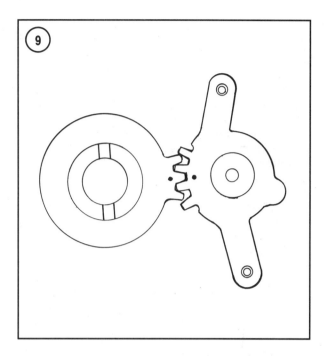

9. Refer to *Throttle/Shift Cable Removal and Installation* to install the cables and the remote control. Check for proper operation before returning the engine into service.

TABLE 1 TIGHTENING TORQUE

	Torque
Remote control back cover	
All side mount models except BF9.9A and BF15A	2.0 N•m (17.7 in.-lb.)
Key switch retaining nut	
All side mount models except BF9.9A and BF15A	4.8 N•m (42.5 in.-lb.)
Emergency stop switch retaining nut	
All side mount models except BF9.9A and BF15A	1.5 N•m (13.3 in.-lb.)
Control handle mounting bolt	
Panel or binnacle mount	17 N•m (12.5 ft.-lb.)
Models BF75A, BF90A, BF115A, BF130A	17 N•m (12.5 ft-lb.)
Throttle plate retaining bolts	
Panel or binnacle mount	
BF75A, BF90A, BF115A, BF130A	4 N•m (35.4 in.-lb.)
Standard tightening torque	

Table 2 STANDARD TIGHTENING TORQUE

Fastener size	Tightening torque
5 mm bolt/nut	4-7 N•m (35-62 in.-lb.)
6 mm bolt/nut	8-12 N•m (71-106 in.-lb.)
8 mm bolt/nut	20-28 N•m (15-21 in.-lb.)
10 mm bolt/nut	35-40 N•m (26-30 ft.-lb.)

Index

B

Base engine 103-111
   break-in procedure 373-374
   cylinder head 308-331
   disassembly 335-359
   flywheel 287-294
   inspection and measurement 359-373
   oil pump 331-335
   primary gearcase repair 373
   removal and installation 270-287
   rocker arm removal/installation 308
   timing belt 294-308
Basic hand tools 21-26
Battery maintenance and testing 261-267
Bearing housing
   installation 473-474
   removal 471-473
Bleeding procedure 504
Break-in procedure 373-374

C

Carburetor
   adjustments 187-193
   repair 225-230
Charging system 89-93, 253-255
Cooling system 111-114
   maintenance 155-156
Correcting steering torque 474
Cylinder head 308-331

E

EFI components 230-240
Electric trim/tilt motor
   removal/installation 497-499
   repair 500-503
Electrical and ignition system 153-155
   battery maintenance and testing 261-267
   charging system 253-255

   ignition system 255-260
   starting system 242-253
   warning system components 261
Electronic fuel injection system 117-129
Engine operation 2

F

Fasteners 2-8
Filling procedure 503-504
Flywheel 287-294
Fuel system 156-159
   repair
     carburetor repair 225-230
     EFI components 230-240
     fuel tank and fuel hose components ... 203-215
     silencer cover and carburetor/
       throttle body 215-225
     testing 46-57
Fuel tank and fuel hose components 203-215
Fuses and wire harnesses 93-94

G

Galvanic corrosion 11-13
Gas-assisted manual tilt system
   removal/installation 490-492
Gasket sealant 10-11
Gearcase 114-116
   operation 395-397
   removal and installation 400-410
   repair 415-463
     propeller 397-400
     water pump 410-415
General information
   engine operation 2
   fasteners 2-8
   galvanic corrosion 11-13
   gasket sealant 10-11
   lubricants 8-10
   manual organization 1

notes, cautions and warnings 1-2
propellers. 14-20
protection from galvanic corrosion. 13-14
torque specifications. 2

I

Ignition system 65-82, 255-260
Impeller
   removal/installation 469
   shimming 469
Intake housing
   liner replacement 469
   removal/installation 468-469

J

Jet drive
   components 465
   operation 465-474
   removal/installation 468
   repair 467-468
   bearing housing
     installation. 473-474
     removal 471-473
   correcting steering torque. 474
   impeller removal/installation 469
   impeller shimming 469
   intake housing liner replacement 469
   intake housing removal/installation 468-469
   thrust control 465-467

L

Lubricants 8-10
Lubrication, maintenance and tune-up
   cooling system maintenance 155-156
   electrical and ignition system 153-155
   fuel system 156-159
   routine maintenance 142-153
   submersion 159-160
   tune-up 160-171

M

Major repairs 507-517
Manual organization. 1
Manual relief valve replacement 500
Mechanic's techniques 31-32
Midsection
   major repairs 507-517
   minor repairs 506-507
   tiller control components 518
Minor repairs. 506-507

N

Neutral start system adjustment 198-200

O

Oil pump 331-335

P

Power trim/tilt systems
   bleeding procedure 504
   electric trim/tilt motor
     removal/installation 497-499
     repair 500-503
   filling procedure 503-504
   gas-assisted manual tilt system
     removal/installation 490-492
   manual relief valve replacement 500
   single hydraulic cylinder trim/tilt systems
     removal/installation 492-494
   three cylinders trim/tilt systems
     removal/installation 494-496
   trim control unit removal/installation 497
   trim position sender removal/installation 496-497
   trim/tilt system components 496
Primary gearcase repair 373
Propeller. 14-20, 397-400
Protection from galvanic corrosion. 13-14

R

Remote control
   disassembly and assembly 524-529
   throttle/shift cable removal/installation 521-524
Rewind starter
   disassembly, inspection and assembly 483-489
   operation 475-477
   removal, repair, assembly and installation ... 477-483
Rocker arm removal/installation 308
Routine maintenance. 142-153

S

Safety first 21
Service hints 28-30
Shifting system adjustments 193-198
Silencer cover and carburetor/ throttle body . . . 215-225
Single hydraulic cylinder trim/tilt systems
   removal/installation 492-494
Special tips 30-31
Starting difficulty 44-46
Starting system 57-64, 242-253
Submersion 159-160

T

Test equipment 26-28
Three cylinders trim/tilt systems
   removal/installation 494-496
Throttle control/cable adjustments 178-187
Throttle/shift cable removal/installation 521-524
Thrust control 465-467

INDEX

Tiller control components 518
Timing adjustments 177-178
Timing belt tensioner 200
Timing belt 294-308
Timing, synchronization and adjustment
   carburetor adjustments 187-193
   neutral start system adjustment 198-200
   shifting system adjustments 193-198
   throttle control/cable adjustments 178-187
   timing adjustments 177-178
   timing belt tensioner 200
   trim sender adjustment 200
Tools and techniques
   basic hand tools 21-26
   mechanic's techniques 31-32
   safety first 21
   service hints 28-30
   special tips 30-31
   test equipment 26-28
Torque specifications 2
Trim control unit removal/installation 497
Trim position sender removal/installation 496-497
Trim sender adjustment 200
Trim system troubleshooting 94-103

Trim/tilt system components 496
Troubleshooting
   base engine 103-111
   charging system 89-93
   cooling system 111-114
   electronic fuel injection system 117-129
   fuel system testing 46-57
   fuses and wire harnesses 93-94
   gearcase 114-116
   ignition system 65-82
   starting difficulty 44-46
   starting system 57-64
   preparation 41-44
   test equipment 33-41
   trim system troubleshooting 94-103
   warning systems 82-89
Tune-up 160-171

W

Warning system 82-89
   components 261
Water pump 410-415
Wiring diagrams 534

MODEL BF20, BF2A (2HP)

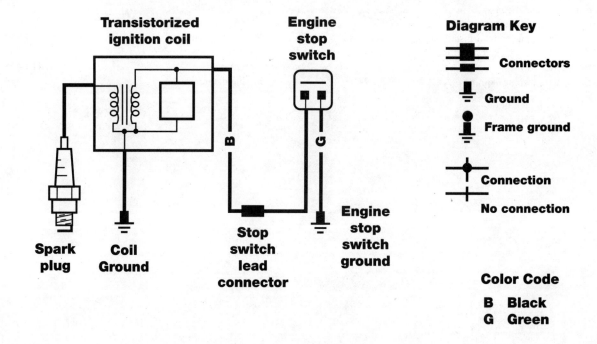

WIRING DIAGRAMS

MODEL BF50, BF5A (5HP)

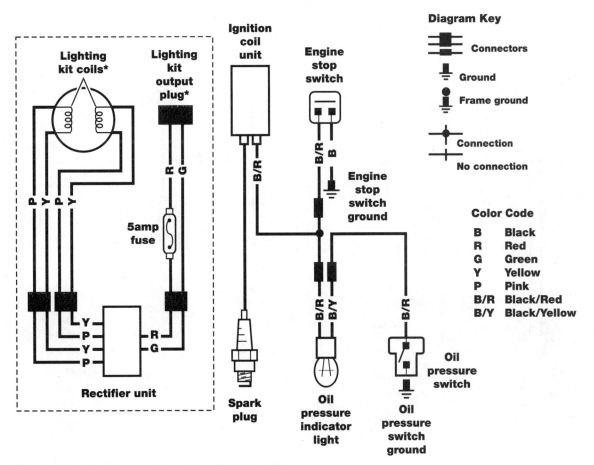

*Used only on engines with optional lighting kit

WIRING DIAGRAMS

MODEL BF75, BF100 (7.5, 9.9HP)

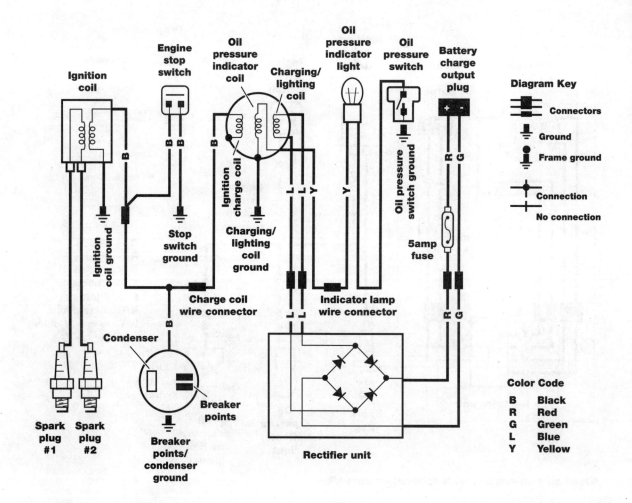

Wiring Diagrams

537

MODEL BF75 & BF100 (SERIAL NO. 120,000-ON) AND BF8A (SERIAL NO. 1099999 AND PRIOR)

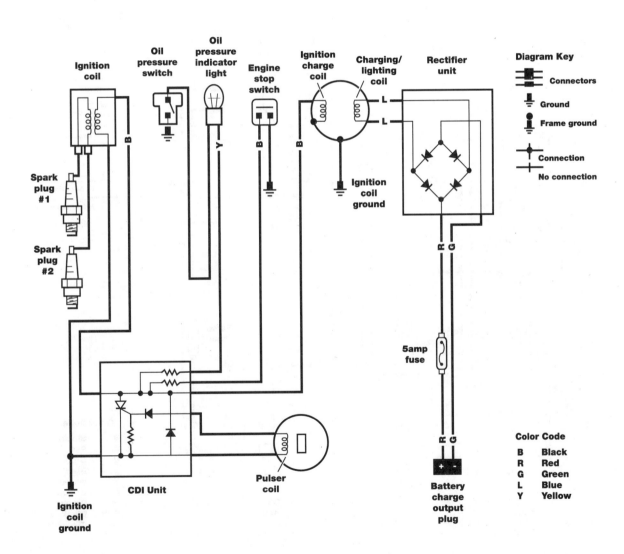

WIRING DIAGRAMS

MODEL BF8A (SERIAL NO. 1100001-ON)

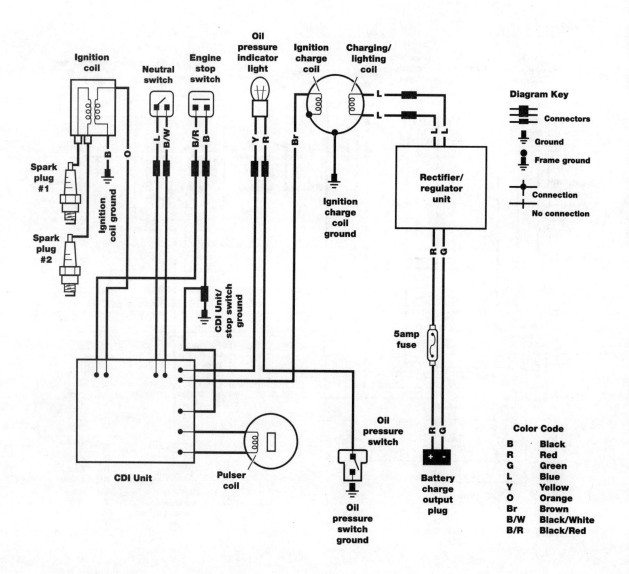

WIRING DIAGRAMS

MODEL BF9.9 AND BF15
(ELECTRIC START SERIAL NO. 1199999 AND PRIOR)

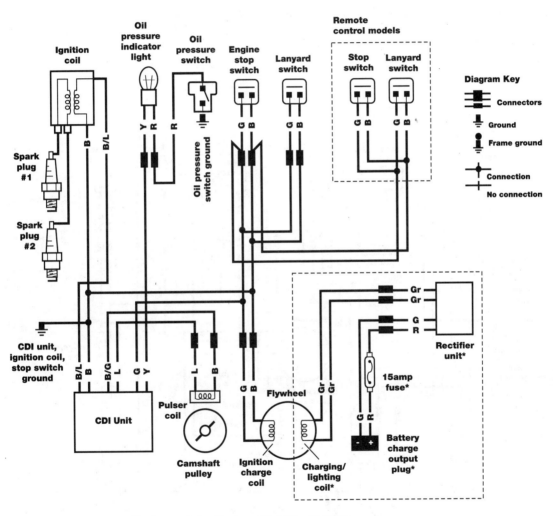

WIRING DIAGRAMS

MODEL BF9.9 AND BF15
(ELECTRIC START SERIAL NO. 1199999 AND PRIOR)

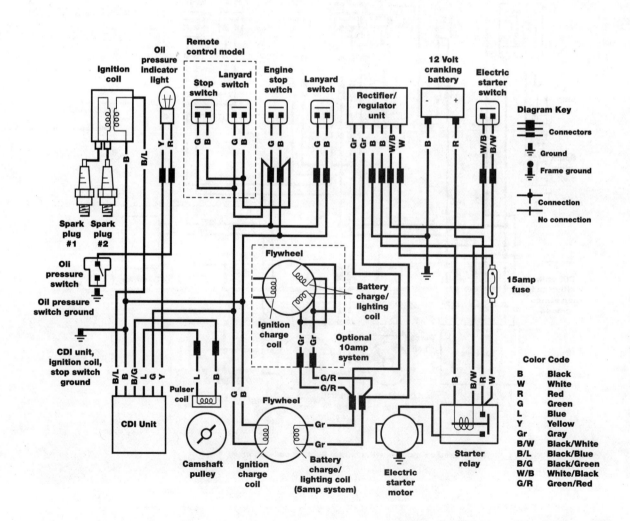

WIRING DIAGRAMS

541

MODEL 9.9 AND BF15 (MANUAL START SERIAL NO. 1200001-ON)

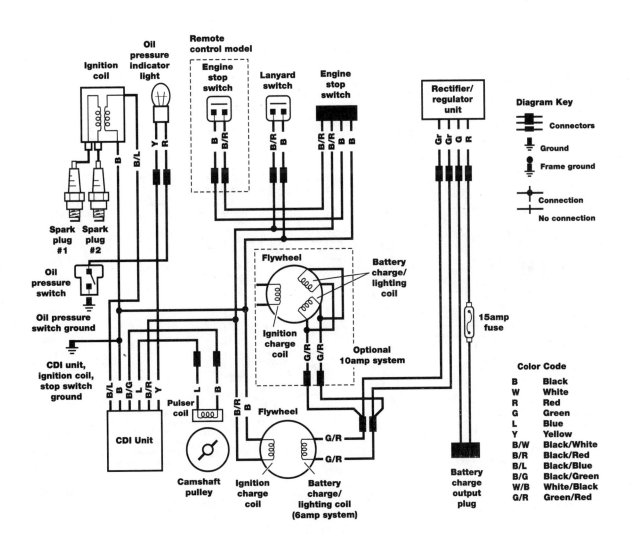

16

MODEL BF9.9 AND BF15
(ELECTRIC START SERIAL NO. 120001-ON)

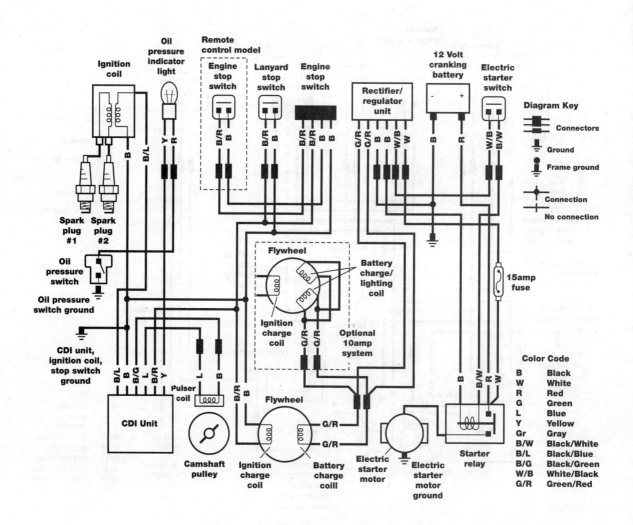

WIRING DIAGRAMS

MODEL BF25 AND BF30 (MANUAL START TILLER CONTROL)

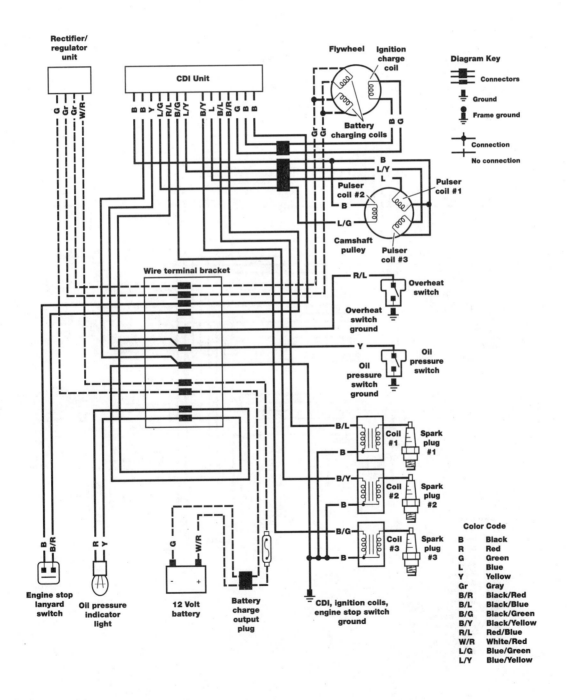

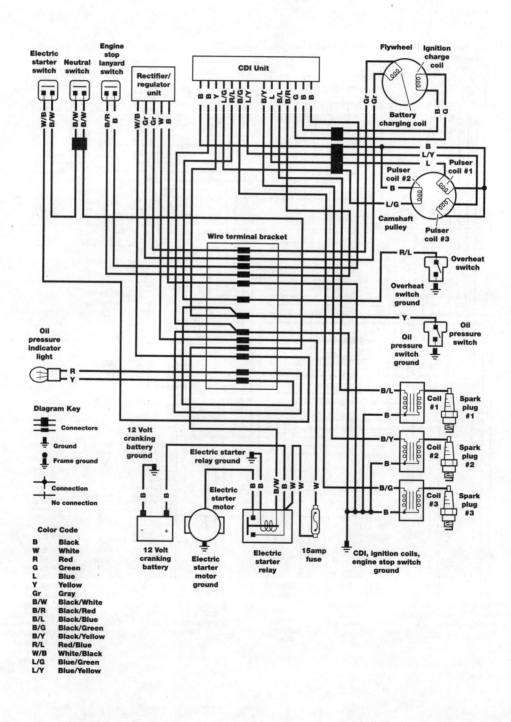

WIRING DIAGRAMS

545

MODEL BF35, BF40, BF45 AND BF50 (TILLER HANDLE CONTROL)

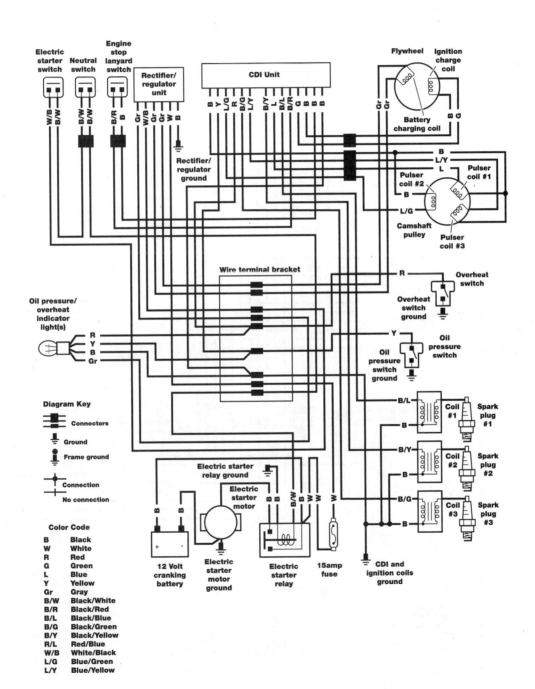

16

MODEL BF25 AND BF30 (ELECTRIC START REMOTE CONTROL)

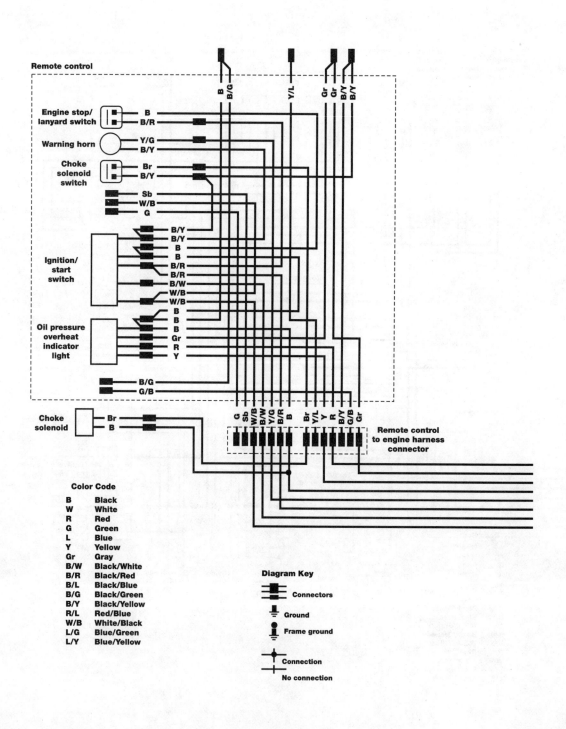

WIRING DIAGRAMS

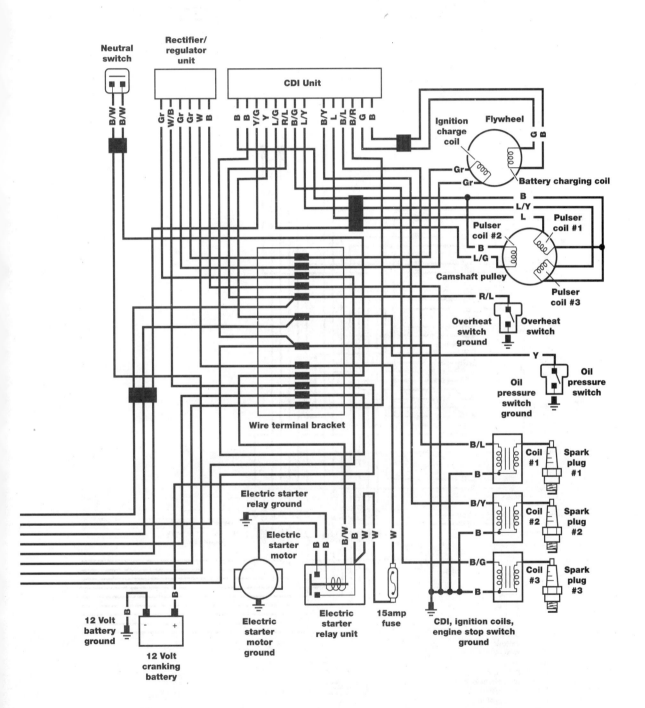

WIRING DIAGRAMS

MODEL BF35, BF40, BF45 AND BF50
(REMOTE CONTROL, WITHOUT POWER TRIM)

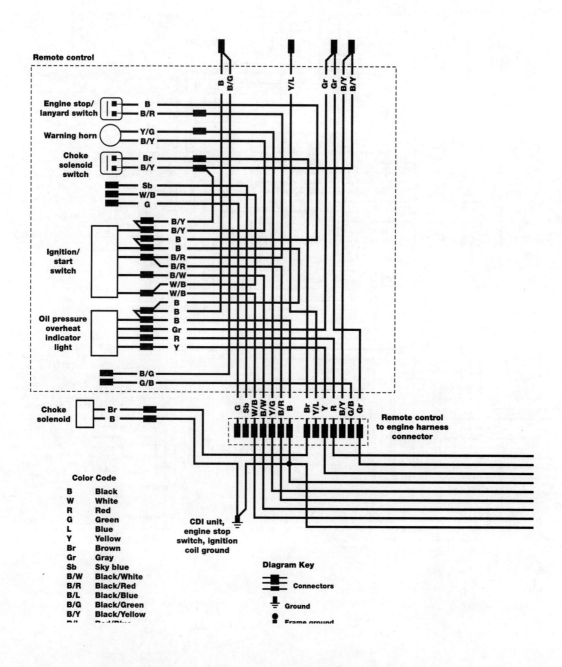

WIRING DIAGRAMS

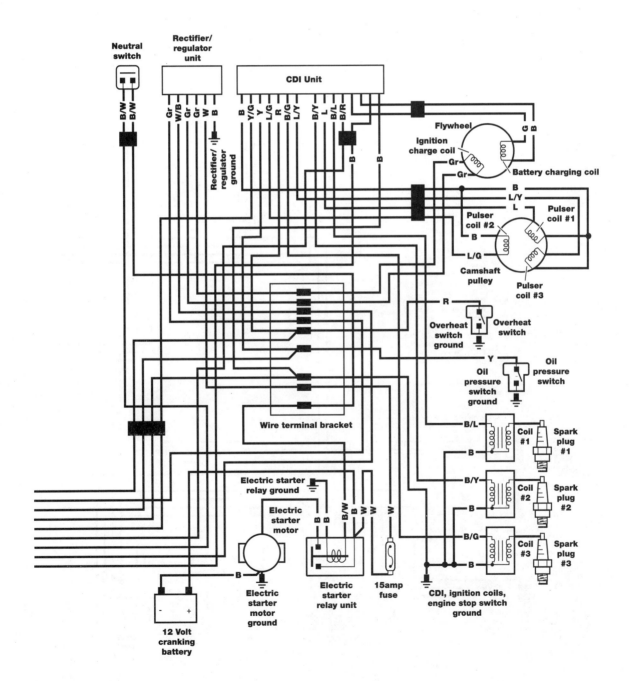

WIRING DIAGRAMS

MODEL BF35, BF40, BF45 AND BF50
(REMOTE CONTROL WITH POWER TRIM)

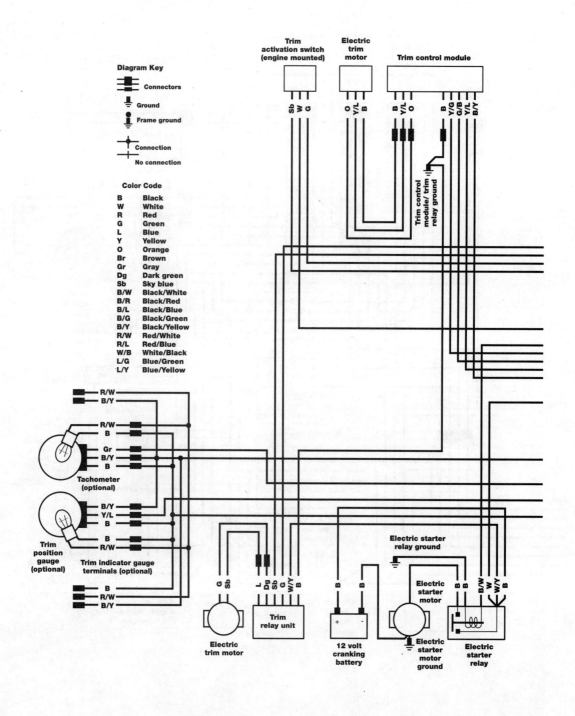

WIRING DIAGRAMS

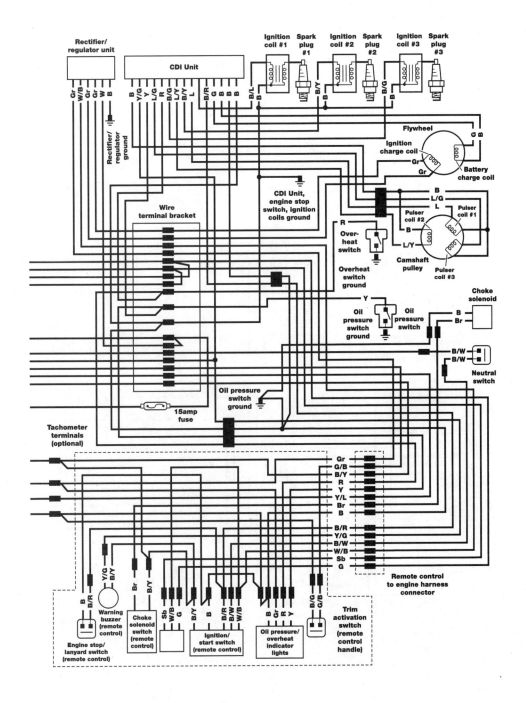

WIRING DIAGRAMS

MODEL BF75 AND BF90 (TILLER HANDLE CONTROL)

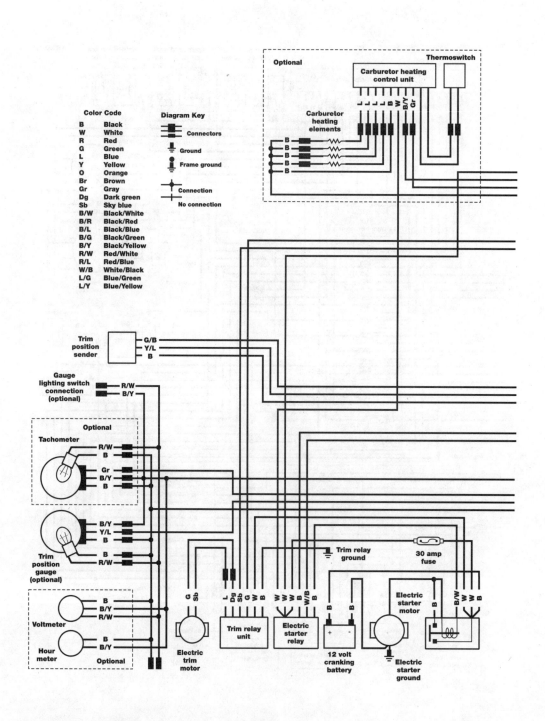

WIRING DIAGRAMS

553

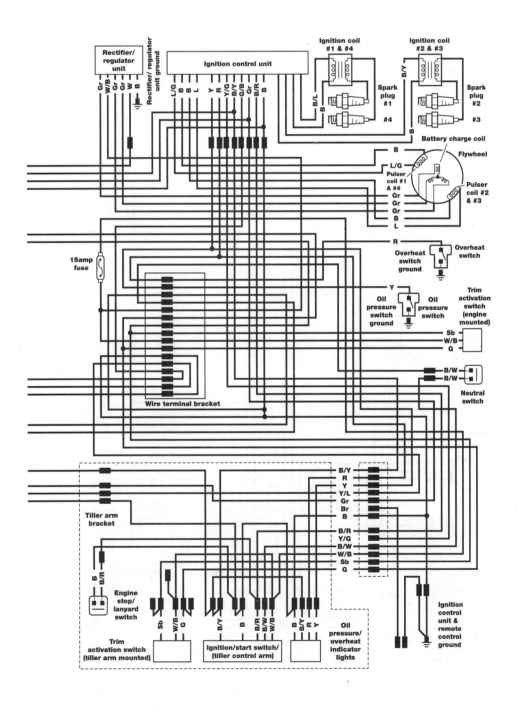

16

MODEL BF75 AND BF90 (REMOTE CONTROL)

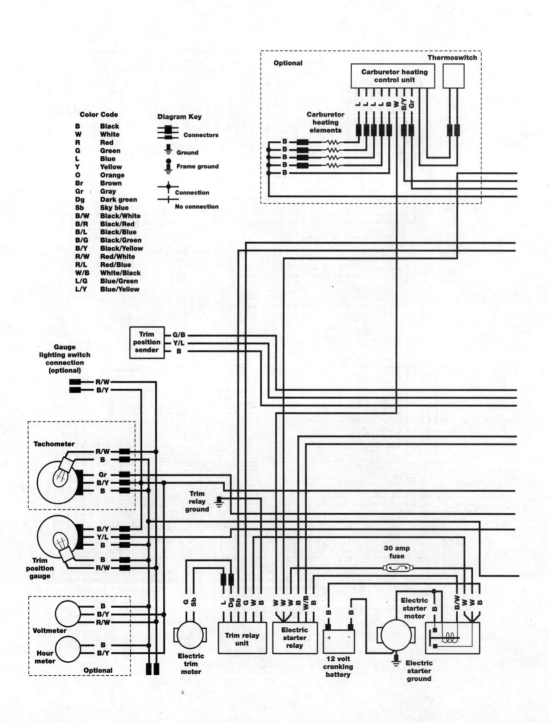

WIRING DIAGRAMS

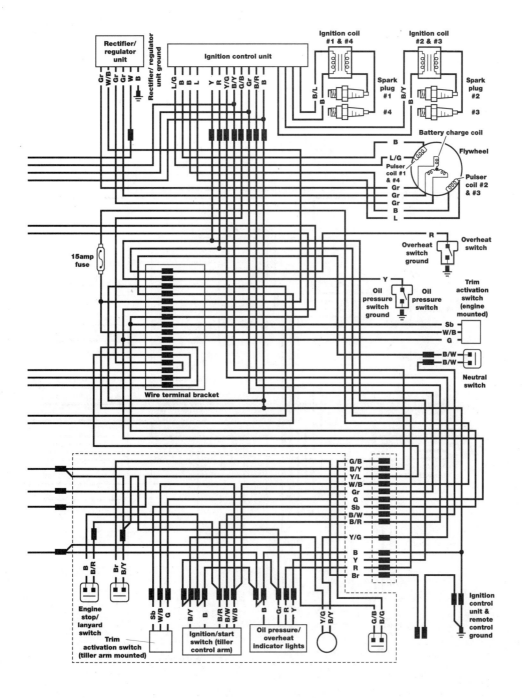

WIRING DIAGRAMS

MODEL BF115 AND BF130 (EFI EQUIPPED)

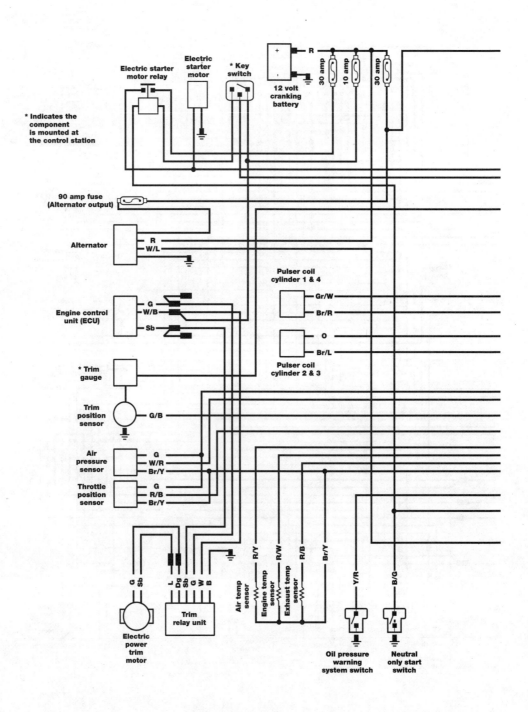

WIRING DIAGRAMS

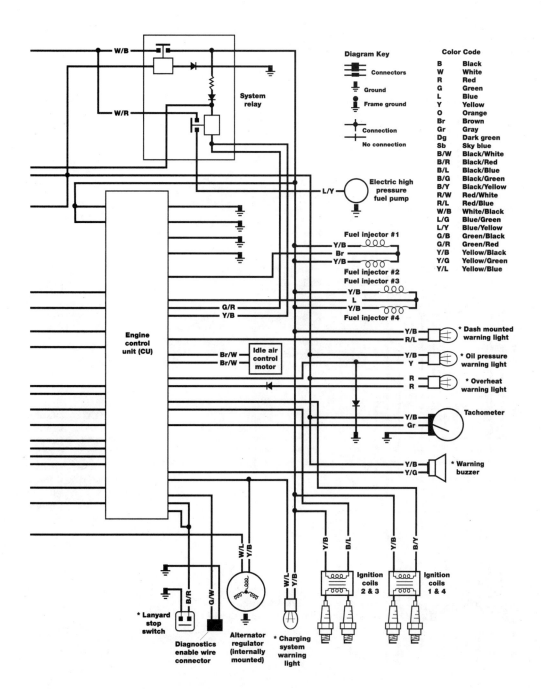

WIRING DIAGRAMS

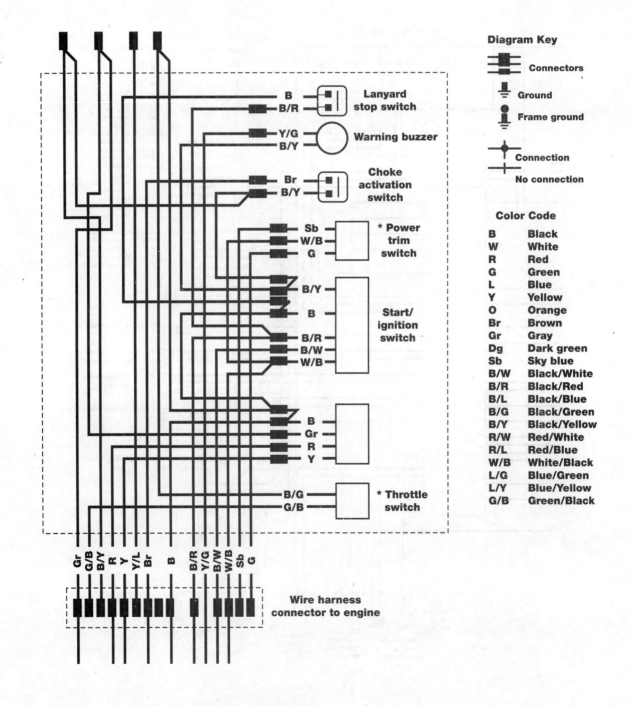

NOTES

MAINTENANCE LOG

Date	Maintenance Performed	Engine Hours